R. Gupta's®

POPULAR MASTER GUIDE

SBI-SCO

SPECIALIST CADRE OFFICERS

Assistant Manager

Recruitment Exam

Strictly based on Current Pattern of Exam

by

RPH Editorial Board

RAMESH PUBLISHING HOUSE, NEW DELHI

Published by
O.P. Gupta *for* Ramesh Publishing House

Admin. Office
12-H, New Daryaganj Road, Opp. Officer' Mess,
New Delhi-110002 ✆ 23275224, 23245124

E-mail: info@rameshpublishinghouse.com
For Online Shopping: www.rameshpublishinghouse.com

Showroom
• Balaji Market, Nai Sarak, Delhi-6 ✆ 23253720, 23282525
• 4457, Nai Sarak, Delhi-6, ✆ 23918938

Book Code: R-2769

ISBN: 978-93-5477-982-4

Price: ₹ 340

Printed at: Deepak Offset, Delhi

CONTENTS

SCHEME OF ONLINE WRITTEN EXAMINATION

Test		No. of Questions	Marks	Time
General Aptitude*	Test of Reasoning	15	15*	45 min
	Quantitative Aptitude	15	15*	
	English Language	20	20*	
Professional Knowledge	General IT Knowledge	60	100	75 min

* Qualifying in nature and marks scored will not be reckoned for arriving at the Merit.

Note: There will be no negative marks for wrong answers in Online Written Examination.

- Except Professional Knowledge (PK) paper, other will be qualifying in nature. Candidates must score minimum qualifying marks in these papers. The minimum qualifying marks will be decided by the Bank or may be waived at the discretion of the Bank.

Tentative pattern for online written exam for Professional Knowledge Paper:

Sl. No.	Subject	Number-of Question	Total Marks
(i)	Software Development	20	33
(ii)	Infra Support	20	33
(iii)	Networking	10	17
(iv)	Cloud Operations	10	17
	Total	**60**	**100**

SBI-SCO—Assistant Manager
Recruitment Exam

TEST OF REASONING

1. How many such pairs of letters are in the word "BONAFIDE" which has as many letters between them as there are in the English alphabetical series (both forward and backward)?
   A. Three B. Four
   C. Five D. Six
   E. More than six

2. If we form a four-letter meaningful word by using the 2nd, 5th, 7th, and 9th letters from the left end of the word "SHOWERING", then which of the following will be the last letter of the meaningful word thus formed? If more than one meaningful word is formed mark Y as your answer. If no meaningful word is formed, mark X as your answer.
   A. H B. G
   C. I D. Y
   E. X

Directions (Qs. No. 3 and 4): *In the question below, there are three statements followed by two conclusions numbered I and II. You have to take the given statements to be true even if they seem to be at variance with commonly known facts. Read all the conclusions and then decide which of the given conclusions logically follows them from the given statements disregarding commonly known facts.*

3. **Statements:**
   Some puzzle are inequality.
   No puzzle is coding.
   Some coding is not input.
   Conclusions:
   I. All inequality can be coding.
   II. Some puzzle is not input.
   A. Both follow
   B. Only II follow
   C. Neither I nor II follow
   D. Only I follow
   E. Either I or II follow

4. **Statements:**
   Only a few true are false.
   No false is correct.
   All wrong are correct.
   Conclusions:
   I. Some false can be wrong.
   II. Some true can be correct.
   A. Both I and II follow
   B. Only I follows
   C. None follows
   D. Either I or II follows
   E. Only II follows

Directions (Qs. No. 5-9): *Study the following information carefully and answer the questions given below:*

Ten persons live on different floors in the same building. The building has ten floors, ground floor is numbered 1 and the topmost floor is numbered 10.

N lives on an even number floor above the sixth floor. Only two persons live between N and A. Only three floors are there between A and J who does not live on the ninth floor. More than four floors between J and B who lives below N. Only three persons live between B and H. The number of floors between N and H same as the number of floors between J and F. G lives on the prime number floor. G lives below D and above E. C does not live on the sixth floor.

5. Which of the following is true with respect to C as per the given information?
   A. N lives immediately below C.
   B. C lives immediately below D.
   C. C lives on floor number 9.
   D. Two floors are there between C and D.
   E. C lives on an even-numbered floor.

1. D	**2.** E	**3.** C	**4.** E	**5.** E

6. Who lives on the floor immediately above D?
A. No one B. A
C. H D. J
E. G

7. Who among the following lives on floor number 6?
A. F B. E
C. D D. G
E. Cannot be determined

8. How many persons live between the floors of G and B?
A. Four B. Seven
C. Five D. Six
E. None of the above

9. Who amongst the following live on the floors exactly between F and H?
A. A and C B. E and A
C. E and D D. D and A
E. C and E

Directions (Qs. No. 10-13): *Study the following information carefully and answer the questions given below:*

In a certain code language:
"work is worship" is coded as "jk rt pq"
"work hard always" is coded as "jk mn uv"
"always do worship" is coded as "uv st pq"
"hard time passes" is coded as "mn ab ef"

10. Which among the following words is coded as "rt"?
A. work B. is
C. hard D. time
E. None of these

11. Which among the following words is coded as "ab"
A. time B. passes
C. is D. Either (A) or (B)
E. None of these

12. Which of the following words is correctly matched with its code?
A. word - rt B. is - jk
C. worship - mn D. do - rt
E. hard - mn

13. What is the code of "time passes" as per the given code language?
A. ab uv B. ef jk
C. ab ef D. ef rt
E. Cannot be determined

Directions (Qs. No. 14 and 15): *Read the following information and answer the questions accordingly.*

Seven boys P, Q, R, S, T, U and V have different weights. V is heavier than Q. P is heavier than only three people. Q is heavier than P. T is heavier than S but lighter than R. U is heavier than R but lighter than Q.

14. How many boys are lighter than U?
A. Five B. Four
C. Two D. Three
E. None of these

15. Who is the third lightest boy?
A. T B. U
C. R D. P
E. None of these

QUANTITATIVE APTITUDE

16. A invested ₹ 15000 and B invested ₹ (15000 + Y) in a business. After 4 months B withdraw 40% of his investment. If the total profit earned at the end of the year is ₹ 4700 and the profit share of B is ₹ 2200. Find the value of 2Y.
A. 210000/23 B. 105000/23
C. 107000/23 D. 205000/23
E. 115000/23

17. A person rows a distance of 20 km upstream and 15 km downstream in a total time of $2\frac{5}{12}$ hours. If the speed of the current is 4 km/h, then in how many hours can he row a distance of 64 km upstream?
A. $5\frac{1}{3}$ B. $4\frac{2}{3}$
C. $5\frac{1}{2}$ D. $4\frac{1}{4}$
E. $4\frac{1}{5}$

18. P, Q and R together can do a piece of work in 16(4/11) days. P and Q together can do the same work in 20 days. In how many days will 'R' alone finish the 60% of the work?
A. 51 days B. 59 days
C. 54 days D. 53 days
E. 50 days

6. B	**7.** C	**8.** D	**9.** D	**10.** B	**11.** D	**12.** E
13. C	**14.** B	**15.** C	**16.** A	**17.** A	**18.** C	

19. In a classroom consisting of boys and girls, the average marks obtained by the boys is 90. If the average of the whole class is 92, and the ratio of the number of boys to that of girls is 3 : 2, what is the average marks scored by the girls?

A. 97 B. 94
C. 96 D. 95
E. None of these

20. Vessel 'A' contains a total of 45 liters of a mixture of milk and water such that milk is 80% of water. Some quantity of milk is taken out from the vessel and the same quantity of water is also taken out and these are added to honey in vessel 'B' to form a mixture 'P', which contains 4 liters of honey. If mixture 'P' contains 40% of water, then in total what percent of the mixture is taken out from vessel 'A'?

A. Between 24% to 28%
B. Between 28% to 32%
C. Between 32% to 36%
D. Between 36% to 40%
E. Between 40% to 44%

21. The length and breadth of a rectangle are in the ratio 3 : 2. If the length is increased by 5 m keeping the breadth same, the new area of rectangle is 2600 m^2. What is the perimeter of the original rectangle?

A. 320 m B. 300 m
C. 295 m D. 200 m
E. None of these

Directions (Qs. No. 22 and 23): *What should come in place of question Mark '?' in the following number series?*

22. 300, ?, 148, 221, 441, 1101.5

A. 115.5 B. 150.5
C. 149 D. 151
E. None of these

23. 25, ?, 256, 476, 745, 1050

A. 60 B. 100
C. 125 D. 65
E. None of these

Directions (Qs. No. 24-28): *Read the following directions carefully and answer the following question.*

Line graph represents the total number of population visited in Museum A, B and C on Sunday.

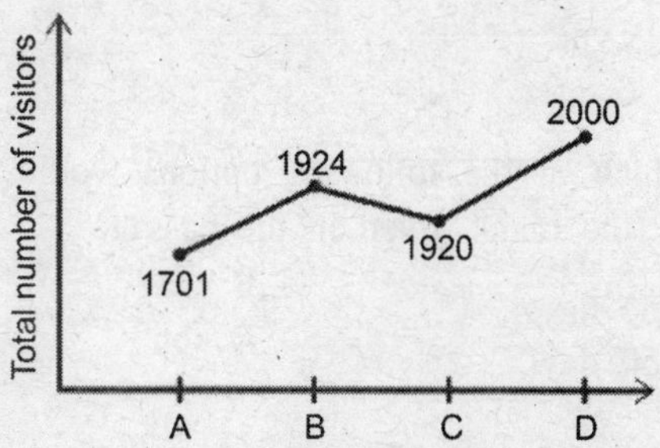

Table represent the number of male visited in Museum out of total population.

Museum	Number of Male out of total people who visited in Museum
A	2/9
B	11/13
C	13/16
D	19/50

24. If the number of male and number in Museum E are 7.69% more than the number of male who visited in Museum C and the number of female are 300 less than the number of Male visited in Museum B. Then find the difference between the number of male and female who visited Museum E?

A. 600 B. 560
C. 628 D. 678
E. 700

25. Museum A is in village Rampur where the number of population was 1,24,000 and the ratio of male and female 15 : 16. Then, find the percentage of total female on Sunday in Rampur village to the total number of male in Museum B?

A. More than 4043%
B. Between 3508% to 4040%
C. Less than 3886%
D. Both option (A) and (C)
E. None of these

26. What are the difference between male who visited museum B and C together to the average of female who visited museum A, B and C together? (approx value)

A. 1962 B. 1700
C. 1882 D. 1688
E. None of these

27. If the cost price of male ticket and the female ticket is ₹ X and ₹ (X-5). And the museum B get the revenue ₹ 94720. Find the total revenue getting from male ticket from museum A?

A. 18900 B. 20800
C. 20600 D. 18700
E. None of these

28. Find the average number of visitors in B, C and D?

A. 1176 B. 2096
C. 1556 D. 1948
E. None of these

19. D	20. C	21. D	22. C	23. B	24. C	25. B	26. D	27. A	28. D

Directions (Qs. No. 29 and 30): *In the given questions, two equations numbered I and II are given. Solve both the equations and mark the appropriate answer.*

29. I. $x^2 + 2x - 35 = 0$
II. $y^2 - 2y - 48 = 0$
A. $x > y$
B. $x < y$
C. $x \geq y$
D. $x \leq y$
E. $x = y$ or relation between x and y can not be established.

30. I. $x^2 - 10x + 16 = 0$
II. $y^2 - 5y - 24 = 0$
A. $x > y$
B. $x < y$
C. $x \geq y$
D. $x \leq y$
E. $x = y$ or relation between x and y can not be established.

ENGLISH LANGUAGE

Directions (Qs. No. 31-39): *Carefully read the provided passage to respond to the subsequent questions. Each question will present five answer options. Select the appropriate option as your answer.*

Pink Tax is commonly used to describe a situation wherein things associated with women are priced higher than those with men. Generally speaking, women pay more than males for similar items. The pink tax is not enforced by the government but by the businesses selling the products. According to experts, the pricing disparity is due to market forces. The pink tax has long imposed an economic burden on women around the world—especially **since** women continue to earn less than men.

According to a study _____ the New York City Department of Consumer Affairs in 2015, women's products are typically more expensive than men's without a proper reason. The study concluded that products explicitly marketed for women cost seven per cent more on average than products sold for men. This discrepancy includes apparel, toys, and healthcare products, among other things. The largest discrepancy came to personal care/hygiene products, where women's products cost 13 per cent more than men's.

Several countries have investigated the pink tax, including Argentina, France, Germany, the UK, Australia, and Italy. For example, in the UK, it was found that women and girls were being charged, on average, 37 per cent more for toys, cosmetics, and clothes than their male counterparts. In the UK, girls' school uniforms were also 12 per cent more expensive than boys' uniforms. In Singapore, a check by the Sunday Times on 10 companies found that women pay more for some products and services, such as dry cleaning and razors, offered by around half of these companies. Additionally, women in Singapore have to pay more premiums for Careshield Life, a national long-term care insurance scheme introduced by the government.

Examples of pink tax in India include salon services, personal care goods such as shampoos, soaps, and deodorants, as well as clothing, toys, and accessories such as jewelry. Presently, women are heavily exploited by vegan products and non-animal-tested cosmetics that are significantly more expensive, a **form** of taxation.

31. What's the synonym of the word **'since'** as used in the passage?
A. until
B. before
C. as
D. till
E. therefore

32. Select the most appropriate synonym of the given word.

Form
A. Damage
B. Demolish
C. Collapse
D. Type
E. Scatter

33. Which of the following options would be suitable for the blank given in the passage?
A. in
B. to
C. by
D. on
E. with

29. E	**30.** E	**31.** C	**32.** D	**33.** C

34. Which of the following statements is **true** as per the passage?

A. The pink tax is enforced by the government but not by the businesses selling the products.

B. Women in Singapore have to pay less premiums for Careshield Life, a national long-term care insurance scheme introduced by the government.

C. Several countries have investigated the pink tax, including Argentina, France, Germany, the UAE, Australia, and Italy.

D. Some of the products that are included under the pink tax in India are salon services, personal care goods such as shampoos, soaps, and deodorants, as well as clothing, toys, and accessories such as jewelry.

E. As per the study by the New York City Department of Consumer Affairs in 2015-2016, women's products are typically more expensive than men's without a proper reason.

35. Find **true** statement(s) from the following:

(*a*) The discrepancy in tax includes apparel, toys, and healthcare products, among other things.

(*b*) The pink tax has long imposed an economic burden on women and men around the world.

(*c*) Currently, women bear a significant financial burden due to the high costs of vegan products and non-animal-tested cosmetics, which can be considered a type of economic imposition.

A. (*a*) and (*b*) are true B. (*c*) and (*a*) are true

C. Only (*c*) is true D. Only (*b*) is true

E. All are true.

36. According to the passage, what is the primary reason for the pricing inequality known as the "pink tax"?

A. The pricing disparity is primarily a result of government regulations that enforce gender-based pricing on products marketed to women.

B. Market forces, driven by supply and demand dynamics, are the primary factors behind the pricing disparity known as the "pink tax."

C. Gender-based taxation, imposed by governments, directly contributes to the higher prices of products associated with women.

D. International trade agreements have established pricing guidelines that result in women's products being priced higher than men's.

E. Consumer preferences, influenced by advertising and social factors, play the central role in the pricing disparity termed the "pink tax".

37. Which of the following expresses the same meaning of the word given in bold?

in the UK, it was found that women and girls were being **charged**

A. confronted

B. imposed

C. limited

D. absolved

E. altered

38. Based on the study by the New York City Department of Consumer Affairs, where was the largest product pricing discrepancy between men and women observed?

A. Clothing

B. Toys

C. Personal care/hygiene products

D. Accessories such as jewelry

E. Vegan products

39. According to the information in the passage, what is the "Pink Tax"?

A. It's an additional tax charged by the government on women's products.

B. It's inequality in the amount payable for insurance based on gender.

C. It's a taxation form enforced by businesses where female products cost more than their male counterparts.

D. It's a type of business tax focused only on clothing, toys, and accessories.

E. It's a tax levied on vegan and non-animal-tested cosmetics.

Directions (Qs. No. 40 and 41): *The given sentence is divided into four parts: (a), (b), (c), and (d). Choose the part that contains an error as your answer. If the sentence is error-free, mark (e) i.e. No error as your answer.*

40. People develop a attachment **(*a*)**/ to a city because they find **(*b*)**/ a sense of belonging **(*c*)**/ within like-minded individuals. **(*d*)**/ No error **(*e*)**

A. (*a*) B. (*b*)

C. (*c*) D. (*d*)

E. (*e*)

34. D	35. B	36. B	37. B	38. C	39. C	40. A

41. These are just small **(*a*)**/ alterations with our lifestyle **(*b*)**/ that will help us achieve **(*c*)**/ that perfect body. **(*d*)**/ No error **(*e*)**

A. (*a*) B. (*b*)
C. (*c*) D. (*d*)
E. (*e*)

Directions (Qs. No. 42 and 43): *In the given sentence, four words, given in bold are marked as (a), (b), (c) and (d). These words may or may not be placed in their right places. Four options with different arrangements of these words are given below, mark the option with the correct arrangement as your answer. If no change is required mark 'No rearrangement required' as your answer.*

42. As data and technology play a **effectively (*a*)**/ role in the **delivery (*b*)**/ of services, human development systems should **ensure (*c*)**/ they are **crucial (*d*)** used.

A. (*d*), (*b*), (*c*), (*a*)
B. (*b*), (*c*), (*a*), (*d*)
C. (*c*), (*a*), (*b*), (*d*)
D. (*a*), (*b*), (*d*), (*c*)
E. No rearrangement required

43. Pandemics, economic **succession (*a*)**/ and **rapid (*b*)**/ weather events were once tail-end risks, but all three have hit South Asia in **extreme (*c*)**/ **slumps (*d*)** since 2020.

A. (*d*), (*b*), (*c*), (*a*)
B. (*a*), (*c*), (*b*), (*d*)
C. (*d*), (*c*), (*b*), (*a*)
D. (*b*), (*a*), (*d*), (*c*)
E. No rearrangement required

Directions (Qs. No. 44 and 45): *Choose the most appropriate word to fill in the given black.*

44. The Budget aims to fulfil the long-term ______ goals of the country along with being the world's fastest-growing large economy.

A. implausible
B. challenging
C. obnoxious
D. sustainable
E. untenable

45. For youngsters, smartwatches are a way to ______ another accessory, for working professionals they are a watch-cum-reminder machine, and for the elderly, they are used to monitor vitals.

A. Recruit B. Flaunt
C. Efface D. Impel
E. Replace

Directions (Qs. No. 46-50): *Below, you will find a set of five sentences. You need to arrange these sentences in the correct sequence to form a coherent paragraph. After doing so, answer the questions that follow.*

(*a*) However, the influencer is not a buzzword anymore. Considering macro and celeb influencers, today's new-gen celebs, these individuals

(*b*) The rise of social media has certainly revolutionised various aspects, including how we connect, share, and consume information.

(*c*) The emergence of influencers is one of the most significant changes brought about by social media in the realm of marketing.

(*d*) Furthermore, with their substantial online followings and persuasive skills, they have emerged as critical players in determining consumers' buying behaviour

(*e*) Can significantly impact the psychology of potential consumers through their recommendations, opinions, and ideas, thereby shaping their purchasing decisions.

46. Which of the following will be the **FIRST** sentence after rearrangement?

A. (*b*) B. (*a*)
C. (*d*) D. (*c*)
E. (*e*)

47. Which of the following will be the **SECOND** sentence after rearrangement?

A. (*a*) B. (*c*)
C. (*e*) D. (*b*)
E. (*d*)

48. Which of the following will be the **THIRD** sentence after rearrangement?

A. (*b*) B. (*c*)
C. (*a*) D. (*d*)
E. (*e*)

49. Which of the following will be the **FOURTH** sentence after rearrangement?

A. (*d*) B. (*c*)
C. (*b*) D. (*e*)
E. (*a*)

50. Which of the following will be the **LAST** sentence after rearrangement?

A. (*d*) B. (*a*)
C. (*b*) D. (*c*)
E. (*e*)

41. B	**42.** A	**43.** C	**44.** D	**45.** B	**46.** A	**47.** B	**48.** C	**49.** D	**50.** A

GENERAL IT KNOWLEDGE

51. Which of the following is a collection of heterogeneous elements?
A. Array
B. Structure
C. Stack
D. Queue
E. None of these

52. Based on the graph below, which of the following is NOT true?

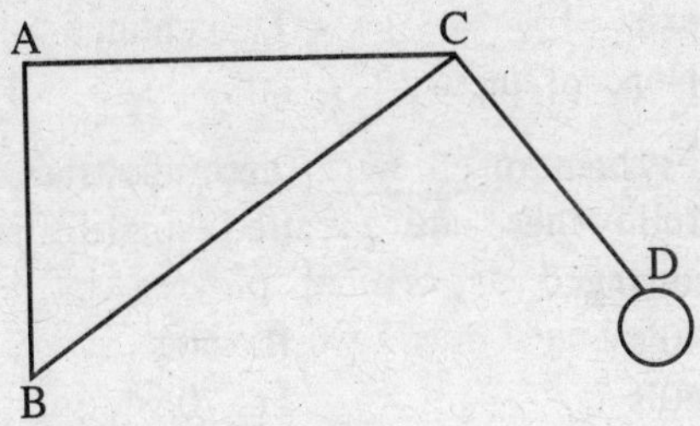

A. There are 5 edges
B. A is adjacent to D
C. There are 2 loops
D. Both (B) and (C)
E. Both (A) and (C)

53. An element of structure can be a Pointer; which points to a structure of the same type is called:
A. Referential Pointer
B. Structure Pointer
C. Pointer Structure
D. Self-Referential Structure
E. None of these

54. In a Stack the elements are entered from ....
A. End
B. Top
C. Random
D. Bottom
E. None of these

55. Which option best describes this tree?

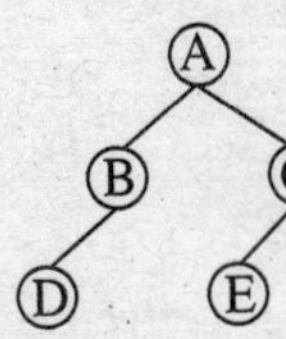

A. Not a tree
B. A binary tree
C. A proper binary tree
D. A complete binary tree
E. None of these

56. The numbers of null pointer are there in N number binary tree is ______.
A. N
B. N + 1
C. N/2
D. N − 1
E. None of these

57. The Collection of data, that contains information about one particular enterprise is known as?
A. DBMS
B. Database
C. Data Dictionary
D. Data file
E. None of these

58. .... is preferred method for enforcing data integrity.
A. Constraints
B. Stored Procedure
C. Triggers
D. Cursors
E. None of these

59. Which of the following contains a complete record of all activity that affected the contents of a database during a certain period of time?
A. Report Writer
B. Query Language
C. Data Manipulation Language
D. Transaction Log
E. None of these

60. Which join refers to join records from the write table that have no matching key in the left table are included in the result set:
A. Left outer join
B. Right outer join
C. Full outer join
D. Half outer join
E. None of these

61. While using encapsulation, which among the following is possible?
A. Code modification can be additional overhead
B. Data member's data type can be changed without changing any other code
C. Data member's type can't be changed, or whole code have to be changed
D. Member functions can be used to change the data type of data members
E. None of these

51. B	52. D	53. D	54. B	55. B	56. B
57. B	58. A	59. D	60. B	61. B	

62. How can you make the private members inheritable?
A. By making their visibility mode as public only
B. By making their visibility mode as protected only
C. By making their visibility mode as private in derived class
D. It can be done both by making the visibility mode public or protected
E. None of these

63. Which one of the following models is not suitable for accommodating any change?
A. Build & Fix Model
B. Prototyping Model
C. RAD Model
D. Waterfall Model
E. None of these

64. Efficiency in a software product does not include ………… .
A. responsiveness
B. licensing
C. memory utilization
D. processing time
E. None of these

65. Identify the software whose vulnerability is exploited the most?
A. Android
B. Browser
C. Adobe Flash Player
D. Microsoft Office
E. None of these

66. An attacker may use automatic brute forcing tool to compromise your _______.
A. username B. employee ID
C. system/PC name D. password
E. None of these

67. Which of the following is not a layer of TCP protocol stack?
A. Application B. Transport
C. Network D. Presentation
E. None of these

68. When a DNS server accepts and uses incorrect information from a host that has no authority giving that information, then it is called _______.
A. DNS lookup B. DNS hijacking
C. DNS spoofing D. DNS authorizing
E. None of these

69. Which tag allows you to add a row in a table?
A. <td> and </td>
B. <cr> and </cr>
C. <th> and </th>
D. <tr> and </tr>
E. None of these

70. Which of these jump statements can skip processing the remainder of the code in its body for a particular iteration?
A. break B. return
C. exit D. continue
E. None of these

71. The system of _______ generally ran one job at a time. These were called single stream batch processing.
A. 40's B. 50's
C. 60's D. 70's
E. None of these

72. ……… is a large operating system core that provides a wide range of services.
A. Multilithic kernel
B. Monolithic kernel
C. Micro kernel
D. Macro kernel
E. None of these

73. ………. is a special type of programming language used to provide instructions to the monitor simple batch processing schema.
A. Job control language (JCL)
B. Processing control language (PCL)
C. Batch control language (BCL)
D. Monitor control language (MCL)
E. None of these

74. Which of the following is not the approach to dealing with deadlock?
A. Prevention B. Avoidance
C. Detection D. Deletion
E. None of these

75. …………. are very effective because a mode switch is not required to switch from one thread to another.
A. Kernel-level threads
B. User-level threads
C. Alterable threads
D. Application level threads
E. None of these

62. D	63. D	64. B	65. B	66. D	67. D	68. C
69. D	70. D	71. B	72. D	73. A	74. D	75. B

76. The sum of the seek time, and the rotational delay is called the ....
A. reached time B. access time
C. arrived time D. common time
E. None of these

77. The mechanism that brings a page into memory only when it is needed is called ....
A. segmentation
B. fragmentation
C. demand paging
D. page replacement
E. None of these

78. A program responsible for assigning the CPU to the process that has been selected by the short term scheduler is known as ....
A. scheduler B. dispatcher
C. debugger D. compiler
E. None of these

79. An arrangement of record in a sequence in which they arrive is known as a ....
A. pile B. file
C. disk D. directory
E. None of these

80. Which technique was introduced because a single job could not keep both the CPU and I/O devices busy?
A. Time-sharing
B. Spooling
C. Preemptive scheduling
D. Multiprogramming
E. None of these

81. Which of the following is crucial time while accessing data on the disk?
A. Seek time
B. Rotational time
C. Transmission time
D. Waiting time
E. None of these

82. In .... condition, processes are allowed to request for new resources without releasing the resources that they are currently holding.
A. Mutual exclusion
B. Hold and wait
C. No preemption
D. Circular wait
E. None of these

83. In computer security, ... means that computer system assets can be modified only by authorized parties.
A. Confidentiality B. Integrity
C. Availability D. Authenticity
E. None of these

84. .... are used in denial of service attacks, typically against targeted web sites.
A. Worm B. Zombie
C. Virus D. Trojan horse
E. None of these

85. An optimal scheduling algorithm in terms of minimizing the average waiting time of a given set of process is ....
A. FCFS scheduling
B. Round robin scheduling algorithm
C. Shortest job first scheduling algorithm
D. Priority scheduling algorithm
E. None of these

86. Mutual exclusion is referred as ....
A. if one process is in a critical region others are excluded
B. prevents deadlock
C. requires semaphore to implement
D. is found only in the Windows NT operating system
E. None of these

87. The principle of locality of reference justifies the use of:
A. virtual memory
B. interrupts
C. main memory
D. cache memory
E. None of these

88. Input transfers are done in advance and output transfers are done after sometimes in which of these technique?
A. Spooling B. Buffering
C. Swapping D. Paging
E. None of these

89. Virtual memory is _______.
A. an extremely large main memory
B. an extremely large secondary memory
C. an illusion of extremely large main memory
D. a type of memory used in super computers
E. None of these

76. B	77. C	78. B	79. A	80. D	81. A	82. B
83. B	84. B	85. C	86. A	87. D	88. B	89. C

90. In kernel model, the operating system services such as process management, memory management are provided by the kernel.

A. monolithic B. micro
C. macro D. complex
E. None of these

91. Which one of the following extends a private network across public networks?

A. local area network
B. virtual private network
C. enterprise private network
D. storage area network
E. None of these

92. Transmission data rate is decided by:

A. network layer
B. physical layer
C. data link layer
D. transport layer
E. None of these

93. The data link layer takes the packets from .... and encapsulates them into frames for transmission.

A. network layer
B. physical layer
C. transport layer
D. application layer
E. None of these

94. CRC stands for:

A. cyclic redundancy check
B. code repeat check
C. code redundancy check
D. cyclic repeat check
E. None of these

95. The .... translates internet domain and host names to IP address.

A. domain name system
B. routing information protocol
C. network time protocol
D. internet relay chat
E. None of these

96. The entire hostname has a maximum of:

A. 255 characters
B. 127 characters
C. 63 characters
D. 31 characters
E. None of these

97. URL stands for:

A. unique reference label
B. uniform reference label
C. uniform resource locator
D. unique resource locator
E. None of these

98. StarBand provides:

A. FTTH internet access
B. Cable access
C. Telephone access
D. Satellite access
E. None of these

99. Which one of the following is a cryptographic protocol used to secure HTTP connection?

A. stream control transmission protocol (SCTP)
B. transport layer security (TSL)
C. explicit congestion notification (ECN)
D. resource reservation protocol (RRP)
E. None of these

100. Which of the following is not applicable for IP?

A. Error reporting
B. Handle addressing conventions
C. Datagram format
D. Packet handling conventions
E. None of these

101. Websocket protocol uses which communication model:

A. Publish-Subscribe
B. Request Response
C. Push-Pull
D. Exclusive Pair
E. None of these

102. What is the primary computing engine behind open stack ....?

A. NOVA B. Swift
C. Cinder D. Switch
E. None of these

103. If the IP address or hostname of a data node changes:

A. The namenode updates the mapping between file name and block name
B. The data in that data node is lost forever
C. The namenode need not update mapping between file name and block name
D. There namenode has to be restarted
E. None of these

90. A	**91.** B	**92.** B	**93.** A	**94.** A	**95.** A	**96.** A
97. C	**98.** D	**99.** B	**100.** A	**101.** A	**102.** A	**103.** C

104. Which of the following is used for Web performance management and load testing?
A. VMware Hyperic
B. Webmetrics
C. Univa UD
D. Tapinsystems
E. None of these

105. .... is the process of making an archival or backup copy of the entire contents of a hard drive.
A. Investigation
B. Disk imaging
C. Formatting
D. S/w Installation
E. None of these

106. Which of the following is a message queue or transaction system for distributed Internet-based applications?
A. Amazon Elastic Compute Cloud
B. Amazon Simple Queue Service
C. Amazon Simple Notification Service
D. Amazon Simple Storage System
E. None of these

107. Which of the following is relational database service provided by Amazon?
A. SimpleDB
B. SQL Server
C. Oracle
D. RDS
E. None of these

108. Which of the following is not the component of a SCADA system?
A. Database server
B. I/O system
C. PLC controller
D. Sparger controller
E. None of these

109. The number of binding of a node to other actors of the graph in the graph representation of a network is called as ....
A. node degree
B. path length
C. social circle
D. bridge
E. None of these

110. Calculating the location of a mobile device from signals sent by the device to base stations:
A. Personal Area Network (PAN)
B. Terminal-based positioning
C. Pervasive computing
D. Network-based positioning
E. None of these

EXPLANATORY ANSWERS

1. (D): BONAFIDE

ON → No letter
BF → 3 letters
AD → 2 letters
DE → No letter
FD → 1 letter
AE → 3 letters

Hence, there are six such pairs of letters are in the word BONAFIDE which has as many letters between them as there are in the English alphabetical series (both forward and backward).

2. (E): "SHOWERING"

HEIG —— X

No meaningful word is formed.

For Qs. No. (5-9):

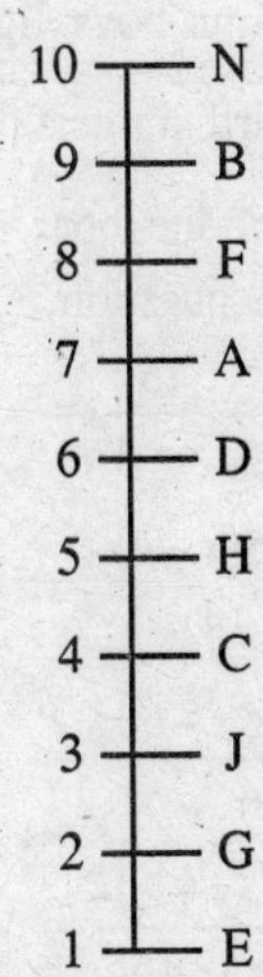

104. B	105. B	106. B	107. D	108. D	109. A	110. B

5. (E): C lives on an even-numbered floor.

6. (B): A lives immediately above D.

7. (C): D lives on floor number 6.

8. (D): There are six persons live between the floors of G and B.

9. (D): D and A live on the floors exactly between F and H

For Qs. No. (10-13):

In a certain code language.
"Work is worship" is coded as "jk rt pq"
"Work hard always" is coded as "jk mn uv"
"always do worship" is coded as "uv st pq"
"hard time passes" is coded as "mn ab ef"

10. (B): 'is' word is coded as "rt".

11. (D): Either 'time' or 'passes' word is coded as "ab".

12. (E): hard-mn word is correctly matched with its code.

13. (C): The code of "time passes" is "ab ef".

For Qs. No. (14-15):

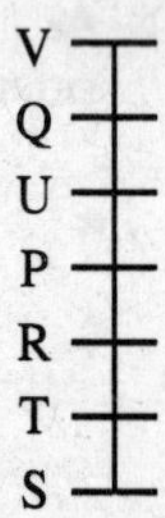

14. (B): There are four boys lighter then U.

15. (C): R is the third lightest boy.

17. (A): Let speed of the boat = x km/hr.
According to the question,

$$\frac{20}{x-4}+\frac{15}{x+4} = \frac{29}{12}$$

$$\Rightarrow \frac{20(x+4)+15(x-4)}{(x-4)(x+4)} = \frac{29}{12}$$

$$\Rightarrow \frac{20x+80+15x-60}{x^2-16} = \frac{29}{12}$$

$$\Rightarrow \frac{35x+20}{x^2-16} = \frac{29}{12}$$

$$\Rightarrow 29x^2 - 464 = 420x + 240$$

$$\Rightarrow 29x^2 - 420x - 704 = 0$$

$$\Rightarrow 29x^2 - 464x + 44x - 704 = 0$$

$$\Rightarrow 29x(x - 16)+ 44(x - 16) = 0$$

$$\Rightarrow (x - 16)(29x + 44) = 0$$

$$\Rightarrow (x - 16) = 0 \text{ or } 29x + 44 = 0$$

$$\Rightarrow x = 16 \text{ or } x = -\frac{44}{29}$$

$$\therefore x = 16$$

Speed of boat = 16 km/hr.

$$\text{Time taken} = \frac{64}{16-4} \text{ hrs.}$$

$$= \frac{64}{12}=\frac{16}{3}=5\frac{1}{3} \text{ hrs.}$$

18. (C): (P + Q + R)'s 1 day work $= \frac{11}{180}$

(P + Q)'s 1 day work $= \frac{1}{20}$

$$\therefore \text{R's 1 day work} = \frac{11}{180}-\frac{1}{20}$$

$$= \frac{11-9}{180}=\frac{2}{180}$$

$$= \frac{1}{90}$$

R can do whole work in 90 days

$$60\% \text{ of } 90 = \frac{60}{100}\times 90 = 54$$

Hence, R can do 60% of work in 54 days.

19. (D): Let, No. of boys = $3x$
and No. of girls = $2x$
Total marks obtained by boys = 90 × 3 = 270
Total marks obtained by boys and girls
= 92 × 5
= 460
Total marks obtained by girls = 460 − 270 = 190
Average marks obtained by girls $= \frac{190}{2} = 95$.

21. (D): Let length of rectangle = $3x$ m
and breadth of rectangle = $2x$ m
New length = $(3x + 5)$ m
and breadth = $2x$ m
New area of rectangle = $2x(3x + 5)$
$= 6x^2 + 10x$
According to the question,

$$6x^2 + 10x = 2600$$

$$\Rightarrow 6x^2 + 10x - 2600 = 0$$

$\Rightarrow 3x^2 + 5x - 1300 = 0$

$\Rightarrow 3x^2 - 60x + 65x - 1300 = 0$

$\Rightarrow 3x(x - 20) + 65(x - 20) = 0$

$\Rightarrow (x - 20)(3x + 65) = 0$

$\Rightarrow x = 20 \text{ or } x = -\frac{65}{3}$

Length of rectangle $= 3x = 3 \times 20 = 60$ m

Breadth of rectangle $= 2x = 2 \times 20 = 40$ m

Perimeter of original rectangle $= 30$ m

$= 2(l + b)$

$= 2(60 + 40)$

$= 2 \times 100$

$= 200$ m.

22. (C): 300 [149] 148 221 441 1101.5

$\times\frac{1}{2} - 1$ $\times 1 - 1$ $\times\frac{3}{2} - 1$ $\times 2 - 1$ $\times\frac{5}{2} - 1$

Hence, 149 will come at the place of question mark.

23. (B): 25 [100] 256 476 745 1050

+75 +156 +220 +269 +305

+81 +64 +49 +36

9^2 8^2 7^2 6^2

Hence, 100 will come at the place of question mark.

25. (B): Number of female was in Rampur before Sunday

$= \frac{16}{31} \times 124000$

$= 64000$

Total no. of female population in village Rampur on Sunday

$= 64000 + 1323$

$= 65323$

Required % $= \frac{65323}{1628} \times 100$

$= 4012.46\%$.

27. (A): $\because$ Revenue generating by male in museum B

$= 1628 \times x$

Revenue generating by female in museum B

$= 296(x - 5)$

Total revenue $= 1628x + 296(x - 5) = 94720$

$\Rightarrow 1628x + 296x - 1480 = 94720$

$\Rightarrow 1924x = 94720 + 1480 = 96200$

$\Rightarrow x = \frac{96200}{1924} = 50$

$\therefore$ Total revenue getting from male ticket from museum A $= 378 \times 50 =$ ₹ 18900.

28. (D): Total number of visitors in B, C and D

$= 1924 + 1920 + 2000$

$= 5844$

Average number of visitors $= \frac{5844}{3} = 1948.$

29. (E): I. $x^2 + 2x - 35 = 0$

$\Rightarrow x^2 + 7x - 5x - 35 = 0$

$\Rightarrow x(x + 7) - 5(x + 7) = 0$

$\Rightarrow (x + 7)(x - 5) = 0$

$\Rightarrow x = 5 \text{ or } -7$

II. $y^2 - 2y - 48 = 0$

$\Rightarrow y^2 - 8y + 6y - 48 = 0$

$\Rightarrow y(y - 8) + 6(y - 8) = 0$

$\Rightarrow (y - 8)(y + 6) = 0$

$\Rightarrow y = 8, -6$

Clearly, relation between x and y can not be established.

30. (E): I. $x^2 - 10x + 16 = 0$

$\Rightarrow x^2 - 2x - 8x + 16 = 0$

$\Rightarrow x(x - 2) - 8(x - 2) = 0$

$\Rightarrow (x - 2)(x - 8) = 0$

$\Rightarrow x = 2, 8$

II. $y^2 - 5y - 24 = 0$

$\Rightarrow y^2 - 8y + 3y - 24 = 0$

$\Rightarrow y(y - 8) + 3(y - 8) = 0$

$\Rightarrow (y - 8)(y + 3) = 0$

$\Rightarrow y = 8, -3$

Relation between x and y can not be established.

31. (C): In the passage, "since" is used to indicate a reason, similar to "because." The synonym "as" also serves this purpose, whereas "until", "before", "till" and "therefore" do not fit this context.

32. (D): "Form" in the context of the passage refers to a category or variety of something. "Type" is the synonym that best matches this meaning. The other options like "Damage", "Demolish", "Collapse", and "Scatter" do not fit the intended meaning.

33. (C): The correct phrase is "a study by the New York City Department of Consumer Affairs." This means the study was conducted by this department. "In", ""to", "on" and "with" would not be grammatically correct in this context.

34. (D): Some of the products that are included under the pink tax in India are salon services, personal care goods such as shampoos, soaps, and deodorants, as well as clothing, toys, and accessories such as jewelry. This statement accurately reflects the passage, which mentions these specific examples of products subjected to the pink tax in India. The other statements either contain incorrect information or are not mentioned in the passage.

35. (B): (*c*) and (*a*) are true

(*a*) The passage states, "This discrepancy includes apparel, toys, and healthcare products, among other things."

(*c*) The passage states, "Presently, women are heavily exploited by vegan products and non-animal-tested cosmetics that are significantly more expensive, a form of taxation."

(*b*) is false because the pink tax imposes an economic burden on women, not on both women and men.

36. (B): Market forces, driven by supply and demand dynamics, are the primary factors behind the pricing disparity known as the "pink tax." The passage mentions that "According to experts, the pricing disparity is due to market forces." This indicates that market dynamics, not government regulations or international trade agreements, are responsible for the pink tax.

37. (B): "Charged" in this context means being asked to pay a certain amount. "Imposed" fits this context as it implies facing a demand or requirement. The other options do not convey the same meaning.

38. (C): The passage states, "The largest discrepancy came to personal care/hygiene products, where women's products cost 13 per cent more than men's." This directly answers the question.

39. (C): It's a taxation form enforced by businesses where female products cost more than their male counterparts. The passage explains that the pink tax is not enforced by the government but by businesses and results in women's products costing more than similar men's products. The other options do not correctly define the pink tax as described in the passage.

40. (A): The error in the given sentence lies in part (*a*). The phrase "a attachment" should be "an attachment" because "attachment" begins with a vowel sound.

41. (B): The error in the given sentence lies in part (*b*). The phrase "with our lifestyle" should be "to our lifestyle" because the correct preposition to use with "alterations" in this context is "to."

44. (D): Among the options provided: Sustainable means able to be maintained or continued over a long period of time. It fits perfectly in describing long-term goals that are in the best interest of the country.

45. (B): The word "flaunt" means to display something ostentatiously or with pride in order to impress others. Using "flaunt" in this sentence implies that youngsters use smartwatches not just as a functional item but also as a fashion statement or accessory to show off or display in a noticeable way.

46. (A): The rise of social media has certainly revolutionized various aspects, including how we connect, share, and consume information.

47. (B): The emergence of influencers is one of the most significant changes brought about by social media in the realm of marketing.

48. (C): However, the influencer is not a buzzword anymore. Considering macro and celeb influencers, today's new-gen celebs, these individuals.

49. (D): Can significantly impact the psychology of potential consumers through their recommendations, opinions, and ideas, thereby shaping their purchasing decisions.

50. (A): Furthermore, with their substantial online followings and persuasive skills, they have emerged as critical players in determining consumers' buying behaviour.

51. (B): A structure in programming is used to store a collection of heterogeneous elements, meaning it can contain variables of different types (like int, float, char) grouped together under a single name. Arrays, on the other hand, consist of homogeneous elements, where all elements must be of the same type. Stacks and queues are data structures designed for specific types of data handling (LIFO and FIFO operations respectively) and typically hold elements of a single data type for consistency in operations. Therefore, the correct answer is B, as structures uniquely allow the combination of different data types in one defined entity.

52. (D): Analyzing each statement against the graph: Option A states there are 5 edges, which is correct as we see AB, AC, BC, CD, and a loop at D.

Option B, "A is adjacent to D," is incorrect because there is no direct edge connecting A and D; they are not adjacent. Option C, "There are 2 loops," is also incorrect as there is only one loop, evident at D. Given the inaccuracies in both B and C, option D, stating that both (B) and (C) are not true, is the correct choice. This approach confirms the accuracy of the answer by counting edges, identifying adjacency through direct connections, and observing loops directly on the graph.

53. **(D):** A self-referential structure is a structure that includes at least one element that is a pointer to a structure of the same type. This is crucial in creating complex data structures like linked lists, where each node points to the next node of the same structure type, enabling dynamic memory management and efficient data organization.

54. **(B):** In a stack, elements are added and removed from the top only, adhering to the Last In, First Out (LIFO) principle. This characteristic is foundational for functionalities like undo mechanisms in software, call stack management in programming, and for solving problems like bracket matching or reversing data.

55. **(B):** The provided diagram still represents a binary tree. Each node in the tree has at most two children, which aligns with the definition of a binary tree. Specifically, node A has two children, B and C. Node B has one child, D, and node C has one child, E. Nodes D and E have no children. A binary tree allows each node to have zero, one, or two children, and the given structure fits within this rule. It is not a proper binary tree because not every node has either zero or two children, nor is it a complete binary tree, where all levels except possibly the last are fully filled.

56. **(B):** In a binary tree with N nodes, there are always N+1 null pointers. This assertion is grounded in the property that in a binary tree, the number of edges (connections between nodes) is one less than the number of nodes, and each leaf node (node without children) has two null pointers, forming the structure's boundary.

57. **(B):** A database is a collection of data that holds information about a particular enterprise. It is an organized, digital store of data and its relationships. Unlike a DBMS (Database Management System), which is the software that manages databases, a database itself is simply the data and its structure.

58. **(A):** Constraints are the preferred method for enforcing data integrity in database systems. They maintain the correctness and validity of the data within the database by enforcing rules on data fields, commonly used constraints include primary keys, foreign keys, and unique constraints.

59. **(D):** A transaction log is a file that contains a record of all transactions and the database modifications made by each transaction handled by a DBMS. It is crucial for maintaining data integrity and is used in the recovery of the database to a known state in case of system failure.

60. **(B):** In a right outer join, records from the right table (right-side in the SQL join clause) that do not have matching keys in the left table are still included in the result set. This type of join ensures that if no matching keys are found in the left table, the result will still include the rows from the right table, filling in with null values for the select columns from the left table that do not have matches.

61. **(B):** Encapsulation allows changes to the data type of a data member without affecting the external code that interacts with it, as long as the interface through which interactions occur remains unchanged. This is possible because encapsulation hides the implementation details from the outside world, allowing internal modifications without external impacts.

62. **(D):** Private members of a class are not inheritable in their private state. To make them inheritable, they can be declared either as protected or public. Protected makes them accessible within the class itself and its derived classes but not outside, while public makes them accessible universally.

63. **(D):** The Waterfall model is a sequential design process, often used in software development processes, in which progress is seen as flowing steadily downwards (like a waterfall) through the phases of conception, initiation, analysis, design, construction, testing, deployment, and maintenance. This model is not suitable for accommodating changes once a phase is completed, making it inflexible compared to other iterative models like RAD or Prototyping, which allow for ongoing revisions and updates.

64. (B): Efficiency in software product design generally refers to how well the product performs under specific conditions and how well it utilizes resources like memory and processing power. Licensing does not affect the operational efficiency of the software but is related to legal and usage terms of the software.

65. (B): Historically, web browsers have been a significant target for exploits due to their ubiquity and complexity, as well as the sensitive data they handle. Browsers often serve as a vector for attacks due to their role in processing untrusted web content, making them vulnerable to a wide range of exploits.

66. (D): Automatic brute forcing tools are commonly used by attackers to compromise passwords. These tools systematically check all possible passwords until the correct one is found. This method exploits the vulnerability of systems that use password-based authentication without sufficient lockout policies or complexity requirements.

67. (D): The TCP/IP protocol stack, which forms the backbone of internet communication, does not include a 'Presentation' layer. The four layers typically recognized in the TCP/IP model are the Application, Transport, Internet (or Network), and Link layers. The Presentation layer is actually a concept from the OSI model, which is a different networking framework.

68. (C): DNS spoofing occurs when a DNS server accepts incorrect information from a host that does not have the authority to provide that information, leading to the server caching falsified data. This can redirect a user to malicious sites instead of the intended destinations, effectively deceiving the user about the identity of the server to which they are connecting.

69. (D): The <tr> tag in HTML is used to define a row in a table. Each row can contain one or more cells, which can be defined using <td> (table data) or <th> (table header) tags. The correct use of the <tr> tag is crucial for structuring the rows of a table in HTML documents.

70. (D): The continue statement in programming languages like C, C++, Java, and Python is used to skip the remaining code in the current iteration of a loop and proceed to the next iteration. This statement is particularly useful in controlling the flow of loops when certain conditions are met, allowing the loop to efficiently skip unnecessary processing.

71. (B): In the 1950s, computing systems were characterized by single stream batch processing, a method where computers ran one job at a time without any interactive processing. This period is noted for its early use of computers for large-scale, automated batch processing for tasks such as payroll.

72. (D): A macro kernel is a large operating system core that provides a wide range of services. Unlike micro kernels, which keep only essential services within the kernel and run other services in user space, macro kernels include more functionality in the kernel space, thereby increasing their size and scope but potentially improving efficiency and performance by reducing the number of context switches needed between user space and kernel space.

73. (A): Job Control Language (JCL) is a special type of programming language used in mainframe systems to instruct and manage job processing. It's particularly associated with systems that support batch processing, allowing for the setup of job flows and management of the system's tasks such as executing programs, handling files, and other job streams.

74. (D): Approaches to dealing with deadlock in computing include prevention, avoidance, and detection. Deletion is not a recognized strategy for handling deadlocks. Deadlocks are typically managed by ensuring they do not occur in the first place (prevention), by carefully allocating resources (avoidance), or by detecting them when they occur and resolving them (detection).

75. (B): User-level threads are managed without the need for kernel intervention, which makes them very effective as switching between these threads does not require a mode switch to kernel space. This leads to faster context switches compared to kernel-level threads, where the operating system kernel manages and schedules threads, necessitating a mode switch each time a thread change occurs.

76. (B): The sum of the seek time and the rotational delay is known as the access time. This measure is crucial in evaluating the performance of disk drives, as it represents the time it takes to locate the data on the disk and begin reading or writing.

77. (C): The mechanism that loads a page into memory only when it is needed is called demand paging. This efficient approach reduces the amount of memory used and avoids loading pages until they are required by a program, thereby improving the system's overall performance and resource utilization.

78. (B): A program responsible for assigning the CPU to the process selected by the short-term scheduler is known as the dispatcher. The dispatcher handles the task of context switching between processes, managing the transition of process states from ready to running, and then back to ready or another state as necessary.

79. (A): An arrangement of records in the sequence in which they arrive is known as a pile. This term reflects a simple storage structure where records are kept in the order they were added without any reordering or sorting, typically allowing fast insertions but potentially slower retrievals.

80. (D): The technique introduced to keep both the CPU and I/O devices busy by having multiple jobs in memory at the same time is called multiprogramming. This approach improves the utilization of both the CPU and peripheral devices by ensuring that the CPU can switch to another job when one job is waiting for I/O operations to complete, thus reducing idle time and increasing system efficiency.

81. (A): Seek time is crucial while accessing data on a disk as it represents the time it takes for the disk's read/write head to move to the position over the correct track on the disk platters where the data is stored. This movement is critical in determining how quickly data can be accessed from the disk.

82. (B): In the hold and wait condition, processes are allowed to request new resources without releasing the resources that they are currently holding. This condition is one of the four necessary conditions for deadlock, where processes continue to hold onto resources while requesting additional ones, potentially leading to a cycle where no progress is possible.

83. (B): In computer security, integrity means that computer system assets can only be modified by authorized parties. This ensures that the data is accurate, reliable, and can only be altered in authorized ways, thus protecting the data from unauthorized changes or corruption.

84. (B): Zombies are computers that have been compromised by hackers and are used in denial of service attacks, typically against targeted websites. A zombie computer is remotely controlled by an attacker and used to perform malicious tasks without the owner's knowledge.

85. (C): The shortest job first (SJF) scheduling algorithm is optimal in terms of minimizing the average waiting time of a given set of processes. This algorithm prioritizes processes based on the shortest next CPU burst, allowing shorter tasks to finish quicker, which reduces the average time each process waits to complete.

86. (A): Mutual exclusion is a concurrency control property that ensures that if one process is in a critical region—part of the code where shared resources are accessed—then all other processes are excluded from executing that same critical region at the same time. This is fundamental to prevent concurrent access that could lead to errors or inconsistent state of the shared resource.

87. (D): The principle of locality of reference justifies the use of cache memory. This principle states that programs tend to reuse data and instructions close to those they have used recently. Cache memory takes advantage of this by storing data that has been recently accessed or is likely to be accessed soon, significantly speeding up data access times.

88. (B): Buffering is a technique where input transfers are done in advance, and output transfers are done afterward. This method is used to manage data transmission smoothly by temporarily holding data in a buffer while it is being transferred between devices or processes, helping to handle speed differences between producers and consumers of the data.

89. (C): Virtual memory is a system that gives users the illusion of having a very large main memory by using disk space to extend the actual physical memory of a computer. This allows for larger programs to be run and for more programs to be run concurrently than would otherwise be possible with the available physical memory.

90. (A): In a monolithic kernel model, the operating system services such as process management, memory management, and device management are all provided within one large kernel. This model contrasts with micro kernel architectures, where the kernel provides only the most fundamental services such as low-level address space management, thread management, and inter-process communication.

91. (B): A Virtual Private Network (VPN) extends a private network across public networks. It allows a device to connect through the internet to a private network, ensuring that the data transmitted remains private through encryption and other security measures.

92. (B): The transmission data rate is decided by the physical layer of the OSI model. This layer is responsible for the transmission and reception of unstructured raw data between a device and a physical transmission medium, including the bit rate control.

93. (A): The data link layer takes the packets from the network layer and encapsulates them into frames for transmission. This process includes framing, physical addressing, and error handling to ensure reliable data transfer across physical networks.

94. (A): CRC stands for Cyclic Redundancy Check, which is a method used to detect accidental changes to raw data in digital networks and storage devices. CRC is used in the data link layer to ensure that the frames transmitted over the network are free from errors.

95. (A): The Domain Name System (DNS) translates internet domain and host names to IP addresses. It functions like a phone directory for the internet by translating the domain name that people can read and remember into the numerical IP addresses needed for the purpose of locating and identifying computer services and devices with the underlying network protocols.

96. (A): The entire hostname, as defined in Internet standards (RFC 1035), has a maximum of 255 characters. This includes the actual name and the dots that separate the different levels of the domain.

97. (C): URL stands for Uniform Resource Locator. It is the address used to access a resource on the internet, providing the methods for retrieving it, such as HTTP or FTP, and the location of the resource, expressed as a host name and path.

98. (D): StarBand provides satellite internet access. This service enables internet connectivity through a satellite dish, allowing data to be transmitted to and from a satellite orbiting the Earth, useful especially in remote or rural areas where traditional cable or fiber-optic connections are not available.

99. (B): While the answer provided is TSL, the correct term and abbreviation is TLS, which stands for Transport Layer Security. This cryptographic protocol is used to secure HTTP connections, ensuring that data transferred between web servers and browsers remains private and secure.

100. (A): IP (Internet Protocol) does handle addressing conventions, datagram formats, and packet handling conventions, but it does not provide error reporting. Error reporting and diagnostics are handled by additional protocols like ICMP (Internet Control Message Protocol), not by IP itself.

101. (A): The WebSocket protocol uses the publish-subscribe communication model, enabling open connections between clients and servers for two-way ongoing communications. In this model, servers can "publish" messages to clients subscribing to those messages without a specific request being made for each message, facilitating real-time web applications.

102. (A): The primary computing engine behind OpenStack for handling compute resources is NOVA. It is responsible for creating and managing large numbers of virtual servers and instances through OpenStack's API interfaces.

103. (C): If the IP address or hostname of a data node changes, the namenode does not need to update the mapping between the file name and block name. This is because the namenode tracks blocks by their IDs within the file system's metadata, not by the IP address or hostname of the data nodes.

104. (B): Webmetrics is used for web performance management and load testing. This tool specializes in monitoring and testing the performance of websites, applications, and services to ensure they operate at optimal levels under various load conditions.

105. (B): Disk imaging is the process of making an archival or backup copy of the entire contents of a hard drive. This includes the system, applications, and all files, creating a complete replica that can be restored in case of a system failure or other data loss events.

106. (B): Amazon Simple Queue Service (SQS) is a message queue system designed for distributed Internet-based applications. It supports programmatic sending of messages via web service applications as a way to communicate over the Internet.

107. (D): Amazon Relational Database Service (RDS) is a relational database service provided by Amazon. It simplifies setup, operation, and scaling of a relational database for use in applications. Common database management tasks such as migration, backup, recovery, and patching are managed by RDS.

108. (D): A Sparger controller is not a component of a SCADA (Supervisory Control and Data Acquisition) system. SCADA systems typically consist of components like database servers, I/O systems, and PLC (Programmable Logic Controller) controllers that manage field data interfaces, not sparger controllers which are more specific to certain types of industrial applications involving gas dispersion.

109. (A): The number of bindings of a node to other actors in the graph representation of a network is called the node degree.

It quantifies the number of edges connected to the node, which can indicate the node's connectivity and influence within the network.

110. (B): Calculating the location of a mobile device from signals sent by the device to base stations is known as terminal-based positioning. This method involves the mobile device calculating its own position based on the signals from multiple nearby base stations and using methods such as time of arrival (TOA) or time difference of arrival (TDOA).

YOUR SPACE

Professional Knowledge

GENERAL IT KNOWLEDGE

SOFTWARE DEVELOPMENT

1. What is Data Structure?

A. Addresses of the variables
B. Subset of all variables
C. The memory representation of data
D. The type of the variables

2. A tool for specifying logical properties of a data type is:

A. Abstract Data Type
B. Logical Data Type
C. Non Abstract Data Type
D. Linear Data Type

3. The Separation of data structures and their operations from the implementation of the data structures in memory and functions is called _______.

A. Data Abstraction B. Data Hiding
C. Data Extraction D. Data Insertion

4. An example of a dynamic data structure is:

1. array
2. record
3. list
4. index

A. 1 and 3 B. 2 and 4
C. Only 2 D. Only 4

5. Which of the following is a collection of heterogeneous elements?

A. Array B. Structure
C. Stack D. Queue

6. Which Data Structure is used to manage Printer Buffer?

A. Stack B. Queue
C. Linked List D. Tree

7. Which one of the following is a hierarchical data structure?

1. Linked list
2. Stack
3. Tree
4. None

A. 1 and 3 B. 2 and 4
C. Only 2 D. Only 4

8. Complexity in terms of machine cycles of a data structure is measured in terms of:

A. Time Complexity
B. Space Complexity
C. Mean Complexity
D. (A) and (B)

9. Which data structure is used in evaluating mathematical expressions with parentheses?

A. Stack B. Queue
C. Tree D. Graph

10. Which of the following occupies more memory with same number of elements?

A. Array B. Single Linked list
C. Doubly Linked list D. Queue

11. Recursive function implements which mechanism?

1. Queue
2. Lifo
3. Filo
4. Fifo

A. Only 1 B. 2 and 3
C. 1 and 4 D. All of these

12. Which of the following abstract data types cannot be used to represent a many to many relation?

1. Binary Tree
2. Graph
3. Stack

A. 1 and 2 B. 2 and 3
C. 1 and 3 D. All of these

13. An example of linear Data structures ?

1. Array
2. Stack
3. Linked List

A. 1 and 2 B. 2 and 3
C. 1 and 3 D. All of these

14. The logical picture of data type plus the specification of operations required to create & manipulate objects of this type is known _______.

A. Structure B. Pointer
C. ADT D. Class

15. Which of the following diagram(s) describe a problem solving process correctly?

A. [Mathematical model / Pseudo code Language] → [Abstract data type / Informal Algorithm] → [Data Structure / Java program]

B. [Mathematical model / Informal Algorithm] → [Abstract data type / Pseudo-code Language] → [Data Structure / Java program]

C. [Mathematical model / Informal Algorithm] → [Abstract data type / Java program] → [Data Structure / Pseudo code Language]

D. [Mathematical model / Abstract data type] → [Pseudo code Language / Java program] → [Data Structure / Informal Algorithm]

16. Consider the following program segment:

```
public void swap()
{
int x, y, z;
...... (i) ......
...... (ii) ......
...... (iii) ......
}
```

Identify suitable statements to fill in the blank lines of the above algorithm so that it will interchange the values of the two variables x and y.

A. (*i*) $x = y$; (*ii*) $z = y$; (*iii*) $y = z$;
B. (*i*) $z = x$; (*ii*) $x = y$; (*iii*) $y = z$;
C. (*i*) $z = x$; (*ii*) $z = y$; (*iii*) $y = x$;
D. (*i*) $z = y$; (*ii*) $y = x$; (*iii*) $x = z$;

17. Consider the following characteristics connected with a program.

(*i*) The input to the program
(*ii*) The time complexity of the algorithm underlying the program
(*iii*) The quality of the compiler
(*iv*) The nature and speed of the machine

The knowledge of which of the above is needed to calculate the exact running time of a program?

A. (*i*) and (*ii*) only
B. (*i*), (*ii*) and (*iii*) only
C. (*i*), (*ii*) and (*iv*) only
D. (*i*), (*iii*) and (*iv*) only

18. The following are operations regarding a data structure.

(*i*) Traversing: accessing each record exactly once so that certain items in the record may be processed
(*ii*) Searching: finding the location of the record with a given key value
(*iii*) Inserting: appending a new record to a structure only in the end.
(*iv*) Deleting: removing a record from the structure

Which of them are correctly described?

A. (*i*) and (*iii*) only B. (*ii*), (*iii*) and (*iv*) only
C. (*i*), (*ii*) and (*iv*) only D. (*i*) and (*iv*) only

19. {2,8,6,1,10,15,3,12,11} is a set of integers. If you create a maximum heap and store it in an array, what would be the final values in the array?

A. 1,2,3,6,8,10,11,12,15
B. 15,12,11,10,8,6,3,2,1
C. 15,12,6,11,10,2,3,8,1
D. 15,12,10,11,2,6,3,1,8

20. Consider the following polynomial.

$f(n) = n^2 + 100n + \log_{10}n + 1000$

What would be the Big–O value of the above polynomial?

A. n B. $\log n$
C. $n^2 + \log n$ D. n^2

21. Which of the following graphs is a tree?

A.
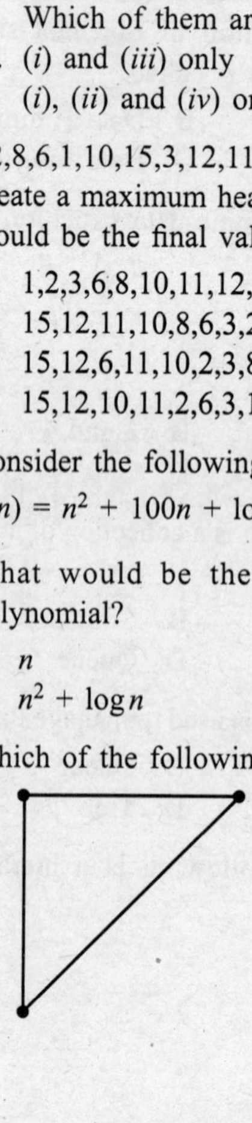

B.
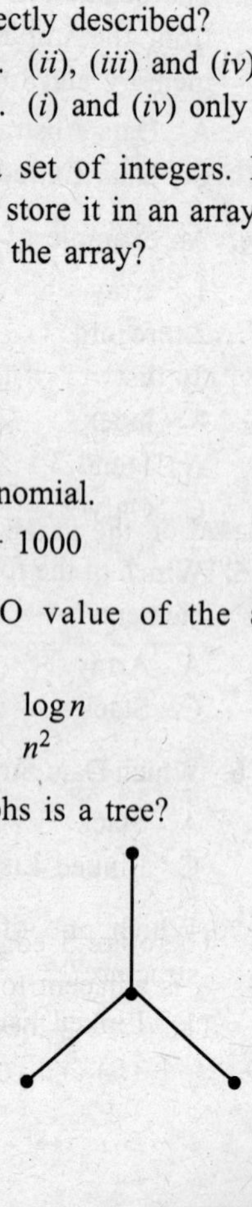

C. 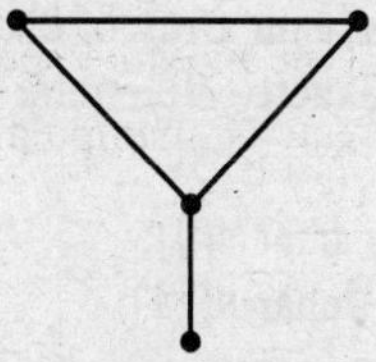

D. Both (B) and (C)

22. Given the rooted tree below, which of the following is FALSE?

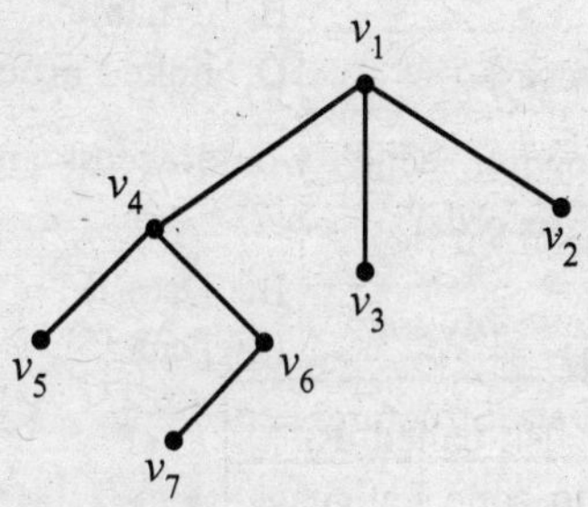

A. The root of the tree is v_1.
B. The height of the tree is 3.
C. v_1 is a descendent of v_1.
D. Both (B) and (C)

23. Given the binary tree below, the preorder traversal is ________.

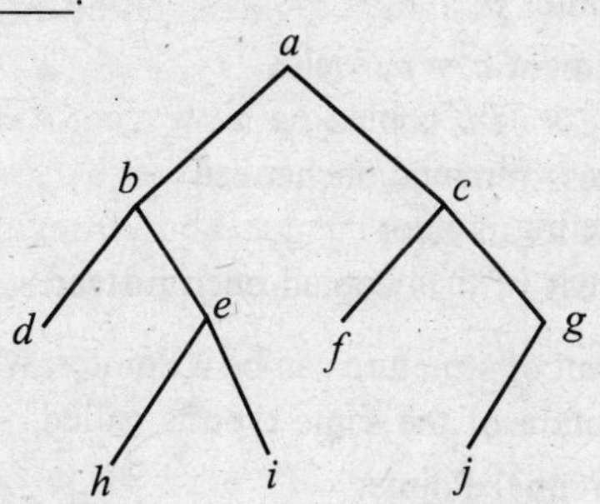

A. abehidcgjf　　B. dbheiafcjg
C. jgfcihedba　　D. abdehicfgj

24. Given the fully parenthesized expression ((A + B) – C), the prefix form of this expression would be________.

A. +–ABC　　B. –A+BC
C. A_B+C　　D. –+ABC

25. Based on the graph below, which of the following is NOT true?

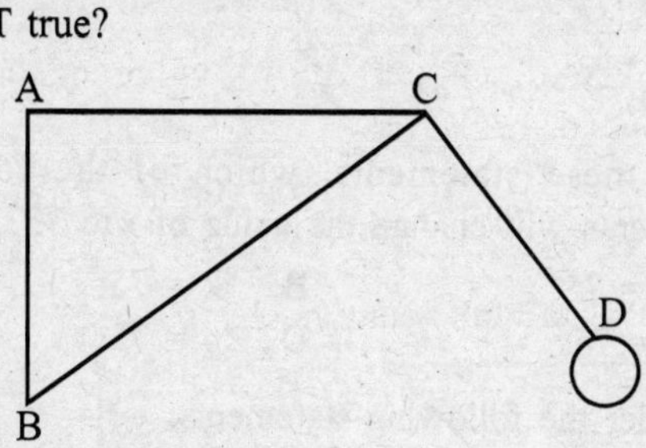

A. There are 5 edges
B. A is adjacent to D
C. There are 2 loops
D. Both (B) and (C)

26. Based upon the graph below, which of the following is true?

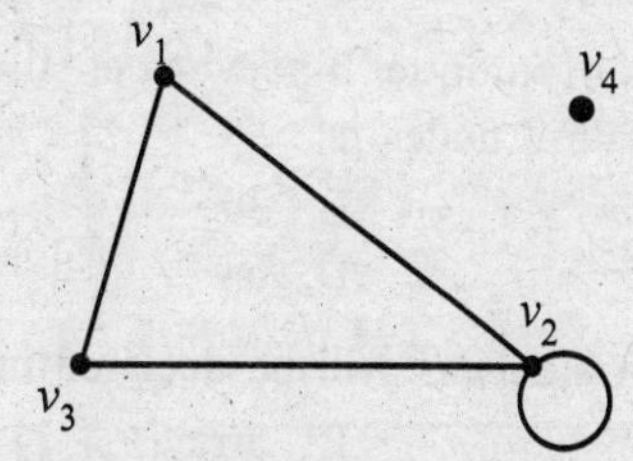

A. $\deg(v_1) > \deg(v_3)$
B. $\deg(v_2) = 3$
C. v_1 is an isolated vertex
D. Both (A) and (C)

27. A complete graph G is known to have 10 edges. Then the number of vertices must be:

A. 20　　B. 11
C. 5　　D. 6

28. Consider the graph below. Which of the following is the correct adjacency matrix for this graph?

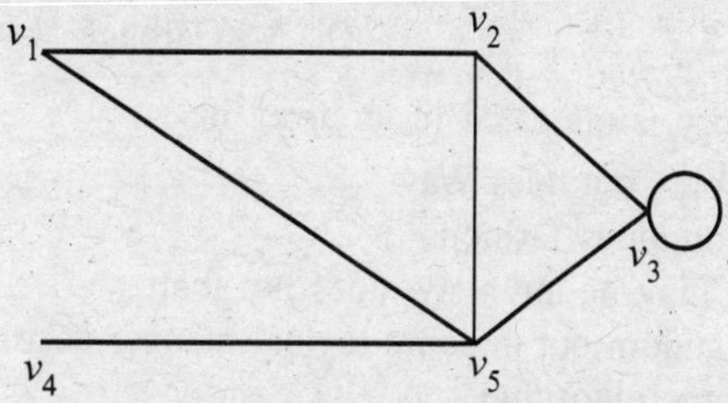

A. $\begin{pmatrix} 1 & 0 & 1 & 1 & 0 \\ 0 & 1 & 0 & 1 & 0 \\ 1 & 0 & 0 & 1 & 0 \\ 1 & 1 & 1 & 1 & 0 \\ 0 & 0 & 0 & 0 & 1 \end{pmatrix}$　　B. $\begin{pmatrix} 0 & 1 & 0 & 0 & 1 \\ 1 & 0 & 1 & 0 & 1 \\ 0 & 1 & 1 & 0 & 1 \\ 0 & 0 & 0 & 0 & 1 \\ 1 & 1 & 1 & 1 & 0 \end{pmatrix}$

C. $\begin{pmatrix} 0 & 1 & 0 & 0 & 1 \\ 1 & 0 & 1 & 0 & 1 \\ 0 & 1 & 0 & 0 & 1 \\ 0 & 0 & 0 & 0 & 1 \\ 1 & 1 & 1 & 1 & 0 \end{pmatrix}$　　D. $\begin{pmatrix} 2 \\ 3 \\ 3 \\ 1 \\ 4 \end{pmatrix}$

29. The output of the following program is?

```
main ()
    {
    Char p[]="string";
    Char t;
    Int i,j;
    for (i=0,j=strlen(p);i<j;i++)
    {
    t=p[i]; p[i]=p[j-i]; p[j-i]=t;
    }
    printf("%s",p);
    }
```

A. Gnirts B. String
C. Nothing is printed D. Gnirt

30. The number of unique binary trees that can be constructed with 3 nodes is:

A. 5 B. 30
C. 10 D. 6

31. An array of *n* elements will be declared in *c* as:

A. array[*n*] B. array[*n* – 1]
C. array[*n* + 1] D. array

32. The first element of a 0 based array can be accessed by:

A. array B. array[0]
C. array[*n* – 1] D. array[*n*]

33. What will be the piece of code reveal... int a[] = {1,2,3,4,5,6,7,8,9,0}; printf("%d",a[2]); printf("%d",2[a]);
** Regarding the fact that there are no syntax errors.

A. 3 8 B. Logical error
C. 3 3 D. 3 <Garbage Value>

34. Memory is allocated in an array in:

A. Non Continues Way
B. Continues fashion
C. It may be any way, does not matter
D. Random but in some logical manner according to some algorithm.

35. How is this resolved.. Arr[2];

A. *(&Arr + 2)
B. Arr[0] + 2
C. The Second position from Arr[0]
D. *(Arr + 2)

36. Lower bound and Upper bound of an Array represent the following element..

A. Largest and Smallest Resp.
B. Smallest and Largest + 1
C. Smallest and Largest – 1
D. Smallest and Largest Resp.

37. In an Array the range specifies...

A. Scope of the Array
B. Nos. of Elements in the Array
C. The Group of the Array
D. Size – 1 of the Array

38. If Upper bound is represented by 99 and lower bound by 0 in a O based array, then the range of the array is....

A. 0 B. 99
C. 100 D. 101

39. A string is ended by.....

A. The Last Character B. The Null Character
C. The Dot Character D. The First Character

40. Suppose that you want to declare an array of characters to hold a C++ string with exactly 9 letters. Which declaration is best?

A. char s[8]; B. char s[9];
C. char s[10]; D. char s[11];

41. Which of the following can be used to describe arrays as well as hard disks?

A. static B. dynamic
C. direct access D. linked access

42. Of the following, which would access an element of an array of records?

A. Data[i] B. Data(i)
C. Data(i,j) D. Data.i

43. Arrays are also called as:

1. Dense lists
2. Predefined variables
3. Static data structures

A. 1 and 2 B. 2 and 3
C. 1 and 3 D. All of these

44. If *a* is an array (which actually is a pointer as such) and a pointer *p*;
The statement *a* = *p*, yields

A. Address of *p* copied on *a*
B. Address remains unchanged
C. Leads to an error
D. Address of *a* is copied on *p* instead.

45. An element of structure can be a Pointer; which points to a structure of the same type is called:

A. Referential Pointer
B. Structure Pointer
C. Pointer Structure
D. Self-Referential Structure

46. Consider the following statements:

```
int *p;
int i;
int k;
i = 42;
k = i;
p = &i;
```

After these statements, which of the following statements will change the value of i to 75?

A. K = 75 B. *k = 75;
C. p = 75; D. *p = 75;

47. Consider the following statements:

```
int i = 42;
int j = 80;
int *p1;
int *p2;
```

```
p1 = &i;
p2 = &j;
*p1 = *p2;
printf("%d%d",i,j);
```

What numbers are printed by the output statement?

A. 42 and then another 42
B. 42 and then 80
C. 80 and then 42
D. 80 and then another 80

48.
```
void main()
{
        int *p1,*p2;
        p1=(int *)malloc(sizeof(int));
        p2=(int *)malloc(sizeof(int));
        *p1=17;
        *p2=153;
1st O/p printf("\n%d.....%d..",*p1,*p2);
        free( p1);
        p1=p2;
2nd O/p printf("\n%d....%d..",*p1,*p2);
        *p1=253;
3rd O/p printf("\n%d....%d..",*p1,*p2);
        *p2=355;
4th O/p printf("\n%d.....%d..",*p1,*p2);
}
```

What will be the O/p at O/p 4.

A. 17....153 B. 253....253
C. 253....353 D. 353....353

49. What is printed by these statements?

```
int i = 1;
int k = 2;
int *p1;
int *p2;
p1 = &i;
p2 = &k;
p1 = p2;
*p1 = 3;
*p2 = 4;
printf("%d",i);
```

A. 1 B. 2
C. 3 D. 4

50. What is printed by these statements?

```
int i = 1;
int k = 2;
int* p1;
int* p2;
p1 = &i;
p2 = &k;
p1 = p2;
*p1 = 3;
*p2 = 4;
printf("%d", k);
```

A. 1 B. 2
C. 3 D. 4

51. What is printed by these statements?

```
int i = 1;
int k = 2;
int* p1;
int* p2;
p1 = &i;
p2 = &k;
*p1 = *p2;
*p1 = 3;
*p2 = 4;
printf("%d",i);
```

A. 1 B. 2
C. 3 D. 4

52. In which location do dynamic variables reside?

A. The code segment. B. The data segment.
C. The heap. D. The run-time stack.

53. Suppose you have the following function prototype and variable declaration:

```
void goop(int z[ ]);
int x[10];
```

Which is the correct way to call the goop function with x as the argument:

A. goop(x); B. goop(x[ ]);
C. goop(x[10]); D. goop(&x);

54. What's wrong with this code?

```
char *p;
*p = malloc(10);
```

A. No Error B. Logical Error
C. Syntax Error D. All of the above

55. Is there a problem with this code…if yes then what?

```
typedef struct {
        char *item;
                NODEPTR next;
        } *NODEPTR;
```

A. No Problem
B. The struct ptr cannot be defined inside the same struct
C. Problem with typedef
D. The struct has to be defined first

56. Does *p++ increment p, or what it points to

A. equivalent to *(p++)
B. equivalent to (*p)++
C. Gives Error
D. Equivalent to *(++p)

57. Here is a function declaration:

```
void goo(int* x)
{
    *x = 1;
}
```

Suppose that a is an int* variable pointing to some integer, and *a is equal to zero. What is printed if you print *a after the function call goo(a)?

A. 0 B. 1
C. address of a D. address of x

58. What is the problem if any...

```
int array[5], i, *ip;
for(i = 0; i < 5; i++) array[i] = i;
ip = array;
printf("%d\n", *(ip + 3 * sizeof(int)));
```

A. No Error
B. Prints 3
C. Prints Garbage (Logical Error)
D. Syntax Error

59. In the statement

Char * p1, p2;

A. Both are pointers
B. Only p1 is a char pointer but p2 is not
C. Neither p1 nor p2 are pointers
D. Syntax Error

60. What's wrong if any :

```
    struct abc{
    int a = 40;
    struct abc *n;
};
```

A. Nothing's Wrong
B. Error because of initialization
C. Error because of the pointer
D. Syntax Error

61. The '&' is known as________.

A. Referencing Operator
B. Dereferencing Operator
C. Memory Allocation Operator
D. Memory freeing operator

62. The '*' is known as ________.

A. Referencing Operator
B. Dereferencing Operator
C. Memory Allocation Operator
D. Memory freeing operator

63. Consider the code

```
int A;
    int * ptr = &A;
    int** ptp = &ptr;
```

ptp will yield:

A. The same value as in ptr
B. Value of A
C. The address of ptr
D. Will give an error, a pointer cannot be pointed

64. A Stack is a _______ DS

A. LIFO B. FIFO
C. LILO D. FILO

65. In a Stack the elements are entered from _____.

A. End B. Top
C. Random D. Bottom

66. The basic Operations on the Stack are

A. Push & Pop B. Insert & Delete
C. Enter & Remove D. Add & Subtract

67. Condition Checked before Pushing:

A. Stack Overflow
B. Stack Underflow
C. No Condition to be checked
D. Both the conditions

68. Consider the following statements.

(*i*) A stack is a list with the restriction that items are inserted or removed/deleted only at one position, namely the end of the list.
(*ii*) The general model is that one where there is some element that is at the top of the stack, and it is the only element that is visible.
(*iii*) A pop or top on an empty stack is generally considered an error in the stack ADT.
(*iv*) The fundamental operations on stacks are push and pop, where push is relevant to the removal of the most recently inserted element and pop is equivalent to an insertion.
(*v*) A stack is a list; insertion and deletion can be performed from both ends.

Which of the above statements is/are valid for stacks?

A. (*i*) and (*ii*) only
B. (*i*), (*ii*) and (*iv*) only
C. (*i*), (*ii*), (*iii*) and (*iv*) only
D. (*i*), (*ii*) and (*iii*) only

69. The following shows a series of stack operations.

(*i*) Push(5)
(*ii*) Push(8)
(*iii*) Isempty( )
(*iv*) Pop( )
(*v*) Push(3)
(*vi*) Pop( )
(*vii*) Pop( )
(*viii*) Pop( )
(*ix*) Isfull( )
(*x*) Push(3)

If the above series of operations is performed, what would be the set returned values?

A. {false, 8, 3, 5, error, false, 3}
B. {5, 8, false, 8, 3, 5, error, false, 3}
C. {false, 8, 3, 5, error, false}
D. {false, 8, 3, 5, false}

70. Consider the following operations and their definitions.

(*i*) Clear( ) :- Clear the stack.
(*ii*) Is_Empty( ) :- Remove all items from the stack.
(*iii*) Insert(x) :- Insert element x in to any location of the stack.
(*iv*) Delete(p) :- Delete the element from the position p.
(v) Top( ) :- Return and remove the topmost element from the stack.

Which of the above operations is/are valid in stacks according to the basic definitions?

A. (*i*), (*ii*) and (*v*) only B. (*i*) and (*v*) only
C. (*i*) only D. (*i*) and (*ii*) only

71. Consider the following infix expression.

((A+B)*C-(D-E))^(F+G)

Note: ^ denotes the power.

Equivalent postfix and prefix expressions are respectively

A. AB+C*DE--FG+^, ^-*ABC-DE+FG
B. AB+C*DE-FG+^, ^-*+ABC-DE+FG
C. AB+C*DE--FG+^, ^-*+ABC-DE+FG
D. AB+C*DE-FG+^, ^-*+ACB-DE+FG

72. One difference between a queue and a stack is:

A. Queues require dynamic memory, but stacks do not.
B. Stacks require dynamic memory, but queues do not.
C. Queues use two ends of the structure; stacks use only one.
D. Stacks use two ends of the structure, queues use only one.

73. If the characters 'D', 'C', 'B', 'A' are placed in a queue (in that order), and then removed one at a time, in what order will they be removed?

A. ABCD B. ABDC
C. DCAB D. DCBA

74. Suppose we have a circular array implementation of the queue class, with ten items in the queue stored at data[2] through data[11]. The CAPACITY is 42. Where does the push member function place the new entry in the array?

A. data[1] B. data[2]
C. data[11] D. data[12]

75. Consider the implementation of the queue using a circular array. What goes wrong if we try to keep all the items at the front of a partially-filled array (so that data[0] is always the front).

A. The constructor would require linear time.
B. The get_front function would require linear time.
C. The insert function would require linear time.
D. The is_empty function would require linear time.

76. In the circular array version of the queue (with a fixed-sized array), which operations require linear time for their worst-case behaviour?

A. front
B. push
C. empty
D. None of these operations require linear time.

77. If data is a circular array of CAPACITY elements, and last is an index into that array, what is the formula for the index after last?

A. (last % 1) + CAPACITY
B. last % (1 + CAPACITY)
C. (last + 1) % CAPACITY
D. last + (1 % CAPACITY)

78. I have implemented the queue with a circular array, keeping track of first, last, and count (the number of items in the array). Suppose first is zero, and last is CAPACITY-1. What can you tell about count?

A. count must be zero.
B. count must be CAPACITY.
C. count could be zero or CAPACITY, but no other values could occur.
D. None of the above

79. I have implemented the queue with a linked list, keeping track of a front pointer and a rear pointer. Which of these pointers will change during an insertion into a NONEMPTY queue?

A. Nothing changes B. Only front_ptr changes
C. Only rear_ptr changes D. Both change

80. Suppose top is called on a priority queue that has exactly two entries with equal priority. How is the return value of top selected?

A. The implementation gets to choose either one.
B. The one which was inserted first.
C. The one which was inserted most recently.
D. This can never happen (violates the precondition)

81. In which queue we can utilize location of deleted element again is called

A. Circular Queue B. Tree
C. Stack D. None of these

82. The time complexity of Deleting an element from a queue of *n* elements is?

A. O(1) B. O(*n*)
C. O(*n***n*) D. None of these

83. Consider the following queue with the indicated initial states and series of queue operations

								2	4
								q-front	q-rear

(*i*) Enqueue(1); (*iv*) Dequeue;
(*ii*) Enqueue(3); (*v*) Dequeue;
(*iii*) Dequeue; (*vi*) Dequeue;

If the above series of operations is performed, what is the final status of the queue?

A.

	q.front q.rear								

B.

q.front	q.rear								

C.

q.rear	q.front								

D.

	q.rear	q.front							

84. Consider the following statements:

(*a*) The queue can be implemented by a linked list.
(*b*) The queue can be implemented only by stack.
(*c*) There are references kept at both the front and the back of the list.
(*d*) The Queue can be implemented only by an array-based method.

Which of the above statement(s) is/are valid for the queues?

A. (*i*) only B. (*i*), (*ii*) and (*iii*) only
C. (*i*) and (*iii*) only D. (*i*), (*iii*) and (*iv*) only

85. Consider the following paragraph in connection with priority queues.

The priority queue is a ___(*i*)___ in which the intrinsic ordering of elements does determine the result of its basic operations. An ascending/descending priority queue is a collection of items which can be inserted ___(*ii*)___ and from which only the ___(*iii*)___ item can be removed.

Correct answers for the blank positions are

A. (*i*) tree (*ii*) highest (*iii*) smallest
B. (*i*) data structure (*ii*) arbitrary (*iii*) largest
C. (*i*) data structure (*ii*) arbitrary (*iii*) smallest
D. (*i*) data structure (*ii*) largest (*iii*) smallest

86. The following shows a series of queue operations:

(*i*) enqueue(5);
(*ii*) enqueue(3);
(*iii*) dequeue( );
(*iv*) enqueue(7);
(*v*) dequeue( );
(*vi*) front();
(*vii*) dequeue( );
(*viii*) dequeue( );
(*ix*) isempty( );
(*x*) enqueue(9);
(*xi*) enqueue(7);
(*xii*) size( );
(*xiii*) enqueue(3);
(*xiv*) enqueue(5)
(*xv*) dequeue( );

If the above series of operation is executed, what is/are the intermediate output values(s) that is/are not returned?

A. 11 B. Error
C. False D. 6

87. Which of the following operation(s) is/are supporting Priority queues?

A. Remove the largest item.
B. Replace the largest with a new item (unless the new item is the largest).
C. Change the priority of an item.
D. Remove any item.

88. The basic queue operations are given in List-A and definitions is given in List-B as follows:

List-A	List-B
1. Makeempty( )	(*p*) Construct the empty queue
2. enqueue(x)	(*q*) Delete item from the front of the queue
3. dequeue( )	(*r*) Insert item x to back end of the queue
4. getfront( )	(*s*) Return the back element of the queue
	(*t*) Return the front element of the queue
	(*u*) Delete element from the back end of the queue

Choose the best definition from List-B for each of the above four operations respectively in List-A.

A. 1 — (*p*), 2 — (*r*), 3 — (*q*), 4 — (*t*)
B. 1 — (*p*), 2 — (*r*), 3 — (*u*), 4 — (*s*)
C. 1 — (*p*), 2 — (*r*), 3 — (*u*), 4 — (*t*)
D. 1 — (*p*), 2 — (*r*), 3 — (*q*), 4 — (*s*)

89. Which option best describes this tree?

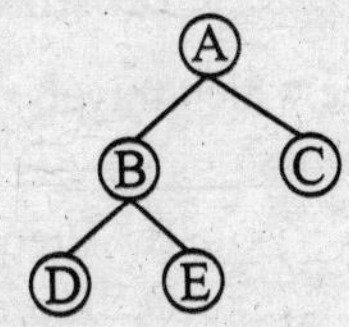

A. Not a tree B. A binary tree
C. A proper binary tree D. A complete binary tree

90. Which option best describes this tree?

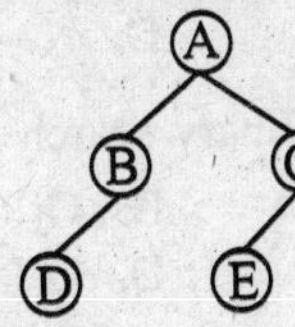

A. Not a tree
B. A binary tree
C. A proper binary tree
D. A complete binary tree

91. Which option best describes this tree:

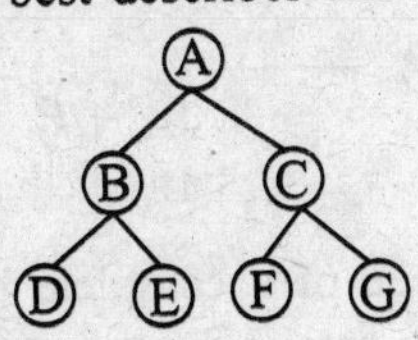

A. A binary tree
B. A proper binary tree
C. A complete binary tree
D. A perfectly balanced binary tree

92. Which option best describes this tree?

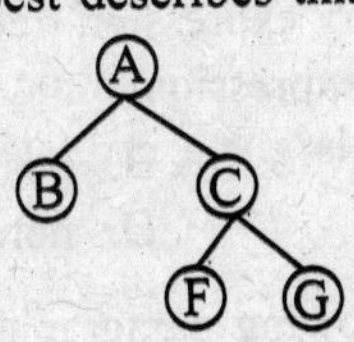

A. Not a tree
B. A binary tree
C. A proper binary tree
D. A complete binary tree

93. Which option best describes this tree?

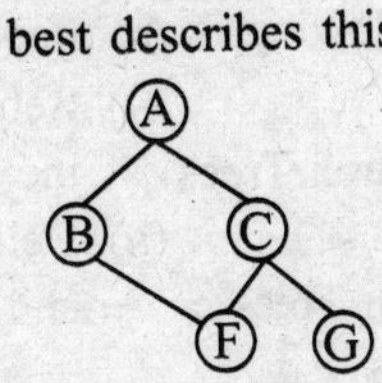

A. Not a tree
B. A binary tree
C. A proper binary tree
D. A complete binary tree

94. Which traversal around the tree will give the order D - E - B - F - G - C - A:

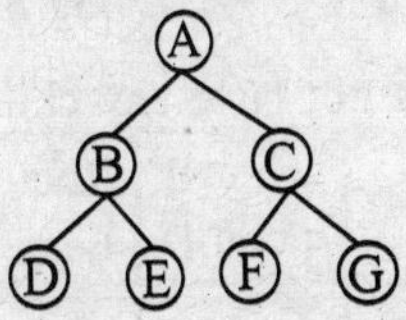

A. Pre-order traversal B. Post-order traversal
C. In-order traversal D. None of these

95. Which traversal around the tree will give the order D - B - E - A - F - C – G

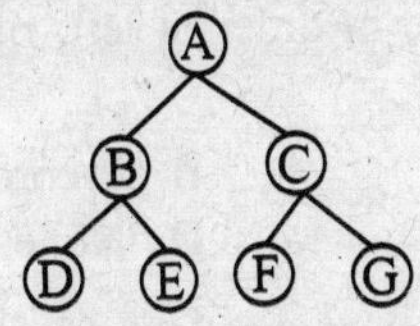

A. Pre-order traversal B. Post-order traversal
C. In-order traversal D. None of these

96. Which trees are heaps, with the heap ordering taken as <= on integers:

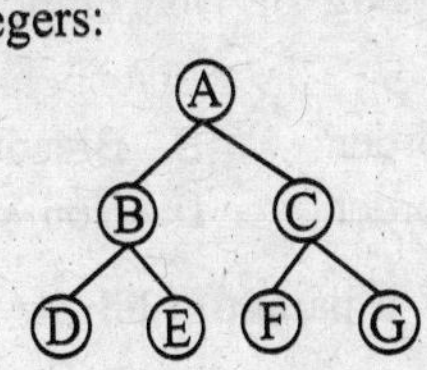

A. A, B, C B. A, C
C. A, C, D D. B

97. A Pre Order Traversing of Non empty Binary Tree is called ______.

A. BFS B. Depth-First Order
C. Linear D. Sequential

98. The Non leaf nodes of a tree are also known as ______ nodes.

A. internal B. external
C. outer D. root

99. A Binary Tree of height *h*, that contains exactly $2h - 1$ is called a ______.

A. B tree B. Complete binary tree
C. Fully Binary Tree D. AVL tree

100. A collection of one or more trees is ______.

A. Forest B. Graph
C. Complete binary tree D. Full binary tree

101. A balanced order-*n* multi way search tree in which each non-root node contains as least $(n - 1)/2$ keys is called as ______.

A. B Tree
B. Complete binary tree
C. Full binary tree
D. AVL tree

102. Height of a Complete Binary Tree that contains n elements is _______.

A. $\log(n*n)$
B. $\log_2(n + 1)$
C. $\log(n + 1)$
D. $\log(n)$

103. A node that does not have any child nodes is called:

A. Empty
B. Root
C. Child
D. Leaf

104. Tree with a difference of one in height of left and right sub-trees is called:

A. Binary tree
B. Binary search tree
C. AVL tree
D. Balanced binary tree

105. Traversing a tree in order of left, right and then root is called:

A. Inorder
B. Preorder
C. Postorder
D. None of these

106. What is the Level of the Root of a Tree:

A. 0
B. 1
C. –1
D. None of these

107. In Order Traversing of Non empty Binary Tree is called:

A. Depth-first order
B. Breadth-first order
C. Symmetric order
D. Non symmetric order

108. A node which is a parent of all the nodes is called:

A. Empty
B. Root
C. Child
D. Leaf

109. Of the following tree structure, which is efficient considering space and time complexities?

A. Incomplete Binary Tree
B. Binary Tree
C. Full Binary Tree
D. Complete Binary Tree

110. Traversing a tree in order of root, left and then right is called:

1. Preorder
2. Depth-first order
3. Inorder

A. 1 and 2
B. 2 and 3
C. 1 and 3
D. All of the above

111. Traversing a tree in order of left, root and then right is called:

1. Symmetric order
2. Depth-first order
3. Inorder

A. 1 and 2
B. 2 and 3
C. 1 and 3
D. All of these

112. Which of the following remarks about tree indexing are true?

1. It is efficient in dealing with strings of variable length
2. It is efficient if there are few member of data items
3. The number of disk accesses can't exceed the length of the particular string that is searched

A. 1 and 2
B. 2 and 3
C. 1 and 3
D. All of the above

113. In binary search tree which traversal is used for getting ascending order values _______.

A. Reverse order
B. Preorder
C. Postorder
D. Inorder

114. The numbers of null pointer are there in N number binary tree is _______.

A. N
B. N + 1
C. N/2
D. N – 1

115. The complexity of Binary search is _______.

A. $O(\log n*n)$
B. $O(\log (n + 1))$
C. $O(\log n)$
D. $O(\log n/2)$

116. The number of different trees are possible with n nodes are _______.

A. $n - 1$
B. $n + 1$
C. n
D. $n/2$

117. B-tree (failure nodes at same level) of nodes in k-ary tree of depth n is _______.

A. $1/n$
B. $1/k$
C. $1 + k$
D. $1 + n$

118. Consider the node of a complete binary tree whose value is stored in data[i] for an array implementation. If this node has a left child, where will the left child's value be stored?

A. data[i + 1]
B. data[i + 2]
C. data[2*i + 1]
D. data[2*i + 2]

119. Traversing a binary expression trees in preorder yields _______ form of expression.

A. prefix
B. postfix
C. infix
D. none of these

120. Consider the following paragraph.

A tree is a data structure consisting of nodes connected to each other with references. Each node in a tree may be connected to one or two nodes. Each node contains one or more data fields and two references.

Which of the following is/are properly describing the above paragraph?

A. Multiway search Trees
B. Binary Trees
C. Binary Search Trees
D. General Trees

121. Consider the following rules.

Rule 1: ***For Loop:*** The running time of a for loop is at most the running time of the statements inside the for loop (including test) times the number of iterations.

Rule 2: ***Nested Loop:*** The total running time of a statement inside a group of nested loops is the running time of the statement multiplied by the product of the sizes of all the loops.

Rule 3: ***IF/ELSE:*** For the fragment if(condition)

S1

else S2

the running time of an if/else statement is never more than the running time of the test plus the larger of the two numbers namely, the running time of S1 and that of S2.

Which of the following is a/are valid rule(s) in connection with analysis of algorithms?

A. Rule 3 only
B. Rule 1 and Rule 3 only
C. Rule 2 and Rule 3 only
D. All of these

122. Consider the following paragraph with blank positions.

If one finds a node with a/an ...... *(i)*......, he should stop the trace at that point. Consider the node with imbalance and ......*(ii)*...... on the layers immediately below this point on the path back to the new node. If these three nodes lie in a ......*(iii)*...... apply a ......*(iv)*...... rotation. If these three nodes lie in a dog-leg pattern (bend in the path), apply ......*(v)*...... rotation to correct the imbalance.

The above sentences are in connection with insertion of new nodes in to an AVL tree. Which of the following are correct words for the above blank positions?

A. *(i)* balance *(ii)* two nodes *(iii)* straight line *(iv)* single *(v)* double
B. *(i)* imbalance *(ii)* three nodes *(iii)* straight line *(iv)* single *(v)* double
C. *(i)* imbalance *(ii)* two nodes *(iii)* dog-leg *(iv)* single *(v)* double
D. *(i)* imbalance *(ii)* two nodes *(iii)* straight line *(iv)* single *(v)* double

123. Consider the following AVL tree.

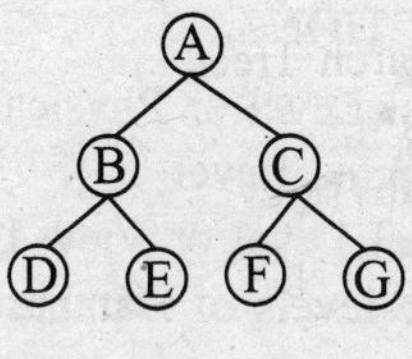

If one performs a left single rotation considering the Node A, what would be correct from among the following.

A. New root is Node C.
B. New root is Node B.
C. Node A's right child is Node F.
D. Node G's left child and right child are null.

124. Consider the following tree.

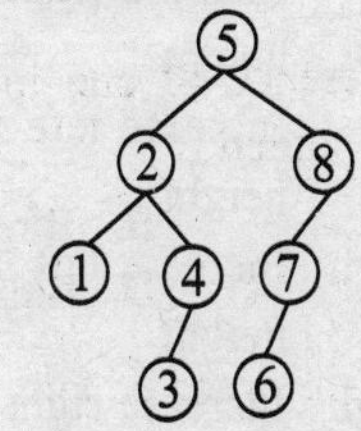

The above tree is a/an

A. AVL tree.
B. Binary Search Tree.
C. Binary Tree.
D. General Tree.

Directions (Qs. No. 125 to 127): *Given below a Binary Search Tree. Read the figure carefully and answer the questions that follow.*

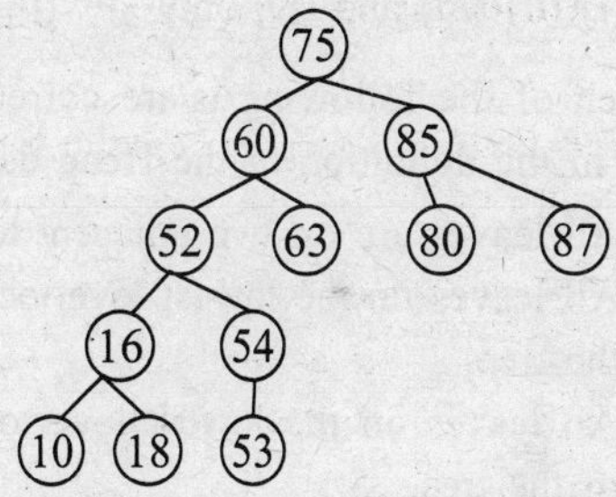

125. In above fig, if one wants to insert a new node p = 55, what is the correct insertion point without violating the binary search property?

A. Right child of node number 18
B. Right child of node number 53
C. Left child of node number 63
D. Right child of node number 54

126. In the above fig, if one wants to insert a new node p = 84 after inserting the new node p = 55, to the above tree, what is the correct insertion point without violating the binary search property?

A. Left child of node number 65
B. Left child of node number 63
C. Left child of node number 80
D. Right child of node number 80

127. In the above fig, if one wants to delete node number 60 from the tree after inserting the new node p = 55 and thereafter another at p = 84, what is/are the suitable replacing node(s) without violating the binary search properties?

A. Node number 63 B. Node number 54
C. Node number 52 D. Node number 53

128. Consider the following table.

	State on node	Effect of new node	Action of new state
(*i*)	Balanced	Increase left sub tree height	Left-high
(*ii*)	Balanced	Increase right sub tree height	Right-high
(*iii*)	Left-high	Increase left sub tree height	Left balance
(*iv*)	Right-high	Increase left sub tree height	Balanced
(*v*)	Right-high	Increase right sub tree height	Left balance

Which of the above would be correct for inserting a new node into an AVL tree?

A. (*i*) only
B. (*i*) and (*ii*) only
C. (*i*), (*ii*) and (*iii*) only
D. (*i*) (*ii*) (*iii*) and (*iv*) only

129. Which of the following is/are correctly describing a step in the definition of the Heap data structure?

A. All leaves are on two adjacent levels.
B. All leaves on the lowest level occur at the left of the tree.
C. All leaves on the lowest level occur at the right of the tree.
D. All levels above the lowest are completely filled.

130. Which of the following is/are AVL tree (s) ?

(*i*)
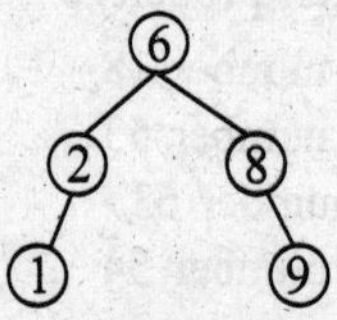
(*ii*)
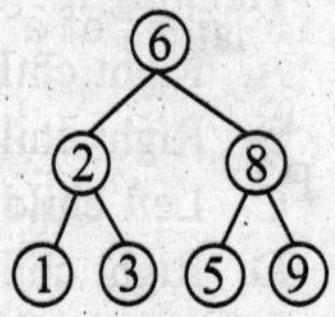
(*iii*)
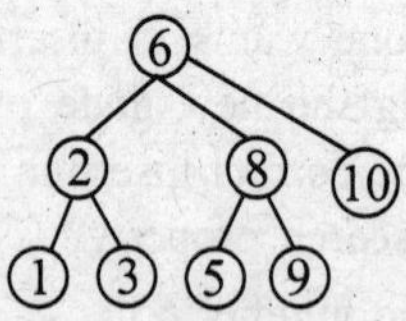
(*iv*)
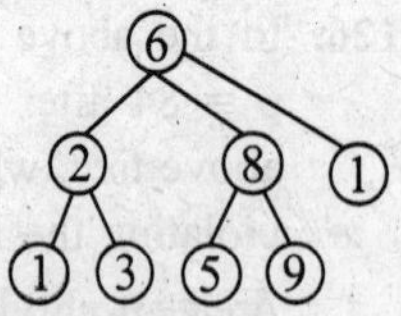

A. (*i*) only B. (*ii*) only
C. (*iii*) only D. (*iv*) only

131. {2, 8, 13, 6, 7, 27, 18}

If the maximum heap is created using the above set of integers, what would be the value at the 6th position of the heap?

A. 2 B. 8
C. 6 D. 13

132. The function that transforms a key into a table index is called a _______.

A. Hash function
B. Key function
C. Transformation function
D. Table function

133. One of the techniques of dealing with the hash collision is:

A. Chaining B. Addressing
C. Resolving D. Probing

134. ______ builds a linked list of all items whose keys hash to the same values.

A. Chaining B. Addressing
C. Resolving D. Probing

135. ______ involves using a secondary hash function on the hash key of the item.

A. Probing B. Addressing
C. Resolving D. Rehashing

136. The Collection of data, that contains information about one particular enterprise is known as?

A. DBMS B. Database
C. Data Dictionary D. Data file

137. The data dictionary tells the DBMS:

A. what files are in database
B. what attributes are possessed by data
C. what these file contain
D. All of the above

138. Data Dictionary contains detail of:

A. Data Structure B. Data flows
C. Data stores D. All of the above

139. Duplication of Data is known as?

A. Data Redundancy
B. Data Integrity
C. Data Inconsistency
D. Corrupt Data

140. Which of the following is not the objective of DBMS?

A. reducing DATA REDUNDANCY
B. controlling DATA INCONSISTANCY
C. facilitating sharing of data, ensuring data security and standards
D. All are the objectives of DBMS

141. Which of the following is not the level of DATABASE ABSTRACTION?

A. Internal Level or Physical Level or Low Level
B. Conceptual Level
C. External Level or View Level
D. All are levels of Database Abstraction

142. Database programs can do all of the following EXCEPT:

A. store and organize data.
B. create graphics.
C. communicate data.
D. manage information.

143. A key field must:

A. uniquely identify a record.
B. be used to connect two tables in the database.
C. be located in a minimum of three tables.
D. be common and used in many records.

144. In a(n) ________, data from more than one table can be combined.

A. key field B. relational database
C. file manager D. XML

145. _______ processing is used when a large mail-order company accumulates orders and processes them together in one large set.

A. Interactive B. Group
C. Real-time D. Batch

146. In a relational schema, each tuple is divided into fields called:

A. Relations B. Domains
C. Queries D. All of the above

147. In an ER model, ______ is described in the database by storing its data.

A. Entity B. Attribute
C. Relationship D. Notation

148. A top-to-bottom relationship among the items in a database is established by a

A. Hierarchical schema
B. Network schema
C. Relational Schema
D. All of the above

149. _______ table store information about database or about the system.

A. SQL B. Nested
C. System D. None of these

150. The candidate key is that you choose to identify each row uniquely is called ________.

A. Alternate Key
B. Primary Key
C. Foreign Key
D. None of the above

151. To eliminate duplicate rows ________ is used:

A. NODUPLICATE B. ELIMINATE
C. DISTINCT D. None of these

152. State true or false:

(*i*) A candidate key is a minimal super key.
(*ii*) A candidate key can also refer to as surrogate key.

A. (*i*) – true, (*ii*) – false B. (*i*) – false, (*ii*) – true
C. (*i*) – true, (*ii*) – true D. (*i*) – false, (*ii*) – false

153. _______ is the process of organizing data into related tables.

A. Normalization B. Generalization
C. Specialization D. None of the above

154. A _______ does not have a distinguishing attribute if its own and mostly are dependent entities, which are part of some another entity.

A. Weak entity B. Strong entity
C. Non attributes entity D. Dependent entity

155. _______ is the complex search criteria in the where clause.

A. Substring B. Drop Table
C. Predict D. Predicate

156. _______ is preferred method for enforcing data integrity.

A. Constraints B. Stored Procedure
C. Triggers D. Cursors

157. The number of tuples in a relation is called its _______. While the number of attributes in a relation is called it's ________.

A. Degree, Cardinality B. Cardinality, Degree
C. Rows, Columns D. Columns, Rows

158. State true or false.

(*i*) Select operator is not a unary operator.
(*ii*) Project operator chooses subset of attributes or columns of a relation.

A. (*i*) – true, (*ii*) – false B. (*i*) – true, (*ii*) – true
C. (*i*) – false, (*ii*) – true D. (*i*) – false, (*ii*) – false

159. ______ operator is basically a join followed by a project on the attributes of first relation.

A. Join B. Semi-Join
C. Full Join D. Inner Join

160. Which of the following is/are the DDL statements?

A. Create B. Drop
C. Alter D. All of the above

161. In snapshot, ______ clause tells oracle how long to wait between refreshes.

A. Complete B. Force
C. Next D. Refresh

162. _______ defines rules regarding the values allowed in columns and is the standard mechanism for enforcing database integrity.

A. Column B. Constraint
C. Index D. Trigger

163. The number of attributes in relation is called as its ________.

A. Cardinality B. Degree
C. Tuples D. Entity

164. The DBMS utility, ________ allows to reconstruct the correct state of database from the backup and history of transactions.

A. Backup B. Recovery
C. Monitoring D. Data loading

165. In RDBMS, Data is presented as a collection of ________.

A. Table B. Attributes
C. Relations D. Entities

166. To select all column from the table the syntax is:

A. select all from table_name
B. select * from table_name
C. select from table_name
D. None of the above

167. Identify the criteria for designing database from the point of view of user:

A. No redundancy
B. No inapplicable attributes
C. Uniformity in naming & definitions of the data items
D. D. All of the above

168. The ________ operator preserves unmatched rows of the relations being joined.

A. Inner join B. Outer join
C. Union D. Union join

169. The reasons leading to popularity of client-server systems are:

A. More powerful workstations on LANs
B. Needed for graphical user interfaces of end users.
C. Remove computing load for presentation services from the system managing a shared database resource
D. All of the above

170. The relational model is based on the concept that data is organized and stored in two-dimensional tables called ________.

A. Fields B. Records
C. Relations D. Keys

171. ______ contains information that defines valid values that are stored in a column or data type.

A. View B. Rule
C. Index D. Default

172. Which of the syntax is correct for insert statement?

(*i*) insert into <table_name> values <list of values>
(*ii*) insert into <table_name> (column list) values <list of values>

A. Only (*i*) B. Only (*ii*)
C. Both of them D. None of them

173. Drop Table cannot be used to drop a table referenced by a ______ constraint.

A. Local Key B. Primary Key
C. Composite Key D. Foreign Key

174. Which of the following fields in a student file can be used as a primary key?

A. Class B. Social Security Number
C. GPA D. Name

175. Which of the following is not an advantage of the database approach:

A. Elimination of data redundancy
B. Ability of associate deleted data
C. Increased security
D. All of the above

176. Which of the following contains a complete record of all activity that affected the contents of a database during a certain period of time?

A. Report Writer
B. Query Language
C. Data Manipulation Language
D. Transaction Log

177. In the DBMS approach, application programs perform the:

A. Storage function B. Processing functions
C. Access Control D. All of the above

178. A set of programs that handle a firm's database responsibilities is called:

A. Data Base Management System (DBMS)
B. Data Base Processing System (DBPS)
C. Data Management System (DMS)
D. All of the above

179. How many types of data structures are used in hierarchical model:

A. 2 B. 3
C. 4 D. 5

180. ______ commands in SQL allow controlling access to data within database:

A. Database B. Data
C. Data control D. All of these

181. SQL has how many main commands for DDL:

A. 1 B. 2
C. 3 D. 4

182. Which are main commands for DDL in SQL:

A. CREATE B. ALTER
C. DROP D. All of these

183. A ________ is a query that retrieves rows from more than one table or view:

A. Start B. End
C. Join D. All of these

184. A condition is referred to as ________:

A. Join in SQL B. Join condition
C. Both D. None

185. How many join types in join condition:

A. 2 B. 3
C. 4 D. 5

186. Which are the join types in join condition:

A. Cross join
B. Natural join
C. Join with USING clause
D. All of these

187. How many tables in a join query have no join condition:

A. 2 B. 3
C. 4 D. None of these

188. Which product is returned in a join query have no join condition:

A. Equijoins B. Cartesian
C. Both (A) and (B) D. None of these

189. Which is a join condition contains an equality operator:

A. Equijoins B. Cartesian
C. Both (A) and (B) D. None of these

190. Which command defines its columns, integrity constraint in create table:

A. Create command B. Drop table command
C. Alter table command D. All of these

191. It refers to set of one or more columns that designates the ________ key in a referential integrity constraint:

A. Select key B. Foreign key
C. Write key D. None of these

192. Which constraint that requires that the column contain a value when it is initially inserted into the table:

A. IS NULL B. NOT NULL
C. UNIQUE D. None of these

193. Which constraint that identifies a column or combination of columns as a unique key:

A. IS NULL B. NOT NULL
C. UNIQUE D. None of these

194. Which command is used for removing a table and all its data from the database:

A. Create command
B. Drop table command
C. Alter table command
D. All of these

195. Which command allows the removal of all rows from a table but flushes a table more efficiently since no rollback information is retained:

A. TRUNCATE command
B. Create command
C. Drop table command
D. Alter table command

196. Which join refers to join records from the write table that have no matching key in the left table are included in the result set:

A. Left outer join B. Right outer join
C. Full outer join D. Half outer join

197. Which view contains more than one table in the top-level FROM clause of the SELECT statement:

A. Join view
B. Datable join view
C. Updatable join view
D. All of these

198. Which option is used to create a view as a constrained view and prohibit specific insert and update operations with the view:

A. DATABASE
B. WITH CHECK OPTION
C. WITH WRITE OPTION
D. WITH OPTION

199. Which command is used to add the views to the database:

A. DATABASE VIEW B. CREATE VIEW
C. CREATE OPTION D. None of these

200. Which option is used with the WHERE clause:

A. DATABASE
B. WITH CHECK OPTION
C. WITH WRITE OPTION
D. WITH OPTION

201. Which was the first purely object oriented programming language developed?

A. Java B. C++
C. SmallTalk D. Kotlin

202. Which of the following best defines a class?

A. Parent of an object
B. Instance of an object
C. Blueprint of an object
D. Scope of an object

203. Who invented OOP?

A. Alan Kay B. Andrea Ferro
C. Dennis Ritchie D. Adele Goldberg

204. What is the additional feature in classes that was not in structures?

A. Data members B. Member functions
C. Static data allowed D. Public access specifier

205. Which is not a feature of OOP in general definitions?

A. Code reusability
B. Modularity
C. Duplicate/Redundant data
D. Efficient Code

206. Pure OOP can be implemented without using class in a program. (True or False)

A. True
B. False

207. Which feature of OOP illustrated the code reusability?

A. Polymorphism B. Abstraction
C. Encapsulation D. Inheritance

208. Which language does not support all 4 types of inheritance?

A. C++ B. Java
C. Kotlin D. SmallTalk

209. How many classes can be defined in a single program?

A. Only 1 B. Only 100
C. Only 999 D. As many as you want

210. When OOP concept did first came into picture?

A. 1970's B. 1980's
C. 1993 D. 1995

211. Which among the following best defines abstraction?

A. Hiding the implementation
B. Showing the important data
C. Hiding the important data
D. Hiding the implementation and showing only the features

212. Hiding the implementation complexity can ______.

A. Make the programming easy
B. Make the programming complex
C. Provide more number of features
D. Provide better features

213. Class is ______ abstraction.

A. Object B. Logical
C. Real D. Hypothetical

214. Object is ______ abstraction.

A. Class B. Logical
C. Real D. Hypothetical

215. Abstraction gives higher degree of ______.

A. Class usage B. Program complexity
C. Idealized interface D. Unstable interface

216. Which among the following best describes encapsulation?

A. It is a way of combining various data members into a single unit
B. It is a way of combining various member functions into a single unit
C. It is a way of combining various data members and member functions into a single unit which can operate on any data
D. It is a way of combining various data members and member functions that operate on those data members into a single unit

217. If data members are private, what can we do to access them from the class object?

A. Create public member functions to access those data members
B. Create private member functions to access those data members
C. Create protected member functions to access those data members
D. Private data members can never be accessed from outside the class

218. While using encapsulation, which among the following is possible?

A. Code modification can be additional overhead
B. Data member's data type can be changed without changing any other code
C. Data member's type can't be changed, or whole code have to be changed
D. Member functions can be used to change the data type of data members

219. Which feature can be implemented using encapsulation?

A. Inheritance B. Abstraction
C. Polymorphism D. Overloading

220. Find which of the following uses encapsulation?

A. void main(){ int a; void fun(int a=10; cout<<a); fun(); }
B. class student{ int a; public: int b;};
C. class student{int a; public: void disp(){ cout<<a;} };
D. struct topper{ char name[10]; public : int marks; }

221. Which among the following would destroy the encapsulation mechanism if it was allowed in programming?

A. Using access declaration for private members of base class
B. Using access declaration for public members of base class

C. Using access declaration for local variable of main() function
D. Using access declaration for global variables

222. Which among the following can be a concept against encapsulation rules?
A. Using function pointers
B. Using char* string pointer to be passed to non-member function
C. Using object array
D. Using any kind of pointer/array address in passing to another function

223. Consider the following code and select the correct option.

```
class student
{
    int marks;
    public : int* fun()
    {
        return &marks;
    }
};
main()
{
    student s;
    int *ptr=c.fun(); return 0;
}
```

A. This code is good to go
B. This code may result in undesirable conditions
C. This code will generate error
D. This code violates encapsulation

224. Consider the code and select the correct option.

```
class hero
{
    char name[10];
    public : void disp()
    {
        cout<<name;
    }
};
```

A. This code maintains encapsulation
B. This code doesn't maintain encapsulation
C. This code is vulnerable
D. This code gives error

225. Encapsulation is the way to add functions in a user defined structure.
A. True
B. False

226. Which among the following best describes the Inheritance?
A. Copying the code already written
B. Using the code already written once
C. Using already defined functions in programming language
D. Using the data and functions into derived segment

227. How many basic types of inheritance are provided as OOP feature?
A. 4 B. 3
C. 2 D. 1

228. Which among the following best defines single level inheritance?
A. A class inheriting a derived class
B. A class inheriting a base class
C. A class inheriting a nested class
D. A class which gets inherited by 2 classes

229. Which among the following is correct for multiple inheritance?
A. class student{public: int marks;}s; class stream{int total;}; class topper: public student, public stream {};
B. class student{int marks;}; class stream{ }; class topper: public student{ };
C. class student{int marks;}; class stream: public student{ };
D. class student{ }; class stream{ }; class topper{ };

230. Which programming language doesn't support multiple inheritance?
A. C++ and Java B. C and C++
C. Java and SmallTalk D. Java

231. Which among the following is correct for a hierarchical inheritance?
A. Two base classes can be used to be derived into one single class
B. Two or more classes can be derived into one class
C. One base class can be derived into other two derived classes or more
D. One base class can be derived into only 2 classes

232. Which is the correct syntax of inheritance?
A. class derived_classname : base_classname{ /*define class body*/ };
B. class base_classname : derived_classname{ /*define class body*/ };
C. class derived_classname : access base_classname{ /*define class body*/ };
D. class base_classname :access derived_classname{ /*define class body*/ };

233. Which type of inheritance leads to diamond problem?
A. Single level B. Multi-level
C. Multiple D. Hierarchical

234. Which access type data gets derived as private member in derived class?

A. Private B. Public
C. Protected D. Protected and Private

235. If a base class is inherited in protected access mode then which among the following is true?

A. Public and Protected members of base class becomes protected members of derived class
B. Only protected members become protected members of derived class
C. Private, Protected and Public all members of base, become private of derived class
D. Only private members of base, become private of derived class

236. Members which are not intended to be inherited are declared as ________.

A. Public members
B. Protected members
C. Private members
D. Private or Protected members

237. While inheriting a class, if no access mode is specified, then which among the following is true? (in C++)

A. It gets inherited publicly by default
B. It gets inherited protected by default
C. It gets inherited privately by default
D. It is not possible

238. If a derived class object is created, which constructor is called first?

A. Base class constructor
B. Derived class constructor
C. Depends on how we call the object
D. Not possible

239. The private members of the base class are visible in derived class but are not accessible directly.

A. True
B. False

240. How can you make the private members inheritable?

A. By making their visibility mode as public only
B. By making their visibility mode as protected only
C. By making their visibility mode as private in derived class
D. It can be done both by making the visibility mode public or protected

241. Which among the following best describes polymorphism?

A. It is the ability for a message/data to be processed in more than one form
B. It is the ability for a message/data to be processed in only 1 form
C. It is the ability for many messages/data to be processed in one way
D. It is the ability for undefined message/data to be processed in at least one way

242. What do you call the languages that support classes but not polymorphism?

A. Class based language
B. Procedure Oriented language
C. Object-based language
D. If classes are supported, polymorphism will always be supported

243. Which among the following is the language which supports classes but not polymorphism?

A. SmallTalk B. Java
C. C++ D. Ada

244. If same message is passed to objects of several different classes and all of those can respond in a different way, what is this feature called?

A. Inheritance B. Overloading
C. Polymorphism D. Overriding

245. Which class/set of classes can illustrate polymorphism in the following code?

```
abstract class student
{
    public : int marks;
    calc_grade();
}
class topper:public student
{
    public : calc_grade()
    {
        return 10;
    }
};
class average:public student
{
    public : calc_grade()
    {
        return 20;
    }
};
class failed{ int marks; };
```

A. Only class student can show polymorphism
B. Only class student and topper together can show polymorphism
C. All class student, topper and average together can show polymorphism
D. Class failed should also inherit class student for this code to work for polymorphism

246. Which type of function among the following shows polymorphism?

A. Inline function
B. Virtual function
C. Undefined functions
D. Class member functions

247. In case of using abstract class or function overloading, which function is supposed to be called first?

A. Local function
B. Function with highest priority in compiler
C. Global function
D. Function with lowest priority because it might have been halted since long time, because of low priority

248. Which among the following can't be used for polymorphism?

A. Static member functions
B. Member functions overloading
C. Predefined operator overloading
D. Constructor overloading

249. What is output of the following program?

```
class student
{
    public : int marks;
    void disp()
    {
        cout<<"its base class"
    };
    class topper:public student
    {
        public :
        void disp()
        {
            cout<<"Its derived class";
        }
    }
    void main() { student s; topper t;
    s.disp();
    t.disp();
}
```

A. Its base class; Its derived class
B. Its base class; Its base class
C. Its derived class; Its base class
D. Its derived class; Its derived class

250. Which among the following can show polymorphism?

A. Overloading ||
B. Overloading +=
C. Overloading <<
D. Overloading &&

251. Find the output of the following program.

```
class education
{
    char name[10];
    public : disp()
    {
        cout<<"Its education system";
    }
    class school:public education
    {
        public: void dsip()
        {
            cout<<"Its school education system";
        }
    };
    void main()
    {
        school s;
        s.disp();
    }
}
```

A. Its school education system
B. Its education system
C. Its school education system; Its education system
D. Its education system; Its school education system

252. Polymorphism is possible in C language.

A. True
B. False

253. Which problem may arise if we use abstract class functions for polymorphism?

A. All classes are converted as abstract class
B. Derived class must be of abstract type
C. All the derived classes must implement the undefined functions
D. Derived classes can't redefine the function

254. Which among the following is not true for polymorphism?

A. It is feature of OOP
B. Ease in readability of program
C. Helps in redefining the same functionality
D. Increases overhead of function definition always

255. If 2 classes derive one base class and redefine a function of base class, also overload some operators inside class body. Among these two things of function and operator overloading, where is polymorphism used?

A. Function overloading only
B. Operator overloading only
C. Both of these are using polymorphism
D. Either function overloading or operator overloading because polymorphism can be applied only once in a program

256. Which of this keyword must be used to inherit a class?

A. super B. this
C. extent D. extends

257. A class member declared protected becomes a member of subclass of which type?

A. public member B. private member
C. protected member D. static member

258. Which of these is correct way of inheriting class A by class B?

A. class B + class A {}
B. class B inherits class A {}
C. class B extends A {}
D. class B extends class A {}

259. Which two classes use the Shape class correctly?

A. public class Circle implements Shape
```
{
private int radius;
}
```
B. public abstract class Circle extends Shape
```
{
private int radius;
}
```
C. public class Circle extends Shape
```
{
private int radius;
public void draw();
}
```
D. public abstract class Circle implements Shape
```
{
private int radius;
public void draw();
}
```
E. public class Circle extends Shape
```
{
private int radius;
public void draw()
{
  /* code here */
}
}
```
F. public abstract class Circle implements Shape
```
{
  private int radius;
  public void draw()
  {
    /* code here */
  }
}
```
A. B, E B. A, C
C. C, E D. None of these

260. What will be the output of the following Java code?
```
class A
{
   public int i;
   private int j;
}
class B extends A
{
   void display()
   {
      super.j = super.i + 1;
      System.out.println(super.i + " " + super.j);
   }
}
class inheritance
{
   public static void main(String args[])
   {
      B obj = new B();
      obj.i=1;
      obj.j=2;
      obj.display();
   }
}
```
A. 2 2 B. 3 3
C. Runtime Error D. Compilation Error

261. Build & Fix Model is suitable for programming exercises of ______ LOC (Line of Code).

A. 100-200 B. 200-400
C. 400-1000 D. above 1000

262. RAD stands for:

A. Relative Application Development
B. Rapid Application Development
C. Rapid Application Document
D. None of the above

263. Which one of the following models is not suitable for accommodating any change?

A. Build & Fix Model
B. Prototyping Model
C. RAD Model
D. Waterfall Model

264. Which is not one of the types of prototype of Prototyping Model?

A. Horizontal Prototype
B. Vertical Prototype
C. Diagonal Prototype
D. Domain Prototype

265. Which one of the following is not a phase of Prototyping Model?

A. Quick Design B. Coding
C. Prototype Refinement D. Engineer Product

266. Which of the following statements regarding Build & Fix Model is wrong?

A. No room for structured design
B. Code soon becomes unfixable & unchangeable
C. Maintenance is practically not possible
D. It scales up well to large projects

267. RAD Model has:

A. 2 phases B. 3 phase
C. 5 phases D. 6 phases

268. What is the major drawback of using RAD Model?

A. Highly specialized & skilled developers/designers are required
B. Increases reusability of components
C. Encourages customer/client feedback
D. Both (A) & (B)

269. SDLC stands for:

A. Software Development Life Cycle
B. System Development Life Cycle
C. Software Design Life Cycle
D. System Design Life Cycle

270. Which model can be selected if user is involved in all the phases of SDLC?

A. Waterfall Model
B. Prototyping Model
C. RAD Model
D. Both (B) & (C)

271. Waterfall model is also called as?

A. Agile process model
B. Classic life cycle model
C. Light-Weight Model
D. None of the above

272. Software Requirements Specification document (SRS) might include:

A. Use cases B. Class diagram
C. Sequence diagram D. All of the above

273. Which of the following is not Users of a requirements document:

A. System Customer
B. System Engineer
C. Manager
D. System Architect

274. Which of these are the 5 generic software engineering framework activities?

A. communication, modeling, planning, construction, deployment
B. communication, planning, modeling, construction, deployment
C. analysis, designing, programming, debugging, maintenance
D. analysis, planning, designing, programming, testing

275. Which of the following are umbrella activities of Software Engineering.

A. Risk Management
B. Software quality assurance
C. Formal Technical Review
D. All of the above

276. What are attributes of good software?

A. Software maintainability
B. Software functionality
C. Software development
D. Both (A) & (B)

277. Which of these software engineering activities are not a part of software processes?

A. Software dependence
B. Software development
C. Software validation
D. Software specification

278. Which of these is true?

A. Generic products and customized products are types of software products
B. Generic products are produced by organization and sold to open market
C. Customized products are commissioned by particular customer
D. All of the above

279. _______ is the way in which we produce software.

A. Product B. Process
C. Metric D. Module

280. Which of the following is a phase(s) of software engineering?

A. Software analysis
B. Software Testing
C. Software Maintenance
D. All of the above

281. Efficiency in a software product does not include _______.

A. responsiveness B. licensing
C. memory utilization D. processing time

282. Which of the following is not a factor useful in decision making process?

A. Non availability of ready-made solutions
B. Cost of ready-made solutions
C. Past success or failure in software acquisition
D. Perceived risk

283. Scheduling in project management includes listing of:

A. activities
B. deliverables
C. milestones within a project
D. all of the above

284. Which of the following is not a type of schedules in project management:

A. Master project schedule
B. Milestone schedule
C. Complete project schedule
D. A detailed project schedule

285. Which one is not a step of requirement engineering?

A. Requirements elicitation
B. Requirements analysis
C. Requirements design
D. Requirements documentation

286. Requirements elicitation means:

A. Gathering of requirements
B. Capturing of requirements
C. Understanding of requirements
D. All of the above

287. SRS stands for:

A. Software requirements specification
B. System requirements specification
C. Systematic requirements specifications
D. None of the above

288. SRS document is for:

A. "What" of a system?
B. How to design the system?
C. Costing and scheduling of a system
D. System's requirement.

289. Which one is not a type of requirements?

A. Known requirements
B. Unknown requirements
C. Undreamt requirements
D. Complex requirements

290. Which one is not a requirements elicitation technique?

A. Interviews B. The use case approach
C. FAST D. Data flow diagram

291. Requirements review process is carried out to:

A. Spend time in requirements gathering
B. Improve the quality of SRS
C. Document the requirements
D. None of the above

292. FAST stands for:

A. Functional Application Specification Technique
B. Fast Application Specification Technique
C. Facilitated Application Specification Technique
D. None of the above

293. Code coverage analysis is used to measure which one of the following?

A. Thoroughness of testing
B. Quality of test cases
C. Quality of code
D. Distribution of bugs

294. Which one of the following is not a black box testing technique?

A. Boundary value testing
B. Cause-effect (Decision table) testing
C. Combinatorial testing
D. Basic condition testing

295. Which one of the following is an implicit assumption made in equivalence class testing?

A. A program behaves in similar ways to every input value belonging to an equivalence class.
B. Different equivalence classes of a program contain similar bugs
C. Different equivalence classes of a program contain dissimilar bugs
D. Equivalence classes define the behaviorally similar components of a program

296. Customers typically carry out which one of the following types of testing?

A. Unit testing B. Integration testing
C. Acceptance testing D. Regression testing

297. Which one of the following types of bugs may not get detected in black-box testing, but are very likely to be get detected by white-box testing?

A. Syntax errors B. Behavioral errors
C. Trojans D. Performance errors

298. White-box testing is also called:

A. functional testing
B. structural testing
C. fault oriented testing
D. None of the these

299. Which of the following is not a White box testing technique?

A. Boundary value analysis
B. Statement Testing
C. Decision Testing
D. Condition Coverage

300. Acceptance testing is also known as:

A. Grey box testing B. White box testing
C. Alpha Testing D. Beta testing

301. What was the percentage increase in Zero Day Vulnerabilities in the year 2015?

A. 4% B. 50%
C. 100% D. 125%

302. Which statement is correct in context of hacking attacks?

A. Hacking in French Election
B. ATM Hacking in India
C. Denial of Service attack in Turkish Bank
D. All of the above

303. Identify the software whose vulnerability is exploited the most?

A. Android
B. Browser
C. Adobe Flash Player
D. Microsoft Office

304. The computer vulnerabilities and exploits databases are maintained by _______.

A. Kaspersky Lab
B. Symantec Corporation
C. MITRE Corporation
D. None of the above

305. Which of the following is/are correct with respect to Ransomware?

A. It is a form of Malware
B. It encrypts the whole hard drive of the computer, essentially locking the user out of the entire system.
C. It locks the system's screen or locks the users' files unless a ransom is paid.
D. All of the above

306. Which of the following is considered legal?

A. Hacking a social media account and sending a private message
B. Hacking a bank account and siphoning funds
C. Hacking a company's security system with permission from the management
D. All of the above

307. Which of the following describes monitoring software installed without your consent?

A. Malware B. Adware
C. Spyware D. Ransomware

308. Which type of cyber-attack is commonly performed through emails?

A. Trojans B. Worms
C. Ransomware D. Phishing

309. What is the price for selling Firefox or Safari browser vulnerability in the black market?

A. \$60K – \$100K B. \$60k – \$120K
C. \$60K – \$150K D. \$60000 – \$15000

310. If you share too much information on social media, what may you by at risk of?

A. Identity Theft B. Ransomware
C. Malware D. Adwa

311. ______ framework made cracking of vulnerabilities easy like point and click.

A. .Net B. Metasploit
C. Zeus D. Etterc

312. Nmap is abbreviated as _______.

A. Network Mapper B. New Mappping
C. Network Manager D. Network Mac Address

313. ________ is a popular tool used for discovering networks as well as in security auditing.

A. Ettercap B. Metasploit
C. Nmap D. Burp Suit

314. Which of this Nmap do not check?

A. services different hosts are offering
B. on what OS they are running
C. what kind of firewall is in use
D. what type of antivirus is in use

315. Wireshark is a _______ tool.

A. network protocol analysis
B. network connection security
C. connection analysis
D. defending malicious packet-filtering

316. A DoS attack coming from a large number of IP addresses, making it hard to manually filter or crash the traffic from such sources is known as a ______.

A. GoS attack B. PDoS attack
C. DoS attack D. DDoS attack

317. ______ attacks always need physical access to the system that is having password file or the hacker needs to crack the system by other means.

A. online B. offline
C. password D. non-electronic

318. Which among the following is the least strong security encryption standard?

A. WEP B. WPA
C. WPA2 D. WPA3

319. ______ will encrypt all your system files and will ask you to pay a ransom in order to decrypt all the files and unlock the system.

A. Scareware B. Ransomware
C. Adware D. Spyware

320. ______ are special malware programs written to spy your mobile phones and systems.

A. Scareware B. Ransomware
C. Adware D. Spyware

321. An attacker may use automatic brute forcing tool to compromise your ______.

A. username B. employee ID
C. system/PC name D. password

322. ______ is a code injecting method used for attacking the database of a system/website?

A. HTML Injection
B. SQL Injection
C. Malicious code Injection
D. XML Injection

323. When there is an excessive amount of data flow, which the system cannot handle, ______ takes place.

A. Database crash attack
B. DoS (Denial of Service) attack
C. Data overflow Attack
D. Buffer Overflow attack

324. Which of this is an example of physical hacking?

A. Remote Unauthorised access
B. Inserting malware loaded USB to a system
C. SQL Injection on SQL vulnerable site
D. DDoS (Distributed Denial of Service) attack

325. Which method of hacking will record all your keystrokes?

A. Keyhijacking B. Keyjacking
C. Keylogging D. Keyboard monitoring

326. If we mark the stack and heap segement as non executable,

A. No code will execute.
B. return-oriented programming will also not be able to exploit it.
C. we can prevent overflow code execution.
D. All of the above

327. If we talk about Return Oriented Programming, which of the following statement is true?

A. It is a computer security exploit technique that allows an attacker to execute code in the presence of security defences such as DEP and code signing
B. These types of attacks arise when an adversary manipulates the call stack by taking advantage of a bug in the program, often a buffer overflow.
C. Return-oriented programming is an advanced version of a stack smashing attack.
D. All of the above

328. An hardware device's interrupt request invokes ______, which handles this interrupt.

A. Instruction Set Randomization
B. Information Storage and Retrieval
C. Interrupt Service Routine
D. Intermediate Session Routing

329. Which of the following is a method of randomization?

A. ASLR
B. Sys-call randomization
C. Memory randomization
D. All of the above

330. The below function is part of a program that is running on a 32-bit ×86 system; the compiler does not change the order of variables on the stack.

```
void function(char *input)
    { int i = 1;
    char buffer[8];
    int j = 2;
        strcpy(buffer,input);
        printf("%x %x %s\n",i,j,buffer);
    }
```

What is the minimum length of a string passed to the function through the input parameter that can crash the application?

A. 10 B. 11
C. 12 D. 13

331. Applications developed by programming languages like ______ and ______ have this common buffer-overflow error.

A. C, Ruby B. C, C++
C. Python, Ruby D. C, Python

332. ______ buffer overflows, which are more common among attackers.

A. Memory-based B. Queue-based
C. Stack-based D. Heap-based

333. Malicious code can be pushed into the ______ during ______ attack.

A. stack, buffer-overflow
B. queue, buffer-overflow
C. memory-card, buffer-overflow
D. external drive, buffer-overflow

334. Which of the following string library functions is unsafe for buffer?

A. gets (char * str)
B. strcat (char * destination, const char * source)
C. strcpy (char * destination, const char * source)
D. All of the above

335. Which of the following statements is correct with respect to integer overflow?

A. It is a result of an attempt to store a value greater than the maximum value an integer can store
B. Integer overflow can compromise a program's reliability and security
C. Both (A) and (B)
D. None of the above

336. If an integer data type allows integers up to two bytes or 16 bits in length (or an unsigned number up to decimal 65,535), and two integers are to be added together that will exceed the value of 65,535, the result will be:

A. Buffer Overflow B. Integer Overflow
C. Stack Overflow D. Heap Overflow

337. Integer overflow bugs in programs are difficult to track down and may lead to fatal errors or exploitable vulnerabilities.

A. True
B. False

338. One way of detecting integer overflows is by using a modified compiler to insert runtime checks.

A. True
B. False

339. A format string is a _____ string that contains _____ and _____ parameters.

A. Format, text, ASCII B. Text, ASCII, format
C. ASCII, text, format D. None of the above

340. Which of the following is not a format function in C?

A. fprintf() B. vsfprint()
C. vfprintf() D. vsprintf()

341. What is the purpose of format functions?

A. They are used to convert simple C data types to a string representation
B. They allow to specify the format of the representation
C. They process the resulting string (output to stderr, stdout, syslog, ...)
D. All of the above

342. The behaviour of the _____ is controlled by the _____.

A. format function, format string
B. format string, format function
C. Both (A) and (B)
D. None of the above

343. Identify whether the following code has format string vulnerability or not.

char tmpbuf[512]; snprintf (tmpbuf, sizeof (tmpbuf), "foo: %s", user); tmpbuf[sizeof (tmpbuf) – 1] = '\0'; syslog (LOG_NOTICE, tmpbuf);

A. No
B. Yes

344. Which of the following is an example of control hijacking?

A. Buffer overflow attacks
B. Integer overflow attacks
C. Format string vulnerabilities
D. All of the above

345. The overflows exploits can be detected by:

A. adding runtime code
B. adding vulnerabilities
C. adding buffer
D. None of the above

346. In TCP, sending and receiving data is done as:

A. Stream of bytes B. Sequence of characters
C. Lines of data D. Packets

347. TCP groups a number of bytes together into a packet called:

A. Packet B. Buffer
C. Segment D. Stack

348. Which of these is not applicable for IP protocol?

A. Is connectionless
B. Offer reliable service
C. Offer unreliable service
D. None of the above

349. Which of the following is a function of IP Protocol?

A. Error reporting
B. Fragmentation and Reassembly
C. Routing
D. All of the above

350. Which of the following is not a layer of TCP protocol stack?

A. Application B. Transport
C. Network D. Presentation

351. _____ is a library for formatting raw packets with arbitrary IP headers.

A. Libnet B. HeadLib
C. IPLib D. None of the above

352. Which of the following is correct for Transmission Control Protocol?

A. Connection Oriented
B. Preserves order
C. Both (A) and (B)
D. None of the above

353. Which of the following is a basic security problem?

A. Network packets pass by untrusted hosts
B. TCP state easily obtained by eavesdropping
C. Denial of service vulnerabilities
D. All of the above

354. Which protocol ensures reliable delivery?

A. TCP B. UDP
C. Both (A) and (B) D. None of the above

355. Which protocol uses window flow system?
A. UDP
B. TCP
C. FTP
D. None of the above

356. Which of the following is not a routing protocol?
A. OSPF
B. BGP
C. ARP
D. MGP

357. On the upper layer of SSL, a protocol for initial authentication and transfer of encryption keys, called the ________.
A. SSL handshake protocol
B. SSL authentication protocol
C. SSL record protocol
D. SSL cipher protocol

358. State whether the following statement are true or false.
(*i*) An application-level gateway is often referred to as a proxy.
(*ii*) In proxy, a direct connection is established between the client and destination server.
A. True, False
B. False, True
C. True, True
D. False, False

359. In packet-filtering router, the following information can be external from the packet header.
(*i*) Source IP address
(*ii*) Destination IP address
(*iii*) TCP/UDP source port
(*iv*) ICMP message type
(*v*) TCP/UDP destination port
A. (*i*), (*ii*), (*iii*) and (*iv*) only
B. (*i*), (*iii*), (*iv*) and (*v*) only
C. (*ii*), (*iii*), (*iv*) and (*v*) only
D. All (*i*), (*ii*), (*iii*), (*iv*) and (*v*)

360. ______ mode is used whenever either end of a security association is gateway.
A. Tunnel
B. Encapsulating
C. Transport
D. Gateway

361. IPSec is designed to provide security at the ______.
A. transport layer
B. network layer
C. application layer
D. session layer

362. In tunnel mode, IPSec protects the ______.
A. Entire IP packet
B. IP header
C. IP payload
D. IP trailer

363. Network layer firewall works as a ______.
A. frame filter
B. packet filter
C. signal filter
D. content filter

364. Network layer firewall has two sub-categories called ______.
A. stateful firewall and stateless firewall
B. bit oriented firewall and byte oriented firewall
C. frame firewall and packet firewall
D. network firewall and data firewall

365. WPA2 is used for security in ______.
A. ethernet
B. bluetooth
C. wi-fi
D. e-mail

366. An attempt to make a computer resource unavailable to its intended users is called ______.
A. denial-of-service attack
B. virus attack
C. worms attack
D. botnet process

367. Extensible authentication protocol is authentication framework frequently used in
A. wired personal area network
B. wireless networks
C. wired local area network
D. wired metropolitan area network

368. Pretty good privacy (PGP) is used in ______.
A. browser security
B. email security
C. FTP security
D. wifi security

369. PGP encrypts data by using a block cipher called ______.
A. international data encryption algorithm
B. private data encryption algorithm
C. internet data encryption algorithm
D. local data encryption algorithm

370. When a DNS server accepts and uses incorrect information from a host that has no authority giving that information, then it is called ______.
A. DNS lookup
B. DNS hijacking
C. DNS spoofing
D. DNS authorizing

371. Network layer firewall works as a ______.
A. Frame filter
B. Packet filter
C. Content filter
D. Virus filter

372. Which of the following is non-functional testing?
A. Black box testing
B. Performance testing
C. Unit testing
D. None of the above

373. A firewall is installed at the point where the secure internal network and untrusted external network meet which is also known as ______.
A. Chock point
B. Meeting point
C. Firewall point
D. Secure point

374. Which of the following is/are the types of firewall?
A. Packet Filtering Firewall
B. Dual Homed Gateway Firewall
C. Screen Host Firewall
D. Dual Host Firewall

375. A proxy firewall filters at ______.

A. Physical layer
B. Data link layer
C. Network layer
D. Application layer

376. The tag used to create a hypertext relationship between current document and another URL is:

A. <ISINDEX
B. <A>
C. <LINK>
D. None of these

377. How can you make an e-mail link?

A. <mail href +"xxx@y.com">
B. <a href ="mail to:xxx@y.com">
C. <a href = "xxx@y.com">
D. Both (B) and (C)

378. To create a combo box (drop down box) which tag will you use?

A. <select>
B. <list>
C. <input type="dropdown">
D. All of the above

379. HTML stands for?

A. Hyper Text Markup Language
B. High Text Markup Language
C. Hyper Tabular Markup Language
D. None of these

380. Which of the following tag is used to mark a beginning of Paragraph?

A. <TD>
B.
C. <P>
D. <TR>

381. Correct HTML tag for the largest heading is:

A. <head>
B. <heading>
C. <h6>
D. <h1>

382. The attribute of <form> tag:

A. Method
B. Action
C. Both (A) & (B)
D. None of these

383. Web pages starts with which of the following tag?

A. <Body>
B. <Title>
C. <HTML>
D. <Form>

384. How can you open a link in a new browser window?

A. < a href = "url" target = "new">
B. <a href = "url" target= "_blank">
C. <a href = "url".new>
D. <a href = "url" target ="open">

385. The tag used to create a new list item and also include a hyperlink is:

A. <LI>
B. <DL>
C. <DD>
D. <UL>

386. Which of the tag is used to create a number list?

A. <LI>
B. <OL>
C. <LI> and <OL>
D. None of these

387. The tag used to create a hypertext relationship between current document and another URL is:

A. <ISINDEX>
B. <A>
C. <LINK>
D. None of these

388. The text inside the <TEXT AREA> tag works like:

A. <P> formatted text
B. <T> formatted text
C. <PRE> formatted text
D. None of these

389. What is the correct HTML for adding a background colour?

A. <background>yellow<Background>
B. <body color = "yellow">
C. <body bgcolor = "yellow">
D. <body bg ="yellow"

390. Which tag allows you to add a row in a table?

A. <td> and </td>
B. <cr> and </cr>
C. <th> and </th>
D. <tr> and </tr>

391. How can you make a bulleted list?

A. <list>
B. <nl>
C. <ul>
D. <ol>

392. Choose the correct HTML tag to make a text italic:

A. <ii>
B. <italics>
C. <italic>
D. <i>

393. Choose the correct HTML tag to make a text bold?

A. <b>
B. <bold>
C. <bb>
D. <bld>

394. Which tag creates a check box for a form in HTML?

A. <checkbox>
B. <input type="checkbox">
C. <input=checkbox>
D. <input checkbox>

395. To create a combo box (drop down box) which tag will you use?

A. <select>
B. <list>
C. <input type="dropdown">
D. All of the above

396 Which of the following attributes is used to specify elements to bind style rules to?

A. Id
B. Class
C. Tag
D. All of the above

397. Which selector is used to specify a rule to bind a particular unique element?

A. Id B. Class
C. Tag D. Both (B) & (C)

398. _______ has introduced text, list, box, margin, border, colour, and background properties.

A. CSS B. selector
C. declaration D. text colour

399. The _______ property is used to set the colour of the text.

A. CSS B. selector
C. declaration D. text colour

400. The CSS _______ properties is used to define the background effects.

A. CSS B. selector
C. background D. text colour

401. ________ is a platform independent light weighted object based scripting language.

A. java script
B. head
C. number, string & boolean
D. None of these

402. Java Script support three primitive data types:

A. java script, string & head
B. head, boolean & number
C. number, string & boolean
D. None of the these

403. Java Script allows two composite data types:

A. objects & array B. head & title
C. number & boolean D. None of these

404. The script tag must be placed in the _______.

A. title B. head
C. body D. None of these

405. __________ keyword is used to declare variables in java script.

A. dim B. head
C. var D. None of these

406. DOM stand for _______.

A. document object model
B. document object memory
C. document oriented memory
D. None of these

407. Assignment operators are used to assign values to Java Script variables.

A. true B. false

408. Break statement indicates the end of that many case.

A. true
B. false

409. A string simply stores a series of characters.

A. true
B. false

410. Which of the following is not used in measuring the size of the software:

A. Size of module B. KLOC
C. Function Points D. None of the above

411. ________ is a platform independent object based scripting language.

A. java script
B. Object based scripting language
C. navigator
D. live wire

412. ________ java script is also called client side java script:

A. Function
B. Object based scripting language
C. Navigator
D. Live wire

413. _______ java script is also called server side java script:

A. Function
B. Object based scripting language
C. Navigator
D. Live wire

414. Increment operator, increases the value of variable by what number?

A. 1 B. 2
C. 3 D. 4

415. FUNCTION is a block of statements that performs certain task.

A. true
B. false

416. Central computer which is powerful than other computer in the network to called _______.

A. Client B. HUB
C. Server D. Switch

417. The application of the client and server model are _______.

A. World wide web B. network printing
C. E-mail D. All of the above

418. A client can use the _______ request to get a web resource form the server.

A. Put B. POST
C. Get D. Head

419. The First line of the header is called the ______ followed by optional request headers.

A. Status line　B. Request line
C. Header　D. Body

420. HTTP is a ________ protocol.

A. Connectionless　B. Connection oriented
C. Object oriented　D. None of these

421. Javascript is ______ language.

A. Scripting　B. Programming
C. Application　D. None of these

422. ______ javascript is also called as client side script.

A. Navigator　B. Microsoft
C. Livewire　D. Native

423. Navigator java-script is also called as client side script.

A. True
B. False

424. Decrement operator, decreases the value of variable by what no.

A. 1　B. 2
C. 0　D. 5

425. ______ is a block of statements that performs certain task.

A. Function　B. Procedure
C. Program　D. None of these

426. Which data type value is returned by all transcendental math functions?

A. int　B. float
C. double　D. long

427. Which of these coding types is used for data type characters in Java?

A. ASCII　B. ISO-LATIN-1
C. UNICODE　D. None of the above

428. Which of these values can a boolean variable contain?

A. True & False　B. 0 & 1
C. Any integer value　D. true

429. Which of these operators is used to allocate memory to array variable in Java script?

A. malloc　B. alloc
C. new　D. new malloc

430. Which of these is an incorrect array declaration?

A. int x[] = new int[5]
B. int [] arr = new int[5]
C. intarr[] = new int[5]
D. int x[] = int [5] new

431. Decrement operator, decreases the value of variable by what number?

A. 1　B. 2
C. 3　D. 4

432. Which of these is not a bitwise operator?

A. &　B. &=
C. |=　D. <=

433. Which right shift operator preserves the sign of the value?

A. <<　B. >>
C. <<=　D. >>=

434. What is the output of relational operators?

A. Integer　B. Boolean
C. Characters　D. Double

435. Which of these is returned by "greater than", "less than" and "equal to" operators?

A. Integers
B. Floating – point numbers
C. Boolean
D. None of the above

436. Which of these selection statements test only for equality?

A. if　B. switch
C. if & switch　D. None of the above

437. Which of the following loops will execute the body of loop even when condition controlling the loop is initially false?

A. do-while　B. while
C. for　D. None of these

438. Which of these jump statements can skip processing the remainder of the code in its body for a particular iteration?

A. break　B. return
C. exit　D. continue

439. Which of the following is not a decision making statement?

A. if　B. if-else
C. switch　D. do-while

440. Which of the following is not a valid flow control statement?

A. exit()　B. break
C. continue　D. return

441. The CSS background properties are used to define the ________ effects.

A. background　B. customize
C. class　D. id rule

442. CSS border properties allow us to _____ the borders.

A. background　B. customize
C. class　D. id rule

443. By applying an ______ a style can be applied to just a single tag.

A. background B. customize
C. class D. id rule

444. ______ selectors are used to specify a group of elements.

A. background B. customize
C. class D. id rule

445. In CSS, "font-size" can be called as ______.

A. property name B. selector
C. declaration D. text colour

446. In CSS, h1 can be called as ______.

A. property name B. selector
C. declaration D. text colour

447. In CSS, "colour: red" can be called as ______.

A. property name B. selector
C. declaration D. text colour

448. Reset (button): it is used to reset the button (cancel the data) to upload

A. <reset> B. checkbox
C. <textarea> D. <text>

449. CSS different the tags and data it menace it store the data in different file and store the tags in different file it minimize the size of the file.

A. CSS B. html
C. <textarea> D. <text>

450. ______ describes how HTML elements are to be displayed on screen, paper, or in other media

A. CSS B. html
C. <textarea> D. <text>

451. Central computer which is powerful than other computers in the network is called as:

A. server B. protocol
C. network D. Internet

452. HTTP is a ______ protocol.

A. server B. protocol
C. connection oriented D. Internet

453. The FTP is a protocol that is used to transfer files between two computers over a ______.

A. server & protocol
B. protocol & internet
C. connection & oriented
D. network & Internet

454. A client can use the ______ request to get a web resource from the server.

A. PUT B. POST
C. GET D. HEAD

455. Websites are uploaded ______.

A. address B. server
C. cache D. client

456. HTML web pages can be read and rendered by ______.

A. web browser B. server
C. empty D. head tag

457. The ______ tag is an inline container used to mark up a part of a text, or a part of a document.

A. <map> B. <span>
C. <img> D. <tt>

458. <INPUT> is ______ tag.

A. web browser B. server
C. empty D. head tag

459. The HTML tag to left align the content inside a table cell is

<td align = "left">.

A. true
B. false

460. The body tag usually used after ______.

A. web browser B. server
C. empty D. head tag

461. Tags and text that are not directly displayed on the page are written in ______ section.

A. web browser B. title
C. empty D. head

462. Some tags enclose the text. Those tags are known as ______.

A. single tag B. paired tag
C. empty D. head

463. The <strike> tag is used to ______ the text or sentence.

A. single tag B. paired tag
C. strikeout D. head

464. The <del> tag is used to display ______ text form a document:

A. single tag B. paired tag
C. strikeout D. deleted

465. ______ is used to give additional information.

A. title tag B. paired tag
C. strikeout D. deleted

466. Java script is ______ weighted.

A. light B. heavy
C. large D. None of these

467. Javascript is case sensitive language.

A. True B. False
C. Can not say D. None of these

468. Every statement in Java Script must be terminated by ________.

A. semicolon B. colon
C. $ sign D. # sign

469. Java script does not have any multithreading capabilities.

A. True B. False
C. Can not say D. None of these

470. _______ is used to show the output in java script.

A. Document.write B. Printf
C. Cout D. None of these

471. In java script, === is called as identical equal.

A. True B. False
C. Can not say D. None of these

472. In java script, ! is called as _______.

A. Not B. Equal
C. Not equal D. OR

473. In Java script if else statement is end by end statement:

A. True B. False
C. Cannot say D. None of these

474. _______ is used to execute one of the statements from many blocks of statements.

A. switch statement B. if else statement
C. else if statement D. None of these

475. _______ loop is used to execute the program first and then check the condition.

A. do while B. while loop
C. for loop D. None of these

ANSWERS

1	2	3	4	5	6	7	8	9	10
C	A	A	A	B	B	A	A	A	C
11	**12**	**13**	**14**	**15**	**16**	**17**	**18**	**19**	**20**
B	C	D	C	B	B, D	A	C	D	D
21	**22**	**23**	**24**	**25**	**26**	**27**	**28**	**29**	**30**
B	B	D	D	D	D	C	B	C	A
31	**32**	**33**	**34**	**35**	**36**	**37**	**38**	**39**	**40**
A	A & B	C	A	A	D	B	C	B	C
41	**42**	**43**	**44**	**45**	**46**	**47**	**48**	**49**	**50**
C	A	C	C	D	D	D	D	A	D
51	**52**	**53**	**54**	**55**	**56**	**57**	**58**	**59**	**60**
C	C	A	C	C	A	B	C	B	B
61	**62**	**63**	**64**	**65**	**66**	**67**	**68**	**69**	**70**
A	B	C	A, D	B	A	A	D	C	C
71	**72**	**73**	**74**	**75**	**76**	**77**	**78**	**79**	**80**
C	C	D	D	C	B	C	B	C	D
81	**82**	**83**	**84**	**85**	**86**	**87**	**88**	**89**	**90**
A	B	D	C	B,C	A,C,D	A,B,C,D	A	D	B
91	**92**	**93**	**94**	**95**	**96**	**97**	**98**	**99**	**100**
D	C	A	B	C	B	B	A	C	A
101	**102**	**103**	**104**	**105**	**106**	**107**	**108**	**109**	**110**
A	B	D	B	C	B	C	B	D	A
111	**112**	**113**	**114**	**115**	**116**	**117**	**118**	**119**	**120**
C	C	D	B	C	A	B	C	A	B
121	**122**	**123**	**124**	**125**	**126**	**127**	**128**	**129**	**130**
D	D	A,C,D	B,C	D	D	A	D	A,B,D	A
131	**132**	**133**	**134**	**135**	**136**	**137**	**138**	**139**	**140**
B	A	A	A	D	B	A	D	A	D
141	**142**	**143**	**144**	**145**	**146**	**147**	**148**	**149**	**150**
D	B	A	B	D	B	A	A	C	B

151	**152**	**153**	**154**	**155**	**156**	**157**	**158**	**159**	**160**
C	C	A	A	D	A	B	C	B	D
161	**162**	**163**	**164**	**165**	**166**	**167**	**168**	**169**	**170**
D	B	B	B	C	B	D	B	D	C
171	**172**	**173**	**174**	**175**	**176**	**177**	**178**	**179**	**180**
C	C	D	B	D	D	B	D	A	C
181	**182**	**183**	**184**	**185**	**186**	**187**	**188**	**189**	**190**
C	D	C	B	D	D	A	B	A	A
191	**192**	**193**	**194**	**195**	**196**	**197**	**198**	**199**	**200**
B	B	C	B	A	B	C	B	B	B
201	**202**	**203**	**204**	**205**	**206**	**207**	**208**	**209**	**210**
C	C	A	B	C	B	D	B	D	A
211	**212**	**213**	**214**	**215**	**216**	**217**	**218**	**219**	**220**
D	A	B	C	C	D	A	B	B	C
221	**222**	**223**	**224**	**225**	**226**	**227**	**228**	**229**	**230**
A	D	D	A	B	D	A	B	A	D
231	**232**	**233**	**234**	**235**	**236**	**237**	**238**	**239**	**240**
C	C	C	A	A	C	C	A	A	D
241	**242**	**243**	**244**	**245**	**246**	**247**	**248**	**249**	**250**
A	C	D	C	C	B	B	A	A	C
251	**252**	**253**	**254**	**255**	**256**	**257**	**258**	**259**	**260**
A	A	C	D	D	D	B	C	A	D
261	**262**	**263**	**264**	**265**	**266**	**267**	**268**	**269**	**270**
A	B	D	C	B	D	C	D	A	C
271	**272**	**273**	**274**	**275**	**276**	**277**	**278**	**279**	**280**
B	D	D	B	D	D	A	D	B	D
281	**282**	**283**	**284**	**285**	**286**	**287**	**288**	**289**	**290**
B	A	D	C	C	D	A	D	D	D
291	**292**	**293**	**294**	**295**	**296**	**297**	**298**	**299**	**300**
B	C	B	D	A	C	C	B	A	D
301	**302**	**303**	**304**	**305**	**306**	**307**	**308**	**309**	**310**
D	D	B	C	D	C	C	D	C	A
311	**312**	**313**	**314**	**315**	**316**	**317**	**318**	**319**	**320**
B	A	C	D	A	D	B	A	B	D
321	**322**	**323**	**324**	**325**	**326**	**327**	**328**	**329**	**330**
D	B	D	D	C	C	D	C	D	C
331	**332**	**333**	**334**	**335**	**336**	**337**	**338**	**339**	**340**
B	C	A	D	C	B	A	A	C	B
341	**342**	**343**	**344**	**345**	**346**	**347**	**348**	**349**	**350**
D	A	B	D	A	B	C	B	D	D
351	**352**	**353**	**354**	**355**	**356**	**357**	**358**	**359**	**360**
A	C	D	A	B	D	A	A	D	A
361	**362**	**363**	**364**	**365**	**366**	**367**	**368**	**369**	**370**
B	A	B	A	C	A	B	B	A	C
371	**372**	**373**	**374**	**375**	**376**	**377**	**378**	**379**	**380**
B	B	A	A	D	C	B	A	A	C

381 D	382 C	383 C	384 B	385 A	386 C	387 C	388 C	389 C	390 D
391 C	392 D	393 A	394 B	395 A	396 D	397 A	398 A	399 D	400 C
401 A	402 C	403 A	404 B	405 C	406 A	407 A	408 B	409 A	410 A
411 A	412 C	413 D	414 A	415 A	416 C	417 B	418 C	419 A	420 B
421 A	422 A	423 A	424 A	425 A	426 C	427 C	428 A	429 C	430 D
431 A	432 D	433 B	434 B	435 C	436 A	437 A	438 D	439 D	440 A
441 A	442 B	443 D	444 C	445 A	446 B	447 C	448 A	449 A	450 A
451 A	452 C	453 D	454 C	455 B	456 A	457 B	458 C	459 A	460 D
461 D	462 A	463 C	464 D	465 A	466 A	467 A	468 A	469 A	470 A
471 A	472 A	473 A	474 A	475 A					

INFRA SUPPORT

1. Which of the following is/are the part of operating system?
   A. Kernel services
   B. Library services
   C. Application level services
   D. All of the above

2. The system of _______ generally ran one job at a time. These were called single stream batch processing.
   A. 40's   B. 50's
   C. 60's   D. 70's

3. In _____ generation of operating system, operating system designers develop the concept of multiprogramming in which several jobs are in main memory at once.
   A. First   B. Second
   C. Third   D. Fourth

4. State True or False.
   (*i*) In spooling high speed device like a disk is interposed between running program and low-speed device in Input/output.
   (*ii*) By using spooling for example instead of writing directly to a printer, outputs are written to the disk.
   A. (*i*) – True, (*ii*) – False
   B. (*i*) – True, (*ii*) – True
   C. (*i*) – False, (*ii*) – True
   D. (*i*) – False, (*ii*) – False

5. Which of the following is/are the functions of operating system?
   (*i*) Sharing hardware among users.
   (*ii*) Allowing users to share data among themselves.
   (*iii*) Recovering from errors.
   (*iv*) Preventing users from interfering with one another.
   (*v*) Scheduling resources among users.
   A. (*i*), (*ii*), (*iii*) and (*iv*) only
   B. (*ii*), (*iii*), (*iv*) and (*v*) only
   C. (*i*), (*iii*), (*iv*) and (*v*) only
   D. All (*i*), (*ii*), (*iii*), (*iv*) and (*v*)

6. ______ must executes frequently and makes the fine grained decision of which process to execute the next.
   A. Long-term scheduling
   B. Medium-term scheduling
   C. Short-term scheduling
   D. None of the above

7. With _________ a page is brought into main memory only when the reference is made to a location on that page.
   A. demand paging   B. main paging
   C. prepaging   D. postpaging

8. ______ provides a larger size of virtual memory but require virtual memory which provides multidimensional memory.
   A. Paging method
   B. Segmentation method
   C. Paging and segmentation method
   D. None of these

9. ______ is a large kernel containing virtually the complete operating system, including, scheduling, file system, device drivers and memory management.
   A. Multilithic kernel   B. Monolithic kernel
   C. Micro kernel   D. Macro kernel

10. ______ is a large operating system core that provides a wide range of services.
    A. Multilithic kernel   B. Monolithic kernel
    C. Micro kernel   D. Macro kernel

11. Which of the following is not the function of Microkernel?
    A. File management
    B. Low-level memory management
    C. Inter-process communication
    D. I/O interrupts management

12. Match the following.

(*i*) Mutual exclusion	(*a*) A process may hold allocated resources while waiting assignment.
(*ii*) Hold and wait	(*b*) No resource can be forcibly removed from a process holding it.
(*iii*) No preemption	(*c*) Only one process may use a resource at a time.

A. (*i*) - (*a*), (*ii*) - (*b*), (*iii*) - (*c*)
B. (*i*) - (*a*), (*ii*) - (*c*), (*iii*) - (*b*)
C. (*i*) - (*b*), (*ii*) - (*c*), (*iii*) - (*a*)
D. (*i*) - (*c*), (*ii*) - (*a*), (*iii*) - (*b*)

13. A direct method of deadlock prevention is to prevent the occurrences of ________.

A. Mutual exclusion B. Hold and wait
C. Circular waits D. No preemption

14. The methods or algorithms which are used to increase the performance of disk storage sub-system is called ________.

A. Disk performing B. Disk scheduling
C. Disk storing D. Disk extending

15. ________ is the time required to move the disk arm to the required track.

A. Seek time B. Rotational delay
C. Latency time D. Access time

16. The ________ policy restricts scanning to one direction only.

A. SCAN B. C-SCAN
C. N-Step SCAN D. Both (A) and (B)

17. ________ policy selects the disk I/O request that requires the least movement of the disk arm from its current position.

A. FSCAN B. SSTF
C. SCAN D. C-SCAN

18. ________ refers to the ability of an operating system to support multiple threads of execution with a single process.

A. Multithreading B. Multiprocessing
C. Multiexecuting D. Bi-threading

19. State whether the following statement is true or false.

(*i*) It takes less time to terminate a thread than a process.
(*ii*) Threads enhance efficiency in communication between different executing programs.

A. (*i*) - True, (*ii*) - False
B. (*i*) - True, (*ii*) - True
C. (*i*) - False, (*ii*) - True
D. (*i*) - False, (*ii*) - False

20. ________ is a special type of programming language used to provide instructions to the monitor simple batch processing schema.

A. Job control language (JCL)
B. Processing control language (PCL)
C. Batch control language (BCL)
D. Monitor control language (MCL)

21. The first batch operating system was developed in the ________ by General Motors for use on an IBM 701.

A. mid 1940's B. mid 1950's
C. mid 1960's D. mid 1970's

22. Process is ________.

A. A program in execution
B. An instance of a program running on a computer.
C. The entity that can be assigned to and executed
D. All of the above.

23. ________ is a facility that allows programmers to address memory from a logical point of view, without regard to the main memory, physically available.

A. Visual memory B. Real memory
C. Virtual memory D. Secondary memory

24. ________ is a large kernel, including scheduling file system, networking, device drivers, memory management and more.

A. Monolithic kernel B. Micro kernel
C. Macro kernel D. Mini kernel

25. A ________ architecture assigns only a few essential functions to the kernel, including address spaces, Inter process communication (IPC) and basic scheduling.

A. Monolithic kernel B. Micro kernel
C. Macro kernel D. Mini kernel

26. State whether true or false.

(*i*) Multithreading is useful for application that perform a number of essentially independent tasks that do not be serialized.
(*ii*) An example of multithreading is a database server that listens for and process numerous client request.

A. (*i*) – True, (*ii*) – False
B. (*i*) – True, (*ii*) – True
C. (*i*) – False, (*ii*) – True
D. (*i*) – False, (*ii*) – False

27. With ________ only one process can execute at a time; meanwhile all other process are waiting for the processer. With ________ more than one process can be running simultaneously each on a different processer.

A. Multiprocessing, Multiprogramming
B. Multiprogramming, Uniprocessing

C. Multiprogramming, Multiprocessing
D. Uniprogramming, Multiprocessing

28. The two central themes of modern operating system are ________.

A. Multiprogramming and Distributed processing
B. Multiprogramming and Central Processing
C. Single Programming and Distributed processing
D. None of the above

29. ________ refers to the ability of multiple process (or threads) to share code, resources or data in such a way that only one process has access to shared object at a time.

A. Synchronization B. Mutual Exclusion
C. Dead lock D. Starvation

30. ________ is the ability of multiple process to co-ordinate their activities by exchange of information.

A. Synchronization B. Mutual Exclusion
C. Dead lock D. Starvation

31. ________ refers to a situation in which a process is ready to execute but is continuously denied access to a processor in deference to other processes.

A. Synchronization B. Mutual Exclusion
C. Dead lock D. Starvation

32. Which of the following is not the approach to dealing with deadlock?

A. Prevention B. Avoidance
C. Detection D. Deletion

33. Which of the following are the states of a five state process model?

(*i*) Running (*ii*) Ready
(*iii*) New (*iv*) Exit
(*v*) Destroy

A. (*i*), (*ii*), (*iii*) and (*v*) only
B. (*i*), (*ii*), (*iv*) and (*v*) only
C. (*i*), (*ii*), (*iii*), and (*iv*) only
D. All (*i*), (*ii*), (*iii*), (*iv*) and (*v*)

34. State which statement is true for Suspended process?

(*i*) The process is not immediately available for execution.
(*ii*) The process may be removed from suspended state automatically without removal order.

A. (*i*) only B. (*ii*) only
C. (*i*) and (*ii*) only D. None of these

35. Following is/are the reasons for process suspension.

A. Swapping parent process
B. Inter request
C. Timing
D. All of the above

36. The different types of tables maintained by the operating system are ________.

A. memory, logical, I/O, file
B. memory, I/O, file, physical
C. memory, I/O, file, process
D. memory, logical, I/O, physical

37. Which of the following information is not included in memory table?

A. The allocation of main memory to process.
B. The allocation of secondary memory to process
C. Any information needed to manage virtual memory
D. Any information about the existence of file

38. Process Management function of an operating system kernel includes.

A. Process creation and termination.
B. Process scheduling and dispatching
C. Process switching
D. All of the above

39. The typical elements of process image are ________.

(*i*) User data (*ii*) System data
(*iii*) User program (*iv*) System stack

A. (*i*), (*iii*) and (*iv*) only
B. (*i*), (*ii*) and (*iv*) only
C. (*ii*), (*iii*) and (*iv*) only
D. All (*i*), (*ii*), (*iii*) and (*iv*)

40. Match the following mechanisms for interrupting the execution of a process and their uses.

(*i*) Interrupt	(*a*) Call to an operating system function
(*ii*) Trap	(*b*) Reaction to an asynchronous external event
(*iii*) Supervisor Call	(*c*) Handling of a error or an exception condition

A. (*i*) - (*a*), (*ii*) - (*b*), (*iii*) - (*c*)
B. (*i*) - (*c*), (*ii*) - (*a*), (*iii*) - (*b*)
C. (*i*) - (*b*), (*ii*) - (*c*), (*iii*) - (*a*)
D. (*i*) - (*a*), (*ii*) - (*c*), (*iii*) - (*b*)

41. The unit of dispatching is usually referred to as a ______.

A. Thread B. Lightweight process
C. Process D. Both (A) and (B)

42. ______ is an example of an operating system that support single user process and single thread.

A. UNIX B. MS-DOS
C. OS/2 D. Windows 2000

43. State true or false.

(*i*) Unix, support multiple user process but only support one thread per process.

(*ii*) A java run time environment is an example of a system of one process with multiple threads.

A. True, False B. True, True
C. False, True D. False, False

44. ______ are very effective because a mode switch is not required to switch from one thread to another.

A. Kernel-level threads
B. User-level threads
C. Alterable threads
D. Application level threads

45. ______ is a condition in which there is a set of concurrent processes, only one of which is able to access a given resource or perform a given function at any time.

A. Mutual Exclusion B. Busy Waiting
C. Deadlock D. Starvation

46. ______ techniques can be used to resolve conflicts, such as competition for resources, and to synchronize processes so that they can cooperate.

A. Mutual Exclusion B. Busy Waiting
C. Deadlock D. Starvation

47. ______ can be defined as the permanent blocking of a set of processed that either complete for system resources or communicate with each other.

A. Deadlock B. Permanent lock
C. Starvation D. Mutual exclusion

48. The following conditions of policy must be present for a deadlock to be possible.

(*i*) Mutual exclusion (*ii*) Hold and wait
(*iii*) No preemption (*iv*) Circular wait

A. (*i*), (*ii*) and (*iii*) only
B. (*ii*), (*iii*) and (*iv*) only
C. (*i*), (*iii*) and (*iv*) only
D. All (*i*), (*ii*), (*iii*) and (*iv*)

49. A direct method of deadlock prevention is to prevent the occurrence of ________.

A. Mutual exclusion B. Hold and wait
C. Circular waits D. No preemption

50. State true or false.

(*i*) With paging, each process is divided into relatively small, fixed-size pages.
(*ii*) Segmentation provides for the use of pieces of varying size.

A. True, False
B. True, True
C. False, True
D. False, False

51. ________ involves treating main memory as a resource to be allocated to and shared among a number of active processes.

A. Partition management
B. Memory management
C. Disk management
D. All of the above

52. A process that execute only in main memory is referred to as ________ and that allocated in disk is referred to as ________.

A. Virtual memory, true memory
B. Virtual memory, real memory
C. Real memory, virtual memory
D. Imaginary memory, real memory

53. In process scheduling, ________determines when new processes are admitted to the system.

A. long term scheduling
B. medium term scheduling
C. short term scheduling
D. None of the above

54. In process scheduling, ________determines which ready process will be executed next by processor.

A. long term scheduling
B. medium term scheduling
C. short term scheduling
D. None of the above

55. The sum of the seek time, and the rotational delay is called the ________.

A. reached time B. access time
C. arrived time D. common time

56. The ________ policy segments the disks request queue into sub queues of the length N.

A. SCAN B. C-SCAN
C. N-Step SCAN D. FSCAN

57. Which of the following are the functions of operating system?

(*i*) recovering from errors
(*ii*) facilitating input/output
(*iii*) facilitating parallel operation
(*iv*) sharing hardware among users
(*v*) implementing user interface

A. (*i*), (*ii*), (*iii*) and (*v*) only
B. (*i*), (*ii*), (*iii*) and (*iv*) only
C. (*ii*), (*iii*), (*iv*) and (*v*) only
D. All (*i*), (*ii*), (*iii*), (*iv*) and (*v*)

58. File management function of the operating system includes

(*i*) File creation and deletion
(*ii*) Disk scheduling

(*iii*) Directory creation
(*iv*) Mapping file in secondary storage.
A. (*i*), (*ii*) and (*iii*) only
B. (*i*), (*iii*) and (*iv*) only
C. (*ii*), (*iii*) and (*iv*) only
D. All (*i*), (*ii*), (*iii*) and (*iv*)

59. The _______ determines when a page should be brought into main memory.
A. Fetch policy
B. Placement policy
C. Replacement policy
D. Resident set management

60. With _________ a page is written out to secondary memory only when it has been selected for replacement.
A. pre-cleaning B. demand cleaning
C. required cleaning D. fast cleaning

61. The process is _______.
A. an instance of a program in execution
B. a program only
C. a processor state
D. the kernel state

62. The mechanism that brings a page into memory only when it is needed is called _______.
A. segmentation B. fragmentation
C. demand paging D. page replacement

63. The two paradigms if IPC are _______ and _______.
A. call, reply
B. shared memory, message passing
C. send, receive
D. call by value, call by reference

64. A program is passive while a process is _______.
A. inactive B. spontaneous
C. active D. impulse

65. FIFO scheduling is _______.
A. preemptive scheduling
B. non preemptive scheduling
C. deadline scheduling
D. fair share scheduling

66. _________ ensures that once transaction completes successively, the results of the operations become permanent.
A. serializability B. synchronizability
C. atomicity D. durability

67. A process is created and is initially put in the _______.
A. ready queue B. device queue
C. i/o queue D. waiting queue

68. Which directory implementation is used in most of the Operating System?
A. single level directory structure
B. two level directory structure
C. tree directory structure
D. acyclic directory structure

69. Isolation property is also known as _______.
A. Performance B. Serializability
C. Durability D. Atomicity

70. A thread is a _______.
A. task B. process
C. program D. light weight process

71. The interval from the fine submission of a process to the time of completion is the _______.
A. waiting time B. blocked time
C. turnaround time D. response time

72. The term "Operating System" means _______.
A. a set of programs which controls computer working
B. the way a computer operator works
C. conversion of high-level language in to machine level language
D. the way a floppy disk drive operates

73. Generally we have user level threads and _______.
A. programmer level thread
B. kernel level thread
C. program level thread
D. process level thread

74. To ensure that the _______ condition never occurs in the system, we must guarantee that, whenever a process requests a resource, it does not have any other resource.
A. mutual exclusion B. no-preemption
C. circular waits D. hold and wait

75. Resource locking _______.
A. allows multiple tasks to simultaneously use resource
B. forces only on takes to use any resource at any time
C. can easily cause a dead lock condition
D. is not used for disk drives

76. A program responsible for assigning the CPU to the process that has been selected by the short term scheduler is known as _______.
A. scheduler B. dispatcher
C. debugger D. compiler

77. The _______ instruct Kernel to do various operations of the calling program and exchange data between the Kernel at the program.

A. shell B. editors
C. system calls D. commands

78. Which of the following buffering strategies are used in interprocess communication?
A. null pointer
B. single message buffer
C. multiple message buffer
D. all of the above

79. The process of splitting of data into equal size partitions over multiple disks is known as _______.
A. data stripping B. array of disks
C. RAID D. SCAN

80. Pipes allow transfer of data between processor in a _______ manner.
A. last in first out B. shortest job first
C. multilevel queue D. first in first out

81. The process of storing extra or duplicate information used for rebuilding the lost information in event of disks failure is known as _______.
A. stripping B. redundancy
C. disk array D. RAID

82. A thread that is to be cancelled is often referred to as the _______.
A. target thread
B. thread cancellation
C. asynchronous cancellation
D. defined cancellation

83. _______ ensures the every message sent to a group of receivers will be delivered to either all of them or none of them.
A. Ordered delivery B. Atomicity
C. Survivability D. Reliability

84. An arrangement of record in a sequence in which they arrive is known as a _______.
A. pile B. file
C. disk D. directory

85. _______ is also known as monitor mode.
A. User mode B. System mode
C. Unprivileged mode D. Process mode

86. The technique, for sharing the time of a computer among several jobs, which switches jobs so rapidly such that each job appears to have the computer to itself, is called _______.
A. time sharing B. time out
C. time domain D. multitasking

87. For batch and payroll applications which of the following file organization is better _______.
A. random file B. sequential file
C. indexed file D. hashed file

88. Name the scheduler that selects among the processes that are ready to execute and allocates the CPU to one of them.
A. Long term scheduler
B. Medium term scheduler
C. Job scheduler
D. Short term scheduler

89. Failure during inter-process communication may be due to _______.
A. loss of request transfer unit
B. single datagram messages
C. multi datagram messages
D. message passing

90. The process of direct mapping by using some faster algorithms is called as _______.
A. hashing B. searching
C. sorting D. indexing

91. Name the system in which the processors do not share memory and each processor that its own local memory.
A. Tightly coupled system
B. Parallel processing system
C. Loosely coupled system
D. Batch processing system

92. Which technique was introduced because a single job could not keep both the CPU and I/O devices busy?
A. Time-sharing
B. Spooling
C. Preemptive scheduling
D. Multiprogramming

93. Those directories in which the root directory has all system file and no other sub-directory is known as _______.
A. flat directory
B. single directory
C. hierarchical directory
D. indexed directory

94. Which is responsible for maintaining all the important abstractions of the operating system?
A. Kernel B. System libraries
C. System utilities D. Daemons

95. A four message reliable IPC protocol for client server communication works as _______.
A. request, reply, acknowledgement, request
B. reply, acknowledgement, request, acknowledgement
C. request, acknowledgement, reply, acknowledgement
D. request, request, reply, acknowledgement

96. A path name that starts at root directory is _______.

A. absolute B. relative
C. hybrid D. hierarchical

97. Where does the problem of fragmentation occur?

A. Static storage allocation
B. Static allocation storage
C. Stack allocation with dynamic binding
D. Heap allocation

98. Idempotency basically means _______.

A. reliability B. repeatability
C. survivability D. flexibility

99. All path names are specified relative to the working directory _______.

A. absolute path name
B. relative path name
C. hybrid path name
D. hierarchical path name

100. The time taken by the disk arm to locate the specific address of a sector for getting information is called _______.

A. rotational latency B. seek time
C. search time D. response time

101. Which of the following is crucial time while accessing data on the disk?

A. Seek time B. Rotational time
C. Transmission time D. Waiting time

102. What is the primary job of the operating system in a computer?

A. Command resources B. Manage resources
C. Provide utilities D. Be user friendly

103. The _______ is a user process that initiates a remote procedure call.

A. client B. server
C. network D. operating system

104. Which of the following memory allocation scheme suffers from external fragmentation?

A. Segmentation B. Pure demand paging
C. Swapping D. Paging

105. Which of the following is used in removal of process from active contention of CPU and reintroduce them into memory later?

A. Interrupt B. Swapping
C. Signal D. Thread

106. The operating system manages _______.

A. memory B. processor
C. disk and I/O devices D. all of the above

107. Information about a process is maintained in a _______.

A. stack
B. translation looks a side buffer
C. process control block
D. program control block

108. Paging _______.

A. solves the memory fragmentation problem
B. allows modular programming
C. allows structured programming
D. avoids deadlock

109. Which is not the layer of the Operating system?

A. Kernel B. Shell
C. Application program D. Critical Section

110. Distributed OS works on the _______ principle.

A. file foundation B. single system image
C. multi system image D. networking image

111. The collection of processes on the disk that is waiting to be brought into memory for execution forms the _______.

A. ready queue B. device queue
C. input queue D. priority queue

112. In _______ condition, processes are allowed to request for new resources without releasing the resources that they are currently holding.

A. Mutual exclusion B. Hold and wait
C. No preemption D. Circular wait

113. The time taken by the disk arm to locate the specific address of a sector for getting information is called _______.

A. rotational delay B. seek time
C. search time D. response time

114. The principle of locality of reference justifies the use of _______.

A. virtual memory B. interrupts
C. main memory D. cache memory

115. In _________ condition, a resource that has been allocated to a process becomes available for allocation to another process only after it has been voluntarily released by the process holding it.

A. Mutual exclusion B. Hold and wait
C. No preemption D. Circular wait

116. Identify the odd thing in the services of operating system _______.

A. Accounting
B. Protection
C. Error detection and correction
D. Dead lock handling

117. Multiprocessing _______.
A. makes the operating system simpler
B. allows multiple processes to run simultaneously
C. is completely understood by all major computer vendors
D. allows the same computer to have the multiple processors

118. In _______condition, two or more processes must form a circular chain in which each process is waiting for a resource that is held by the next member of the chain.
A. Mutual exclusion B. Hold and wait
C. No preemption D. Circular waits

119. Which of the following is not advantage of multiprogramming?
A. Increased throughput
B. Shorter response time
C. Decreased operating system overhead
D. Ability to assign priorities of jobs

120. Which is not a state of the process?
A. Blocked B. Running
C. Ready D. Privileged

121. In computer security, _______ means that computer system assets can be modified only by authorized parties.
A. Confidentiality B. Integrity
C. Availability D. Authenticity

122. In computer security, _______ means that the information in a computer system only be accessible for reading by authorized parties.
A. Confidentiality B. Integrity
C. Availability D. Authenticity

123. The type of threats on the security of a computer system or network are _______.
(*i*) Interruption (*ii*) Interception
(*iii*) Modification (*iv*) Creation
(*v*) Fabrication
A. (*i*), (*ii*), (*iii*) and (*iv*) only
B. (*ii*), (*iii*), (*iv*) and (*v*) only
C. (*i*), (*ii*), (*iii*) and (*v*) only
D. All (*i*), (*ii*), (*iii*), (*iv*) and (*v*)

124. Which of the following is independent malicious program that need not any host program?
A. Trap doors B. Trojan horse
C. Virus D. Worm

125. The _________ is code that recognizes some special sequence of input or is triggered by being run from a certain user ID of by unlikely sequence of events.
A. Trap doors B. Trojan horse
C. Logic Bomb D. Virus

126. The _________ is code embedded in some legitimate program that is set to "explode" when certain conditions are met.
A. Trap doors B. Trojan horse
C. Logic Bomb D. Virus

127. Which of the following malicious program do not replicate automatically?
A. Trojan Horse B. Virus
C. Worm D. Zombie

128. _________ programs can be used to accomplish functions indirectly that an unauthorized user could not accomplish directly.
A. Zombie B. Worm
C. Trojan Horses D. Logic Bomb

129. State whether true of false.
(*i*) A worm mails a copy of itself to other systems.
(*ii*) A worm executes a copy of itself on another system.
A. True, False B. False, True
C. True, True D. False, False

130. A _________ is a program that can infect other programs by modifying them, the modification includes a copy of the virus program, which can go on to infect other programs.
A. Worm B. Virus
C. Zombie D. Trap doors

131. ________ are used in denial of service attacks, typically against targeted web sites.
A. Worm B. Zombie
C. Virus D. Trojan horse

132. Select the correct order for the different phases of virus execution.
(*i*) Propagation phase
(*ii*) Dormant phase
(*iii*) Execution phase
(*iv*) Triggering phase
A. (*i*), (*ii*), (*iii*) and (*iv*)
B. (*i*), (*iii*), (*ii*) and (*iv*)
C. (*ii*), (*i*), (*iv*) and (*iii*)
D. (*ii*), (*iii*), (*iv*) and (*i*)

133. A ________ attaches itself to executable files and replicates, when the infected program is executed, by finding other executable files to infect.
A. Stealth Virus B. Polymorphic Virus
C. Parasitic Virus D. Macro Virus

134. ________ is a form of virus explicitly designed to hide itself from detection by antivirus software.
A. Stealth Virus B. Polymorphic Virus
C. Parasitic Virus D. Macro Virus

135. A ________ creates copies during replication that are functionally equivalent but have distinctly different bit patterns.

A. Boot Sector Virus B. Polymorphic Virus
C. Parasitic Virus D. Macro Virus

136. A portion of the Polymorphic virus, generally called a ________, creates a random encryption key to encrypt the remainder of the virus.

A. mutual engine B. mutation engine
C. multiple engine D. polymorphic engine

137. State which of the following statement is true.

(*i*) A macro virus is platform independent.
(*ii*) Macro viruses infect documents, not executable portions of code.

A. Only (*i*)
B. Only (*ii*)
C. Both (*i*) and (*ii*)
D. None of these

138. The type(s) of auto executing macros, in Microsoft word is/are

A. Auto execute B. Auto macro
C. Command macro D. All of the above

139. In ________, the virus places an identical copy of itself into other programs or into certain system areas on the disk.

A. Dormant phase B. Propagation phase
C. Triggering phase D. Execution phase

140. A ________ is a program that secretly takes over another Internet-attached computer and then uses that computer to launch attacks.

A. Worm B. Zombie
C. Virus D. Trap doors

141. An optimal scheduling algorithm in terms of minimizing the average waiting time of a given set of process is ________.

A. FCFS scheduling
B. Round robin scheduling algorithm
C. Shortest job first scheduling algorithm
D. Priority scheduling algorithm

142. The hardware mechanism that enables a device to notify the CPU is called ________.

A. polling B. interrupts
C. system call D. None of the above

143. In the running state ________.

A. only the process which has control of the processor is found
B. all the process waiting for I/O to be completed are found
C. all the processes waiting for the processor are found
D. None of the above

144. Which technique was introduced because a single job could keep both the CPU and the I/O devices busy?

A. Time sharing
B. Spooling
C. Preemptive scheduling
D. Multiprogramming

145. RMA works on static priorities while EDF algorithm works on ________.

A. starvation B. dynamic priorities
C. RR scheduling D. FIFO scheduling

146. In the ________ method of data transfer, the participation of the processor is eliminated during data transfer.

A. buffering
B. caching
C. direct memory access
D. indirect memory access

147. Inter process communication can be done through ________.

A. mails B. messages
C. system calls D. traps

148. RR scheduling is most suitable for ________.

A. time shared OS B. distributed OS
C. real time OS D. an ordinary OS

149. The aim of ________ transparency is to ensure that the movement of the object is handled automatically by the system in a user transparent manner.

A. location B. name
C. migration D. scaling

150. ________ is a memory management scheme that permits the physical address space of a process to be non contiguous.

A. Paging B. Segmentation
C. Virtual memory D. Main memory

151. Context switching is ________.

A. part of spooling
B. part of polling
C. part of interrupt handling
D. part of paging

152. The normal functioning of an RPC may get disrupted due to ________.

A. call message gets lost
B. response message gets lost
C. called node and caller node crashes and is restarted
D. all of the above

153. Mutual exclusion is referred as ________.

A. if one process is in a critical region others are excluded
B. prevents deadlock
C. requires semaphore to implement
D. is found only in the Windows NT operating system

154. IFO scheduling is ________.

A. preemptive B. non-preemptive
C. deadline scheduling D. RR scheduling

155. ________ deals with the process of deciding which process should be assigned to which processor.

A. Process migration B. Processor allocation
C. Threads D. None of the above

156. Which scheduler controls the degree of multi-programming?

A. Short term scheduler
B. Long term scheduler
C. Middle term scheduler
D. Pre term scheduler

157. Safe state is ________.

A. deadlock state B. non-deadlocked state
C. polling state D. spooling state

158. ________ time is defined as the time period for which the execution of the process is stopped for transferring its information to the destination node.

A. turn around B. latency
C. freezing D. execution

159. The principle of locality of reference justifies the use of:

A. virtual memory B. interrupts
C. main memory D. cache memory

160. For a multiple instances of resource type which algorithm is used ________.

A. divide and conquer algorithm
B. banker's algorithm
C. partition algorithm
D. sorting algorithm

161. In memory management, a technique called as paging, the physical memory is broken into fixed sized blocks called ________.

A. pages B. frames
C. blocks D. segments

162. Which method is used to recover from deadlock?

A. Process termination
B. Resource preemption
C. Resource non-preemption
D. Process termination and Resource preemption

163. Saving the state of the old process and loading the saved state of the new process is called ________.

A. context switch B. static
C. multi programming D. None of the above

164 The degree of Multiprogramming is controlled by ________.

A. CPU scheduler
B. context switching
C. long term scheduler
D. medium term scheduler

165. Input transfers are done in advance and output transfers are done after sometimes in which of these technique?

A. Spooling B. Buffering
C. Swapping D. Paging

166. A binary semaphore ________.

A. has the values one or zero
B. is essential to binary computers
C. is used only for synchronization
D. is used only for mutual exclusion

167. A scheduling algorithm is fair ________.

A. if no process faces starvation.
B. if a process is starved, detect it and run it with high priority
C. if it uses semaphores
D. only if a queue is used for scheduling

168. Which of the following is also known as double buffering?

A. anticipated buffering
B. buffer swapping
C. circular buffering
D. swapping buffering

169. ________ is the ability of a system to continue functioning in the event of partial system failure.

A. fault avoidance B. fault tolerance
C. fault detection D. fault recovery

170. Virtual memory is ________.

A. an extremely large main memory
B. an extremely large secondary memory
C. an illusion of extremely large main memory
D. a type of memory used in super computers

171. Error handling and I/O interrupt handling are the functions of......

A. I/O device Handler B. I/O traffic controller
C. I/O scheduler D. I/O buffer

172. In a multithreaded environment ________.

A. each thread is allocated with new memory from main memory

B. main thread terminates after the termination of child threads
C. every process can have only one thread
D. None of the above

173. The kernel keeps track of the state of each task by using a data structure called ________.

A. process control block
B. user control block
C. memory control block
D. hardware control block

174. A virtual device is a ________.

A. dedicated for none purpose
B. shared device converted to a dedicated device
C. dedicated device converted to a shared device
D. shared device

175. CPU scheduling is the basis of ________ operating system.

A. batch
B. real time
C. multiprogramming
D. monoprogramming

176. ________ is a high speed cache used to hold recently referenced page table entries a part of paged virtual memory?

A. Translation looks a side buffer
B. Inverse page table
C. Segmented page table
D. Indexed page table

177. A technique that smoothes out peaks in I/O demand is ________.

A. spooling
B. buffering
C. swapping
D. paging

178. In kernel model, the operating system services such as process management, memory management are provided by the kernel.

A. monolithic
B. micro
C. macro
D. complex

179. A process is said to be in ________ state if it was waiting for an event that will never occur.

A. safe
B. unsafe
C. starvation
D. dead lock

180. Which of the following is an example of spooled device?

A. The terminal used to enter the input data for a program being executed
B. The secondary memory device in a virtual memory system
C. A line printer used to print the output of a number of jobs
D. None of the above

ANSWERS

1	2	3	4	5	6	7	8	9	10
D	B	C	B	D	C	A	B	B	D
11	**12**	**13**	**14**	**15**	**16**	**17**	**18**	**19**	**20**
A	D	C	B	A	A	B	A	B	A
21	**22**	**23**	**24**	**25**	**26**	**27**	**28**	**29**	**30**
B	D	C	A	B	B	C	A	B	A
31	**32**	**33**	**34**	**35**	**36**	**37**	**38**	**39**	**40**
D	D	C	A	D	C	D	D	A	C
41	**42**	**43**	**44**	**45**	**46**	**47**	**48**	**49**	**50**
D	B	B	B	A	A	A	D	C	B
51	**52**	**53**	**54**	**55**	**56**	**57**	**58**	**59**	**60**
B	C	A	C	B	C	D	B	A	B
61	**62**	**63**	**64**	**65**	**66**	**67**	**68**	**69**	**70**
A	C	B	C	B	D	A	C	B	D
71	**72**	**73**	**74**	**75**	**76**	**77**	**78**	**79**	**80**
C	A	B	D	B	B	C	D	A	D
81	**82**	**83**	**84**	**85**	**86**	**87**	**88**	**89**	**90**
B	A	B	A	B	A	B	D	B	A
91	**92**	**93**	**94**	**95**	**96**	**97**	**98**	**99**	**100**
C	D	A	A	C	A	D	B	B	D

101	102	103	104	105	106	107	108	109	110
A	B	A	A	B	D	C	A	D	B
111	**112**	**113**	**114**	**115**	**116**	**117**	**118**	**119**	**120**
C	B	B	D	C	C	D	D	C	D
121	**122**	**123**	**124**	**125**	**126**	**127**	**128**	**129**	**130**
B	A	C	D	A	C	A	C	C	B
131	**132**	**133**	**134**	**135**	**136**	**137**	**138**	**139**	**140**
B	C	C	A	B	B	C	D	B	B
141	**142**	**143**	**144**	**145**	**146**	**147**	**148**	**149**	**150**
C	B	A	D	C	C	B	A	B	A
151	**152**	**153**	**154**	**155**	**156**	**157**	**158**	**159**	**160**
C	D	A	B	B	B	B	C	D	B
161	**162**	**163**	**164**	**165**	**166**	**167**	**168**	**169**	**170**
B	D	A	C	B	A	A	B	B	C
171	**172**	**173**	**174**	**175**	**176**	**177**	**178**	**179**	**180**
A	B	A	B	C	A	B	A	D	C

NETWORKING

1. When collection of various computers seems a single coherent system to its client, then it is called:

A. computer network
B. distributed system
C. both (A) and (B)
D. none of the above

2. Two devices are in network if:

A. a process in one device is able to exchange information with a process in another device
B. a process is running on both devices
C. PIDs of the processes running of different devices are same
D. none of the above

3. Which one of the following computer network is built on the top of another network?

A. prior network   B. chief network
C. prime network   D. overlay network

4. In computer network nodes are:

A. the computer that originates the data
B. the computer that routes the data
C. the computer that terminates the data
D. all of the above

5. Communication channel is shared by all the machines on the network in:

A. broadcast network   B. unicast network
C. multicast network   D. none of the above

6. Bluetooth is an example of:

A. personal area network
B. local area network
C. virtual private network
D. none of the above

7. A ________ is a device that forwards packets between networks by processing the routing information included in the packet.

A. bridge   B. firewall
C. router   D. all of the above

8. A list of protocols used by a system, one protocol per layer, is called:

A. protocol architecture
B. protocol stack
C. protocol suit
D. none of the above

9. Network congestion occurs:

A. in case of traffic overloading
B. when a system terminates
C. when connection between two nodes terminates
D. none of the above

10. Which one of the following extends a private network across public networks?

A. local area network
B. virtual private network
C. enterprise private network
D. storage area network

11. OSI stands for:

A. open system interconnection
B. operating system interface
C. optical service implementation
D. none of the above

12. The OSI model has ________ layers.

A. 4   B. 5
C. 6   D. 7

13. TCP/IP model does not have ________ layer but OSI model have this layer.

A. session layer   B. presentation layer
C. application layer   D. both (A) and (B)

14. Which layer links the network support layers and user support layers:

A. session layer B. data link layer
C. transport layer D. network layer

15. Which address is used in an internet employing the TCP/IP protocols?

A. physical address and logical address
B. port address
C. specific address
D. all of the above

16. TCP/IP model was developed ________ the OSI model.

A. prior to B. after
C. simultaneous to D. none of the above

17. Which layer is responsible for process to process delivery?

A. network layer B. transport layer
C. session layer D. data link layer

18. Which address identifies a process on a host?

A. physical address B. logical address
C. port address D. specific address

19. Which layer provides the services to user?

A. application layer B. session layer
C. presentation layer D. none of the above

20. Transmission data rate is decided by:

A. network layer B. physical layer
C. data link layer D. transport layer

21. The physical layer concerns with:

A. bit-by-bit delivery
B. process to process delivery
C. application to application delivery
D. none of the above

22. Which transmission media has the highest transmission speed in a network?

A. coaxial cable B. twisted pair cable
C. optical fiber D. electrical cable

23. Bits can be send over guided and unguided media as analog signal by:

A. digital modulation B. amplitude modulation
C. frequency modulation D. phase modulation

24. The portion of physical layer that interfaces with the media access control sublayer is called:

A. physical signalling sublayer
B. physical data sublayer
C. physical address sublayer
D. none of the above

25. Physical layer provides:

A. mechanical specifications of electrical connectors and cables
B. electrical specification of transmission line signal level
C. specification for IR over optical fiber
D. all of the above

26. In asynchronous serial communication the physical layer provides:

A. start and stop signalling
B. flow control
C. both (A) and (B)
D. none of the above

27. The physical layer is responsible for

A. line coding B. channel coding
C. modulation D. all of the above

28. The physical layer translates logical communication requests from the ________ into hardware specific operations.

A. data link layer B. network layer
C. trasnport layer D. application layer

29. A single channel is shared by multiple signals by:

A. analog modulation B. digital modulation
C. multiplexing D. none of the above

30. Wireless transmission can be done via:

A. radio waves B. microwaves
C. infrared D. all of the above

31. The data link layer takes the packets from ________ and encapsulates them into frames for transmission.

A. network layer B. physical layer
C. transport layer D. application layer

32. Which one of the following task is not done by data link layer?

A. framing B. error control
C. flow control D. channel coding

33. Which sublayer of the data link layer performs data link functions that depend upon the type of medium?

A. logical link control sublayer
B. media access control sublayer
C. network interface control sublayer
D. none of the above

34. Header of a frame generally contains:

A. synchronization bytes
B. addresses
C. frame identifier
D. all of the above

35. Automatic repeat request error management mechanism is provided by:

A. logical link control sublayer
B. media access control sublayer

C. network interface control sublayer
D. none of the above

36. When 2 or more bits in a data unit has been changed during the transmission, the error is called:
A. random error B. burst error
C. inverted error D. none of the above

37. CRC stands for:
A. cyclic redundancy check
B. code repeat check
C. code redundancy check
D. cyclic repeat check

38. Which one of the following is a data link protocol?
A. ethernet
B. point to point protocol
C. HDLC
D. all of the above

39. Which one of the following is the multiple access protocol for channel access control?
A. CSMA/CD B. CSMA/CA
C. both (A) and (B) D. none of the above

40. The technique of temporarily delaying outgoing acknowledgements so that they can be hooked onto the next outgoing data frame is called
A. piggybacking
B. cyclic redundancy check
C. fletcher's checksum
D. none of the above

41. The network layer concerns with:
A. bits B. frames
C. packets D. none of the above

42. Which one of the following is not a function of network layer?
A. routing B. inter-networking
C. congestion control D. none of the above

43. The 4 byte IP address consists of:
A. network address B. host address
C. both (A) and (B) D. none of the above

44. In virtual circuit network each packet contains:
A. full source and destination address
B. a short VC number
C. both (A) and (B)
D. none of the above

45. Which one of the following routing algorithm can be used for network layer design?
A. shortest path algorithm
B. distance vector routing
C. link state routing
D. all of the above

46. Multidestination routing:
A. is same as broadcast routing
B. contains the list of all destinations
C. data is not sent by packets
D. none of the above

47. A subset of a network that includes all the routers but contains no loops is called:
A. spanning tree B. spider structure
C. spider tree D. none of the above

48. Which one of the following algorithm is not used for congestion control?
A. traffic aware routing
B. admission control
C. load shedding
D. none of the above

49. The network layer protocol of internet is:
A. ethernet
B. internet protocol
C. hypertext transfer protocol
D. none of the above

50. ICMP is primarily used for:
A. error and diagnostic functions
B. addressing
C. forwarding
D. none of the above

51. Transport layer aggregates data from different applications into a single stream before passing it to:
A. network layer B. data link layer
C. application layer D. physical layer

52. Which one of the following is a transport layer protocol used in internet?
A. TCP B. UDP
C. Both (A) and (B) D. None of the above

53. User datagram protocol is called connectionless because:
A. all UDP packets are treated independently by transport layer
B. it sends data as a stream of related packets
C. both (A) and (B)
D. none of the above

54. Transmission control protocol is:
A. connection oriented protocol
B. uses a three way handshake to establish a connection
C. receives data from application as a single stream
D. all of the above

55. An endpoint of an inter-process communication flow across a computer network is called:

A. socket B. pipe
C. port D. none of the above

56. Socket-style API for windows is called
A. wsock B. winsock
C. wins D. none of the above

57. Which one of the following is a version of UDP with congestion control?
A. datagram congestion control protocol
B. stream control transmission protocol
C. structured stream transport
D. none of the above

58. A ________ is a TCP name for a transport service access point.
A. port B. pipe
C. node D. none of the above

59. Transport layer protocols deals with:
A. application to application communication
B. process to process communication
C. node to node communication
D. none of the above

60. The ________ translates internet domain and host names to IP address.
A. domain name system
B. routing information protocol
C. network time protocol
D. internet relay chat

61. Teredo is an automatic tunneling technique. In each client the obfuscated IPv4 address is represented by bits:
A. 96 to 127 B. 0 to 63
C. 80 to 95 D. 64 to 79

62. Which one of the following allows a user at one site to establish a connection to another site and then pass keystrokes from local host to remote host?
A. HTTP B. FTP
C. telnet D. none of the above

63. Application layer protocol defines:
A. types of messages exchanged
B. message format, syntax and semantics
C. rules for when and how processes send and respond to messages
D. all of the above

64. Which one of the following protocol delivers/stores mail to reciever server?
A. simple mail transfer protocol
B. post office protocol
C. internet mail access protocol
D. hypertext transfer protocol

65. The ASCII encoding of binary data is called:
A. base 64 encoding B. base 32 encoding
C. base 16 encoding D. base 8 encoding

66. Which one of the following is an internet standard protocol for managing devices on IP network?
A. dynamic host configuration protocol
B. simple network management protocol
C. internet message access protocol
D. media gateway protocol

67. Which one of the following is not an application layer protocol?
A. media gateway protocol
B. dynamic host configuration protocol
C. resource reservation protocol
D. session initiation protocol

68. Which protocol is a signalling communication protocol used for controlling multimedia communication sessions?
A. session initiation protocol
B. session modelling protocol
C. session maintenance protocol
D. none of the above

69. Which one of the following is not correct?
A. application layer protocols are used by both source and destination devices during a communication session
B. application layer protocols implemented on the source and destination host must match
C. both (A) and (B)
D. none of the above

70. When displaying a web page, the application layer uses the:
A. HTTP protocol B. FTP protocol
C. SMTP protocol D. none of the above

71. The entire hostname has a maximum of:
A. 255 characters B. 127 characters
C. 63 characters D. 31 characters

72. A DNS client is called:
A. DNS updater B. DNS resolver
C. DNS handler D. None of the above

73. Servers handle requests for other domains:
A. directly
B. by contacting remote DNS server
C. it is not possible
D. none of the above

74. DNS database contains
A. name server records

B. hostname-to-address records
C. hostname aliases
D. all of the above

75. If a server has no clue about where to find the address for a hostname then:
A. server asks to the root server
B. server asks to its adjacent server
C. request is not processed
D. none of the above

76. Which one of the following allows client to update their DNS entry as their IP address change?
A. dynamic DNS
B. mail transfer agent
C. authoritative name server
D. none of the above

77. Wildcard domain names start with label:
A. @ B. *
C. & D. #

78. The right to use a domain name is delegated by domain name registers which are accredited by:
A. internet architecture board
B. internet society
C. internet research task force
D. internet corporation for assigned names and numbers

79. The domain name system is maintained by:
A. distributed database system
B. a single server
C. a single computer
D. none of the above

80. Which one of the following is not true?
A. multiple hostnames may correspond to a single IP address
B. a single hostname may correspond to many IP addresses
C. a single hostname may correspond to a single IP address
D. none of the above

81. Telnet protocol is used to establish a connection to:
A. TCP port number 21
B. TCP port number 22
C. TCP port number 23
D. TCP port number 24

82. Which one of the following is not true?
A. telnet defines a network virtual terminal (NVT) standard
B. client programs interact with NVT
C. server translates NVT operations
D. none of the above

83. All telnet operations are sent as:
A. 4 bytes B. 8 bytes
C. 16 bytes D. 32 bytes

84. Absolute Telnet is a telnet client for:
A. windows B. linux
C. mac D. none of the above

85. The decimal code of interpret as command (IAC) character is:
A 252 B. 253
C. 254 D. 255

86. In character mode operation of telnet implementation
A. each character typed is sent by the client to the server
B. each character typed is discarded by the server
C. both (A) an (B)
D. none of the above

87. In telnet, the client echoes the character on the screen but does not send it until a whole line is completed in:
A. default mode B. character mode
C. server mode D. none of the above

88. Which one of the following is not correct?
A. telnet is a general purpose client-server program
B. telnet lets user access an application on a remote computer
C. telnet can also be used for file transfer
D. none of the above

89. Which operating mode of telnet is full duplex?
A. default mode B. server mode
C. line mode D. none of the above

90. If we want that a character be interpreted by the client instead of server:
A. escape character has to be used
B. control functions has to be disabled
C. it is not possible
D. none of the above

91. A piece of icon or image on a web page associated with another webpage is called:
A. url B. hyperlink
C. plugin D. none of the above

92. Dynamic web page
A. is same every time whenever it displays
B. generates on demand by a program or a request from browser
C. both (A) and (B)
D. none of the above

93. What is a web browser?

A. a program that can display a web page
B. a program used to view html documents
C. it enables user to access the resources of internet
D. all of the above

94. Common gateway interface is used to:

A. generate executable files from web content by web server
B. generate web pages
C. stream videos
D. none of the above

95. URL stands for:

A. unique reference label
B. uniform reference label
C. uniform resource locator
D. unique resource locator

96. A web cookie is a small piece of data:

A. sent from a website and stored in user's web browser while a user is browsing a website
B. sent from user and stored in the server while a user is browsing a website
C. sent from root server to all servers
D. none of the above

97. Which one of the following is not used to generate dynamic web pages?

A. PHP   B. ASP.NET
C. JSP   D. none of the above

98. An alternative of javascript on windows platform is:

A. VBScript   B. ASP.NET
C. JSP   D. none of the above

99. What is document object model (DOM)?

A. convention for representing and interacting with objects in html documents
B. application programming interface
C. hierarchy of objects in ASP.NET
D. none of the above

100. AJAX stands for:

A. asynchronous javascript and xml
B. advanced JSP and xml
C. asynchronous JSP and xml
D. advanced javascript and xml

101. Multiple object can be sent over a TCP connection between client and server in

A. persistent HTTP   B. nonpersistent HTTP
C. both (A) and (B)   D. none of the above

102. HTTP is _______ protocol.

A. application layer
B. transport layer
C. network layer
D. none of the above

103. In the network HTTP resources are located by:

A. uniform resource identifier
B. unique resource locator
C. unique resource identifier
D. none of the above

104. HTTP client requests by establishing a ________ connection to a particular port on the server.

A. user datagram protocol
B. transmission control protocol
C. broader gateway protocol
D. none of the above

105. In HTTP pipelining:

A. multiple HTTP requests are sent on a single TCP connection without waiting for the corresponding responses
B. multiple HTTP requests can not be sent on a single TCP connection
C. multiple HTTP requests are sent in a queue on a single TCP connection
D. none of the above

106. FTP server listens for connection on port number:

A. 20   B. 21
C. 22   D. 23

107. In FTP protocol, client contacts server using ________ as the transport protocol.

A. transmission control protocol
B. user datagram protocol
C. datagram congestion control protocol
D. stream control transmission protocol

108. In which mode FTP, the client initiates both the control and data connections.

A. active mode   B. passive mode
C. both (A) and (B)   D. none of the above

109. The file transfer protocol is built on:

A. data centric architecture
B. service oriented architecture
C. client server architecture
D. none of the above

110. In file transfer protocol, data transfer can be done in

A. stream mode   B. block mode
C. compressed mode   D. all of the above

111. Ethernet frame consists of:

A. MAC address   B. IP address
C. both (A) and (B)   D. none of the above

112. What is stat frame delimeter (SFD) in ethernet frame?

A. 10101010 B. 10101011
C. 00000000 D. 11111111

113. MAC address is of:

A. 24 bits B. 36 bits
C. 42 bits D. 48 bits

114. What is autonegotiation?

A. a procedure by which two connected devices choose common transmission parameters
B. a security algorithm
C. a routing algorithm
D. none of the above

115. Ethernet in metropolitan area network (MAN) can be used as:

A. pure ethernet B. ethernet over SDH
C. ethernet over MPLS D. all of the above

116. A point-to-point protocol over ethernet is a network protocol for:

A. encapsulating PPP frames inside ethernet frames
B. encapsulating ethernet frames inside PPP frames
C. for security of ethernet frames
D. for security of PPP frames

117. High speed ethernet works on:

A. coaxial cable B. twisted pair cable
C. optical fiber D. none of the above

118. The maximum size of payload field in ethernet frame is:

A. 1000 bytes B. 1200 bytes
C. 1300 bytes D. 1500 bytes

119. What is interframe gap?

A. idle time between frames
B. idle time between frame bits
C. idle time between packets
D. none of the above

120. An ethernet frame that is less than the IEEE 802.3 minimum length of 64 octets is called:

A. short frame B. run frame
C. mini frame D. man frame

121. Which of this is not a constituent of residential telephone line?

A. A high-speed downstream channel
B. A medium-speed downstream channel
C. A low-speed downstream channel
D. None of the above

122. In DSL telco provides these services

A. Wired phone access B. ISP
C. Both the above D. None of the above

123. The function of DSLAM is:

A. Convert analog signals into digital signals
B. Convert digital signals into analog signals
C. Amplify digital signals
D. None of the above

124. The following term is not associted with DSL:

A. DSLAM B. CO
C. Splitter D. CMTS

125. HFC contains:

A. Fibre cable
B. Coaxial cable
C. Both the above
D. None of the above

126. Choose the statement which is not applicable for cable internet access

A. It is a shared broadcast medium
B. It includes HFCs
C. Cable modem connects home PC to Ethernet port
D. Analog signal is converted to digital signal in DSLAM

127. Among the optical-distribution architectures that is essentially switched ethernet is:

A. AON B. PON
C. NON D. None of the above

128. StarBand provides:

A. FTTH internet access
B. Cable access
C. Telephone access
D. Satellite access

129. Home Access is provided by:

A. DSL B. FTTP
C. Cable D. All of the above

130. ONT is connected to splitter using:

A. High speed fibre cable
B. HFC
C. Optical cable
D. None of the above

131. The sharing of a medium and its link by two or more devices is called ______.

A. Fully duplexing B. Multiplexing
C. Both (A) and (B) D. None of the above

132. Multiplexing is used in ______.

A. Packet switching
B. Circuit switching
C. Data switching
D. None of the above

133. Which multiplexing technique transmits digital signals?
A. FDM B. TDM
C. WDM D. None of the above

134. If there are n signal sources of same data rate than TDM link has ________ slots:
A. n B. $n/2$
C. $n*2$ D. 2^n

135. If link transmits 4000 frames per second, and each slot has 8 bits, the transmission rate of circuit this TDM is:
A. 32kbps B. 500bps
C. 500kbps D. None of the above

136. The state when dedicated signals are idle are called
A. Death period B. Poison period
C. Silent period D. None of the above

137. Multiplexing can provide
A. Efficiency B. Privacy
C. Anti jamming D. Both (A) and (B)

138. In TDM, the transmission rate of the multiplexed path is usually ________ the sum of the transmission rates of the signal sources.
A. Greater than B. Lesser than
C. Equal to D. Equal to or greater than

139. In TDM, slots are further divided into:
A. Seconds B. Frames
C. Packets D. None of the above

140. Multiplexing technique that shifts each signal to a different carrier frequency:
A. FDM B. TDM
C. Either (A) or (B) D. Both (A) and (B)

141. Physical or logical arrangement of network is:
A. Topology B. Routing
C. Networking D. None of the above

142. In this topology there is a central controller or hub:
A. Star B. Mesh
C. Ring D. Bus

143. This topology requires multipoint connection:
A. Star B. Mesh
C. Ring D. Bus

144. Data communication system spanning states, countries, or the whole world is
A. LAN B. WAN
C. MAN D. None of the above

145. Data communication system within a building or campus is:
A. LAN B. WAN
C. MAN D. None of the above

146. Expand WAN:
A. World area network
B. Wide area network
C. Web area network
D. None of the above

147. A local telephone network is an example of a ________ network:
A. Packet switched
B. Circuit switched
C. both the above
D. none of the above

148. Most packet switches use this principle:
A. Stop and wait
B. Store and forward
C. Both the above
D. None of the above

149. If there are N routers from source to destination, total end to end delay in sending packet P(L→ number of bits in the packet R→ transmission rate):
A. N B. (N*L)/R
C. (2N*L)/R D. L/R

150. Method(s) to move data through a network of links and switches:
A. Packet switching B. Circuit switching
C. Line switching D. Both (A) and (B)

151. The resources needed for communication between end systems are reserved for the duration of session between end systems in ________.
A. Packet switching B. Circuit switching
C. Line switching D. Frequency switching

152. As the resources are reserved between two communicating end systems in circuit switching, this is achieved ________.
A. authentication B. guaranteed constant rate
C. reliability D. store and forward

153. What is internet?
A. a single network
B. a vast collection of different networks
C. interconnection of local area networks
D. none of the above

154. To join the internet, the computer has to be connected to a:
A. internet architecture board
B. internet society
C. internet service provider
D. none of the above

155. Internet access by transmitting digital data over the wires of a local telephone network is provided by:

A. leased line B. digital subscriber line
C. digital signal line D. none of the above

156. ISP exchanges internet traffic between their networks by:

A. internet exchange point
B. subscriber end point
C. ISP end point
D. none of the above

157. Which one of the following protocol is not used in internet?

A. HTTP B. DHCP
C. DNS D. None of the above

158. IPv6 address have a size of:

A. 32 bits B. 64 bits
C. 128 bits D. 265 bits

159. Internet works on:

A. packet switching B. circuit switching
C. both (A) and (B) D. none of the above

160. Which one of the following is not an application layer protocol used in internet?

A. remote procedure call
B. internet relay chat
C. resource reservation protocol
D. none of the above

161. Which protocol assigns IP address to the client connected in the internet?

A. DHCP B. IP
C. RPC D. None of the above

162. Which one of the following is not used in media access control?

A. ethernet
B. digital subscriber line
C. fiber distributed data interface
D. none of the above

163. In cryptography, what is cipher?

A. algorithm for performing encryption and decryption
B. encrypted message
C. both (A) and (B)
D. none of the above

164. In asymmetric key cryptography, the private key is kept by:

A. sender
B. receiver
C. sender and receiver
D. all the connected devices to the network

165. Which one of the following algorithm is not used in asymmetric key cryptography?

A. RSA algorithm
B. diffie-hellman algorithm
C. electronic code book algorithm
D. none of the above

166. In cryptography, the order of the letters in a message is rearranged by:

A. transpositional ciphers
B. substitution ciphers
C. both (A) and (B)
D. none of the above

167. What is data encryption standard (DES)?

A. block cipher B. stream cipher
C. bit cipher D. none of the above

168. Cryptanalysis is used:

A. to find some insecurity in a cryptographic scheme
B. to increase the speed
C. to encrypt the data
D. none of the above

169. Which one of the following is a cryptographic protocol used to secure HTTP connection?

A. stream control transmission protocol (SCTP)
B. transport layer security (TSL)
C. explicit congestion notification (ECN)
D. resource reservation protocol (RRP)

170. Voice privacy in GSM cellular telephone protocol is provided by:

A. A5/2 cipher B. b5/4 cipher
C. b5/6 cipher D. b5/8 cipher

171. ElGamal encryption system is:

A. symmetric key encryption algorithm
B. asymmetric key encryption algorithm
C. not an encryption algorithm
D. none of the above

172. Cryptographic hash function takes an arbitrary block of data and returns:

A. fixed size bit string
B. variable size bit string
C. both (A) and (B)
D. none of the above

173. The attackers of a network of compromised devices known as:

A. Internet B. Botnet
C. Telnet D. D-net

174. Which of the following is a form of DoS attack ?

A. Vulnerability attack
B. Bandwidth flooding
C. Connection flooding
D. All of the above

175. The DoS attack in which the attacker establishes a large number of half-open or fully open TCP connections at the target host is:
A. Vulnerability attack B. Bandwidth flooding
C. Connection flooding D. All of the above

176. The DoS attack in which the attacker sends deluge of packets to the targeted host is:
A. Vulnerability attack B. Bandwidth flooding
C. Connection flooding D. All of the above

177. Packet sniffers involve:
A. Active receiver
B. Passive receiver
C. Both the above
D. None of the above

178. Sniffers can be deployed in:
A. Wired environment B. WiFi
C. Ethernet LAN D. All of the above

179. Firewalls are often configured to block:
A. UDP traffic
B. TCP traffic
C. Both the above
D. None of the above

180. DHCP (dynamic host configuration protocol) provides ________ to the client.
A. IP address B. MAC address
C. Url D. None of the above

181. DHCP is used for:
A. IPv6 B. IPv4
C. Both (A) and (B) D. None of the above

182. The DHCP server
A. maintains a database of available IP addresses
B. maintains the information about client configuration parameters
C. grants an IP address when receives a request from a client
D. all of the above

183. IP assigned for a client by DHCP server is:
A. for a limited period
B. for unlimited period
C. not time dependent
D. none of the above

184. DHCP uses UDP port _______ for sending data to the server.
A. 66 B. 67
C. 68 D. 69

185. The DHCP server can provide the ________ of the IP addresses.
A. dynamic allocation B. automatic allocation
C. static allocation D. all of the above

186. DHCP client and servers on the same subnet communicate via:
A. UDP broadcast B. UDP unicast
C. TCP broadcast D. TCP unicast

187. After obtaining the IP address, to prevent the IP conflict the client may use:
A. internet relay chat
B. broader gateway protocol
C. address resolution protocol
D. none of the above

188. What is DHCP snooping?
A. techniques applied to ensure the security of an existing DHCP infrastructure
B. encryption of the DHCP server requests
C. algorithm for DHCP
D. none of the above

189. If DHCP snooping is configured on a LAN switch, then clients having specific ________ can access the network.
A. MAC address B. IP address
C. both (A) and (B) D. none of the above

190. Real-time transport protocol (RTP) is mostly used in
A. streaming media B. video teleconference
C. television services D. all of the above

191. RTP is used to:
A. carry the media stream
B. monitor transmission statistics of streams
C. monitor quality of service of streams
D. none of the above

192. RTP provides the facility of jitter ________.
A. compensation B. expansion
C. both (A) and (B) D. none of the above

193. Which protocol provides the synchronization between media streams?
A. RTP B. RTCP
C. RPC D. None of the above

194. An RTP session is established for:
A. each media stream
B. all media streams
C. some predefined number of media streams
D. none of the above

195. RTP can use:
A. unpreviledged UDP ports
B. stream control transmission protocol
C. datagram congestion control protocol
D. all of the above

196. Which one of the following multimedia formats can not be supported by RTP?

A. MPEG-4 B. MJPEG
C. MPEG D. None of the above

197. An RTP header has a minimum size of:

A. 12 bytes B. 16 bytes
C. 24 bytes D. 32 bytes

198. Which one of the following is not correct?

A. RTCP provides canonical end-point identifiers to all session participants
B. RTCP reports are expected to be sent by all participants
C. Both (A) and (B)
D. None of the above

199. Which protocol defines a profile of RTP that provides cryptographic services for the transfer of payload data?

A. SRTP B. RTCP
C. RCP D. None of the above

200. Ping can:

A. Measure round-trip time
B. Report packet loss
C. Report latency
D. All of the above

201. Suppose two IPv6 nodes want to interoperate using IPv6 datagrams but are connected to each other by intervening IPv4 routers. The best solution here is

A. Use dual-stack approach
B. Tunneling
C. No solution
D. Replace the system

202. Ping sweep is a part of:

A. Traceroute B. Nmap
C. Route D. Ipconfig

203. ICMP is used in:

A. Ping B. Traceroute
C. Ifconfig D. Both (A) and (B)

204. _______ command is used to manipulate TCP/IP routing table.

A. route B. Ipconfig
C. Ifconfig D. Traceroute

205. If you want to find the number of routers between a source and destination, the utility to be used is.

A. route B. Ipconfig
C. Ifconfig D. Traceroute

206. Which of the following is related to ipconfig in Microsoft Windows?

A. Display all current TCP/IP network configuration values
B. Modify DHCP settings
C. Modify DNS settings
D. All of the above

207. This allows to check if a domain is available for registration.

A. Domain Check B. Domain Dossier
C. Domain Lookup D. None of the above

208. Choose the wrong statement:

A. Nslookup is used to query a DNS server for DNS data
B. Ping is used to check connectivity
C. Pathping combines the functionality of ping with that of route
D. Ifconfig can configure TCP/IP network interface parameters

209. Expansion of FTP is:

A. Fine Transfer Protocol
B. File Transfer Protocol
C. First Transfer Protocol
D. None of the above

210. FTP is built on ________ architecture.

A. Client-server
B. P2P
C. Both of the above
D. None of the above

211. FTP uses ________ parallel TCP connections to transfer a file:

A. 1 B. 2
C. 3 D. 4

212. Identify the incorrect statement:

A. FTP stands for File Transfer Protocol
B. FTP uses two parallel TCP connections
C. FTP sends its control information in-band
D. FTP sends exactly one file over the data connection

213. If 5 files are transfered from server A to client B in the same session. The number of TCP connection between A and B is:

A. 5 B. 10
C. 2 D. 6

214. FTP server:

A. Mantains state
B. Is stateless
C. Has single TCP connection for a file transfer
D. None of the above

215. The commands, from client to server, and replies, from server to client, are sent across the control connection in ________ bit ASCII format:

A. 8 B. 7
C. 3 D. 5

216. Find the FTP reply whose message is wrongly matched:
A. 331 – Username OK, password required
B. 425 – Can't open data connection
C. 452 – Error writing file
D. 452 – Can't open data connection

217. Mode of data transfer in FTP, where all is left to TCP:
A. Stream mode B. Block mode
C. Compressed mode D. None of the above

218. The password is sent to the server using ______ command:
A. PASSWD B. PASS
C. PASSWORD D. None of the above

219. The number of objects in a Web page which consists of 4 jpeg images and HTML text is:
A. 4 B. 1
C. 5 D. None of the above

220. The default connection type used by HTTP is ______.
A. Persistent
B. Non-persistent
C. Either of the above
D. None of the above

221. The time taken by a packet to travel from client to server and then back to the client is called ______.
A. STT B. RTT
C. PTT D. None of the above

222. The HTTP request message is sent in ______ part of three-way handshake.
A. First B. Second
C. Third D. None of the above

223. In the process of fetching a web page from a server the HTTP request/response takes ______ RTTs.
A. 2 B. 1
C. 4 D. 3

224. The first line of HTTP request message is called ______.
A. Request line B. Header line
C. Status line D. Entity line

225. The values GET, POST, HEAD etc. are specified in ______ of HTTP message:
A. Request line B. Header line
C. Status line D. Entity body

226. The ______ method when used in the method field, leaves entity body empty.
A. POST
B. GET
C. Both the above
D. None of the above

227. The HTTP response message leaves out the requested object when ______ method is used:
A. GET B. POST
C. HEAD D. PUT

228. Find the oddly matched HTTP status codes:
A. 200 OK
B. 400 Bad Request
C. 301 Moved permanently
D. 304 Not Found

229. Which of the following is not correct?
A. Web cache doesn't has its own disk space
B. Web cache can act both like server and client
C. Web cache might reduce the response time
D. Web cache contains copies of recently requested objects

230. Which of the following is present in both an HTTP request line and a status line?
A. HTTP version number
B. URL
C. Method
D. None of the above

231. Which of the following is not applicable for IP?
A. Error reporting
B. Handle addressing conventions
C. Datagram format
D. Packet handling conventions

232. Which of the following field in IPv4 datagram is not related to fragmentation?
A. Flags B. Offset
C. TOS D. Identifier

233. The TTL field has value 10. How many routers (max) can process this datagram?
A. 11 B. 5
C. 10 D. 1

234. If the value in protocol field is 17, the transport layer protocol used is ______.
A. TCP
B. UDP
C. Either of the above
D. None of the above

235. The data field can carry which of the following?
A. TCP segemnt B. UDP segment
C. ICMP messages D. None of the above

236. What should be the flag value to indicate the last fragment?

A. 0
B. 1
C. TTl value
D. None of the above

237. Which of these is not applicable for IP protocol?

A. is connectionless
B. offer reliable service
C. offer unreliable service
D. none of the above

238. Fragmentation has following demerits:

A. complicates routers
B. open to DOS attack
C. overlapping of fragments
D. all of the above

239. Which field helps to check rearrangement of the fragments?

A. Offset
B. Flag
C. TTL
D. Identifier

240. The size of IP address in IPv6 is:

A. 4 bytes
B. 128 bits
C. 8 bytes
D. 100 bits

241. The header length of an IPv6 datagram is ________.

A. 10 bytes
B. 25 bytes
C. 30 bytes
D. 40 bytes

242. In the IPv6 header,the traffic class field is similar to which field in the IPv4 header?

A. Fragmentation field
B. Fast-switching
C. ToS field
D. Option field

243. IPv6 does not use ________ type of address:

A. Broadcast
B. Multicast
C. Anycast
D. None of the above

244. These are the features present in IPv4 but not in IPv6.

A. Fragmentation
B. Header checksum
C. Options
D. All of the above

245. The ________ field determines the lifetime of IPv6 datagram:

A. Hop limit
B. TTL
C. Next header
D. None of the above

246. Dual-stack approach refers to:

A. Implementing Ipv4 with 2 stacks
B. Implementing Ipv6 with 2 stacks
C. Node has both IPv4 and IPv6 support
D. None of the above

ANSWERS

1	2	3	4	5	6	7	8	9	10
B	A	D	D	A	A	C	B	A	B
11	**12**	**13**	**14**	**15**	**16**	**17**	**18**	**19**	**20**
A	D	D	C	D	A	B	C	A	B
21	**22**	**23**	**24**	**25**	**26**	**27**	**28**	**29**	**30**
A	C	A	A	D	C	D	A	C	D
31	**32**	**33**	**34**	**35**	**36**	**37**	**38**	**39**	**40**
A	D	B	D	A	B	A	D	C	A
41	**42**	**43**	**44**	**45**	**46**	**47**	**48**	**49**	**50**
C	D	C	B	D	C	A	D	B	A
51	**52**	**53**	**54**	**55**	**56**	**57**	**58**	**59**	**60**
A	C	A	D	A	B	A	A	B	A
61	**62**	**63**	**64**	**65**	**66**	**67**	**68**	**69**	**70**
A	C	D	A	A	B	C	A	C	A
71	**72**	**73**	**74**	**75**	**76**	**77**	**78**	**79**	**80**
A	B	B	D	A	A	B	D	A	C
81	**82**	**83**	**84**	**85**	**86**	**87**	**88**	**89**	**90**
C	D	B	A	D	A	A	C	C	A
91	**92**	**93**	**94**	**95**	**96**	**97**	**98**	**99**	**100**
B	B	D	A	C	A	D	A	A	A

101	102	103	104	105	106	107	108	109	110
A	A	A	B	A	B	A	B	C	D
111	112	113	114	115	116	117	118	119	120
A	B	D	A	D	A	C	D	A	B
121	122	123	124	125	126	127	128	129	130
C	C	A	D	C	D	A	D	D	C
131	132	133	134	135	136	137	138	139	140
B	B	B	A	A	C	D	A	B	A
141	142	143	144	145	146	147	148	149	150
A	A	D	B	A	B	A	B	B	D
151	152	153	154	155	156	157	158	159	160
B	B	B	C	B	A	D	C	A	C
161	162	163	164	165	166	167	168	169	170
A	D	A	B	C	A	A	A	B	A
171	172	173	174	175	176	177	178	179	180
B	A	B	D	C	B	B	D	A	A
181	182	183	184	185	186	187	188	189	190
C	D	A	B	D	A	C	A	C	D
191	192	193	194	195	196	197	198	199	200
A	A	B	A	D	D	A	D	A	D
201	202	203	204	205	206	207	208	209	210
B	B	D	A	D	D	A	C	B	A
211	212	213	214	215	216	217	218	219	220
B	C	D	A	B	D	A	B	C	A
221	222	223	224	225	226	227	228	229	230
B	C	B	A	A	B	C	D	A	A
231	232	233	234	235	236	237	238	239	240
A	C	C	B	C	A	B	D	A	B
241	242	243	244	245	246				
D	C	A	D	A	C				

CLOUD OPERATIONS

1. Cloud model relies on:
   A. Communication API B. Middleware
   C. Web documents D. Embedded device

2. What widely used service is built on cloud-computing technology?
   A. Twitter B. Skype
   C. Gmail D. All of the above

3. HTTP is a _______ protocol.
   A. stateful B. unidirectional
   C. bidirectional D. full dulpex

4. Websocket is a _______ Protocol.
   A. stateful
   B. bidirectional
   C. connection oriented
   D. all of the above

5. Websocket protocol uses which communication model:
   A. Publish-Subscribe B. Request Response
   C. Push-Pull D. Exclusive Pair

6. Which of these techniques is vital for creating cloud-computing centers:
   A. Virtualization B. Transubstantiation
   C. Cannibalization D. Insubordination

7. An internal cloud is _______.
   A. An overhanging threat
   B. A career risk for a CIO
   C. A cloud that sits behind a corporate
   D. The group of knowledge workers who use a social network for water- cooler gossip

8. Which of these is not an antecedent of the cloud?
   A. Software as a service
   B. Utility computing
   C. Grid computing
   D. Desktop computing

9. Which of the following subject area deals with pay-as-you-go usage model?
   A. Accounting Management
   B. Compliance
   C. Data Privacy
   D. All of the above

10. Point out the correct statement:
    A. Except for tightly managed SaaS cloud providers
    B. Cloud computing vendors run very reliable networks
    C. The low barrier to entry cannot be accompanied by a low barrier to provisioning
    D. All of the above

11. ________captive requires that the cloud accommodate multiple compliance regimes.
    A. Licensed B. Policy-based
    C. Variable D. All of the above

12. Security methods such as private encryption, VLANs and firewalls comes under _______subject area.
    A. Accounting Management
    B. Compliance
    C. Data Privacy
    D. All of the above

13. Which of the following captive area deals with monitoring?
    A. Licensed
    B. Variable but under control
    C. Law
    D. All of the above

14. Network bottlenecks occur when _________ data sets must be transferred.
    A. large B. small
    C. big D. all of the above

15. Amazon AWS Consists of following services

A. Iaas B. Paas
C. Saas D. All of the above

16. RDS is a ________ type of database.

A. SQL B. NonSQL
C. Simple storage D. All of the above

17. Dynamodb is ________ type of storage.

A. NonSQL B. SQL
C. Simple storage D. All of the above

18. Cloud __________ are standardized in order to appeal to the majority of its audience.

A. SVAs B. SLAs
C. SALs D. None of the above

19. The reputation for cloud computing services for the quality of those services is shared by _________.

A. replicas B. shards
C. tenants D. all of the above

20. _______ is a function of the particular enterprise and application in an on-premises deployment.

A. Vendor lock B. Vendor lock-in
C. Vendor lock-ins D. None of the above

21. _______ computing refers to applications and services that run on a distributed network using virtualized resources.

A. Distributed B. Cloud
C. Soft D. Parallel

22. _______ as a utility is a dream that dates from the beginning of the computing industry itself

A. Model B. Computing
C. Software D. All of the above

23. Amazon Elastic Compute Cloud (Amazon EC2) is a web service based on:

A. Iaas B. Paas
C. Saas D. All of the above

24. Which of the following is essential concept related to Cloud?

A. Reliability B. Productivity
C. Abstraction D. All of the above

25. Point out the wrong statement:

A. applications benefit from deployment in the cloud
B. start very small and become big very fast
C. technology it is built on is evolutionary
D. None of the above

26. Which of the cloud concept is related to pooling and sharing of resources:

A. Polymorphism B. Abstraction
C. Virtualization D. None of the above

27. _______ has many of the characteristics of what is now being called cloud computing.

A. Internet B. Softwares
C. Web Service D. All of the above

28. Which of the following can be identified as cloud:

A. Web Applications B. Intranet
C. Hadoop D. All of the above

29. Which of the following is Cloud Platform by Amazon?

A. Azure B. AWS
C. Cloudera D. All of the above

30. Which of the following is the deployment model?

A. public B. private
C. hybrid D. all of the above

31. Which of the following is best known service model?

A. SaaS B. IaaS
C. PaaS D. All of the above

32. Which of the following is the highest degree of integration in cloud computing?

A. SaaS B. IaaS
C. PaaS D. All of the above

33. Which of the architectural layer is used as a front end in cloud computing?

A. client B. cloud
C. soft D. all of the above

34. Which of the following benefit is provided by the PaaS service provider?

A. A larger pool of qualified developers
B. More reliable operation
C. A logical design methodology
D. All of the above

35. Communication between services is done widely using _______ protocol.

A. REST B. SOAP
C. RESTful D. None of the above

36. Which of the following provider rely on the virtual machine technology to deliver servers?

A. CaaS B. AaaS
C. PaaS D. IaaS

37. Which of the following component is called hypervisor?

A. VGM B. VMc
C. VMM D. All of the above

38. Applications such as a Web server or database server that can run on a virtual machine image are referred to as _________.

A. virtual server B. virtual appliances
C. machine imaging D. all of the above

39. Amazon Machine Images are virtual appliances that have been packaged to run on the grid of ______ nodes.

A. Ben B. Xen
C. Ken D. Zen

40. _______ is a CPU emulator and virtual machine monitor.

A. Imaging B. Parallels
C. QEMU D. None of the above

41. What is the primary computing engine behind open stack ______?

A. NOVA B. Swift
C. Cinder D. Switch

42. Block Storage Service provides ______.

A. Cinder-api and Cinder-Scheduler
B. Api-Scheduler
C. Volume-block
D. Cinder-cinder

43. The block storage service contains the following component:

A. Back –end storage Devices user and Tenants (projects)
B. Software & hardware
C. Back-end and Front-end
D. User-Server

44. Open Stack Networking supports the following types ________.

A. Projects
B. Network isolation and overlay technologies
C. API
D. VLAN

45. Which HTTP error code would you get if the keystone token has expired?

A. Error 404 B. Error 403
C. Error 402 D. Error 401

46. Which of the following provide system resource access to virtual machine?

A. VMC B. VMM
C. VMN D. VNN

47. Which is not an approach to virtualization?

A. Partial virtualization
B. Lightweight virtualization
C. Full virtualization
D. Para virtualization

48. Cloud Service Consist of:

A. Software, Hardware, infrastructure
B. Platform, Software, infrastructure
C. Platform, Hardware, infrastructure
D. Platform , infrastructure

49. oVirt nodes are servers using ________with installed libvit demon and VDSM.

A. Linux x86-64 B. Linux x84-68
C. Linux x88-67 D. OS

50. oVirt Engine is a set of:

A. Software & operating system
B. Software & Hardware
C. Software & Service
D. Service and process

51. Benefits of using KVM:

A. Service and process
B. Hard 70 acess
C. Software and operating system
D. It support for any kind of guest os

52. Cons of virtualization:

A. It can have a high cost of implementation
B. It can have a low cost
C. It still has no limitation
D. It support security

53. Which of the following algorithm is used by Google to determine the importance of a particular page?

A. SVD B. PageRank
C. Fast Map D. PBD

54. Which of the following programming language solves problems by acting on constraints and inputs?

A. 3GL B. 4GL
C. 5GL D. 2GL

55. How many aspects need to be considered while assessing network capacity?

A. one B. two
C. three D. four

56. _______ scaling allows you to use a virtual system to run more virtual machines.

A. Horizontal B. Vertical
C. Out D. Virtue

57. Which of the following allows merchants to fill orders through Amazon.com fulfilment service?

A. Amazon Elastic Compute Cloud
B. Amazon Fulfilment Web Services
C. Amazon Relational Database Service
D. Amazon Simple Storage System

58. Which of the following uses an authentication device?

A. Amazon Elastic MapReduce
B. Amazon Mechanical Turk
C. Amazon DevPay
D. Multi-Factor Authentication

59. AMIs are operating systems running on the _______ virtualization hypervisor.

A. Yen
B. Xen
C. Ben
D. Multi-Factor Authentication

60. Which of the following instance class is best used for applications that are processor or compute-intensive?

A. Standard Instances B. High Memory Instances
C. High CPU Instances D. Programming

61. The source of HDFS architecture in Hadoop originated as:

A. Google distributed filesystem
B. Yahoo distributed filesystem
C. Facebook distributed file system
D. Amazon S3 storage

62. What is HDFS?

A. Storage layer
B. Batch processing engine
C. Resource management layer
D. All of the above

63. Which among the following command is used to copy a directory from one node to another in HDFS?

A. rcp B. distcp
C. dcp D. drcp

64. Which utility is used for checking the health of an HDFS file system?

A. fsck B. fchk
C. fsch D. fcks

65. Which among the following is the correct statement?

A. Datanode manage file system namespace
B. Namenode stores metadata
C. Namenode stores actual data
D. All of the above

66. What is default replication factor?

A. 1 B. 2
C. 3 D. 5

67. The namenode knows that the datanode is active using a mechanism known as:

A. Active pulse B. Data pulse
C. Heartbeats D. h-signal

68. What is the default size of HDFS Data Block?

A. 16 MB B. 32 MB
C. 64 MB D. 128 MB

69. What is HDFS Block in Hadoop?

A. It is the logical representation of data
B. It is the physical representation of data
C. Both the above
D. None of the above

70. Which of the following is the correct statement?

A. DataNode is the slave/worker node and holds the user data in the form of Data Blocks
B. Each incoming file is broken into 32 MB by default
C. NameNode stores user data in the form of Data Blocks
D. None of the above

71. The need for data replication can arise in various scenarios like:

A. Replication Factor is changed
B. DataNode goes down
C. Data Blocks get corrupted
D. All of the above

72. A file in HDFS that is smaller than a single block size:

A. Cannot be stored in HDFS
B. Occupies the full block's size.
C. Can span over multiple blocks
D. Occupies only the size it needs and not the full block

73. Which among the following are the duties of the NameNodes?

A. Manage file system namespace
B. It is responsible for storing actual data
C. Perform read-write operation as per request for the clients
D. None of the above

74. If the IP address or hostname of a data node changes:

A. The namenode updates the mapping between file name and block name
B. The data in that data node is lost forever
C. The namenode need not update mapping between file name and block name
D. There namenode has to be restarted

75. For the frequently accessed HDFS files the blocks are cached in:

A. The memory of the data node
B. In the memory of the namenode
C. Both the above
D. None of the above

76. Which scenario demands highest bandwidth for data transfer between nodes?

A. Different nodes on the same rack
B. Nodes on different racks in the same data center.
C. Nodes in different data centers
D. Data on the same node

77. When a client contacts the namenode for accessing a file, the namenode responds with:

A. Size of the file requested
B. Block ID and hostname of all the data nodes containing that block
C. Block ID of the file requested
D. All of the above

78. In HDFS the files cannot be:

A. Read B. Deleted
C. Executed D. Archived

79. Which among the following is the duties of the Data Nodes?

A. Manage file system namespace
B. Stores meta-data
C. Regulates client's access to files
D. Perform read-write operation as per request for the clients

80. NameNode and DataNode do communicate using:

A. Active pulse B. Heartbeats
C. h-signal D. Data pulse

81. Amazon EC2 provides virtual computing environments, known as:

A. chunks B. instances
C. messages D. none of the above

82. Data stored in ________ domains doesn't require maintenance of a schema.

A. SimpleDB B. SQL Server
C. Oracle D. RDS

83. Which of the following is a system for creating block level storage devices that can be used for Amazon Machine Instances in EC2?

A. CloudWatch
B. Amazon Elastic Block Store
C. AWS Import/Export
D. All of the above

84. Which of the following type of virtualization is also characteristic of cloud computing?

A. Storage B. Application
C. CPU D. All of the above

85. Which of the following is most important feature of cloud storage listed below?

A. Logon authentication
B. Bare file
C. Multiplatform support
D. Adequate bandwidth

86. Which of the following is open cloud storage management standard by SNIA?

A. CDMI B. OCCI
C. CEA D. Adequate bandwidth

87. Which of the following system does not provision storage to most users?

A. Paas B. Iaas
C. Caas D. Saas

88. Which of the following service is provided by Google for online storage?

A. Drive B. SkyDrive
C. Dropbox D. All of the above

89. Which of the following backup create a cloned copy of your current data or drive?

A. Continuous Data Protection
B. Open file backup
C. Reverse Delta backup
D. None of the above

90. Which of the following storage devices exposes its storage to clients as Raw storage that can be partitioned to create volumes?

A. block B. file
C. disk D. all of the above

91. Which of the following should be used considering factors shown in the figure?

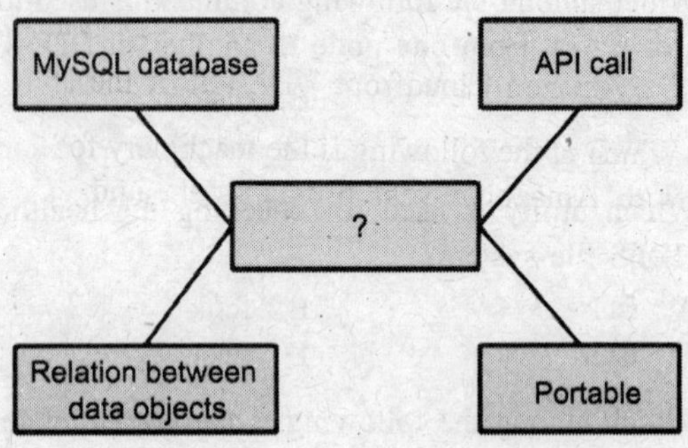

A. SimpleDB B. RDS
C. Amazon EC2 D. All of the above

92. Point out the wrong statement.

A. The metrics obtained by CloudWatch may be used to enable a feature called Auto Scaling
B. A number of tools are used to support EC2 services
C. Amazon Machine Instances are sized at various levels and rented on a computing/hour basis
D. None of the above

93. Which of the following is an edge-storage or content-delivery system that caches data in different physical locations?

A. Amazon Relational Database Service
B. Amazon SimpleDB
C. Amazon Cloudfront
D. Amazon Associates Web Services

94. Which of the following allows you to create instances of the MySQL database to support your Web sites?

A. Amazon Elastic Compute Cloud
B. Amazon Simple Queue Service
C. Amazon Relational Database Service
D. Amazon Simple Storage System

95. Which of the following is not a type of cybercrime?
A. Data theft
B. Forgery
C. Damage to data and systems
D. Installing antivirus for protection

96. Which are the following are data compression techniques?
A. LZW B. Huffman coding
C. RLE D. All of the above

97. Point out the correct statement.
A. Amazon Elastic Cloud is a system for creating virtual disks (volume)
B. SimpleDB interoperates with both Amazon EC2 and Amazon S3
C. EC3 is an Analytics as a Service provider
D. None of the above

98. Which of the following is a structured data store that supports indexing and data queries to both EC2 and S3?
A. Cloud Watch B. Amazon SimpleDB
C. Amazon Cloudfront D. All of the above

99. Which of the following is the machinery for interacting with Amazon's vast product data and eCommerce catalog function?
A. Amazon Elastic Compute Cloud
B. Amazon Associates Web Services
C. Alexa Web Information Service
D. All of the above

100. Which of the following is a billing and account management service?
A. Amazon Elastic Map Reduce
B. Amazon Mechanical Turk
C. Amazon DevPay
D. Multi-Factor Authentication

101. Which of the following is not the feature of Network management systems?
A. Accounting B. Security
C. Performance D. None of the above

102. Which of the following service provider provides the least amount of built in security?
A. SaaS B. PaaS
C. IaaS D. All of the above

103. Point out the correct statement.
A. Different types of cloud computing service models provide different levels of security services
B. Adapting your on-premises systems to a cloud model requires that you determine what security mechanisms are required
C. Data should be transferred and stored in an encrypted format for security purpose
D. All of the above

104. Which of the following services that need to be negotiated in Service Level Agreements?
A. Logging
B. Auditing
C. Regulatory compliance
D. All of the above

105. The following flowchart is intended to evaluate ________ in any cloud.

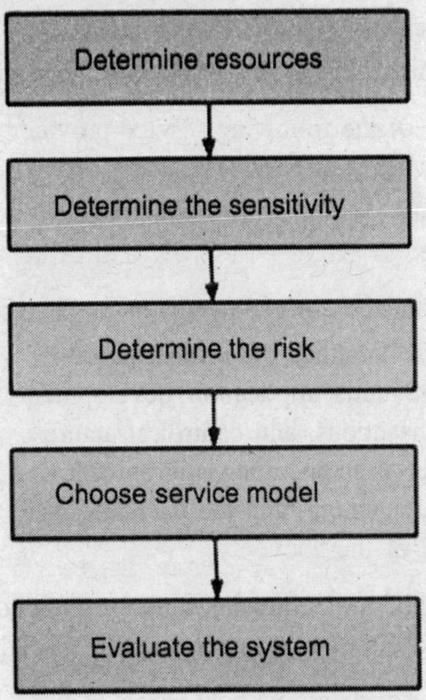

A. risk B. errors
C. inconsistencies D. none of the above

106. Point out the wrong statement.
A. You can use proxy and brokerage services to separate clients from direct access to shared cloud storage
B. Any distributed application has a much greater attack surface than an application that is closely held on a Local Area Network
C. Cloud computing doesn't have vulnerabilities associated with Internet applications
D. All of the above

107. Which of the following area of cloud computing is uniquely troublesome?
A. Auditing
B. Data integrity
C. e-Discovery for legal compliance
D. All of the above

108. Which of the following is the operational domain of CSA(Cloud Security Alliance)?

A. Scalability
B. Portability and interoperability
C. Flexibility
D. None of the above

109. Which of the following is considered an essential element in cloud computing by CSA?

A. Multi-tenancy
B. Identity and access management
C. Virtualization
D. All of the above

110. Which of the following is used for Web performance management and load testing?

A. VMware Hyperic B. Webmetrics
C. Univa UD D. Tapinsystems

111. Which of the following service provider provides the highest level of service?

A. SaaS B. PaaS
C. IaaS D. All of the above

112. Point out the correct statement.

A. PaaS supplies the infrastructure
B. IaaS adds application development frameworks, transactions, and control structures
C. SaaS is an operating environment with applications, management, and the user interface
D. All of the above

113. Which of the following functional cloud computing hardware/software stack is the Cloud Reference Model?

A. CAS B. CSA
C. SAC D. All of the above

114. For the _______ model, the security boundary may be defined for the vendor to include the software framework and middleware layer.

A. SaaS B. PaaS
C. IaaS D. All of the above

115. Which of the following model allows vendor to provide security as part of the Service Level Agreement?

A. SaaS B. PaaS
C. IaaS D. All of the above

116. Which of the following cloud does not require mapping?

A. Public B. Private
C. Hybrid D. None of the above

117. Which of the following service model is owned in terms of infrastructure by both vendor and customer?

A. Public B. Private
C. Hybrid D. None of the above

118. Which of the following model type is not trusted in terms of security?

A. Public B. Private
C. Hybrid D. None of the above

119. Which of the following has infrastructure security managed and owned by the vendor?

A. Hybrid B. Private/Community
C. Public D. None of the above

120. Point out the wrong statement.

A. Each different type of cloud service delivery model creates a security boundary
B. Any security mechanism below the security boundary must be built into the system
C. Any security mechanism above the security boundary must be maintained by the customer
D. All of the above

121. ________ is an application for collecting messages sent in RSS and Atom format from information providers.

A. Google Reader B. Yahoo Mail
C. EmailRackspace D. All of the above

122. Which of the following application is a newsreader?

A. Google Reader
B. Bloglines
C. Newsgator Online
D. All of the above

123. Which of the following was developed an alternative to XML syndication by IETF?

A. Atom Publishing Protocol
B. Atom Subscribing Protocol
C. Atom Subscribe Protocol
D. None of the above

124. How many technologies are used for most of the syndicated content on the Internet?

A. 1 B. 2
C. 3 D. 4

125. Which of the following technology is used for syndicated content?

A. AJAX B. RSS
C. Javascript D. All of the above

126. The full form of AJAX is:

A. Asynchronous Javascript and XML
B. Another Java and XML Library
C. Abstract JSON and XML
D. None of the above

127. The advantages of AJAX is:

A. Bandwidth utilization
B. More interactive
C. Speeder retrieval of data
D. All of these

128. Which of the following are the controls of Ajax?

A. Script Manager
B. Script Manager Proxy
C. Update Progress
D. All of the above

129. Which of the following type of virtualization is also characteristic of cloud computing?

A. Storage B. Application
C. CPU D. All of the above

130. Virtualization assigns a logical name for a physical resource and then provides a pointer to that physical resource when a request is made:

A. TRUE
B. FALSE

131. Virtual Machines (VMs) are offered in cloud by:

A. SaaS B. PaaS
C. IaaS D. None of these

132. The technology used to distribute service requests to resources is referred to as ________.

A. load performing B. load scheduling
C. load balancing D. all of the above

133. _________ computing refers to applications and services that run on a distributed network using virtualized resources.

A. Distributed B. Cloud
C. Soft D. Parallel

134. Cloud computing is an abstraction based on the notion of pooling physical resources and presenting them as a ________ resource.

A. real B. virtual
C. cloud D. none of the above

135. Amazon's Elastic Compute Cloud (EC2) is a well known ________.

A. Virtual machine B. Cloud Storage
C. PaaS D. SoA

136. ________ virtualization abstracts networking hardware and software into a virtual network that can be managed.

A. Storage B. Network
C. Software D. None of the above

137. _________ is used by Amazon Web Services to store copies of a virtual machine.

A. AMI B. EMI
C. IMI D. Application services

138. In para-virtualization, VMs run on hypervisor that interacts with the hardware.

A. True
B. False

139. Which of the following provide system resource access to virtual machines?

A. VMM B. VMC
C. VNM D. All of the above

140. An operating system running on a Type_VM is a full virtualization.

A. 1 B. 2
C. 3 D. All of the above

141. Point out the wrong statement.

A. In Gmail, you can construct searches with multiple operators using the Advanced Search feature
B. RSS and Atom are prototypes of a class of XML specifications called synchronized markup languages
C. A typical RSS document or feed contains text and metadata that can be used to indicate publication dates
D. None of the above

142. Which of the following file format is used by RSS module?

A. XML B. SMIL
C. JSON D. All of the above

143. What makes Ajax unique?

A. It works as a stand- alone Web-development tool
B. It works the same with all Web browsers
C. It uses C++ as its programming language
D. It makes data requests asynchronously

144. ________ JavaScript is also called server-side JavaScript.

A. Microsoft B. Navigator
C. LiveWire D. None of these

145. Which of the following visualization is most commonly achieved through a mapping mechanism where a logical storage address is translated into a physical storage address?

A. Storage B. Network
C. Software D. None of the above

146. Point out the wrong statement.

A. A virtual network can create virtual network interfaces

B. Instantiating a virtual machine is a very slow process
C. You can make machine images of systems in the configuration that you want to deploy or take snapshots of working virtual machines
D. All of the above

147. AMI (Amazon Machine Image) imaging service is provided by Amazon for:

A. private use B. public use
C. pay-per-use D. all of the above

148. Which of the following runs on Xen Hypervisor?

A. Azure B. AWS EC2
C. AWS EC3 D. All of the above

149. Virtualization allows sharing the resources of hardware across multiple an environments.

A. True
B. False

150. A virtual machine running on a server of a particular make cannot be relocated to the server of another make.

A. True
B. False

151. Amazon Web Services (AWS) is an example of ___________.

A. Software as a service (SaaS)
B. Infrastructure as a service (IaaS)
C. Platform as a Service (PaaS)
D. None of the above

152. Which of the following is Type 1 Hypervisor?

A. Wind River Simics
B. Virtual Server 2005 R2
C. KVM
D. LynxSecure

153. Which of the following is Type 2 VM?

A. VirtualLogix VLX B. VMware ESX
C. Xen D. LynxSecure

154. In _________ the virtual machine simulates hardware, so it can be independent of the underlying system hardware.

A. paravirtualization B. full virtualization
C. emulation D. none of the above

155. In a ___________ scheme, the VM is installed as a Type 1 Hypervisor directly onto the hardware.

A. paravirtualization B. full virtualization
C. emulation D. none of the above

156. Full virtualization:

A. Simulates hardware within software
B. Has VMs with the same OS
C. Clones images
D. Alters the guest OS

157. What are the goals of Hypervisor design?

A. Scalability B. Reliability
C. Isolation D. All of the above

158. Bare metal hypervisor sits on top of:

A. Physical Hardware B. Virtualized hardware
C. Operating System D. None of the above

159. If virtualization occurs at application level, OS level and hardware level, then such service in cloud is:

A. IaaS B. SaaS
C. PaaS D. no such service

160. Order of Virtual Machine Life Cycle (*i*) Release Ms (*ii*) IT Service Request (*iii*) VM in operation (*iv*) VM Provision:

A. (*ii*), (*i*), (*iii*), (*iv*)
B. (*i*), (*ii*), (*iii*) and (*iv*)
C. (*ii*), (*iii*), (*iv*) and (*i*)
D. (*ii*), (*iv*), (*iii*) and (*i*)

161. Which of the following should be replaced with the question mark in the following figure?

A. Abstraction B. Virtualization
C. Mobility Pattern D. All of the above

162. Which type of Hypervisor is shown in the following figure?

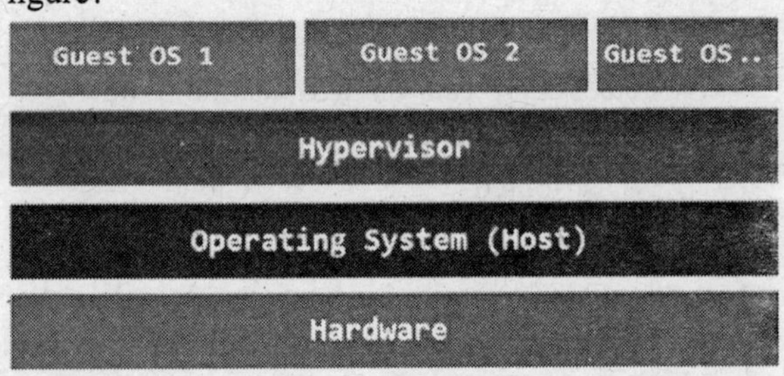

A. Type 1 B. Type 2
C. Type 3 D. All of the above

163. ___________ where a VM can be moved from one physical machine to another even as it continues to execute.

A. Load Balancing B. Migration
C. Live Migration D. Server Consolidation

164. ______ is the process of making an archival or backup copy of the entire contents of a hard drive.

A. Investigation B. Disk imaging
C. Formatting D. S/w Installation

165. Point out the wrong statement:

A. Load balancing virtualizes systems and resources by mapping a logical address to a physical address

B. Multiple instances of various Google applications are running on different hosts
C. Google uses hardware virtualization
D. All of the above

166. Which of the following should be placed in second lowermost layer for the following figure?

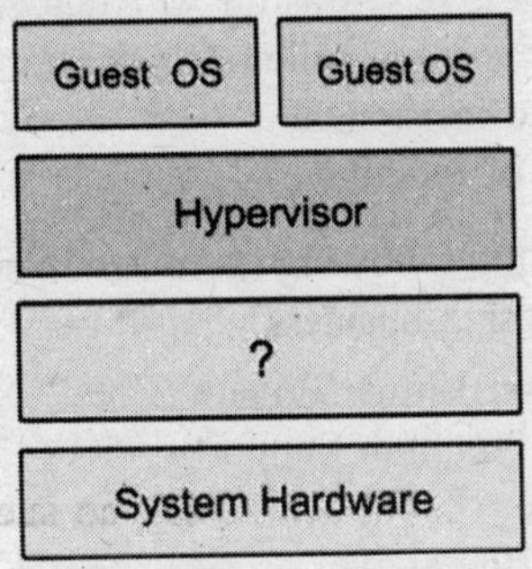

A. Host Operating System
B. Software
C. VM
D. None of the above

167. Point out the wrong statement:

A. Some hypervisors are installed over an operating system and are referred to as Type 2 or hosted VM
B. All CPUs support virtual machines
C. On a Type 2 VM, a software interface is created that emulates the devices with which a system would normally interact
D. All of the above

168. Which of the following type of virtualization is found in hypervisor such as Microsoft's Hyper-V?

A. paravirtualization
B. full virtualization
C. emulation
D. none of the above

169. Point out the wrong statement:

A. Full virtualization requires that the host operating system provide a virtual machine interface for the guest operating system and that the guest access hardware through that host VM
B. Guest operating systems in full virtualization systems are generally faster than other virtualization schemes
C. A process virtual machine instantiates when a command begins a process
D. All of the above

170. Which of the following operating system support operating system virtualization?

A. Windows NT B. Sun Solaris
C. Windows XP D. Compliance

171. __________ is a service that creates and manages virtual network interfaces.

A. VMware vStorage B. VMware vNetwork
C. VMware vCompute D. Application services

172. Which of the following allows a virtual machine to run on two or more physical processors at the same time?

A. Virtual SMP
B. Distributed Resource Scheduler
C. vNetwork Distributed Switch
D. Storage Vmotion

173. VMM is:

A. A virtual machine B. Hardware
C. Host OS D. A layer of software

174. VMM facilitates sharing of:

A. Memory & I/O B. CPU, memory & I/O
C. CPU & memory D. I/O & CPU

175. The BEST way to define Virtualization in cloud computing is:

A. Virtualization enables simulating compute, network, and storage service platforms from the underlying virtual hardware
B. Virtualization enables abstracting compute, network, and storage service platforms from the underlying physical hardware
C. Virtualization enables realization of compute, network, and storage service platforms from the underlying virtual hardware
D. Virtualization enables emulating compute, network, and storage service platforms from the underlying virtual hardware

176. Which one is NOT generally a change after Virtualization?

A. Virtual machines can be provisioned to any system
B. Hardware- independence of operating system and applications
C. Can manage OS and application as a single unit by encapsulating them into virtual machines.
D. Software and hardware tightly coupled

177. Which one of the statement is generally NOT correct for Microkernelized Hypervisor?

A. Drivers run within guests
B. Simple partitioning functionality
C. Increase reliability and minimize lowest level of the TCB
D. Contains its own drivers model

178. In multiple VM processing, CPU is alloted to the different processes in form of:

A. Space slices by the OS

B. Different CPUs are allocated to different processes
C. Time slices by the OS
D. Frequecy slices by the OS

179. Appear IQ, Mendix, Amazon Web Services (AWS) Elastic Beanstalk, Google App Engine and Heroku, are some of the example of providing services for:

A. IaaS B. SaaS
C. PaaS D. None of these

180. Which one of the cases not impacting major system availability?

A. Service performance degrade
B. Service outage by unplanned downtime
C. Live migration of VM for load balancing
D. Service outage by planned downtime

181. A valid definition of digital evidence is:

A. Data stored or transmitted using a computer
B. Information of probative value
C. Digital data of probative value
D. Any digital evidence on a computer

182. Which of the following is the machinery for interacting with Amazon's vast product data and eCommerce catalog function?

A. Amazon Elastic Compute Cloud
B. Amazon Associates Web Services
C. Alexa Web Information Service
D. All of the above

183. Which of the following is the central application in the AWS portfolio?

A. Amazon Elastic Compute Cloud
B. Amazon Simple Queue Service
C. Amazon Simple Notification Service
D. Amazon Simple Storage System

184. Which of the following is a message queue or transaction system for distributed Internet-based applications?

A. Amazon Elastic Compute Cloud
B. Amazon Simple Queue Service
C. Amazon Simple Notification Service
D. Amazon Simple Storage System

185. Which of the following feature is used for scaling of EC2 sites?

A. Auto Replica B. Auto Scaling
C. Auto Ruling D. All of the above

186. Which of the following provides a bridge between a company's existing network and the AWS cloud?

A. Amazon Virtual Private Cloud
B. AWS Premium Support
C. Amazon Fulfillment Web Services
D. All of the above

187. Point out the wrong statement.

A. Between FBA and FWS, you can create a nearly virtual store on Amazon.com
B. Amazon plans to extend the capabilities of VPC to integrate with other systems in the Amazon cloud computing portfolio
C. FPS is exposed as an API that sorts transactions into packages called Quick Starts that makes it easy to implement
D. None of the above

188. Which of the following is Amazon's technical support and consulting business?

A. Amazon Virtual Private Cloud
B. AWS Premium Support
C. Amazon Fulfillment Web Services
D. All of the above

189. Which of the following is a method for bidding on unused EC2 capacity based on the current spot price?

A. On-Demand Instance
B. Reserved Instances
C. Spot Instance
D. All of the above

190. Point out the wrong statement.

A. The standard instances are not suitable for standard server applications
B. High memory instances are useful for large data throughput applications such as SQL Server databases and data caching and retrieval
C. FPS is exposed as an API that sorts transactions into packages called Quick Starts that makes it easy to implement
D. None of the above

191. Which of the following instance has an hourly rate with no long-term commitment?

A. On-Demand Instance
B. Reserved Instances
C. Spot Instance
D. All of the above

192. Which of the following tool is used for measuring I/O of your systems to estimate these transaction costs?

A. EBS B. IOSTAT
C. ESW D. All of the above

193. Point out the wrong statement.

A. The cost of creating an EBS volume is lesser than creating a similarly sized S3 bucket
B. An EBS volume can be used as an instance boot partition
C. EBS boot partitions can be stopped and started, and they offer fast AMI boot times
D. None of the above

194. Which of the following is also referred to edge computing?

A. CloudWave B. CloudFront
C. CloudSpot D. All of the above

195. Computer forensics involves all of the following stated activities except:

A. extraction of computer data
B. preservation of computer data
C. interpretation of computer data
D. manipulation of computer data

196. Which of the following is a system for creating block level storage devices that can be used for Amazon Machine Instances in EC2?

A. CloudWatch
B. Amazon Elastic Block Store
C. AWS Import/Export
D. All of the above

197. Amazon EC2 provides virtual computing environments, known as:

A. chunks B. instances
C. messages D. none of the above

198. Amazon EMR uses Hadoop processing combined with several __________ products.

A. AWS B. ASQ
C. AMR D. AWES

199. What is a virtual server platform that allows users to create and run virtual machines on Amazon's server farm.

A. Azure B. EC2
C. EC5 D. None of the above

200. _________ is the central application in the AWS portfolio.

A. Amazon Simple Queue Service
B. Amazon Elastic Compute Cloud
C. Amazon Simple Notification Service
D. All of the above

201. Which of the following allows you to create instances of the MySQL database to support your Web sites?

A. Amazon Elastic Compute Cloud
B. Amazon Simple Queue Service
C. Amazon Relational Database Service
D. Amazon Simple Storage System

202. Point out the correct statement.

A. Amazon Elastic Cloud is a system for creating virtual disks(volume)
B. SimpleDB interoperates with both Amazon EC2 and Amazon S3
C. EC3 is an Analytics as a Service provider
D. None of the above

203. Which of the following is a billing and account management service?

A. Amazon Elastic MapReduce
B. Amazon Mechanical Turk
C. Amazon DevPay
D. Multi-Factor Authentication

204. Which of the following is a means for accessing human researchers or consultants to help solve problems on a contractual or temporary basis?

A. Amazon Elastic MapReduce
B. Amazon Mechanical Turk
C. Amazon DevPay
D. Multi-Factor Authentication

205. Point out the wrong statement.

A. Virtual private servers can provision virtual private clouds connected through virtual private networks
B. Amazon Web Services is based on SOA standards
C. Starting in 2012, Amazon.com made its Web service platform available to developers on a usage-basis model
D. All of the above

206. Point out the correct statement.

A. SQL Server is having enormous impact on cloud computing
B. Amazon.com's services represent the largest pure Infrastructure as a Service (IAAS)
C. EC2 is a Platform as a Service (PaaS) market
D. None of the above

207. In this phase from the collection data identify and extract the pertinent information using proper forensic tools.

A. Collection B. Examination
C. Analysis D. Reporting

208. Which of the following allows merchants to fill orders through Amazon.com fulfillment service?

A. Amazon Elastic Compute Cloud
B. Amazon Fulfillment Web Services
C. Amazon Relational Database Service
D. Amazon Simple Storage System

209. Point out the correct statement.

A. With EC2, you can launch and run server instances called Amazon Machine Images (AMIs) running different operating systems such as Red Hat Linux
B. A machine image is the software and operating system running on top of the instance
C. A machine image may be thought of as the contents of a boot drive
D. All of the above

210. Which of the following provides access for developers to charge Amazon's customers for their purchases?

A. FWS B. FAS
C. FPS D. All of the above

211. Which of the following uses an authentication device?

A. Amazon Elastic MapReduce
B. Amazon Mechanical Turk
C. Amazon DevPay
D. Multi-Factor Authentication

212. Which of the following is a batch processing application?

A. IBM sMash
B. IBM WebSphere Application Server
C. Condor
D. Windows Media Server

213. Point out the correct statement.

A. Security can be set through passwords, Kerberos tickets, or certificates
B. Secure access to your EC2 AMIs is controlled by passwords, Kerberos, and 509 Certificates
C. Most of the system image templates that Amazon AWS offers are based on Red Hat Linux
D. All of the above

214. How many EC2 service zones or regions exist?

A. 1 B. 2
C. 3 D. 4

215. Amazon __________ cloud-based storage system allows you to store data objects ranging in size from 1 byte up to 5GB.

A. S1 B. S2
C. S3 D. S4

216. CloudFront supports ________ data by performing static data transfers and streaming content from one CloudFront location to another.

A. table caching
B. geocaching
C. index caching
D. windows Media Server

217. Point out the correct statement.

A. A volume is mounted on a particular instance and is available to all instances
B. The advantages of an EBS boot partition are that you can have a volume up to 1TB
C. You cannot mount multiple volumes on a single instance
D. All of the above

218. What things are not recover while investigating the computer fraud:

A. Financial and asset record
B. Accounting software and files
C. Photos and diaries of the victim
D. Credit card data

219. Amazon Web Services falls into which of the following cloud-computing category?

A. Platform as a Servic
B. Software as a Service
C. Infrastructure as a Service
D. Back-end as a Service

220. AWS reaches customers in ________ countries.

A. 137 B. 182
C. 190 D. 86

221. This attack uses a killer packet to flood a system:

A. DNS DoS attack
B. The Ping of death attack
C. SYN/LAND attack
D. Teardrop attacks

222. Point out the wrong statement.

A. Amazon Machine Instances are sized at various levels and rented on a computing/hour basis
B. The metrics obtained by CloudWatch may be used to enable a feature called Auto Scaling
C. A number of tools are used to support EC2 services
D. None of the above

223. Which of the following is an edge-storage or content-delivery system that caches data in different physical locations?

A. Amazon Relational Database Service
B. Amazon SimpleDB
C. Amazon Cloudfront
D. Amazon Associates Web Services

224. Which of the following is built on top of a Hadoop framework using the Elastic Compute Cloud?

A. Amazon Elastic MapReduce
B. Amazon Mechanical Turk
C. Amazon DevPay
D. Multi-Factor Authentication

225. Which of the following correctly describes components roughly in their order of importance from top to down?

A. 1. Amazon Elastic Compute Cloud 2. Amazon Simple Storage System 3. Amazon Elastic Block Store
B. 1. Amazon Elastic Block Store 2. Amazon Elastic Compute Cloud 3. Amazon Simple Storage System

C. 1. Amazon Simple Storage System 2. Amazon Elastic Block Store 3. Amazon Elastic Compute Cloud
D. None of the above

226. Which of the following is a Web service that can publish messages from an application and deliver them to other applications or to subscribers?
A. Amazon Elastic Compute Cloud
B. Amazon Simple Queue Service
C. Amazon Simple Notification Service
D. Amazon Simple Storage System

227. Which of the following metrics are used to support Elastic Load Balancing?
A. CloudWatch
B. Amazon Elastic Block Store
C. AWS Import/Export
D. All of the above

228. Which of the following is an online backup and storage system?
A. Amazon Elastic Compute Cloud
B. Amazon Simple Queue Service
C. Amazon Simple Notification Service
D. Amazon Simple Storage System

229. ________ is a virtual server platform that allows users to create and run virtual machines on Amazon's server farm.
A. EC2 B. Azure
C. EC5 D. None of the above

230. AMIs are operating systems running on the ________ virtualization hypervisor.
A. Yen
B. Xen
C. Ben
D. Multi-Factor Authentication

231. Which of the following instance class is best used for applications that are processor or compute-intensive?
A. Standard Instances
B. High Memory Instances
C. High CPU Instances
D. None of the above

232. Which of the following can be done with S3 buckets through the SOAP and REST APIs?
A. Upload new objects to a bucket and download them
B. Create, edit, or delete existing buckets
C. Specify where a bucket should be stored
D. All of the above

233. Which of the following operation retrieves the newest version of the object?
A. PUT B. GET
C. POST D. COPY

234. Which of the following statement is wrong about Amazon S3?
A. Amazon S3 is highly reliable
B. Amazon S3 provides large quantities of reliable storage that is highly protected
C. Amazon S3 is highly available
D. None of the above

235. Which of the following is relational database service provided by Amazon?
A. SimpleDB B. SQL Server
C. Oracle D. RDS

236. Which of the following can be considered as a distributed caching system?
A. CND B. CDN
C. CWD D. All of the above

237. Amazon Relational Database Service is a variant of the ________ 5.1 database system.
A. Oracle B. MySQL
C. SQL Server D. All of the above

238. What are the different types of instances?
A. General purpose B. Computer Optimized
C. Storage Optimized D. All of the above

239. The types of AMI provided by AWS are:
A. Instance store backed
B. EBS backed
C. Both (A) & (B)
D. None of the above

240. Storage classes available with Amazon S3 are:
A. Amazon S3 standard
B. Amazon S3 standard - infrequent Access
C. Amazon Glacier
D. All of the above

241. IBM's Blue Cloud uses a special software for monitoring of virtual cluster operations and acts as a provisioning manager is known as ________.
A. Web Sphere B. Tivoli
C. Nebula D. Altix

242. Cloud system from SGI is functionally considered as an ________.
A. on-demand cloud computing service
B. on-demand cloud storage service
C. on-demand cloud accessing service
D. on-demand

243. Cyclone is available in two service models as follows:

A. Paas and Iaas B. Saas and Paas
C. SaaS and Iaas D. All of the above

244. NASA created __________ can be fifty percent more energy efficient as it turns off the computers on the network to make cloud computing efficient.

A. Nebula Cloud B. Cyclone Cloud
C. Force.com Cloud D. CERN Cloud

245. To establish scalability for the analysis of huge research data, CERN uses LSF i.e. a ________ grid and workload management solution of cloud computing platform.

A. Load Setting Facility
B. Load Sharing Facility
C. Load Setting Faculty
D. Load assigning Faculty

246. One of the reasons of widespread of cloud is its ability to provide resource allocation dynamically from a pool of VM resources. State True or False.

A. TRUE
B. FALSE

247. A mashup cloud can be designed by utilizing the Scalability of AWS and ________ of GAE platforms.

A. Accessibility B. Mobility
C. Agility D. Scalability

248. The Cloudlets have a ________ ownership unlike that of Clouds.

A. centralized B. decentralized
C. global D. None of the above

249. The Data-Intensive Scalable Computing(DISC) utilizes a ________ data-center clusters to gather and maintain data.

A. HTC B. HPC
C. HCC D. HAC

250. Performance metrics for HPC/HTC systems include:

A. Multitasking Scalability
B. Security Index
C. Cost Effectiveness
D. All of the above

251. [π = n/Ttotal = n/[kTo + Te(n, m)]

The above equation calculates the value of which of the following?

A. Scalability B. Throughput
C. Availability D. Effectiveness

252. ________ refers to an increase in the performance by the addition of more resources along the service layers.

A. Horizontal Scalability
B. Vertical Scalability
C. Diagonal Scalability
D. None of the above

253. The percentage of time the system is up and running smoothly is referred as ________.

A. system up time B. system scalability
C. system availability D. system efficiency

254. ________ is the technology used to search tagged objects and mobile devices with the help of browsing an IP address or using the database entry.

A. GPS B. Cloud
C. IoT D. RFID

255. RFID stand for ________.

A. Rangeable Frequency Identification
B. Radio Fragment Identification
C. Radio Frequency Identification
D. Rangeable Fragment Identification

256. The architecture of IoT consists of different layers including which of the following?

(*i*) Application Layer
(*ii*) Sensing Layer
(*iii*) Combination Layer
(*iv*) Network Layer.

A. (*i*), (*ii*), (*iv*) B. (*i*), (*iii*), (*iv*)
C. (*ii*), (*iii*), (*iv*) D. (*i*), (*ii*), (*iii*)

257. ________ tags contain battery and transmit signals autonomously.

A. Acitve RFID
B. Passive RFID
C. Battery-assisted passive RFID
D. Battery-assisted RFID

258. ________ tags needs an external source to wake up the battery.

A. Acitve RFID
B. Passive RFID
C. Battery-assisted passive RFID
D. Battery-assisted active RFID

259. The three major components of RFID hardware based on functionality include:

A. RFID Reader
B. Reader Antenna
C. Reader
D. All of the above

260. Types of Zigbee devices are available as follows:

(*i*) ZigBee Coordinator
(*ii*) ZigBee Router
(*iii*) ZigBee End Device
(*iv*) ZigBee Accessor

A. (*i*), (*ii*), (*iii*) B. (*i*), (*ii*), (*iii*), (*iv*)
C. (*ii*), (*iii*), (*iv*) D. (*i*), (*ii*), (*iv*)

261. Even with two-factor authentication, users may still be vulnerable to ________ attacks.

A. Scripting
B. Cross attack
C. Man-in-the-middle
D. Radiant

262. Process of identifying any individual:

A. Auditing B. Authorisation
C. Authentication D. Accounting

263. Process that prevents someone from denying that she accessed resource:

A. Accounting B. Non-repudiation
C. Sniffing D. Authorisation

264. What security threats do employee-owned devices pose by storing corporate data and accessing corporate networks?

A. Making infrastructure vulnerable to malware
B. Potential for noncompliance
C. Data Loss
D. All of the above

265. Which of the following is not a correct way to secure communication layer?

A. Cloud initiated communication
B. TLS/SSL
C. IPS (Intrusion Prevention System)
D. Firewalls

266. Which of the following is not the component of IoT Endpoint?

A. Sensor
B. Gateway
C. Communication Module
D. MCU

267. Which of the following makes sure that data is not changed when it not supposed to be?

A. Integrity B. Availability
C. Confidentiality D. Accounting

268. Which of the following terms indicates that information is to be read only by those people for whom it is intended?

A. Availability B. Accounting
C. Integrity D. Confidentiality

269. What is the full form of SCADA?

A. Supervisory Control and Document Acquisition
B. Supervisory Control and Data Acquisition
C. Supervisory Column and Data Assessment
D. Supervisory Column and Data Acquisition

270. DCS is a ___________.

A. Distributed Control System
B. Data Control System
C. Data Column System
D. Distributed Column System

271. What is SCADA?

A. Software B. Process
C. System D. Hardware

272. The control in SCADA is:

A. Online control B. Direct control
C. Supervisory control D. Automatic control

273. When did the SCADA start?

A. 1980s B. 1990s
C. 1970s D. 1960s

274. Which of the following is not the component of a SCADA system?

A. Database server B. I/O system
C. PLC controller D. Sparger controller

275. Which of the following is the heart of a SCADA system?

A. PLC B. HMI
C. Alarm task D. I/O task

276. RFID stands for?

A. Random frequency identification
B. Radio frequency identification
C. Random frequency information
D. Radio frequency information

277. Which of the following is not involved in working of IoT?

A. RFID B. Sensor
C. Nano tech D. Server

278. M2M is a term introduced by:

A. IoT service providers
B. Fog computing service providers
C. Telecommunication service providers
D. None of these

279. Which of these statements regarding sensors is TRUE?

A. Sensors are input devices.
B. Sensors can be analog as well as digital
C. Sensors respond to some external stimuli.
D. All of these

280. Smart Dust can be used to measure the:

A. Temperature of the industrial lathe machine

B. Heat inside a computer's CPU
C. Chemical in the soil
D. Strength of a solid material

281. In threat modeling, what methodology used to perform risk analysis:

A. DREAD B. OWASP
C. STRIDE D. DAR

282. Out of the following which is not element of threat modelling:

A. Asset B. Vulnerability
C. Threat D. Time

283. Request field is present in which message format?

A. Request message
B. Response message
C. Both request and response
D. Neither request nor response

284. CoAP is specialized for:

A. Internet applications
B. Device applications
C. Wireless applications
D. Wired applications

285. Which layer is CoAP?

A. Control layer B. Transport layer
C. Service layer D. Application layer

286. CoAP provides which of the following requirements?

A. Multicast support and simplicity
B. Low overhead and multicast support
C. Simplicity and low overhead
D. Multicast support, Low over head and simplicity

287. CoAP is a specialized ________ protocol.

A. Web Transfer B. Power
C. Application D. Resource

288. URI and content type support is which protocol feature?

A. Http B. UDP
C. CoAP D. SPI

289. What is the full form of WLAN?

A. Wide Local Area Network
B. Wireless Local Area Network
C. Wireless Land Access Network
D. Wireless Local Area Node

290. Which of the following specifies a set of media access control (MAC) and physical layer specifications for implementing WLANs?

A. IEEE 802.16 B. IEEE 802.3
C. IEEE 802.11 D. IEEE 802.15

291. Which of the following is not a characteristic of a ZigBee network?

A. Low power consumption
B. Easy installation.
C. High data rates.
D. Unlicensed radio bands.

292. Which of the following IEEE standards provides the lowest level of the ZigBee software stack?

A. IEEE 802.11.
B. IEEE 802.15.1.
C. IEEE 802.15.3.
D. IEEE 802.15.4.

293. Which of the following layers are defined by the ZigBee stack?

A. Transport layer
B. Physical layer.
C. Application Support sub-layer
D. Medium Access layer

294. What is the typical range of transmission distance in a ZigBee network?

A. 5 m B. 50 m
C. 500 m D. 5 km

295. ________ is an attack which forces an end user to execute unwanted actions on a web application in which he/she is currently authenticated.

A. Cross-site scoring scripting
B. Cross-site request forgery
C. Two-factor authentication
D. Cross-site scripting

296. Representational State Transfer (REST) is the standard interface between:

A. Two machines in a LAN
B. HTTP client and user
C. HTTP client and servers
D. None of the above

297. Which of the following is not a messaging mode in CoAP?

A. Confirmable B. Separate
C. Direct D. Piggyback

298. Which of the following is the full form of XMPP?

A. Extension Messaging and Presence Protocol
B. Extensible Messaging and Presence Protocol
C. Extension Messaging and Privacy Protocol
D. Extensible Messaging and Privacy Protocol

299. In 6LoWPAN address, how many bits are globally unique?

A. 16 bits B. 32 bits
C. 64 bits D. 128 bits

300. IEEE 802.15.4 uses which of the following for accessing the channel?
A. Carrier sense multiple access (CSMA)
B. Carrier sense multiple access with collision detection (CSMA-CD)
C. Carrier sense multiple access with collision avoidance (CSMA-CA)
D. None of these

301. Three parts of GPS include:
A. space segment B. control segment
C. user segment D. all of the above

302. In case of ________, the GPS works as a receiver, not a transmitter.
A. active tracking B. passive tracking
C. assisted tracking D. receiver tracking

303. ________ is an embedded system which meshes the computing process with the physical world in the form of an interactive as well as intelligent system.
A. Cloud-Physical System
B. Cyber-Space System
C. Cyber-Physical System
D. None of the above

304. The number of binding of a node to other actors of the graph in the graph representation of a network is called as ________.
A. node degree B. path length
C. social circle D. bridge

305. ________ is the degree to which nodes have a common set of connections to other nodes.
A. Structural hole B. Structural equivalence
C. Structural cohesion D. None of the above

306. The degree to which actors are directly linked to one another through cohesive bonds is called as ________.
A. closeness B. cohesion
C. centralized D. path length

307. The social circles are loosely coupled if there is ________ stringency of direct contact.
A. less B. more
C. equal D. no

308. The measures of centrality include:
A. Betweenness B. Closeness
C. Degree D. All of the above

309. Arrange the stages in supply chain management:
(*i*) Material and Equipment Supplies
(*ii*) Delivery of Products
(*iii*) After Sale Service and Returns
(*iv*) Planning and Coordination
(*v*) Manufacturing and Testing
A. (*iv*), (*v*), (*i*), (*ii*), (*iii*)
B. (*iv*), (*i*), (*v*), (*iii*), (*ii*)
C. (*iv*), (*i*), (*v*), (*ii*), (*iii*)
D. (*i*), (*ii*), (*iv*), (*v*), (*ii*)

310. Nodes in the network analysis graph represent the ________ and the edges represent the relationships between nodes.
A. actors B. nodes
C. users D. Both (A) and (B)

311. Which is the latest Operating System?
A. Real-time OS B. Desktop OS
C. Mainframe OS D. Cloud OS

312. JOES stands for ________.
A. Joint Expensive Operating System
B. Just Expensive Operating System
C. Just Enough Operating System
D. Joined Environmental Operating System

313. Responsibility of OS developers to add new feature in existing OS are ________.
A. More reliability
B. Convenience and security
C. Compatibility
D. All of the above

314. In future, companies wont worry about the capital for large data center because of ________.
A. SaaS solution B. PaaS solution
C. IaaS solution D. None of the above

315. ________ is an autonomic cloud engine whose basic aim is to realize a virtual component of cloud with computing capability.
A. CometCloud B. AsteroidCloud
C. StarCloud D. PlanetCloud

316. CometCloud supports policy based autonomic and ________.
A. CloudBursting B. CloudBridging
C. None D. Both (A) and (B)

317. Which are the three conceptual layers in CometCloud?
A. Development, Application, Physical
B. Infrastructure, Dynamic, Static
C. Transport, Network, Programming
D. Programming, Service, Infrastructure

318. In Comet, a tuple is a simple ________ string.
A. Java B. Python
C. XML D. HTML

319. Which of the following policies is not above in 'not to violate' regarding CloudBurst?
A. Deadline-based B. Budget-based
C. Quality-based D. Workload-based

320. The cloud media services are:
A. Cloud gaming
B. Experiencing multi-screens
C. Image Processing
D. All of the above

321. KPI stands for ________.
A. Key Practices in Industry
B. Key Performance Index
C. Key Performance Indicators
D. Key Parameters in Information

322. SEEP is used in ________.
A. Energy optimization
B. Multimedia
C. Information leakage
D. Cost reduction

323. SEEP stands for ________.
A. System End to End Protocol
B. Static Environmental Execution Process
C. Symbolic Execution and Energy Profiles
D. State Execution And Energy Profiles

324. Keywords in Docker are ________.
A. Develop, ship, run anywhere
B. Create, export
C. Transport, cloud
D. User, data, privacy

325. Docker can simplify both, ________ and ________.
A. Process, state
B. Behaviour, aspect
C. Workflows, communication
D. All of the above

326. Basic approach of Docker as a company is:
A. "batteries included but removable"
B. "batteries included but non-removable"
C. "batteries but chargeable"
D. "battery less execution"

327. Which containers are used by Docker servers?
A. Windows B. Android
C. Linux D. Mac

328. Two main components in Docker are:
A. Master, slave B. Client, server
C. Client, master D. All of the above

329. Docker is generally configured to use TCP port ________ while executing unencrypted traffic.
A. 3306 B. 53378
C. 2375 D. 2376

330. Docker is generally configured to use TCP port ______ while managing encrypted traffic.
A. 3306 B. 53378
C. 2375 D. 2376

331. Containers require less disk space as compared to virtual machine:
A. True
B. False

332. There is no built-in framework in Docker for testing.
A. True
B. False

333. Docker provides simple one-line deployment strategy.
A. True
B. False

334. The examples of deployment tools are:
A. Docker's storm B. New Relic's Centurion
C. Spotify's Helios D. All of the above

335. CNS stands for ________.
A. Consumption Near Sweet-Spot
B. Continuous Network System
C. Compact Neural System
D. Compound Near Sweet-SpoT

336. Systems used to track and identify the location of objects in real time:
A. Geolocation
B. Geographical information system (GIS)
C. Wireless Application Protocol (WAP)
D. Real-time location system (RTLS)

337. Gateway to the Internet optimized for mobility:
A. Voice portal B. WiMax
C. Mobile enterprise D. Mobile Portal

338. Automatically identifying a Web user's location:
A. Voice portal B. Geolocation
C. Sensor network D. WiMax

339. Computing capabilities embedded into objects around us (mobile and stationary):
A. Pervasive computing
B. Ubiquitous computing (ubicom)
C. Context-aware computing
D. Geolocation

340. Computing capabilities embedded in the environment but typically not mobile:
A. Mobile Portal
B. Pervasive computing
C. Context-aware computing
D. Voice portal

341. Vehicle mount solutions
- Handheld solutions
- Hands-free and voice solutions

A. Mobile enterprise
B. Wireless wide area network (WWAN)
C. Typical Mobile Devices Used in Warehouses
D. Interactive voice response (IVR)

342. A collection of nodes capable of environmental sensing, local computation, and communication with its peers or with other higher performance nodes:

A. Voice portal
B. Mobile Portal
C. Geolocation
D. Sensor network

343. CIA triad is also known as ________.

A. NIC (Non-repudiation, Integrity, Confidentiality)
B. AIC (Availability, Integrity, Confidentiality)
C. AIN (Availability, Integrity, Non-repudiation)
D. AIC (Authenticity, Integrity, Confidentiality)

344. A technology that offers Internet browsing from wireless devices:

A. Real-time Location System (RTLS)
B. Wireless Wide Area Network (WWAN)
C. Wireless Local Area Network (WLAN)
D. Wireless Application Protocol (WAP)

345. Delivery of m-commerce transactions to individuals in a specific location, at a specific time:

A. Location-based m-commerce (l-commerce)
B. Context-aware computing
C. Ubiquitous computing (ubicom)
D. Network-based positioning

346. Calculating the location of a mobile device from signals sent by the device to base stations:

A. Personal Area Network (PAN)
B. Terminal-based positioning
C. Pervasive computing
D. Network-based positioning

347. A wireless technology, designed to provide Internet access across metro areas to fixed (not moving) users. It is considered wireless broadband technology:

A. Voice Portal B. Mobile Portal
C. WiMax D. Geolocation

348. A website with an audio interface that can be accessed through a telephone call:

A. WiMax B. Geolocation
C. Mobile Portal D. Voice Portal

349. A wireless version of the Ethernet networking standard:

A. Wireless wide area network (WWAN)
B. Wireless Local Area Network (WLAN)
C. Personal Area Network (PAN)
D. Wireless Application Protocol (WAP)

350. Computer system capable of integrating, storing, editing, analyzing, sharing, and displaying geographically referenced (spatial) information:

A. Personal Area Network (PAN)
B. Interactive Voice Response (IVR)
C. Real-time Location System (RTLS)
D. Geographical Information System (GIS)

351. A voice system enables users to request/receive info, enter/change data through a telephone to a computerized system:

A. Pervasive Computing
B. Real-time Location System (RTLS)
C. Personal Area Network (PAN)
D. Interactive Voice Response (IVR)

352. A telecommunications network that offers wireless coverage over a large geographical area, typically over a cellular phone network:

A. Personal Area Network (PAN)
B. Wireless Application Protocol (WAP)
C. Wireless Wide Area Network (WWAN)
D. Wireless Local Area Network (WLAN)

353. Application of mobile computing inside the enterprise (e.g., for improved communication among employees):

A. Sensor network B. Mobile enterprise
C. Voice portal D. Mobile Portal

354. A wireless telecommunications network for device-to-device connections within a very short range:

A. Wireless Wide Area Network (WWAN)
B. Personal Area Network (PAN)
C. Wireless Local Area Network (WLAN)
D. Sensor Network

355. Ability to detect and react to a set of environmental variables that is described as context (which can be sensor info or users' attitudes):

A. Mobile Portal
B. Context-aware computing
C. Pervasive computing
D. Network-based positioning

356. Which of the following is a specification for multicast discovery on a LAN?

A. WS-Agent
B. WS-Discovery
C. WS-SOAP
D. All of the above

357. The use of cloud computing is limited to a ______. service at time.

A. Single B. Multiple
C. Same D. Both (B) & (C)

358 Hybrid Cloud is combination of ________.
A. Public B. Private
C. Public & private D. Public & hybrid

359. Characteristic of cloud computing ________.
A. Service oriented B. Cloud
C. Connection base D. Platform oriented

360. ______ Model consists of the particular types of services that you can Access on a cloud computing platform.
A. Service B. Deployment
C. Application D. Software

361. Point out the correct statement________.
A. The use of the word "cloud" makes reference to the two essential concepts
B. Cloud computing abstracts systems by pooling and sharing resources
C. Cloud computing is nothing more than the Internet
D. Cloud computing is protocol

362. Distributed system consists of large number of ________ module.
A. Hardware B. Software
C. Hardware & Software D. Application

363. Web 2.0 is the term used to describe a variety of ____.
A. Web sites B. Application
C. Networks D. Process

364. Distributed system should be perceived by ________ developers.
A. User B. Application
C. User and application D. Code

365. Which two are most popular sides for videos and photographs?
A. YouTube WWW.YouTube.com and Flickr WWW.Flickr.com
B. Only YouTube WWW.YouTube.com
C. Only Flickr WWW.Flickr.com
D. Internet

366. Business process represented by ________.
A. Source B. Service
C. Documents D. Source & documents

367. Which of the following is the deployment model?
A. Public B. Web
C. Cloud D. Services

368. Which of the following is best known service model
A. Software as a service (SAAS)
B. Hardware as a service (HAAS)
C. Web service (WS)
D. Infrastructure platform (IP)

369. ______ has many of characteristics of what is now being called cloud computing
A. Internet B. Software
C. Web service D. Hardware

370. Cloud Computing System are classified________.
A. Single Instruction, Single Data (SISD)
B. Multiple Data, Single Data (MDSD)
C. Single Data Multiple Instruction (SDMI)
D. Multiple Instruction Double Data (MIDD)

371. Which of the Cloud platform by amazon ________.
A. Azure B. AWS
C. Cloudera D. Google

372. MIMD systems that shares a common memory is known as ________.
A. Multiple Units B. Multiple Data
C. Multiprocessor D. Processors

373. Utility Computing resources are modelled as a ______ to electric power.
A. Utility analogous B. Utility
C. Digital D. Session

374 A computer system is said to be ________.
A. Parallel computer B. Serial computer
C. Processor D. Memory

375. Virtualization allows the creation of separate________.
A. Process B. Computing environment
C. Networks D. Routers

376. Server Virtualization is most ______of virtualization industry.
A. Active segment B. Passive segment
C. Both (A) & (B) D. Hybrid

377. Advantages of Network Virtualization ______.
A. Lower cost less space consumption
B. Less devices
C. High Risk
D. Non- flexible

378. KVM is short for ______.
A. Kernel-base virtual machine
B. Kernel Machine
C. Virtualization
D. VMware

379. Security and Privacy of data are the main challenges in ________.
A. Cloud computing B. DBMS
C. Process D. Peer to peer model

380. KVM is ________.
A. Close Source Software
B. Open Source Software
C. Processor
D. Input-output Device

ANSWERS

1	2	3	4	5	6	7	8	9	10
A	D	B	D	A	A	D	D	A	B
11	12	13	14	15	16	17	18	19	20
B	C	B	A	D	A	A	B	C	B
21	22	23	24	25	26	27	28	29	30
B	B	A	C	C	C	A	C	B	D
31	32	33	34	35	36	37	38	39	40
D	A	A	D	C	D	C	B	B	C
41	42	43	44	45	46	47	48	49	50
A	A	A	B	D	B	A	B	A	C
51	52	53	54	55	56	57	58	59	60
D	A	B	C	C	B	B	D	B	C
61	62	63	64	65	66	67	68	69	70
A	A	B	A	B	C	C	D	B	A
71	72	73	74	75	76	77	78	79	80
D	D	A	C	A	C	B	C	D	B
81	82	83	84	85	86	87	88	89	90
B	A	B	D	A	A	B	A	A	A
91	92	93	94	95	96	97	98	99	100
B	D	C	C	D	D	B	B	B	C
101	102	103	104	105	106	107	108	109	110
D	C	D	D	A	C	D	B	A	B
111	112	113	114	115	116	117	118	119	120
A	C	A	B	A	A	C	A	B	D
121	122	123	124	125	126	127	128	129	130
A	D	A	B	B	A	D	D	D	A
131	132	133	134	135	136	137	138	139	140
C	C	B	B	A	B	A	B	A	A
141	142	143	144	145	146	147	148	149	150
B	A	D	C	A	B	D	B	A	B
151	152	153	154	155	156	157	158	159	160
B	D	C	C	B	A	D	A	B	D
161	162	163	164	165	166	167	168	169	170
B	B	C	B	C	A	B	A	A	B
171	172	173	174	175	176	177	178	179	180
B	A	D	B	B	D	D	A	C	C
181	182	183	184	185	186	187	188	189	190
C	B	A	B	B	A	B	B	C	A
191	192	193	194	195	196	197	198	199	200
A	B	A	B	D	B	B	A	B	B
201	202	203	204	205	206	207	208	209	210
C	B	C	B	C	B	B	B	D	C
211	212	213	214	215	216	217	218	219	220
D	C	D	D	C	B	B	C	C	C

221	222	223	224	225	226	227	228	229	230
B	D	C	A	A	C	A	D	A	B
231	232	233	234	235	236	237	238	239	240
C	D	B	C	D	B	B	D	C	D
241	242	243	244	245	246	247	248	249	250
B	A	C	A	B	A	C	B	A	D
251	252	253	254	255	256	257	258	259	260
B	B	C	D	C	A	A	C	D	A
261	262	263	264	265	266	267	268	269	270
C	C	B	D	A	B	A	D	B	A
271	272	273	274	275	276	277	278	279	280
B	C	B	D	D	B	D	C	D	C
281	282	283	284	285	286	287	288	289	290
A	D	A	A	C	D	A	C	B	C
291	292	293	294	295	296	297	298	299	300
C	D	D	B	D	C	C	B	C	C
301	302	303	304	305	306	307	308	309	310
D	B	C	A	C	B	A	D	C	D
311	312	313	314	315	316	317	318	319	320
D	C	D	B	A	D	D	C	C	D
321	322	323	324	325	326	327	328	329	330
C	A	C	A	C	A	C	B	C	D
331	332	333	334	335	336	337	338	339	340
A	A	A	D	A	D	D	B	B	B
341	342	343	344	345	346	347	348	349	350
C	D	D	D	A	B	C	D	B	D
351	352	353	354	355	356	357	358	359	360
D	C	B	B	B	B	A	C	A	A
361	362	363	364	365	366	367	368	369	370
B	C	A	C	A	B	A	A	A	A
371	372	373	374	375	376	377	378	379	380
B	C	A	A	B	A	A	A	A	B

ELEMENTARY MATH

CHAPTER 1

Numbers System

Whole Numbers

In our System of numeration, numbers are written by using the symbols 0, 1, 2, 3, 4, 5, 6, 7, 8 and 9 with each symbol getting a value depending on the place it occupies. These symbols are called digits. A number related to the objects in a collection gives an idea of how many objects are there in the collection.

The number 789345126 can be represented as:

Ten crores	Crores	Ten Lacs (Millions)	Lacs	Ten Thousands	Thousands	Hundreds	Tens	Units
10^8	10^7	10^6	10^5	10^4	10^3	10^2	10^1	10^0
7	8	9	3	4	5	1	2	6

This number can be read as: "Seventy-eight crores, ninety-three lacs, forty-five thousands, one hundred twenty six".

1. **Natural Numbers or Positive Integers (N = 1, 2, 3, 4, 5 .....):** These are also called counting numbers. When two natural numbers are added or multiplied together, the result is always a natural number. Therefore, all positive integers, used for counting objects, are always **natural numbers** whereas zero together with negative integers and fractional numbers are not natural numbers.

2. **Whole Numbers: (W = 0, 1, 2, 3, 4, 5, ...):** The number '0' together with the natural numbers gives us the numbers which are called **whole numbers,** e.g., 0, 1, 2, 3, 4 ..... etc. whereas –10, –15, –12 ..... or $\frac{1}{5}, \frac{2}{9}, \frac{4}{5}$..... etc. are not whole numbers.

3. **Integers: (I = ..., –5, –4, –3, –2, –1, 0, 1, 2, 3, 4, 5, ...):** The negative numbers together with the whole numbers are called integers. The numbers –1, –2, –3, –4, –5, ... are called negative integers and 1, 2, 3, 4, 5, ..., *i.e.,* natural numbers are called positive integers. The number 0 is simply an integer, *i.e.,* it is neither positive nor negative.

4. **Rational Numbers:** A rational number is a number that can be put in the form $\frac{p}{q}$ where p and q are both integers and $q \neq 0$, e.g., 8, $-\frac{7}{5}$, $-\frac{3}{4}$, $\frac{1}{7}$, 0 .... are all rational numbers i.e. a rational number may be positive, zero or negative.

5. **Irrational Numbers:** An irrational number is a number that can not be put in the form $\frac{p}{q}$ where p and q are both integers and $q \neq 0$, e.g., $\sqrt[3]{5}, \sqrt{11}, \sqrt{15}$, $3 + \sqrt{5}$ .... etc. are all irrational numbers.

6. **Real Numbers:** All those numbers which are either rational or irrational, are called real numbers, e.g., $\frac{11}{17}$, $\frac{19}{21}$, $-\frac{7}{8}$, $\sqrt{7}$, $8 + \sqrt{3}$ etc. are real numbers.

7. **Even Numbers:** All those numbers which are exactly divisible by 2, are called 'even numbers', e.g., 2, 8, 14, 28, 52 etc. are even numbers.

8. **Odd Numbers:** All those numbers which are not exactly divisible by 2, are called 'odd numbers', e.g., 1, 3, 5, 7, 9, 19 etc. are odd numbers.

9. **Composite Numbers:** The numbers which are divisible not only by 1 or themselves, but by some other numbers also, are called the 'composite numbers'. In other words, the numbers which have more than two factors are called 'composite numbers.', e.g., 4, 9, 15, 18, 27, ... etc. are composite numbers.

10. **Prime Numbers:** The numbers which have only two factors, 1 and the number itself are called 'prime numbers', e.g., 2, 5, 11, 19, 23, 31, ... etc. are prime numbers.

11. **Co-primes:** Two numbers which have only 1 as the common factor are called 'co-primes'. 5 and 7 are co-primes. So are 15 and 16.

12. **Twin Primes:** Two prime numbers which differ by 2, are called 'twin primes', e.g., 3, 5; 5, 7; 11, 13; 71, 73 are some pairs of twin primes.

13. **Consecutive Numbers:** The numbers which are following or coming after other numbers in regular order, are called consecutive numbers. 4, 6, 8, 10 are consecutive even numbers and 9, 11, 13, 15 are consecutive odd numbers. 3, 4, 5, 6, 7 ..... etc. are consecutive numbers in the natural order of the number series.

TESTS FOR DIVISIBILITY OF NUMBERS

1. **Divisibility by 2:** A number is divisible by 2, if its units digit is 0, 2, 4, 6 or 8. For example, each of the numbers 130, 244, 566, 278, ... etc. is divisible by 2.

2. **Divisibility by 3:** A number is divisible by 3, if the sum of its digits is a multiple of 3. For example, each of the numbers 312, 213, 456 is divisible by 3 since sum of digits in each of these numbers is $(3 + 1 + 2 = 6)$, $(2 + 1 + 3 = 6)$ and $(4 + 5 + 6 = 15)$ respectively, each of which is a multiple of 3.

3. **Divisibility by 4:** A number is divisible by 4, if the number formed by its digits in ten's and unit's places is divisible by 4. For example, numbers formed by ten's and unit's digits of 1132, 1312, 1400 and 1348 are 32, 12, 00 and 48 respectively which are divisible by 4. Hence, these numbers also are divisible by 4.

4. **Divisibility by 5:** A number is divisible by 5, if its unit's digit is either 0 or 5. For example, each of the numbers 100, 205, 315, 435 is divisible by 5 since unit's digit in each of these numbers is either 0 or 5.

5. **Divisibility by 6:** A number is divisible by 6, if it is divisible by both 2 and 3.

6. **Divisiblity by 8:** A number is divisible by 8, if the number formed by its digits in hundred's, ten's and unit's places is divisible by 8. For example, numbers formed by hundred's, ten's and unit's digits of 1864, 1024, 2008 and 5000 are 864, 024, 008 and 000 respectively which are divisible by 8. Hence, these numbers also are divisible by 8.

7. **Divisibility by 9:** A number is divisible by 9, if the sum of its digits is a multiple of 9. For example, each of the numbers 23409, 454554, 66636 is divisible by 9 since sum of digits in each of these numbers is $(2 + 3 + 4 + 0 + 9 = 18)$, $(4 + 5 + 4 + 5 + 5 + 4 = 27)$ and $(6 + 6 + 6 + 3 + 6 = 27)$ respectively, each of which is a multiple of 9.

8. **Divisibility by 10:** A number is divisible by 10, if its unit's digit is zero. For example, each of the numbers 50, 80, 1310, 1400 is divisible by 10 since unit's digit in each of these numbers is 0.

9. **Divisibility by 11:** A number is divisible by 11, if the difference of the sum of its digits in even places and the sum of its digits in odd places (starting from unit's place) is either 0 or a multiple of 11. For example, each of the numbers 909183, 540045 and 184712 is divisible by 11 since in each of the numbers difference of the sum of digits in even places and sum of the digits in odd places is $[(9 + 9 + 8) - (0 + 1 + 3) = 22]$, $[(5 + 0 + 4) - (4 + 0 + 5) = 0]$ and $[(8 + 7 + 2) - (1 + 4 + 1) = 11]$ respectively, each of which is either '0' or a multiple of '11'.

10. **Divisibility by 12:** A number is divisible by 12, if it is divisible by 3 and 4 both.

    For example, take a number 769824

    (*i*) Sum of digits $= 7 + 6 + 9 + 8 + 2 + 4 = 36$, it is divisible by 3.

    (*ii*) The number has 24 as its last two digits, which is divisible by 4.

    Hence, 769824 is divisible by 3 and 4 both, so it is divisible by 12.

11. **Divisibility by 14:** A number is divisible by 14, if it is divisible by 2 and 7 both.

12. **Divisibility by 15:** A number is divisible by 15, if it is divisible by 3 and 5 both.

13. **Divisibility by 16:** A number is divisible by 16, if the number formed by its last four digits is divisible by 16.

    For example, take a number 9877856, the number formed by its last four digits is 7856, which is divisible by 16. Hence, the number 9877856 is divisible by 16.

14. **Divisibility by 24:** A number is divisible by 24, if it is divisible by 3 and 8 both.

15. **Divisibility by 40:** A number is divisible by 40, if it is divisible by 5 and 8 both.

16. **Divisibility by 80:** A number is divisible by 80, if it is divisible by 5 and 16 both.

[**Note:** If a number is divisible by two co-primes separately, then the number will be also divisible by the product of co-primes.]

EXERCISE

1. The difference between the squares of two consecutive numbers is 25. The numbers are—
   A. 11, 12　B. 12, 13
   C. 15, 14　D. 14, 13

2. The sum of two digits of a number is 15. If 9 is added to the number, the digits are reversed. The number is—
   A. 78　B. 87
   C. 69　D. 96

3. A number which when multiplied by 11 is as much above 180 as it was originally below it. The number is—
   A. 25　B. 30
   C. 40　D. 45

4. Divide ₹ 53 among X, Y, Z so that X may receive ₹ 7 more than Y, and Y may receive ₹ 8 more than Z.
   A. 10, 15, 18
   B. 18, 10, 25
   C. 20, 12, 27
   D. 25, 18, 10

5. If $a = 16$ and $b = 15$, then what is the value of $\frac{a^2+b^2+ab}{a^3-b^3} = ?$
   A. $\frac{1}{2}$　B. $\frac{1}{3}$
   C. 1　D. 2

6. Find the number which when multiplied by 16 is increased by 225.
   A. 13　B. 14
   C. 15　D. 16

7. What is the largest number of four digits which is exactly divisible by 88?
   A. 9999　B. 9988
   C. 9944　D. 9998

8. If $\frac{a}{b} = \frac{4}{3}$, then $\frac{3a+2b}{3a-2b} = ?$
   A. 2　B. 3
   C. 4　D. 5

9. If $\frac{x}{y} = \frac{3}{4}$, then the value of $\frac{6}{7}+\frac{y-x}{y+x} = ?$
   A. 1　B. 2
   C. 3　D. 4

10. If the number $(10^n - 1)$ is divisible by 11, then n is—
    A. odd number　B. even number
    C. any number　D. multiple of 11

ANSWERS

1	2	3	4	5	6	7	8	9	10
B	A	B	B	C	C	C	B	A	B

EXPLANATORY ANSWERS

1. Let the numbers are x and $(x + 1)$

$$\therefore \quad (x+1)^2 - x^2 = 25$$
$$\Rightarrow \quad x^2 + 1 + 2x - x^2 = 25$$
$$\Rightarrow \quad 2x + 1 = 25$$
$$\Rightarrow \quad 2x = 25 - 1 = 24$$
$$\therefore \quad x = \frac{24}{2} = 12$$
$$\therefore \quad x + 1 = 12 + 1 = 13$$

Hence, the numbers are 12, 13.

2. Let x be the digit in units place. Digit in ten's place is then $15 - x$.

$\therefore$ The number = $10(15 - x) + x$

The new number with reverse digits

$$= 10 \times x + (15 - x)$$
$$\therefore \quad 10(15 - x) + x + 9 = 10x + 15 - x$$
$$\Rightarrow \quad 150 - 10x + x + 9 = 9x + 15$$
$$\Rightarrow \quad 18x = 144$$
$$x = \frac{144}{18} = 8$$

The digit of ten's place = 15 – 8 = 7

$\therefore$ The required number = 78.

3. Let the number is x

$$\therefore \quad 180 - x = 11x - 180$$
$$\Rightarrow \quad 180 + 180 = 11x + x$$
$$\Rightarrow \quad 360 = 12x,$$
$$\Rightarrow \quad x = \frac{360}{12} = 30.$$

4. Let Y receives ₹ a. Then X receives ₹ $(a + 7)$ and Z receives ₹ $(a - 8)$

But, $a + 7 + a + a - 8 =$ ₹ 53

$$\Rightarrow \quad 3a - 1 = 53,$$
$$\Rightarrow \quad 3a = 53 + 1$$
$$\Rightarrow \quad 3a = 54,$$
$$\therefore \quad a = \frac{54}{3} = ₹\ 18. = \text{Y's share}$$

X's share = $a + 7 = 18 + 7 =$ ₹ 25

Z's share = $a - 8 = 18 - 8 =$ ₹ 10.

5. Given $a = 16$ and $b = 15$, then $\frac{a^2+b^2+ab}{a^3-b^3}$

$$= \frac{a^2+b^2+ab}{(a-b)(a^2+b^2+ab)} = \frac{1}{a-b} = \frac{1}{16-15} = 1$$

6. Let the required no. = x

then, $16x - x = 225$

$\Rightarrow$ $15x = 225 \therefore x = 15$

7. The greatest no. of 4 digit = 9999

Now, after dividing 9999 by 88, we get Remainder = 55

Hence, the largest 4 digit no. = 9999 – 55 = 9944

8. $$\frac{3a+2b}{3a-2b} = \frac{3\frac{a}{b}+2}{3\frac{a}{b}-2} = \frac{3\times\frac{4}{3}+2}{3\times\frac{4}{3}-2} = \frac{6}{2} = 3$$

9. $$\frac{6}{7}+\frac{y-x}{y+x} = \frac{6}{7}+\frac{1-x/y}{1+x/y}$$

$$= \frac{6}{7}+\frac{1-3/4}{1+3/4} = \frac{6}{7}+\frac{1}{7} = 1$$

10. n is even number.

Decimal Fraction

FRACTION

The relation to represent some part of the body to the whole body is known *Fraction*. For example $\frac{2}{5}$ is a fraction where 2 is the numerator and 5 is the denominator.

Important Facts :

(*i*) A fraction is also called a rational number.

(*ii*) A fraction is unity when its numerator and denominator are equal.

(*iii*) When a fraction is reduced in its lowest term, its numerator and denominator are prime to each other, *i.e.*, they have no common factor.

(*iv*) The value of fraction is not altered by multiplying or dividing the numerator and the denominator by the same number.

Vulgar or Common Fraction : The fraction such as $\frac{2}{9}, \frac{7}{11}, \frac{3}{10}, \frac{9}{100}$ are called vulgar fraction.

Decimal Fraction : Fractions in which denominators are power of 10 are called decimal fractions.

For example : $\frac{1}{10}, \frac{1}{100}, \frac{7}{1000}$ etc.

Here, $\frac{1}{10}$ is 1 tenths, written as .1

$\frac{1}{100} = .01$

$\frac{7}{1000} = .007$

$\frac{13}{100} = .13$ and so on.

Converting a Decimal into a Vulgar Fraction

First of all write down the given number as numerator without the decimal point, and for the denominator write 1 followed by as many zeros as many are there figures after the decimal point. Now reduce the fraction to its lowest terms.

Ex : (*i*) $0.63 = \frac{63}{100}$

(*ii*) $3.013 = 3\frac{013}{1000} = 3\frac{13}{1000}$

Addition and Subtraction of Decimal Fractions

First of all write down the numbers under one another. Other than the decimal point lies in one column. After arranging in this way, we add or subtract in usual fashion.

An example : Add 521 + 52.1 + 5.21 + 0.521

Sol : 521.000
52.100
5.210
0.521 After adding we get 578.831

Multiplication of decimal fraction

1. To multiply by 10, 100, 1000, etc

Example : (*i*) 63.02 × 10 = 630.2

(*ii*) 63.02 × 100 = 6302

(*iii*) 63.02 × 1000 = 63020

2. To multiply of two or more decimal fractions.

An example : (*i*) 5.91 × 13 = 76.83

(*ii*) 6.32 × 0.59 = 3.7288

(*iii*) 63.2 × 0.01 = 0.632

Conclusion: First of all multiply the given numbers assuming them without the decimal point. Now mark off the decimal point from extreme right in the product as many places of decimal as is the sum of the number of decimal places in the given numbers.

DIVISION OF DECIMALS

1. When the divisor is a counting number

Example : (*i*) 4.309 ÷ 10 = 0.4309

(*ii*) 0.0182 ÷ 14 = 0.0013

(*iii*) 9.586 ÷ 100 = 0.09586

(iv) $0.05 \div 10^3 = 0.00005$

(v) $0.49 \div 7 = 0.07$

Conclusion : *(i)* When divisor is the power of 10, then shift the decimal point to the left by as many places of decimal as is the power of 10, prefixing zero if necessary.

(ii) When divisor is other than power of 10, then divide as in the case of integers, and in quotient, put the decimal point to give as many places of decimal as are there in the dividend.

2. When the divisor is a decimal

Example:

(i) $0.00066 \div 0.11 = \dfrac{0.00066}{0.11} = \dfrac{0.066}{11} = 0.006$

(ii) $42 \div 0.07 = \dfrac{42}{0.07} = \dfrac{4200}{7} = 600$

(iii) $32.5 \div 0.0064 = \dfrac{32.5}{0.0064} = \dfrac{325000}{64} = 5078.125$

Recurring Decimal : If in a decimal number a digit or a set of digits is repeated again and again, the decimal is known as recurring decimal.

For example:

(i) $2.666... = 2.\dot{6}$

(ii) $1.363636... = 1.\dot{3}\dot{6}$ or $1.\overline{36}$

(iii) $7.3424242... = 7.3\dot{4}\dot{2}$ or $7.3\overline{42}$

Recurring decimal numbers are of two types:

(i) **Pure recurring decimals :** A decimal fraction in which all the figures after the decimal point are repeated is called a pure recurring decimal. For example, $0.\overline{3}$, $0.\overline{37}$, $3.\overline{4579}$ etc

(ii) **Mixed recurring decimals :** A decimal fraction in which at least one figure after the decimal point is not repeated is called a mixed recurring decimal. For example, $0.3\overline{59}$, $0.29\overline{54}$, $0.2\dot{7}$ etc.

Conversion of Recurring into Vulgar Fraction

1. Pure recurring decimals

Rule : Put as many 9's in the denominator at the number of digits under recurring and delete the recurring sign.

For example, $0.\overline{5} = \dfrac{5}{9}$

$$0.\overline{35} = \frac{35}{99}$$

$$0.\overline{24} = \frac{24}{99} = \frac{8}{33}$$

2. Mixed Recurring Decimals

For example,

(i) $0.1\overline{8}$

Here, numerator $= 18 - 1 = 17$

and denominator $= 9 \times 10 = 90$

$$\therefore \quad 0.1\dot{8} = \frac{18-1}{90} = \frac{17}{90}$$

(ii) $0.2\dot{7}\dot{9}$

Here, numerator $= 279 - 2 = 277$

and denominator $= 99 \times 10 = 990$

$$\therefore \quad 0.2\overline{79} = \frac{279-2}{990} = \frac{277}{990}$$

(iii) $$0.3\overline{56} = \frac{356-3}{99 \times 10} = \frac{353}{990}$$

(iv) $$2.53\dot{6} = 2 + \frac{536-53}{9 \times 100} = 2 + \frac{483}{900}$$

$$= 2 + \frac{161}{300} = 2\frac{161}{300}$$

(v) $$0.43\overline{213} = \frac{43213-43}{999 \times 100}$$

$$= \frac{43170}{99900} = \frac{4317}{9990}$$

Addition and Subtraction of recurring decimals

Example : *(i)* Add $3.\overline{76}$ and $1.4\overline{576}$ and subtract also.

3.7	676767	67
1.4	576576	57
(+) 5.2	253344	24 ⇒ $5.2\overline{253344}$
(–) 2.3	100191	10 ⇒ 2.3100191

(ii) Subtract $3.\overline{75}$ from $25.5\overline{473}$.

25.5	473473	47
3.7	575757	57
21.7	897715	90

Hence, the required subtract = $21.7\overline{897715}$

Multiplication and Division of Recurring Decimal

Example 1:

(i) $7.\overline{63} \times 11 = 7\dfrac{63}{99} \times 11$

$$= 7\frac{7}{11} \times 11 = \frac{84}{11} \times 11 = 84$$

(ii) $0.\overline{09} \times 7.\overline{3} = \dfrac{9}{99} \times 7\dfrac{3}{9}$

$$= \frac{1}{11} \times \frac{66}{9} = \frac{6}{9} = 0.\overline{6}$$

(iii) $0.\overline{6} \times 7.\overline{3} = \dfrac{6}{9} \times 7\dfrac{3}{9}$

$$= \frac{6}{9} \times \frac{66}{9} = \frac{44}{9} = 4.\overline{8}$$

(iv) $0.\overline{06} \div 100 = 0.060606... \div 100 = 0.00\overline{06}$

(v) $0.7\overline{32} \div 0.02\dot{7} = 0.73\dot{2}\dot{3} \div 0.027\dot{7}$

$= \dfrac{7323-73}{99 \times 100} \div \dfrac{277-2}{99 \times 100}$

$= \dfrac{7250}{9900} \div \dfrac{275}{9900}$

$= \dfrac{7250}{275} = \dfrac{290}{11} = 26.\overline{36}$.

EXERCISE

1. Which of the following is equivalent to $\frac{15}{25}$?

A. $\frac{150}{25}$ B. $\frac{15}{250}$
C. $\frac{3}{5}$ D. $\frac{60}{75}$

2. If $\frac{9*3}{3*7}$ is equivalent to $\frac{9}{7}$, the sign * is replaced by

A. ÷ B. ×
C. + D. –

3. $\frac{5}{6}$ of an hour is equal to

A. half an hour B. 40 minutes
C. 50 minutes D. 55 minutes

4. An aircraft uses 2/5 of its fuel in flying 1,250 kilometres. The distance travelled on remaining fuel is

A. 1875 km B. 2125 km
C. 250 km D. 475 km

5. If $\frac{4}{3} * \frac{3}{4} = \frac{16}{9}$, then * means

A. + B. –
C. × D. ÷

6. Which of the following is the largest fraction?

$\frac{3}{15}, \frac{5}{20}, \frac{8}{64}, \frac{25}{1000}$

A. $\frac{3}{15}$ B. $\frac{5}{20}$
C. $\frac{8}{64}$ D. $\frac{25}{1000}$

7. Six times x increased by 12 is equal to

A. $\frac{x}{2}$ B. $2x$
C. $6x + 12$ D. $12x + 6$

8. Five times y diminished by 20 is equal to

A. $5y - 20$ B. $5y + 20$
C. $y/4$ D. $4y$

9. The number less than 15 by 7 is

A. $15x - 7$ B. 15/7
C. 15 D. 8

ANSWERS

1	2	3	4	5	6	7	8	9
C	B	C	A	D	B	C	A	D

EXPLANATORY ANSWERS

1. $\frac{15}{25} = \frac{3 \times 5}{5 \times 5} = \frac{3}{5}$

2. $\frac{9*3}{3*7} = \frac{9}{7}$, or, $\frac{9 \times 3}{7 \times 3} = \frac{9}{7}$, ∴ The sign * is ×.

3. $\frac{5}{6}$ of 1 hr. $= \frac{5}{6} \times 60$ minutes $= 50$ minutes.

4. Remaining fuel $= 1 - \frac{2}{5} = \frac{5-2}{5} = \frac{3}{5}$

Distance flown by $\frac{2}{5}$ of fuel = 1250 km.

Distance flown by full fuel $= \frac{1250}{2/5} = \frac{1250 \times 5}{2}$ km.

Distance flown by $\frac{3}{5}$ of fuel

$= \frac{1250 \times 5 \times 3}{2 \times 5} = 1875$ km.

6. $\frac{3}{15} = \frac{1}{5}, \frac{8}{64} = \frac{1}{8}, \frac{5}{20} = \frac{1}{4}, \frac{25}{1000} = \frac{1}{40}$

Now, the fractions are $\frac{1}{5}, \frac{1}{4}, \frac{1}{8}, \frac{1}{40}$.

∴ The largest fraction is $\frac{1}{4} = \frac{5}{20}$

7. $x \times 6 + 12 = 6x + 12$

8. $5 \times y - 20 = 5y - 20$

9. $15 - 7 = 8$

Relation Between Numbers

Simplification is a mathematical operation by which a complex expression of numbers or fractions is converted into a simpler or less difficult form. It is erroneous to solve this type of questions on random basis and a very appropriate method is to apply BODMAS Rule for arriving at the solution of such problems. Each of the letters of the word 'BODMAS' when explained serially, has following implications:

1.	B	→	Bracket	[{ ($\bar{\ }$) }]
2.	O	→	of	of
3.	D	→	Division	÷
4.	M	→	Multiplication	×
5.	A	→	Addition	+
6.	S	→	Subtraction	–

Therefore, for simplification, we should remove the brackets first. Thereafter operation for 'of', then for 'division', after that the operation for 'multiplication' and thereafter for 'addition' and at last operation for 'subtraction' should be carried out.

Important Notes

A. In mathematical operations the word 'of' indicates multiplication.

B. While removing brackets, first of all bar bracket '–' and after that small bracket '( )' is removed. Thereafter the curly bracket '{ }' and at last square bracket [ ] is removed.

EXERCISE

1. The value of 51 ÷ 17 ÷ 3 is:
A. 9 B. 4
C. 3 D. 1

2. What will be the value of
40 × 2 ÷ 10 + 5 – 4?
A. 5 B. 8
C. 11 D. 9

3. The value of 28 × 104 ÷ (18 + 6) + 3 is:
A. $124\frac{1}{3}$ B. $104\frac{1}{3}$
C. $125\frac{1}{3}$ D. 128

4. If $75^2 - 65^2 = 2x$, then value of x is:
A. 715 B. 700
C. 688 D. 711

5. The value of 99 × 14 ÷ 11 ÷ 0.7 is:
A. 2.9 B. 1.6
C. 1.8 D. 2.8

6. If 45 – [28 – {37 – (15 – ?) }] = 58, then which of the following should replace the sign of interrogation (?)?
A. 18 B. 17
C. 13 D. 19

7. The value of $8\frac{1}{3}+5\frac{1}{4}\times13\frac{1}{5}\div6\frac{3}{5}$ is:
A. $19\frac{1}{3}$ B. $18\frac{5}{6}$
C. $21\frac{1}{3}$ D. $22\frac{1}{2}$

8. The value of $\frac{14}{3}$ of $\frac{5}{8}$ of 72 is:
A. 209 B. 217
C. 210 D. 199

9. What will be the value of
10 × 10 × 10 ÷ (20 ÷ 10 × 10 – 10) + 6?
A. 108 B. 111
C. 106 D. 114

10. What will be the value of $\dfrac{\frac{1}{3}\times20\div4}{\frac{1}{4}\times25\div5}$?
A. 7/3 B. 4/3
C. 5/3 D. 10/3

11. Which of the following is the standard form of $\dfrac{(24\times13)+(28\div7)}{(24+13)-\left(\frac{14}{3}\text{ of }\frac{5}{8}\right)}$?
A. $\frac{3792}{409}$ B. $\frac{4792}{309}$
C. $\frac{3792}{411}$ D. $\frac{3092}{409}$

12. If $\dfrac{144+32\div?-8}{35\div\frac{1}{2}\text{ of }\frac{1}{2}}=1$, then which of the following should replace the sign of interrogation?
A. 7 B. 6
C. 10 D. 8

13. What is the value of
$\dfrac{2.70\times2.70+4.30\times4.30+8.60\times2.70}{2.70+4.30}$?
A. 6.8 B. 7.0
C. 7.6 D. 8.5

14. What will be the value of $\dfrac{\left(\sqrt{6}+\frac{1}{\sqrt{6}}\right)^2}{\frac{1}{2}\text{ of }18+4}+\frac{2}{3}$?
A. 101/78 B. 104/71
C. 101/88 D. 99/57

15. 1150 ÷ 50 ÷ 23 + 15 = ?
A. 16 B. 20
C. 22 D. 18

ANSWERS

1	2	3	4	5	6	7	8	9	10
D	D	A	B	C	D	B	C	C	B
11	**12**	**13**	**14**	**15**					
A	D	B	A	A					

EXPLANATORY ANSWERS

1. $\because$ $51 \div 17 \div 3 = \frac{51}{17} \div 3 = 3 \div 3 = \frac{3}{3} = 1$

2. $\because$ $40 \times 2 \div 10 + 5 - 4$

$= 40 \times \frac{2}{10} + 5 - 4 = 8 + 5 - 4 = 9.$

3. $\because$ $28 \times 104 \div (18 + 6) + 3$

$= 28 \times 104 \div 24 + 3$

$= 28 \times \frac{104}{24} + 3 = 28 \times \frac{13}{3} + 3$

$= \frac{364}{3} + 3 = \frac{373}{3} = 124\frac{1}{3}$

4. $\because$ $75^2 - 65^2 = 2x$

$\Rightarrow (75 + 65)(75 - 65) = 2x$

$[\because a^2 - b^2 = (a + b)(a - b)]$

$\Rightarrow 140 \times 10 = 2x \Rightarrow x = 70 \times 10 = 700$

$\therefore$ Value of x is 700.

5. $\because$ $.99 \times 14 \div 11 \div 0.7$

$= .99 \times \frac{14}{11} \div 0.7 = \frac{.99 \times 14}{11 \times 0.7} = 1.8$

6. $\because$ $45 - [28 - \{37 - (15 - ?)\}] = 58$

$\Rightarrow 45 - [28 - \{37 - 15 + ?\}] = 58$

$\Rightarrow 45 - [28 - \{22 + ?\}] = 58$

$\Rightarrow 45 - [28 - 22 - ?] = 58$

$\Rightarrow 45 - 28 + 22 + ? = 58$

$\Rightarrow 39 + ? = 58$

$\Rightarrow ? = 58 - 39 = 19$

Therefore, the interrogation sign should be replaced by 19.

7. $\because$ $8\frac{1}{3} + 5\frac{1}{4} \times 13\frac{1}{5} \div 6\frac{3}{5}$

$= \frac{25}{3} + \frac{21}{4} \times \frac{66}{5} \div \frac{33}{5} = \frac{25}{3} + \frac{21}{4} \times \frac{66}{5} \times \frac{5}{33}$

$= \frac{25}{3} + \frac{21}{2} = \frac{50 + 63}{6} = \frac{113}{6} = 18\frac{5}{6}$

8. $\because$ $\frac{14}{3}$ of $\frac{5}{8}$ of $72 = \frac{14 \times 5 \times 72}{3 \times 8} = 210$

9. $10 \times 10 \times 10 \div (20 \div 10 \times 10 - 10) + 6$

$= 10 \times 10 \times 10 \div \left(\frac{20}{10} \times 10 - 10\right) + 6$

$= 10 \times 10 \times 10 \div (20 - 10) + 6$

$= 10 \times 10 \times 10 \div 10 + 6$

$= 10 \times 10 \times \frac{10}{10} + 6$

$= 10 \times 10 \times 1 + 6 = 100 + 6 = 106$

10. $\because$ $\dfrac{\frac{1}{3} \times 20 \div 4}{\frac{1}{4} \times 25 \div 5} = \dfrac{\frac{1}{3} \times 5}{\frac{1}{4} \times 5} = \dfrac{\frac{5}{3}}{\frac{5}{4}} = \frac{4}{3}$

11. $\because$ $\dfrac{(24 \times 13) + (28 \div 7)}{(24 + 13) - \left(\frac{14}{3} \text{ of } \frac{5}{8}\right)} = \dfrac{312 + 4}{37 - \frac{35}{12}} = \dfrac{316}{\frac{409}{12}} = \dfrac{3792}{409}$

12. If $\dfrac{144 + 32 \div ? - 8}{35 \div \frac{1}{2} \text{ of } \frac{1}{2}} = 1 \Rightarrow \dfrac{144 + \frac{32}{?} - 8}{35 \div \frac{1}{4}} = 1 \Rightarrow \dfrac{136 + \frac{32}{?}}{\frac{35}{\frac{1}{4}}} = 1$

$\Rightarrow 136 + \frac{32}{?} = 35 \times 4 = 140$

$\Rightarrow \frac{32}{?} = 140 - 136 = 4 \Rightarrow ? = \frac{32}{4} = 8$

$\therefore$ Sign of interrogation (?) will be replaced by 8.

13. $\dfrac{2.70 \times 2.70 + 4.30 \times 4.30 + 8.60 \times 2.70}{2.70 + 4.30}$

$= \dfrac{(2.70)^2 + (4.30)^2 + 2 \times 4.30 \times 2.70}{2.70 + 4.30}$

$= \dfrac{(2.70 + 4.30)^2}{2.70 + 4.30}$ $[\because a^2 + b^2 + 2ab = (a + b)^2]$

$= 2.70 + 4.30 = 7.00$

14. $\therefore$ $\dfrac{\left(\sqrt{6} + \frac{1}{\sqrt{6}}\right)^2}{\frac{1}{2} \text{ of } 18 + 4} + \frac{2}{3} = \dfrac{(\sqrt{6})^2 + \left(\frac{1}{\sqrt{6}}\right)^2 + 2.\sqrt{6}\frac{1}{\sqrt{6}}}{9 + 4} + \frac{2}{3}$

$= \dfrac{6 + \frac{1}{6} + 2}{13} + \frac{2}{3} = \dfrac{\frac{49}{6}}{13} + \frac{2}{3} = \frac{49}{78} + \frac{2}{3} = \frac{101}{78}$

15. $1150 \div 50 \div 23 + 15$

$= \frac{1150}{50} \div 23 + 15 = 23 \div 23 + 15 = \frac{23}{23} + 15$

$= 1 + 15 = 16.$

CHAPTER 2

Comparing Quantities

Percentage

The word 'per cent' or 'percentage' means 'for every one hundred'. In other words, it gives an indication of rate per hundred. It is denoted by the symbol %.

For example, 5% means 5 out of one hundred or $\frac{5}{100}$.

Remember:

(*i*) For converting a per cent into a fraction, divide it by 100.

(*ii*) For converting a fraction into a per cent, multiply it by 100.

(*iii*) For converting a per cent into a decimal, shift the decimal point two places to the left.

(*iv*) For converting one given quantity (*x*) as a percentage of another given quantity (*y*), find $\frac{x}{y} \times 100$.

(*v*) There is no unit of percentage.

Important Facts—For quickly solving the problems related to percentage, remember following rules:

Rule 1:

(*a*) Of the given two numbers if the first is $x\%$ more than the second, then the second will be $\left(\frac{100 \times x}{100 + x}\right)\%$ less than the first.

(*b*) Of the given two numbers if the first is $x\%$ less than the second, then the second will be $\left(\frac{100 \times x}{100 - x}\right)\%$ more than the first.

(*c*) If two numbers are respectively $x\%$ and $y\%$ more than a third number, then the first number will be $\left(\frac{100 + x}{100 + y} \times 100\right)\%$ of the second.

(*d*) If two numbers are respectively $x\%$ and $y\%$ less than a third number, then the first number will be $\left(\frac{100 - x}{100 - y} \times 100\right)\%$ of the second.

Rule 2:

(*a*) If a number or quantity is increased by $x\%$ then in order to restore its original value it must be decreased by $\left[\frac{100 \times x}{100 + x}\right]\%$.

(*b*) If a number or quantity is decreased by $x\%$ then in order to restore its original value it must be increased by $\left[\frac{100 \times x}{100 - x}\right]\%$.

Rule 3:

(*a*) If a number is successively increased by $x\%$ and $y\%$ then a single equivalent increase in that number will be $\left(x + y + \frac{xy}{100}\right)\%$

(*b*) If two successive discounts of $x\%$ and $y\%$ are allowed on a particular amount, then a single discount that is equivalent to the two successive discounts will be $\left(x + y - \frac{xy}{100}\right)\%$

(*c*) If a number is successively increased by $x\%$, $y\%$ and $z\%$, then a single equivalent increase in that number will be

$$\left[(x + y + z) + \left(\frac{xy + yz + zx}{100}\right) + \frac{(xyz)}{10000}\right]\%$$

(*d*) If three successive discounts of $x\%$, $y\%$ and $z\%$ are allowed on an amount, then a single discount that is equivalent to the three successive discounts will be

$$\left[x + y + z - \frac{(xy + yz + zx)}{100} + \frac{xyz}{10000}\right]\%$$

Rule 4:

(*a*) If a number is increased by $x\%$ and thereafter reduced by $x\%$, then the number will be reduced by $\left(\frac{x^2}{100}\right)$ per cent.

(b) If a number is reduced by $x\%$ and thereafter increased by $x\%$ then the number will be reduced by $\left(\frac{x^2}{100}\right)$ per cent.

(c) If due to an increase of $x\%$ in the selling price of certain commodity the sell/consumption of the commodity decreases by $y\%$, then gross receipts on account of sale of that commodity will be increased or decreased by $\left(x-y-\frac{xy}{100}\right)\%$, where $x > y$ and will be decreased by $\left(y-x+\frac{xy}{100}\right)\%$, where $y > x$.

EXERCISE

1. In the expression xy^2, the values of both variables x and y are decreased by 20%. By this, the value of the expression is decreased by

A. 40% B. 48.8%
C. 51.2% D. 80%

2. 15 litres of mixture contains 20% alcohol and rest water. If 3 litres of water be mixed in it, the percentage of alcohol in the new mixture will be:

A. 15 B. $16\frac{2}{3}$
C. 17 D. $18\frac{1}{2}$

3. The difference between 70% and 55% of a number is 72. The number is:

A. 370 B. 460
C. 480 D. 520

4. 20% of a number is 10% of:

A. half the number
B. double the number
C. ten times the number
D. twenty times the number

5. 75% of what area is 15 sq. metres?

A. 10 sq. metres B. 15 sq. metres
C. 20 sq. metres D. 25 sq. metres

6. In an examination 80% of the students passed in Mathematics and 70% passed in English, while 10% students failed in both the subjects. If 360 students passed in both the subjects, find the total number of students who appeared in the examination.

A. 400 B. 600
C. 630 D. 640

7. In an election, there are two candidates. A candidate secured 57% of the total votes polled and elected by a margin of 2100 votes. Find the total number of votes polled.

A. 15000 B. 17500
C. 18000 D. 21000

8. Electric tax is increased by 20% and its consumption is decreased by 20%. The change in the expenditure is:

A. 4% decrease B. 4% increase
C. 5% decrease D. 5% increase

9. A man loses 10% of his money, after spending 20% of the remainder he is left with ₹ 2160. Initially the man had:

A. ₹ 1800 B. ₹ 2500
C. ₹ 3000 D. ₹ 3200

10. In a school 55% of the students are below 9 years of age and the remaining 153 above 9 years of age. The total number of students in the school is:

A. 296 B. 300
C. 340 D. 1000

ANSWERS

1	2	3	4	5	6	7	8	9	10
B	B	C	B	C	B	A	A	C	C

EXPLANATORY ANSWERS

1. Decrease in expression

$$= xy^2 - \frac{80}{100}\times x\left(\frac{80}{100}y\right)^2 = xy^2 - \frac{64}{125}xy^2 = \frac{61xy^2}{125}$$

Hence, decrease per cent

$$= \frac{61xy^2}{125\times xy^2}\times 100 = 48.8\%$$

2. Amount of alcohol $= \frac{20}{100}\times 15 = 3$ litre

Hence, required percentage $= \frac{3}{18}\times 100 = 16\frac{2}{3}\%$

3. Let the number be x; then

$$(70-55)\times\frac{1}{100}\times x = 72$$

$\therefore \quad x = \frac{100 \times 72}{15} = 480$

4. Let number be 100, then 20% and 10% of the number be 20 and 10 respectively.

Hence, 20% of a number is 10% of double the number.

5. Let required area be x sq. metre; then

$\frac{75}{100} \times x = 15$

$\therefore \; x = \frac{15 \times 100}{75} = 20$ sq metre

6. Here, percentage of students failed in Mathematics and English be 30% and 20% respectively.

Percentage of students failed either one or both subjects = 30 + 20 – 10 = 40%

Hence, percentage of pass students = 100 – 40 = 60%

Now, 60% = 360

$\therefore \quad 100\% = \frac{360}{60} \times 100 = 600$

7. Let total number of votes be x; then

$(57 - 43) \times \frac{1}{10} x = 2100$

$\therefore \quad x = \frac{100 \times 2100}{14} = 15000$

8. Let initially electric tax is ₹ 100 and consumption = 100 units

Decrease in consumption

= 100 × 100 – 120 × 80 = ₹ 400

Hence, decrease percentage = $\frac{400 \times 100}{100 \times 100} = 4\%$

9. Let initally the man had ₹ x, then

amount of money loses = $\frac{10}{100} \times x = ₹\frac{x}{10}$

Remaining amount of money = $x - \frac{x}{10} = ₹\frac{9x}{10}$

Money spent = $\frac{20}{100} \times \frac{9x}{10} = ₹\frac{9x}{50}$

Now, $\frac{9x}{10} - \frac{9x}{50} = 2160$

$\Rightarrow \frac{36x}{50} = 2160$

$\therefore \; x = \frac{2160 \times 50}{36} = ₹\ 3000$

10. Let total number of students be x, then

$\frac{45}{100} \times x = 153 \;\therefore\; x = \frac{100 \times 153}{45} = 340$

Discount

Market Price (M.P.)—The attached price is called the market price (M.P.) or list price (L.P.) of the article and the reduction allowed in the price is called the **discount**.

(*i*) Discount = M.P. – S.P.

(*ii*) Discount % = $\frac{\text{Discount} \times 100}{\text{M.P.}}$

(*iii*) S.P. = M.P. – $\frac{\text{Discount\%} \times \text{M.P.}}{100}$

(*iv*) S.P. = M.P. × $\left(1 - \frac{\text{Discount\%}}{100}\right)$

(*v*) M.P. = $\frac{100 \times \text{S.P.}}{100 - \text{Discount\%}}$

S.P. = M.P. $\left(\frac{100 - \text{Discount\%}}{100}\right)$

M.P. – S.P. = $\frac{\text{M.P.} \times \text{Discount\%}}{100}$

Discount% = $\left(\frac{\text{M.P.} - \text{S.P.}}{\text{M.P.}}\right) \times 100$

EXERCISE

1. A cloth merchant offers 15% festival discount on every saree sold. If a certain saree is sold for ₹ 680, what is its marked price?

A. ₹ 800　　B. ₹ 900
C. ₹ 1250　　D. ₹ 1300

2. A shopkeeper offers 10% discount on an article and still makes a profit of 20%. What is the C.P. of the article if the marked price is ₹ 350?

A. ₹ 259.20　　B. ₹ 262.50
C. ₹ 265.75　　D. ₹ 272.5

3. A manufactures marks his goods in such a way that after allowing 20% discount, he makes a profit of 18%. What is the marked price of an item which costs him ₹ 200?

A. ₹ 295　　B. ₹ 310
C. ₹ 315　　D. ₹ 375

4. The marked price of a brand of coffee is ₹ 35 for 100g. But the shopkeeper gives a cup costing ₹ 7.50 free with it. Even then he gets a gain of 10%. What is the cost price of 100g of coffee?

A. ₹ 15 B. ₹ 25
C. ₹ 35 D. ₹ 65

5. A car is marked at ₹ 2,25,000. The manufacturer gives a discount of 10%. The dealer also gives a discount of 5%. What is the S.P. of the car?
A. ₹ 1,72,369 B. ₹ 1,64,370
C. ₹ 1,52,393 D. ₹ 1,92,375

6. A cycle merchant allows 25% commission on his advertised price and still makes a profit of 20%. If he gains ₹ 60 over the sale of one cycle. What is his advertised price?
A. ₹ 290 B. ₹ 310
C. ₹ 480 D. ₹ 520

7. The marked price of a shirt was ₹ 165 and it was at a discount of 12%. What the selling price of the shirt?
A. ₹ 145.20 B. ₹ 155.30
C. ₹ 165.20 D. ₹ 175.25

8. A trader marks his goods 40% above the cost price and gives a discount of 20% on the marked price. What is his gain per cent?
A. 8% B. 9%
C. 12% D. 15%

9. How much per cent more than the C.P. should a manufacturer mark his goods so that after allowing a discount of 20% on the marked price, he gains 10%.
A. 34.5% B. 27.5%
C. 37.5% D. 38.5%

10. A shopkeeper allows a discount of 10% to his customers and still gains 20%. What is the marked price of an article which costs ₹ 450 to the shopkeeper?
A. ₹ 600 B. ₹ 700
C. ₹ 800 D. ₹ 900

ANSWERS

1	2	3	4	5	6	7	8	9	10
A	B	A	B	D	C	A	C	C	A

EXPLANATORY ANSWERS

1. S.P. = ₹ 680, Discount = 15%

$$\text{M.P.} = \frac{100 \times \text{S.P.}}{100 - \text{Discount\%}}$$

$$= \frac{100 \times 680}{100 - 15} = \frac{100 \times 680}{85} = ₹\ 800$$

2. C.P. = ₹ x, 120% of x = 350 − 350 × 10%

$$\frac{120}{100} \times x = 350 - 35 = 315.$$

$$x = \frac{315 \times 5}{6} = \frac{525}{2},\ \text{C.P.} = ₹\ 262.50.$$

3. Let M.P. = ₹ x

80% x = 118% of 200

$$\frac{80}{100} \times x = \frac{118}{100} \times 200 \Rightarrow x = \frac{236 \times 5}{4} = ₹\ 295.$$

4. Let C.P. of 100 gm coffee = ₹ x

110% of x = 35 − 7.50 = 27.50

$$\frac{110}{100} \times x = 27.50$$

$$x = \frac{27.50 \times 100}{110 \times 100}$$

C.P. = ₹ 25.

5. M.P. = ₹ 225000

$$\text{1st S.P.} = 225000 - 225000 \times \frac{10}{100}$$

$$= 225000 - 22500 = 202500$$

$$\text{2nd S.P.} = 202500 - 202500 \times \frac{5}{100}$$

$$= 202500 - 10125 = ₹\ 192375$$

6. Let M.P. = 100

Commission = 25%

S.P. = 100 − 25 = 75

Profit = 20%

$$\text{C.P.} = \frac{100}{120} \times 75 = \frac{375}{6} = 62.50$$

Gain = 75 − 62.50 = ₹ 12.50

$$\text{M.P.} = \frac{100}{12.50} \times 60 = ₹\ 480$$

7. $$\text{S.P.} = \frac{\text{M.P.}(100 - \text{Discount})}{100}$$

$$= \frac{165 \times (100 - 12)}{100} = \frac{165 \times 88}{100}$$

= 33 × 4.4 = ₹ 145.20

8. Let C.P. = 100, M.P. = 140, Discount = 20%

$$\text{S.P.} = 140 - 140 \times \frac{20}{100} = 140 - 28 = 112$$

Profit = 112 − 100 = 12

$$\text{Profit \%} = \frac{12 \times 100}{100} = 12\%$$

9. Let C.P. = ₹ x, S.P. = 110% of $x = \frac{110}{100} \times x = \frac{11}{10} x.$

Discount = 20%

$$\text{M.P.} = \frac{100 \times \frac{11}{10} x}{100 - 20} = \frac{100 \times \frac{11}{10} x}{80} = \frac{11}{8} x.$$

$$\text{Required \%} = \frac{\frac{11x}{8} - x}{x} \times 100 = \frac{3x \times 100}{8x} = 37.5\%$$

10. C.P. = 450, Gain = 20%

$$\text{S.P.} = 450 + 450 \times \frac{20}{100} = 450 + 90 = 540$$

Discount = 10%

$$\text{M.P.} = \frac{100 \times \text{S.P.}}{100 - \text{Discount}} = \frac{100 \times 540}{100 - 10}$$

$$= \frac{100 \times 540}{90} = ₹\ 600$$

Profit & Loss

A consumer who goes to the market and buys certain goods. The buyer is called a customer and the shopkeeper who sells the goods to him is called a retailer. The retailer purchases goods in turn in bulk from a wholesaler who keeps a large stock of good and in this case, the retailer becomes the customer.

1. **Cost price (C.P.):** Cost price is that price at which a particular article is bought. Profit and loss both are marked at cost price.
2. **Selling Price (S.P.):** Selling price is that price at which a particular article is sold.
3. **Overheads:** The expenses incurred on transportation, maintenance, packaging, advertisements and the like are included as *Overhead.* These overheads and the profit when added to the cost price determine the selling price.
4. **Profit or Gain** : Whenever a person sells an article at price greater than the cost price he is said to have made a profit or gain.
   Profit or Gain = S.P. – C.P.
5. **Loss** : If S.P. is less than the C.P. there is loss.
   Loss = C.P – S.P

Some Basic Formulae:

(i) Gain = S.P. – C.P.

(ii) Loss = C.P. – S.P.

(iii) $\text{Gain\%} = \dfrac{\text{Gain} \times 100}{\text{C.P.}}$

(iv) $\text{Loss\%} = \dfrac{\text{Loss} \times 100}{\text{C.P.}}$

From these we can write direct expressions for S.P. and C.P.

(v) $\text{S.P.} = \left(\dfrac{100 + \text{Gain\%}}{100}\right) \times \text{C.P.}$ in case of gain or profit

(vi) $\text{S.P.} = \left(\dfrac{100 - \text{Loss\%}}{100}\right) \times \text{C.P.}$ in case of loss

These can be rewritten as

$$\text{C.P.} = \frac{100}{100 + \text{Gain\%}} \times \text{S.P.} \text{ in case of profit}$$

$$\text{C.P.} = \frac{100}{100 - \text{Loss\%}} \times \text{S.P.} \text{ in case of loss}$$

(vii) If the C.P. of x goods = S.P. of y goods, then

(a) $\text{Gain\%} = \dfrac{x - y}{y} \times 100$ [In case of $x > y$]

(b) $\text{Loss\%} = \dfrac{y - x}{y} \times 100$ [In case of $y > x$]

(viii) When a man sells two things at the same price each and in this process his loss on first things is $x\%$ and gain on second things is $x\%$, then in such a type question, there is always a loss.

$$\text{Loss\%} = x\% \text{ of } x = \frac{x^2}{100} = \left(\frac{x}{10}\right)^2$$

$$\text{and Loss} = \frac{2 \times \text{S.P.}}{\left(\frac{100}{x}\right)^2 - 1}$$

(ix) An article is sold at a profit of $x\%$. Had it been sold for ₹ a some more, $y\%$ would have gained. Then,

$$\text{C.P. of an article} = \frac{\text{More gain} \times 100}{\text{Difference in percentage profit}}$$

(x) A dishonest shopkeeper prefers to sell goods at his cost price but uses a false weight of x grams for each kilogram. Then his gain per cent,

$$\text{gain\%} = \frac{\text{Error}}{\text{True value} - \text{Error}} \times 100$$

$$= \frac{1000 - x}{x} \times 100$$

$$\text{or, gain\%} = \frac{\text{True weight} - \text{False weight}}{\text{False weight}} \times 100.$$

EXERCISE

1. Ashok bought 25 kg of rice at the rate of ₹ 6 per kg and 35 kg of rice at the rate of ₹ 7 per kg. He mixed the two and sold the mixture at the rate of ₹ 6.75 per kg. What was his gain or loss in the transaction?
   A. ₹ 16 gain B. ₹ 16 loss
   C. ₹ 10 gain D. None of these

2. A horse and a cow were sold for ₹ 12000 each. The horse was sold at a loss of 20% and the cow at a gain of 20%. The entire transaction resulted in
   A. no loss no gain B. loss of ₹ 1000
   C. gain of ₹ 1000 D. loss of ₹ 2000

3. Profit after selling a commodity for ₹ 425 is same as loss after selling it for ₹ 355. The cost of the commodity is :

A. ₹ 285 B. ₹ 390
C. ₹ 295 D. ₹ 400

4. Bhajan Singh purchased 120 reams of paper at ₹ 80 per ream. He spent ₹ 280 on transportation, paid octroi at the rate of 40 paise per ream and paid ₹ 72 to the coolie. If he wants to have a gain of 8%, what must be the selling price per ream?

A. ₹ 86 B. ₹ 86.48
C. ₹ 79 D. ₹ 90

5. Ram bought 4 dozen apples at ₹ 12 per dozen and 2 dozen at ₹ 16 per dozen. He sold all of them to earn 20%. At what price per dozen did he sell the apples?

A. ₹ 14.40 B. ₹ 16.00
C. ₹ 16.80 D. ₹ 16.20

6. Jimmy bought paper sheets for ₹ 7200 and spent ₹ 200 in transport. Paying ₹ 600 he had 330 boxes made, which he sold at ₹ 28 each. What is his profit percentage?

A. 15.5 B. 40
C. 50 D. None of these

7. A owns a house worth ₹ 10000. He sells it to B at a profit of 10% based on the worth of the house. B sells the house back to A at a loss of 10%. In this transaction A gets:

A. no profit no loss B. profit of ₹ 1000
C. profit of ₹ 1100 D. profit of ₹ 1200

8. At what price must Kantilal sell a mixture of 80 kg sugar at ₹ 6.75 per kg with 120 kg at ₹ 8 per kg to gain 20%?

A. ₹ 7.50 per kg B. ₹ 8.20 per kg
C. ₹ 8.35 per kg D. ₹ 9 per kg

9. Subhash purchased a taperecorder at $\frac{9}{10}$ of its selling price and sold it at 8% more than its S.P. His gain is:

A. 8% B. 10%
C. 18% D. 20%

10. A dealer marks his goods 20% above cost price. He then allows some discount on it and makes a profit of 8%. The rate of discount is :

A. 12% B. 10%
C. 6% D. 4%

ANSWERS

1	2	3	4	5	6	7	8	9	10
C	B	B	D	B	A	C	D	D	B

EXPLANATORY ANSWERS

1. C.P. of 60 kg mixture = ₹ (25 × 6 + 35 × 7) = ₹ 395

S.P. of 60 kg mixtire = ₹ (60 × 6.75) = ₹ 405

∴ Gain = ₹ (405 − 395) = ₹ 10

2. Loss% = $\left(\frac{20}{10}\right)^2 = (2)^2 = 4\%$ Total S.P. = ₹ 24000

and Total C.P. = ₹$\left(\frac{100}{96} \times 24000\right)$ = ₹ 25000

∴ Loss = ₹ (25000 − 24000) = ₹ 1000

3. Let C.P. = ₹ x, Then, $425 - x = x - 355$

⇒ $2x = 780$ ∴ x = ₹ 390

4. C.P. of 1 ream = $80 + \frac{280}{120} + \frac{72}{120} + 0.40$

$= 80 + \frac{7}{3} + \frac{3}{5} + \frac{2}{5}$ = ₹ $\frac{250}{3}$

∴ S.P. of 1 ream = ₹$\left(\frac{108}{100} \times \frac{250}{3}\right)$ = ₹ 90

5. C.P. of 6 dozen apples = ₹ (12 × 4 + 16 × 2) = ₹ 80

∴ S.P. = ₹$\left(\frac{120}{100} \times 80\right)$ = ₹ 96

∴ S.P. per dozen = ₹$\left(\frac{96}{6}\right)$ = ₹ 16

6. C.P. of 1 box = $\frac{7200+200+600}{330}$ = ₹ $\frac{800}{33}$

Hence, Gain% = $\frac{28 - \frac{800}{33}}{800/33} \times 100 = \frac{124}{800} \times 100 = 15.5\%$

7. Final C.P. for A = $\frac{110}{100} \times \frac{90}{100} \times$ ₹ 10000 = ₹ 9900

Hence, profit for A

= $\frac{10}{100}$ × ₹ 10,000 + ₹ (10,000 − 9900) = ₹ 1100

8. C.P. of 1 kg sugar = $\frac{80 \times 6.75 + 120 \times 8}{200}$ = ₹ 7.50

∴ S.P. of 1 kg = ₹$\left(\frac{120}{100} \times 7.50\right)$ = ₹ 9 per kg

9. Let S.P. = ₹ 100;

C.P. for Subhash = $\frac{9}{10} \times 100$ = ₹ 90 and S.P. = ₹ 108

Hence, gain% for Subhash = $\frac{108-90}{90} \times 100 = 20\%$

10. Let C.P. be ₹ 100; then Marked price = ₹ 120 and S.P. = ₹ 108

∴ Discount = $\left(\frac{12}{120} \times 100\right)\% = 10\%$

Simple Interest

Interest is the money paid for the use of money borrowed, *i.e.*, extra money paid for using other's money is called *interest.*

The sum borrowed is called the principal. The sum of interest and principal is called the *Amount.*

If the interest on a certain sum borrowed for a certain period is reckoned uniformly, then it is called simple interest, denoted by S.I.

Thus, if A = Amount, P = Principal,

I = Interest, T = Time (in year),

R = Rate per cent per annum, then

(*a*) $I = \frac{P \times R \times T}{100}$ (*b*) $P = \frac{100 \times I}{R \times T}$

(*c*) $T = \frac{100 \times I}{P \times R}$ (*d*) $R = \frac{100 \times I}{P \times T}$

(*e*) $P = \frac{100\,A}{100 + RT}$ (*f*) A = P + I.

EXERCISE

1. If the simple interest on a certain sum of money at 6% per annum for 3 years is ₹ 90, the sum will be:

A. ₹ 500 B. ₹ 450
C. ₹ 525 D. ₹ 560

2. If the simple interest on ₹ 1 for 1 month is 1 paise, the rate per cent p.a. will be :

A. 10% B. 8%
C. 12% D. 6%

3. A sum of money doubles itself in 20 years. In how many years will it triple itself at the same rate of simple interest?

A. 30 years B. 50 years
C. 40 years D. 45 years

4. If the simple interest on ₹ 500 for 4 years is ₹ 40, find the rate per cent p.a.

A. 3½% B. 2%
C. 2½% D. 3%

5. After what time will the sum of ₹ 2000 become ₹ 2240 at 4% per annum simple interest?

A. 3 years B. 2 years
C. 5 years D. 4 years

6. The simple interest on a certain sum of money is $\frac{25}{64}$ of the sum and the number of years equals the rate per cent p.a. The rate per cent p.a. will be :

A. $7\frac{1}{2}\%$ B. $5\frac{1}{4}\%$
C. $6\frac{3}{4}\%$ D. $6\frac{1}{4}\%$

7. A sum of money amounts to ₹ 1150 in 3 years and to ₹ 1250 in 5 years at a certain rate per cent p.a. simple interest. The rate per cent p.a. will be :

A. 5% B. 8%
C. 7% D. 6%

8. The simple interest on a sum of ₹ 892 lent out at 6% p.a. for 8 months will be :

A. ₹ 36.68 B. ₹ 35.68
C. ₹ 48.58 D. ₹ 33.38

9. If the simple interest on a certain sum of money at 6% p.a. for 4½ years is ₹ 81, the sum will be:

A. ₹ 325 B. ₹ 225
C. ₹ 300 D. ₹ 340

10. A sum of ₹ 1850 lent out for 5 years at 3% p.a. simple interest will amount to:

A. ₹ 2227.75 B. ₹ 2127.50
C. ₹ 2137.50 D. ₹ 2086.50

ANSWERS

1	2	3	4	5	6	7	8	9	10
A	C	C	B	A	D	A	B	C	B

EXPLANATORY ANSWERS

1. $P = \frac{90 \times 100}{6 \times 3} = ₹\ 500$

2. $\text{Rate} = \frac{1 \times 100}{100 \times \frac{1}{12}} = 12\%.$

3. Let principal = ₹ x; Amount = ₹ $2x$;

then $I = 2x - x = ₹\ x$

$\therefore R = \frac{x \times 100}{x \times 20} = 5\%$

Again, if principal = ₹ x;

Amount = ₹ $3x$; then I = $3x - x$ = ₹ $2x$

Hence, $T = \dfrac{2x \times 100}{x \times 5} = 40$ years.

4. Rate $= \dfrac{40 \times 100}{500 \times 4} = 2\%$

5. Here, I = 2240 – 2000 = ₹ 240

$\therefore \quad T = \dfrac{240 \times 100}{2000 \times 4} = 3$ years

6. Let, $\quad R = T = x$; then

$\dfrac{25}{64}P = \dfrac{P \times x \times x}{100} \Rightarrow x^2 = \dfrac{25 \times 100}{64}$

$\therefore \quad x = \dfrac{5 \times 10}{8} = \dfrac{25}{4}$; $R = 6\dfrac{1}{4}\%$

7. Here, Simple interest for 2 years

= ₹ 1250 – ₹ 1150 = ₹ 100

$\therefore$ Simple interest for 3 years $= \dfrac{100 \times 3}{2}$ = ₹ 150

Hence, P = ₹ 1150 – ₹ 150 = ₹ 1000

$\therefore \quad$ Rate $= \dfrac{50 \times 100}{1000 \times 1} = 5\%$

8. Here, $\quad I = \dfrac{892 \times 6 \times \frac{2}{3}}{100}$ = ₹ 35.68

9. $\quad P = \dfrac{81 \times 100 \times 2}{6 \times 9}$ = ₹ 300

10. $I = \dfrac{1850 \times 3 \times 5}{100}$ = ₹ 277.50

$\therefore \quad$ Amount = ₹ 1850 + ₹ 277.50

= ₹ 2127.50

Compound Interest

In business transaction if interest as it becomes due is not paid to the lender but is added on to the principal, the money is said to be lent at *compound interest* and the total sum owed after a given time is called the amount at compound interest for that time.

After a certain period, the difference between the amount and the original principal is called the compound Interest (C.I.).

Some Important Formulae :

Let $\quad$ Principal = P, Time = n years

Rate = r% p.a.

then, the amount,

(*a*) when interest is compounded annually:

then, $\quad \text{Amount} = P\left(1+\dfrac{r}{100}\right)^n$

(*b*) when interest is compounded half yearly:

then, $\quad \text{Amount} = P\left(1+\dfrac{r/2}{100}\right)^{2n}$

(*c*) when interest is compounded quarterly :

then, $\quad \text{Amount} = P\left(1+\dfrac{r/4}{100}\right)^{4n}$

(*d*) when time is fraction of a year, say $4\dfrac{1}{3}$ years,

then, $\text{Amount} = P\left(1+\dfrac{r}{100}\right)^4 \times \left(1+\dfrac{\frac{1}{3}r}{100}\right)$

(*e*) when rates are $r_1\%$, $r_2\%$ and $r_3\%$ for Ist, IInd and IIIrd year respectively; then,

$\text{Amount} = P\left(1+\dfrac{r_1}{100}\right)\left(1+\dfrac{r_2}{100}\right)\left(1+\dfrac{r_3}{100}\right)$

EXERCISE

1. What will be the compound interest on ₹ 8000 for 3 years at 5% p.a.?

A. ₹ 1361 B. ₹ 1261
C. ₹ 1260 D. ₹ 1250

2. What will be the amount if a sum of ₹ 2500 is invested for 1 year at 4% per annum compound interest, interest being compounded half-yearly?

A. ₹ 2625 B. ₹ 2601
C. ₹ 2830 D. ₹ 2901

3. Find the compound interest on ₹ 2560 for ½ year at 12½% per annum, interest payable quarterly.

A. ₹ 3720.50 B. ₹ 2722.50
C. ₹ 2752.50 D. ₹ 2250.50

4. After how many years will ₹ 3375 become ₹ 4096 at $6\dfrac{2}{3}\%$ per annum compound interest?

A. 4 years B. 2 years
C. 2½ years D. 3 years

5. A certain sum of money placed at compound interest amounts to ₹ 110 in 1 year and to ₹ 121 in 2 years. The rate of interest per annum is :

A. 5% B. 10%
C. 8% D. 4%

6. The present population of a city is 80,000. If the rate of growth is 5% per year, find its population after 3 years.
A. 88,100 B. 95,600
C. 92,610 D. 84,600

7. First year's interest on a sum of money placed at compound interest at the rate of 8% per annum is ₹ 72. What will be interest for the second year?
A. ₹ 77.76 B. ₹ 78.66
C. ₹ 85.66 D. ₹ 78.76

8. The difference between compound and simple interest on a certain sum of money for 2 years at 5% per annum is ₹ 21. Find the sum.
A. ₹ 7200 B. ₹ 8400
C. ₹ 9200 D. ₹ 8500

9. In how many years will a sum of ₹ 19200 placed at 10% per annum compound interest yield an interest of ₹ 4032?
A. 1½ years B. 2½ years
C. 2 years D. 3 years

10. The compound interest on a certain sum of money invested for 3 years at 5% per annum is ₹ 1891.50. What will be the simple interest on the same sum at the same rate for 2 years?
A. ₹ 1700 B. ₹ 1200
C. ₹ 1500 D. ₹ 2100

ANSWERS

1	2	3	4	5	6	7	8	9	10
B	B	B	D	B	C	A	B	C	B

EXPLANATORY ANSWERS

1. ∴ $\text{C.I.} = 8000\left[\left(1+\frac{5}{100}\right)^3 - 1\right]$

$= 8000\left[\left(\frac{21}{20}\right)^3 - 1\right] = \frac{8000 \times 1261}{8000} = ₹\ 1261$

2. $A = 2500\left(1+\frac{2}{100}\right)^2 = 2500\left(\frac{51}{50}\right)^2 = \frac{2500 \times 51 \times 51}{50 \times 50}$

= ₹ 2601.

3. Amount $= 2560\left(1+\frac{25}{8 \times 100}\right)^2 = \frac{2560 \times 33 \times 33}{32 \times 32}$

= ₹ 2722.50

4. Here, $4096 = 3375\left(1+\frac{20}{3 \times 100}\right)^n$

$\Rightarrow \frac{4096}{3375} = \left(1+\frac{1}{15}\right)^n \Rightarrow \left(\frac{16}{15}\right)^3 = \left(\frac{16}{15}\right)^n$

∴ $n = 3$ years

5. Here, simple interest of ₹ 110 for 1 year
= 121 – 110 = ₹ 11

Hence, rate $= \frac{11 \times 100}{110 \times 1} = 10\%$

6. Population of the city after 3 years

$= 80{,}000\left(1+\frac{5}{100}\right)^3 = 80{,}000 \times \frac{21}{20} \times \frac{21}{20} \times \frac{21}{20} = 92610$

7. Second year's interest = 72 + 8% of 72

$= 72 + \frac{72 \times 8}{100} = 72 + 5.76 = ₹\ 77.76$

8. Here, $P\left[\left(1+\frac{5}{100}\right)^2 - 1\right] - \frac{P \times 5 \times 2}{100} = 21$

$\Rightarrow P\left[\frac{441}{400} - 1\right] - \frac{P}{10} = 21$

$\Rightarrow P\left[\frac{41}{400} - \frac{1}{10}\right] = 21 \Rightarrow P \times \frac{1}{400} = 21$

∴ P = 21 × 400 = ₹ 8400

9. Amount = ₹ 19200 + ₹ 4032 = ₹ 23232

Now, $23232 = 19200\left(1+\frac{10}{100}\right)^n$

$\Rightarrow \frac{23232}{19200} = \left(\frac{11}{10}\right)^n \Rightarrow \frac{121}{100} = \left(\frac{11}{10}\right)^n$

$\Rightarrow \left(\frac{11}{10}\right)^2 = \left(\frac{11}{10}\right)^n$

∴ $n = 2$ years

●●●

CHAPTER 3

Ratio and Proportion

RATIO

In ratio we compare two quantities of the same kind and consider what multiple, part or parts one is of the other. In comparing 8 with 4, observe that it is 2 times 4. This comparison can be represented as $8 \div 4$ or $\frac{8}{4}$.

Hence, *ratio is that relation between two numbers which is expressed by the fraction, the numerator is which is the measure of the first quantity and denominator is the measure of the second quantity.*

If the terms of a ratio be multiplied or divided by the same quantity the value of the ratio remains unaltered.

Thus, 3 : 4 is the same as 9 : 12 and 9 : 12 is the same as 3 : 4.

PROPORTION

The equality of two ratio is called proportion.

Consider the two ratios:

Ist ratio	2nd ratio
5 : 15	7 : 21

Since, 5 is one-third of 15 and 7 is one-third of 21, the two ratios are equal. The equality of two ratios is called proportion and the numbers 5, 15, and 7, 21 are said to be in **proportion.**

The proportion may be written as 5 : 15 : : 7 : 21 (5 is to 15 as 7 is to 21)

$\Rightarrow \quad 5 : 15 = 7 : 21$

$\Rightarrow \quad \frac{5}{15} = \frac{7}{21}$

The numbers 5, 15, 7 and 21 are called the terms. 5 is the first term, 15 the second, 7 the third, and 21 the fourth.

The first and fourth terms, *i.e.*, 5 and 21 are called extremes (end terms), and the second and the third terms, *i.e.*, 15 and 7 are called the **means** (middle terms), 21 is called the fourth proportional.

Some Important Facts:

1. If a and b are two quantities, then

(*a*) Duplicate ratio of $a : b = a^2 : b^2$

(*b*) Sub-duplicate ratio of $a : b = \sqrt{a} : \sqrt{b}$

(*c*) Triplicate ratio of $a : b = a^3 : b^3$

(*d*) Sub-triplicate ratio $a : b = \sqrt[3]{a} : \sqrt[3]{b}$

(*e*) Inverse or reciprocal ratio of $a : b = \frac{1}{a} : \frac{1}{b}$

(*f*) Third proportional to 'a' and 'b' $= \frac{b^2}{a}$

2. If $A : B = x : y$ and $B : C = p : q$, then

(*a*) $A : C = \frac{x \times p}{y \times q}$

(*b*) $A : B : C = px : py : qy$

3. In what *ratio* the two kinds of tea must be mixed together one at ₹ x per kg and another at ₹ y per kg, so that the mixture may cost ₹ z per kg?

$$\text{Ratio} = \frac{z - y}{x - z}$$

4. A grey hound persues a hare as takes J_1 leaps for every J_2 leaps of the hare. If K_1 leaps of the hound are equal to K_2 leaps of the hare, then the Ratio of speeds of the hound and hare is

$$\frac{J_2 \times K_1}{J_1 \times K_2}$$

5. The incomes of two persons are in the ratio of $a : b$ and their expenditure are in the ratio of $x : y$. If the saving of each person is ₹ s, then income of each is ₹ $\frac{as(y - x)}{ay - bx}$ and ₹ $\frac{bs(y - x)}{ay - bx}$ respectively.

6. In a mixture of z litre, the ratio of milk and water is $x : y$. If another p litres of water is added to the mixture, the ratio of milk and water in the resulting mixture $= \dfrac{xz}{yz + p(x+y)}$

7. There are four members a, b, c and d, then formula for

(a) What should be added to each of these numbers so that the remaining numbers may be proportional $= \dfrac{ad - bc}{(b+c)-(a+d)}$

(b) What should be subtracted from each of these numbers so that the remaining numbers may be proportional $= \dfrac{ad - bc}{(a+d)-(b+c)}$

8. In a mixture the ratio of milk and water is $a : b$. If in this mixture another K litre of water is added, then the ratio of milk and water in the resulting mixture becomes $a : m$. Then the quantity of milk in the original mixture $= \dfrac{ak}{m-b}$ and quantity of water $= \dfrac{bk}{m-b}$

EXERCISE

1. If A : B = 6 : 7 and B : C = 8 : 9, then A : B : C is:
   A. 24 : 28 : 63 B. 48 : 28 : 63
   C. 48 : 56 : 63 D. None of these

2. The sum of two numbers is 20 and their difference is $2\frac{1}{2}$. What is the ratio of the numbers?
   A. 11 : 7 B. 9 : 11
   C. 9 : 7 D. None of these

3. If 0.7 of one number is equal to 0.075 of another, what is the ratio of the two numbers?
   A. 6 : 14 B. 3 : 28
   C. 5 : 7 D. None of these

4. If 10% of x is the same as 20% of y, then $x : y$ is equal to :
   A. 1 : 2 B. 2 : 1
   C. 5 : 1 D. 10 : 1

5. Two numbers are in the ratio 3 : 5. If each number is increased by 10, the ratio becomes 5 : 7. The numbers are:
   A. 3, 5 B. 7, 9
   C. 13, 22 D. 15, 25

6. The mean proportional between 0.32 and 0.02 is:
   A. 0.34 B. 0.3
   C. 0.16 D. 0.08

7. The sum of three numbers is 98. If the ratio between the first and second be 2 : 3 and that between the second and third be 5 : 8, then what is the second number?
   A. 20 B. 30
   C. 10 D. 40

ANSWERS

1	2	3	4	5	6	7
C	C	B	B	D	D	B

EXPLANATORY ANSWERS

1. A : B = 6 : 7
   B : C = 8 : 9
   ∴ A : B : C = 6 × 8 : 7 × 8 : 7 × 9 = 48 : 56 : 63

2. Ratio $= \dfrac{20 + \frac{5}{2}}{20 - \frac{5}{2}} = \dfrac{22.5}{17.5} = \dfrac{225}{175} = \dfrac{9}{7} = 9 : 7$

3. We have, $0.7x = 0.075\,y$

$$\frac{x}{y} = \frac{0.075}{0.7} = \frac{75}{700} = \frac{3}{28} = 3 : 28$$

4. 10% of x = 20% of y

$$\Rightarrow \frac{10}{100}x = \frac{20}{100}y$$

$$\therefore \frac{x}{10} = \frac{y}{5} \Rightarrow \frac{x}{y} = \frac{10}{5} = \frac{2}{1} \Rightarrow x : y = 2 : 1$$

5. Let the number be $3x$ and $5x$.

Then, $\dfrac{3x+10}{5x+10} = \dfrac{5}{7} \Rightarrow 7(3x + 10) = 5(5x + 10)$

$\Rightarrow 21x + 70 = 25x + 50$

$\Rightarrow 4x = 20$

$\Rightarrow x = 5$

So, the numbers are 15, 25.

6. Mean proportional $= \sqrt{0.32 \times 0.02} = \sqrt{0.0064} = 0.08$

7. The ratio among the three numbers is

2 : 3
5 : 8
and 10 : 15 : 24

∴ The second number $= \dfrac{98}{10+15+24} \times 15 = 30$

•••

CHAPTER 4

Algebra

Square Roots

Points To Remember

- A number n is a perfect square number, if $n = m^2$
- A perfect square number is never negative.
- A square number never ends in 2, 3, 7 or 8.
- The number of zeros at the end of a perfect square is even.
- The square of an even number is even.
- The square of an odd number is odd.
- There are no natural number p and q such that $p^2 = 2q^2$.
- A number m is a square root of n, if $n = m \times m = m^2$. Positive square root of n is written as $\sqrt{n}$.
- If p and q are perfect squares ($q \neq 0$), then
  (*i*) $\sqrt{p \times q} = \sqrt{p} \times \sqrt{q}$
  (*ii*) $\sqrt{\frac{p}{q}} = \frac{\sqrt{p}}{\sqrt{q}}$
- A perfect squares leaves remainder 0 or 1 on division by 3.
  The following table gives the possible remainders for some other prime divisors.

Divisor	Possible Remainders
3	0, 1
5	0, 1, 4
7	0, 1, 2, 4
11	0, 1, 3, 4, 5, 9
13	0, 1, 3, 4, 9, 10, 12

- The unit's digit of the square of a natural number is the unit's digit of the square of the digit at unit's place of the given natural number.

Unit's digit of the number	Unit's digit of the square of the number
0	0
1 or 9	1
2 or 8	4
3 or 7	9
4 or 6	6
5	5

- For every natural number n,
  $(n + 1)^2 - n^2 = (n + 1) + n$
  e.g.; $9^2 - 8^2 = 9 + 8 = 17$
  $19^2 - 18^2 = 19 + 18 = 37$
- The square of a natural number n is equal to the sum of first n odd natural numbers.
  e.g.; $2^2 = 1 + 3$
  $4^2 = 1 + 3 + 5 + 7 = 16$
  n^2 = Sum of first n odd natural numbers.
- A triplet (m, n, p) of three natural numbers m, n and p is called a pythagorean triplet if $m^2 + n^2 = p^2$
- The square root of a perfect square number can be obtained by :
  (*i*) the prime factorization. (*ii*) the division method.
- If n is not a perfect square, then $\sqrt{n}$ is not a rational number.
- Squares of natural numbers having all digits 1 have a following pattern:
  $1^2 = 1$
  $11^2 = 1\,\mathbf{2}\,1$
  $111^2 = 1\,2\,\mathbf{3}\,2\,1$
  $1111^2 = 1\,2\,3\,\mathbf{4}\,3\,2\,1$

$11111^2 = 1\ 2\ 3\ 4\ \mathbf{5}\ 4\ 3\ 2\ 1$

$111111^2 = 1\ 2\ 3\ 4\ 5\ \mathbf{6}\ 5\ 4\ 3\ 2\ 1$

⋮ ⋮ ⋮

$111111111^2 = 1\ 2\ 3\ 4\ 5\ 6\ 7\ 8\ \mathbf{9}\ 8\ 7\ 6\ 5\ 4\ 3\ 2\ 1$

In this pattern the sum of the digits of every number on the right hand side is a perfect square at given below:

$1 + 2 + 1 = 4 = 2^2$

$1 + 2 + 3 + 2 + 1 = 9 = 3^2$

$1 + 2 + 3 + 4 + 3 + 2 + 1 = 16 = 4^2$

....

$1 + 2 + 3 + 4 + 5 + 6 + 7 + 8 + 9 + 8 + 7 + 6 + 5 + 4 + 3 + 2 + 1 = 81 = 9^2$.

- Observe the following pattern

$11^2 = 121$

$101^2 = 10201$

$1001^2 = 1002001$

$10001^2 = 100020001$

- Observe the following pattern

$11^2 = 121$

$101^2 = 10201$

$10101^2 = 102030201$

$1010101^2 = 1020304030201$

$101010101^2 = 10203040504030201$

- **Short Cut Method to find Squares Column Method**

Using $(a + b)^2 = a^2 + 2ab + b^2$.

Make three columns: What is square of 86

$a = 8,\ b = 6$

Step	Column I (a^2)	Column II $2ab$	Column III b^2
I	$(8)^2 = 64$	$2 \times 8 \times 6 = 96$	$(6)^2 = 36$
II	64	96 + 3 **99**	3**6**
III	64 + 9 **73**	**9**9	**6**

The bold digits give the required square $86^2 = 7396$.

Square Root

Square root of a given number is that number which is multiplied by itself is equal to the given number.
For example, square root of 81 is 9 because
92 = 9 × 9 = 81.

Methods of Finding the square root

(a) Prime Factorization Method

(i) Prime Factorization Method

(ii) Group the Factors in Paris

(iii) Take one number from each pair of factors and then multiply them together.

Example: Find the square root of 4761?

Solution: $4761 = \underbrace{23 \times 23} \times \underbrace{3 \times 3}$

$\therefore \quad \sqrt{4761} = 23 \times 3 = 69.$

(b) Method of Division: This method is used when the number is large and the factors cannot be easily determined.

Example: Find the square root of 226576?

Solution:

```
          476
     4  226516
          16
    87    665
     7    609
   946     5676
     6     5676
              ×
```

$\sqrt[2]{226576} = 476.$

EXERCISE

1. $\sqrt{53824} = ?$

A. 202 B. 232
C. 242 D. 332

2. The value of $\sqrt{10+\sqrt{25+\sqrt{108+\sqrt{154+\sqrt{255}}}}}$ is:

A. 4 B. 6
C. 8 D. 10

3. Evaluate : $\sqrt{41-\sqrt{21+\sqrt{19-\sqrt{9}}}}$.

A. 3 B. 5
C. 6 D. 6.4

4. $\left(\frac{\sqrt{625}}{11} \times \frac{14}{\sqrt{25}} \times \frac{11}{\sqrt{196}}\right)$ is equal to:

A. 5
B. 6
C. 8
D. 11

5. If $x * y = x + y + \sqrt{xy}$, the value of 6*24 is:

A. 41 B. 42
C. 43 D. 44

6. $\sqrt{\frac{25}{81}-\frac{1}{9}} = ?$

A. $\frac{2}{3}$ B. $\frac{4}{9}$

C. $\frac{16}{81}$ D. $\frac{25}{81}$

7. The value of $\sqrt{0.01}+\sqrt{0.81}+\sqrt{1.21}+\sqrt{0.0009}$ is:

A. 2.03 B. 2.1

C. 2.11 D. 2.13

8. If $\sqrt{18225} = 135$, then the value of $\left(\sqrt{182.25}+\sqrt{1.8225}+\sqrt{0.018225}+\sqrt{0.00018225}\right)$ is:

A. 1.49985 B. 14.9985

C. 149.985 D. 1499.85

9. If $\sqrt{3^n} = 729$, then the value of n is:

A. 6 B. 8

C. 10 D. 12

10. If $\sqrt{1+\frac{x}{169}} = \frac{14}{13}$, then x is equal to:

A. 1 B. 13

C. 27 D. None of these

ANSWERS

1	2	3	4	5	6	7	8	9	10
B	A	C	A	B	B	D	B	D	C

EXPLANATORY ANSWERS

1.
```
  2 | 53824 (232
    | 4
 43 | 138
    | 129
462 |  924
    |  924
    |   ×
```

$\therefore \sqrt{53824} = 232.$

2. Given exp. $= \sqrt{10+\sqrt{25+\sqrt{108+\sqrt{154+15}}}}$

$= \sqrt{10+\sqrt{25+\sqrt{108+\sqrt{169}}}}$

$= \sqrt{10+\sqrt{25+\sqrt{108+13}}} = \sqrt{10+\sqrt{25+\sqrt{121}}}$

$= \sqrt{10+\sqrt{25+11}} = \sqrt{10+\sqrt{36}}$

$= \sqrt{10+6} = \sqrt{16} = 4$

3. Given exp. $= \sqrt{41-\sqrt{21+\sqrt{19-3}}}$

$= \sqrt{41-\sqrt{21+\sqrt{16}}} = \sqrt{41-\sqrt{21+4}}$

$= \sqrt{41-\sqrt{25}} = \sqrt{41-5} = \sqrt{36} = 6$

4. Given exp. $= \frac{25}{11}\times\frac{14}{5}\times\frac{11}{14} = 5$

5. $6*24 = 6 + 24 + \sqrt{6\times 24} = 30+\sqrt{144} = 30+12 = 42$

6. $\sqrt{\frac{25}{81}-\frac{1}{9}} = \sqrt{\frac{25-9}{81}} = \sqrt{\frac{16}{81}} = \frac{\sqrt{16}}{\sqrt{81}} = \frac{4}{9}$

7. Given exp.

$= \sqrt{\frac{1}{100}}+\sqrt{\frac{81}{100}}+\sqrt{\frac{121}{100}}+\sqrt{\frac{9}{10000}}$

$= \frac{1}{10}+\frac{9}{10}+\frac{11}{10}+\frac{3}{100}$

$= 0.1 + 0.9 + 1.1 + 0.03 = 2.13$

8. Given exp.

$= \sqrt{\frac{18225}{10^2}}+\sqrt{\frac{18225}{10^4}}+\sqrt{\frac{18225}{10^6}}+\sqrt{\frac{18225}{10^8}}$

$= \frac{\sqrt{18225}}{10}+\frac{\sqrt{18225}}{10^2}+\frac{\sqrt{18225}}{10^3}+\frac{\sqrt{18225}}{10^4}$

$= \frac{135}{10}+\frac{135}{100}+\frac{135}{1000}+\frac{135}{10000}$

$= 13.5 + 1.35 + 0.135 + 0.0135 = 14.9985$

9. $\sqrt{3^n} = 729 = 3^6$

$\Leftrightarrow \left(\sqrt{3^n}\right)^2 = (3^6)^2$

$\Leftrightarrow 3^n = 3^{12}$

$\Leftrightarrow n = 12$

10. $\sqrt{1+\frac{x}{169}} = \frac{14}{13} \Rightarrow 1+\frac{x}{169} = \frac{196}{169}$

$\Rightarrow \frac{x}{169} = \left(\frac{196}{169}-1\right) = \frac{27}{169}$

$\Rightarrow x = 27.$

Basic Algebraic Identities of School Algebra & Elementary Surds

Algebric Identies

Some Important Formula

(i) $(a + b)^2 = a^2 + 2ab + b^2$

(ii) $(a - b)^2 = a^2 - 2ab + b^2$

(iii) $a^2 - b^2 = (a - b)(a + b)$

(iv) $(a + b + c)^2 = a^2 + b^2 + c^2 + 2ab + 2bc + 2ca$

(v) $(a + b - c)^2 = a^2 + b^2 + c^2 + 2ab - 2bc - 2ca$

(vi) $(a - b + c)^2 = a^2 + b^2 + c^2 - 2ab - 2bc + 2ca$

(vii) $(-a + b + c)^2 = a^2 + b^2 + c^2 - 2ab + 2bc - 2ca$

(viii) $(a + b)^3 = a^3 + b^3 + 3ab(a + b)$ or
$= a^3 + b^3 + 3a^2b + 3ab^2$

(ix) $(a - b)^3 = a^3 - b^3 - 3ab\,(a - b)$ or
$= a^3 - b^3 - 3a^2b + 3ab^2$

(x) $a^3 + b^3 = (a + b)\,(a^2 + b^2 - ab)$ or
$= (a + b)^3 - 3ab(a + b)$

(xi) $a^3 - b^3 = (a - b)\,(a^2 + b^2 + ab)$ or
$= (a - b)^3 + 3ab\,(a - b)$

(xii) $a^3 + b^3 + c^3 - 3abc$
$= (a + b + c)(a^2 + b^2 + c^2 - ab - bc - ca)$
If $a + b + c = 0$
$a^3 + b^3 + c^3 = 3abc$

(xiii) $(x + a)\,(x + b) = x^2 + (a + b)x + ab$

(xiv) $(a + b)^2 + (a - b)^2 = 2(a^2 + b^2)$

(xv) $(a + b)^2 - (a - b)^2 = 4ab$

(xvi) $(a + b)^3 + (a - b)^3 = 2(a^3 + 3ab^2)$

(xvii) $(a + b)^3 - (a - b)^3 = (2(b^3 + 3a^2b)$

(xviii) If $x+\frac{1}{x}=t$ Then, $x^2+\frac{1}{x^2}=t^2-2$

(xix) If $x-\frac{1}{x}=t$ Then, $x^2+\frac{1}{x^2}=t^2+2$

(xx) $x^3+\frac{1}{x^3}=\left(x+\frac{1}{x}\right)^3-3\left(x+\frac{1}{x}\right)$

(xxi) $x^2-\frac{1}{x^3}=\left(x-\frac{1}{x}\right)^3+3\left(x-\frac{1}{x}\right)$

(xxii) $x+\frac{1}{x}=\sqrt{x^2+\frac{1}{x^2}+2}$

(xxiii) $x-\frac{1}{x}=\sqrt{x^2+\frac{1}{x^2}-2}$

Factorization of Algebraic Expressions

Factorization : The process of writing an algebraic expression as the product of two or more algebraic expressions is called factorization.

Factors : The algebraic expressions that may be multiplied to obtain the given algebraic expressions are called factors of the given expression.

Factor Theorem : If $f(x)$ is completely divisible by $(x - a)$ then $f(a) = 0$, $(x - a)$ is called factor of $f(x)$, if and only if $f(a) = 0$

Remainder Theorem : If an expression $f(x)$ is divided by $(x - a)$ then the remainder is $f(a)$.

e.g., $f(x) = ax^3 + bx + cx + d$

$f(a) = a\,.\,a^3 + b\,.\,a + c\,.\,a + d$ is known as remainder of the given polynomials.

Surds

Given a number, it is not always possible to find some whole number which when multiplied by itself will give the given number. In other words all given numbers are not perfect square numbers. For example, square root of 9, *i.e.*, $\sqrt{9}$ is 3, which is a whole number. But square root of 15, *i.e.*, $\sqrt{15}$ = 3.873, which is not a whole number.

Hence square roots of natural numbers which are not perfect squares are not rational numbers. These are irrational numbers and are called **Surds**.

For example, $\sqrt{3}$, $\sqrt{7}$, $2+\sqrt{11}$, $4+\sqrt{13}$ ..... etc. are Surds.

Given below are a few formulas which are quite helpful in solving the problems related to surds:

1. $\sqrt{a}\times\sqrt{a}=a$

2. $\sqrt{a}\times\sqrt{b}=\sqrt{ab}$

3. $\left(\sqrt{a}+\sqrt{b}\right)^2 = a + b + \sqrt[2]{ab}$

4. $\left(\sqrt{a}-\sqrt{b}\right)^2 = a + b - \sqrt[2]{ab}$

5. $x\sqrt{a}+x\sqrt{b}=x\left(\sqrt{a}+\sqrt{b}\right)$

6. $\frac{1}{\sqrt{a}+\sqrt{b}}=\frac{1}{\sqrt{a}+\sqrt{b}}\times\frac{\sqrt{a}-\sqrt{b}}{\sqrt{a}-\sqrt{b}}=\frac{\sqrt{a}-\sqrt{b}}{a-b}$

7. $\frac{1}{\sqrt{a}-\sqrt{b}}=\frac{1}{\sqrt{a}-\sqrt{b}}\times\frac{\sqrt{a}+\sqrt{b}}{\sqrt{a}+\sqrt{b}}=\frac{\sqrt{a}+\sqrt{b}}{a-b}$

8. $a+\sqrt{b}=c+\sqrt{d} \Rightarrow a = c$ and $b = d$

9. $\sqrt{2}$ = 1.41421, $\sqrt{3}$ = 1.73205, $\sqrt{5}$ = 2.23607,
$\sqrt{6}$ = 2.4494 $\sqrt{7}$ = 2.64575, $\sqrt{8}$ = 2.82842,
$\sqrt{10}$ = 3.16227, $\sqrt{11}$ = 3.31662

EXERCISE

1. $(28)^3 + (-15)^3 + (-13)^3 = ?$

A. 16380 B. 16250
C. 16420 D. 16280

2. If $x+\frac{1}{x} = 5$, What is the value of $x^3+\frac{1}{x^3}$:

A. 120 B. 210
C. 110 D. 105

3. If $x^2+\frac{1}{x^2}=83$, what is the value of $x^3-\frac{1}{x^3} = ?$

A. 756 B. 754
C. 856 D. 932

4. $23^3 - 17^3 = ?$

A. 7254 B. 7153
C. 7271 D. 7154

5. If $x + \frac{1}{x} = 15$, then the value of $x^2 + \frac{1}{x^2}$ will be:

A. 228 B. 230
C. 323 D. 223

6. If $x = 12$ and $y = 4$, the value of $(x+y)^{x/y}$ will be:

A. 4096 B. 3896
C. 4196 D. 5086

7. If $x + y = 2z$, then the value of $\left(\frac{x}{x-z}+\frac{z}{y-z}\right)$ will be:

A. 1 B. 4
C. 3/2 D. 2

8. If $x + y + z = 0$, then the value of $\frac{(x+y)(y+z)(z+x)}{xyz}$ will be:

A. –3 B. –2
C. 0 D. –1

9. If $x + \frac{1}{x} = 3$, the value of $x^4 + \frac{1}{x^4}$ will be:

A. 49 B. 47
C. 37 D. 42

10. If $\left(x+\frac{1}{x}\right)^2 = 0$, then the value of $\left(x^2+\frac{1}{x^2}\right)$ will be:

A. 1 B. –1
C. 2 D. –2

ANSWERS

1	2	3	4	5	6	7	8	9	10
A	C	A	A	D	A	A	D	B	D

EXPLANATORY ANSWERS

1. Let $a = 28$, $b = -15$ and $c = -13$. Then

$$a + b + c = 28 - 15 - 13 = 0$$
$$a^3 + b^3 + c^3 = 3abc$$
$$(28)^3 + (-15)^3 + (-13)^3 = 3 \times 28 \times (-15) \times (-13) = 16380$$

2. $$x^3+\frac{1}{x^3} = \left(x+\frac{1}{x}\right)^3 - 3\left(x+\frac{1}{x}\right)$$
$$= (5)^3 - 3 \times 5 = 125 - 15 = 110.$$

3. If $x^2+\frac{1}{x^2}=83$, what is the value of $x^3-\frac{1}{x^3} = ?$

$$\left(x-\frac{1}{x}\right)^2 = x^2+\frac{1}{x^2}-2$$
$$x-\frac{1}{x} = \sqrt{83-2} = \sqrt{81}$$
$$x-\frac{1}{x} = 9$$
$$\therefore \left(x^3-\frac{1}{x^3}\right) = \left(x-\frac{1}{x}\right)^3 + 3\left(x-\frac{1}{x}\right)$$
$$= (9)^3 + 3 \times 9 = 729 + 27 = 756$$

4. $23^3 - 17^3 = (20 + 3)^3 - (20 - 3)^3 = 2(3^3 + 3 \times 20^2 \times 3)$

$[\because (a + b)^3 - (a - b)^3 = 2(b^3 + 3a^2b)]$

$= 2\ (27 + 3600) = 54 + 7200 = 7254$

5. $\because x+\frac{1}{x} = 15 \Rightarrow \left(x+\frac{1}{x}\right)^2 = (15)^2$

$$\Rightarrow x^2+\frac{1}{x^2}+2.x\frac{1}{x} = 225$$
$$\therefore \quad x^2+\frac{1}{x^2} = 225 - 2 = 223.$$

6. $(x+y)^{x/y} = (12+4)^{12/4} = (16)^3 = 4096.$

$[\because x = 12, y = 4]$

7. $\because x + y = 2z \Rightarrow x - z = z - y = -(y - z)$

$$\therefore \frac{x}{x-z}+\frac{z}{y-z} = \frac{x}{-(y-z)}+\frac{z}{y-z} = \frac{z-x}{y-z} = 1.$$

$[\because x - z = z - y]$

8. $\because$
$$x + y + z = 0 \Rightarrow x + y = -z$$
$$x + y + z = 0 \Rightarrow y + z = -x$$
and
$$x + y + z = 0 \Rightarrow z + x = -y$$

$$\therefore \quad \frac{(x+y)(y+z)(z+x)}{xyz} = \frac{(-z)(-x)(-y)}{xyz}$$
$$= -1.$$

9. $\because x + \frac{1}{x} = 3 \Rightarrow \left(x + \frac{1}{x}\right)^2 = (3)^2$

$$\Rightarrow \quad x^2 + \frac{1}{x^2} + 2.x.\frac{1}{x} = 9$$

$$\Rightarrow \quad x^2 + \frac{1}{x^2} = 9 - 2 = 7$$

$$\because \quad x^2 + \frac{1}{x^2} = 7 \Rightarrow \left(x^2 + \frac{1}{x^2}\right)^2 = (7)^2$$

$$\Rightarrow \quad x^4 + \frac{1}{x^4} + 2.x^2.\frac{1}{x^2} = 49$$

$$\therefore \quad x^4 + \frac{1}{x^4} = 49 - 2 = 47.$$

10. $\left(x + \frac{1}{x}\right)^2 = 0 \Rightarrow x^2 + \frac{1}{x^2} + 2x.\frac{1}{x} = 0$

$$\Rightarrow \quad x^2 + \frac{1}{x^2} = -2.$$

Graphs of Linear Equations

Linear Equation in One Variable

Definition: A linear equation in one variable is an equation of the form $ax + b = 0$ or, $ax = c$ where, a, b, c are real numbers, $a \neq 0$ and x is a variable. Its graph is a straight line.

(*i*) If equation is on X-axis, then Y = 0

(*ii*) If equation is on Y-axis, then X = 0

Linear Equation in Two Variables

Definition: An equation of the form $ax + by + c = 0$ or, $ax + by = c$ where, a, b, c are real numbers, $a \neq 0$, $b \neq 0$ and x, y are variables, is called a linear equation in two variables.

For example: (*i*) $2x + 3y = 12$ (*ii*) $x + 2y = 8$

The System of Equations

$a_1x + b_1y + c_1 = 0$ and $a_2x + b_2y + c_2 = 0$ may be either unique solution or no solution or infinitely many solutions.

Unique solution is known as consistent or not parallel. No solution is known as inconsistent or parallel, while many solutions are known as coincident or dependent.

(*a*) **For unique solution:** $\frac{a_1}{a_2} \neq \frac{b_1}{b_2}$

(*b*) **For no solution:** $\frac{a_1}{a_2} = \frac{b_1}{b_2} \neq \frac{c_1}{c_2}$

(*c*) **For many solutions:** $\frac{a_1}{a_2} = \frac{b_1}{b_2} = \frac{c_1}{c_2}$

Graph of linear equations

Graph of a linear equation in two variables x and y *i.e.*, the graph of the equation of the form

$$ax + by + c = 0, \; a \neq 0, \; b \neq 0$$

we consider the equation,

$$2x + y = 6$$

then, $$y = 6 - 2x$$

We find different values of this equation

x	0	1	2	3
y	6	4	2	0

Now, we plot these points (x, y) on a graph paper and then join these points

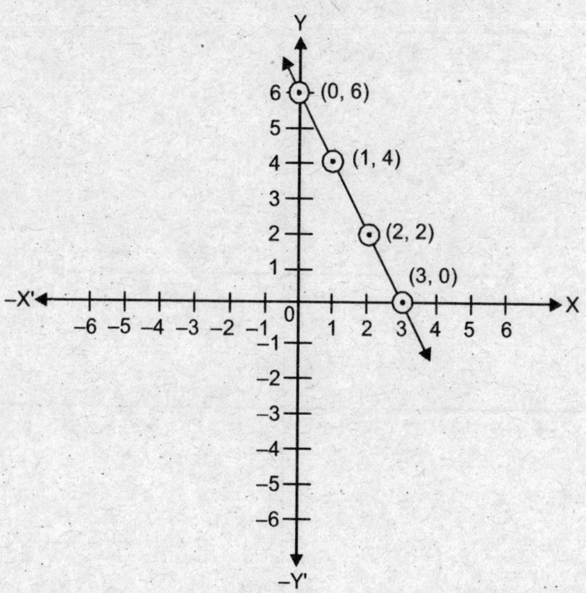

Hence, the line l is called the graph of the equation

$$2x + y = 6$$

Example 1: Draw the graph:

(*i*) $x = 2$, (*ii*) $y = 3$, (*iii*) $y = 0$

Solution: (*i*) The given equation, $x = 2$ does not contain y

Table of values

x	2	2	2	fixed
y	1	3	4	any value

ploting the points (2, 1), (2, 3) and (2, 4) and joining them

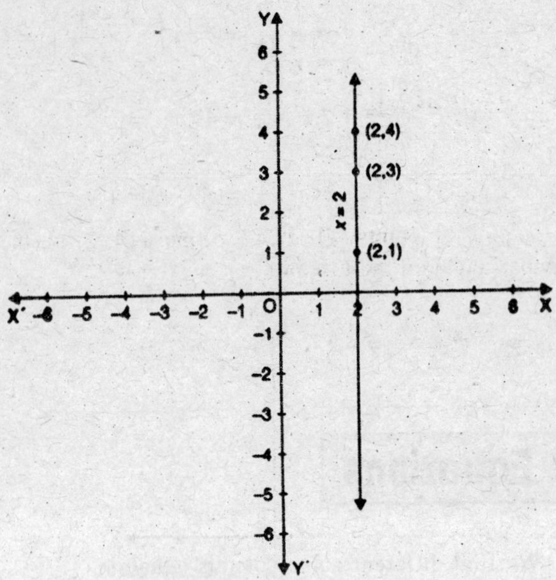

Hence, the graph of the given equation is a line parallel to y-axis

(*ii*) The given equation $y = 3$ does not contain x

Table of values

x	1	2	4	any value
y	3	3	3	fixed

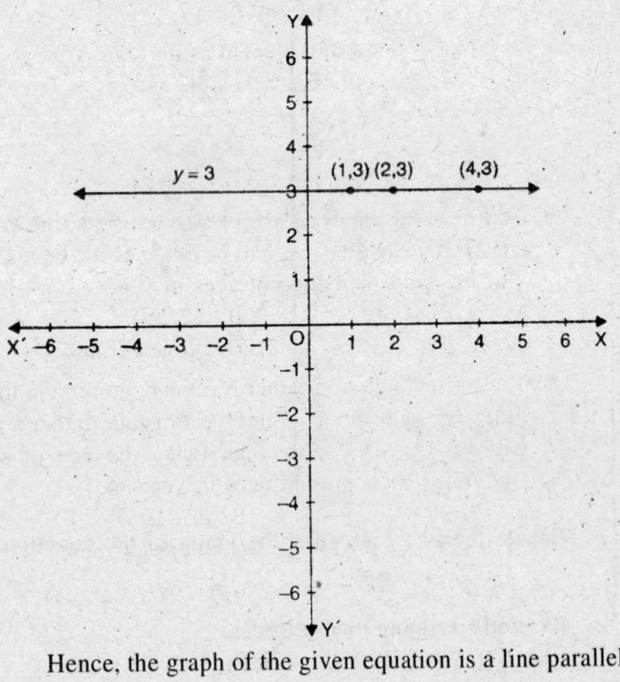

Hence, the graph of the given equation is a line parallel to x-axis.

(*iii*) The given equation is $y = 0$

Table of values

x	1	2	3	any value
y	0	0	0	fixed

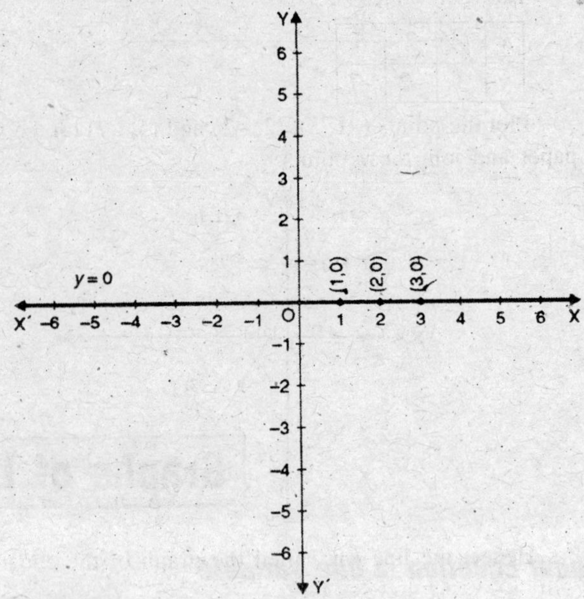

Hence, $y = 0$ is the equation of x-axis.

Example 2. Draw the graph of the line $x - 2y = 3$. From the graph find co-ordinates of the points when

(*i*) $x = -5$, (*ii*) $y = 0$

Solution: The given equation is $x - 2y = 3$

Table of value

x	3	5	1
y	0	1	–1

$$\because \quad 2y = x - 3$$

$$\therefore \quad y = \frac{x-3}{2}$$

Plotting the points (3, 0), (5, 1) and (1, –1) on the graph paper and joining these points.

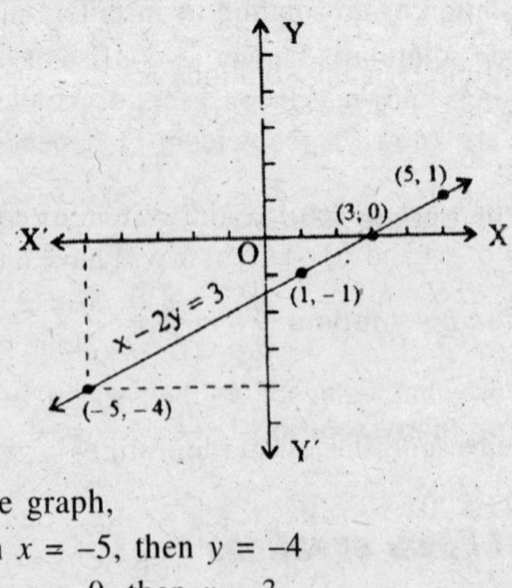

From the graph,

(*i*) when $x = -5$, then $y = -4$

(*ii*) when $y = 0$, then $x = 3$

Example 3. Draw the graph of the equations $5x + 3y = 4$.

Solution: The given equation is $5x + 3y = 4$

$$\Rightarrow \quad y = \frac{4-5x}{3}$$

Table of values

x	-1	2	5
y	3	-2	-7

Plot the points $(-1, 3)$, $(2, -2)$ and $(5, -7)$ on the graph paper and join these points.

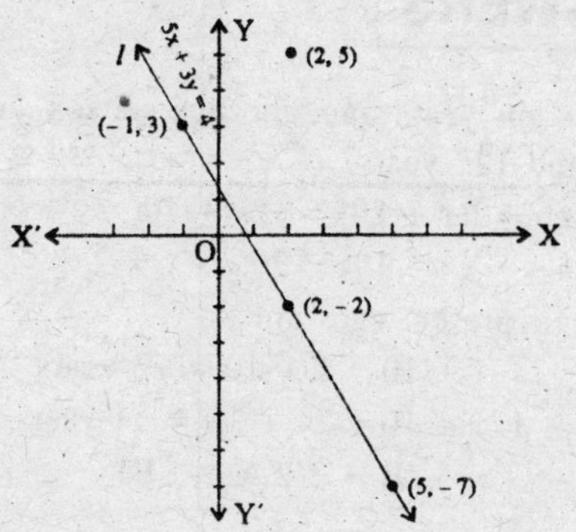

Hence, the line l is called the graph of the equation,

$$5x + 3y = 4$$

Example 4. Draw the graph of the equation

$$2x - 3y = -11.$$

Solution: The given equation is

$$2x - 3y = -11$$

$$\Rightarrow \quad 3y = 2x + 11$$

$$\Rightarrow \quad y = \frac{2x+11}{3}$$

Table of values

x	-1	2	-4
y	3	5	1

plot the points $(-1, 3)$, $(2, 5)$ and $(-4, 1)$ on the graph paper and join these points

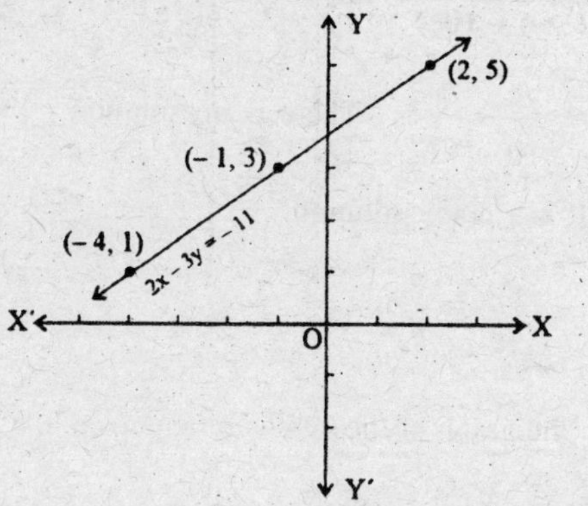

Hence, this line l is called the graph of the equation $2x - 3y = -11$.

EXERCISE

1. The system of linear equations $2x + 3y = 7$ and $4x + 6y = 10$ has:
   A. no solution
   B. unique solution
   C. infinite solution
   D. no conclusion can be drawn

2. The value of k for which the system of equations $x + 2y + 7 = 0$ and $2x + ky + 14 = 0$ will have infinitely many solutions is:
   A. 2 B. 4
   C. 6 D. 8

3. For what value of α, the system of equations $\alpha x + 3y = \alpha - 3$ and $12x + \alpha y = \alpha$ will have a unique solution?
   A. $\alpha \neq \pm 6$ B. $\alpha \neq \pm 3$
   C. $\alpha \neq \mp 6$ D. None of these

4. For what value of k, the system of equations will represent the coincident lines $x+5y-7=0$ and $4x+20y+k=0$?
   A. 28 B. –28
   C. –26 D. None of these

5. A lady has 50 paise and ₹ 1 coins in her purse. If in all, she has 40 coins totally ₹ 25.50 how many of each type of coins does she have?
   A. 26, 11 B. 11, 29
   C. 29, 11 D. None of these

6. A father is three times as old as his son. After twelve years his age will be twice as the age of his son. Find their present ages in years.
   A. 12, 26 B. 24, 36
   C. 36, 12 D. None of these

7. Ten years ago, father was twelve times as old as his son. Ten years after, he will be twice as old as his son will be. Find their present ages in years.
   A. 12, 36 B. 12, 24
   C. 12, 34 D. None of these

8. The present age of a father is 3 years more than three times the age of son. Three years hence father's age will be 10 years more than twice the age of son. Determine their present ages in years.
   A. 10, 33 B. 33, 10
   C. 10, 30 D. None of these

9. In a triangle ABC, $\angle C = 3\angle B = 2(\angle A + \angle B)$. Find three angles in degrees.
   A. 20°, 50°, 120° B. 30°, 40°, 120°
   C. 20°, 40°, 120° D. None of these

10. The fraction becomes 2 when 1 is added to both the numerator and the denominator, and it becomes 3 when 1 is subtracted from both the numerator and denominator. The given fraction is :
    A. 7/3 B. 4/7
    C. 3/7 D. 7/4

ANSWERS

1	2	3	4	5	6	7	8	9	10
A	B	A	B	C	C	C	A	C	A

EXPLANATORY ANSWERS

1. $\frac{2}{4} = \frac{3}{6} \neq \frac{7}{10} \Rightarrow \frac{1}{2} = \frac{1}{2} \neq \frac{7}{10}$

$\frac{a_1}{a_2} = \frac{b_1}{b_2} \neq \frac{c_1}{c_2}$ ∴ There is no solution.

2. Since, it has many solutions.

$$\therefore \quad \frac{a_1}{a_2} = \frac{b_1}{b_2} = \frac{c_1}{c_2}$$

$$\frac{1}{2} = \frac{2}{K} = \frac{7}{14}$$

$$\frac{1}{2} = \frac{2}{K} \Rightarrow K = 4.$$

3. Since, the given equations have unique solution.

$$\therefore \quad \frac{a_1}{a_2} \neq \frac{b_1}{b_2}$$

$$\frac{\alpha}{12} \neq \frac{3}{\alpha}$$

$$\Rightarrow \quad \alpha^2 \neq 36 \Rightarrow \alpha \neq \pm 6$$

4. Since, the given set of equations represent coincident lines.

then, $\frac{1}{4} = \frac{5}{20} = \frac{-7}{K} \Rightarrow K = -28$

5. Let, x be the number of 50 paise coins and y be the number of ₹ 1 coins.

According to the question,

$x + y = 40$ ...(*i*)

and $\frac{x}{2} + y = 25.50$

$\Rightarrow \quad x + 2y = 51$ ...(*ii*)

Subtracting equation (*i*) from (*ii*) and solving we get, $x = 29, y = 11$

6. Let, age of son = x years.

∴ age of father = $3x$ years.

According to the question,

$2(x + 12) = 3x + 12 \Rightarrow x = 12$

∴ Son's age = 12 years; Father's age = 36 years.

7. Let ten years ago, the age of son and father were x and $12x$ years.

Then, $2(x + 20) = 12x + 20$

$\Rightarrow \quad 10x = 20 \Rightarrow x = 2$

Their present ages are

$x + 10 = 2 + 10 = 12$ years

$12x + 10 = 24 + 10 = 34$ years.

9. ∴ $\angle C = 3\angle B = 2(\angle A + \angle B)$

$$\angle A + \angle B = \frac{\angle C}{2}$$

We have, $\angle A + \angle B + \angle C = 180°$

(Sum of angles of a triangle is 180°)

$$\frac{\angle C}{2} + \angle C = 180°$$

$$3\angle C = 2 \times 180°$$

$$\angle C = \frac{2 \times 180°}{3} = 120°$$

$$3\angle B = \angle C$$

$$\angle B = \frac{\angle C}{3} = \frac{120°}{3} = 40°$$

$$\therefore \quad \angle A = 180° - (120° + 40°) = 180° - 160° = 20°.$$

10. Let the fraction be $\frac{x}{y} \Rightarrow \frac{x+1}{y+1} = 2$

$\Rightarrow \quad x + 1 = 2y + 2$

$\Rightarrow \quad x - 2y = 1$ ...(*i*)

Again $\frac{x-1}{y-1} = 3$

$\Rightarrow \quad x - 1 = 3y - 3$

$\Rightarrow \quad x - 3y = -2$ ...(*ii*)

from (*i*) and (*ii*)

$$\begin{array}{r} x - 2y = 1 \\ x - 3y = -2 \\ - \quad + \quad + \\ \hline y = 3 \end{array}$$

Putting the value of y in (*i*) then we get, $x = 7$

∴ fraction = $\frac{x}{y} = \frac{7}{3}$

●●●

CHAPTER 5

Average

The average of any number of quantities of the same kind can be found by dividing their sum by their number.

Thus,

$$\text{Average} = \frac{\text{Sum of quantities}}{\text{No. of quantities}}$$

Sum of quantities = Their average × Their number

$$\text{Number of quantities} = \frac{\text{Sum of quantities}}{\text{Their average}}$$

When a body coveres the same distance at two different speeds p km/hr and q km/hr, then its average speed for the whole journey is $\frac{2pq}{p+q}$ km/hr.

EXERCISE

1. The average of the fractions $1\frac{1}{2}$, $2\frac{1}{3}$, $3\frac{1}{3}$ and $4\frac{5}{6}$ is:

A. 2 B. $2\frac{1}{2}$

C. 3 D. 4

2. The average of first nine multiples of 3 is

A. 12.0 B. 12.5

C. 15.0 D. 18.5

3. The average of 13 numbers is 68, the average of first 7 numbers is 63 and the average of last 7 numbers is 70. What is the 7th number?

A. 43 B. 45

C. 47 D. 49

4. One-third of a certain journey was covered at the rate of 25 km per hour, one-fourth at the rate of 30 km per hour and the rest at the 50 km per hour. What is the average speed per hour for whole journey?

A. $33\frac{1}{3}$ kmph B. $44\frac{1}{4}$ kmph

C. $22\frac{1}{2}$ kmph D. 33 kmph

5. Nine men went to a hotel. Eight of them spent ₹ 3 for each over their meals and the ninth spent ₹ 2 more than the average expenditure of all the nine. What is the total money spent by them?

A. ₹ 29.25 B. ₹ 29.50

C. ₹ 29 D. ₹ 30

6. An establishment is permitted an average monthly contingency expenditure of ₹ 500 per month during the financial year. When a trial check was made at the end of the first nine months of the year it was found that the average monthly contingency expenditure worked out to be ₹ 511. What average monthly expenditure for the next three months should be aimed at in order to attain the permissible average of ₹ 500 per month for the whole year?

A. ₹ 567 B. ₹ 467

C. 367 D. ₹ 667

7. Average age of 8 persons increased by 2 years, when two men whose ages are 20 and 24 years are replaced by two women. What is the average age of women?

A. 30 years B. 31 years

C. 28 years D. 33 years

ANSWERS

1	2	3	4	5	6	7
C	C	C	A	A	B	A

EXPLANATORY ANSWERS

1. Average = $\frac{1}{4}\left(\frac{3}{2}+\frac{7}{3}+\frac{10}{3}+\frac{29}{6}\right)$

$= \left(\frac{9+14+20+29}{24}\right) = \frac{72}{24} = 3$

2. Average = $\frac{3(1+2+3+4+5+6+7+8+9)}{9} = \frac{135}{9}$

$= 15$

3. Average of 13 numbers = 68

$\therefore$ Total of 13 numbers = 13 × 68 = 884

Average of last 7 numbers = 70

$\therefore$ Total of last 7 numbers = 7 × 70 = 490

$\therefore$ Average of first 6 numbers

= 884 – 490 = 394

$\therefore$ Average of first 7 numbers = 63.

$\therefore$ Total of first 7 numbers = 63 × 7 = 441

$\therefore$ 7th number = 441 – 394 = 47

4. Let the total distance covered during journey = 60 km

$\frac{1}{3}$ of the distance covered during journey

$= 60 \times \frac{1}{3} = 20$ km

$\frac{1}{4}$ of the distance covered during journey

$= \frac{1}{4} \times 60 = 15$ km

$\therefore$ The distance covered during the rest of journey = 60 – (20 + 15) = 25 km

Time taken to cover 20 km at 25 km/h

$= \frac{20}{25}$ hours $= \frac{4}{5}$ hour

Time taken to cover 15 km at 30 km/h

$= \frac{15}{30}$ hours $= \frac{1}{2}$ hour

Time taken to cover 25 km at 50 km/h

$= \frac{25}{50}$ hours $= \frac{1}{2}$ hour

Total time taken = $\frac{4}{5}+\frac{1}{2}+\frac{1}{2} = \frac{9}{5}$ hours

Hence average speed per hour

$= 60 \div \frac{9}{5} = \frac{60 \times 5}{9}$

$= \frac{100}{3}$ km / h $= 33\frac{1}{3}$ km / h

5. Let the average expenditure of all the nine

= ₹ x

Now amount spent by eight

= ₹ 3 × 8 = ₹ 24

and total spent by the ninth = ₹ $x + 2$

$\Rightarrow \quad \frac{26+x}{9} = x$

$\therefore$ Average amount spent by nine = $\frac{26+x}{9}$

Total amount spent by nine = 24 + x + 2 = 26 + x

$\Rightarrow \quad 9x = 26 + x$

or, $\quad 8x = 26$

$\Rightarrow \quad x = \frac{26}{8}$ = ₹ 3.25

Hence total money spent

= ₹ (3.25 × 9) = ₹ 29.25

6. Average monthly expenditure permitted = ₹ 500

Total expenditure permitted for 12 months

= ₹ 500 × 12 = ₹ 6000

Expenditure incurred during the first nine months

= ₹ 511 × 9 = ₹ 4,599

Expenditure for the last three month

= ₹ (6000 – 4599) = ₹ 1,401

$\therefore$ Average monthly expenditure for the three months

= ₹ $\frac{1401}{3}$ = ₹ 467

7. Total increase in the age of 8 persons

= 2 × 8 = 16 years

Total age of two men being replaced

= 20 + 24 = 44 years

Total of the age of two women = 44 + 16 = 60 years

$\Rightarrow$ The average age of women

$= \frac{60}{2} = 30$ years.

●●●

CHAPTER 6

Partnership Business

When two or more than two persons agree to invest money to run a business jointly, this association or deal is called *partnership* and those who invest money are called *pertners.* The total investment is called the *capital.*

Kind of partners : There are two kinds of partners.

1. **Working or active partner :** When a partner devotes his time for the business in addition to invest his money, he is called a working partner.
   With mutual agreement, the active partners get some fixed percentage of profit as *working allowance.*
2. **Sleeping or non-active partner :** A partner who simply invests money, but does not attend to the business is called a sleeping partner.

Kind of partnership :

(i) **Simple partnership :** If the capitals of several partners are invested for the same period, it is called a simple partnership.

(ii) **Compound or complex partnership :** If the capitals of the partners are invested for diffrent intervals of time, the partnership is called compound or complex.

EXERCISE

1. A and B started a business with the investment of ₹ 80000 and ₹ 60000 respectively. At the end of the year total profit in the business will be divided between them in the ratio of :

A. 2 : 3 B. 3 : 4
C. 2 : 1 D. 4 : 3

2. A and B started a business in partnership with the investment of ₹ 4000 and ₹ 6000 respectively. If at the end of the year total profit is ₹ 2250, what will each of them get?

A. ₹ 900, ₹ 1350 B. ₹ 800, ₹ 1450
C. ₹ 1000, ₹ 1250 D. ₹ 1200, ₹ 1050

3. Sonu, Monu and Mohit together start a business with the investment of ₹ 1800, ₹ 1500 and ₹ 1600 respectively. If at the end of the year, Monu gains a profit of ₹ 900 the total profit in the business is :

A. ₹ 2880 B. ₹ 2940
C. ₹ 3200 D. ₹ 3240

4. Omdutt started a business with a capital of ₹ 8000. After six months, Sanjay joined him with investment of some capital. If at the end of the year each of them gets equal amount as profit, how much did Sanjay invest in the business?

A. ₹ 18000 B. ₹ 17500
C. ₹ 16000 D. ₹ 16500

5. A, B and C buy a farm for ₹ 100000. A contributes ₹ 40000 in it. They sell it, and from the profit B gets ₹ 2750 and C gets ₹ 1750. What would be the profit of A?

A. ₹ 2780 B. ₹ 3000
C. ₹ 3280 D. ₹ 2785

6. A and B jointly invest ₹ 2100 and ₹ 3100 respectively in a firm. A is an active partner and hence he gets 25% of the profit separately. If their business yields them total ₹ 1040 as profit, what will be the gain of each of them?

A. ₹ 415, ₹ 625 B. ₹ 575, ₹ 465
C. ₹ 515, ₹ 525 D. ₹ 560, ₹ 480

7. Two partners invested ₹ 12500 and ₹ 8500 respectively in a business and decided that 60% of the profit incurred from the business will be equally divided between them while remaining profit will be assumed as interest on their capitals. If one of the partners gets ₹ 300 more profit than the other, what is the total profit in the business?

A. ₹ 3937.50 B. ₹ 4940.50
C. ₹ 3936.50 D. ₹ 4156

8. Neeraj and Birju are partners in a business. They divide between them the profit incurred in the business in such a proportion that $\frac{2}{5}$th portion of the profit gained by Neeraj is equal to $\frac{1}{3}$rd portion of the profit gained by Birju. If total profit in the business is ₹ 1210, find the profit earned by Birju.

A. ₹ 780 B. ₹ 660
C. ₹ 680 D. ₹ 590

9. A, B and C together took under lease a pasture ground for ₹ 888. If in this pasture ground A put his 20 sheep out to graze for 2½ months, B put his 30 sheep out to graze for 4 months and C put his 36 sheep out to graze for 3½ months, find the lease amount paid by each of them.

A. ₹ 205, ₹ 315, ₹ 378 B. ₹ 150, ₹ 360, ₹ 378
C. ₹ 170, ₹ 360, ₹ 358 D. ₹ 228, ₹ 360, ₹ 300

ANSWERS

1	2	3	4	5	6	7	8	9
D	A	B	C	B	B	A	B	B

EXPLANATORY ANSWERS

1. Ratio between their profits = 80000 : 60000 = 4 : 3.

2. Ratio of capitals of A and B = 4000 : 6000 = 2 : 3

A's share in the profit = $\frac{2}{5} \times 2250$ = ₹ 900

B's share in the profit = $\frac{3}{5} \times 2250$ = ₹ 1350

3. Ratio of their capitals
= 1800 : 1500 : 1600 = 18 : 15 : 16
Sum of proportionals = 18 +15 + 16 = 49
Monu's profit = ₹ 900

∴ Total profit in the business = $\frac{900}{15} \times 49$ = ₹ 2940

4. Investment by Omdutt for 1 month
= ₹ 8000 × 12 = ₹ 96000
Let Sanjay invested ₹ x for 6 months
∴ Capital of Sanjay for 1 month = ₹ $x \times 6$ = ₹ $6x$
Now, $6x = 96000$
∴ x = ₹ 16000

5. Here, ratio of capitals of A and (B + C)
= 40000 : 60000 = 2 : 3
Profit of (B + C) = 2750 + 1750 = ₹ 4500

Hence, A's profit = $\frac{4500}{3} \times 2$ = ₹ 3000

6. Separate profit for A = $\frac{1040 \times 25}{100}$ = ₹ 260

Remaining profit = ₹ (1040 – 260) = ₹ 780
Ratio of capitals of A and B = 2100 : 3100 = 21 : 31

A's profit = $\frac{21}{52} \times 780$ = ₹ 315

B's profit = $\frac{31}{52} \times 780$ = ₹ 465

Total profit of A = ₹ (315 + 260) = ₹ 575
Therefore A and B will make profit of ₹ 575 and ₹ 465 respectively.

7. Ratio of their capitals = 12500 : 8500 = 25 : 17
Hence, sum of their ratios = 25 + 17 = 42 and difference of ratios = 25 – 17 = 8
Now total profit taken as interest

= $\frac{300}{8} \times 42$ = ₹ 1575

Hence, total profit in the business

= $\frac{100}{40} \times 1575$ = ₹ 3937.50

8. Let shares of Neeraj and Birju in profit are ₹ x and ₹ y respectively; then,

$\frac{2}{5}x = \frac{1}{3}y \quad \therefore \; x : y = 5 : 6$

Hence, share of Birju = $\frac{6}{11} \times 1210$ = ₹ 660

9. Ratio of their shares = (20 × 5/2) : (30 × 4) : (36 × 7/2) = 25 : 60 : 63
Sum of proportionals = 25 + 60 + 63 = 148
Total lease amount = ₹ 888

∴ Amount paid by A = $\frac{25}{148} \times 888$ = ₹ 150

Amount paid by B = $\frac{60}{148} \times 888$ = ₹ 360

Amount paid by C = $\frac{63}{148} \times 888$ = ₹ 378

●●●

CHAPTER 7

Mixture and Alligation

Alligation deals with calculation of values or properties of a mixture. Alligation is the rule that enables us—

(1) to find the proportion in which the two or more ingredients at the given prices must be mixed to yield a mixture at the given price. This is termed as "Alligation Alternate".

(2) to calculate the average or mean value of a mixture when the prices of two or more ingredients which are to be mixed together and proportion in which they are to be mixed are given. This is termed as "Alligation Medial".

1. Rule of Alligation:

$$\frac{\text{Amount of Cheaper ingredient}}{\text{Amount of Dearer ingredient}} = \frac{\text{Cost price of Dearer} - \text{Mean Price}}{\text{Mean Price} - \text{Cost Price of Cheaper}}$$

Here cost price of unit quantity of the mixture is called the *Mean Price.*

The above rule may be represented schematically as under:

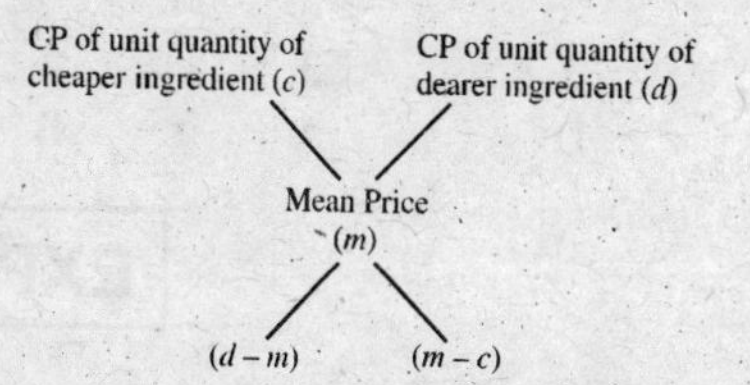

(Cheaper quantity) : (Dearer quantity) $= (d - m) : (m - c)$

This relationship is very helpful in solving problems on mixture involving percentage values, rates, prices, speeds etc.

2. *m* gm of sugar solution has *x*% sugar in it. To increase the sugar content in the solution to *y*%, quantity of sugar need to be added $= \frac{m(y-x)}{100-y}$

3. A vessel contains *x* litres of liquid A. *y* litres are withdrawn and replaced by liquid B. Next *y* litres of the mixture is withdrawn and again replaced by liquid B. This operation is repeated *n* times.

$$\frac{\text{Quantity of liquid A left after } n\text{th operation}}{\text{Whole quantity of liquid A initially present}} = \left(\frac{x-y}{x}\right)^n \text{ or } \left(1-\frac{y}{x}\right)^n$$

EXERCISE

1. In what proportion must tea at ₹ 62 per kg be mixed with tea at ₹ 72 per kg in order to obtain the mixture worth ₹ 65 per kg?

A. 4 : 6 B. 7 : 3
C. 2 : 3 D. 4 : 7

2. Find the quantity of rice @ ₹ 10 per kg. which should be mixed with 25 kgs of rice @ ₹ 8 per kg, so that on selling the mixture @ 15 per kg there is 80% profit.

A. 6 kgs B. 7 kgs
C. 3 kgs D. 5 kgs

3. A shopkeeper buys 26 kgs of milk @ ₹ 16 per kg. He also buys from another source an inferior quality of milk @ ₹ 10 per kg. How much quantity of the latter should he buy to mix it with the former so that he can sell the mixture @ ₹ 14 per kg without making any loss?

A. 13 kgs B. 12 kgs
C. 14 kgs D. 16 kgs

4. Two vessels A and B contain milk and water in the ratio 7 : 5 and 17 : 7 respectively. In what ratio mixtures from two vessels should be mixed to get a new mixture containing milk and water in the ratio 5 : 3?

A. 1 : 2 B. 2 : 1
C. 2 : 3 D. 3 : 2

5. Two vessels A and B contain mixture of milk and water in the ratio 4 : 1 and 9 : 11 respectively. They are mixed in the ratio of 3 : 2. Find the ratio of milk : water in the resulting mixture.

A. 34 : 16 B. 33 : 17
C. 16 : 34 D. 17 : 33

6. A person has two solutions of sugar with 30% and 50% concentration respectively. In what proportion should he mix two solutions to get 45% concentration in the resulting mixture?

A. 1 : 3 B. 3 : 1
C. 2 : 3 D. 3 : 2

7. 6 litres of milk and water mixture has 75% milk in it. How much milk should be added to the mixture to make it 90% pure?

A. 8 litres B. 9 litres
C. 10 litres D. 12 litres

8. In what ratio must water be added to spirit to gain 25% by selling it at cost price?

A. 1 : 4 B. 4 : 1
C. 3 : 4 D. 4 : 3

ANSWERS

1	2	3	4	5	6	7	8
B	D	A	B	B	A	B	A

EXPLANATORY ANSWERS

1.

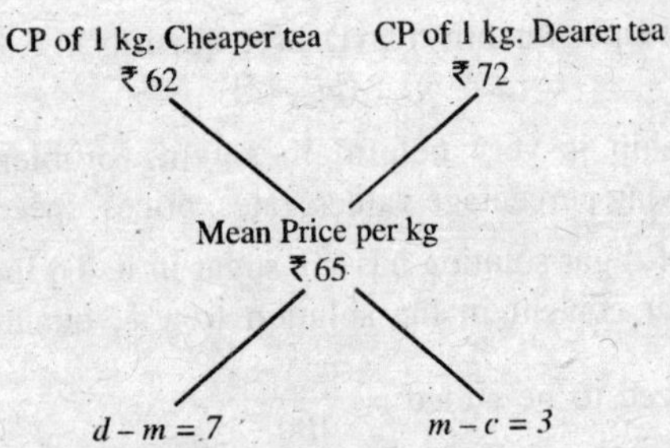

Using Alligation rule,

$$\frac{\text{Quantity of cheaper tea}}{\text{Quantity of dearer tea}} = \frac{d-m}{m-c} = \frac{7}{3}$$

Therefore, they must be mixed in the ratio of 7 : 3.

3.

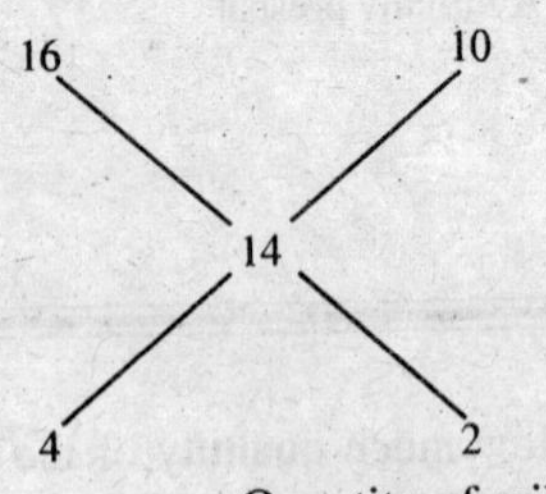

or 2 : 1 $\frac{\text{Quantity of milk @ ₹ 10 per kg}}{\text{Quantity of milk @ ₹ 16 per kg}} = \frac{1}{2}$.

So, quantity of milk @ ₹ 10 per kg. = $\frac{26}{2}$ = 13 kgs.

5. Fraction is

	Milk	*Water*
A :	$\frac{4}{5}$	$\frac{1}{5}$
B :	$\frac{9}{20}$	$\frac{11}{20}$

$$(3A + 2B) = A \text{ and } B : \left(\frac{12}{5}+\frac{9}{10}\right) \left(\frac{3}{5}+\frac{11}{10}\right)$$

$$\frac{33}{10} \qquad \frac{17}{10}$$

So, Ratio of milk : water in the resulting mixture = 33 : 17.

6.

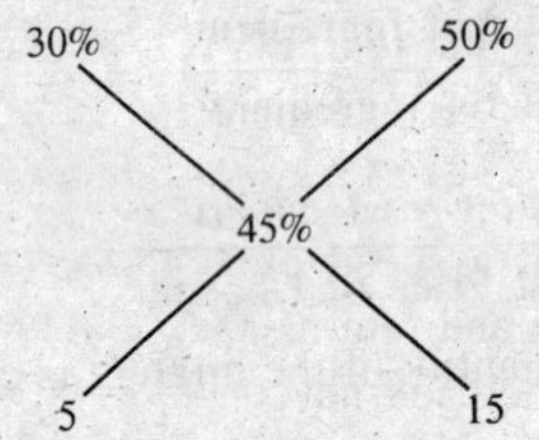

He should mix 30% and 50% in the ratio 5 : 15 or 1 : 3.

$$\frac{\text{30\% Solution}}{\text{50\% Solution}} = \frac{1}{3} \text{ or } 1 : 3$$

7. The given solution has 75% milk.

Milk to be added has 100% milk.

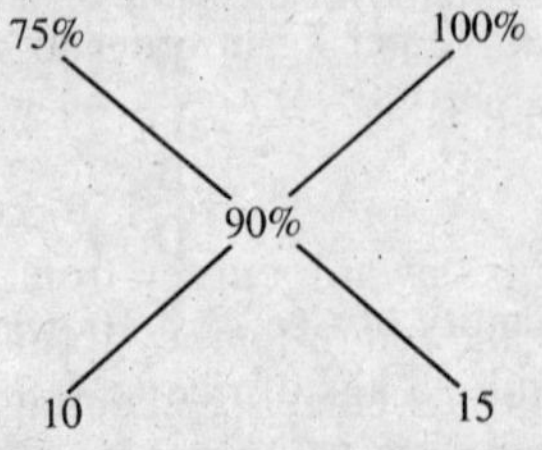

Milk should be added to the given mixture in the ratio 15 : 10 or 3 : 2.

∴ Quantity of milk to be added = $\frac{3}{2} \times 6$ = 9 litres.

●●●

CHAPTER

8 Time and Distance

Important Formulae:

1. Speed = Distance ÷ Time
2. Distance = Time × Speed
3. Time = Distance ÷ Speed
4. x km/hr = $\left(x \times \frac{5}{18}\right)$ m/sec
5. x metres/sec = $\left(x \times \frac{18}{5}\right)$ km/hr.
6. If the speed of a body is changed in the ratio $m : n$, then the ratio of the time taken changes in the ratio $n : m$.
7. When a man covers a certain distance with a speed of x km/h and another equal distance at the rate of y km/h, then for the whole journey, the average speed is given by

   Average speed = $\frac{2xy}{x+y}$ km/h.

EXERCISE

1. A car moving at 48 km/hr completes a journey in 10 hours. By how much the speed of this car should be increased so as to do this journey in 8 hours?
   A. 8 km/hr. B. 12 km/hr
   C. 10 km/hr D. 15 km/hr
2. Starting from a point at a speed of 4 km/hr a man reaches at a cerain place and returns back to the point from where he had started journey on bicycle at the speed of 16 km/hr. His average speed during the entire journey will be:
   A. 6.4 km/h B. 8.4 km/h
   C. 5.4 km/h D. 10 km/h
3. A motorist covers a certain distance at a average speed of 48 km/h in 45 minutes. What speed in km/h he must maintain to cover the same distance in 30 minutes?
   A. 66 km/h B. 79 km/h
   C. 80 km/h D. 72 km/h
4. Two points A and B are 150 km apart. A man completes his onward journey from A to B in 3 hours 20 minutes and return journey from B to A in 4 hours 10 minutes. His average speed during the entire journey will be less than his average speed during the journey from A to B by:
   A. 5 km/h B. 7.5 km/h
   C. 9 km/h D. 3 km/h
5. A policeman saw a thief at a distance of 200 m. The policeman and the thief started running at the same time. If the policeman runs at a speed of $4\frac{1}{6}$ m per second and the thief at a speed of $3\frac{1}{3}$m per second, after what time the policeman will catch the thief?
   A. 12 min B. 10 min
   C. 9 min D. 4 min
6. Kanchan walks from her home at 4 kms per hour and reaches her school 5 minutes late. If she walks at 5 kms per hour, she reaches the school 2½ minutes earlier. How far is the school from her home?
   A. 3.5 kms B. 2.5 kms
   C. 2.75 kms D. 3.2 kms
7. A monkey wants to climb up a glazed pole. He climbs 12 metres in 1 minute and then he slips back 3 metres in the next minute. If the pole is 63 metre high, how long does he take to climb at the top of the pole?
   A. $11\frac{1}{4}$ min B. $12\frac{1}{2}$ min
   C. $12\frac{3}{4}$ min D. $14\frac{3}{4}$ min
8. A and B start walking at the same time on a circular path with circumference 35 metre. If they walk in the same direction at 4 km/hr and 5 km/hr respectively, after what time will they meet together?

A. 35 hours
B. 27 hours
C. 24 hours
D. 40 hours

9. While walking at $\frac{3}{5}$ of his usual speed Kamalkant reaches at his destination late by 30 minutes. His usual time consumed in reaching to his destination is:

A. 32 min
B. 40 min
C. 45 min
D. 42 min

10. The distance between two stations A and B is 300 km. A train leaves the station A with a speed of 40 km/hr. At the same time another train departs from the station B with a speed of 50 km/hr. How much time will these two trains take to cross each other?

A. 3 hrs 40 min
B. 3 hrs 20 min
C. 2 hrs 20 min
D. 3 hrs 45 min

ANSWERS

1	2	3	4	5	6	7	8	9	10
B	A	D	A	D	B	C	A	C	B

EXPLANATORY ANSWERS

1. Let he has to increase his speed by x km/hr for given condition; then,

$$(48 + x) \times 8 = 48 \times 10$$

$$\Rightarrow \quad 48 + x = 60 \therefore x = 12 \text{ km/hr}$$

2. Average speed during the entire journey

$$= \frac{2xy}{x+y} = \frac{2\times4\times16}{4+16} = \frac{8\times16}{20} = 6.4 \text{ km/hr.}$$

3. Let required speed be x km/hr; then

$$x \times \frac{1}{2} = 48 \times \frac{3}{4} \quad \therefore x = 48 \times \frac{3}{4} \times 2 = 72 \text{ km/hr}$$

4. During onward journey from A to B:

$$\text{Average speed} = \frac{150}{10/3} = \frac{150\times3}{10} = 45 \text{ km/hr.}$$

During entire jouney:

$$\text{Average speed} = \frac{300}{\frac{10}{3}+\frac{25}{6}} = \frac{300\times6}{45} = 40 \text{ km/hr.}$$

Hence, difference of average speed

$$= 45 - 40 = 5 \text{ km/hr.}$$

5. Suppose the policeman will catch the thief after t sec

$$\text{then, } \left(\frac{25}{6}-\frac{10}{3}\right)t = 200 \Rightarrow \frac{5}{6}t = 200$$

$$\therefore t = \frac{200\times6}{5} = 240 \text{ sec} = 4 \text{ min.}$$

6. Suppose the distance between her house to the school $= x$ km

$$\text{Difference of time} = \frac{5}{2} - (-5) = \frac{15}{2} \text{ min} = \frac{1}{8} \text{ hr.}$$

$$\frac{x}{4}-\frac{x}{5} = \frac{1}{8} \Rightarrow \frac{x}{20} = \frac{1}{8}$$

$$\therefore x = \frac{20}{8} = 2.5 \text{ km}$$

7. The monkey climbs 12 metres in 1 minute and then he slips back 3 metres in the next minute

$\therefore$ The monkey climbs in the first 2 minutes = 12 – 3 = 9 metres

$\therefore$ In the first 12 minutes the monkey climbs = 9 × 6 = 54 metres

Remaining height of the pole to be covered by the monkey = 63 – 54 = 9 metre

$\therefore$ The monkey will climb the height of 9 metres in the 13th minute

$\because$ The monkey climbs 12 metres in 1 minute

$\therefore$ The monkey will climb 9 metres in

$$\frac{1}{12}\times9 = \frac{3}{4} \text{ minute}$$

$\therefore$ Time spent in climbing at the top of the pole

$$= \left(12+\frac{3}{4}\right) \text{ minutes} = 12\frac{3}{4} \text{ minutes}$$

8. The two persons walk in the same direction

$\therefore$ Their relative speed = 5 – 4 = 1 km/hr

Distance covered in 1 round on the circular path = 35 km

$$\therefore \text{They will meet after } \frac{35}{1} = 35 \text{ hours.}$$

9. Suppose usual speed of Kamalkant is v km/hr and his destination is at a distance of x kms; then usual time taken $= \frac{x}{v}$ hours.

$$\frac{x}{3v/5}-\frac{x}{v} = \frac{1}{2} \Rightarrow \frac{2x}{3v} = \frac{1}{2} \quad \therefore \frac{x}{v} = \frac{3}{4} \text{ hour} = 45 \text{ min.}$$

10. The two trains are moving in the opposite directions

$\therefore$ Relative speed = 40 + 50 = 90 km/hr.

$\therefore$ Time taken to cross each other

$$= \frac{300}{90} = 3\frac{1}{3} \text{ hours or, 3 hours 20 minutes.}$$

●●●

CHAPTER 9

Time and Work

IMPORTANT FACTS:

1. If A can do a piece of work in n days, then work done by A in 1 day $= \frac{1}{n}$.
2. If work done by A in 1 day $= \frac{1}{n}$; then A can finish the whole work in n days.
3. If A is twice as good a workman as B then; Ratio of work done by A and B = 2 : 1
   Ratio of times taken by A and B to finish a work = 1 : 2.

EXERCISE

1. 12 boys can do a piece of work in 16 days. In how many days can 6 boys do the same work?
   A. 16 days B. 32 days
   C. 23 days D. 24 days
2. A can do a piece of work in 8 days while B can do the same work in 16 days. If they start working together, how long would they take to complete half portion of this work?
   A. $2\frac{2}{3}$ days B. $3\frac{5}{7}$ days
   C. $4\frac{1}{2}$ days D. $3\frac{1}{2}$ days
3. A can do a piece of work in 4 days. B is 50% more efficient than A. How long would B alone take to finish this work?
   A. $3\frac{1}{3}$ days B. $5\frac{1}{4}$ days
   C. $2\frac{2}{3}$ days D. $1\frac{2}{3}$ days
4. A and B working together complete a work in 35 days. If A takes 60 days to complete it, how long would B alone take to complete it?
   A. 64 days B. 72 days
   C. 81 days D. 84 days
5. A few children working together can do a piece of work in 18 days. If the number of children employed on the work is made double, how long would they take to complete half of the work?
   A. $4\frac{1}{2}$ days B. $2\frac{1}{3}$ days
   C. $8\frac{3}{4}$ days D. $6\frac{1}{2}$ days
6. 10 men or 18 boys can do a piece of work in 15 days. In how many days would 25 men and 15 boys complete the same work working together?
   A. $5\frac{1}{2}$ days B. $4\frac{1}{2}$ days
   C. $6\frac{2}{3}$ days D. $2\frac{1}{3}$ days
7. A can do a piece of work in 40 days. He starts working, but having some other engagements he drops out after 5 days. Thereafter B completes this work in 21 days. How many days would A and B take to complete this work working together?
   A. 15 days B. 16 days
   C. 17 days D. 11 days
8. Two persons A and B can complete a piece of work in 8 hours and 16 hours respectively. If they work at it alternately for an hour, A starting first, in how many hours will the work be finished?
   A. $9\frac{1}{3}$ hours B. $10\frac{1}{2}$ hours
   C. $11\frac{1}{2}$ hours D. $8\frac{1}{2}$ hours

9. 15 men can complete a work in 210 days. They started the work but at the end of 10 days 15 additional men, with double efficiency, were inducted. How many days, in whole, did they take to finish the work?

A. $76\frac{2}{3}$ days B. $84\frac{3}{4}$ days

C. $72\frac{1}{2}$ days D. 70 days

ANSWERS

1	2	3	4	5	6	7	8	9
B	A	C	D	A	B	A	B	A

EXPLANATORY ANSWERS

1. $\because$ 12 boys can do a piece of work in 16 days.

$\therefore$ 1 boy will do the same piece of work in 16 × 12 days.

$\therefore$ 6 boys will do the same piece of work in

$\frac{16\times12}{6}$ days = 32 days.

2. (A + B)'s 1 day's work $= \frac{1}{8}+\frac{1}{16}=\frac{3}{16}$

Hence, (A + B) will do the whole work in $\frac{16}{3}$ days

So, they will do the half portion of the work in

$\frac{16}{3\times2}$ days $= \frac{8}{3}=2\frac{2}{3}$ days.

3. A's 1 day's work $=\frac{1}{4}$;

Hence, B's 1 day's work $= \frac{150}{100}\times\frac{1}{4}=\frac{3}{8}$

So, B will do the whole work in $\frac{8}{3}=2\frac{2}{3}$ days.

4. (A + B)'s 1 day's work $= \frac{1}{35}$

and also, A's 1 day's work $= \frac{1}{60}$

Hence, B's 1 day's work

$= \frac{1}{35}-\frac{1}{60}=\frac{5}{420}=\frac{1}{84}$

So, B will do the whole work in 84 days.

5. Let number of children be x;

Now x children can do the work in 18 days.

Hence, $2x$ children will do $\frac{1}{2}$ of the work in

$\frac{18\times x}{2x\times2}=\frac{9}{2}$ days $= 4\frac{1}{2}$ days.

6. 10 men $\equiv$ 18 boys; 25 men $\equiv \frac{18}{10}\times25 = 45$ boys

Hence, 25 men + 15 boys = 45 + 15 = 60 boys

Now, 18 boys can do a piece of work in 15 days.

Hence, 60 boys will do a piece of work in

$\frac{15\times18}{60}=\frac{9}{2}$ days $= 4\frac{1}{2}$ days.

7. A's 5 days' work $= 5\times\frac{1}{40}=\frac{1}{8}$

Remaining work $= 1-\frac{1}{8}=\frac{7}{8}$, which is done by B in 21 days.

Hence, B's 1 day's work $= \frac{7}{8\times21}=\frac{1}{24}$

Now, (A + B)'s 1 day's work $= \frac{1}{40}+\frac{1}{24}=\frac{8}{120}=\frac{1}{15}$

Hence, (A + B) will complete the work in 15 days.

8. In 2 hours the part of work $= \frac{1}{8}+\frac{1}{16}=\frac{3}{16}$ will be completed.

Hence, in 5 pairs of hours the part of work

$= 5\times\frac{3}{16}=\frac{15}{16}$ will be completed

Remaining work $= 1-\frac{15}{16}=\frac{1}{16}$ which will be done by A.

Time taken by A to complete the $\frac{1}{16}$ work

$= \frac{1/16}{1/8}=\frac{1}{2}$ hour.

Hence, required number of hours

$= 10+\frac{1}{2}=10\frac{1}{2}$ hours.

9. 15 men's 10 days' work $= 10\times\frac{1}{210}=\frac{1}{21}$

Remaining work $= 1-\frac{1}{21}=\frac{20}{21}$

Now, (15 men + 15 men having double efficiency)'s

1 day's work $= \frac{1}{210}+\frac{2}{210}=\frac{3}{210}=\frac{1}{70}$

Hence, number of days

$= \frac{20/21}{1/70}=\frac{20}{21}\times70=\frac{200}{3}=66\frac{2}{3}$ days

So, required number of total days

$= 10+66\frac{2}{3}=76\frac{2}{3}$ days.

•••

CHAPTER 10

Geometry

Triangle and Its Various Kinds of Centres

There are 4 very important ways of viewing the center of a triangle. We can look at its CENTROID, ORTHOCENTER, CIRCUMCENTER, and the INCENTER.

Centroid

The centroid is the first center and is obtained by locating the intersection of the three medians of the triangle. The median of a triangle is obtained by joining each vertex with the midpoint of the opposite side.

- It is the point of the intersection of the three median of the triangle. It is denoted by G.
- A centroid divides the area of the triangle in exactly three parts.

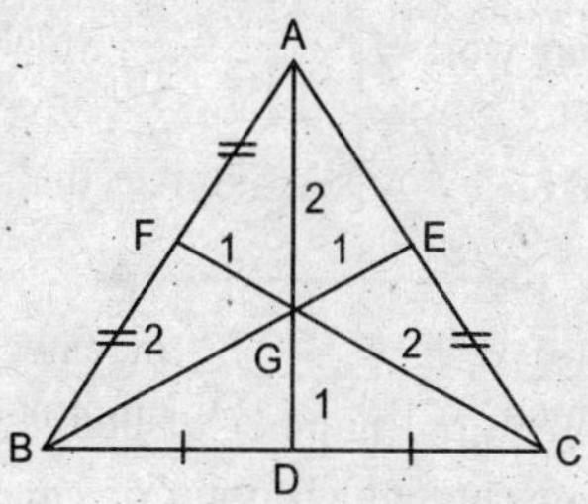

Medians:

- A line segment joining the midpoint of the side with the opposite vertex is called median.
- Median bisects the opposite side as well as divide the area of the triangle in two equal parts.

Orthocenter

The second center of a triangle is the orthocenter. It is obtained by finding the intersection of the 3 altitudes of the triangle. An altitude is found by joining each vertex with the point on the opposite side that creates a perpendicular line with the opposite side.

It is the point of intersection of all the three altitudes of the triangle.

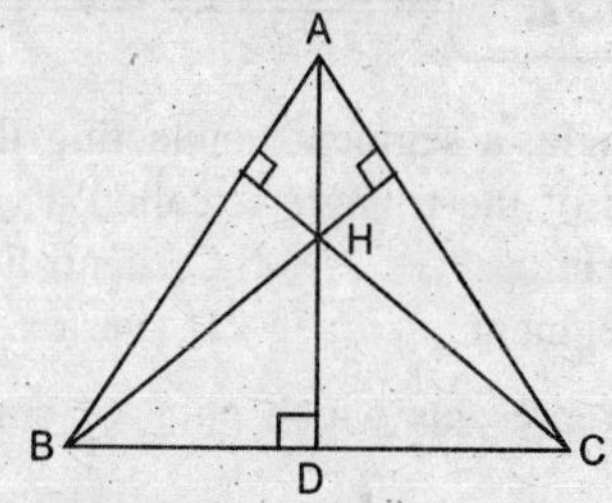

$\angle BHC = 180 - \angle A$

$\angle AHB = 180 - \angle C$

$\angle AHC = 180 - \angle B$

Position of orthocentre inside the triangle:

Acute angled triangle: lies inside the triangle.

Obtuse angle triangle: lies outside the triangle on the backside of the obtuse angle. Orthocentre and circumcentre lie opposite to each other in obtuse angle triangle.

Circumcenter

The third center is the circumcenter. The circumcenter is the intersection of the perpendicular bisectors of each side of the triangle. We can also think of this center as the point that is equidistant from each of the vertices. Since it is equidistant from each vertex, we can also construct a circle that passes through each vertex with the center being the circumcenter.

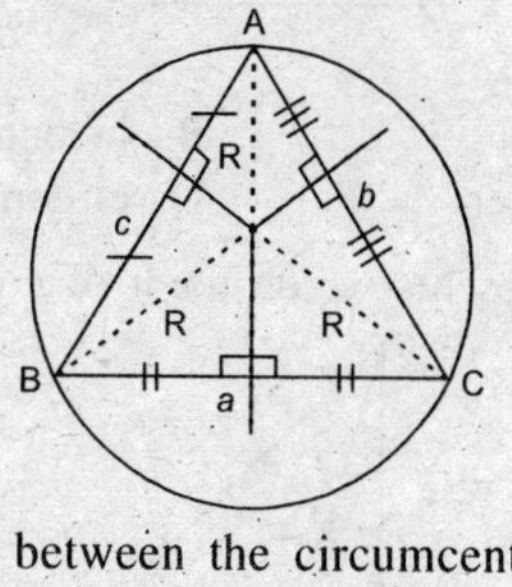

The distance between the circumcentre and the three vertices of a triangle is always equal.

OA = OB = OC = R (circumradius) = $abc/4A$

$\angle BOC = 2\angle A$

$\angle AOC = 2\angle B$

$\angle AOB = 2\angle C$

Location of circumcentre in various types of triangle:

Acute angle triangle: Lies inside the triangle

Obtuse angle triangle: Lies outside the triangle

Right angle triangle: Lies at the midpoint of the hypotenuse.

Incenter

The last center is the incenter. The incenter is found by first constructing the angle bisectors of each of the three angles. The incenter is the intersection of these 3 segments.

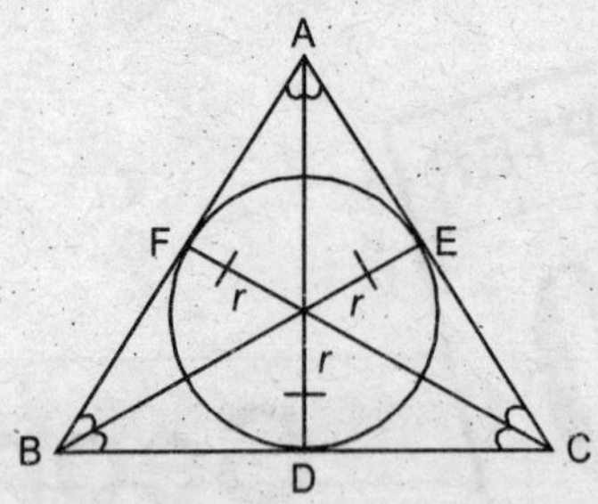

The distance of the in-centre from the all the three sides is equal (ID = IE = IF = inradius "r")

In-radius (r) = Area of triangle/Semiperimetre = A/S

$\angle BIC = 90 + \angle A/2$

$\angle AIC = 90 + \angle B/2$

$\angle AIB = 90 + \angle C/2$

EXERCISE

1. In a triangle, a segment connecting the midpoints of two sides of the triangle is called a _____.

A. shortcut C. centroid
B. midsegment D. vertex

2. Point Q represents which point of concurrency?

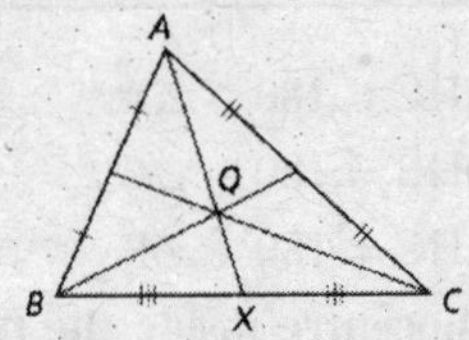

A. centroid C. orthocenter
B. incenter D. circumcenter

3. Point P represents which point of concurrency?

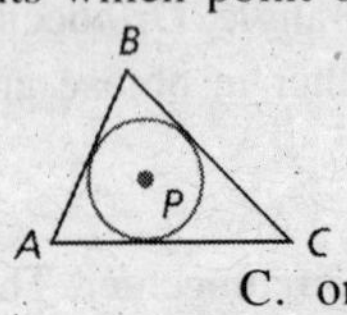

A. centroid C. orthocenter
B. incenter D. circumcenter

4. Point P represents which point of concurrency?

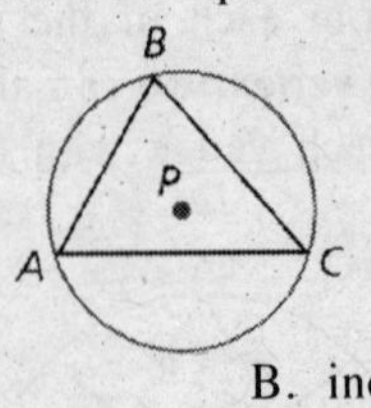

A. centroid B. incenter
C. orthocenter D. circumcenter

5. Point T represents which point of concurrency?

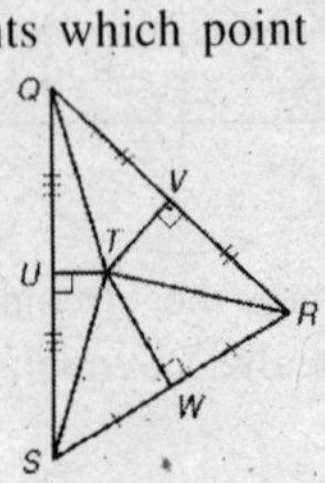

A. centroid B. incenter
C. orthocenter D. circumcenter

6. Point M represents which point of concurrency?

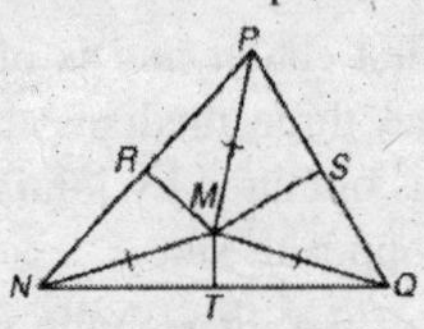

A. centroid B. incenter
C. orthocenter D. circumcenter

7. Point M represents which point of concurrency?

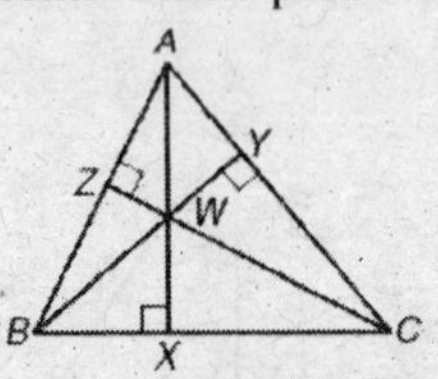

A. centroid B. incenter
C. orthocenter D. circumcenter

8. Point L represents which point of concurrency?

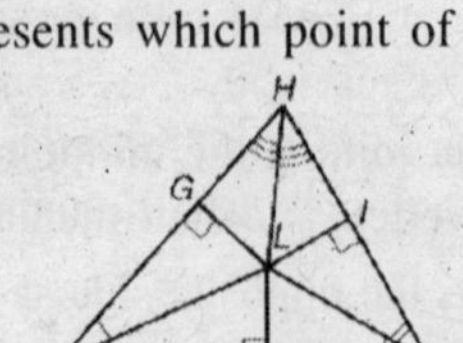

A. centroid B. incenter
C. orthocenter D. circumcenter

9. Which point of concurrency is the intersection of the medians of the triangle?

A. centroid B. incenter
C. orthocenter D. circumcenter

10. Which point of concurrency is the intersection of the altitudes of the triangle?

A. centroid B. incenter
C. orthocenter D. circumcenter

ANSWERS

1	2	3	4	5	6	7	8	9	10
B	A	B	D	D	D	C	B	A	C

Congruence and Similarity of Triangles

Congruence of triangle: Two triangles having same shape and measurement but different positions are called congruent triangle.

Congruence criterion

(*i*) **Side-Side-Side (SSS) Congruence criterion:** Two triangles are congruent if the three sides of one triangle are equal to the three sides of the other triangle.

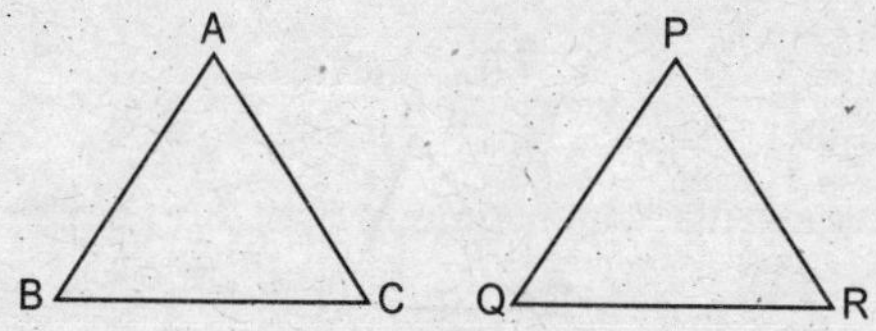

Here, $AB = PQ$, $BC = QR$ and $AC = PR$

$\therefore$ $\Delta ABC \cong \Delta PQR$

(*ii*) **Side-Angle-Side (SAS) Congruence criterion:** Two triangles are congruent if two sides and the included angle of one are equal to the corresponding sides and the included angles of the other.

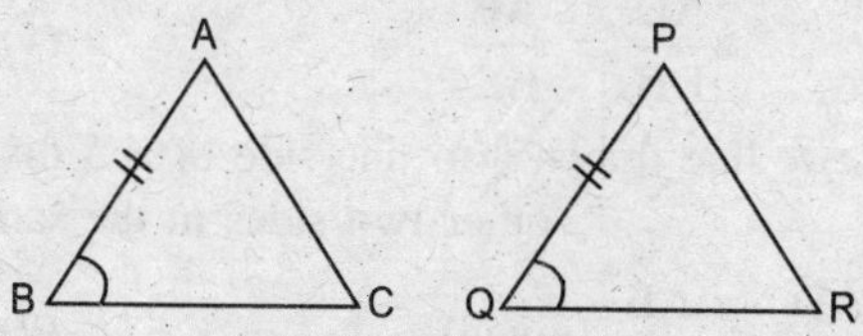

Here, $AB = PQ$, $\angle B = \angle Q$ and $BC = QR$

$\therefore$ $\Delta ABC \cong \Delta PQR$

(*iii*) **Angle-Side-Angle (ASA) Congruence criterion:** Two triangles are congruent if two angles and the included side of one triangle are equal to the corresponding two angles and the included side of the triangle.

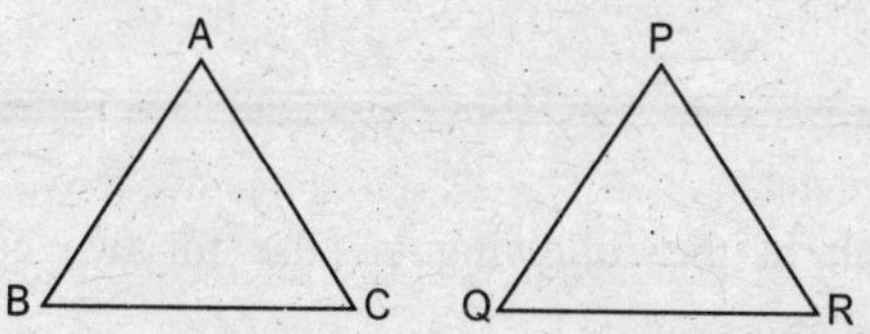

$\because$ $\angle B = \angle Q$, $\angle C = \angle R$ and $BC = QR$

$\therefore$ $\Delta ABC \cong \Delta PQR$

(*iv*) **Right Angle-Hypotenuse-Side (RHS) congruence criterion:** Two right triangles are congruent. If the hypotenuse and one side of one triangle are respectively equal to the hypotenuse and one side of the other triangle.

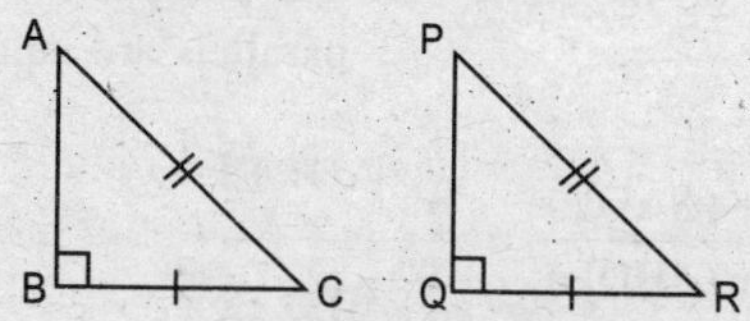

$\because$ $\angle B = \angle Q = 90°$, $AC = PR$, $BC = QR$

$\therefore$ $\Delta ABC \cong \Delta PQR$.

Similar Triangles: Two triangles having same shape but not necessarily of the same size, called similar triangle.

Basic properties of similar triangles:

(*i*) The corresponding angles of similar triangles are equal.

(*ii*) The corresponding sides of similar triangles are proportional.

The symbol for similar or is similar to is ~

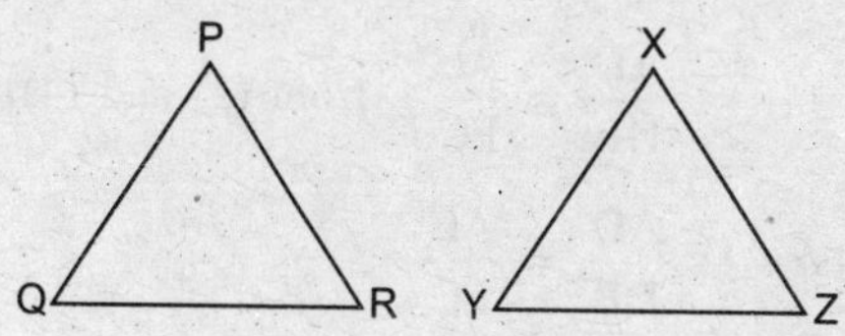

$\angle P = \angle X$, $\angle Q = \angle Y$ and $\angle R = \angle Z$

Then, $\frac{PQ}{QR} = \frac{XY}{YZ}$ or, $\frac{PR}{PQ} = \frac{XZ}{XY}$

Thus, $\Delta PQR \sim \Delta XYZ$

→ Congruent triangles are always similar but similar triangles may or may not be congruent.

→ Any two equilateral triangles are always similar triangles.

SOME IMPORTANT THEOREMS

Basic Proportionality Theorem: (Thalse Theorem)

Theorem 1: *In a triangle, a line drawn parallel to one side to intersect the other sides in distinct points divides the two sides in the same ratio.*

Given: A ΔABC in which DE is drawn parallel to side BC.

To prove. $\frac{AD}{DB} = \frac{AE}{EC}$.

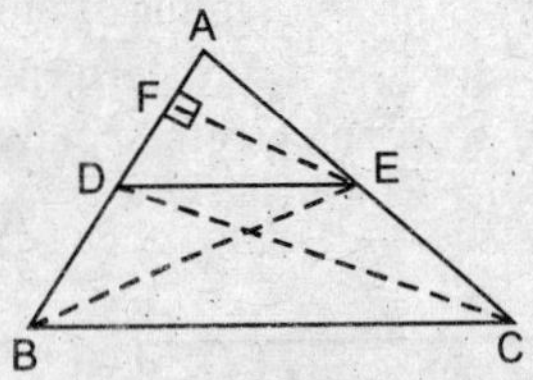

Const.: Join BE and CD. Draw EF ⊥ AB.

Proof: ar.(ΔBDE) = ar.(ΔCDE) ...(1)

[∵ Δs on the same base DE and between the same parallels are equal in area]

$$\frac{\text{ar.}(\Delta ADE)}{\text{ar.}(\Delta BDE)} = \frac{\frac{1}{2}\times AD\times EF}{\frac{1}{2}\times BD\times EF}$$

[∵ Area of Δ = $\frac{1}{2}$ base × height]

$$\Rightarrow \frac{\text{ar.}(\Delta ADE)}{\text{ar.}(\Delta BDE)} = \frac{AD}{DB} \quad ...(2)$$

Similarly, $$\frac{\text{ar.}(\Delta ADE)}{\text{ar.}(\Delta CDE)} = \frac{AE}{EC} \quad ...(3)$$

$$\therefore \frac{\text{ar.}(\Delta ADE)}{\text{ar.}(\Delta BDE)} = \frac{AE}{EC} \quad \text{[from (1) and (3)]} \quad ...(4)$$

$$\therefore \frac{AD}{DB} = \frac{AE}{EC} \quad \text{[from (2) and (4)]}$$

Corollary 1: $\frac{AD}{DB} = \frac{AE}{EC}$

Adding 1 to both sides, we get

$$\frac{AD}{DB}+1 = \frac{AE}{EC}+1$$

$$\Rightarrow \frac{AD+DB}{DB} = \frac{AE+EC}{EC}$$

Corollary 2: $\frac{AD}{DB} = \frac{AE}{EC}$

$$\Rightarrow \frac{DB}{AD} = \frac{EC}{AE}$$

Adding 1 to both sides, we get

$$1+\frac{DB}{AD} = 1+\frac{EC}{AE}$$

$$\Rightarrow \frac{AD+DB}{AD} = \frac{AE+EC}{AE}$$

$$\Rightarrow \frac{AB}{AD} = \frac{AC}{AE}.$$

Converse of Basic Proportionality Theorem

Theorem 2: *If a line divides any two sides of a triangle in the same ratio, prove that it is parallel to the third side.*

Given: A ΔABC, DE is st. line such that

$$\frac{AD}{DB} = \frac{AE}{EC}.$$

To Prove. DE || BC

Const.: If DE is not || BC, draw BK || DE meeting AC produce in.

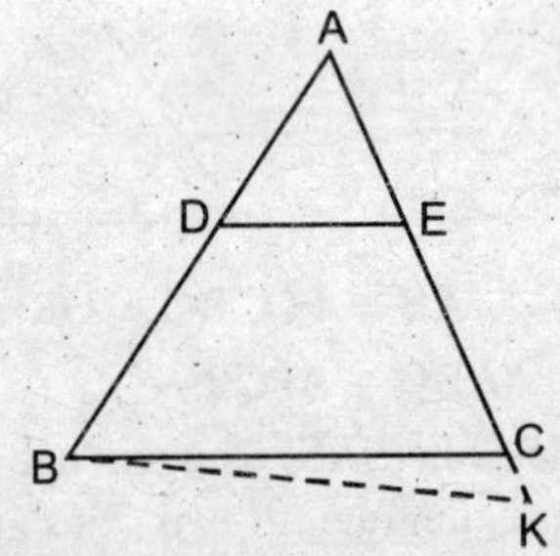

Proof: In DABK, DE || BK

$$\therefore \frac{AD}{DB} = \frac{AE}{EK} \quad ...(1)$$

[∵ A line drawn || to one side of a Δ divides the other two sides in the same ratio]

But, $\frac{AD}{DB} = \frac{AE}{EC}$ (given) ...(2)

From (1) and (2), we get

$\frac{AE}{EK} = \frac{AE}{EC}$ or, EK = EC

which is possible only when C and K coincides.

Hence, DE || BC.

EXERCISE

1. Two similar triangles have
 A. equal sides B. equal areas
 C. equal angles D. None of these

2. Two congruent triangles have
 A. proportional sides
 B. equal sides
 C. equal corresponding sides
 D. equal corresponding angles

3. Which of the following is false for two congruent triangles?
 A. Corresponding angles are equal.
 B. Two sides and included angles are equal.
 C. Corresponding sides are equal.
 D. Two angles and one side are equal.

4. If the sides of a triangle are 8 cm, 12 cm and 15 cm then the angle is

A. Right angle B. Obtuse angle
C. Acute angle D. None of these

5. If two triangles are on the same base and between the parallel lines then they will be
A. equilaterals B. right angled
C. equal in area D. congruent

6. If the three heights of a traingle are equal then it is
A. right angled triangle B. obtuse angled triangle
C. equilateral triangle D. None of these

7. If two corresponding sides and the angle between them of a traingle are equal to another triangle. Then the angles are :
A. congruent but not similar
B. similar but not congruent
C. neither congruent nor similar
D. congruent and similar.

8. Ratio of areas of two similar triangles is equal to :
A. ratio of squares of the corresponding altitudes
B. ratio of squares of corresponding medians.
C. Either (A) or (B)
D. (A) and (B) both

9. If the areas of two similar triangles are equal then the triangles :
A. are congruent
B. have equal length of corresponding sides
C. (A) and (B)
D. None of these

10. Two isosceles triangles have equal vertical angles and their areas are in the ratio of 9 : 25 then the ratio between their corresponding heights is :
A. 5 : 3 B. 25 : 9
C. 3 : 5 D. 16 : 9

ANSWERS

1	2	3	4	5	6	7	8	9	10
C	C	D	C	C	C	C	D	C	C

EXPLANATORY ANSWERS

10. According to equestion

$\angle A = \angle D$ and $\dfrac{ar\,(\Delta\,ABC)}{ar\,(\Delta\,DEF)} = \dfrac{9}{25}$

Since, $AB = AC$ (given) ....(*i*)

$DE = DF$ (given) ....(*ii*)

Dividing (i) by (ii)

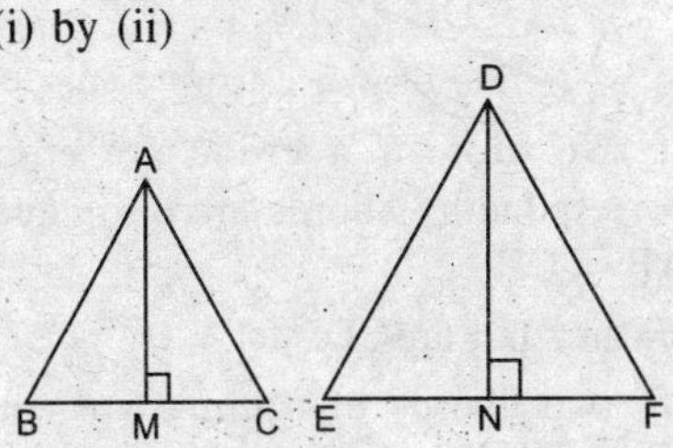

$$\frac{AB}{DE} = \frac{AC}{DF} \quad ...(iii)$$

Hence, $\Delta ABC \sim \Delta DEF$

[By SAS criterion of similar Δs]

In ΔAMC and ΔDNF

$\angle AMC = \angle DNF = 90°$

$\angle C = \angle F$ (because $\Delta ABC \sim \Delta DEF$)

$\therefore \angle AMC \sim DNF$

(By AA Criterion of similar Δs)

$$\therefore \quad \frac{AC}{DF} = \frac{AM}{DN}$$

and, $$\frac{ar\,(\Delta\,ABC)}{ar\,(DEF)} = \frac{AC^2}{DF^2} = \frac{AM^2}{DN^2}$$

$$\therefore \quad \frac{AM^2}{DN^2} = \frac{9}{25}$$

$$\Rightarrow \quad \frac{AM}{DN} = \frac{3}{5}$$

Hence required ratio = 3 : 5

Circle and Its Chord

A circle is a set of those points in a plane that are at a given constant distance from a given fixed point in the plane. The fixed point is called the **centre of the circle** and the constant distance of every point on the circle from its centre of called the **radius of the circle**.

Things to Remember

1. Locus of a point moving in a plane such that its distance from a fixed point in the same plane remains constant is called a circle.

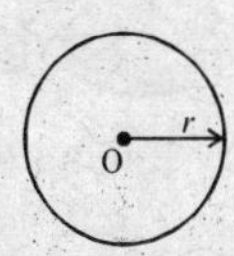

2. The fixed point O is called its centre and the constant distance r is called the radius.

3. The path traced by the moving point as described above is called the circumference of the circle.
4. The part of the plane containing the circle that consists the circle and its interior is called the circular region.

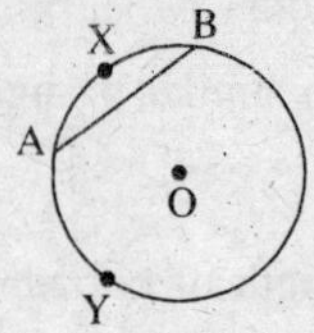

5. Line segment joining any two points on the circumference is called a chord of the circle. In the above figure AB is a chord of the circle.

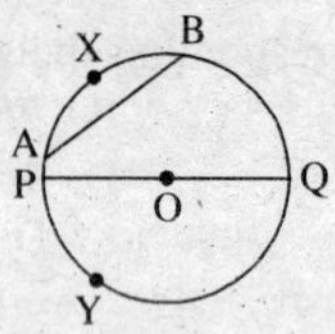

6. The chord passing through the centre of the circle is called its diameter.
   In the above figure PQ is a diameter of the circle.
7. Diameter is the longest chord of the circle.
8. Any fraction of the circumference is called an arc of the circle.
9. The remaining part of the circumference is called the alternate segment of the circle with respect to the arc.
10. An arc of a circle smaller in length than the semicircle is called a minor arc. In the above figure arc AXB is a minor arc.
11. An arc of a circle more in length than the semicircle is called a major arc. In the above figure arc AYB is a major arc.

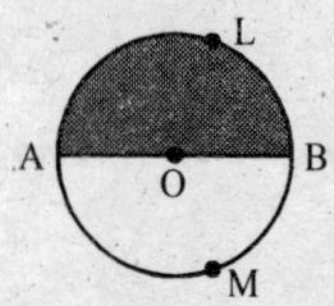

12. Diameter of a circle divides its circumference into two equal arcs. Each of them is called a semicircle.
13. The part of the plane containing the semicircle that consists the semicircle, the enclosing diameter and its interior is called the semicircular region.
    In the above figure region ALB and region BMA are semicircular regions.

14. The angle formed by joining the end points of an arc to the centre of the circle is said to be the angle subtended by an arc at the centre of the circle. In the above figure, θ is the degree measure of arc AB.
15. The part of the plane containing the circle that consists of the arc enclosing radii and its interior is called the sector of the circle. In the above figure AOB is sector of the circle.
16. A chord of the circle other than a diameter divides the circular region into two unequal parts.
    Each of these parts is called a segment. The larger part is called the major segment and the smaller is called the minor segment.

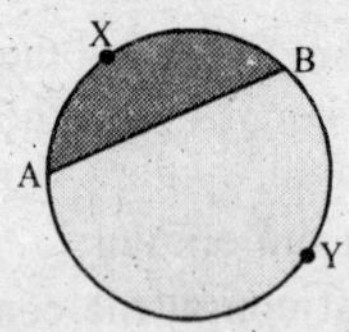

In the above figure segment AXB is a minor segment and segment BYA is the major segment.

17. Two circles in a plane are said to be concentric if they have same centre but different radii.
18. The chord formed by joining the end points of an arc of a circle is called its corresponding chord.

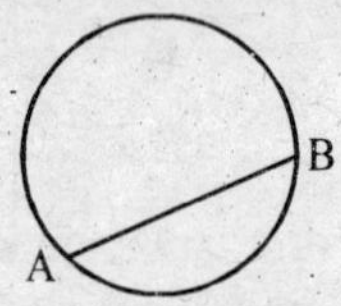

In the given figures chord AB is the corresponding chord of arc AB.

Important Theorems on Circles

1.

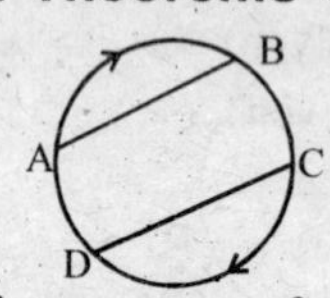

(*a*) If two arcs of a circle are equal then their corresponding chords are also equal.
AB = CD
$\Leftrightarrow$ arcAB = arcCD.

(*b*) If two chords of a circle are equal then their corresponding arcs are also equal.

2.

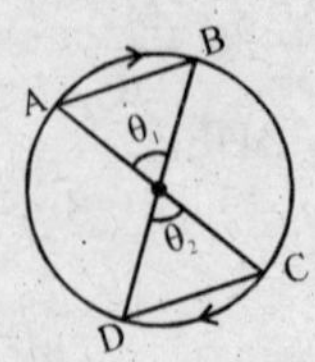

(*a*) If two chords of a circle are equal then they subtend equal angles at the centre of the circle.

(*b*) If two chords of a circle subtend equal angles at the centre of a circle then they are equal
$AB = CD \Leftrightarrow \theta_1 = \theta_2$

3.

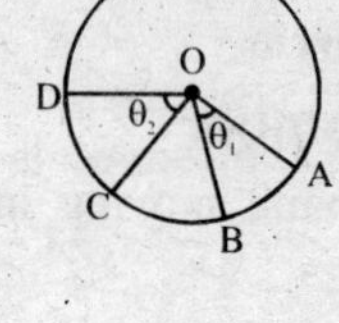

(*a*) If two arcs of a circle have same degree measure then they are equal.
arc AB = arc CD

$\Leftrightarrow \theta_1 = \theta_2$

(*b*) If two arcs of a circle are equal then their degree measures are also equal.

4.

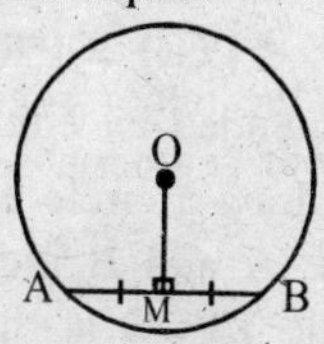

(*a*) Perpendicular to a chord from the centre of the circle bisects the chord.

(*b*) Line segment joining the centre of the circle to the mid point of the chord is perpendicular to the chord.

$OM \perp AB \Leftrightarrow M$ is the mid point of AB.

5.

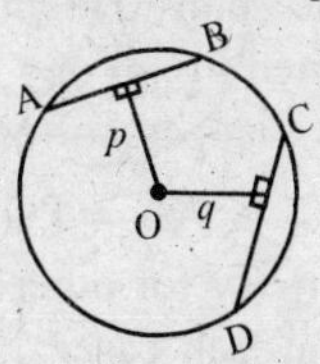

(*a*) If two chords of a circle are equidistant from the centre of the circle, they are equal.

(*b*) If two chords of a circle are equal then they are equidistant from the centre of the circle

$AB = CD \Leftrightarrow p = q$

6.

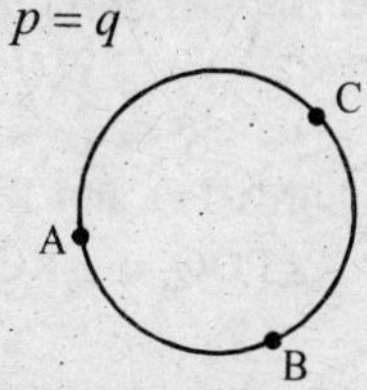

Through any three non collinear points, passes one and only one circle. A, B and C are three non-collinear points in a plane then one and only one circle passes through them.

7. Perpendicular bisector of a chord of a circle passes through the centre of the circle.

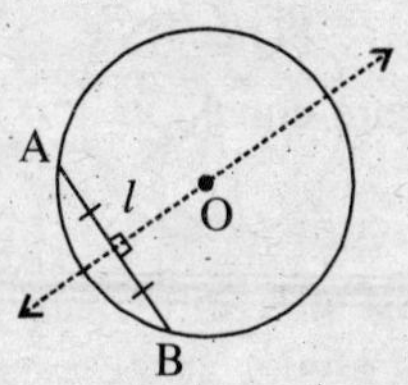

l is the $\perp$ bisector of AB $\Leftrightarrow$ l passes through O.

8.

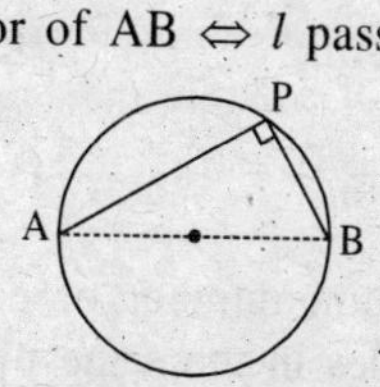

(*a*) **Theorem of Thales:** Angle in a semicircle is a right angle.

(*b*) If an arc subtends a right angle at any point in its alternate segment then it is a semicircle.

$\overparen{APB}$ is a semicircle $\Leftrightarrow \angle APB = 90°$

9. Angles in the same segment of a circle are equal

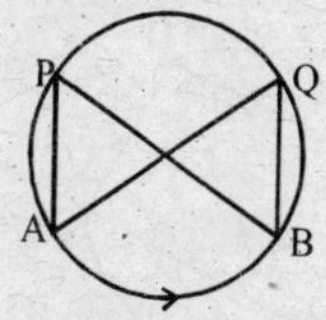

In the above figure $\angle APB = \angle AQB$

10.

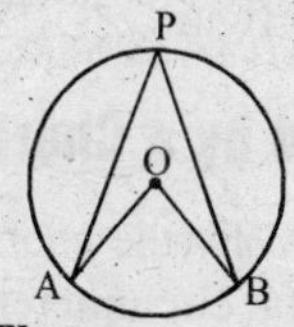

Degree Measure Theorem : Degree measure of an arc is twice the angle subtended by it at any point on the alternate segment of the circle with respect to the arc. In the above figure $\angle AOB = 2\angle APB$

11. If a line segment joining two points subtends equal angles at two other points on same side of the line containing the two points then the four points are concyclic.

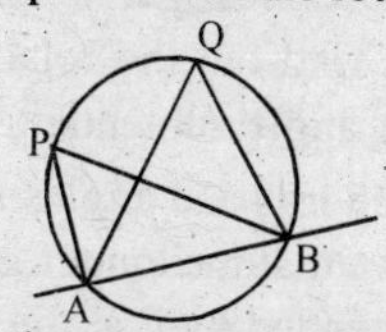

In the above figure $\angle APB = \angle AQB$, then A,B,Q and P are concylic.

Definition

A quadrilateral is said to be cyclic if all of its four vertices lie on the circle, ABCD is a cyclic quadrilateral.

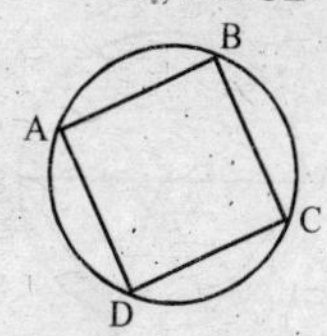

12. If in a quadrilateral the pair of opposite angles is supplementary then the quadrilateral is cyclic.
In the above figure

$\angle A + \angle C = 180°$

or $\angle B + \angle D = 180°$.

$\Rightarrow$ ABCD is cyclic quadrilateral.

13. Sum of each pair of opposite angles of a cyclic quadrilateral is 180°.

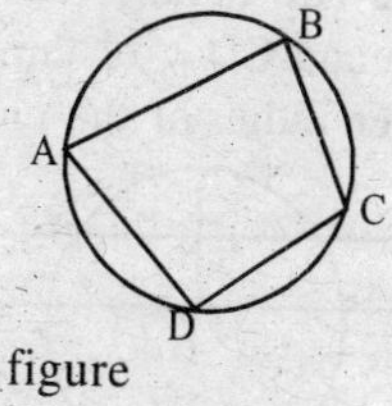

In the above figure
ABCD is cyclic quadrilateral

$\Rightarrow \quad \angle A + \angle C = 180°$

and $\angle B + \angle D = 180°$.

14. Exterior angle of a cyclic quadrilateral is equal to its opposite interior angle.

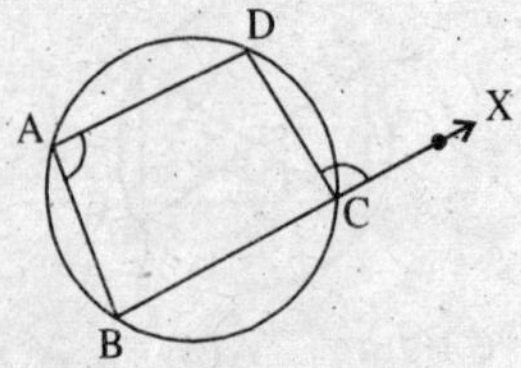

In the above figure, $\angle DCX = \angle A$

Angle subtended by a Chord

The angle subtended by the chord AB at a point C (not on the chord AB) on the circumference of the circle is $\angle ACB$. The angle subtended by chord AB at the centre O is $\angle AOB$.

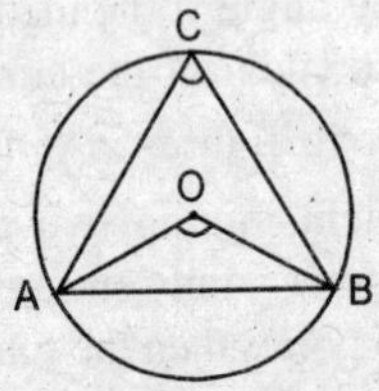

Activity: Let us find out the relation between the size of the chord and the angle subtended by it at the centre.

We draw many chords and angles subtended by them at the centre. We observe that the longer is the chord the bigger will be the angle subtended by it at the centre. We draw two equal chords and measure the angles subtended by them at the centre. We find that the angles subtended by them at the centre are equal.

Theorem 1. Equal chords of a circle subtend equal angles at the centre.

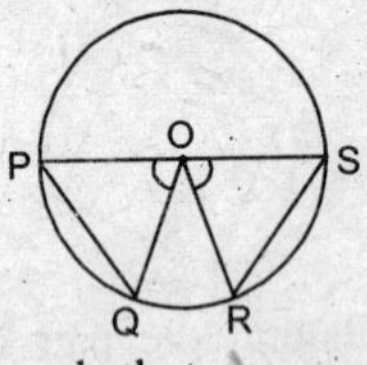

Given. A circle such that

Chord PQ = Chord RS

To prove, $\angle POQ = \angle ROS$

Proof. In ΔPOQ and ΔROS,

$PQ = RS$

$OP = OS$ = radius

$OQ = OR$ = radius

$\therefore \quad \Delta POQ \cong \Delta ROS$

(By SSS Theorem of congruence)

$\Rightarrow \quad \angle POQ = \angle ROS$ (C.P.C.T.)

$\Rightarrow$ Angles subtended by equal chords are equal.

Activity, We draw a circle with centre O and draw an angle AOB, where A and B are the points on the circle. Draw another angle $\angle POQ$ at the centre equal to $\angle AOB$. Separate these two angles AOB and POQ. If we put segment AOB on the segment POQ of the circle, we find that they cover each other.

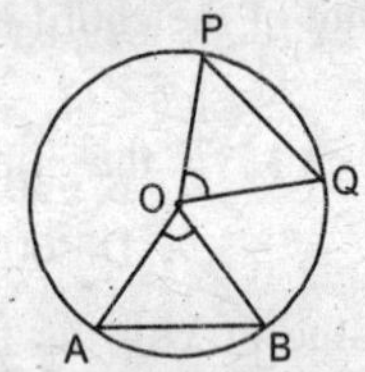

So, $AB = PQ$

Repeat this activity for other equal angles. We find the chords are equal in each case.

Theorem 2. If the angles subtended by the two chords at the centre of a circle are equal, then the chords are equal.

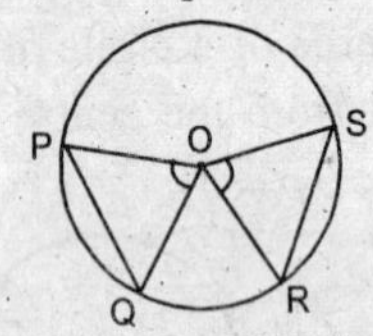

Given. Two chords PQ and RS of a circle in which,

$\angle POQ = \angle ROS$; $PQ = RS$

To prove.

Proof. In ΔPOQ and ΔROS

$OP = OR$ = radius

$\angle POQ = \angle ROS$

$OQ = OS$ = radius

$\therefore \quad \Delta POQ \cong \Delta ROS$

[By SAS Theorem of congruence]

$\Rightarrow \quad PQ = RS$ (C.P.C.T.)

Hence, Chords are equal.

EXERCISE

1. AB and CD are two parallel chords of a circle such that AB = 5 cm and CD = 11 cm. If distance between them is 3 cm then radius of the circle is

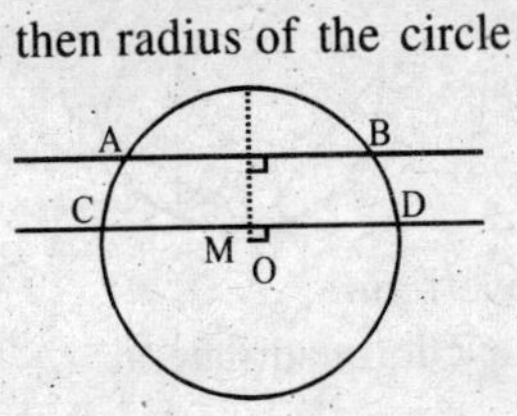

A. $2\sqrt{146}$ cm B. $\sqrt{146}$ cm

C. $\frac{\sqrt{146}}{2}$ cm D. None of these

2. The maximum number of common tangents to any pair of circles in the same plane is :

A. 4 B. 5

C. 2 D. 3

3. Find the length of a chord which is at a distance of 3 cm from the centre of a circle of radius 5 cm.

A. 2 cm B. 6 cm
C. 8 cm D. 10 cm

4. If AB and AC are two chords of a circle of radius 5 cm such that AB = AC = $4\sqrt{5}$ cm then the length of the chord BC is :

A. 8 cm B. 8.4 cm
C. 9 cm D. None of these

5. In the given figure AB is the diameter of the circle, PM bisects ∠APB then the measure of ∠ABM is :

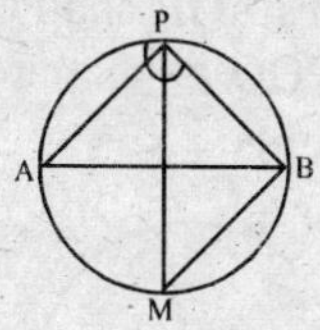

A. 45° B. 30°
C. 15° D. 60°

6. Determine the value of x in the figure given below.

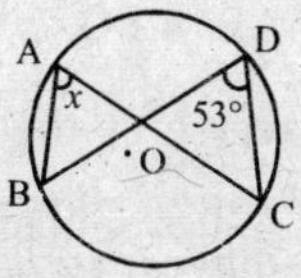

A. 53° B. 106°
C. 26.5° D. 100°

7. Determine the value of x in the figure given below.

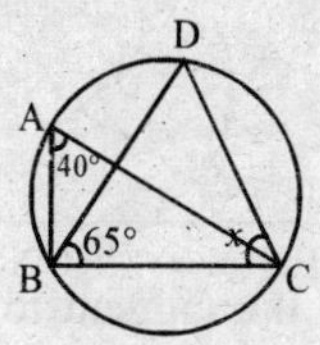

A. 40° B. 75°
C. 65° D. 105°

8. Determine the value of x in the figure given below.

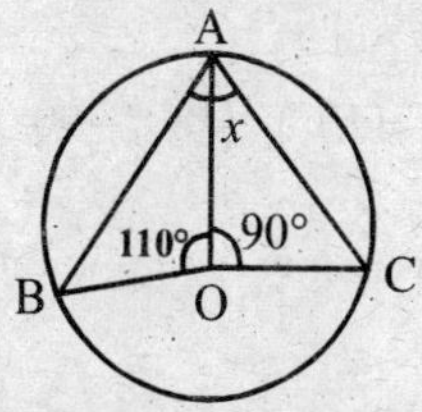

A. 80° B. 100°
C. 90° D. 110°

9. PQ is a diameter and PQRS is a cyclic quadrilateral. If ∠PSR = 150°, then measure of ∠RPQ is :

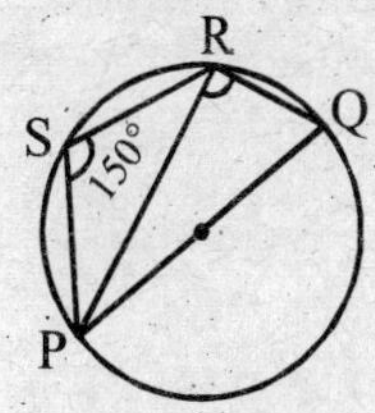

A. 90° B. 60°
C. 30° D. None of these

10. Determine the value of x in the figure given below.

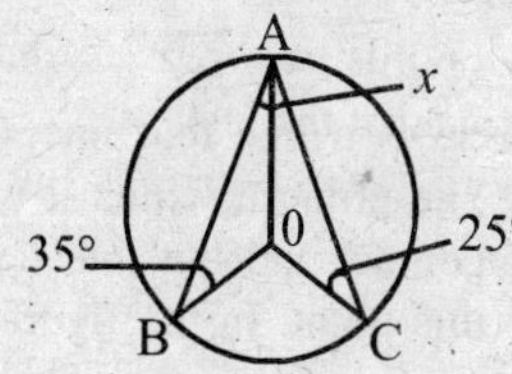

A. 35° B. 25°
C. 30° D. 60°

ANSWERS

1	2	3	4	5	6	7	8	9	10
C	A	C	A	A	A	B	A	B	D

EXPLANATORY ANSWERS

1. Let OM = x

Then $x^2 + \left(\frac{11}{2}\right)^2 = r^2$ and $(x+3)^2 + \left(\frac{5}{2}\right)^2 = r^2$

Then, $x^2 + 6x + 9 + \frac{25}{4} = x^2 + \frac{121}{4}$

$\Rightarrow 6x = 15 \Rightarrow x = 2.5$ cm

Thus, $r^2 = (2.5)^2 + \frac{121}{4} = \frac{146}{4} \Rightarrow r = \frac{\sqrt{146}}{2}$ cm

3. Length of chord = $2.\sqrt{5^2 - 3^2} = 8$ cm.

4. Let OP = x and BP = y

Then $x^2 + y^2 = 25$ and $(5+x)^2 + y^2 = 80$

Solving these two, we get, y = BP = 4 cm

Thus, BC = 8 cm.

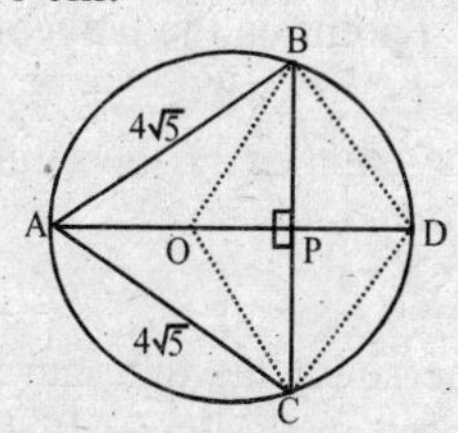

5. $\angle ABM = \angle APM = \frac{1}{2}\angle APB = \frac{1}{2} \times 90° = 45°$

6. As angle in the same segment are equal.

$x = 53°$

7. $x + 65° + 40° = 180°$

$x = 75°$

8. $x = \frac{1}{2}[(180° - 110°) + (180° - 90°)]$

$= \frac{1}{2}(70° + 90°) = 80°$

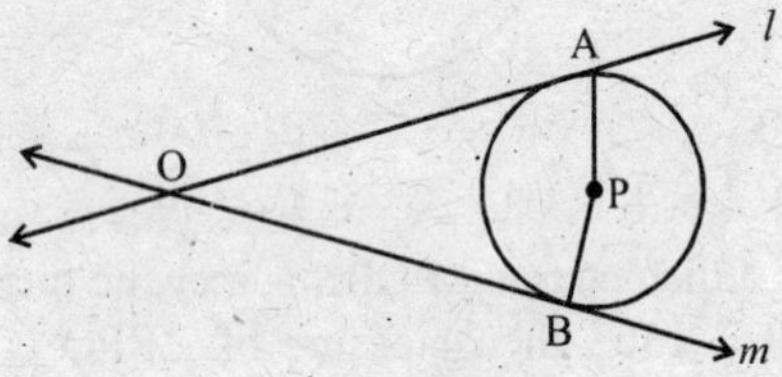

Let P be the centre of a circle touching l and m. Clearly, AP = BP.

Hence, P lies on angle bisector of ∠AOB. Hence, locus of P will be the angle bisectors of the angles formed by these intersecting lines.

9. $\angle PQR = 180° - 150° = 30°$

$\angle PRQ = 90°$ (Angle of a semicircle)

$\angle RPQ + 90° + 30° = 180°$

$\Rightarrow \angle RPQ = 60°$

10. $\angle OAB = \angle OBA (\because OA = OB)$

$\angle OAB = 35°$

Similarly, $\angle AOC = 25°$

$\therefore \angle x = 35° + 25° = 60°$

Tangent

Secant

A line which interesects a circle in two distinct points is called a **secant** of the circle. In the fig. the line l intersects the circle in two distinct points A and B. The line l is a secant to the circle.

Tangent

A tangent to a circle is a line that intersects the circle at exactly one point. The point at which it meets the circle is called its point of contact and the line (tangent) is said to touch the circle at this point. In the figure, the line l meets the circle at only point A. Here A is the point of contact.

Some Important theorems on tangent

Theorem 1: *A tangent to a circle is perpendicular to the radius throught the point of contact.*

Given: A tangent AB to a circle C(O, r) with the point P as its point of contact.

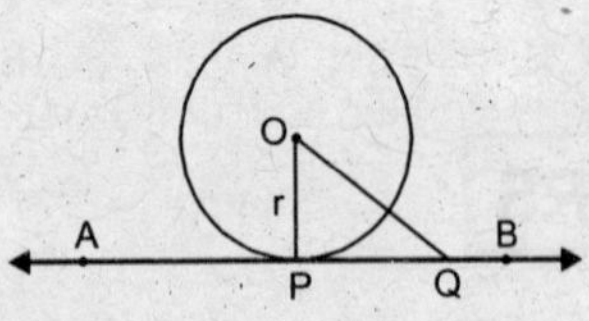

To prove: OP ⊥ AB.

Construction: Let Q be any point other that P, an AB. join OQ.

Proof: ∵ Q is a point on the tangent AB other than the point of contact P.

∴ Q lies in the exterior of the circle.

∴ OQ > OP

i.e., OP < OQ

Thus, of all the segments that can be drawn from the centre O to any point on the line AB, OP is the shortest.

We know that the shortest segment that can be drawn from a given point to a given line perpendicular from the given point to the given line.

Hence OP ⊥ AB.

Theorem 2: (Converse of theorem 1)

A line drawn through the end of a radius and perpendicular on it is tangent to the circle.

Given: A radius OP of a circle C(O, r) and a line APB perpendicular to OP.

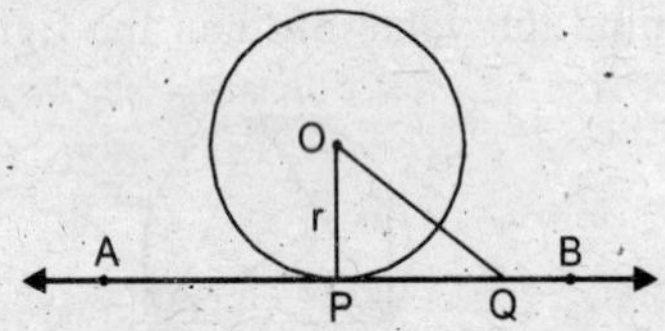

To prove: AB is the tangent to the circle at A.

Proof: Take a point Q, different from P, on line AB, since OP ⊥ AB, OQ > OP.

∴ The point Q lies outside the circle (since OP is the shortest line segment from O to AB).

Thus every point on the line AB, other P, lies outside the circle and therefore AB meets the circle only at the point P.

Hence AB is a tangent to the circle.

Theorem 3: *The lengths of the two tangents drawn from an external point to a circle are equal.*

Given: A is an external point to the circle C(O, r). AP and AQ are two tangent segments from A to the circle.

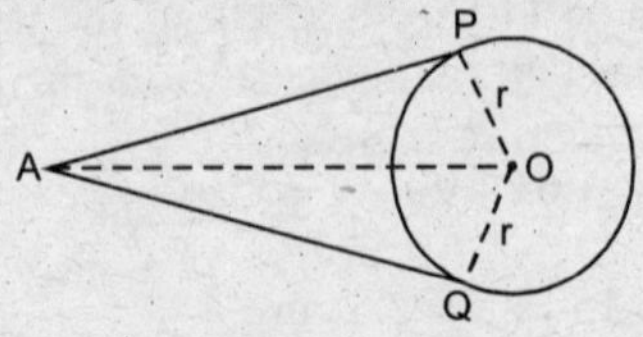

To prove: AP = AQ.

Construction: Draw line segments AP, OP and OQ.

Proof: A tangent to a circle is perpendicular to the radius through the point of contact.

∴ $\angle OPA = \angle OQA = 90°$

Now in right Δs OPA and OQA,

	OP = OQ	[each = r]
	OA = OA	[common]
∴	ΔOPA ≅ ΔOQA	[by RHS congruence rule]
∴	AP = AQ	[c.p.c.t.c.]

Common Tangents to Two circles

(*i*) Where the two circles neither intersect nor touch each other, there are FOUR common tangents, two of them are transverse & the others are direct common tangents.

(*ii*) When they intersect there are two common tangents, both of them being direct.

(*iii*) When they touch each other:

(*a*) **Externally:** there are three common tangents, two direct and one is the tangent at the point of contact.

(*b*) **Internally:** only one common tangent possible at their point of contact.

(*iv*) Length of an external common tangent & internal common tangent to the two circles is given by:

$$L_{ext} = \sqrt{d^2 - (r_1 - r_2)^2} \text{ \& } L_{int} = \sqrt{d^2 - (r_1 + r_2)^2}$$

Where d = distance between the centres of the two circles. r_1 & r_2 are the radii of the two circles.

(*v*) The direct common tangents meet at a point which divides the line joining centre of circles externally in the ratio of their radii.

Transverse common tangents meet at a point which divides the line joining centre of circles internally in the ratio of their radii.

In a plane, two circles can intersect in two points, one point, or no points. Coplanar circles that intersect in one point are called **tangent circles.** Coplanar circles that have a common center are called **concentric.**

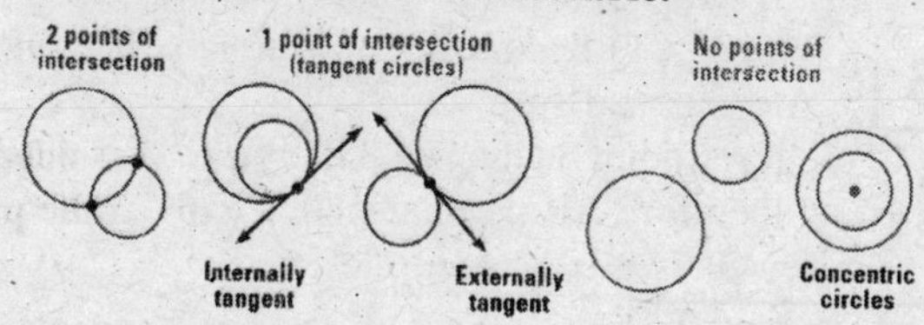

A line or segment that is tangent to two coplanar circles is called a **common tangent.** A *common internal tangent* intersects the segment that joins the centers of the two circles. A *common external tangent* does not intersect the segment that joins the centers of the two circles.

Example: Tell whether the common tangents are internal or external.

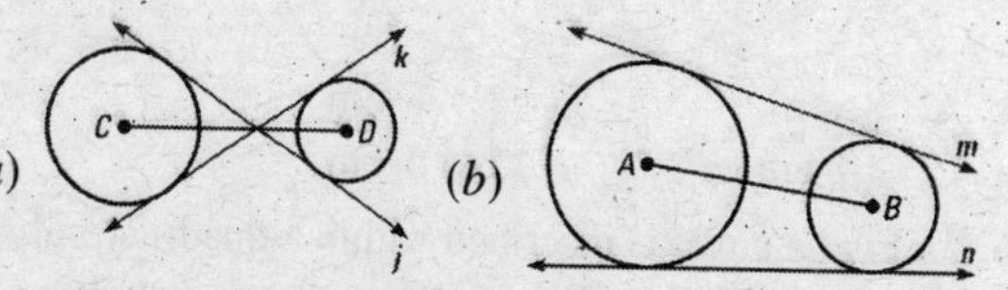

Solution: (*a*) The lines j and k intersect $\overline{CD}$, so they are common internal tangents.

(*b*) The lines m and n do not intersect $\overline{AB}$, so they are common external tangents.

In a plane, the **interior of a circle** consists of the points that are inside the circle. The **exterior of a circle** consists of the points that are outside the circle.

Example: Give the center and the radius of each circle. Describe the intersection of the two circles and describe all common tangents.

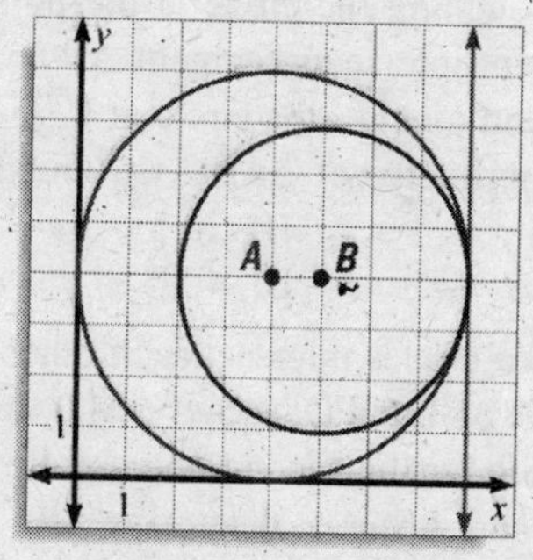

Solution: The center of ⊙A is A(4, 4) and its radius is 4. The center of ⊙B is B(5, 4) and its radius is 3. The two circles have only one point of intersection. It is the point (8, 4). The vertical line $x = 8$ is the only common tangent of the two circles.

EXERCISE

1. From a point Q, the length of the tangent to a circle is 24 cm and the distance from the centre is 25 cm. The radius of the circle is

A. 7 cm B. 12 cm
C. 15 cm D. 24.5 cm

2. In the given figure, if TP and TQ are the two tangents to a circle with centre O and that ∠POQ = 110°, then ∠PTQ is equal to

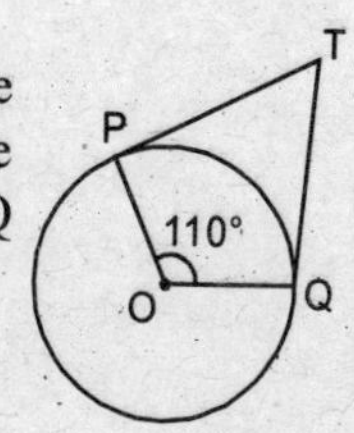

A. 60° B. 70°
C. 80° D. 90°

3. If tangents PA and PB from a point P to a circle with centre O are inclined to each other at angle of 80°, then ∠POA is equal to

A. 50° B. 60°
C. 70° D. 80°

4. In Fig., a circle touches all the four sides of a quadrilateral ABCD whose sides AB = 6 cm, BC = 7 cm and CD = 4 cm. Find AD

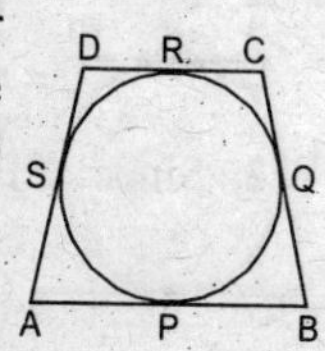

A. 2 cm B. 5 cm
C. 3 cm D. 4 cm

5. If AB, AC, PQ are tangents in the figure and AB = 5 cm. The perimeter of ΔAPQ is

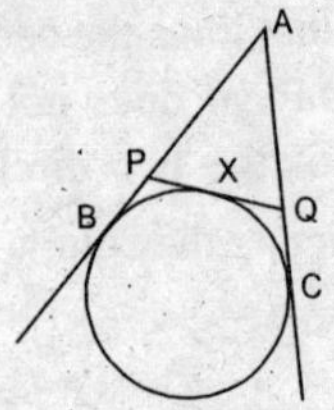

A. 8 cm B. 6 cm
C. 10 cm D. 5 cm

6. In Fig., a circle is inscribed within a quadrilateral ABCD. Given that BC = 38 cm, BQ = 27 cm and DC = 25 cm and that AD is perpendicular to DC. The radius of the circle is

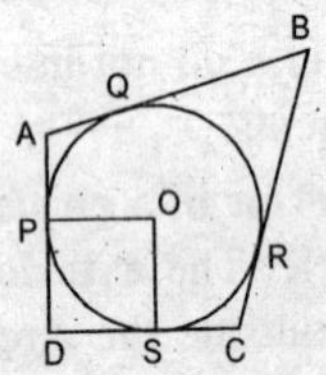

A. 10 cm B. 14 cm
C. 8 cm D. 12 cm

7. Two tangents are drawn to a circle from an external point A, touching the circle at the points P and Q. A third tangent intersects segment AP at B and segment AQ at C and touches the circle at R. If AQ = 10 units, then the perimeter of ΔABC (in units) is
A. 22.0 B. 20.5
C. 20.0 D. 40.0

8. In Fig., two circles intersect each other at points P and Q. From A on line PQ, secant AMD for one circle and secant ASR for the second one are drawn. If AM = 3, MD = 5 and AS = 4, determine SR.

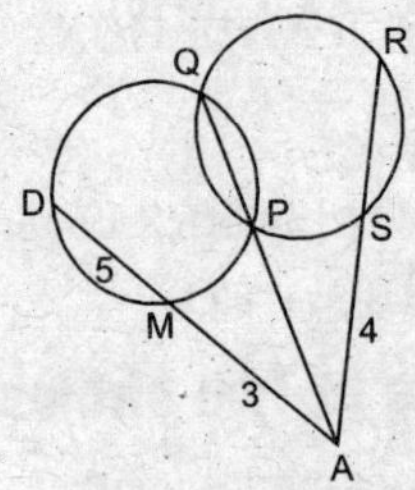

A. 2 cm B. 4 cm
C. 3 cm D. 1 cm

9. In the figure, KLMN is a cyclic quadrilateral and PQ is a tangent to the circle at K. If LN is a diameter of the circle. $\angle KLN = 30°$ and $\angle MNL = 60°$. Determine $\angle QKN$

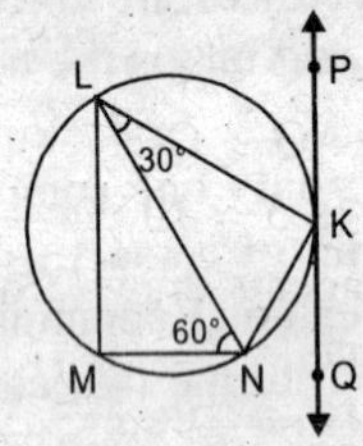

A. 30° B. 60°
C. 90° D. 100°

10. In the given Fig., PQ is tangent and O is the centre of the circle. Find EP is OP = 21, OQ = 9 and OM $\sqrt{80}$.

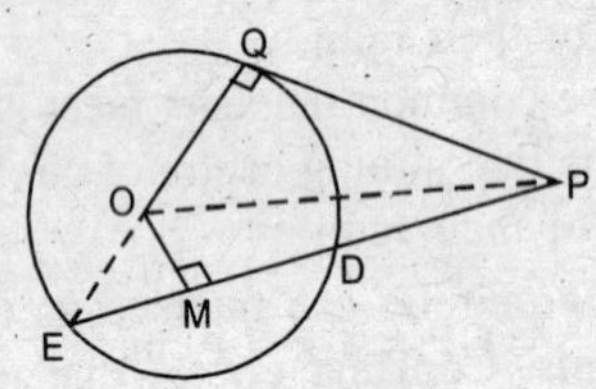

A. 10 B. 20
C. 30 D. 40

ANSWERS

1	2	3	4	5	6	7	8	9	10
A	B	A	C	C	B	C	A	A	B

EXPLANATORY ANSWERS

1. In rt. $\angle d$ ΔOTQ,

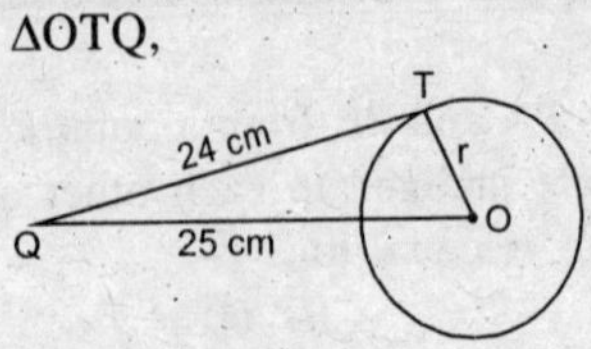

$$OT = \sqrt{OQ^2 - OT^2}$$
$$= \sqrt{25^2 - 24^2} = \sqrt{625 - 576} = \sqrt{49} = 7 \text{ cm.}$$

2. Since $\angle POQ + \angle PTQ = 180°$

[$\because$ $\angle OPT = 90°$, $\angle OQT = 90°$]

$\Rightarrow$ $110° + \angle PTQ = 180°$

$\Rightarrow$ $\angle PTQ = 180° - 110° = 70°$.

3. Since $\angle APB = 80°$

$\angle AOB = 180° - 80° = 100°$

$\angle PAO = \angle PBO = 90°$

Since OP bisects $\angle AOB$

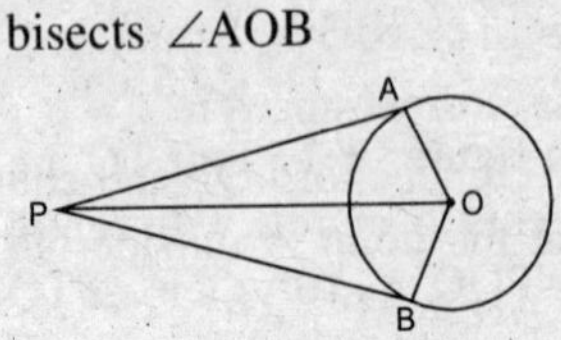

$$\angle AOP = \frac{1}{2}(100°) = 50° \text{ i.e. } \angle POA = 50°.$$

4. AD = AS + DS = AP + DR

[∵ AS = AP and DS = DR]

= (AB – BP) + (CD – RC)

= AB + CD – (BP + RC)

= AB + CD – (BQ + CQ)

[∵ BP = BQ, RC = CQ]

= AB + CD – BC = 6 + 4 – 7 = 3 cm.

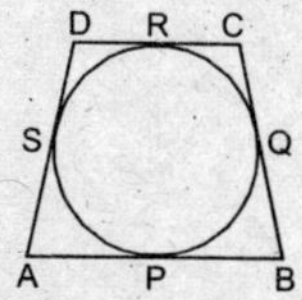

5. Since AB and AC are the tangents from the same point A

∴ AB = AC = 5 cm

Similarly, BP = PX and XQ = QC

Perimeter of ΔAPQ

= AP + AQ + PQ

= AP + AQ + (PX + XQ)

= (AP + PX) + (AQ + XQ)

= (AP + BP) + (AQ + QC)

= AB + AC = 5 + 5 = 10 cm.

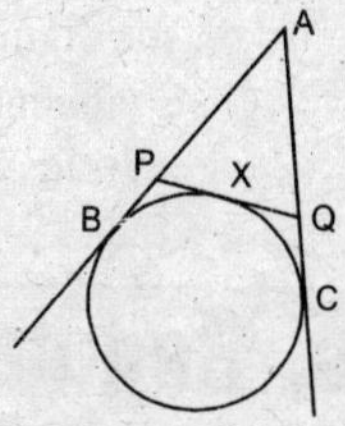

6. ∵ Lengths of tangents drawn from an external point to a circle are equal

∴ BQ = BR = 27 cm

Let x be the radius of the circle

∴ OP = OS = PD = x

CR = BC – BR

= 38 – 27 = 11 cm

Now CS = CR = 11 cm

[∵ Length of tangents from an external point to a circle are equal]

∴ DS = CD – CS

= 25 cm – 11 cm = 14 cm

But DS = OP = x = 14 cm.

Hence radius = OP = 14 cm.

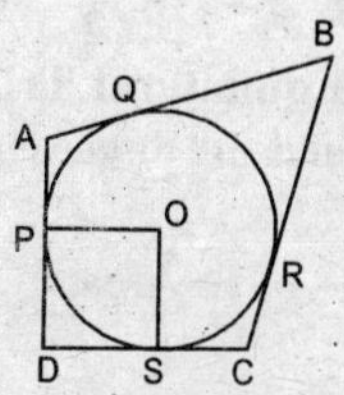

7. Since the tangents to a circle from an external point are equal in length

AP = AQ = 10 units

and BP = BR, CQ = CR

Adding these, we get,

BP + CQ = BR + CR = BC

Adding AB and AC to both sides, we get

BP + CQ + AB + AC = BC + AB + AC

⇒ (BP + AB) + (CQ + AC) = AB + BC + AC

⇒ AP + AQ = Perimeter of ΔABC

⇒ (10 + 10) units = Perimeter of ΔABC

∴ Perimeter of ΔABC = 20 units.

∴ (*iii*) is the correct answer.

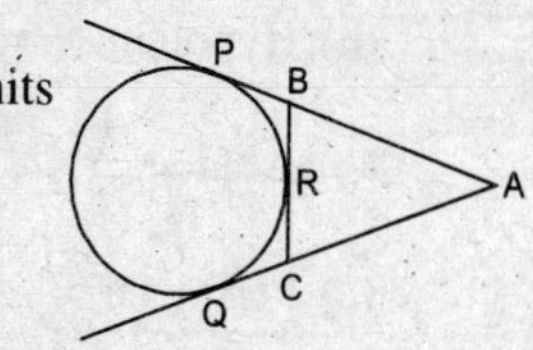

8. In the larger circle, chord QP and chord DM intersect each other at the point A outside the circle

∴ AM × AD = AP ...(1)

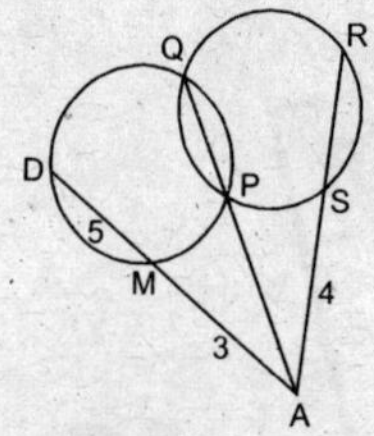

Again in the smaller circle, chord QP and chord RS intersect each other at the point A outside the circle.

∴ AS × AR = AP × AQ ...(2)

∴ AM × AD = AS × AR ...(3)

[From (1) and (2)]

Now AD = AM + MD

= 3 + 5 = 8

∴ From (3), 3 × 8 = 4 × AR

⇒ $AR = \frac{24}{4} = 6$

But AS + SR = AR

∴ 4 + SR = 6,

SR = 6 – 4 = 2.

9. KN is a chord through the point of contact K.

∴ ∠QKN = ∠KLN = 30°

[∠*s* in the alt. segment are equal]

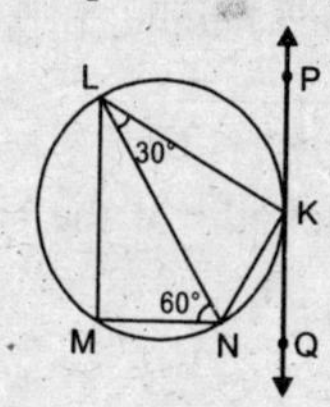

10. Join OQ and OE

In ΔOPQ, m ∠OQP = 90°

∴ $OQ^2 + QP^2 = OP^2$ [By Pythagoras Theorem]

⇒ $(9)^2 + QP^2 = (21)^2$

⇒ $QP^2 = (21)^2 - (9)^2 = 360$

In rt. ∠*d* ΔOME,

$OM^2 + EM^2 = OE^2$

⇒ $80 + (EM)^2 = (9)^2$

⇒ $EM^2 = 81 - 80 = 1$

⇒ $EM = +\sqrt{1} = 1$

∴ ED = 2EM = 2 × 1 = 2

Let EP = x

Then $PQ^2 = PD \times PE$

[Tangent secant second point theorem]

∴ $360 = (x - 2)x$

⇒ $x^2 - 2x - 360 = 0$

⇒ $(x - 20)(x + 18) = 0$

⇒ $x = 20, -18$

But $x \neq -18$

Hence EP = 20.

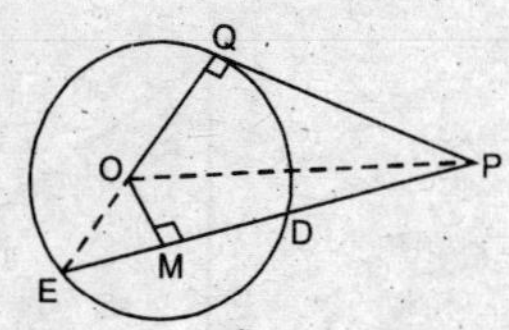

CHAPTER 11

Mensuration

Triangle, Quadrilaterals, Regular Polygons

In mensuration we often have to deal with the problem of finding the areas and perimeters of plane figures.

Triangle

1. Perimeter = 3 × side

2. Area = $\frac{1}{2} \times \text{base} \times \text{height}$, or

Area = $\sqrt{s(s-a)(s-b)(s-c)}$

where a, b, c, are the lengths of the sides of triangle and $s = \frac{a+b+c}{2}$

Right Angled Triangle : It is one where one of the angles is right angle, i.e., 90°.

1. $(\text{Hypotenuse})^2 = (\text{Perpendicular})^2 + (\text{Base})^2$

2. Area = $\frac{1}{2} \times \text{Base} \times \text{Perpendicular}$

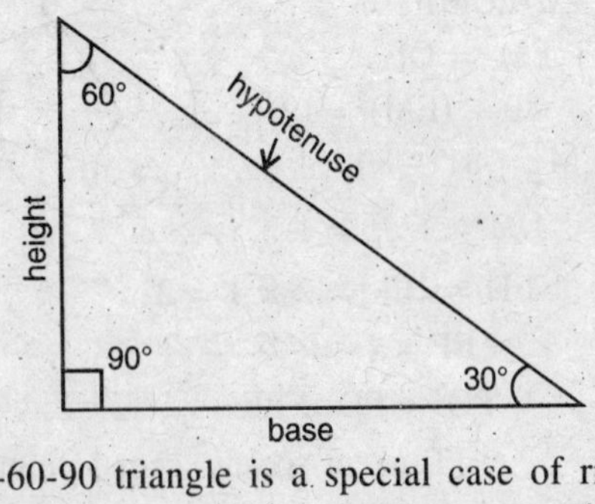

N.B. : 30-60-90 triangle is a special case of right angled triangle, where the three angles are equal to 30°, 60° and 90°.

Here,

3. Side opposite to the angle 30° $= \frac{1}{2} \times \text{Hypotenuse}$

4. Side opposite to the angle 60° $= \frac{\sqrt{3}}{2} \times \text{Hypotenuse}$

Equilateral Triangle : All three sides are equal in length and all three angles are equal to 60°

1. Area = $\frac{\sqrt{3}}{4} \times (\text{Side})^2$ 2. Area = $\frac{(\text{Height})^2}{\sqrt{3}}$

3. Height = $\frac{\sqrt{3}}{2} \times \text{side}$ 4. Perimeter = 3 × side

Isosceles Triangle : Two sides are equal in lengths.

1. Area = $\frac{b}{4}\sqrt{4a^2 - b^2}$

   where a = lengths of opposite sides

   b = length of unequal side

2. In an isosceles right triangle,

   (*a*) Hypotenuse = $\sqrt{2} \times \text{congruent side (a)}$

   (*b*) Area = $\frac{1}{2} \times a^2$

   (*c*) Perimeter = $\sqrt{2} \times a(\sqrt{2}+1)$

Quadrilaterals

Rectangle:

1. Area = length(l) × breadth(b)
2. Perimeter = $2(l + b)$
3. Diagonal = $\sqrt{l^2 + b^2}$
4. Area of the path (inside of the rectangle) $= 2x\ (l + b - 2x)$
   where, x is the width of path.
5. Area of the path (Outside of the rectangle) = $2x\ (l + b + 2x)$

Square:

1. Area = $(\text{Side})^2$
2. Perimeter = 4 × side
3. Diagonal = $\text{side} \times \sqrt{2}$
4. Area of path (outside of square) = $4x \times (a + x)$ [where a = side, x = width of path]
5. Area of path (inside of square) = $4x \times (a - x)$

Parallelogram: In parallelogram opposite sides are parallel and equal. The two diagonals are not always equal but they bisect each other at the point of intersection.

Area = Base × Height.

Trapezium : It is a quadrilateral whose one pair of opposite sides is parallel. Other two opposite sides are oblique.

1. Area = $\frac{1}{2} \times \text{Height} \times (\text{Sum of parallel sides})$. Here, height is the distance between the two parallel sides.
2. Median = $\left(\frac{1}{2} \times \text{Sum of parallel side}\right)$. Here, median is the segment joining the midpoints of oblique sides.
3. Height = $\frac{2}{K}\sqrt{s(s-k)(s-c)(s-d)}$

(where $k = a - b$, *i.e.*, the difference between the parallel sides and c and d are the two non-parallel sides.)

Also $s = \frac{k+c+d}{2}$

Rhombus : It is parallelogram whose all sides are equal and diagonals are bisect each other at right angle.

1. Area = $\frac{1}{2} \times \text{Product of diagonals}$
2. Side = $\sqrt{\left(\frac{d_1}{2}\right)^2 + \left(\frac{d_2}{2}\right)^2}$,

where d_1 and d_2 are diagonals
3. Perimeter = 4 × side
4. Area of a rhombus (with one side and one diagonal given)

$= \text{diagonal} \times \sqrt{(\text{side})^2 - \left(\frac{\text{diagonal}}{2}\right)^2}$

5. Other diagonal

$= 2 \times \sqrt{(\text{side})^2 - \left(\frac{\text{diagonal}}{2}\right)^2}$

Quadrilateral : Area = $\frac{1}{2} \times \text{One diagonal} \times$

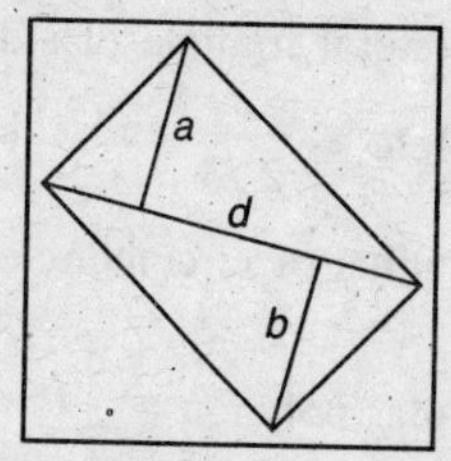

(Sum of perpendicular to it from the opposite vertices)

$= \frac{1}{2} \times d \times (a+b)$

Circle :

1. Diameter = 2 × Radius
2. Area = $\pi r^2 = \frac{\pi}{4} d^2$

[where d = diameter = $\sqrt{\frac{4A}{\pi}}$
3. Circumference = $2\pi r = \pi d$
4. Radius = $\frac{\text{Circumference}}{2\pi} = \frac{\sqrt{\text{Area}}}{\pi}$
5. Length of an Arc = $\frac{\theta}{360°} \times 2\pi r$
6. Area of sector = $\frac{\theta}{360°} \times \pi r^2 = \frac{1}{2} \times \text{Arc} \times r$
7. Area of the ring or circular path $= \pi (R + r)(R - r)$

Remember some tricks for plane figures.

(*i*) If area related each side is increased by $a\%$, then

(*a*) Percentage increase in the area

$= 2a + \frac{a^2}{100}$

(*b*) $\frac{\text{New Area}}{\text{Old Area}} = \left(1 + \frac{a}{100}\right)^2$

(*ii*) If area related to each side is decreased by $a\%$, then

(*a*) Percentage decrease in area = $2a - \frac{a^2}{100}$

(*b*) $\frac{\text{New Area}}{\text{Old Area}} = \left(1 - \frac{a}{100}\right)^2$

(*iii*) If the perimeter of a rectangle, circle, quadrilateral and triangle are same, then area of the circle will be the largest.

Polygon

1. Interior angle + Exterior angle = 180°
2. Each interior angle = $\left(\frac{2n-4}{n}\right) \times 90°$

where n = number of sides
3. Sum of Exterior angles = 360°
4. Perimeter = Number of sides × Length of side.

5. For an equilateral triangle of side 'a' (*a*) radius of inscribed circle = $\frac{a}{2\sqrt{3}}$ and side of the triangle = $2\sqrt{3}r$, (*b*) radius of circumcircle = $\frac{a}{\sqrt{3}}$

6. Area of regular polygon = $\frac{1}{2}$(No. of sides) (Radius of the incribed circle)

7. Area of regular hexagon

$$= \frac{3\sqrt{3}}{2}(\text{side})^2 = 2.598\ (\text{side})^2$$

8. Area of a regular octagon

$$= 2(\sqrt{2}+1)(\text{side})^2 = 4.828\ (\text{side})^2$$

9. Area of cyclic quadrilateral A

$$= \sqrt{s(s-a)(s-b)(s-c)(s-d)}$$

where, $s = \frac{a+b+c+d}{2}$ and,

$\angle A + \angle C = \angle B + \angle D = 180°$

10. For circum-circle, if a is the length of each side of a regular polygon and R is the circum-radius, then

(*a*) $R = \frac{a}{2}\text{cosec}\left(\frac{180°}{n}\right)$

(*b*) Area of the polygon = $\frac{1}{4}na^2\cot\left(\frac{180°}{n}\right)$, or

(*c*) Area of the polygon

$$= nR^2\sin\left(\frac{180°}{n}\right)\cos\left(\frac{180°}{n}\right)$$

(*d*) Area of the circum-circle of n-sided regular polygon

$$= \frac{\pi}{4}a^2\text{cosec}^2\left(\frac{180°}{n}\right)$$

11. For in-circle, if a is the length of a side of a regular polygon and r is the radius of the in-circle, then

(*a*) $r = \frac{a}{2}\cot\left(\frac{180°}{n}\right)$

(*b*) Area of the polygon = $\pi r^2\cot\left(\frac{180°}{n}\right)$

(*c*) Area of the in-circle of an n-sided regular polygon

$$= \frac{\pi}{4}a^2\cot^2\left(\frac{180°}{n}\right)$$

(*d*) Radius of the in-circle of a regular hexagon = $\frac{\sqrt{3}}{4}\times a^2$

(*e*) Area of the in-circle = $\frac{3}{4}\pi a^2$

EXERCISE

1. A rectangle measures 50 cm × 25 cm. Its area is
   A. 1150 sq. cm B. 1250 sq. cm
   C. 1275 sq. cm D. 1280 sq. cm

2. A field is in the form of a square whose perimeter is 580 m. Area of this field is
   A. 20025 sq. m B. 20225 sq. m
   C. 30025 sq. m D. 19975 sq. cm

3. Find the area of the square whose each side measures 20 cm.
   A. 300 sq. cm B. 380 sq. cm
   C. 360 sq. cm D. 400 sq. cm

4. Area of a circle is 154 sq. cm. Its circumference will be
   A. 44 cm B. 48 cm
   C. 54 cm D. 68 cm

5. The base and the height of a triangle is 8 cm and 10 cm respectively. Its area will be
   A. 40 sq. cm B. 20 sq. cm
   C. 49 sq. cm D. 64 sq. cm

6. If it is given that the parallel sides of a trapezium are 15 m and 25 m while the distance between them is 10 m. its area will be
   A. 150 sq. m B. 225 sq. m
   C. 200 sq. m D. 270 sq. m

7. Perimeter of a rectangular field is 760 m and its length and breadth are in the ratio 11 : 8. Area of this rectangular field is
   A. 35200 sq. m B. 34700 sq. m
   C. 35600 sq. m D. 45200 sq. m

8. If side of a square is reduced by 50%, its area will be reduced by
   A. 50% B. 75%
   C. 80% D. 60%

9. If area of a square is equal to the area of a rectangle 6.4 m long and 2.5 m wide, then each side of this square measures
   A. 8 m B. 5.4 m
   C. 3.8 m D. 4 m

10. If perimeter of a right angled triangle is six times its smallest side, then the three sides of this triangle are in the ratio of
    A. 13 : 5 : 12 B. 13 : 12 : 5
    C. 12 : 5 : 13 D. 13 : 5 : 10

ANSWERS

1	2	3	4	5	6	7	8	9	10
B	A	D	A	A	C	A	B	D	B

EXPLANATORY ANSWERS

1. Area of the rectangle

$= l \times b = 50 \times 25 = 1250$ sq. cm

2. Perimeter of the square $= 4 \times$ side

According to question :

$$4 \times \text{side} = 580 \Rightarrow \text{side} = \frac{580}{4} = 145 \text{ m}$$

$\therefore$ Area $= (\text{side})^2 = (145)^2 = 20025$ sq. m.

3. Area of the square $= (\text{side})^2 = (20)^2 = 400$ sq. cm.

4. Area of the circle $= \pi r^2$

$$\therefore \quad \pi r^2 = 154$$

$$\Rightarrow \quad r^2 = \frac{154 \times 7}{22}$$

$$\Rightarrow \quad r^2 = 7 \times 7 \Rightarrow r = 7 \text{ cm}$$

$\therefore$ Circumference of the circle

$$= 2\pi r = 2 \times \frac{22}{7} \times 7 = 44 \text{ cm.}$$

5. Area of the triangle

$$= \frac{1}{2} \times \text{base} \times \text{height} = \frac{1}{2} \times 8 \times 10 = 40 \text{ sq. cm.}$$

6. Area of the trapezium

$$= \frac{1}{2} \times (\text{sum of the parallel sides}) \times \text{distance between them}$$

$$= \frac{1}{2} \times (15 + 25) \times 10 = \frac{1}{2} \times 40 \times 10 = 200 \text{ sq. m.}$$

7. Suppose length and breadth of the rectangular field are $11x$ m and $8x$ m.

$\therefore$ Perimeter of the field

$$= 2(11x + 8x) = 2 \times 19x = 38x \text{ m.}$$

According to question :

Perimeter of the field = 760 m

$$\therefore \quad 38x = 760 \Rightarrow x = \frac{760}{38} = 20$$

$\therefore$ Length of the field $= 11 \times 20 = 220$ m

Breadth of the field $= 8 \times 20 = 160$ m

$\therefore$ Area of the field $= 220 \times 160 = 35200$ sq.m.

8. Suppose side of the square $= x$ m

In the first case :

Area of the square $= x^2$ sq. m.

In the second case :

On effecting 50% reduction in the side of the square,

Side of the new square $= x - 50\%$ of $x = \frac{x}{2}$ m

$\therefore$ Area of the new square $= \left(\frac{x}{2}\right)^2 = \frac{x^2}{4}$ sq.m.

$\therefore$ Reduction in area of the square

$$= x^2 - \frac{x^2}{4} = \frac{3x^2}{4} \text{ sq. m.}$$

$$\therefore \text{ Percentage reduction} = \frac{3x^2/4}{x^2} \times 100 = 75\%$$

Hence, area of the square will be reduced by 75%.

9. Area of the rectangle $= 6.4 \times 2.5 = 16.00$ sq.m.

According to question :

Area of the square = Area of the rectangle

$\therefore$ Area of the square = 16 sq. m.

$\therefore$ Side of the square $= \sqrt{16} = \sqrt{4 \times 4} = 4$ m.

10. Suppose, the three sides of the triangle are a, b and c and a is the largest while c is the smallest side of the triangle.

$$\therefore \quad a^2 = b^2 + c^2 \quad \text{... (i)}$$

Perimeter of the triangle $= a + b + c$

According to question :

$$(a + b + c) = c \times 6$$

$$\Rightarrow \quad a + b = 5c \quad \text{... (ii)}$$

From equation *(i)*, $a^2 - b^2 = c^2$

$$\Rightarrow (a + b)(a - b) = c^2$$

$$\Rightarrow \quad 5c(a - b) = c^2$$

$$\Rightarrow \quad a - b = \frac{c}{5} \quad [\because a + b = 5c] \quad \text{... (iii)}$$

From equation *(ii)* and *(iii)*,

$$a + b = 5c, \; a - b = \frac{c}{5}$$

$$\Rightarrow \quad 2a = 5c + \frac{c}{5}$$

$$= \frac{26c}{5} \Rightarrow a = \frac{26c}{10} = \frac{13}{5}c$$

$$\Rightarrow \quad a : c = 13 : 5$$

on substituting the value of a in equation *(ii)*

$$b = 5c - \frac{13c}{5} = \frac{12c}{5}$$

$$\Rightarrow \quad b : c = 12 : 5$$

$$\therefore \quad a : b : c = 13 : 12 : 5$$

Hence, the three sides of the right angled triangle are in the ratio of 13 : 12 : 5.

Prism; Right Circular Cone; Right Circular Cylinder; Sphere; Hemisphere; Right Pyramid; Rectangular Parallelepiped

In mensuration we often have to deal with the problem of finding the volume of solid figure.

Cuboid : A cuboid has six faces, each one a ractangle. It has 12 edges. For example, a rectangular brick.

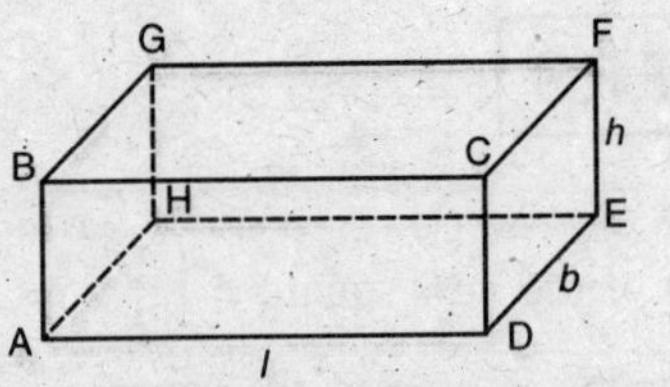

Let length = l, Breadth = b and height = h, then,

1. Volume = (Length × Breadth × Height)
2. Whole surface = $2(lb + bh + lh)$
3. Diagonal = $\sqrt{l^2+b^2+h^2}$
4. Area of 4 walls of a room = $2 \times h\ (l + b)$

Cube : In a cube, Length = Breadth = Height

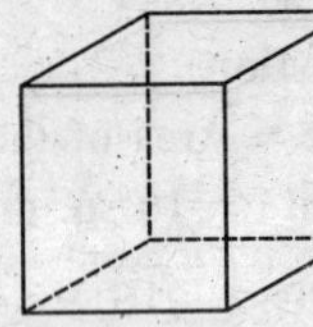

1. Volume = $(l)^3$
2. Length = $\sqrt[3]{\text{Volume}}$
3. Whole Surface area = $6\ l^2$
4. Diagonal = $l \times \sqrt{3}$
5. Lateral surface area = $4\ l^2$

Cylinder :

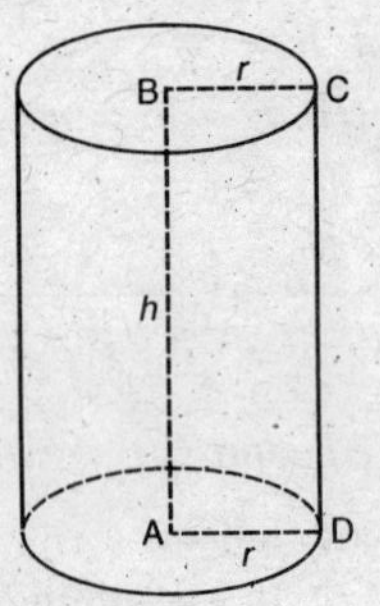

1. Volume = $\pi r^2 h$
2. Curved surface Area = $2\pi rh$
3. Total surface area = $2\pi r(r + h)$
   where r = radius, h = height
4. Curved surface of hollow cylinder
   $= 2\pi h\ (r_1 + r_2)$
5. Total surface of hollow cylinder
   $= 2\pi h\ (r_1 + r_2) + 2\pi\ (r_1^2 - r_2^2)$
6. Volume of hollow cylinder
   $= \pi h\left(r_1^2 - r_2^2\right)$
   where r_1 = outer radius
   r_2 = inner radius

Spherical Cell :

1. Volume = $\frac{4}{3}\pi\left(R^3 - r^3\right)$
2. Total surface area= $4\pi(R^2 - r^2)$
   where R = Outer radius
   r = Inner radius

Sphere

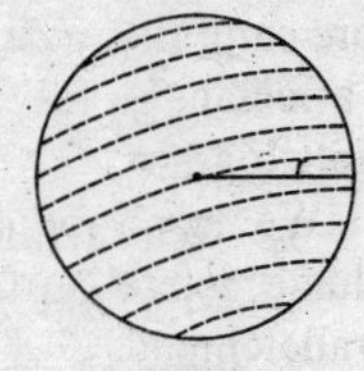

1. Volume = $\frac{4}{3}\pi r^3$
2. Surface area = $4\pi r^2$

Semi-Sphere

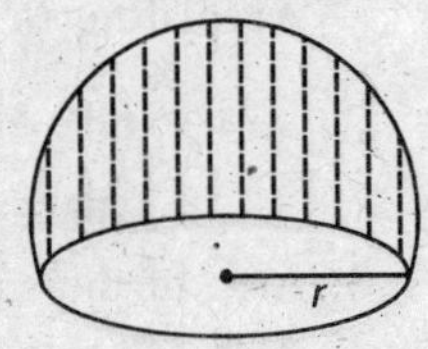

1. Volume = $\frac{2}{3}\pi r^3$
2. Curved surface area = $2\pi r^2$
3. Total surface area = $3\pi r^2$

Cone :

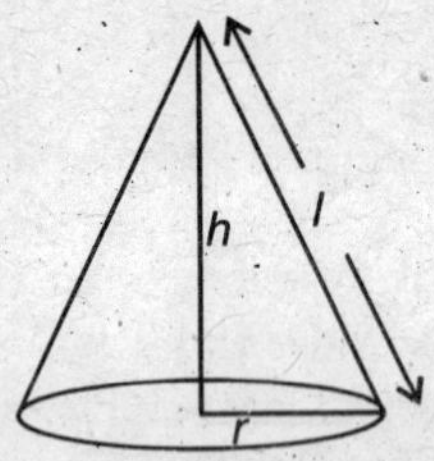

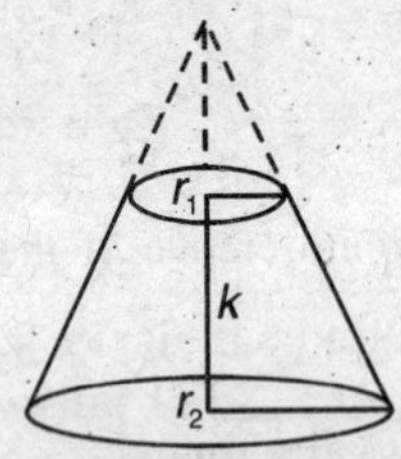

1. Slant height $(l) = \sqrt{r^2+h^2}$
2. Volume = $\frac{1}{3}\pi r^2 h$
3. Curved surface area = πrl
4. Total surface area = $\pi r\ (l + r)$
5. If the thickness of the frustum of a cone be k and the radii of its ends are r_1 and r_2, then
   (i) Slant height of the frustum of cone
   $= \sqrt{K^2+(r_1-r_2)^2}$
   (ii) Curved surface of the frustum = $\pi(r_1 + r_2)\ l$.
   (iii) Volume = $\frac{\pi K}{3}\left(r_1^2+r_1r_2+r_2^2\right)$

Right Pyramid

1. Volume = $\frac{1}{3}$(area of the base) × height
2. Lateral surface area
   $= \frac{1}{2}$(Perimeter of the base) × Slant height
3. Total surface area = 2 (Area of one end) + Lateral surface area

Right Prism

1. Volume = Area of the base × Height
2. Lateral surface Area = Perimeter of the Base × Height
3. Total surface Area = 2 (Area of one end) + Lateral surface area.

Rectangular Parallelepiped

Sometimes also referred to as "Rhomboid", a parallelepiped is a 3-D shape moulded by 6 parallelograms. If observed more carefully, as a cube relates to a square, a cuboid relates to a rectangle, the same way a parallelepiped is related to parallelogram.

We have the following formula for finding out the volume, lateral surface area and surface area of rectangular parallelepiped.

The formulas are:

Volume = abc

Surface area = $2ab + 2bc + 2ac$

Diagonal = $\sqrt{a^2 + b^2}$

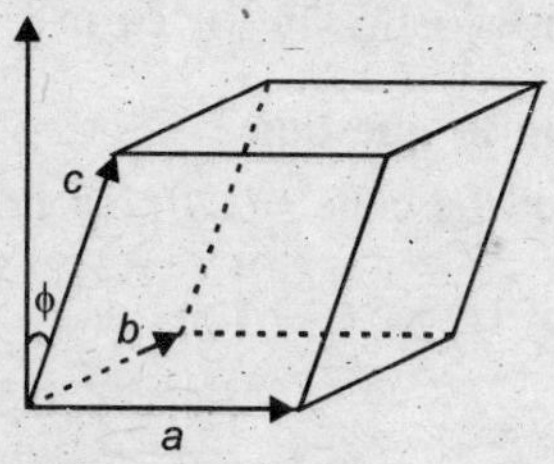

Example: Counting 38 cu. ft. of coal to a ton, how many tons will a coal bin 19 ft. long, 6 ft. wide, and 9 ft. deep contain, when level full?

Solution: The volume of a rectangular parallelepiped is given by the formula

$$V = L \times W \times H$$

Substitute the values of length, width and height of a tin, we have

$$V = L \times W \times H$$
$$V = (19ft)\ (6R.)\ (9\ ft.)$$
$$V = 1026\ R^3$$

The density of a substance is given by the formula

$$\rho = \frac{W}{V}$$

where, ρ is the density, W is the weight, and V is the volume of a substance respectively.

$$W = V \times \rho$$

Therefore, the weight of a coal in a bin is:

$$W = (1026\,R^3)\left(\frac{1\ \text{ton}}{38n^3}\right)$$

W = 27 tons.

Example: The base face of a parallelepiped has opposite sides measuring 5 inches and 10 inches. The height of the parallelepiped is 4 inches. Find the cost of painting its walls from outside at a cost of INR 1.5 per square inch.

Solution: We need to find the lateral surface area first, therefore;

LSA = Perimeter of base × height

LSA = 2 (5 + 10) + 6

LSA = 180 sq. inch

Cost of painting = Lateral surface area × cost per square inch

Cost of painting the walls = 180 × 1.5 = ₹ 270.

EXERCISE

1. A solid in the form of a cuboid is 4 cm × 3 cm × 2 cm. Its volume will be
A. 20 cu cm B. 22 cu cm
C. 28 cu cm D. 24 cu cm

2. A reservoir is 3 m long, 2 m wide and 1 m deep. Its capacity in litres is
A. 8000 litres B. 10000 litres
C. 6500 litres D. 6000 litres

3. Surface area of a cube is 1014 sq. cm. Its volume will be
A. 2197 cu cm B. 2297 cu cm
C. 2179 cu cm D. 2117 cu cm

4. If the volumes of two cubical blocks are in the ratio of 8 : 1, what will be the ratio of their edges?
A. 1 : 2 B. 2 : 1
C. 4 : 1 D. 2 : 3

5. Two spheres have their surface areas in the ratio 9 : 16. Their volumes are in the ratio of
A. 64 : 27 B. 27 : 64
C. 16 : 27 D. 11 : 27

6. The length of the longest rod that can be place in a room 12 m long, 9 m broad and 8 m high is
A. 17 m *(b)* 18 m
C. 25 m D. 16 m

7. The radius and the height of a right circular cone are in the ratio of 3 : 5. If its volume is 120π cu m, its slant height is
A. $3\sqrt{34}$m B. $2\sqrt{28}$m
C. $2\sqrt{44}$m D. $2\sqrt{34}$m

8. Circumference of the base of a cylinder is 88 cm and height of the cylinder is 42 cm. Its volume is
A. 25872 cu cm B. 28572 cu cm
C. 25870 cu cm D. 22584 cu cm

9. It fwo cubes each of 10 cm side are kept close to each other, then the cuboid so formed will have surface area equal to
A. 1200 sq. cm B. 5000 sq. cm
C. 1000 sq. cm D. 1250 sq. cm

ANSWERS

1	2	3	4	5	6	7	8	9
D	D	A	B	B	A	D	A	C

EXPLANATORY ANSWERS

1. Volume of the cuboid
$= l \times b \times h = 4 \times 3 \times 2 = 24$ cu. cm.

2. Volume of the reservoir
$= l \times b \times h = 3 \times 2 \times 1 = 6$ cu. cm
($\because$ 1 cu m = 1000 litre)
$\therefore$ Capacity of the reservoir
$= 6 \times 1000 = 6000$ litre.

3. Surface area of a cube $= 6 \times (\text{side})^2$
$\therefore \quad 6 \times (\text{side})^2 = 1014$
$\Rightarrow \quad (\text{side})^2 = \frac{1014}{6} = 169$
$\Rightarrow \quad \text{side} = \sqrt{169} = 13$ cm
$\therefore$ Volume of the cube $= (\text{side})^3 = (13)^3$
$= 2197$ cu cm.

4. Suppose sides of the two cubical blocks are a_1 and a_2 respectively
$\therefore$ Volume of the two cubical blocks will be $(a_1)^3$ and $(a_2)^3$ rspectively
According to question :
$$a_1^3 : a_2^3 = 8 : 1 \therefore \frac{a_1^3}{a_2^3} = \frac{8}{1}$$
$$\therefore \left(\frac{a_1}{a_2}\right)^3 = \left(\frac{2}{1}\right)^3 \Rightarrow a_1 : a_2$$
$$= 2 : 1$$
Therefore ratio of their edges = 2 : 1.

5. Suppose radii of the two spheres are r_1 and r_2 respectively.
$\therefore$ Surface areas of the two spheres are $4\pi r_1^2$ and $4\pi r_2^2$ respectively
According to question :
$4\pi r_1^2 : 4\pi r_2^2 = 9 : 16 \Rightarrow r_1^2 : r_2^2 = 9 : 16$
$$\Rightarrow \frac{r_1^2}{r_2^2} = \frac{9}{16} \Rightarrow \left(\frac{r_1}{r_2}\right)^2 = \left(\frac{3}{4}\right)^2$$
$$\Rightarrow r_1 : r_2 = 3:4 \Rightarrow \left(\frac{r_1}{r_2}\right)^3 = \left(\frac{3}{4}\right)^3$$
$$\Rightarrow \frac{r_1^3}{r_2^3} = \frac{27}{64} \Rightarrow r_1^3 : r_2^3 = 27 : 64.$$
Therefore ratio of their volumes
$$= \frac{4}{3}\pi r_1^3 : \frac{4}{3}\pi r_2^3 = r_1^3 : r_2^3 = 27 : 64$$

6. The longest rod that can be placed in the cuboidal room = Length of the diagonal
$$= \sqrt{l^2 + b^2 + h^2} = \sqrt{(12)^2 + (9)^2 + (8)^2}$$
$$= \sqrt{144 + 81 + 64} = \sqrt{289} = 17 \text{ m}$$

7. Suppose the base radius and the height of the right circular cone are $3x$ m and $5x$ m respectively.
$\therefore$ Volume of the cone
$$= \frac{1}{3}\pi r^2 h = \frac{1}{3}\pi (3x)^2 \times 5x \text{ cu m}$$
According to question :
Volume of the cone = 120π cu m (given)
$$\therefore \frac{1}{3}\pi \times 9x^2 \times 5x = 120\pi$$
$$\Rightarrow x^3 = \frac{120 \times 3}{9 \times 5}$$
$$\Rightarrow x^3 = 8 \Rightarrow x^3 = (2)^3$$
$$\Rightarrow x = 2 \text{ m}$$
$\therefore$ The radius and the height of the cone will be $3 \times 2 = 6$ m and $5 \times 2 = 10$ m respectively.
$\therefore$ Slant height of the cone
$$= \sqrt{r^2 + h^2} = \sqrt{(6)^2 + (10)^2}$$
$$= \sqrt{36 + 100} = \sqrt{136} = 2\sqrt{34}\text{m}.$$

8. Suppose the base radius of the cylinder = r cm
$\therefore$ Circumference of the base of the cylinder = $2\pi r$ cm
According to question :
$$2\pi r = 88$$
$$\therefore r = \frac{88}{2\pi} = \frac{88 \times 7}{2 \times 22} = 14 \text{ cm}$$
$\therefore$ Volume of the cylinder
$$= \pi r^2 h = \frac{22}{7} \times (14)^2 \times 42$$
$$= 22 \times 2 \times 14 \times 42$$
$$= 25872 \text{ cu cm.}$$

9. Candidates should note that in such type of questions where two cubes of equal edges are kept close to each other, only the length of the cuboid so form increases and breadth and height of the cuboid remain same as that of the cube.
$\therefore$ Length of the cuboid = Edge of the first cube + Edge of the second cube
$= 10 + 10 = 20$ cm
$\therefore$ Surface area of the cuboid
$= 2(20 \times 10 + 10 \times 10 + 10 \times 20)$
$= 2(200 + 100 + 200)$
$= 5 \times 500 = 1000$ sq. cm.

●●●

CHAPTER 12

Trigonometry

Trigonometrical Ratios; Degree and Radian Measures; Standard Identities; Complementary Angles

Measurement of Angles: In general, the angles are measured in degrees or in radians which are defined as follows:

(a) ***Degrees***: A right angle is divided into 90 equal parts and each part is called a degree. Thus a right angle is equal to 90 degrees. One degree is denoted by $1°$.

A degree is divided into sixty equal parts and each part is called a minute and is denoted by $1'$.

A minute is divided into sixty equal parts and each part is called a second and is denoted by $1''$.

Thus, we have

1 right angle = $90°$ (read as 90 degrees)

$1° = 60'$ (read as 60 minutes)

$1' = 60''$ (read as 60 seconds)

(b) ***Radians***: A radian is the angle subtended at the centre of a circle by an arc equal in length to the radius of the circle.

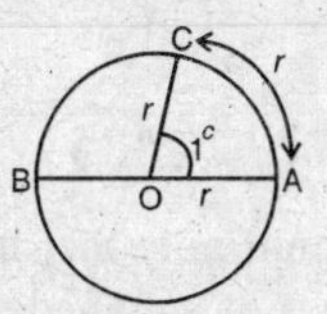

In the adjacent figure OA = OC = arc AC = r = radius of the circle, then measurement of $\angle$ AOC is one radian and is denoted by 1^c. Thus $\angle$ AOC = 1^c.

A Constant Number π: The ratio of the circumference to the diameter of a circle is always equal to a constant and this constant is denoted by the Greek letter π.

Thus π = circumference/diameter.

$\therefore$ If r is the radius of a circle, then its circumference $= 2\pi\, r$.

The constant π is an irrational number and its approximate value is taken as 22/7.

Relation Between an Arc and an Angle: If s is the length of an arc of a circle of radius r, then the angle θ (in radians) subtended by this arc at the centre of the circle is given by $\theta = s/r$ or $s = r\,\theta$

i.e., arc = radius × angle in radians

Given in the figure,

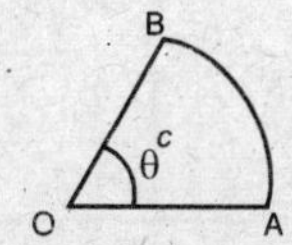

$$\angle \text{ AOB} = \frac{\text{arc ACB}}{r} \text{ (in radians)}$$

$$= \frac{\pi r}{r} = \pi \text{ radians.}$$

Thus we have, π radians = $180°$ = 2 right angles

or 1 radian $= \frac{180}{\pi}$ degrees $= \frac{180}{22} \times 7$ degrees = $57°\ 17'\ 44.8''$ (Appr.)

Sectorial Area: Let OAB be a sector having central angle θ^c and radius r. Then area of the sector OAB is given by $\frac{1}{2} r^2\,\theta$.

Trigonometrical Ratios: In a right angled triangle ABC, if $\angle$ CAB = θ, then BC = side opposite to the angle θ = Perpendicular = p (say), AC = side opposite to the right angle = Hypotenuse = h (say) and AB = b (say).

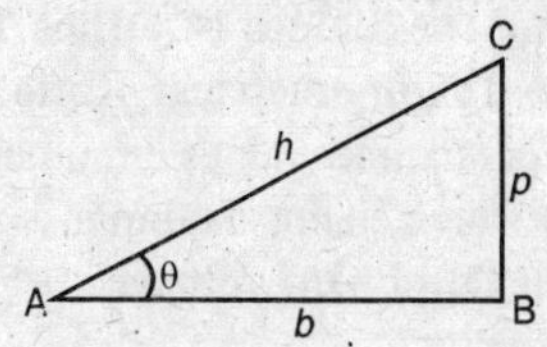

The six trigonometrical ratios are given as follows: $\sin\theta = p/h$, $\cos\theta = b/h$, $\tan\theta = p/b$.
(Also $\tan\theta = \sin\theta/\cos\theta$, $\operatorname{cosec}\theta = 1/\sin\theta$, $\sec\theta = 1/\cos\theta$, $\cot\theta = 1/\tan\theta$,)

Basic Formulae Connecting Six Trigonometrical Ratios

The formulae connecting the six trigonometrical ratios are:

(i) $\sin^2\theta + \cos^2\theta = 1$ or $\cos^2\theta = 1 - \sin^2\theta$ or $\sin^2\theta = 1 - \cos^2\theta$.

(ii) $1 + \tan^2\theta = \sec^2\theta$ or $\sec^2\theta - \tan^2\theta = 1$

(iii) $1 + \cot^2\theta = \operatorname{cosec}^2\theta$ or $\operatorname{cosec}^2\theta - \cot^2\theta = 1$.

Sign of Trigonometrical Ratios:

1st quadrant $0 < \theta < 90°$, all trigonometrical ratios +ve,

2nd quadrant $90° < \theta < 180°$, only $\sin\theta$ and $\operatorname{cosec}\theta$, +ve

3rd quadrant $180° < \theta < 270°$, only $\tan\theta$ and $\cot\theta$, +ve

4th quadrant $270° < \theta < 360°$, only $\cos\theta$ and $\sec\theta$, +ve.

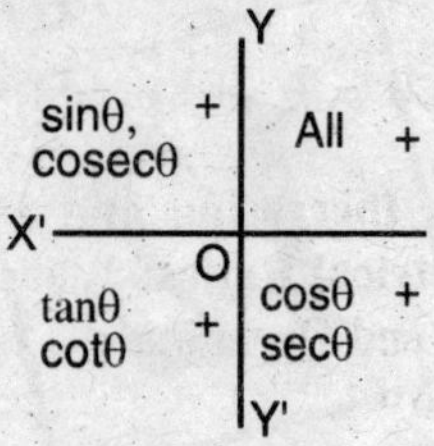

Trigonometrical Ratios of Related Angles:

$\sin(-\theta) = -\sin\theta$	$\cos(-\theta) = \cos\theta$	$\tan(-\theta) = -\tan\theta$
$\sin(90° - \theta) = \cos\theta$	$\sin(180° + \theta) = -\sin\theta$	$\sin(270° + \theta) = -\cos\theta$
$\cos(90° - \theta) = \sin\theta$	$\cos(180° + \theta) = -\cos\theta$	$\cos(270° + \theta) = \sin\theta$
$\tan(90° - \theta) = \cot\theta$	$\tan(180° + \theta) = \tan\theta$	$\tan(270° + \theta) = -\cot\theta$
$\sin(90° + \theta) = \cos\theta$	$\sin(270° - \theta) = -\cos\theta$	$\sin(360° + \theta) = \sin\theta$
$\cos(90° + \theta) = -\sin\theta$	$\cos(270° - \theta) = -\sin\theta$	$\cos(360° + \theta) = \cos\theta$
$\tan(90° + \theta) = -\cot\theta$	$\tan(270° - \theta) = \cot\theta$	$\tan(360° + \theta) = \tan\theta$

Table giving sine, cosine and tangent of some angles less than 90°:

	0°	15°	18°	22.5°	30°	36°	45°	60°	67.5°	90°
sin	0	$\frac{\sqrt{6}-\sqrt{2}}{4}$	$\frac{\sqrt{5}-1}{4}$	$\frac{\sqrt{2-\sqrt{2}}}{2}$	$\frac{1}{2}$	$\frac{\sqrt{10-2\sqrt{5}}}{4}$	$\frac{1}{\sqrt{2}}$	$\frac{\sqrt{3}}{2}$	$\frac{\sqrt{\sqrt{2}+1}}{\sqrt{(2\sqrt{2})}}$	1
cos	1	$\frac{\sqrt{6}+\sqrt{2}}{4}$	$\frac{\sqrt{10+2\sqrt{5}}}{4}$	$\frac{\sqrt{\sqrt{2}+1}}{\sqrt{(2\sqrt{2})}}$	$\frac{\sqrt{3}}{2}$	$\frac{\sqrt{5}+1}{4}$	$\frac{1}{\sqrt{2}}$	$\frac{1}{2}$	$\frac{\sqrt{2-\sqrt{2}}}{2}$	0
tan	0	$2-\sqrt{3}$	$\frac{\sqrt{25-10\sqrt{5}}}{5}$	$\sqrt{2}-1$	$\frac{1}{\sqrt{3}}$	$\sqrt{5-2\sqrt{5}}$	1	$\sqrt{3}$	$\sqrt{2}+1$	not defined

Bounds of T-Ratios: Since $\sin^2\theta + \cos^2\theta = 1$, the absolute values of $\sin\theta$ and $\cos\theta$ can never be greater than 1.

Thus $0 < |\sin\theta| < 1$, $0 < |\cos\theta| < 1$,
i.e., $-1 < \sin\theta$; $\cos\theta < 1$, or $0 < \sin^2\theta$; $\cos^2\theta < 1$.

Also $\sec\theta$; $\operatorname{cosec}\theta > 1$ or < -1
i.e., $\sec\theta$, $\operatorname{cosec}\theta$ can never lie between -1 and 1.

It should be noted that $-\infty < \tan\theta$; $\cot\theta < \infty$.

To Determine the Values of Other Trigonometrical Ratios when one Trigonometrical Ratio is given: If one of the *t*-ratio is given, the values of other *t*-ratios can be found by using formulae. For example, $\sin\theta = 1/3$. Since sine is positive in Q_1 or Q_2, we have

$\cos\theta = \sqrt{1-(1/9)}$

or $-\sqrt{1-(1/9)}$, *i.e.*, $2\sqrt{2}/3$

or $-2\sqrt{2}/3$ according to $\theta \in Q_1$ or $\theta \in Q_2$.

We can also find other ratios by forming right angled triangle, *e.g.*, Let $\tan\theta = 1/2$, $\pi < \theta < 3\pi/2$, then since θ in Q_3, sine and cosine both are negative,

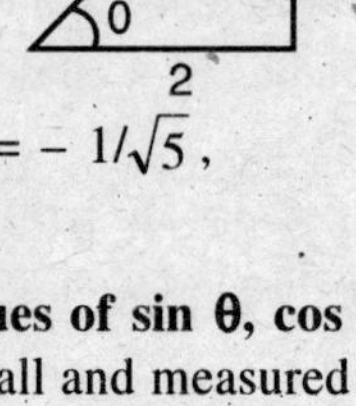

∴ We have $\sin\theta = -1/\sqrt{5}$,

$\cos\theta = -2/\sqrt{5}$.

Approximate Values of sin θ, cos θ and tan θ when θ is Small: Let θ be small and measured in radians, then sin

$\theta \approx \theta$, $\cos \approx 1$, $\tan \theta \approx \theta$. These are first degree approximations. The second degree approximations are given by

$\sin \theta \simeq \theta$, $\cos \theta \simeq 1 - \frac{1}{2}\theta^2$, $\tan \theta = \theta$.

Increasing and Decreasing Behaviour of Trigonometrical Ratios: When $-\pi/2 < \theta < \pi/2$, $\sin \theta$ increases in Q_1 and Q_4 with angle while in Q_2, Q_3, $\sin \theta$ decreases from 1 to –1.

Thus $\theta_1 < \theta_2$

$\Rightarrow \sin \theta_1 < \sin \theta_2$ $(\theta_1, \theta_2 \in Q_1 \text{ or } Q_4)$

$\Rightarrow \sin \theta_1 > \sin \theta_2$ $(\theta_1, \theta_2 \in Q_2 \text{ or } Q_3)$

We can decide the behaviour of other ratios in a similar manner. If we denote ↑ for increasing and ↓ for decreasing, we have the following chart:

	Left of y-axis		Right of y-axis	
Above x-axis	sin	↓	sin	↑
	cos	↓	cos	↓
	tan	↑	tan	↑
	cot	↓	cot	↓
	sec	↑	sec	↑
	cosec	↑	cosec	↓
Below x-axis	sin	↓	sin	↑
	cos	↑	cos	↑
	tan	↑	tan	↑
	cot	↓	cot	↓
	sec	↓	sec	↓
	cosec	↑	cosec	↓

(Axes: y (top), y′ (bottom), x′ (left), x (right), origin O.)

EXERCISE

1. The angles of a triangle are in A.P. and the radian measure of the smallest to the degree measure of the mean is $\pi : 200$. The greatest angle in radians is:
A. $(11/30)\pi$ B. $\pi/3$
C. $\pi/2$ D. None of these

2. The moon's distance from the earth is 3,50,000 kilometres and its diameter subtends an angle of 31′ at the eye of the observer. The diameter of the moon is:
A. 3157 (11/27) km B. 315 (11/27) km
C. 3050 (11/27) km D. None of these

3. If $\sin \theta = -3/5$ and θ lies in the third quadrant, then the value of $\cos(\theta/2)$ is:
A. 1/5 B. $-1/\sqrt{(10)}$
C. –1/5 D. $1/\sqrt{(10)}$

4. If $\tan \theta = -4/3$, then $\sin \theta$ is:
A. – 4/5 but not 4/5 B. –4/5 or 4/5
C. 4/5 but not – 4/5 D. None of these

5. If the angle θ is in the third quadrant and $\tan \theta = 3$, then the value of $\sin \theta$ is:
A. $1/\sqrt{(10)}$ B. $-1/\sqrt{(10)}$
C. $-3/\sqrt{(10)}$ D. $3/\sqrt{(10)}$

6. If $(\sec \alpha + \tan \alpha)(\sec \beta + \tan \beta)(\sec \gamma + \tan \gamma) = \tan \alpha \tan \beta \tan \gamma$, then $(\sec \alpha - \tan \alpha)(\sec \beta - \tan \beta)(\sec \gamma - \tan \gamma) = ?$
A. $\cot \alpha \cot \beta \cot \gamma$
B. $\tan \alpha \tan \beta \tan \gamma$
C. $\cot \alpha + \cot \beta + \cot \gamma$
D. $\tan \alpha + \tan \beta + \tan \gamma$

7. Which of the following is correct?
A. $\sin 1° > \sin 1$
B. $\sin 1° < \sin 1$
C. $\sin 1° = \sin 1$
D. $\sin 1° = (\pi/180) \sin 1$

8. Which of the following is correct?
A. $\tan 1 > \tan 2$ B. $\tan 1 = \tan 2$
C. $\tan 1 < \tan 2$ D. $\tan 1 = 1$

9. The value of $\log \tan 1° + \log \tan 2° + ... + \log \tan 89°$ is:
A. 0 B. 1
C. ∞ D. None of these

ANSWERS

1	2	3	4	5	6	7	8	9
A	A	B	B	C	A	B	A	A

EXPLANATORY ANSWERS

1. Let the angles in degrees in A.P. be taken as

$A = \theta - \phi$, $B = \theta$, $C = \theta + \phi$

$\therefore A + B + C = 180° = 3\theta$

$\Rightarrow B = \theta = 60°$

Now $\frac{\pi}{200} = \frac{\text{A in radian}}{\text{B in degrees}}$

$= \frac{(60-\phi)(\pi/180)}{60}$

$\Rightarrow \qquad \phi = 6°$

$\therefore$ Greatest angle $C = \theta + \phi = 66°$

$= 66 \times (\pi/180)$

$= (11/30)\ \pi$ radians.

2. Let l be the diameter of moon and a its distance from the earth. If the moon subtends an angle θ at the eye of the observer, then

$$l = a\theta = 350000 \times \left(\frac{31}{60} \times \frac{\pi}{180}\right)$$

$$= \frac{3500 \times 31}{6 \times 18} \times \frac{22}{7} = 3157\ \frac{11}{27} \text{ km.}$$

3. $\because$ θ lies in the third quadrant

$\because \quad \cos\theta$ is –ve

$\because \quad \sin\theta = -3/5$

$\Rightarrow \quad \cos\theta = -\sqrt{(1 - \sin^2\theta)} = -4/5$

Now, $\quad \cos^2 \frac{1}{2}\theta = \frac{1}{2}(1 + \cos\theta)$

$= \frac{1}{2}(1 - 4/5) = 1/10$

$\Rightarrow \quad \cos\frac{1}{2}\theta = +1/\sqrt{(10)}$

But given that, $180° < \theta < 270°$

$\Rightarrow 90° < \theta/2 < 135°$

i.e., θ/2 lies in the second quadrant

$\Rightarrow \cos\frac{1}{2}\theta$ is –ve

Hence $\cos\frac{1}{2}\theta = -1/\sqrt{10}$.

4. $\tan\theta = -4/3$

$\Rightarrow$ θ lies in 2nd or 4th quadrant.

$\therefore$ sin θ is positive or negative according as θ lie in 2nd or 4th quadrant respectively, *i.e.*, sin θ may be positive or negative.

Now $\quad \sin\theta = \tan\theta/\sqrt{(1 + \tan^2\theta)} = 4/5$

Hence $\quad \sin\theta = -4/5$ or $4/5$.

5. $\because$ θ is in the third quadrant,

$\because \sin\theta < 0$.

Thus $\quad \sin\theta = -\tan\theta/\sqrt{(1 + \tan^2\theta)}$

$= -3/\sqrt{(10)}$.

6. Multiplying both sides of the given expression by $(\sec\alpha - \tan\alpha).(\sec\beta - \tan\beta).(\sec\gamma - \tan\gamma)$, we get, 1.1.1 $= (\sec\alpha - \tan\alpha).(\sec\beta - \tan\beta).(\sec\gamma - \tan\gamma).\tan\alpha\tan\beta\tan\gamma$

$\Rightarrow (\sec\alpha - \tan\alpha).(\sec\beta - \tan\beta).(\sec\gamma - \tan\gamma)$ $= \cot\alpha.\cot\beta.\cot\gamma$.

7. 1 radian = $(180/\pi)$ Degrees = 57° (appr.)

$\therefore \sin 1° < \sin 57° \Rightarrow \sin 1° < \sin 1$.

8. 1 radian = 57° (appr.)

which lie in first quadrant. $\therefore \tan 1 > 0$,

and 2 radians = 114° (appr.), which lie in second quadrant $\therefore \tan 2 < 0$

Hence $\tan 1 > \tan 2$.

9. $\log\tan 1° + \log\tan 2° + ... + \log\tan 89°$

$= \log[\tan 1°.\tan 2° ... \tan 45° ... \tan 88°.\tan 89°]$

$= \log[\tan 1°.\tan 2° ... \tan 45° ... \tan(90°-2°)\tan(90°-1°)]$

$= \log[\tan 1°.\cot 1°.\tan 2°.\cot 2° ... 1]$

$= \log 1 = 0$

Heights and Distance

Angle of Elevation and Depression: Let O and P be two points such that P is at higher level than O. Let PQ, OX be horizontal lines through P and O, respectively.

If an observer (or eye) is at O and the object is at P, then ∠XOP is called the angle of elevation of P as seen from O.

This angle is also called the angular height of P from O.

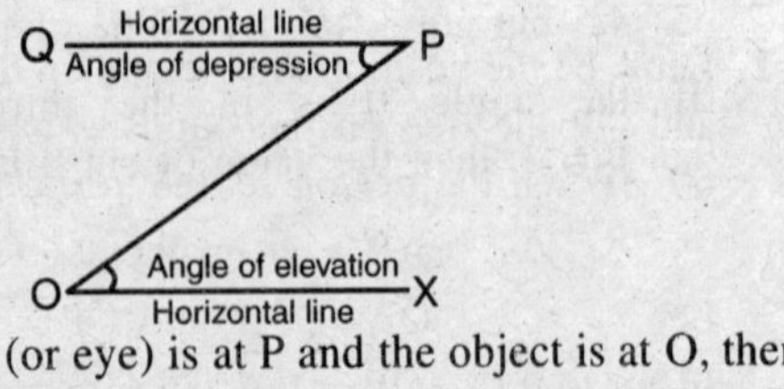

If an observer (or eye) is at P and the object is at O, then ∠QPO is called the angle of depression of O as seen from P.

EXERCISE

1. A person standing on the bank of a river observes that the angle subtended by a tree on the opposite bank is 60°, when he retires 40 metres from the bank he finds the angle to be 30°. Then the breadth of the river is:

A. 40 m B. 60 m
C. 20 m D. 30 m

2. At a point on a level plane a tower subtends an angle θ and a flag-staff a ft. in length at the top of the tower subtends an angle ϕ. The height of the tower is:

A. $\dfrac{a\sin\theta\cos\phi}{\cos(\theta+\phi)}$ B. $\dfrac{a\sin\theta\cos(\theta+\phi)}{\sin\phi}$

C. $\dfrac{a\cos(\theta+\phi)}{\sin\theta\sin\phi}$ D. None of these

3. The angle of elevation of the top of a tower standing on a horizontal plane from a point A is α. After walking a distance a towards the foot of the tower the angle of elevation is found to be β. The height of the tower is:

A. $\dfrac{a\sin\alpha\sin\beta}{\sin(\beta-\alpha)}$ B. $\dfrac{a\sin\alpha\sin\beta}{\sin(\alpha-\beta)}$

C. $\dfrac{a\sin(\beta-\alpha)}{\sin\alpha\sin\beta}$ D. $\dfrac{a\sin(\alpha-\beta)}{\sin\alpha\sin\beta}$

4. The angle of elevation of the top of a TV tower from the three points A, B, C in a straight line (in the horizontal plane) through the foot of the tower are α, 2α, 3α respectively. If AB = a, the height of the tower is:

A. $a\tan\alpha$ B. $a\sin\alpha$
C. $a\sin 2\alpha$ D. $a\sin 3\alpha$

5. The height of the centre of the round balloon of radius r, which subtend an angle α at the eye of an observer and the elevation of whose centre from the eye is β, is given by:

A. $r\sin\alpha\sin\beta$ B. $r\operatorname{cosec}\frac{1}{2}\alpha\sin\beta$
C. $r\operatorname{cosec}\alpha\sin\beta$ D. None of these

6. ABCD is a square plot. The angle of elevation of the top of a pole standing at D from A or C is 30° and that from B is θ, then $\tan\theta$ is equal to:

A. $\sqrt{6}$ B. $1/\sqrt{6}$
C. $\sqrt{3}/\sqrt{2}$ D. $\sqrt{2}/\sqrt{3}$

7. The angle of elevation of the top of two vertical towers as seen from the middle point of the line joining the foot of the towers are 60° and 30° respectively. The ratio of the heights of the towers is:

A. 2 : 1 B. $\sqrt{3}$: 1
C. 3 : 2 D. 3 : 1

8. ABC is a triangular park with AB = AC = 100 metres. A clock tower is situated at the mid-point of BC. The angles of elevation of the top of the tower of A and B are $\cot^{-1}(3.2)$ and $\operatorname{cosec}^{-1}(2.6)$ respectively. The height of the tower in metres is:

A. 25/2 B. 25
C. 50 D. None of these

9. The angles of elevation of the top of a vertical tower from two points, distant a and b ($a > b$) from the base and in the same straight line with it are complementary. Then the height of the tower is:

A. $\sqrt{(ab)}$ B. $\sqrt{(a^2+b^2)}$
C. $\sqrt{(a^2-b^2)}$ D. $\sqrt{a(a-b)}$

ANSWERS

1	2	3	4	5	6	7	8	9
C	B	A	C	B	B	D	B	A

EXPLANATORY ANSWERS

1. Let A be the position of a person on the bank of a river and OP the tree on the opposite bank and $\angle OAP$ = 60°. When the person retires to the position B, s.t.

AB = 40 m then $\angle$ OBP = 30°

Let OA = x m and OP = h m

In Δ OAP, OP = OA tan 60° = $x\sqrt{3}$

and in Δ OBP, OP = OB tan 30° = $(x + 40)/\sqrt{3}$

$\therefore$ $(x + 40)/\sqrt{3} = x\sqrt{3} \Rightarrow x = 20$ m

2. Let OP be the tower of height h (say) and PQ the flag-staff of height a, such that

$\angle OAP = \theta$ and $\angle PAQ = \phi$

In ΔOAP and ΔOAQ

OA = OP $\cot\theta = h\cot\theta$

and OA = OQ $\cot(\theta+\phi)$

$= (h + a)\cot(\theta+\phi)$

$\therefore$ $h\cot\theta = (h+a)\cot(\theta+\phi)$

$$\Rightarrow h = \frac{a\cot(\theta+\phi)}{\cot\theta-\cot(\theta+\phi)} = \frac{a\sin\theta\cos(\theta+\phi)}{\sin\phi}.$$

3. Let OP be the tower of height h (say) and A and B be the two positions on the horizontal line through O, such that

$\angle$ OAP = α, $\angle$ OBP = β and OB = x

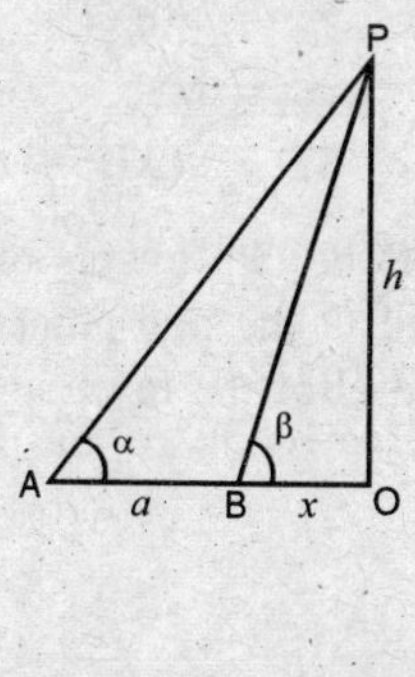

In ΔOBP, $OB = x = h \cot \beta$, and
in ΔOAP, $OA = a + x = h \cot \alpha$
$\therefore a = h (\cot \alpha - \cot \beta)$
$\Rightarrow h = a \sin \alpha \sin \beta / \sin (\beta - \alpha)$

4. OP is vertical tower. The elevations of the top of P from A, B, C are α, 2α, 3α respectively

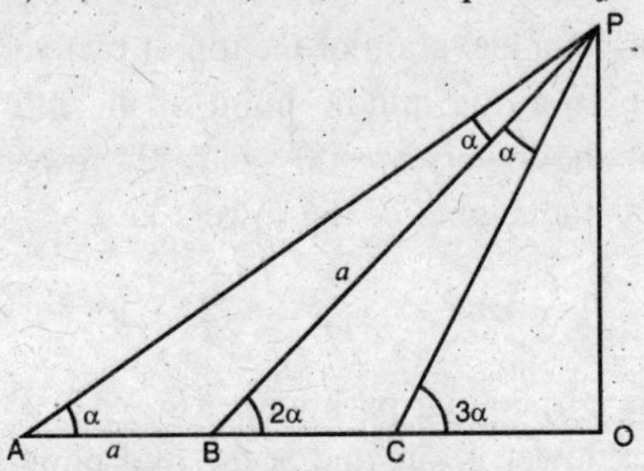

$$\angle OAP = \angle APB = \alpha$$
$$\therefore \quad AB = PB = a$$
In ΔOBP, $\quad OP = PB \sin 2\alpha = a \sin 2\alpha$

5. Let O be the centre of the balloon of radius r which subtend an angle α at the eye of an observer at E.

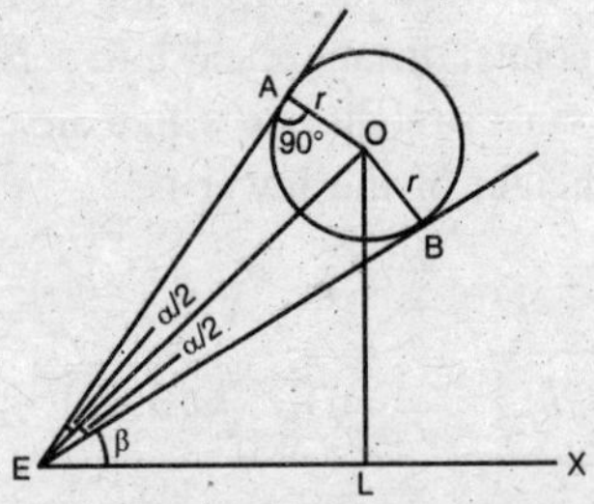

If EA and EB are the tangents to the balloon,

then $\quad \angle OEA = \angle OEB = \dfrac{\alpha}{2}$

In ΔOAE, $\sin \dfrac{1}{2}\alpha = OA/OE \therefore OE = r \operatorname{cosec} \dfrac{1}{2}\alpha$

In ΔOEL, height of the centre of the balloon

$= h = OE \sin \beta = r \operatorname{cosec} \dfrac{1}{2}\alpha \sin \beta$.

6. Let a be the length of a side of square plot ABCD and h, the height of the pole standing at D. Since elevations of P from A or C is 30° and that from B is θ,

$\therefore$ In ΔPCD, $\tan 30° = h/a$

i.e., $\quad h/a = 1/\sqrt{3}$

And in ΔPBD,

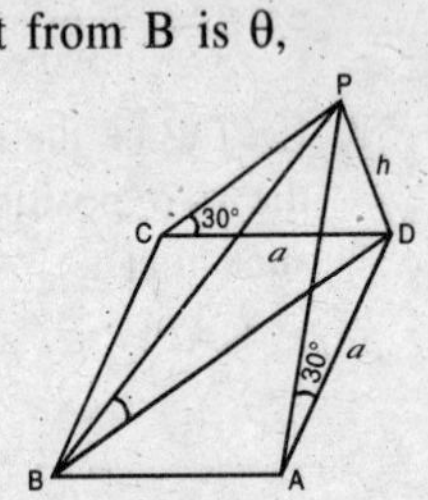

$$\tan \theta = PD/BD$$
$$= h/(a\sqrt{2})$$
$$= 1/\sqrt{6}$$
$$\therefore \quad BD = \sqrt{(AB^2 + AD)^2} = a\sqrt{2}.$$

7. Let AB and CD be two towers of heights h_1 and h_2 respectively and O the mid-point of the line joining the foots A and C of the towers.

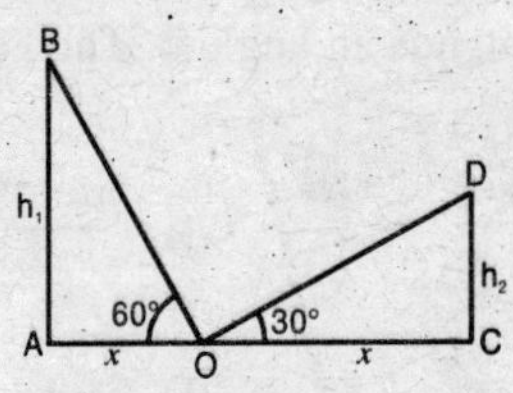

Let $\quad OA = OC = x$
Then $\quad h_1 = x \tan 60° = x\sqrt{3}$
and $\quad h_2 = x \tan 30° = x/\sqrt{3}$

$\therefore \dfrac{h_1}{h_2} = \dfrac{3}{1}$, Hence, $h_1 : h_2 = 3 : 1$.

8. Given $\alpha = \cot^{-1} (3.2)$, $\beta = \operatorname{cosec}^{-1} (2.6)$

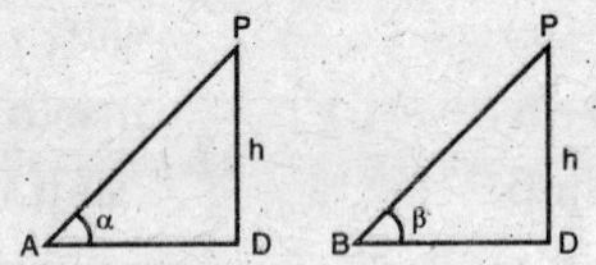

In ΔPAD, $AD = h \cot \alpha$,
In ΔPBD, $BD = h \cot \beta$

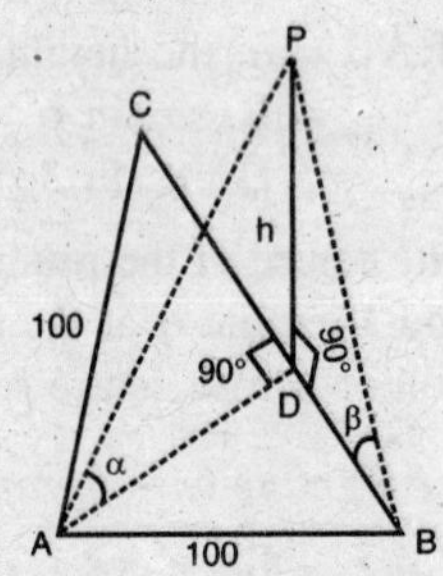

In ΔABD, $\quad AB^2 = AD^2 + BD^2$
$$= h^2 (\cot^2 \alpha + \cot^2 \beta)$$
$$\Rightarrow 100^2 = h^2 \{\cot^2 \alpha + (\operatorname{cosec}^2 \beta - 1)\}$$
$$\Rightarrow 100^2 = h^2 [(3.2)^2 + (2.6)^2 - 1] = 16h^2$$
$$\Rightarrow \quad h = 25 \text{ m}.$$

9. Let $CD = h$ unit be the height of the tower and A and B be the two points on the ground, such that $DA = a$; $DB = b$; $\angle DAC = \alpha$ and $\angle DBC = 90° - \alpha$

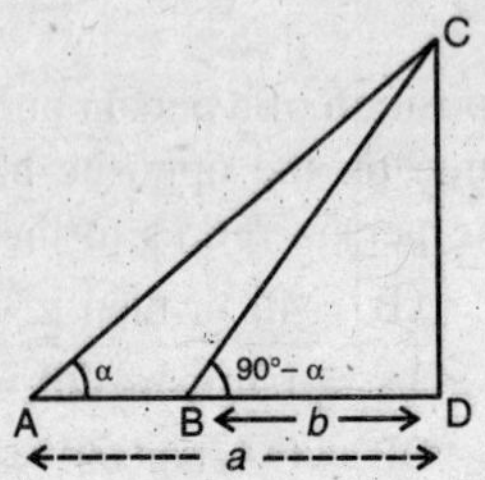

From right triangle ADC,
$$CD = h = a \tan\alpha \quad ...(i)$$
From right triangle BDC,
$$CD = h = b \tan (90° - \alpha)$$
$$= b \cot\alpha \quad ...(ii)$$
Multiplying equations (*i*) and (*ii*), we get
$$h^2 = a \tan\alpha \,.\, b\cot\alpha$$
Hence, $h = \sqrt{ab}$

●●●

CHAPTER 13

Data Handling

Histogram; Frequency Polygon; Bar Diagram & Pie-Chart

Graphical Representation of Statistical Data

One of the most convincing and appearing ways in which statistical result may be presented is through diagrams and graphs. The impressions created by diagrams last much longer than those created by the figures presented in a tabular form.

Rather than present data numerically in the form of a table it can sometimes be better to illustrate the information through the use of graphs, charts, diagrams and so on.

The frequency distribution of a discrete value is best represented by a bar diagram. The height of the bars is proportional to the frequency of each variate-value. The bars must be kept distinct to show that the variate-values are distinct.

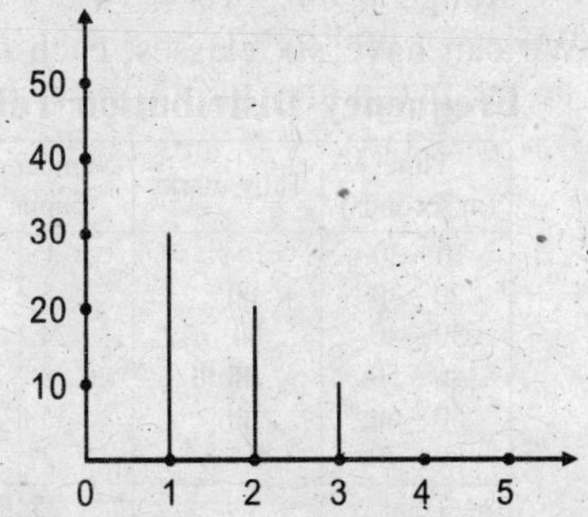

A simple bar chart is used to illustrate a frequency distribution. The lengths of the bars are proportional to the frequency and the bars are of equal width.

Some Important Types of Diagrams and Graphs

The different types of Diagrams and Graphs

(1) Bar diagram
(2) Histogram
(3) Frequency circle
(4) Cumulative frequency curve of the ogive
(5) Pie diagram.

Bar Diagram

Bar diagram is the easiest and most adaptable general purpose chart. In this, bars or rectangles of uniform width are drawn with equal spaces in between on the axis. Along the y-axis is shown, the scale of the height of the rectangles.

Thickness of bars is not taken into account, they should be so constructed that they look attractive and beautiful. This can be done by colouring them or by preparing designs in them.

However, the colour or designs of all bars representing one type of data should be identical. The bars may be vertical or horizontal. Some of the main bar diagrams are:

(*i*) Simple Bar-Diagram
(*ii*) Sub-divided Bar-Diagram
(*iii*) Multiple Bar-Diagram

The following Examples of Illustrate :

Example: The following table gives the population of India (in millions). Draw a bar diagram of the data:

Population (in million) of India 1931-1971

Year	Population (*in millions*)
1931	275.5
1941	312.1
1951	356.9
1961	439.9
1971	546.9

Solution: The above data is represented by a simple bar diagram as follows :

Simple Bar Diagram Showing Population (in Millions)

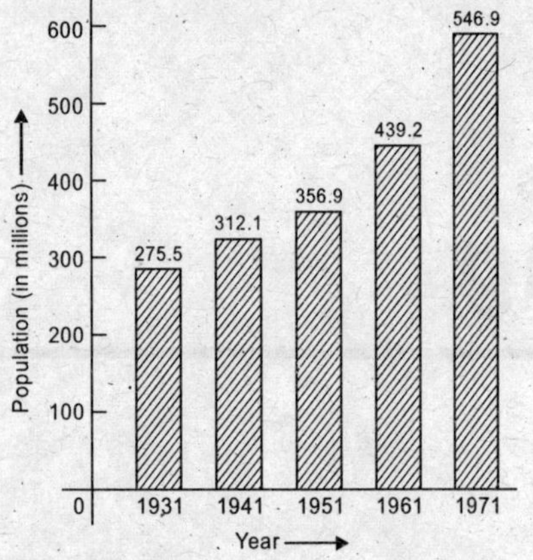

Here years are denoted on the x-axis and population (in millions) on the y-axis. The length of each bar corresponds to the number representing population on the y-axis.

Sub-Divided or Component Bar Diagram

The sub-divided bar diagram is used where the total magnitude of the given variable is to be divided into various parts or sub-classes. The bars are drawn proportional in length to the total and divided in the ratios of their components. Different colours, shades, designs, etc. are used to distinguish the various components.

Example: Represent the following data of sex-wise distribution of students in a school by a bar diagram.

Year	No. of Students		Total
	Male	*Female*	
1978	800	250	1050
1979	900	300	1200
1980	950	375	1325
1981	1000	400	1400
1982	1150	450	1600

Solution: The above data are represented by a sub-divided bar diagram, as follows.

Sub-Divided Bar Diagram showing Sex-wise Distribution of Students

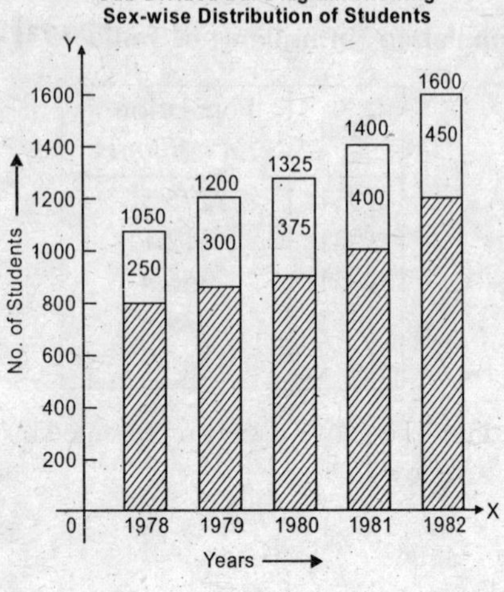

In a multiple bar diagram two or more sets of inter-related data are presented. The technique of drawing such a diagram is basically the same as that of simple bar diagram.

Histograms

The histogram is most popularly used for graphical presentation of a frequency distribution. A histogram is a graph that represents the class frequencies in a frequency distribution by vertical adjacent rectangles. After choosing a convenient scale on the axes, mark off the class intervals along x-axis and the frequencies of the respective class intervals along y-axis. Then construct rectangles with each class intervals as breadth and the respective frequency of the class interval as height. The set of the all adjacent rectangles so constructed form a histogram.

Note : A histogram is a development of the bar chart but remember when drawing a histogram it is the Area of each bar which is proportional to the frequency and there are no gaps between the bars because the classes are usually arranged so that there are no gaps.

The following Examples of Illustrates:

Example: The time taken, in seconds, to solve a problem by each of 25 pupils is as follows: 16, 20, 26, 27, 28, 30, 33, 37, 38, 40, 42, 42, 43, 46, 46, 48, 49, 50, 53, 58, 59, 60, 64, 52, 20.

(*a*) Construct a frequency distribution for these data, using a class interval of 10 seconds.

(*b*) Draw a histogram to represent the frequency distribution.

Solution:

(*a*) Lowest observation = 10

Highest observation = 64

Range = 64 − 10 = 54

We can have six classes, each of width 10.

Frequency Distribution Table

Time (in seconds)	Tally marks	Number of pupils
10 – 20	I	1
20 – 30	~~IIII~~	5
30 – 40	IIII	4
40 – 50	~~IIII~~ III	8
50 – 60	~~IIII~~	5
60 – 70	II	2
Total		25

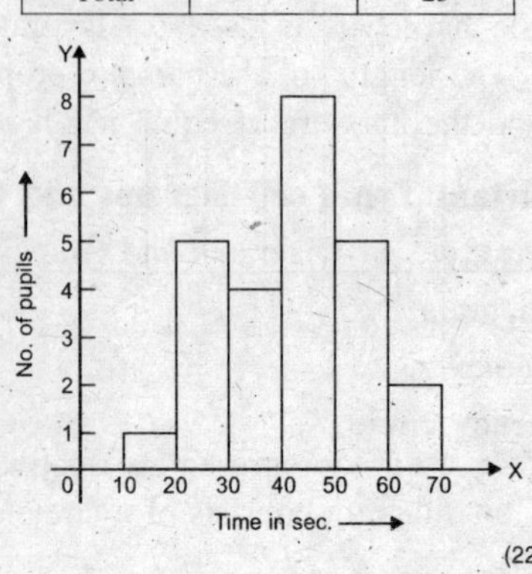

Frequency Polygon

A frequency polygon is a graph of frequency distribution. The steps constructing a frequency polygonal are:

1. Draw a suitable histogram keeping in view all the basic principles.
2. Get the mid-points of the upper horizontal side of each rectangle.
3. Join these mid-points of the adjacent rectangles of the histogram by straight lines taken in order, they form a polygon called frequency polygon.
4. End of frequency polygon preferably extended to the base line.

In a frequency polygon the variables or individuals of each class are assumed to be concentrated at the class-intervals.

Note: If only frequency polygon is to be drawn, first represent the class-marks (x_i) on the x-axis and corresponding frequencies (f_i) on y-axis. Plot all the points (x_i, f_i). Then join these points by line segments. The figure so obtained is known as the frequency polygon. The polygon should be brought down at the ends to the x-axis at each and of the drawn.

The following Examples of Illustrate:

Example: In a city the following weekly observations were made in a study on cost of Living Index for the year 1970–71.

Cost of Living Index	No. of weeks
140 – 150	5
150 – 160	10
160 – 170	20
170 – 180	9
180 – 190	6
190 – 200	2

Draw a histogram and frequency polygon on the same scale.

Solution:

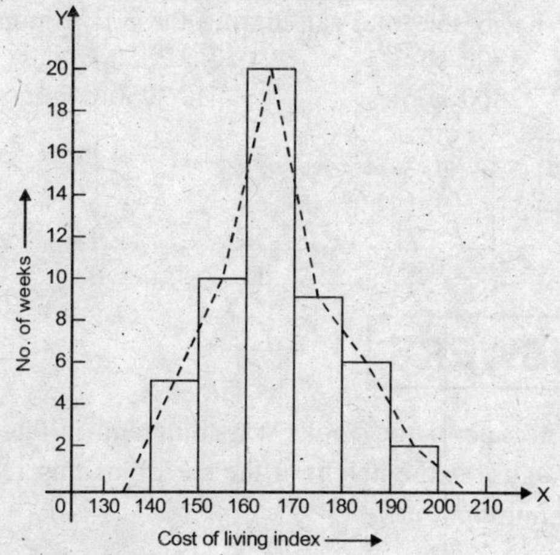

Pie Diagram

Pie-diagrams are used to represent a relative frequency distribution. A pie diagram consists of a circle divided into as many sectors as there are classes in a frequency distribution. The area of each sector is proportional to the relative frequency of the class.

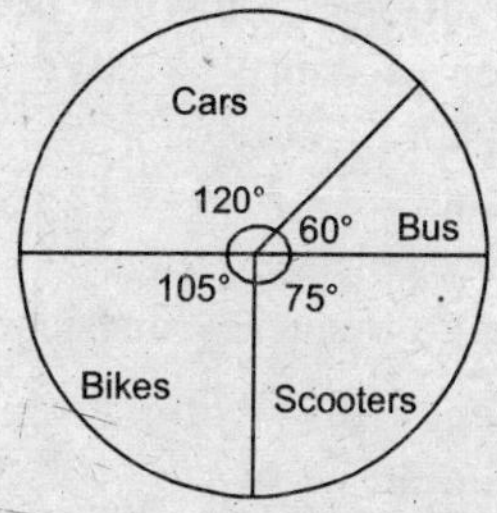

Now we make angles at the centre proportional to the relative frequencies. And in order to get the angles of the disired sectors, we divide 360° in the proportion of the various relative frequencies, *i.e.*,

$$\text{Central angle} = \left[\frac{\text{Frequency} \times 360°}{\text{Total frequency}}\right]$$

Example : The pie-chart provided below gives the distribution of land (in a village) under various food crops. Study the pie-chart carefully and answer the questions that follow.

Distribution of Areas (in Acre) Under various Food Crops

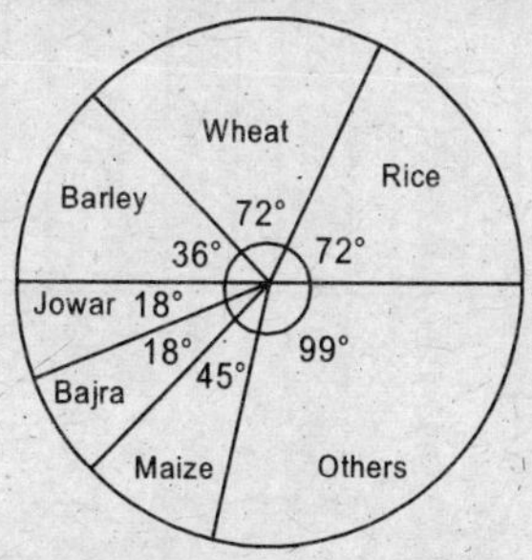

1. Which combination of three crops contribute to 50% of the total area under the food crops?
(*a*) Wheat, Barley and Jowar
(*b*) Rice, Wheat and Jowar
(*c*) Rice, Wheat and Barley
(*d*) Bajra, Maize and Rice

Solution:

1 (*c*): The total of the central angles corresponding to the three crops which cover 50% of the total area, should be 180°. Now, the total of the central angles for the given combinations are:

(*i*) Wheat, Barley and Jowar
= (72° + 36° + 18°) = 126°

(*ii*) Rice, Wheat and Jowar
= (72° + 72° + 18°) = 162°

(*iii*) Rice, Wheat and Barley
= (72° + 72° + 36°) = 180°

(*iv*) Bajra, Maize and Rice
= (18° + 45° + 72°) = 135°

Clearly, (*iii*) is the required combination.

EXERCISE

1. Which one of the following is not the graphical representation of statistical data?
   A. Bar graph
   B. Histogram
   C. Frequency polygon
   D. Cumulative frequency distribution

2. In a frequency distribution, ogives are graphical representation of:
   A. Frequency
   B. Relative frequency
   C. Cumulative frequency
   D. Raw data

3. Read the bar graph shown in figure and answer the following question:

   In which year is the increase of students maximum?

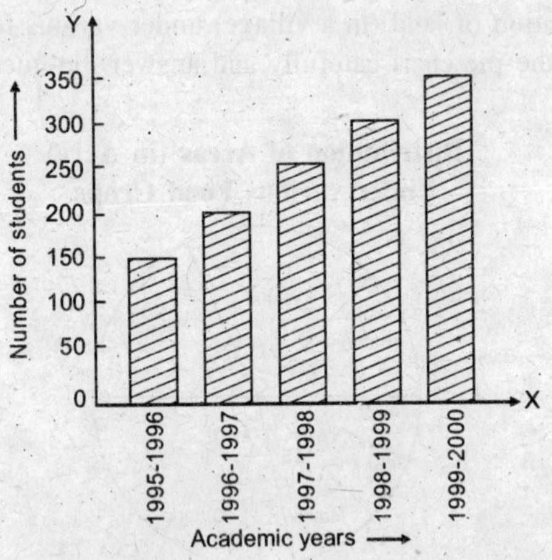

   A. 1996-1997 B. 1997-1998
   C. 1999-2000 D. None of these

4. In a histogram the area of each rectangle is proportional to:
   A. the class mark of the corresponding class interval
   B. the class size of the corresponding class interval
   C. frequency of the corresponding class interval
   D. cumulative frequency of the corresponding class interval

5. In a histogram, each class rectangle is constructed with base as:
   A. frequency B. class-intervals
   C. range D. size of the class

6. A frequency polygon is constructed by plotting frequency of the class interval and the:
   A. upper limit of the class
   B. lower limit of the class
   C. mid value of the class
   D. any values of the class

Directions (Qs. 7 to 9) : *Read the following bar graph shown in figure and answer the following questions:*

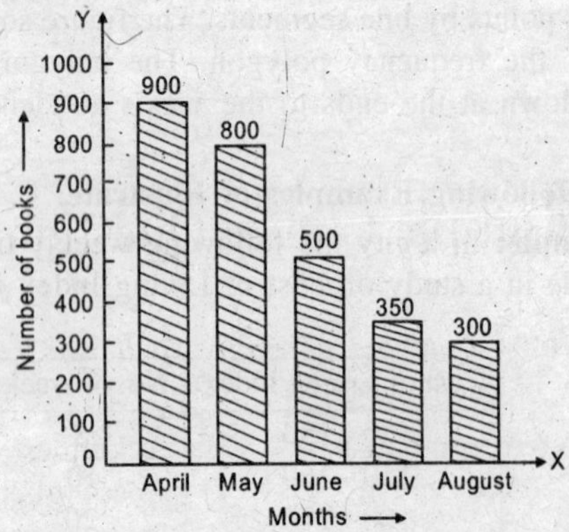

7. In which month was the sale of the books maximum?
   A. April B. May
   C. June D. August

8. In which month was the sale of the books minimum?
   A. April B. May
   C. July D. August

9. What is the total sale during these five months?
   A. 3800 copies B. 2850 copies
   C. 2800 copies D. 2950 copies

ANSWERS

1	2	3	4	5	6	7	8	9
D	C	D	C	B	C	A	D	B

EXPLANATORY ANSWERS

3. The increase in the number of students is uniform as the increase in the heights of bars is uniform. Hence, in this case the increase is not maximum in any of the year.

7. The sale of the books was maximum in the month of April as the height of the rectangle corresponding to April month is maximum.

8. The sale of the books was minimum in the month of August as the height of the corresponding rectangle is minimum.

9. Total sale of the books during 5 months.

   $(900 + 800 + 500 + 350 + 300) = 2850$ copies.

●●●

GENERAL ENGLISH

1 Spelling Errors

The most common errors in English are of spellings of words. Even the most learned men are sometimes confused about the correct spellings of some words. One must keep and use a dictionary religiously. Never ignore and let pass a new word casually.

A number of question to test your knowledge of spellings are compiled here. Try to solve as many as you can.

Multiple Choice Questions

Directions: *Find the correctly spelt word out of the four options in each question.*

1. A. Accompalish B. Ackmplesh C. Acomplush D. Accomplish

2. A. Acommodation B. Acomodation C. Accomodation D. Accommodation

3. A. Astonished B. Astronished C. Astoneshed D. Asstonished

4. A. Benefeted B. Benefitted C. Benifited D. Benefited

5. A. Belligerent B. Beligirent C. Belligarant D. Belligerrent

6. A. Chancelery B. Chancellery C. Chancellary D. Chancelary

7. A. Discriminate B. Discremineta C. Discrimenate D. Discriminat

8. A. Damage B. Dammage C. Damaige D. Dammege

9. A. Efficiant B. Effecient C. Efficient D. Eficient

10. A. Extravagant B. Extreragent C. Extreregant D. Extravegent

11. A. Efflorascence B. Eflorescene C. Effllorescence D. Efflorescence

12. A. Equinimity B. Equanimmity C. Equannimity D. Equanimity

13. A. Farmament B. Farmement C. Fermament D. Fremament

14. A. Grieff B. Grief C. Grieef D. Grrief

15. A. Guarantee B. Garuntee C. Guaruntee D. Gaurantee

16. A. Hypocritical B. Hypocretical C. Hypocriticel D. Hypocirticel

17. A. Humurous B. Humorous C. Humoreus D. Humorrous

18. A. Itenerary B. Itinarery C. Itinarary D. Itinerary

19. A. Indipenseble B. Indispansible C. Indispensable D. Indipensable

20. A. Imprecticability B. Impracticebility C. Impracticibility D. Impracticability

21. A. Incradulous B. Incredulous C. Incridulous D. Incredalous

22. A. Juddicious B. Judiceous C. Judicious D. Judiceus

23. A. Kleptomonia B. Kleptemonia C. Kleptomania D. Klaptomania

24. A. Lackdaisical B. Lackadaisical C. Lckadaisicle D. Lackadisical

25. A. Licentious B. Licontious C. Licenttious D. Licientious

26. A. Meddicine B. Medicine
C. Medicene D. Medicinne

27. A. Meritricious B. Merefrecious
C. Meretricious D. Merritricious

28. A. Missunderstood B. Miesunderstood
C. Misunderstood D. Misunderstod

29. A. Occurad B. Occurred
C. Ocurred D. Occured

30. A. Osttentatious B. Ostentetious
C. Ostentatious D. Ostenttatious

31. A. Obnosious B. Obnoxeous
C. Obnoxious D. Obnoseous

32. A. Omenous B. Ominous
C. Ommineous D. Omineous

33. A. Pecification B. Pacification
C. Pecifacation D. Pecefication

34. A. Prograssive B. Progressive
C. Progresive D. Prograsive

35. A. Pasiveness B. Passiveness
C. Passeveniss D. Passivines

36. A. Polyendry B. Poliendry
C. Pollyendry D. Polyandry

37. A. Puerille B. Puerrile
C. Puerile D. Purrile

38. A. Pesanger B. Passenger
C. Pessenger D. Pasanger

39. A. Querrelsome B. Quarrelsame
C. Quarrelsome D. Querralsome

40. A. Rigourous B. Rigerous
C. Rigorous D. Regerous

41. A. Survellance B. Surveilance
C. Surveillance D. Survaillance

42. A. Schedule B. Schdule
C. Schedale D. Schedeule

43. A. Sepalchrle B. Sepalchral
C. Sepulchrle D. Sepulchral

44. A. Sympathetic B. Smypathetic
C. Sympothetic D. Sympethetic

45. A. Sincerely B. Sencerely
C. Sincerelly D. Sincerrely

46. A. Satellite B. Sattellite
C. Satelite D. Sattelite

47. A. Teracherous B. Treacherous
C. Treacheraus D. Treachereans

48. A. Uncivilized B. Uncevilized
C. Uncivillized D. Uncevelized

49. A. Vainglorious B. Vaniglorious
C. Vaniglerious D. Vaingloreus

50. A. Vulnarable B. Valnerable
C. Velnerable D. Vulnerable

ANSWERS

1	2	3	4	5	6	7	8	9	10
D	D	A	B	A	C	A	A	C	A
11	12	13	14	15	16	17	18	19	20
D	D	C	B	A	A	B	D	C	D
21	22	23	24	25	26	27	28	29	30
B	C	C	B	A	B	C	C	B	C
31	32	33	34	35	36	37	38	39	40
C	B	B	B	B	D	C	B	C	C
41	42	43	44	45	46	47	48	49	50
C	A	D	A	A	A	B	A	A	D

❑❑❑

2 Spotting Errors

The most common errors in English are of spellings, grammar and usage of words. By regular practice, the errors can be easily spotted and minimised.

Common Errors with Nouns and Noun-Phrases

	Incorrect	*Correct*
1.	I have bought new *furnitures.*	I have bought new *furniture.*
2.	The wages of sin *are* death.	The wages of sin *is* death.
3.	She told these *news* to her mother.	She told her mother this *news.*
4.	He took *troubles* to do his work.	He took *trouble* (or pains) over his work.
5.	The *cattles* were grazing.	The *cattle* were grazing.
6.	He showered *many abuses* on me.	He showered *much abuse* on me.
7.	I spent the holidays with my *family members.*	I spent the holidays with my *family.*
8.	There is no *place* in this compartment.	There is no *room* in this compartment.
9.	Write this new *poetry* in your *copy.*	Write this new *poem* in your *note-book.*
10.	He took *insult* at this.	He took *offence* at this.
11.	Put your *sign* here.	Put your *signatures* here.
12.	She is my *cousin sister.*	She is my *cousin.*
13.	*Sunil's* my *neighbour's* house was burgled.	*Sunil* my *neighbour's* house was burgled.
14.	I lost a *ten-rupees* note.	I lost *a ten-rupee* note.
15.	Road closed for *repair.*	Road closed for *repairs.*
16.	His house is out of *repairs.*	His house is out of *repair.*
17.	What is the *reason* of an earthquake?	What is the *cause* of an earthquake?
18.	This building is made of *stones.*	This building is made of *stone.*
19.	I disapprove of *these kinds* of games.	I disapprove of *this kind* of games.
20.	Veena's and Sheela's father is ill.	Veena and Sheela's father is ill.
21.	His *son-in-laws* are doctors.	His *sons-in-law* are doctors.
22.	*Alms* is given to the *poor.*	*Alms* are given to the poor.
23.	He always keeps his words.	He always keeps his *word.*
24.	I carried the *luggages.*	I carried the *luggage.*
25.	*Two-third* of the work is left.	*Two-thirds* of the work is left.

Common Errors with Pronouns

	Incorrect	Correct
1.	Both did not go.	Neither went.
2.	We all did not go.	None of us went.
3.	Each of these boys play.	Each of these boys plays.
4.	Whoever does best he will get a prize.	Whoever does best will get a prize.
5.	One should not waste his time.	A man should not waste his time.
6.	I and she are sisters.	She and I are sisters.
7.	He is wiser than me.	He is wiser than I.
8.	Between you and I, Anil is not to be trusted.	Between you and me, Anil is not to be trusted.
9.	Nobody was there but I.	Nobody was there but me.
10.	Who is there ? It is me.	Who is there ? It is I.
11.	Only he and me can use this card.	Only he and I can use this card.
12.	Let you and I go now.	Let you and me go now.
13.	Everyone got one's pay.	Everyone got his pay.
14.	Everyone is frightened when they see a tiger.	Everyone is frightened when he sees a tiger.
15.	These two friends are fond of one another.	These two friends are fond of each other.
16.	I did not like him coming at that hour.	I did not like his coming at that hour.
17.	Who do you think I met?	Whom do you think I met?
18.	You should avail this opportunity.	You should avail yourself this opportunity.
19.	When you have read these books, please return the same to me.	When you have read the books, please return them to me.
20.	They that are humble need fear no fall.	Those that are humble need fear no fall.

Common Errors with Adjectives

	Incorrect	Correct
1.	These all oranges are good.	All these oranges are good.
2.	He held the book in the both hands.	He held the book in both hands.
3.	Both men have not come.	Neither man has come.
4.	That man should do some or other work.	That man should do some work or other.
5.	He is elder than I.	He is older than I.
6.	Shakespeare is greater than any other poets.	Shakespeare is greater than any other poet.
7.	He is a coward man.	He is a cowardly man.
8.	Many villagers cannot write his own name.	Many villagers cannot write their own name.
9.	Each of us loves our home.	Each of us loves his home.
10.	Much efforts bring their reward.	Much effort brings its reward.
11.	He found hundred rupees.	He found a hundred rupees.
12.	He had leave of four days.	He had four days leave.
13.	This is a worth seeing sight.	This is a sight worth seeing.
14.	He will spend his future life here.	He will spend the rest of his life here.
15.	There is a best teacher in that class.	There is a very good teacher in that class.
16.	Of the two plans this is the best.	Of the two plans this is the better.
17.	He is becoming strong every day.	He is becoming stronger every day.
18.	He is worst than I.	He is worse than I.
19.	Jaipur is hot than Delhi.	Jaipur is hotter than Delhi.
20.	In our library the number of books is less.	In our library the number of books is small.

Common Errors with Verbs

	Incorrect	*Correct*
1.	He asked had we taken our luggage.	He asked if we had taken our luggage.
2.	She asked what are you doing.	She asked what we were doing.
3.	Rama asked to Anil why he is angry.	Rama asked Anil why he was angry.
4.	He does not care for his money.	He does not take care of his money.
5.	He does not care for his work.	He takes no care over his work.
6.	No one cared for him after his mother died.	No one took care of him after his mother died.
7.	He got angry before I said a word.	He got angry before I had said a word.
8.	I met a man who was my tutor 20 years ago.	I met a man who had been my tutor twenty years ago.
9.	I had been for walking yesterday.	I went for a walk yesterday.
10.	If I shall do this I shall be wrong.	If I do this I shall be wrong.
11.	I have left trekking.	I have given up trekking.
12.	I came to know as to how he did this.	I learnt how he did this.
13.	I came to know why he was sad.	I found out why he was sad.
14.	He knows to swim.	He knows how to swim.
15.	The criminal's head was cut.	The criminal's head was cut off.
16.	I said to him to go.	I told him to go.
17.	I told the teacher to excuse me.	I asked the teacher to excuse me.
18.	He is troubling me.	He is giving me trouble.
19.	I have got a hurt on my leg.	I have hurt my leg.
20.	She gave a speech.	She made a speech.

Common Errors in Subject-Verb Agreement

	Incorrect	*Correct*
1.	The owners of this factory *is* very rich.	The owners of this factory *are* very rich.
2.	The pleasures of nature that one can experience at Shimla *is* beyond description.	The pleasures of nature that one can experience at Shimla *are* beyond description.
3.	There *is* no street lights in our colony.	There *are* no street lights in our colony.
4.	He and I *am* entrusted with the job.	He and I *are* entrusted with the job.
5.	Rice and curry *are* his favourite dish.	Rice and curry *is* his favourite dish.
6.	The honour and glory of our country *are* at stake.	The honour and glory of our country *is* at stake.
7.	Time and tide *waits* for none.	Time and tide *wait* for none.
8.	All the passengers with the driver *was* killed.	All the passengers, with the driver, *were* killed.
9.	The teacher, with her students, *were* going out.	The teacher, with her students, *was* going out.
10.	I as well as they *am* tired.	I as well as they *are* tired.
11.	Not only the soldiers but their captain also *were* captured.	Not only the soldiers but their captain also *was* captured.
12.	Neither you nor I *were* selected.	Neither you nor I *was* selected.
13.	Either of these two applicants *are* fit for the job but neither want to accept it.	Either of these two applicants *is* fit for the job but neither wants to accept it.
14.	One of these students are sure to stand first.	One of these students *is* sure to stand first.
15.	Everyone of these workers want a raise.	Everyone of these workers wants a raise.
16.	None of these letters has been answered so far.	None of these letters *have* been answered so far.
17.	None of the girls were present at the party.	None of the girls *was* present at the party.
18.	Many a battle were fought on Indian soil.	Many a battle *was* fought on Indian soil.
19.	A lot of work remain to be done.	A lot of work *remains* to be done.
20.	The majority of these girls likes music.	The majority of these girls *like* music.

Common Errors in the Use of Modals/Auxiliary Verbs

	Incorrect	*Correct*
1.	When I shall see him I shall tell him this.	When I *see* him, I shall tell him this.
2.	If I should do wrong, he would punish me.	If I *did* wrong, he would punish me.
3.	Until he will have confessed his fault, he will be kept in prison.	Until he *has* confessed his fault, he will be kept in prison.
4.	She will obey me.	She *shall* obey me.
5.	You would work hard.	You *should* work hard.
6.	You shall find him in the garden.	You *will* find him in the garden.
7.	He must have died of exposure, but we cannot be certain.	He *might* have died of exposure, but we cannot be certain.
8.	You might not show disrespect to your elders.	You *must* not show disrespect to your elders.
9.	You may take exercise in order to maintain good health.	You *must* take exercise in order to maintain good health.
10.	He must be a crook for all we know.	He *may* be a crook for all we know.

Common Errors in the Use of Adverbs

	Incorrect	*Correct*
1.	He is very much angry.	He is *very* angry.
2.	She was very good enough to help me.	She was *good enough* to help me.
3.	She runs much fast.	She runs *very* fast.
4.	She runs very faster than Seema.	She runs *much* faster than Seema.
5.	It is bitter cold today.	It is *bitterly* cold today.
6.	He is a much learned man.	He is a very learned man.
7.	She is thinking very hardly.	She is thinking very hard.
8.	To tell in brief the film was boring.	*In short* the film was boring.
9.	He told the story in details.	He told the story *in detail.*
10.	I did it anyhow.	I *managed to do* it somehow.
11.	Aeroplanes reach Europe soon.	Aeroplanes reach Europe quickly.
12.	Before long there were dinosaurs on the earth.	*Long ago,* there were dinosaurs on the earth.
13.	This book is too interesting.	This book is *very* interesting.
14.	He lives miserly.	He lives in *a miserly* way.
15.	Just I had gone when she came.	I had just gone when she came.
16.	He sings good.	He sings *well.*
17.	He sings good than I.	He sings *better* than I.
18.	Really speaking it is cold.	*As a matter of fact* it is cold.
19.	He is enough tall to reach the ceiling.	He is *tall enough* to reach the ceiling.
20.	He went directly to his college.	He went *direct* to his college.

Common Errors in the Use of Conjunctions

	Incorrect	*Correct*
1.	As he is fat so he runs slowly.	As he is fat *he* runs slowly.
2.	If he is fat then he will run slowly.	If he is fat, he will run slowly.
3.	Though he is fat still he runs fast.	Though he is fat, *he runs* fast.
4.	*As* I pulled the trigger at the sametime he shook my arm.	As I pulled the trigger, he shook my arm.
5.	No sooner I had spoken than he left.	No sooner *had* I spoken than he left.

	Incorrect	Correct
6.	Not only he will go, but also he will stay there.	Not only *will he* go, but he *will also* stay there.
7.	Neither he comes nor he writes.	Neither *does he* come nor *does he* write.
8.	Scarcely he entered the room than the telephone rang.	Scarcely *had* he entered the room *when the* telephone rang.
9.	Hardly she had left the house than it began to rain.	Hardly *had she* left the house *when* it began to rain.
10.	He is the fastest runner and he comes last.	He is the fastest runner *but* he comes last.
11.	She is as innocent as if she looks.	She is as innocent as she looks.
12.	Until he does not try he must be punished.	He must be punished unless he tries.
13.	I want to know as to why you are late.	I want to know why you are late.
14.	I am fond of Chinese food as for example sweet and sour prawns.	I am fond of Chinese food, for example, sweet and sour prawns.
15.	He was angry therefore I ran away.	He was angry so I ran away.
16.	I was trying to work, at that time he was disturbing me.	While I was trying to work, he was disturbing me.
17.	Supposing if he is late, what will happen?	Supposing he is late (or if he is late) what will happen?
18.	He asked me that why I was late.	He asked me why I was late.
19.	Let us catch a taxi lest we should not get late.	Let us catch a taxi lest we should get late.
20.	She dresses herself like the teacher does.	She dresses herself as the teacher does.
21.	Wait while I come.	Wait *until* (or *till*) I come.
22.	Until, there is corruption in India, there can be little progress.	*As long* as there is corruption in India there can be little progress.
23.	I have never told a lie nor cheated anybody.	I have never told a lie *nor have I* cheated anybody.
24.	Both Mohan as well as Arun are responsible for this action.	Both Mohan *and* Arun are responsible for this action.
25.	Hindus and Muslims both are to blame for the riots.	*Both Hindus* and Muslims are to blame for the riots.

Common Errors in the Use of Prepositions

	Incorrect	*Correct*
1.	I will not listen him.	I will not listen *to* him.
2.	Copy this word by word.	Copy this word *for* word.
3.	He enquired from her where she lived.	He enquired *of* her where she lived.
4.	Sign here with ink.	Sign here *in* ink.
5.	Has she come in train or by foot?	Has she come *by* train or *on* foot?
6.	She said this at his face.	She said this *to* his face.
7.	Open the book on page one.	Open the book *at* page one.
8.	I was invited for lunch.	I was *invited to* lunch.
9.	I am ill since three months.	I have been *ill for* three months.
10.	This paper is inferior than that.	This paper is inferior *to* that.
11.	This resembles to that.	This *resembles* that.
12.	My brother is superior than you in strength.	My brother is superior *to* you in strength.
13.	He wrote me.	He wrote *to* me.
14.	I shall explain them this.	I shall explain this *to* them.
15.	Send this letter on my address.	Send this letter *to* my address.
16.	He suggested me this.	He suggested this *to* me.
17.	He goes *on his* work.	He goes *to his* work.
18.	He *reached to* Nagpur.	He *reached* Nagpur.
19.	He told *to me* to go.	He told *me* to go.
20.	The term begins *from* July 1st.	The term begins *on* July 1st.

Multiple Choice Questions

Directions: *In this section, each sentence has three parts, indicated by (A), (B) and (C). Read each sentence to find out whether there is an error. If you find an error in any one of the parts (A, B, C), indicate your response by marking the letter related to that part. If a sentence has no error, indicate this by marking '(D)' which stands for "No error". Errors may belong to grammar, usage or idiom. Ignore errors of punctuation, if any.*

1. (A) Beware of/(B) a fair-weather friend/(C) who is neither a friend in need nor a friend indeed/(D) No error.
2. (A) Copernicus proved/(B) that Earth/(C) moves round the Sun./(D) No error.
3. (A) Seldom we have been treated/(B) in such a rude manner/(C) by the police personnel./(D) No error.
4. (A) Some men are born great,/(B) some achieve greatness/(C) and some had greatness thrust on them./(D) No error.
5. (A) The property/(B) was divided/(C) among the two brothers./(D) No error.
6. (A) I am quite certain/(B) that the lady is not only greedy/(C) but miserly./(D) No error.
7. (A) The aircraft overloaded/(B) there was something wrong of the battery/(C) and the engine was making a queer noise/(D) No error.
8. (A) A thorough inquiry of the misappropriation of funds/(B) is now imperative/(C) to bring the guilty to book/(D) No error.
9. (A) The brilliant success in the examination/(B) as well as his record in sports/(C) deserves high praise/(D) No error.
10. (A) While travelling by a train/(B) on a cold winter night/(C) an argument rose between two passengers in our compartment/(D) No error.
11. (A) I cannot find/(B) where has he gone/(C) though I have tried may best/(D) No error.
12. (A) If I was/(B) the Prime Minister of India/(C) I would work wonders/(D) No error.
13. (A) Amit's severe bout of flu/(B) debilitated him so much/(C) that he was too tired to do for work for a week./(D) No error.
14. (A) This is the crux of the entire problem;/(B) everything centres on/(C) it being resolved./(D) No error.
15. (A) One of the major aims of the Air Force/(B) was the complete demolition of all means of transportation/(C) by the bombing of rail lines and terminals./(D) No error.
16. (A) His strong voice cut over/(B) the hum of conversation/(C) like a knife through butter./(D) No error.
17. (A) Even though they weren't expecting us/(B) they managed to knock up/(C) a marvellous meal./(D) No error.
18. (A) The celebrated singer was/(B) surrounded by the usual crowd/(C) of lackeys and hanger-ons./(D) No error.
19. (A) If it weren't/(B) for you,/(C) I wouldn't be alive today./(D) No error.
20. (A) He looked like a lion/(B) baulked from/(C) its prey./(D) No error.
21. (A) Widespread flooding/(B) is effecting/(C) large areas of the villages./(D) No error.
22. (A) She regards/(B) negotiating prices with customers/(C) as her special preserve./(D) No error.
23. (A) Often in political campaigns, a point is reached at which/(B) the candidates take out their gloves./(C) and start slugging with bare fists./(D) No error.
24. (A) If we really set to/(B) we can get the whole house/(C) cleaned in an afternoon./(D) No error.
25. (A) Pieces of rock plummeted/(B) down the mountainside/(C) in the ground below./(D) No error.

Answers

1	2	3	4	5	6	7	8	9	10
D	B	A	C	C	C	B	A	D	C
11	12	13	14	15	16	17	18	19	20
B	A	C	C	B	A	A	C	C	C
21	22	23	24	25					
C	A	A	A	C					

❑❑❑

3 Articles

Definite and Indefinite Articles

(*i*) 'A' and 'an' are Indefinite Articles.

(*ii*) 'The' is Definite Article.

(*iii*) 'A' and 'an' modify a noun in a general way.

(*iv*) 'The' particularises it. *e.g.*,

Mohan has **a pen.**

The pen which you gave me was expensive.

Vowel and Consonant Sounds

(*i*) 'A' is used before words starting with the sound of a consonant.

(*ii*) 'An' is used before a vowel sound (vowels a, e, i, o, u) *e.g.*, a book, a cat, a useful thing, a European girl, a university, but an FDR, an MA, an honest boy, an hour, an owl, an egg, an umbrella, etc.

Use of Articles 'A' and 'An'

A cat mews. (*i.e.,* every cat)

The cat of my neighbour mews day and night. (*i.e.,* a particular cat)

He gave me **an** egg. (Here 'an' means 'one')

Use of Article 'The'

1. 'The' is used before names of rivers, mountains, seas, oceans:
   The Himalayas, the Ganga, the Yamuna, the Bay of Bengal, the Indian Ocean, the Nile, the English Channel, *etc.*
2. Names of newspapers and magazines:
   The Times of India, the Tribune, The Sun, *etc.*
3. Names of the famous and holy books:
   The Guru Granth Sahib, The Gita, The Ramayana, *etc.*
4. Names of creations of nature:
   the sun, the earth, the moon, the sky, *etc.*
5. While using Adjectives as Nouns:
   The poor should be helped by **the rich.**
6. Sometimes with the Comparative Degree:
   The more you think, **the more** you worry.
7. With the Superlative Degree:
   She is **the most intelligent** girl in our school.
8. Before the imaginary lines and directions:
   The Latitude, The Equator, the east, the west, etc.
9. Before the names of musical instruments:
   The violin, the piano, the flute, etc.
10. While using a Proper Noun as a Common Noun:
    Mohan is **the Sachin** of our team.

Omission of Article 'The'

1. Before some Nouns used to convey general sense, articles are not used but are used to particularise them:
   Man is mortal.
2. Before Proper Nouns:
   Rakesh is an intelligent boy.
3. With Abstract Noun:
   Childhood is the prime time of one's life.
   The childhood of Sohan was full of sorrow.
4. With Material Nouns:
   Milk is an essential food.
   The milk of the cow is sweet.
5. Usually no article is used before names of diseases:
   Cancer is a fatal disease.
   However, when we talk about a disease figuratively, we use an article before its name, *e.g.*
   Corruption is a cancer.
6. Names of games and language:
   I like football.
   I can speak Punjabi, Hindi and English.
7. Gold is a precious metal.
   NOTE: As you must have noted above, the definite article 'the' has been used where a noun is particularised.

Double Use of Article 'The'

Read the following sentences carefully to understand this :

1. The poet and novelist has been honoured.
   (The same person is the poet as well as novelist)
2. The poet and the novelist have been honoured.
   (The poet and the novelist are two different persons).
3. I have a black and white dog.
   (that is, one dog)
4. I have a black and a white dog.
   (that is, two dogs)

Multiple Choice Questions

Directions : *Fill in the blanks with suitable articles. Mark 'D' if no article required.*

1. Do you know .... boy in white?
A. a B. an
C. the D. No article

2. She is .... girl I am looking for.
A. a B. an
C. the D. No article

3. Have you read .... Mahabharat?
A. a B. an
C. the D. No article

4. ....rich are not always happy.
A. A B. An
C. The D. No article

5. Oranges are sold by .... dozen.
A. a B. an
C. the D. No article

6. Milk is sold by .... litre.
A. a B. an
C. the D. No article

7. .... Amazon is the longest river in the world.
A. A B. An
C. The D. No article

8. .... higher you climb, the colder it gets.
A. A B. An
C. The D. No article

9. She is .... untidy girl.
A. a B. an
C. the D. No article

10. I am .... M.A. is English.
A. a B. an
C. the D. No article

11. I have already spent .... few rupees I had.
A. a B. an
C. the D. No article

12. .... English are very hard-working.
A. A B. An
C. The D. No article

13. April is the fourth month of .... year.
A. a B. an
C. the D. No article

14. Rice is sold by .... kilogram
A. a B. an
C. the D. No article

15. She is .... best of the three girls.
A. a B. an
C. the D. No article

16. .... man in the car is a friend of mine.
A. A B. An
C. The D. No article

17. Brevity is .... soul of wit.
A. a B. an
C. the D. No article

18. .... thing of beauty is a joy for ever.
A. A B. An
C. The D. No article

19. .... little learning is a dangerous thing.
A. A B. An
C. The D. No article

20. .... best sauce for food is hunger.
A. A B. An
C. The D. No article

Answers

1	2	3	4	5	6	7	8	9	10
C	C	C	C	C	C	C	C	B	B
11	**12**	**13**	**14**	**15**	**16**	**17**	**18**	**19**	**20**
C	C	C	C	C	C	C	A	A	C

❑❑❑

4 Prepositions

A Preposition is a word that comes before a Pronoun or a Noun and expresses the relationship between Noun or Pronoun and some part of the remaining sentence.

(*a*) He is busy **with** his work.
(*b*) The boy jumped **into** the river.
(*c*) The birds are chirping **in** the trees.

In these sentences the words **with**, **into** and **in** show the relationship between the verbs **busy, jumped** and **chirping** with the nouns **work, river** and **trees** respectively.

Position of the Preposition

A. A Preposition usually precedes its object.
(*i*) He laughs **at** the poor.
(*ii*) He is angry **with** you.
(*iii*) She agrees **with** me.

B. In the case of Relative Pronouns it comes after the subject.
(*i*) This is the boy whom I was looking **for**.
(*ii*) That is the pen whose mention I was making **of**.

C. In the following cases, the Preposition comes after its object.
(*i*) Where is the boy you were complaining **against**?
(*ii*) What things are there you are looking **for**?
(*iii*) Who is there, you are waiting **for**?

Omission of the Prepositon

In many cases when the sentences contain Nouns of Time or Place, the Prepositions **from**, **in** and **for** are often omitted.
(*i*) He walked many kilometres.
(*ii*) He came to see me last year.
(*iii*) As I could not find my puppy anywhere, I looked here and there.

Prepositions are small words that show the relationship between one word and another. Prepositions in the following sentences show the position of the paper in relation to the desk, the book, hand and the door.

The paper is **on** the desk.
The paper is **under** the book.
The paper is **in** his hand.
The paper is **by** the door.

Common Prepositions

about	at	by
in	onto	toward
above	before	concerning
inside	out	under
across	behind	despite
into	over	until
after	below	down
like	since	up
against	beneath	during
near	through	upon
along	beside	except
of	throughout	with
amid	between	for
off	till	within
among	beyond	from
on	to	without

Multiple Choice Questions

Directions: *Select the most appropriate preposition from the given alternatives to fill in the blanks and make the sentence meaningfully complete.*

1. Don't try to be an advocate ..... these criminals.
A. for B. with
C. across D. in

2. The audience admired him ..... his sweet voice.
A. to B. on
C. for D. at

3. I want to check your bag ..... fake currency notes.
A. to B. for
C. upon D. on

4. The dew drops clung .... the blades of grass.
A. for B. on
C. to D. in

5. The thief was chased ..... by the police.
A. on B. after
C. into D. at

6. Please carry this bag ..... my room.
A. on B. for
C. to D. in

7. A lorry bumped ..... a car.
A. on B. over
C. into D. to

8. They were begging ..... food.
A. for B. on
C. to D. after

9. She always boasts ..... her wealth.
A. of B. for
C. on D. after

10. She banged ..... the door violently.
A. for B. to
C. on D. down

11. I applied ..... the post of a clerk.
A. for B. on
C. in D. to

12. I applied ..... the Principal for the post of a teacher.
A. to B. on
C. with D. for

13. I begged ..... him not to divulge the secret.
A. for B. of
C. with D. to

14. You had better borrow a pen ..... Rakesh.
A. over B. into
C. from D. by

15. I baked a cake ..... the guests.
A. to B. for
C. on D. of

16. She is confident ..... (her) success.
A. with B. on
C. of D. for

17. The doctor will cure you ..... malaria.
A. of B. with
C. for D. from

18. This law is common ..... all.
A. to B. upon
C. over D. at

19. She was condemned ..... her bad hand writing.
A. on B. for
C. into D. of

20. In summer there will be a great demand ..... desert cooler.
A. on B. with
C. for D. of

21. We shall wait ..... you.
A. on B. for
C. towards D. after

22. Tom displayed his injury ..... all his friends.
A. for B. upon
C. to D. at

23. She distributed the sweets ..... the two brothers.
A. among B. between
C. for D. in

24. Please distribute these apples ..... all.
A. among B. to
C. for D. at

25. It rarely happened that he defended ..... an innocent person.
A. against B. for
C. upon D. at

26. The parents were disappointed ..... the performance of their son.
A. on B. with
C. at D. of

27. Common salt dissolves ..... water.
A. for B. in
C. with D. by

28. This medicare is free ..... sugar.
A. on B. to
C. from D. of

29. The manager granted leave ..... the clerk.
A. to B. on
C. into D. for

30. The air was heavy ..... aroma of perfumes.
A. on B. with
C. into D. from

ANSWERS

1	2	3	4	5	6	7	8	9	10
A	C	B	C	B	C	C	A	A	C
11	12	13	14	15	16	17	18	19	20
A	A	B	C	B	C	A	A	B	C
21	22	23	24	25	26	27	28	29	30
B	C	B	A	A	C	B	C	A	B

❑❑❑

5 Synonyms & Antonyms

There are thousands of words in English language. No one can remember their meanings easily but with regular practice one can memorise most of them. A number of words with their Synonyms and Antonyms are compiled here. Try to learn as many as you can and answer the questions thereafter.

Words	*Synonyms*	*Antonyms*
Abandon	Cease, Forsake	Continue
Abhor	Hate, Loathe, Detest	Like, Love
Abiding	Enduring, Durable	Fleeting
Able	Proficient, Competent	Incompetent, Unfit
Ability	Skill, Power	Disability, Inability
Abortive	Fruitless, Futile	Fruitful, Successful
Abolish	Destroy, Undo	Restore, Revive
Abridge	Shorten, Curtail	Lengthen, Expand
Absolve	Forgive, Pardon, Excuse	Condemn
Accelerate	Hasten	Retard
Accord	Agreement, Harmony	Discord, Disagreement
Accumulate	Collect, Store, Amass	Distribute, Scatter
Adamant	Hard, Inflexible	Flexible
Adversity	Misfortune, Distress	Prosperity
Adept	Expert, Skilful	Inexpert, Unskillful
Aggravate	Heighten, Intensify	Quell, Suppress
Agile	Nimble	Clumsy, Undeft
Alert	Vigilant	Heedless
Allay	Calm, Soothe, Assuage	Arouse
Ameliorate	Improve, Advance, Amend	Worsen, Deteriorate
Ambiguous	Vague, Unclear	Clear
Amiable	Lovable, Agreeable	Disagreeable
Annihilate	Destroy	Create
Arduous	Hard, Strenuous	Easy
Attacks	Assault	Defend
Audacity	Boldness	Cowardice
Auspicious	Favourable, Propitious, Lucky	Ominous, Inauspicious, Unlucky
Austere	Harsh, Severe, Rigorous	Easy-going
Authentic	True, Genuine	Spurious, False
Avarice	Greed	Generosity
Averse	Unwilling, Loath, Disinclined	Willing, Inclined
Aversion	Hostility, Hatred	Affinity, Liking

Words	Synonyms	Antonyms
Base	Low, Mean, Ignoble	Noble, Exalted
Boisterous	Noisy, Stormy	Calm, Quiet
Brave	Courageous, Daring, Bold, Plucky	Cowardly, Dastardly, Timid
Brief	Short, Concise, Laconic	Lengthy, Diffuse
Bright	Vivid, Radiant	Dull, Dark
Brutal	Savage, Cruel	Humane, Kindly
Callous	Hard, Cruel, Indifferent	Soft, Tender, Concerned
Cautious	Careful, Wary	Rash, Reckless, Foolhardy
Censure (*n*)	Blame, Condemnation	Praise
Censure (*vb*)	Blame, Condemn	Praise, Commend
Circumscribed	Restricted, Confined, Limited	Unconfined, Unrestricted
Civil	Polite, Courteous, Gracious, Urbane	Rude, Uncivil, Impolite, Ungracious
Coerce	Compel, Force	Volunteer
Compassionate	Pitiful, Sympathetic, Merciful	Unsympathetic, Merciless, Cruel
Compress	Condense, Abbreviate	Expand, Lengthen
Conspicuous	Noticeable, Manifest	Inconspicuous
Constant	Steady, Steadfast, Uniform	Inconstant, Variable
Cordial	Friendly, Warm, Hearty	Cold, Unfriendly
Covert	Hidden, Secret	Overt, Open
Cruel	Savage, Ruthless, Vicious	Kind, Gentle, Benevolent
Cursory	Rapid, Superficial	Thorough, Exhaustive, Intensive
Credible	Believable, Probable, Plausible	Incredible, Unbelievable, Fantastic
Crafty	Cunning, Sly	Artless, Simple, Ingenuous
Costly	Expensive, Dear	Cheap, Inexpensive
Confidence	Trust, Reliance	Distrust, Doubt
Death	Decease, Demise	Existence, Life
Dearth	Scarcity, Lack, Want, Paucity, Shortage	Plenty, Abundance
Decay	Dissolution, Decline, Decomposition, Disintegration	Regeneration
Deference	Respect, Reverence	Disrespect, Irreverence
Deficient	Lacking, Inadequate	Complete, Sufficient
Desolate	Lonely, Deserted	Crowded, Occupied
Destitute	Wanting, Needy	Rich, Affluent
Diligence	Industry, Perseverance	Idleness
Disgrace	Dishonour, Discredit	Honour, Credit
Dwindle	Decrease, Shrink	Grow, Increase
Earthly	Terrestrial, Mundane	Celestial, Heavenly, Unearthly
Eligible	Qualified, Suitable	Ineligible, Unsuitable
Emancipate	Liberate, Free	Enslave
Excited	Impassioned, Stimulated	Composed, Cool, Impassive
Extraordinary	Uncommon, Remarkable, Marvellous	Commonplace, Ordinary
Extravagant	Lavish, Prodigal, Wastrel, Spendthrift	Thrifty, Economical, Frugal
Fabricate	Construct, Make	Destroy
Fabulous	Fictitious, Mythical	Actual, Real
False	Untrue, Mendacious	True, Genuine
Famous	Well-known, Renowned	Obscure, Unknown

Words	Synonyms	Antonyms
Fantastic	Fanciful, Imaginative, Visionary	Practical, Down to earth
Fearful	Nervous, Anxious, Afraid, Scared	Fearless, Dauntless
Felicity	Happiness	Sorrow
Gaiety	Joyousness, Hilarity	Mourning, Dullness
Garrulous	Talkative, Loquacious	Taciturn, Silent, Reserved
Generous	Liberal, Magnanimous	Stingy, Miserly
Gigantic	Huge, Colossal	Minute, Small
Graphic	Vivid, Pictorial, Meaningful	Vague
Guest	Visitor	Host
Guile	Fraud, Trickery	Artlessness, Ingenuousness
Gratitude	Gratefulness	Ingratitude, Ungratefulness
Gratuitous	Voluntary, Spontaneous, Unwarranted	Involuntary, Forced
Hamper	Hinder, Obstruct	Facilitate, Ease
Haughty	Arrogant, Proud	Humble, Modest
Hazardous	Dangerous, Perilous	Safe, Secure Protected
Headstrong	Obstinate, Stubborn	Weak-willed, Flexible
Hope	Belief, Conviction, Expectation	Despair, Hopelessness
Improvident	Prodigal, Carelessness	Provident, Economical
Incessant	Unceasing, Continuous	Discontinuous
Indolent	Slothful, Lethargic	Active, Energetic
Joy	Delight, Pleasure	Sadness, Gloom
Jolly	Jovial, Merry	Gloomy, Sad
Judicious	Discreet, Prudent	Indiscreet, Injudicious
Knowledge	Enlightenment, Learning	Ignorance, Stupidity
Laborious	Industrious, Assiduous	Slothful, Lazy
Laxity	Slackness, Looseness	Firmness
Lenient	Mild, Forbearing	Strict, Stern
Lethal	Deadly, Fatal, Mortal	Life-giving, Vital, Vivifying
Liberal	Generous, Tolerant	Intolerant, Illiberal
Liberty	Freedom, Independence	Slavery, Bondage
Lively	Animated, Active	Dull, Listless
Loyal	Faithful, Devoted	Treacherous, Disloyal, Unfaithful
Lucky	Fortunate	Unlucky, Unfortunate
Lucrative	Profitable	Unprofitable
Magnanimous	Generous, Largehearted	Ungenerous, Stingy
Malady	Illness, Ailment	Health
Manifest	Noticeable, Obvious	Obscure, Puzzling
Meagre	Small	Plentiful, Large
Mean	Low, Abject	Noble, Exalted
Mendacious	False, Untruthful	Truthful
Misery	Sorrow, Distress	Happiness, Joy
Morbid	Sick, Diseased	Healthy
Mournful	Sorrowful, Sad	Joyful, Happy
Negligent	Careless, Heedless	Careful
Notorious	Infamous, Disreputable	Reputable
Obedient	Submissive, Compliant, Docile	Disobedient, Recalcitrant, Wayward

Words	Synonyms	Antonyms
Obsolete	Antiquated, Out-of-Date	Current, Modern
Opportune	Timely, Seasonable	Inopportune
Opulence	Wealth, Riches	Penury, Poverty
Onerous	Heavy, Burdensome	Light, Easy
Palatable	Tasty, Delicious	Unpalatable
Pathetic	Touching	Joyous, Cheery
Persuade	Urge, Induce	Dissuade
Praise (*vb*)	Applaud, Eulogise	Condemn
Praise (*n*)	Applause, Eulogy	Condemnation
Precarious	Risky, Uncertain	Safe, Certain
Pretence	Pretext, Excuse	Candour, Frankness
Propagate	Breed, Circulate	Terminate, Restrict
Quaint	Odd, Singular	Usual, Ordinary
Quell	Suppress, Subdue	Agitate, Arouse
Rare	Uncommon, Scarce	Common, Ordinary
Refined	Polished, Elegant	Crude, Coarse
Remote	Distant	Near, Close
Renown	Fame, Reputation	Infamy, Notoriety
Rigid	Stiff, Unyielding	Flexible, Yielding
Remorseful	Regretful, Repentant	Unrepentant
Rebellion	Revolt, Mutiny, Insurgency	Loyalty
Scared	Holy, Consecrated	Profane, Unholy
Sane	Sensible, Sound	Insane
Scold	Chide, Rebuke	Praise
Serious	Grave, Earnest	Frivolous
Shy	Bashful	Bold, Impudent
Simple	Plain, Artless	Complex, Cunning, Shrewd
Solitary	Single, Lonely, Secluded	Numerous, Multitude
Shallow	Superficial	Deep
Solace	Comfort, Relief	Discomfort, Grief
Spurious	Sham, False	Genuine, Authentic
Stagnant	Still, Motionless	Moving
Surplus	Excess	Deficit, Shortage
Tame	Gentle, Mild, Domesticated	Savage, Wild
Teacher	Instructor, Educator	Student, Pupil
Tedious	Wearisome, Monotonous	Agreeable, Lively
Temporal	Worldly, Secular	Spiritual
Temperate	Moderate	Immoderate, Intemperate
Tortuous	Winding, Circuitous	Straight, Direct
Tough	Hard, Strong	Tender, Soft, Flexible
Transient	Temporary, Fleeting	Lasting, Durable, Permanent
Trusworthy	Reliable	Unreliable, Untrustworthy
Tranquil	Calm	Agitated
Ugly	Unsightly, Repulsive	Beautiful, Attractive
Useful	Advantageous, Serviceable	Useless
Vehemence	Passion, Force	Apathy, Indifference

Words	Synonyms	Antonyms
Vindictive	Revengeful	Forgiving
Wholesome	Healthy	Unwholesome, Morbid, Unhealthy, Diseased
Wicked	Evil, Impious	Pious, Good
Wise	Sagacious, Erudite	Foolish, Stupid
Wrath	Anger, Fury, Rage	Love, Peace, Calm
Wreck	Ruin, Destroy	Create, Construct
Yield	Surrender, Submit	Resist, Revolt
Yielding	Submissive, Supple	Inflexible, Intractable
Yoke	Oppression, Bondage	Freedom
Zeal	Passion, Fervour	Apathy, Indifference
Zest	Relish, Enthusiasm	Distaste, Disrelish

Multiple Choice Questions

Directions (Qs. 1 to 45): *In the following questions choose the word which best expresses the MEANING of the given word.*

1. TEPID
   A. Hot B. Warm
   C. Cold D. Boiling
2. MAYHEM
   A. Jubilation B. Havoc
   C. Excitement D. Defeat
3. TIMID
   A. Fast B. Slow
   C. Medium D. Shy
4. CANTANKEROUS
   A. Quarrelsome B. Rash
   C. Disrespectful D. Noisy
5. PRECARIOUS
   A. Cautious B. Critical
   C. Perilous D. Brittle
6. TACITURNITY
   A. Dumbness B. Changeableness
   C. Hesitation D. Reserve
7. INEBRIATE
   A. Dreamy B. Stupefied
   C. Unsteady D. Drunken
8. HARBINGER
   A. Massenger B. Steward
   C. Forerunner D. Pilot
9. INTIMIDATE
   A. To hint B. Frighten
   C. Bluff D. Harass
10. IRONIC
    A. Inflexible B. Bitter
    C. Good-natured D. Disguisedly sarcastic
11. STRINGENT
    A. Tense B. Stringy
    C. Strict D. Causing to shrink
12. ECSTATIC
    A. Animated B. Bewildered
    C. Enraptured D. Willful
13. COMMENSURATE
    A. Measurable B. Proportionate
    C. Beginning D. Appropriate
14. DESTITUTION
    A. Humility B. Moderation
    C. Poverty D. Beggary
15. ASCEND
    A. Leap B. Grow
    C. Deviate D. Mount
16. UNCOUTH
    A. Ungraceful B. Rough
    C. Slovenly D. Dirty
17. LYNCH
    A. Hang B. Madden
    C. Killed D. Shoot
18. LAUD
    A. Lord B. Eulogy
    C. Praise D. Extolled
19. CORRESPONDENCE
    A. Agreements B. Contracts
    C. Documents D. Letters
20. VENUE
    A. Place B. Agenda
    C. Time D. Duration

21. STERILE
A. Barren B. Arid
C. Childless D. Dry

22. SYNOPSIS
A. Index B. Mixture
C. Summary D. Puzzle

23. GERMANE
A. Responsible B. Logical
C. Possible D. Relevant

24. PONDER
A. Think B. Evaluate
C. Anticipate D. Increase

25. CANNY
A. Obstinate B. Handsome
C. Clever D. Stout

26. ABUNDANT
A. Ripe B. Cheap
C. Plenty D. Absent

27. CONSEQUENCES
A. Results B. Conclusions
C. Difficulties D. Applications

28. SHIVER
A. Shake B. Rock
C. Tremble D. Move

29. DILIGENT
A. Progressive B. Brilliant
C. Inventive D. Hard-working

30. DISTANT
A. Far B. Removed
C. Reserved D. Separate

31. FORAY
A. Excursion B. Contest
C. Ranger D. Intuition

32. FRUGALITY
A. Foolishness B. Extremity
C. Enthusiasm D. Economy

33. GARNISH
A. Paint B. Garner
C. Adorn D. Abuse

34. VIGOUR
A. Strength B. Boldness
C. Warmth D. Enthusiasm

35. CANDID
A. Apparent B. Explicit
C. Frank D. Bright

36. BRIEF
A. Limited B. Small
C. Little D. Short

37. GARRULITY
A. Credulity B. Senility
C. Loquaciousness D. Speciousness

38. FURORE
A. Excitement B. Worry
C. Flux D. Anteroom

39. NEUTRAL
A. Unbiased B. Non-aligned
C. Undecided D. Indifferent

40. LAMENT
A. Complain B. Comment
C. Condone D. Console

41. ADVERSITY
A. Failure B. Helplessness
C. Misfortune D. Crisis

42. TURN UP
A. Land up B. Show up
C. Crop up D. Come up

43. DEIFY
A. Flatter B. Challenge
C. Worship D. Face

44. ERROR
A. Misadventure B. Misgiving
C. Ambiguity D. Blunder

45. SHALLOW
A. Artificial B. Superficial
C. Foolish D. Worthless

ANSWERS

1	2	3	4	5	6	7	8	9	10
B	B	D	A	B	D	D	C	B	D
11	**12**	**13**	**14**	**15**	**16**	**17**	**18**	**19**	**20**
C	C	B	C	D	A	C	C	D	A
21	**22**	**23**	**24**	**25**	**26**	**27**	**28**	**29**	**30**
A	C	D	A	C	C	A	C	D	A
31	**32**	**33**	**34**	**35**	**36**	**37**	**38**	**39**	**40**
A	D	C	A	C	D	C	A	A	A
41	**42**	**43**	**44**	**45**					
C	B	C	D	B					

6 One Word Substitutions

There are many words in English language which can be perfectly used for a number of words. These words help in expressing ideas in a short and correct manner for the right occasion. Such words not only enhance the vocabulary but also enable you to economise in the use of words to a great extent. Try to learn as many as you can.

Denoting Numbers

- A collection of poems — *anthology*
- A number of merchant ships protected by warships (in war-time) — *convoy*
- A number of stars grouped together — *constellation*
- A number of hired applauders, *i.e.* persons paid to clap — *claque*
- A number of people at church — *congregation*
- A number of people gathered together for some common purpose — *gathering, assembly, society*
- A group of people who get together to work for some cause of common interest — *coterie*
- A number of workmen, prisoners, thieves — *gang*
- A number of sheep — *flock*
- A number of geese — *gaggle*
- A number of leopards — *leap*
- A number of lions, monkeys — *pride, troop*
- A number of herrings, mackerel — *shoal*
- A number of fish taken in a net — *catch, haul*
- A number of whales, porpoises — *school, gam*
- A number of oxen or horses (two or more) harnessed together — *team*
- A number of ships, cars, buses — *fleet*

Denoting Places

- A place where bees are kept — *apiary*
- A place where birds are kept — *aviary*
- A place where fishes are kept — *aquarium*
- A dwelling-place of an animal underground — *burrow*
- A squirrel's home — *drey*
- A nest of a bird of prey — *eyrie, aerie*
- A place where spirituous liquors are produced — *distillery*
- A place where clothes are washed and ironed — *laundry*
- A place where Government records are kept — *archives*
- A place where treasures of art, curiosities, etc. are preserved or exhibited — *museum*
- A place where fruit trees are grown — *orchard*

Pertaining to the Literary Sphere

- A work whose writer is unknown *anonymous*
- A record of one's life written by oneself *autobiography*
- The history of the life of a person *biography*
- The heading or short description of a newspaper article, chapter of a book etc. *caption*
- A humorous play, having a happy ending *comedy*
- A list of books in a library *catalogue, bibliography*
- A book in which the events of each day are recorded *diary*
- A books containing the words of a language with their definitions, in alphabetical order *dictionary*
- A book of names and addresses *directory*
- A short speech by a player at the end of a play *epilogue*
- A brief summary of a book *epitome*
- A book containing information on all branches of knowledge *encyclopedia*
- To remove the offensive portions of a book *expurgate*
- A speech delivered without earlier preparation *extempore*
- A noisy or vehement speech intended to excite passions *harangue*
- A written account, usually in book form of the interesting and memorable experiences of one's life *memoirs*
- A note to help the memory *memorandum*
- A declaration of plans and promises put forward by a candidate for election, political party or a sovereign *manifesto*
- A short speech by a player at the beginning of a play *prologue*
- Literary theft, or passing off an author's original work as one's own *plagiarism*
- Speaking aloud to oneself *soliloquy*
- A play with a sad or tragic end *tragedy*

Pertaining to Religion

- One who believes that man can have no knowledge of God but only of natural phenomena *agnostic*
- One who renounces his religious vows or forsakes his religious principles *apostate*
- One who does not believe in existence of God *atheist*
- One intolerantly devoted to a particular creed *bigot*
- To utter profane language against God or anything holy *blaspheme*
- A breaker of church images *iconoclast*
- Worship of images or idols *idiolatory*
- One who believes in God *theist*
- One who believes in only one God *monotheist*
- One who believes in many Gods *polytheist*

Pertaining to Government

- To give up a throne or other office of dignity *abdicate*
- Absence of government *anarchy*
- Government by Sovereign of uncontrolled authority *autocracy, despotism*
- Government by departments of states *bureaucracy*
- Government of the people, for the people and by the people *democracy*
- Government by the nobility *aristocracy*
- The right of self-government *autonomy*
- Government by a few *oligarchy*
- Government by the wealthy *plutocracy*

- Government by divine guidance — *theocracy*
- To decide a political question by the direct vote of the whole electorate — *referendum*
- Sweeping governmental change — *revolution*
- The science of government — *politics*

Pertaining to Professions

- One who attends to the diseases of the eye — *oculist*
- One who tests eyesight and sells spectacles — *optician*
- One who attends to the teeth — *dentist*
- One skilled in the care of hands and feet — *chiropodist*
- A physician who assists women at child-birth — *obstetrician*
- One who drives a motorcar — *chauffeur*
- One who makes or sells candles — *chandler*
- One who preserves the skins of animals and mounts them so as to resemble the living animals — *taxidermist*
- One who compiles a dictionary — *lexicographer*
- One who writes books — *author*
- One skilled in the treatment of diseases of animals — *veterinarian*
- A tradesman who manages funerals — *undertaker*
- One who draws up contracts and lends money on interest — *scrivener*
- One who lends money and keeps goods as security — *pawnbroker*
- A teacher who travels from place to place to give instruction. — *peripatetic*
- One who travels from place to place selling miscellaneous articles — *hawker, pedlar*
- One who collects postage stamps — *philatelist*
- One who lends money at exorbitant interest — *usurer*
- One who takes care of a building — *janitor*
- One who sells sweets and pastries — *confectioner*
- One who works in a coalmine — *collier*
- One who flies an aeroplane — *pilot, aviator*
- One who studies rocks and soils — *geologist*
- One who shoes horses — *farrier*
- A professional rider in horses races — *jockey*
- One who deals in silks, cotton, woollen, and linen goods — *mercer*
- One who deals in wines — *vintner*
- One who deals in fish — *fishmonger*
- One who deals in iron and hardware — *ironmonger*
- One who sells fruits, vegetables, etc. from a barrow — *costermonger*
- One who sets type in a printing office — *compositor*

Pertaining to Medicine

- A substance which destroys or weakens germs — *antiseptic*
- Any medicine which produces insensibility — *anaesthetic*
- A medicine to counteract poison — *antidote*
- Want or poorness of blood — *anaemia*
- A medicine which alleviates pain — *anodyne*
- To cut off a person's body a part which is infected — *amputate*
- One who is recovering from illness — *convalescent*
- To be able to tell the nature of disease by its symptoms — *diagnose*
- A disease affecting many persons at the same place and time — *epidemic*
- A disease confined to a particular district or place — *endemic*
- To disinfect by smoke — *fumigate*

- ❑ Free or exempt from infection — *immune*
- ❑ A person who is sick — *invalid*
- ❑ A cure for all diseases — *panacea*
- ❑ A disease widely epidemic — *pandemic*
- ❑ Confinement to one place to avoid spread of infection — *quarantine*

Pertaining to Characteristics and Actions

- ❑ One who devotes his life to the welfare and interests of other people — *altruist*
- ❑ One who can use both hands with equal ease — *ambidexterous*
- ❑ One who fishes with a rod — *angler*
- ❑ One who kills secretly or by surprise — *assassin*
- ❑ A person who collects things belonging to ancient times — *antiquary*
- ❑ One who is always finding faults — *censorious*
- ❑ One living at the same time as another — *contemporary*
- ❑ One who sneers at the aims and beliefs of his fellowmen — *cynic*
- ❑ One who delights in speaking about oneself — *egotist*
- ❑ One who exalts his own opinion — *egoist*
- ❑ One who dies for a noble cause — *martyr*
- ❑ One who retires from society to live a solitary life — *recluse, hermit*
- ❑ One who maliciously sets fire to buildings — *incendiary*
- ❑ One who is banished from his home or his country — *exile*
- ❑ One who takes refuge in a foreign country — *refugee, alien*
- ❑ One who runs away from justice or the law — *fugitive*
- ❑ One who walks in his sleep — *somnambulist*
- ❑ One who looks on the bright side of things — *optimist*
- ❑ One who looks on the dark side of things — *pessimist*
- ❑ A hater of mankind — *misanthropist*
- ❑ One who knows everything — *omniscient*
- ❑ One who is all powerful — *omnipotent*
- ❑ One who is present everywhere — *omnipresent*
- ❑ One who devotes his service or wealth for the love of mankind — *philanthropist*
- ❑ One new to anything — *novice, tyro, neophyte*
- ❑ One who engages in any pursuit for the love of it, and not for gain — *amateur*
- ❑ One who journeys to a holy place — *pilgrim*
- ❑ A leader of the people who can sway his followers by his oratory — *demagogue*
- ❑ One who has special skill in judging art, music, tastes, etc. — *connoisseur*
- ❑ One whose reasoning is clever yet false — *sophist*
- ❑ One who makes a display of his learning — *pedant*
- ❑ One who is indifferent to pain or pleasure — *stoic*
- ❑ One who loves his country and serves it devotedly — *patriot*
- ❑ One devoted to the pleasures of eating and drinking — *epicure*
- ❑ One who poses to be what he is not — *hypocrite, impostor*
- ❑ One who foretells events — *prophet*
- ❑ One who pretends to know a great deal about everything — *mountebank, charlatan, quack*
- ❑ One versed in many languages — *linguist*
- ❑ One who cannot pay one's debts — *insolvent*
- ❑ One who takes over after another in office or employment — *successor*
- ❑ One who has been before another in office or employment — *predecessor*
- ❑ One who is opposed to intellectual progress — *obscurant*
- ❑ One who abstains from alcoholic drinks — *teetotaller*

- One who hides away on a ship to obtain a free passage — *stowaway*
- One who spends very little — *miser*
- One who spends too much — *spendthrift*

Pertaining to War

- An unprovoked attack by an enemy — *aggression*
- Shells, bombs, military stores — *ammunition*
- A place where naval or military weapons are made or stored — *ordnance*
- An agreement between belligerents to stop fighting — *armistice*
- A general pardon of offenders — *amnesty*
- To reduce to nothing — *annihilate*
- Nations carrying on warfare — *belligerents*
- To surround a place with the intention of capturing — *besiege*
- To camp in the open air without tents or covering — *bivouac*
- To seize for military use — *commandeer*
- A person who is forced by law to become a soldier — *conscript*
- An order prohibiting ships to leave the ports — *embargo*
- A number of firearms being discharged continuously — *fusillade*
- To make an examination or preliminary survey of enemy territory for military objectives — *reconnoitre*

Pertaining to Marriage and Children

- One who marries a second wife or husband while the legal spouse is alive — *bigamist*
- One vowed to a single or unmarried life — *celibate*
- One engaged to be married — *fiancé, fiancee*
- A child whose parents are dead — *orphan*
- A hater of marriage — *misogamist*
- One who has more than two wives at a time — *polygamist*

Pertaining to Death

- Dead and decaying flesh (esp. of animals) — *carrion*
- A monument set up for persons who are buried elsewhere — *cenotaph*
- To preserve a dead body from putrefaction — *embalm*
- Words inscribed on a tomb — *epitaph*
- An examination of dead body — *postmortem, autopsy*
- An account in the newspaper of the funeral of one deceased — *obituary*
- The property left to someone by a will — *legacy*
- Occurring after death — *posthumous*
- The act of killing a human being — *homicide*
- Murder of a new born child — *infanticide*
- Murder of a brother — *fratricide*
- Murder of a sister — *sororicide*
- Murder of a mother — *matricide*
- Murder of a father — *patricide*
- Murder of a parent — *parricide*
- Murder of a king — *regicide*

Pertaining to Sciences and Arts

- The study of all heavenly bodies and the earth in relation to them — *astronomy*
- The science of land management — *agronomics*

- The study of mankind — *anthropology*
- The study of physical life or living matter — *biology*
- The study of plants — *botany*
- The art of beautiful handwriting — *calligraphy*
- The science which deals with the varieties of human race — *ethnology*
- The study of the origin and history of words — *etymology*
- The study of coins — *numismatics*
- The study of human face — *physiognomy*
- The art of making fireworks — *pyrotechnics*
- The study of birds — *ornithology*
- The study of languages — *philology*
- At home equally on land or in water — *amphibious*
- The inside of a nut — *kernel*
- The central or innermost part of fruit — *core*
- The animals of a certain region — *fauna*
- The plants and vegetation of a certain region — *flora*
- Absence of rain for a long time — *drought*
- To supply land with water by artificial means — *irrigate*
- One who studies plant and animal life — *naturalist*
- A cud-chewing animal, *e.g.* the cow — *ruminant*
- A gnawing animal, *e.g.* the rat — *rodent*
- A four-footed animal — *quadruped*
- Animals which carry their young in a pouch, *e.g.* kangaroo — *marsupials*
- Soil composed largely of decayed vegetable matter — *humus*
- A preparation for killing insects — *insecticide*
- A plant or animal growing on another — *parasite*
- Living for many years — *perennial*

Multiple Choice Questions

Directions: *Below are given some statements each of which is capable of being expressed by one word only. Each statement is followed by four such words of which only one is correct. Out of the given alternatives A, B, C and D choose the correct word which very closely fits each definition.*

1. A set of papers giving information about a person or event:
A. editorial B. agenda
C. dossier D. clippings

2. List and explanations of technical, difficult, etc. terms:
A. preface B. glossary
C. bibliography D. appendix

3. One who pays too much care to his clothes and personal appearance:
A. conscious B. dandy
C. cynosure D. leer

4. A child born after death of father:
A. effeminate B. immature
C. fatherless D. posthumous

5. A person who is hard to please:
A. insensible B. hypocrite
C. egoist D. fastidious

6. Complete failure in something attempted:
A. fiasco B. vain
C. falsies D. flop

7. A word which can be interpreted in any way:
A. confusing B. misnomer
C. ambiguous D. precise

8. A group of persons united by common interests:
A. society B. class
C. clique D. coterie

9. A person who is inexperienced and easily deceived:
A. fool B. immature
C. blackhorn D. greenhorn

10. Instruction by question and answer:
A. interrogatory B. catechism
C. bulletin D. alibi

11. Record of events by someone with first hand knowledge:
A. novice B. report
C. memoir D. itinerary

12. A mode of talk familiar to a particular group or profession:
A. jargon B. colloquial
C. slang D. abuses

13. Person who is crazy:
A. lackadaisical B. tarter
C. scrupulous D. loony

14. A person who readily believes others:
A. hasty B. immature
C. credulous D. credible

15. One who eats human flesh:
A. beast B. cannibal
C. maneater D. carnivorous

16. Intentional destruction of racial groups:
A. genocide B. homicide
C. fratricide D. communal riot

17. One with weakness of mind caused by old age:
A. dastard B. dotard
C. fop D. philanderer

18. Study of insects:
A. zoology B. philology
C. entomology D. etymology

19. A critical judge of any art particularly fine arts:
A. connoisseur B. veteran
C. philistine D. dilettante

20. One who introduces items of an entertainment:
A. consort B. compere
C. director D. introducer

21. A combination of business firms:
A. enterprise B. franchise
C. cartel D. autonomous

22. Freeing of suppressed emotions:
A. catastrophe B. catharsis
C. epilogue D. chagrin

23. One who believes in the power of fate:
A. optimist B. pessimist
C. fearful D. fatalist

24. The murder of brother:
A. genocide B. homicide
C. salvage D. fratricide

25. Additional to proper payment:
A. premium B. overtime
C. ex-gratia D. fringe

26. A person or thing used to tempt somebody into a position of danger:
A. decoy B. provocateur
C. jinx D. scapegoat

27. Custom of having more than one husband at the same time:
A. polygamy B. polyandry
C. bigamy D. sexagenary

28. A person of refined taste in food and drink:
A. emeritus B. epicure
C. glutton D. gourmand

29. A tombstone inscription:
A. epithet B. encomium
C. epistle D. epitaph

30. An office which has no work but high salary:
A. fortuitous B. gratuitous
C. sinecure D. ceremonial

31. One who is indifferent to pains and pleasure of life:
A. stoic B. metaphysical
C. pessimist D. sceptic

32. List of names of persons showing duties to be performed by each in turn:
A. notice B. bulletin
C. roster D. agenda

33. Long angry speech of criticism or accusation:
A. track record B. tirade
C. taut D. outburst

34. One who is in favour of never drinking alcoholic drinks:
A. idealist B. uxorious
C. teetotaller D. unalcoholic

35. Trying to win favour by flattery and charm:
A. smarmy B. shrewish
C. toady D. loquacious

ANSWERS

1	2	3	4	5	6	7	8	9	10
C	B	B	D	D	A	C	C	D	B
11	12	13	14	15	16	17	18	19	20
C	A	D	C	B	A	B	C	A	B
21	22	23	24	25	26	27	28	29	30
C	B	D	D	D	A	B	B	D	C
31	32	33	34	35					
A	C	B	C	A					

❑❑❑

7 Idioms and Phrases

- An idiom is a group of words established by usage as having a meaning different from the individual words.
- A phrase is a small group of words standing together as an idiomatic expression.

  Learn and practise as may as you can.

Idioms and Idiomatic Phrases

- **ABC** (basic principles)
  She does not know the ABC of photography.
- **At one's beck and call** (ready to obey)
  He had a dozen men at his beck and call.
- **At sixes and sevens** (in disorder)
  The drawing room articles were lying at sixes and sevens on the floor.
- **A wet blanket** (a discouraging person)
  Don't allow Rakesh to accompany you to the hunting trip because he is a wet blanket.
- **A big gun** (an important person)
  Mr Smith is a big gun in our city.
- **At a stone's throw** (at a short distance from)
  My school is at a stone's throw from my house.
- **A man of word** (a person who keeps his promise)
  Mr Sharma is a man of word.
- **A man of a few words** (a remarkable person)
  Gandhiji was a man of a few words.
- **At arm's length** (to keep away)
  We should always keep bad boys at arm's length
- **A bolt from the blue** (a sudden and unexpected event)
  The news of my friend's death came to me like a bolt from the blue.
- **A man of letters** (a scholar)
  Radha Krishnan was a man of letters.
- **A hard nut to crack.** (a puzzling problem)
  To get a win over American basket ball team is a hard nut to crack for India.
- **A yeoman's service** (service which is beneficial to the human beings)
  He did yeoman's service through his life.
- **A snake in the grass** (a hidden foe)
  Beware of him because he seems to be a snake in the grass.
- **Acid test** (hard test)
  The election will be an acid test for the ruling party.
- **A wolf in sheep's clothing** (a hypocrite)
  You should not keep company with him because he is a wolf in sheep's clothing.
- **At the eleventh hour** (at the last moment)
  The war was about to start but fortunately at the eleventh hour a messenger came to the PM with a message of peace.
- **A great card** (an important person)
  Mr Sood is a great card in the ministry of finance.
- **A fool of the first water** (one completely foolish)
  Being a fool of the first water he could not solve even the simplest sum.
- **A bone of contention** (to be the cause of quarrel)
  Kashmir is the bone of contention between India and Pakistan.
- **A green hand** (not very much experienced)
  We shall pay a little to a green hand.
- **All in all** (completely)
  Rajesh is all in all in this office.
- **A bed of roses** (a comfort)
  Life is not a bed of roses.
- **An apple of discord** (to be the cause of)
  Kashmir is an apple of discord between India and Pakistan.
- **A white elephant** (of no use)
  This sort of glib talker always proves a white elephant in the end.
- **A red letter day** (An important day)
  15th August is a red letter day for the Indians.
- **By hook or by crook** (by any means fair or foul)
- **Black sheep** (a traitor)
  Later on Mr XYZ proved a black sheep.
- **By dint of** (by means of)
  By dint of hard work, she earned a lot of money.
- **Break ones back** (to work hard to get something)
  He broke his back to earn his livelihood.
- **Break the back of** (accomplish the hardest part of a certain job)

There is nothing to be worried about as we've already broken the back of the problem.

- ✦ **Beat about the bush** (to go on talking on some worthless topic)
  Stop this beating about the bush, come to the main task.
- ✦ **Beyond one's means** (beyond one's budget)
  He is living beyond his means, therefore, he is sure to get ruined.
- ✦ **Cut loose** (Keep away)
  India should cut loose from bad politics.
- ✦ **Chips of the same block** (having the same taste)
  They are the chips of the same block.
- ✦ **Cut-throat competition** (a stiff competition)
  There is a cut-throat competition among the publishers in the market.
- ✦ **Come what may** (no matter what happens)
  I'll do it come what may.
- ✦ **Drop someone a line** (send a letter, etc.)
  Please drop me a line of your well-being.
- ✦ **Dull the edge of** (reduce the intensity of)
  Take this pill and it will dull the edge of pain.
- ✦ **From hand to mouth** (without any saving)
  The poor factory worker is living from hand to mouth.
- ✦ **Fair and square** (clean)
  One must be fair and square in one's dealing.
- ✦ **Hard of hearing** (somewhat deaf)
  She is a bit hard of hearing.
- ✦ **In the good books of** (be good in one's mind)
  Jack is in the good books of his teachers.
- ✦ **In black and white** (in written)
  Don't give him anything in black and white.
- ✦ **In cold blood** (mercilessly)
  The old woman was murdered in cold blood.
- ✦ **In a crack** (all of a sudden or rapidly)
  The thief left the place in a crack.
- ✦ **In full swing** (in full force)
  The studies of the students are going on in full swing.
- ✦ **In the twinkling of an eye** (quickly)
  The monkey ate up grams in the twinkling of an eye.
- ✦ **Keep the ball rolling** (to maintain the progress of some activity)
  After the death of his father he had to take the charge of his office to keep the ball rolling.
- ✦ **Neck and neck** (even)
  There is a neck and neck fight between the two boxers.
- ✦ **Once in a blue moon** (seldom)
  She visits her brother once in a blue moon.
- ✦ **Slow and steady** (slowly but continually)
  Slow and steady wins the race.
- ✦ **To cut a sorry figure** (present oneself in a bad way)
  She cut a sorry figure on the stage.
- ✦ **To give a red carpet reception** (to give a warm welcome)
  The PM was given a red carpet reception in America.
- ✦ **To dance one's tune** (to follow someone submissively)
  He always dances to his brother's tune.
- ✦ **To turn a deaf ear to** (to disregard)
  She turned a deaf ear to her parents' advice.
- ✦ **To call a spade a spade** (to speak the truth)
  Gandhiji always called a spade a spade.
- ✦ **To bring to book** (to scold)
  The naughty boy was brought to book by the teacher.
- ✦ **To cut short** (to reduce)
  Smoking will cut short your life.
  He wants to get money by hook or by crook.
- ✦ **To grease the palm of** (to bribe)
  Rohit greased the palm of the clerk and got the file moved.
- ✦ **Through thick and thin.** (under all circumstances)
  We'll stand by you through thick and thin.
- ✦ **To die by inches** (to die a painful death)
  The old man died by inches.
- ✦ **To eat one's words** (to retract one's statement)
  You'll have to eat your words because you have spoken without thinking.
- ✦ **To burn the midnight oil** (to work hard)
  You'll have to burn the midnight oil if you want to get good marks.
- ✦ **To poke one's nose into** (to meddle with)
  It is bad to poke your nose into others' affair.
- ✦ **To fall flat** (to have no effect)
  His father's advice fell flat on him.
- ✦ **To make a clean breast of** (to confess)
  He made a clean breast of his involvement in the bomb blast.
- ✦ **To get the better of** (overcome)
  Anger got the better of him.
- ✦ **To break somebody's back** (to give too much work to him to do)
  She broke his back by giving him so much hard work to do.
- ✦ **Throw cold water on** (to discourage)
  She tried to throw cold water on his plan but he was well-determined.
- ✦ **The long and short of** (in brief)
  The long and short of his lecture is that we should live like brothers.
- ✦ **To burn one's fingers** (to get oneself in trouble)
  You have burnt your fingers by speaking against him.
- ✦ **To turn over a new leaf** (to change the course of life)
  He has turned over a new leaf in his life.
- ✦ **To have one's own axe to grind** (to have vested interest)
  He has his own axe to grind in this matter.

- **To take to one's heels** (to run away)
  The thief took to his heels as soon as he saw the policeman.
- **To move heaven and earth** (to make too much effort)
  The young man moved heaven and earth to find a job.
- **To be caught red handed** (to be caught at the time of committing a crime)
  The clerk was caught red handed when he was accepting bribe from Mr ABC.
- **To receive with open arms** (to give a warm welcome)
  The new president of the club was received with open arms by the members.
- **To be born with a silver spoon in one's mouth** (to be born in a rich family)
  Mr. J. L. Nehru was born with a silver spoon in his mouth.
- **To come to light** (to be known)
  A new disease has recently come to light.
- **To be the apple of one's eye** (be very dear)
  He is the apple of his parent's eye.
- **To make fun of** (laugh at)
  The children made fun of the waiter in the hotel.
- **To let the cat out of the bag** (to divulge secret)
  It was Sohan who let the cat out of the bag by telling the real matter.
- **To open a new chapter** (to start some habit, etc.
  By drinking, you've opened a new chapter in your life.
- **To make the flesh creep** (to terrify)
  The story made my flesh creep.
- **To lose ground** (to retreat)
  After fighting for some time the Pakistani army began to lose ground.
- **To bring to book** (to punish)
  The student was brought to book by the teacher.
- **To show a clean pair of heels** (to run away)
  The thief showed a clean pair of heels as soon as he saw the policeman approaching.
- **To gain ground** (to be established)
  He gained ground in India in a few years.
- **To get wind of** (to get information)
  I got wind of his secret plans.
- **Under a cloud** (be in trouble or in a state of disgrace or suspicion)
  His company seemed to be under a cloud as it had no funds to pay the wages to the workers.

Verbal Phrases

- **Act upon** (to follow)
  I acted upon my father's advice.
- **Act upto** (to perform within limits)
  He acted upto his conscience.
- **Act beyond** (to perform crossing limits)
  We should not act beyond our capacity.
- **Act for** (to perform in place of someone else)
  The vice principal acted for the principal.
- **Back up** (to make a queue)
  The vehicles began to back up.
- **Back down** (withdraw claim in the presence of opposition)
  The leader backed down from his previous statement.
- **Back off** (draw back some plan or action)
  They backed off from building a flyover.
- **Back out** (withdraw from a promise, etc.)
  The government backed out of its promise.
- **Break down** (stop working) My car broke down on the highway.
- **Break into** (enter in certain premises by breaking the door, etc.)
  Last night a thief broke into my neighbour's.
- **Break off** (stop all of a sudden)
  She broke off and began to think over about her/his hand.
- **Break out** (spread)
  Cholera has broken out in the town.
- **Break out of** (escape from)
  A prisoner broke out of the prison last night.
- **Break up** (disperse)
  The cloud of fog began to break up as the sun rose.
- **Break something up** (Cause something to break into small pieces)
  She broke up the chocolate to distribute it among the girls.
- **Break with** (Cut off connection after quarrelling with someone)
  He has broken with his brother.
- **Call on** (pay a visit to somebody)
  I'll call on Mohan's today.
- **Call out** (to start)
  The workers have called out a strike.
- **Call off** (to stop the strike etc.)
  The workers have called off the strike.
- **Call at** (to visit someone's house)
  I called at his house yesterday.
- **Call in** (send for)
  Please call in the doctor.
- **Carry on** (continue)
  Please carry on your work.
- **Carry something out** (perform a task)
  Our company is carrying out a big deal with a foreign company.
- **Carry something over** (postpone)
  The fancy dress competition had to be carried over till Monday)

✦ **Carry someone off** (kill somebody)
Cancer carried her off on the day of her 20th birthday.

✦ **Come of age** (get established)
As our company has come of age, so, there is no problem in selling our goods.

✦ **Come of** (belong to)
She comes of a royal family.

✦ **Come over** (surmount)
We at last came over all our problems.

✦ **Come off** (to take place)
The marriage of my brother comes off in the next month.

✦ **Come round** (agree)
At last he came round to my views.

✦ **Come under** (fall in the category of)
All these animals come under the same species.

✦ **Come down with** (suffer from)
She came down with whopping cough.

✦ **Come from** (be the nature of)
She came from London.

✦ **Come about** (happen)
The explosion came about when the worker struck the match to light a cigarette.

✦ **Cut off** (die)
The princess was cut off in the prime of her life.

✦ **Cut down** (reduce)
The prices of consumer goods should be cut down.

✦ **Cut someone out** (exclude someone)
His father cut him out of his will.

✦ **Fall in**
She fell in love with the prince.

✦ **Fall down** (fail)
The deal fell down for lack of transparency.

✦ **Fall out** (quarrel)
She fell out with his elder brother.

✦ **Fall through** (fail)
The project fell through for lack of funds.

✦ **Get away** (escape)
She got away with her life.

✦ **Get by** (to accomplish something with great difficulty)
She is not rich. She has just enough to get by.

✦ **Get on** (perform)
How are you getting on with your studies?

✦ **Get out** (become known)
The news got out that the PM was paying a visit to Russia.

✦ **Get over** (overcome)
At last I got over all obstacles.

✦ **Get up** (rise)
When do you get up in the morning?

✦ **Give up** (stop)
He gave up smoking.

✦ **Give out** (emit)
Garlic gives out a pungent smell.

✦ **Give in** (collapse)
The bridge gave in under the heavy load.

✦ **Give away** (distribute)
The Principal gave away the prizes.

✦ **Give out** (announce)
It was given out that the President of India would visit the place soon.

✦ **Go off** (explode)
The gun went off suddenly.

✦ **Go on** (continue)
She went on about how she flew the aeroplane.

✦ **Go through** (examine)
I'll go through this book later on.

✦ **Go up** (be built)
The construction of the house is going up.

✦ **Grind on** (continue for a long time in a tedious way)
The discussion over political issues ground on.

✦ **Grind something out** (produce something a tedious way)
She will grind some more short stories.

✦ **Look out** (be careful)
Look out! there is a snake.

✦ **Look down upon** (hate)
We should not look down upon the poor.

✦ **Look at** (watch)
Look at the blackboard.

✦ **Look after** (take care of)
We ought to look after our old parents.

✦ **Look into** (investigate)
The new police inspector will look into the matter.

✦ **Look up** (rise)
The prices of consumer goods are looking up.

✦ **Look back** (think of the past)
It made her feel disolate when she looked back on things of the past.

✦ **Make up** (to fulfil)
I'll make up my deficiency in Mathematics.

✦ **Make out** (understand)
I could not make out what she said.

✦ **Make up one' mind** (to resolve)
I have made up my mind to settle in the USA.

✦ **Make off** (leave hurriedly)
She made off without informing anybody.

✦ **Make something over** (transfer)
She should make her property over to her sons.

✦ **Make over** (hand over)
He made over the charge of the file to Mr Robert.

✦ **Pull back** (retreat)
The government has pulled back from its previous policy.

✦ **Pull something down** (demolish)
The authorities concerned pulled down a few building which were illegally built on government land.

✦ **Pull out** (pluck)
The child pulled out a few petals of the flower.

✦ **Pull through** (recover)
The patient will pull through.

✦ **Push on** (continue a journey)
It was getting darker but we pushed on.

✦ **Push at** (exert force)
He pushed at the bell, but it did not ring.

✦ **Push for** (demand persistently)
The workers have been pushing for the installation of new machines for five years.

✦ **Put out** (extinguish)
She put out the light.

✦ **Put on** (wear)
He put on an overcoat.

✦ **Put off** (postpone)
The plan had to be put off.

✦ **Put by** (spare something for future)
We must put by some money for future.

✦ **Put up with** (stay)
Your aunt is out of town for a couple of days, you may put up with us till she comes.

✦ **Put something down** (record something)
She put a new idea down on the paper.

✦ **Take after** (resemble)
He takes after his father.

✦ **Take off** (remove)
He took off his shoes.

✦ **Take something out** (obtain)
You may take out some money from Rohit if you want to purchase this car.

✦ **Take to** (fall into the habit of)
He took to gambling.

✦ **Turn something down** (reject something)
The judge turned down his appeal.

✦ **Turn on** (attack)
The thief turned on him with a knife.

Multiple Choice Questions

Directions: *Some idioms/phrases are given below with their probable meanings. Select the options with their correct meanings.*

1. Carry out
A. To take from one place to another
B. To continue
C. To obey
D. To make efforts

2. In the same boat
A. A worn out choice
B. Indifferent
C. In identical circumstances
D. Carry off

3. In one's good book
A. A costly book
B. A priceless treasure
C. In one's favour
D. An enchanting beauty

4. Keep a straight face
A. To do make up
B. To change clothes
C. Assume responsibility
D. To remain serious

5. To be above board
A. To have a good height
B. To be honest in any business deal
C. To have no debts
D. To try to be beautiful

6. On the face of it
A. To agree B. From an action
C. More than enough D. Apparently

7. Let the bygones be bygones
A. In one's favour B. To pretend
C. To forget the past D. Other choice

8. To split hairs
A. Major distinctions
B. Hair with two ends
C. To make minute distinction
D. Without distinction

9. Bread and butter
A. Both bread and butter
B. Something essential
C. Livelihood
D. Relevant things

10. To bell the cat
A. To catch a cat and tie a bell round its neck
B. To make an effort
C. To be quick
D. To face a risk

11. Hard and fast
A. Strict B. Solid
C. Fast moving D. Some hard surface

12. Part and parcel
A. The part of a parcel
B. An essential part
C. A missing parcel
D. Some part of a machine sent by parcel

13. Null and void
A. Something invalid
B. Something that can be avoided
C. Something that can be nullified
D. Something evil

14. To make clean breast of
A. To gain prominence
B. To praise oneself
C. To confess without reserve
D. To destroy before it blooms

15. Trump card
A. A powerful means of achieving an object
B. Resourcefulness
C. The best gamble to attain success
D. None of these

16. Tall talk
A. A discussion continued for a long time
B. A high sounding talk
C. A meaningful talk
D. A useless talk

17. Small talk
A. Gossip
B. A discussion carried on for a long time
C. A brief discussion
D. None of these

18. Throw out of gear
A. To replace B. Hinder, disturb
C. To decide D. Take up tune

19. To and fro
A. Back and forth B. Puzzled
C. Amazed D. Reprove

20. To bell the cat
A. To do an easy job
B. To be indifferent to
C. To undertake a difficult job
D. To clarify

21. To be under cloud
A. Puzzle
B. Enjoy the favour
C. Talk thoughtlessly
D. To be under suspicion

22. A labour of love
A. A tragic end
B. A funny thing
C. Not fruitful
D. Work done without payment

23. Follow suit
A. Follow an example B. Wear a new dress
C. Irrelevant D. A gay person

24. Foul play
A. Bad intentions
B. A play not well acted
C. A play not liked by the audience
D. None of these

25. To pick holes
A. To find some reason to quarrel
B. To destroy something
C. To criticise someone
D. To cut some part of an item

26. To smell a rat
A. To see signs of plague epidemic
B. To get bad smell of a dead rat
C. To suspect foul dealings
D. To be in a bad mood

27. To put a spoke in one's wheel
A. To encourage
B. Act without restraint
C. Risk something
D. To obstruct one's progress

28. To pull one's leg
A. To give up B. Take care of
C. To befool D. To know

29. To play with fire
A. Grasp the truth
B. To handle something dangerous
C. To ridicule
D. To flee away

30. To reckon with
A. Take up time
B. Make an inventory
C. To deal with
D. Submit to punishment

ANSWERS

1	2	3	4	5	6	7	8	9	10
C	C	C	D	B	D	C	C	C	D
11	**12**	**13**	**14**	**15**	**16**	**17**	**18**	**19**	**20**
A	B	A	C	C	B	A	B	A	C
21	**22**	**23**	**24**	**25**	**26**	**27**	**28**	**29**	**30**
D	D	A	A	C	C	D	C	B	C

❑❑❑

8 Narration

Direct and Indirect Narration/Speech

The exact words spoken by the speaker are known as Direct Speech.

The words spoken by somebody and expressed by someone else with some modification are known as Indirect Speech.

(*a*) Ram says to me, "You do not help me."

(*b*) Ram tells me that I do not help him.

The sentence (*a*) shows the words spoken by Ram. So, it is a sentence of Direct Speech.

The sentence (*b*) shows the words spoken by Ram and expressed by someone else with certain modification. So, it is a sentence of Indirect Speech.

The following points should be noted while changing Direct Speech into Indirect speech:

1. The verb outside the inverted commas is called the Reporting Verb.
2. The verb or sentence inside the inverted commas is called the Reported Speech.
3. If the Reporting verb is in the Present or Future Tense, there is no change in the tense in the Reported Speech.
4. If the Reporting Verb is in the Past Tense, the Tense in the Reported Speech is changed.
5. The Reporting verb may be in any Tense, in it the Pronouns are changed as under:
   (*i*) First Person according to Subject
   (*ii*) Second Person according to Object
   (*iii*) Third Person, No change.
6. If the Reporting verb is in the Past Tense the Adverb will change as under in the Indirect Speech.

Direct	***Indirect***
now	then
here	there
after	before
today	that day
yesterday	the previous day
these	those
tomorrow	the next day
last week	the previous week
this	that

7. Adjectives/Determiners are changed as under:

Direct	***Indirect***
this	that
these	those

Rules for Change of Tense

Reporting Verb	Reporting Speech	Change of Tense
Present Tense	Any Tense	No change
Future Tense	Any Tense	No change
Past Tense	Present/Future Tense	Change into corresponding Past Tense
Past Tense	Past Indefinite Tense	Change into Past Perfect Tense
Past Tense	Past Continuous Tense	Change into Past Perfect Continuous Tense
Past Tense	Past Perfect/Perfect Continuous Tense	No change
Past Tense	Universal Truth	No change
Past Tense	Proverb	No change

Transformation of Speech Based on Special Rules

1. Rule Related to Interrogative Sentence

- If the answer of an interrogative sentence is possible in yes-no manner.

Illustration.

Dhoni said to Sachin, "Will you help me?"

Dhoni asked Sachin whether he would help him.

(**Note :** The answer of R.S. is possible in yes-no manner)

Rule of Transformation from Direct to Indirect speech

Step I : Change R.V. into ask.

Step II : In place of comma use 'if/whether'.

Step III : Change interrogative sentence into assertive sentence.

- If the answer of an interrogative sentence is not possible in yes-no manner.

Illustration:

Sachin said to Dhoni, "What do you want?"

Sachin asked Dhoni what he wanted.

(**Note :** Only in Step II, you have to avoid comma and inverted comma and rest will be same as mentioned above).

2. Rule related to Imperative Sentence

- Imperative sentence is a sentence which shows Order/ Advice/Request

Illustration:

My teacher said to me, "Go there".

My teacher ordered me to go there.

Rule of Transformation from Direct to Indirect Speech

Step I : Change R.V. as per meaning/sense of R.S. into order/request/advise.

Step II : In place of comma, use 'to'.

Step III : Rest portion will be same.

3. Rule related to Optative Sentence

- Optative sentence is a sentence which expresses the feeling of bless/curse/pray/wish.

Illustration:

Mother said to me, "May you live long!".

Mother blessed me that I might live long.

Rule of Transformation from Direct to Indirect Speech

Step I : Change R.V. as per meaning/sense of R.S. into bless/curse/pray/wish.

Step II : In place of comma, use 'that'.

Step III : Change optative sentence into assertive sentence.

4. Rule related to Exclamatory Sentence

- Exclamatory sentence is a sentence which takes note of exclamatory (!) mark in that sentence showing inner feeling.

Illustration:

She said, "Alas! I am ruined".

She exclaimed with sorrow that she was ruined.

Rule of Transformation from Direct to Indirect Speech

Step I : Change R.V. as per meaning/sense of R.S. into exclaim/exclaims/exclaimed/will or shall exclaim + joy/sorrow/anger/surprise/applause/ contempt.

Step II : Change comma into that.

Step III : Change note of exclamation (!) into full stop (.)

Step IV : Change exclamatory sentence into assertive sentence.

Universal, Historical truth, etc.

If the Reported Speech expresses a Universal or Historical or Habitual truth, its Tense will not change.

1. The teacher said to the students, "The sun rises in the east."

   The teacher told the students that the sun rises in the east.

2. My father said to me, "The First Battle of Panipat was fought in 1526."

   My father told me that the First Battle of Panipat was fought in 1526.

Multiple Choice Questions

Directions (Qs. 1 to 13): *Select the correct Indirect Speech for the following sentences:*

1. I said to him, "I shall help you."

A. I told him that I can help him.
B. I told him that I would help him.
C. I told him that I will help him.
D. I told him that I shall be helping him.

2. My Teacher said to me, "The earth revolves round the sun."

A. My teacher told me that the earth revolves round the sun.
B. My teacher told me that the earth revolve round the sun.
C. My teacher told me that the earth had been revolving round the sun.
D. My teacher told me that the earth has been revolving round the sun.

3. I said to my friend, "My father daily goes for a walk."

A. I told my friend that my father daily goes for a walk.
B. I told my friend that my father daily went for a walk.
C. I told my friend that my father has to go for a walk.
D. I told my friend that my father had gone for a walk.

4. He said to me, "May God bless you!"

A. He requested that God can bless me.
B. He prayed that God can bless me.
C. He prayed that God might bless me.
D. He prayed that God will bless me.

5. The patient said, "Thank you, doctor."

A. The patient thanked the doctor.
B. The patient requested the doctor with thanks.
C. The patient told the doctor thanks.
D. The patient suggested the doctor thanks.

6. Satish said, "No, I shall not talk to him."

A. Satish told that he should not talk to him.

B. Satish suggested that he would not have talked to him.
C. Satish exclaimed with sorrow that he would not talk with him.
D. Satish refused to talk to him.

7. The child said, "What a lovely place!"
A. The child exclaimed with sorrow that it was a lovely place.
B. The child thought that the place was lovely.
C. The child exclaimed with joy that the place was very lovely.
D. The child suggested that the place was lovely.

8. He said, "What a fool I have been!"
A. He told himself with sorrow that he was a fool.
B. He confessed with regret that he had been a great fool.
C. He said himself a fool.
D. He suggested that he could be a fool.

9. He said, "Alas! I am ruined."
A. He told me that he had been ruined.
B. He exclaimed with joy that he had been ruined.
C. He exclaimed with sorrow that he was ruined.
D. He told me that he should not be ruined.

10. The accused said, "I am not guilty."
A. The accused exclaimed with sorrow that I am not guilty.
B. The accused exclaimed with joy that he was not guilty.
C. The accused stated that he was not guilty.
D. The accused told me that he has not been guilty.

11. My teacher said, "The earth is round".
A. My teacher said that the earth was round.
B. My teacher says that the earth is round.
C. My teacher said that the earth is round.
D. My teacher ordered that the earth is round.

12. He said, "What a place it is!"
A. He said that it was a very fine place.
B. He said that is a very fine place.
C. He said that the place is fine.
D. He exclaimed with joy/surprise that it was a very fine place.

13. Ria said, "Shall I thread the needle?"
A. Ria asked if she should thread the needle.
B. Ria asked if she shall thread the needle.
C. Ria ordered if she should thread the needle.
D. Ria says that if she would thread the needle.

Directions (Qs. 14 to 20): *Pick out the correct alternative that completes the incomplete sentence which is changed into Indirect Narration.*

14. She said to me, "I shall see you as soon as I get time."
She told me:
A. that she will see me as soon as she will get time.
B. that she would see me as soon as she would get time.
C. she would see me whenever she got time.
D. that she would see me whenever she gets time.

15. My secretary said to me, "Your plane will leave if you do not go at once."
My secretary told me that:
A. her plane would leave if she did not go at that time.
B. her plane would leave if I do not go at once.
C. my plane would leave if I did not go at that very time.
D. my plane will leave if I did not go at that time.

16. My mother said to me, "Don't quarrel among yourselves".
My mother:
A. forbade me to quarrel among ourselves.
B. asked me not to quarrel among ourselves.
C. asked me that not to quarrel among ourselves.
D. asked me to quarrel not among ourselves.

17. Her father said to her mother, "Excuse the daughter."
Her father:
A. requested her mother to excuse the daughter.
B. asked her mother to excuse the daughter.
C. asked her mother to have excused the daughter.
D. asked her mother to have been excused.

18. He said to his friend, "Wait here till father comes."
He requested his friend:
A. to wait here till father had come.
B. that to wait there till his friend came.
C. to wait there till father came.
D. to wait here until his friend came.

19. She said to her maid, "Run and catch the thief."
She ordered her maid:
A. ran and catch the thief.
B. that to run and to catch the thief.
C. ran and caught the thief.
D. to run and catch the thief.

20. Anita said to Sunita, "What are you doing?"
Anita asked Sunita:
A. what she will be doing.
B. that what she is doing.
C. that what she was doing.
D. what she was doing.

ANSWERS

1	2	3	4	5	6	7	8	9	10
B	A	A	C	A	D	C	B	C	C
11	12	13	14	15	16	17	18	19	20
C	D	A	B	C	A	B	C	D	D

9 Voice

A sentence in active voice focuses on the person or thing doing the action. A sentence in passive voice focuses on the person or thing affected by the action. *e.g.,*

The idol was built. (Active voice)
Someone built the idol. (Passive voice)

Transformation of Voice

- Voice and Tense are closely associated with each other.
- Tense plays an important role while transforming the voice.

On the basis of following points, voice can be transformed from active to passive voice.

The Present Indefinite Tense

Active voice: Subject + V_1 + Object
Passive voice: Subject + is, am, are + V_3 + by + Object

1. **Active voice:** He sings sweet songs.
   Passive voice: Sweet songs are sung by him.
2. **Active voice:** She does not cause any hindrance in my work.
   Passive voice: No hindrance in my work is caused by her.
3. **Active voice:** Do they love their country?
   Passive voice: Is their country loved by them?

The Present Continuous Tense

Active voice: Subject + is/am/are + V_1 + ing + Object.
Passive voice: Subject + is/am/are + being + V_3 + by + Object.

1. **Active voice:** She is cooking food.
   Passive voice: Food is being cooked by her.
2. **Active voice:** Rita is not knitting a sweater.
   Passive voice: A sweater is not being knitted by Rita.
3. **Active voice:** Is Meena baking a cake?
   Passive voice: Is a cake being baked by Meena?

The Present Perfect Tense

Active voice: Subject + has/have + V_3 + Object.
Passive voice: Subject + has/have + been + V_3 + by + Object.

1. **Active voice:** I have written an essay.
   Passive voice: An essay has been written by me.
2. **Active voice:** They have not whitewashed the fence.
   Passive voice: The fence has not been whitewashed by them.
3. **Active voice:** Have you cut the cake?
   Passive voice: Has the cake been cut by you?

The Past Indefinite Tense

Active voice: Subject + V_2 + Object
Passive voice: Subject + was/were + V_3 + by + Object

1. **Active voice:** He composed a new song.
   Passive voice: A new song was composed by him.
2. **Active voice:** He did not operate the computer.
   Passive voice: The computer was not operated by him.
3. **Active voice:** Did she catch a fish?
   Passive voice: Was a fish caught by her?

The Past Continuous Tense

Active voice: Subject + was/were + V_1 + ing + Object
Passive voice: Subject + was/were + being + V_3 + by + Object

1. **Active voice:** The farmers were ploughing the fields.
   Passive voice: The fields were being ploughed by the farmers.
2. **Active voice:** He was not administering the new drug to the patient.
   Passive voice: The new drug was not being administered to the patient by him.
3. **Active voice:** Was she sewing a dress?
   Passive voice: Was a dress being sewn by her?

The Past Perfect Tense

Active voice: Subject + had + V_3 + Object.
Passive voice: Subject + had + been + V_3 + by + Object

1. **Active voice:** He had issued me an import licence.
   Passive voice: I had been issued an import licence.
2. **Active voice:** We had not visited the Taj.
   Passive voice: The Taj had not been visited by us.
3. **Active voice:** Who had taught you English?
   Passive voice: By whom had you been taught English?

The Future Indefinite Tense

Active voice: Subject + will/shall + V_1 + Object.
Passive voice: Subject + will/shall + be + V_3 + by + Object.

1. **Active voice:** He will remove the dust from the shelf.
   Passive voice: The dust from the shelf will be removed by him.
2. **Active voice:** He will not open the main gate.
   Passive voice: The main gate will not be opened by him.
3. **Active voice:** Will you help us?
   Passive voice: Shall we be helped by you?

The Future Perfect Tense

Active voice: Subject + will/shall + have + V_3 + Object.
Passive voice: Subject + will/shall + have + been + V_3 + by + Object.

1. **Active voice:** They will have sold their house by then.
   Passive voice: Their house will have been sold by them by then.
2. **Active voice:** He will not have informed the police about it.
   Passive voice: The police will not have been informed about it by him.
3. **Active voice:** Will they have accepted the deal?
   Passive voice: Will the deal have been accepted by them?

Imperative Sentences

1. **Active voice:** Open the window.
   Passive voice: You are ordered to open the window.
   Or
   Let the window be opened.
2. **Active voice:** Please/kindly open the window.
   Passive voice: You are requested to open the window.
3. **Active voice:** Never make a noise.
   Passive voice: A noise should never be made.

Infinitives

1. **Active voice:** It is time to open the shop.
   Passive voice: It is time for the shop to be opened.
2. **Active voice:** He begged the officer to forgive him.
   Passive voice: He begged the officer to be forgiven.
3. **Active voice:** He has to break the door.
   Passive voice: The door has to be broken by him.

Prepositional Verb

1. **Active voice:** She laughed at the beggar.
   Passive voice: The beggar was laughed at by her.
2. **Active voice:** He listened to the news.
   Passive voice: The news was listened to by him.
3. **Active voice:** They called in the doctor.
   Passive voice: The doctor was called in by them.

Double Object

1. **Active voice:** He gave me a pen.
   Passive voice: A pen was given to me by him.
   Or
   I was given a pen by him.
2. **Active voice:** She told us a story.
   Passive voice: A story was told (to) us by her.
   Or
   We were told a story by her.

Use of Preposition other than 'by'

1. **Active voice:** The jug contains juice.
   Passive voice: Juice is contained in the jug.
2. **Active voice:** The audience thronged the hall.
   Passive voice: The hall was thronged with the audience.
3. **Active voice:** I know her.
   Passive voice: She is known to me.

Quasi Passive Verbs

1. **Active voice:** Quinine tastes bitter.
   Passive voice: Quinine is bitter when tasted.
   Or
   Quinine is bitter when it is tasted.
2. **Active voice:** Sugar is sweet (to taste).
   Passive voice: Sugar is sweet when tasted.
   Or
   Sugar is sweet when it is tasted.

Implied Sentences

1. **Active voice:** The driver drove the bus.
   Passive voice: The bus was driven.
2. **Active voice:** Someone read the news.
   Passive voice: The news was read.
3. **Active voice:** They say work is worship.
   Passive voice: It is said that work is worship.

Multiple Choice Questions

Directions (Qs. 1 to 17): *In the following questions, a sentence has been given in Active/Passive Voice. Out of the four alternatives suggested, select the one that Best Expresses the same sentence in Passive/Active Voice.*

1. Circumstances will oblige me to go.
   A. I will oblige the circumstances and go.
   B. I shall be obliged to go by the circumstances.

C. Under the circumstances, I should go.
D. I shall be obliged by the circumstances to go.

2. We waste much time on trifles.
A. Much time was wasted on trifles.
B. Much time will be wasted on trifles.
C. Much time is wasted by us on trifles.
D. Much time is wasted on trifles.

3. Mohan gave the beggar an old shirt.
A. An old shirt was given to Mohan by the beggar.
B. An old shirt was given to the beggar by Mohan
C. The begger was gave an old shirt by Mohan.
D. An old shirt was gave to the beggar by Mohan.

4. They have made him a king.
A. A king has been made by him.
B. He was made a king by them.
C. They have been made kings by him.
D. He has been made a king by them.

5. Who taught you English?
A. By whom English was taught to you?
B. By whom you were taught English?
C. By whom was English taught to you?
D. By whom are you taught English?

6. Was he knocking at the door?
A. Was the door being knocked at by him?
B. Was the door being knocked by him?
C. Was the door knocked by him?
D. Was the door knocking at him?

7. What was Rani doing?
A. What was done by Rani?
B. What was Rani being done?
C. What was being done by Rani?
D. What was being doing Rani?

8. Why were you wasting your time?
A. Why was your time being wasted?
B. Why was your time being wasted by you?
C. Why was your time wasted by you?
D. Why was your time wasted?

9. She has laid out a small garden.
A. A small garden has been laid by her.
B. A small garden has laid her.
C. A small garden being laid by her.
D. A small garden has been laid out by her.

10. She had already solved all the sums.
A. All the sums had already been solved by her.
B. All the sums have already been solved by her.
C. All the sums have been solved by her.
D. All the sums are solved by her.

11. He will have posted the letter.
A. The letter has been posted by him.
B. The letter will be posted by him.
C. The letter will have been posted by him.
D. The letter is posted by him.

12. They will have sold all the books by 4 P.M.
A. All the books will be sold by 4 P.M.
B. All the books will have been sold by 4 P.M.
C. All the books were being sold by 4 P.M.
D. All the books must be sold by 4 P.M.

13. Do you speak English?
A. Is English spoken by you?
B. Does English spoken by you?
C. Is English being spoken by you?
D. Does English being spoken by you?

14. Had they seen me before?
A. Had myself been seen by them before?
B. Had me being seen by them before?
C. Had I been seen by them before?
D. Had I being seen by them before?

15. May I take this pen?
A. May this pen will be taken by me?
B. May this pen shall be taken by me?
C. May this pen should be taken by me?
D. May this pen be taken by me?

16. Can we send it by air?
A. Can this be sent by air?
B. Can it be sent by air?
C. Can it go by air?
D. Can it be send by air?

17. Who wrote this book?
A. By whom was this book written?
B. By whom is this book written?
C. By whom was this book being written?
D. By whom is this book being written?

ANSWERS

1	2	3	4	5	6	7	8	9	10
D	C	B	D	C	A	C	B	D	A
11	**12**	**13**	**14**	**15**	**16**	**17**			
C	B	A	C	D	B	A			

❑❑❑

10 Sentence Completion

Filling the blanks is such an exercise that starts with the primary schools and continues at the highest level of competitive examinations. One must practise it regularly to score well.

Multiple Choice Questions

Directions: *Pick out the most effective word(s) from the given words to fill in the blanks and make the sentence meaningfully complete.*

1. One requires great .... to teach and handle little children who are restless.
A. patience B. attitude
C. determination D. knowledge

2. The researchers will .... some of the causes of increasing poverty in the state.
A. fund B. investigate
C. promote D. circulate

3. I usually perform .... when nobody is watching me.
A. alone B. good
C. better D. hard

4. It was .... to everyone that the minister had been drinking.
A. observed B. known
C. discovered D. realised

5. I would rather stay indoors .... the rain stops.
A. so B. waiting
C. until D. usually

6. The process should be completed as far as possible within a week, ... which the matter should be brought to notice of the officer concerned.
A. following B. failing
C. realizing D. referring

7. The officers are ..... to regular transfers.
A. free B. open
C. subject D. available

8. All letters received from Government should ..... be acknowledged.
A. suddenly B. obviously
C. immediately D. occasionally

9. Mumbai office ..... a meeting of senior officials to discuss the high incidence of frauds.
A. attended B. convened
C. reported D. registered

10. The note should be ..... to all the concerned departments for their consideration.
A. regulated B. requested
C. carried D. forwarded

11. Your present statement does not .... what you said last week.
A. accord to B. accord in
C. accord with D. accord for

12. I had a vague .... that the lady originally belonged to Scotland.
A. notion B. expression
C. imagination D. theory

13. The prisoner showed no .... for his crimes.
A. hatred B. obstinacy
C. remorse D. anger

14. It is inconceivable that in many schools children are subjected to physical .... in the name of discipline.
A. violation B. exercise
C. violence D. security

15. We have not yet fully realised the .... consequences of the war.
A. happy B. pleasing
C. grim D. exciting

16. Happiness consists in being .... what we have.
A. contented to B. contented with
C. contented for D. contented in

17. His rude behaviour is a .... his organization.
A. disgrace for B. disgrace on
C. disgrace upon D. disgrace to

18. No child is .... understanding. One has to wait and provide proper guidance.
A. dull to B. dull in
C. dull of D. dull for

19. I am fully .... the problems facing the industry.
A. alive with B. alive to
C. alive for D. alive on

20. The Romans were .... science.
A. bad in B. bad to
C. bad for D. bad at

21. Although I was .... of his plans, I encouraged him, because there was no one else who was willing to help.
A. sceptical B. remorseful
C. fearful D. excited

22. You have no business to .... pain on a weak and poor person.
A. inflict B. put
C. direct D. force

23. Her uncle died in a car accident. He was quite rich. She suddenly .... all her uncle's money.
A. succeeded B. caught
C. gave D. inherited

24. There was a major accident. The plane crashed. The pilot .... did not see the tower.
A. likely B. probably
C. scarcely D. hurriedly

25. The car we were travelling in .... a mile from home.
A. broke off B. broke down
C. broke into D. broke up

26. What are you .... in the kitchen cupboard?
A. looking in B. looking on
C. looking to D. looking for

27. I did not see the point of .... waiting for them, so I went home.
A. hanging around B. hang on
C. hang together D. hanging up

28. He lost confidence and .... of the deal at the last minute.
A. backed out B. backed on
C. backed down D. backed onto

29. To the dismay of all the students, the class monitor was ..... berated by the principal at a school assembly.
A. critically B. ignominiously
C. prudently D. fortuitously

30. All attempts to revive the fishing industry were ..... failure.
A. foredoomed to B. heading at
C. predicted for D. estimated to

31. There are ..... parked outside than yesterday.
A. fewer cars B. few cars
C. less cars D. a small number of cars

32. The minister had to ..... some awkward questions from reporters.
A. fend B. fend at
C. fend out D. fend off

33. The ..... of evidence was on the side of the plaintiff since all but one of the witnesses testified that his story was correct.
A. propensity B. force
C. preponderance D. brunt

34. Attention to detail is ..... of a fine craftsman.
A. hallmark B. stamp
C. seal of authority D. authenticity

35. Behaving in a .... and serious way, even in a .... situation, makes people respect you.
A. calm, difficult B. steady, angry
C. flamboyant, tricky D. cool astounding

ANSWERS

1	2	3	4	5	6	7	8	9	10
A	B	C	A	C	B	C	C	B	D
11	12	13	14	15	16	17	18	19	20
C	A	C	C	C	B	D	B	B	D
21	22	23	24	25	26	27	28	29	30
B	C	C	B	C	C	D	A	B	A
31	32	33	34	35					
A	D	D	A	A					

❑❑❑

11 Sentence Improvement

One may use the same words in many ways but the best way is only one that makes the perfect usage of the words and conveys the proper meaning of the expression. Try it yourself in the following questions.

Multiple Choice Questions

Directions: *In these questions, a part of the sentence is bold. Below are given alternatives to the bold part at A, B and C which may improve the sentence. Choose the correct alternative. In case no improvement is needed, your answer is 'D'.*

1. Discreet salience **is extremely important** to create that 'irresistible-yet-unattainable' image for brands that want to take India seriously
A. was extremely important
B. is mainly important
C. was important extremely
D. No Improvement

2. This, over a designer outfit that he wanted for a friend's party and **that his sensitive** parents refused him.
A. which his sensitive
B. which his insensitive
C. that his insensitive
D. No Improvement

3. Goa was full of non-Goa property hunters **rushing about buying up the place** like tomorrow was an expired lease.
A. rushing in buying up the place
B. rushed about buying up the place
C. rushing about to buy up the place
D. No Improvement

4. Property hunting is a **tired and hungry** making business.
A. is a tiresome and hungry
B. is a tiring and hungry
C. is a tiring and waste
D. No Improvement

5. Cultural differences aside, **till luxury need speaks** in a manner that befits.
A. luxury still needs to speak
B. luxury still need to speak
C. luxury till need to speak
D. No Improvement

6. Indian food—the culinary avatar of the subcontinent's social history presented on a platter—**is without doubt the best food** in the world.
A. is undoubtedly the greatest food
B. is without doubt greatest food
C. is best food without doubt
D. No Improvement

7. It must retain the language of poetry. **It needed to create** stories, and not statements.
A. It needed creating B. It needs creating
C. It needs to create D. No Improvement

8. This year, Asia-Pacific has become the first region **to reach aggregate profiting** in biotech.
A. to reach aggregated profitability
B. to reach aggregate profitability
C. to reach aggregate of profit
D. No Improvement

9. India is deviating to embrace the West. If Western luxury brands deviate a little, **albeit selectively**, they will find rich Indian arms open far and wide.
A. though selectively B. however selectively
C. albeit selectedly D. No Improvement

10. China and India continued to attract attention and deals, motivated by the desire to increase access to these **largest and growing** drug markets and by the need to lower the costs of drug development.
A. larger and growing B. large and growing
C. larger and grown D. No Improvement

11. Luxury brands are **still above of the** clover curve here, with their elite (small) audiences.
A. still ahead of the B. still in the
C. still far of the D. No Improvement

12. Agencies **hence needed to be** sure of returns before investing, say admen.
A. hence needs to be B. so needs to be
C. hence need to be D. No Improvement

13. India is still a nascent market and that's the spirit everyone's **looking at it**.
A. looking for it B. looking in it
C. looking with it D. No Improvement

14. Questioning the state's move to allow women to serve liquor but not dance in bars **of the ground that** dançing aroused physical lust.
A. on the grounds that
B. of the grounds that
C. over the grounds that
D. No Improvement

15. For England the positives from their crushing series lose come in the shape of James Anderson and Kevin Pietersen, **both of which** have made significant strides up the rankings.
A. both of which B. both of whom
C. both of who D. No Improvement

16. International campaigns can work well for luxury here, **but context cannot be** ignored.
A. so context cannot be
B. but context cannot
C. but context couldn't
D. No Improvement

17. For one, the Indian luxury context, **while evolved rapidly**, still has its own meaning, and its own implications.
A. while evolved rapid
B. which evolving rapidly
C. while evolving rapidly
D. No Improvement

18. But too much of availability can compromise a luxury brand or **made it lose** its lustre.
A. make her lose B. make him lose
C. make it lose D. No Improvement

19. Still, it's under-the-upper **layers themselves who** are aspiring for slivers of luxury.
A. layers themselves which
B. layer itself who
C. layers themself which
D. No Improvement

20. It is like saying Hindi movies, with skimpily dressed dancers, would **effect public** order.
A. effect your B. affect public
C. affected public D. No Improvement

21. The court held that a few women being involved in prostitution was no **justice to deny other** bar girls the right to livelihood.
A. justification to declare other
B. justification to deny other
C. justice to let other
D. No Improvement

22. All-rounder cricketer has also made some progress **over the** player rankings.
A. above the B. at the
C. up the D. No Improvement

23. Former minister on Sunday **joined hands** with a suspended Lok Sabha member to float a new political outfit.
A. folded hands B. walked hand in hand
C. shaked hands D. No Improvement

24. Pakistan's former ministers will meet in London on Monday **to ask** a strategy to return home from exile.
A. to chalk out B. to negotiate
C. to create D. No Improvement

25. It's a family potboiler, medical thriller and political drama **all in one**—except that it's all too real and all too grim.
A. all 3 in one
B. all coupled into one
C. all rolled into one
D. No Improvement

ANSWERS

1	2	3	4	5	6	7	8	9	10
D	C	D	B	A	D	C	C	D	B
11	**12**	**13**	**14**	**15**	**16**	**17**	**18**	**19**	**20**
C	C	D	A	C	D	C	C	C	C
21	**22**	**23**	**24**	**25**					
B	C	C	A	C					

❑❑❑

12 Reordering Words & Sentences

Different words form a sentence and convey their meaning only when arranged in a proper order. A Paragraph is formed from sentences, it will convey its true meaning and purpose only when the sentences are arranged in a proper manner. Try and practise it in this exercise.

Multiple Choice Questions

Directions (Qs. 1 to 20): *In the following questions, some parts of the sentence have been jumbled up. You are required to rearrange these parts which are labelled P, Q, R and S to produce the correct sentence. Choose the option with proper sequence.*

1. We are doing
P : to the people
Q : to give relief
R : all we can
S : but more funds are needed
The correct sequence should be
A. P Q R S B. R Q P S
C. Q P R S D. S P Q R

2. The man
P : when he was
Q : in the office last evening
R : could not finish
S : all his work
The correct sequence should be
A. P Q R S B. Q R S P
C. R Q P S D. R S P Q

3. The people decided
P : they were going
Q : how much
R : to spend
S : on the construction of the school building
The correct sequence should be
A. Q P R S B. P Q R S
C. P R Q S D. S Q P R

4. The man said that
P : those workers
Q : would be given a raise
R : who did not go on
S : strike last month
The correct sequence should be
A. P Q R S B. P R S Q
C. Q P R S D. R S P Q

5. I think
P : the members
Q : are basically in agreement
R : of the group
S : on the following points
The correct sequence should be
A. R Q P S B. S Q R P
C. P R Q S D. P Q S R

6. While it was true that
P : I had
Q : to invest in industry
R : some lands and houses
S : I did not have ready cash
The correct sequence should be
A. P Q R S B. P R S Q
C. S Q P R D. Q P R S

7. P : But for your help
Q : to finish this work
R : it would not have been possible
S : in time
The correct sequence should be
A. P R Q S B. S P Q R
C. R P Q S D. P Q R S

8. The boy
P : in the competition
Q : who was wearing spectacles
R : won many prizes
S : held in our college

The correct sequence should be

A. P Q R S B. R P S Q

C. Q R P S D. Q P S R

9. About 200 years ago,

P : in the south of India

Q : an old king

R : ruled over a kingdom

S : called Rajavarman

The correct sequence should be

A. Q S R P B. P Q R S

C. Q P S R D. Q S P R

10. P : his land

Q : a wooden plough

R : the Indian peasant still uses

S : to cultivate

The correct sequence should be

A. R Q P S B. Q P S R

C. S R Q P D. R Q S P

11. He was a man,

P : even if he had to starve

Q : who would not beg

R : borrow or steal

S : from anyone

The correct sequence should be

A. P Q R S B. P R Q S

C. Q R S P D. Q P R S

12. P : in the progress of

Q : universities play a crucial role

R : our civilization

S : in the present age

The correct sequence should be

A. S Q P R B. Q R S P

C. Q R P S D. S Q R P

13. P : far out into the sea

Q : for the next two weeks there were further explosions

R : which hurled

S : ashes and debris

The correct sequence should be

A. Q R P S B. R S P Q

C. Q R S P D. S R P Q

14. William Shakespeare,

P : in his lifetime

Q : the great English dramatist

R : wrote thirty-five plays

S : and several poems

The correct sequence should be

A. P Q R S B. R S P Q

C. Q S R P D. Q R S P

15. Whenever I am,

P : with an old friend of mine

Q : in New Delhi

R : to have dinner

S : I always try

The correct sequence should be

A. S Q P R B. Q S R P

C. R P S Q D. P R Q S

16. P : I don't know

Q : must have thought

R : what people sitting next to me

S : but I came away

The correct sequence should be

A. R S Q P B. R Q S P

C. P Q R S D. P R Q S

17. P : in estimating the size of the earth

Q : but they were hampered by the lack of instruments of precision

R : ancient astronomers

S : used methods which were theoretically valid

The correct sequence should be

A. R P Q S B. P R Q S

C. R S Q P D. R P S Q

18. P : It is a pity that

Q : by offering a handsome dowry

R : a number of parents think that

S : they will be able to ensure the happiness of their daughters

The correct sequence should be

A. S Q R P B. P R S Q

C. P S R Q D. P R Q S

19. The common man

P : in nurturing

Q : a more active role

R : communal harmony.

S : should play

The correct sequence should be

A. P R S Q B. S Q P R

C. S Q R P D. P R Q S

20. The doctor

P : able to find out

Q : what has caused

R : the food poisoning

S : has not been

The correct sequence should be

A. S P R Q B. P R Q S

C. P R S Q D. S P Q R

Directions (Qs. 21 to 27): *A number of sentences are given below which when properly sequenced form a coherent paragraph. Each sentence is labelled as abcdef...... Choose the most logical order of sentences from among the given choices to construct a coherent paragraph:*

21. (a) Parts of northern region were pounded by heavy rains today,

(b) Vehicular traffic came to a near halt.

(c) As mid and high altitude areas of Himachal Pradesh were in grip of severe cold wave with snow lashing the tribal areas and mid ranges receiving showers.

(d) As the sky remained heavily overcast with dark clouds reducing the visibility considerably.
(e) A large number of tourists were forced to buy heavy woollens and stay indoors due to inclement weather.
A. ecabd B. adecb
C. edabc D. acbde

22. (a) The idea is that students should be able to find employment for themselves after the course.
(b) The Central Board of Secondary Education is planning a revamp of its vocational courses.
(c) For this it is necessary to tie up with the industry as well as mobilise schools for their support.
(d) While others will be made less academic and more in tune with the needs of the industry.
(e) A number of courses have been identified as 'deadwood' and will be done away with.
A. bedac B. abcde
C. acebd D. baced

23. (a) Clearly, age is not a deterrent in one's choice of learning.
(b) Perhaps, it was because of her childhood desire.
(c) When Rachna came to Delhi eight years back, she had not anticipated a career in the field of art.
(d) She has been successful in the various exhibitions that she has been part of in terms of business.
(e) She had got into expressing her thoughts with the help of a brush and colours only because her daughter refused to get initiated into it.
(f) She feels that her use of colour appeals to people.
A. aedcbf B. cdefba
C. cebadf D. acdebf

24. (a) The rehabilitation record has been dismal.
(b) It has been two years years since the earthquake rudely rattled the people of Gujarat.
(c) And since then, life has been a constant struggle.
(d) The quake set Gujarat's clock back by 10 years.
(e) Things changed forever.
A. bedca B. bcade
C. dbace D. edcba

25. (a) In fact, success in exams depended on rote learning from old notes.
(b) when he was studying civil engineering in a college in Gujarat.
(c) He was detained for lack of attendance.
(d) Lectures were soporific, classes rarely worth attending and 80 per cent attendance compulsory.
(e) The college became a trap he hated.
(f) His is a plight many engineers across India would identify with.
(g) He found the going tough.
A. abcdgef B. bgdacef
C. fabcdge D. abcdefg

26. (a) In a country that has close to 600 recognised engineering colleges, there are only seven IITs.
(b) Barring a few exeptions, the academic atmosphere in these is moribund.
(c) The very best students usually get there.
(d) many waste themselves in frustration.
(e) Most of those who get into engineering are good students.
(f) but about 1.25 lakh others and up in the remaining colleges.
A. aecfbd B. abecdf
C. abcdef D. acfbed

27. (a) Whatever the job market, common wisdom says that IIT graduates will find jobs where others have failed.
(b) The IIT brand name is a ticket to success.
(c) When recruiters go headhunting, the IITs are still top of their list.
(d) Its possessor is understood to have an excellent academic record and the will to succeed.
(e) In the job market, that counts.
A. bdeac B. abcde
C. abdce D. dbace

ANSWERS

1	2	3	4	5	6	7	8	9	10
B	D	A	B	C	C	A	C	A	D
11	12	13	14	15	16	17	18	19	20
C	A	C	D	B	D	C	B	B	D
21	22	23	24	25	26	27			
D	A	C	A	B	D	A			

❑❑❑

13 Comprehension Passages

PASSAGES

Directions: *Read the following passages and answer the questions given below each.*

PASSAGE-1

In the Roman times, defected enemies were generally put to death as criminals for having offended the emperor of Rome. In the middle ages, however, the practice of ransoming of returning prisoners in exchange for money became common. Though some saw this custom as a step towards a most humane society, the primary reasons behind it were economic rather than humanitarian.

In those times, rulers had only a limited ability to raise taxes. They could neither force their subject to fight nor pay them to do so. The promise of material compensation in the form of goods and ransom was therefore the only way of inducing combatants to participate in a war. In the middle ages, the predominant incentive for the individual soldiers was the expectation of spoils. Although collecting ransom clearly brought financial gain, keeping a prisoner and arranging for his exchange had its cost. Consequently, procedures were devised to reduce transaction costs.

One such device was a rule asserting that the prisoner had to assess his own value. This compelled the prisoner to establish a value *without too much distortion;* indicating too low a value would increase, the captive's chances of being killed, while indicating too high a value would either ruin him financially or create a prohibitively expensive ransom that would also result in death.

1. It can be inferred from the passage that a medieval soldier
   A. was less likely to kill captured members of opposing armies than was a soldier of the Roman Empire
   B. was similar to a 20th century terrorist in that he operated on a basically independent level and was motivated solely by economic incentives
   C. had few economic options and chose to fight because it was the only way to earn an adequate living
   D. was motivated to spare prisoners' lives by humanitarian rather than economic ideals

2. Which of the following best describes the change in policy from executing prisoners in Roman times to ransoming prisoners in the middle ages?
   A. The emperors of Rome demanded more respect than did medieval rulers and thus Roman subjects went to greater lengths to defend their nation
   B. It was a reflection of the lesser degree of direct control medieval ruler had over subjects
   C. It became a show of strength and honour warrior of the middles ages to be able to capture and return their enemies
   D. Medieval soldiers were not as hum-anitarian as their ransoming practices might have indicated

3. The primary purpose of the passage is to
   A. discuss the economic basis of the medieval practice of exchanging prisoners for ransom
   B. examine the history of the treatment of prisoner of war
   C. emphasize the importance of a warrior's code of honour during the middle ages
   D. explore a way of reducing the cost of ransom

4. The author uses the phrase *"without too much distortion"* in order to
   A. indicate that prisoners would fairly assess their worth
   B. emphasize the important role medieval prisoners played in determining whether they should be ransomed
   C. explain how prisoners often paid more than an appropriate ransom in order to increase their chances for survival
   D. suggest that captors and captives often had understanding relationships

PASSAGE-2

The world dismisses curiosity by calling it idle or mere idle curiosity—even though curious persons are seldom idle. Parents do their best to extinguish curiosity in their children because it makes life difficult to be faced everyday with a string of unanswerable questions about what makes fire hot or why grass grows. Children whose curiosity survives parental discipline are invited to join our university. With the university, they go on asking their questions and trying to find the answers. In the eyes of a scholar, that is what a university is for. Some of the questions which the scholars ask, seem to the world to be scarcely worth asking, let alone answering. They asked questions too minute specialised for you and me to understand without years of explanation. If the world inquires of one of them why he wants to know the answer to a particular question he may say especially if he is a scientist, that the answer will in some obscure way make possible a new machine or weapon or gadget. He talks that way because he knows that the world understands and respects utility.

But to you who are now part of the university, he will say that he wants to know the answer simply because he does not know it, the way the mountain climber wants to climb a mountain, simply because it is there. Similarly a historian asked by an outsider why he studies history may come out with the argument that he has learnt to repeat on such occasions, something about knowledge of the past making it possible to understand the present and mould the future. But if you really want to know why a historian studies the past, the answer is much simpler, something happened and he would like to know what. All this does not mean that the answers which scholars find to their questions have no consequences. They may have enormous consequences but these seldom form the reason for asking the questions or pursuing the answers. It is true that scholars can be put to work answering questions for the sake of the consequences as thousands are working, now, for example, in search of a cure for cancer. But this is not the primary function of the scholars. For the consequences are usually subordinate to the satisfaction of curiosity.

1. According to the passage, the children make life difficult for their parents
   A. by their ceaseless curiosity
   B. by unceasing bombardment of questions
   C. by asking irrelevant questions
   D. by posing profound questions
2. The common people consider some of the questions that the scholars ask unimportant
   A. as they are too lazy and idle
   B. as they are too modest
   C. as it's beyond their comprehension
   D. as it is considered a waste of time
3. A historian really studies the past
   A. to comprehend the present and to reconstruct the future
   B. to explain the present and plan the future
   C. to understand the present and make fortune
   D. to understand the present and mould the future
4. Children whose curiosity survives parental discipline means
   A. children retaining their curiosity in spite of being discouraged by their parents
   B. children pursuing their mental curiosity
   C. children's curiosity subdued due to parents' intervention
   D. children being disciplined by their parents
5. According to the passage, parents do their best to discourage curiosity in their children
   A. because they have no time
   B. because they have no patience to answer them
   C. because they feel that their children ask stupid questions continuously
   D. because they are unable to answer all their questions

PASSAGE-3

The factor of geographical distribution is equally, possibly even more, significant that English is spoken as first or native language in at least four continents of the world, Russian in two, Chinese and the Indian languages in one. English is without question the closest approach to a world language today. It goes without saying that no two persons ever have an identical command of their common language. Certainly, they have not precisely the same vocabulary. There are at least minor differences in pronunciation, indeed the same individual will not pronounce his vowels and consonants in absolutely identical fashion everytime he utters them. Everyone possesses, in addition, certain individual traits of grammatical form and syntactical order, constituting that peculiar and personal quality of language which we term as style. All of this is implicit in the well-known phrase, 'Style is the man.' No men are identical, no two styles are the same. If this be true of but two persons, the potential of differences resident in a language spoken by more than 200 million truly staggers imagination.

1. The author argues that English is the closest approach to a world language because
   A. there are more native speakers of English than of any other language
   B. English has less number of mutually unintelligible dialects
   C. the geographical distribution of English covers a much greater area
   D. other languages are much too complex to be world languages

2. The fact that the same individual will not pronounce his vowels and consonants identically everytime shows that
   A. literary style varies from person to person
   B. mutual intelligibility is a myth
   C. vocabulary varies from individual to individual
   D. no two persons speak the same language exactly the same way
3. It is evident from the passage that style is
   A. a strange type of language
   B. a language where one does not have to be particular about correctness and grammar
   C. language used in a particular way by an individual
   D. a question of grammatical and syntactic correctness
4. According to some authorities
   A. more people speak Chinese dialect than English
   B. more people speak English as an auxiliary language than as a first language
   C. more people speak English in the UK than in England
   D. about one-fourth of the world's population speaks English
5. The overall implication of the passage is that
   A. to suppose that 230 million people speak English as a native language would certainly be an underestimate
   B. the 55 million inhabitants of the British Isles speak like the 30 million inhabitants of the dominions and colonies
   C. a little less than half the native English speakers in the world live in the US
   D. about one-tenth of the total English-speaking world population lives in British dominions and colonies

PASSAGE-4

What is the future which awaits our children? The underlying assumption of the question, that Indian children have a common future, is itself dubious. It can legitimately be asked whether a student who is well-fed, attending a boarding school in the salubrious climate of the hills and learning to use computers has any future in common with a malnourished child who goes to a school with no blackboards, if indeed he does go to school. The latter may have no worthwhile future at all. And it might be worthwhile to analyse the significance of this marginalisation of more than 75 per cent of the children of this country.

The failure to provide an infrastructure for primary education in the villages of India more than 40 years after independence is in sharp contrast with the sophisticated institutions, for technical institutes of higher education are funded by the government, which essentially means that the money to support them comes from taxes. And, since indirect taxation forms a substantial part of the taxes collected by the government, the financial burden is borne by all the people. L.K. Jha put it graphically when he observed that 25 paise of every rupee spent on educating an IIT student comes from the pockets of men and women whose children may never enter a proper classroom.

1. The author is trying to highlight which of the following?
   A. Faulty system of direct taxes
   B. The greatness of L.K. Jha
   C. Need of sophisticated education for rural poor
   D. Need to have common future for Indian children
2. Which of the following pairs have been termed as 'sharp contrast' by the author?
   (*i*) Infrastructure for technical education
   (*ii*) Lack of infrastructure for rural primary schools
   (*iii*) 25 paise of every rupee earned by Government is spent on education
   (*iv*) The financial burden of higher technical education is borne by all people
   (*v*) 75% of children have limited opportunities
   A. (*ii*) and (*iv*) B. (*ii*) and (*iii*)
   C. (*iii*) and (*iv*) D. (*i*) and (*ii*)
3. Which of the following statements is not true?
   (*i*) The author welcomes Govt.'s initiative on primary education
   (*ii*) 75% of the children have a bright future
   (*iii*) 25% cost of educating a technocrat comes from poor people
   A. Only (*i*) B. Only (*ii*)
   C. Only (*iii*) D. Only (*i*) and (*ii*)
4. According to the author, who among the following does not have a hopeful and prosperous future?
   (*i*) All students from technical institutes
   (*ii*) All students financially supported by the Government
   A. Only (*i*) B. Only (*ii*)
   C. Both (*i*) and (*ii*) D. Neither (*i*) nor (*ii*)
5. What seems to be the likely answer of the author to the question posed by him in the first sentence of the passage?
   (*i*) There is no common future for the Indian children
   (*ii*) The future is worthwhile for majority of Indian children
   (*iii*) The majority may never enter a proper classroom
   A. Only (*i*) B. Only (*ii*)
   C. Only (*iii*) D. Both (*i*) and (*ii*)
6. What seems to be the purpose of the author in writing this passage?
   A. Setting goals for children of upper middle class
   B. Questioning the legitimacy of public schools
   C. Highlighting lack of infrastructural facilities for primary education
   D. Focusing on inequality in educational opportunities

PASSAGE-5

Cyber crime is the branded stigma defacing the culture and magnanimity of computer technology. It is upkeeping the flag with indomitable triumph against developing computer technology worldwide.

Modern age is striding with marching steps of technology revolution beating the past decade of ancestral belief with ultimate care. Computer invention has unfolded the mystery of quick access with the objective of minimum manpower and cutting the time consumption parameters.

As each coin has dual face of its portrait, likewise computer technology is sick of creeping virus. Synthetic man-made dilemma of site hackers activation is causing setback to the expanding anchor of revolutionary device with great loss of time, economy and data profile as suffered by consumers. A recent report from Internet security firm Websense estimates that 85.6 per cent of all the unwanted e-mails contained links to spam sites. The company's data suggests that the number of malicious sites grew 233 per cent in the last six months and saw 671 per cent growth in the number of malicious sites during the last year. In June alone, the total number of e-mails detected as containing viruses increased by 600 per cent compared to May.

Chat rooms, blogs and message-boards where the users post comments have been identified as the top targets of hackers and spammers due to the high traffic these attract. According to Websense, 95 per cent of user-generated comments to blogs, chat rooms and message-boards during the first half of the year were malicious.

It is advisable not to click on spurious links and stay away from keying in passwords at unknown sites as they are most likely to be spammed. Hackers can steal your passwords and log in to your account and access critical information like account numbers and contact details among other things.

1. The above passage is:
A. an advisory for the computer users.
B. an advisory for the Internet users.
C. a warning against possible threat to the Internet users.
D. related to chat rooms, blogs and message boards.

2. People who use chat rooms and blogs,
A. are safe and have no threats from spam.
B. are more prone to malicious e-mails.
C. create virus and hack the accounts of others.
D. are unsafe.

3. According to the writer, it is not safe to:
A. log on to spurious links.
B. access one's own account frequently.
C. have essential information stored in a computer.
D. include data-stealing code.

4. Hackers and spammers, according to the writer, are:
A. a new threat to the Internet users and the economy.
B. only pranksters and not serious threat to the system.
C. trained, professional technocrats who are an asset.
D. not expert professionals.

5. Which word in the passage is synonym of *weblog*?
A. blog B. password
C. site D. e-mail

6. Which agency has assessed the data record with spam sites?
A. Microsoft
B. Internet security from Google
C. Websense
D. Spammers

7. Which month dominates the e-mails detection data record?
A. May B. June
C. Last six months D. Last year

ANSWERS

PASSAGE-1

1	2	3	4
A	B	A	A

PASSAGE-2

1	2	3	4	5
A	C	D	A	D

PASSAGE-3

1	2	3	4	5
A	D	C	D	A

PASSAGE-4

1	2	3	4	5	6
D	A	D	A	A	D

PASSAGE-5

1	2	3	4	5	6	7
A	D	A	A	A	C	B

❑❑❑

14 Cloze Test

A cloze test is a procedure in which a person is asked to supply words that have been removed from a passage as a test of his ability to comprehend text. Practise it regularly to score well.

PASSAGES

Directions: *In each of the following passages some numbered blank spaces are given. For each numbered blank space four answer choices are given. Pick out the one which is the most appropriate for that blank space, keeping the trend of the passage in mind.*

Passage-1

Mankind's most ....(1).... treasure of thoughts is carefully preserved in the golden casket of books. The ....(2).... of books is as vast as the universe, for there is no corner of it which they have left ....(3).... . There is no ....(4).... of books on any topic, be it as simple as the composition of sodium nitrate or as ....(5).... as the mechanism of a spacecraft rocketing towards Mars. The ....(6).... of books is not only most easily available but is enlightened, dependable and lifelong. In times of distress they make us stoically ....(7).... of the object that causes uneasiness and we learn to ....(8).... with the sting of adversity.

Questions

1. A. costly B. important C. valuable D. vast

2. A. area B. scope C. storage D. kingdom

3. A. unexplored B. unseen C. untouched D. unapproached

4. A. lack B. dearth C. shortage D. insufficiency

5. A. extricate B. intricate C. intrinsic D. internecine

6. A. company B. assistance C. friendship D. companionship

7. A. defiant B. defendant C. defensible D. delusive

8. A. adapt B. adopt C. exist D. co-exist

Passage-2

Though the government has tried to ....(1).... Naxalism with all its might, much more needs to be done to totally root out the ....(2).... of Naxalism. The roots of Naxalism ....(3).... economic backwardness and social exploitation of the peasants and the weaker classes. Thus, the best way to ....(4).... Naxalism is to bring the naxals ....(5).... the mainstream. ....(6).... policies and schemes should be implemented effectively ....(7).... the Naxals economically stable. They should be ....(8).... to participate in democratic processes. The government has to ....(9).... the social upliftment of the Naxals. Use of force in ....(10).... Naxalism will yield little success.

Questions

1. A. crush B. handle C. tackle D. suppress

2. A. menace B. whole C. gamut D. stems

3. A. lies in B. are in C. abound in D. exist in

4. A. crash B. crush C. break D. defy

5. A. in B. on
C. into D. within

6. A. Current B. Latest
C. Occurring D. Existing

7. A. so that B. so as to make
C. such that D. to make

8. A. insisted B. brought
C. encouraged D. forced

9. A. assure B. insure
C. guarantee D. ensure

10. A. countering B. defying
C. banishing D. desecrating

Passage-3

We are living in very exciting ....(1).... . The ....(2).... change is dizzying and the impact this progress is having on our present and — more importantly — on our future is difficult to ....(3).... in its ...(4).... . This is the age of ....(5).... micro-processors, sophisticated software, new hardware technology and high bandwidth, high-speed networks. The PC gave us a new way to work, play and ....(6).... . In fact, it brought ....(7).... our desktops computing power, which until a few years ....(8).... had only been available to corporates. With the ....(9).... of the internet, the PC ....(10).... us the most convenient and flexible way to head on to the Net.

Questions

1. A. periods B. days
C. phase D. times

2. A. phase B. pace
C. sphere D. drastic

3. A. guess B. forecast
C. comprehend D. approximate

4. A. whole B. entirety
C. fruition D. fullness

5. A. strong B. changing
C. powerful D. sonorous

6. A. convey B. communicate
C. entertain D. enjoy

7. A. onto B. to
C. on D. at

8. A. back B. earlier
C. behind D. before

9. A. addendum B. adherence
C. afoot D. advent

10. A. allowed B. privileged
C. brought D. offered

Passage-4

What is required today in our country is ....(1).... of a new political culture based on full respect for human liberty, on pluralism and on a better social deal for all. The major ....(2).... facing us today is to carry out democratic transformation in all the ....(3)...., social, cultural, economic and political. The events of the 20th century ....(4).... one thing absolutely clear that human ....(5)...., everywhere, specially in countries whose political structures were ....(6).... to reflect the revolutionary aspirations of the people ....(7).... not only under stress and strain but are ....(8).... vast upheavals because of the ....(9).... of democracy. At the same time it has also to be understood that democracy cannot be ....(10).... into a static mould.

Questions

1. A. growing B. developing
C. creating D. creation

2. A. development B. crisis
C. challenge D. drawback

3. A. corners B. context
C. realm D. spheres

4. A. have made B. has made
C. had made D. made

5. A. travails B. traverse
C. traps D. transverse

6. A. supposed B. meant
C. caused D. forced

7. A. were B. was
C. are D. have been

8. A. developing B. evolving
C. experiencing D. faced with

9. A. denial B. rebuff
C. rebuttal D. absence

10. A. shaped B. flex
C. frozen D. caused

Passage-5

For centuries, women not only in India but all over the world ....(1).... treated as ....(2).... secondary position to men. ....(3).... human history men ....(4).... far greater power then women to name, classify, and order the worlds in which they both live. ....(5).... studies in various parts of the world point out to a wide ....(6).... in male and female roles ....(7).... cultures and demonstrate the possibility of change in these sex-determined roles. The 20th century in particular ....(8).... the cause of gender justice by internationalizing struggles for equality ....(9).... women and other oppressed people. Women's struggles against their ....(10).... were intertwined in ....(11).... degrees with ideologies and movements based on the values of freedom, self-determination, equality, democracy and justice.

Questions

1. A. has been B. have been
   C. had been D. were
2. A. occupying B. taking
   C. possessing D. serving
3. A. All through B. Throughout
   C. Since D. From
4. A. have B. had
   C. have had D. enjoy
5. A. Sociological B. Anthropological
   C. General D. Practical
6. A. concord B. repulsion
   C. disagreement D. variation
7. A. among B. across
   C. between D. of
8. A. developed B. evolved
   C. promoted D. entertained
9. A. for B. to
   C. among D. by
10. A. subsidiary B. subsequent
    C. subservience D. subordination
11. A. various B. varying
    C changing D. differing

Passage-6

Visualisation is a strong ....(1).... to memory. Those persons who ......(2)..... a powerful memory cannot do so without taking the help of visualisation. Such persons have developed the skills to ....(3).... visualisation even in such ....(4).... tasks as remembering names and numbers. These persons have the names and numbers ....(5).... in their brain even after hearing those names and figures only once. On the other hand those who take the help of revising to memorise ....(6).... to forget it once they have ....(7).... the practice of revising ....(8).... the ones who have applied visualisation to memorise. Psychologists ....(9).... in visualisation a powerful tool for personality development. The more you visualise, the more you are ....(10).... your attitude and behaviour to the blue prints of your vision and ....(11).... more you are inching towards success.

Questions

1. A. way B. path
   C. aid D. symptom
2. A. command B. master
   C. rule D. enjoy
3. A. use B. apply
   C. put D. place
4. A. trivial B. difficult
   C. mundane D. unscrupulous
5. A. impress B. imprinted
   C. impinge D. store
6. A. bent B. incline
   C. prone d. tend
7. A. dropped B. left
   C. gave up D. given up
8. A. unlike B. opposite
   C. contrary D. not like
9. A. found B. have found
   C. sees D. finds
10. A. shaping B. moulding
    C. making D. attuning
11. A. actually B. factually
    C. subsequently D. consequently

Passage-7

The development of an area depends on the resources ....(1).... in the area, the needs and ....(2).... of the people living there and the technological skill ....(3).... by them. Humans play an important and decisive role in the ....(4).... of development of an area. We choose the ....(5).... of resources which could be developed to our ....(6).... . The natural ....(7).... available in an area ....(8).... value as a resource only when people find a use for them. There are ....(9).... where large potential resources are available, but they ....(10).... developed for economic reasons. Lack of capital for investments, roads and railway lines, and other ....(11).... facilities may stand in the way of resource development.

Questions

1. A. present B. prevalent
   C. available D. exist
2. A. inspirations B. aspirations
   C. ambitions D. curiosity
3. A. handled B. practised
   C. availed D. possessed
4. A. system B. design
   C. pattern D. style
5. A. class B. group
   C. variety D. types
6. A. good B. advantage
   C. approach D. favour
7. A. secrets B. phenomenon
   C. products D. endowments
8. A. get B. acquire
   C. possess D. takes
9. A. instances B. events
   C. circumstances D. happenings
10. A. have not yet been B. haven't been
    C. are not yet D. yet have not been

11. A. common B. general
C. infrastructural D. structural

Passage-8

The Naxal problem in India is basically socio-economic in ....(1).... . The main reasons ....(2).... the Naxal movement in India are the ....(3).... of peasants and their weak social and economic position. ....(4).... of the peasants are landless labourers whose lands have been ....(5).... occupied by the landlords. Moreover, the landlords give ....(6).... wages to the peasants. Their ....(7).... suffering at the hands of the landlords thus encourage many peasants to take law ....(8).... their own hands. Due to their poor economic condition the peasants easily ....(9).... the trap of the naxal leaders who have their ....(10).... interests. Illiteracy, unemployment, police excesses, corruption and ....(11).... administration further ....(12).... this complex problem.

Questions

1. A. form B. shape
C. behaviour D. nature
2. A. for B. of
C. in D. behind
3. A. complaisance B. exploitation
C. domination D. exculpation
4. A. Many B. Much
C. Most D. All
5. A. imperiously B. imperatively
C. forcefully D. forcibly
6. A. improper B. small
C. inadequate D. insufficient
7. A. long B. brutal
C. pathetic D. great
8. A. in B. into
C. on D. by
9. A. fall into B. fall in
C. fell in D. fell into
10. A. selfish B. vested
C. vicious D. vindictive
11. A. failed B. improper
C. inefficient D. bureaucratic
12. A. heighten B. deepen
C. add D. worsen

ANSWERS

PASSAGE-1

1	2	3	4	5	6
C	D	A	B	B	D
7	8				
A	D				

PASSAGE-2

1	2	3	4	5	6
C	A	A	B	C	D
7	8	9	10		
B	C	D	A		

PASSAGE-3

1	2	3	4	5	6
D	B	C	B	C	B
7	8	9	10		
A	D	D	D		

PASSAGE-4

1	2	3	4	5	6
D	C	D	A	A	B
7	8	9	10		
C	C	A	C		

PASSAGE-5

1	2	3	4	5	6
B	A	B	C	B	D
7	8	9	10	11	
B	C	D	D	B	

PASSAGE-6

1	2	3	4	5	6
C	A	B	C	B	D
7	8	9	10	11	
A	A	B	D	D	

PASSAGE-7

1	2	3	4	5	6
C	B	D	C	D	B
7	8	9	10	11	
D	B	A	A	C	

PASSAGE-8

1	2	3	4	5	6
D	A	B	C	D	C
7	8	9	10	11	12
A	B	A	B	C	D

GENERAL INTELLIGENCE

VERBAL

CHAPTER 1

Analogies

NUMBER ANALOGY

In number analogy also, the relationship between the given numbers is detected and then applied to the second part to find the missing numbers. This relationship between the numbers can be based on any of the following patterns : *(i)* numbers can be odd/even/prime numbers; *(ii)* numbers can be multiples of one number; *(iii)* numbers can be squares/cubes of different numbers; *(iv)* some numbers can be added to/subtracted from/multiplied to/divided into the first number to get the second number; *(v)* the second number can be the sum/product/difference of the digits of first number; and *(vi)* combinations of any mathematical calculations given above can apply to the relationship between the two given numbers.

MULTIPLE CHOICE QUESTIONS

Directions : *In the following questions, select the number from the given options which follows the same relationship as shared between the first two numbers.*

1. 1 : 11 : : 2 : ?
(*a*) 20 (*b*) 22
(*c*) 24 (*d*) 44

2. 18 : 27 : : 22 : ?
(*a*) 42 (*b*) 39
(*c*) 33 (*d*) 54

3. 14 : 20 : : 16 : ?
(*a*) 23 (*b*) 10
(*c*) 48 (*d*) 32

4. 8 : 27 : : 64 : ?
(*a*) 277 (*b*) 125
(*c*) 250 (*d*) 99

5. 0.16 : 0.0016 : : 1.02 : ?
(*a*) 10.20 (*b*) 0.102
(*c*) 0.0102 (*d*) 1.020

EXPLANATORY ANSWERS

1. (*b*) : The first number is repeated to obtain the second number.

2. (*c*) : In the given set, the numbers are multiples of 9 and in the second set, multiples of 11.

18	:	27	: :	22	:	33
↓		↓		↓		↓
9 × 2		9 × 3		11 × 2		11 × 3

3. (*a*) : The relationship between the numbers is :

14	:	20	: :	16	:	23
↓		↓		↓		↓
7 × 2		(7 × 3) – 1		8 × 2		(8 × 3) – 1

4. (*b*) : The numbers are cubes of different numbers.

8	:	27	: :	64	:	125
↓		↓		↓		↓
2^3		3^3		4^3		5^3

5. (*c*) : The decimals are divided by 100.

LETTER ANALOGY

In this type of analogy the relationship between two given set of letters is established and then applied to the other set to obtain the required set of letters as the answer. These letters can be moved some steps backward or forward; reversed in whole or in sections or have some common identity between each other.

MULTIPLE CHOICE QUESTIONS

Directions : *In the questions given below one term is missing. Based on the relationship of the two given terms find the missing term from the given options.*

1. GFC : CFG : : RPJ : ?
(*a*) JRP (*b*) JPR
(*c*) PJR (*d*) RJP

2. BCF : DEG : : MNQ : ?
(*a*) OPR (*b*) PQS
(*c*) OPP (*d*) QRT

3. NATION : ANITNO : : HUNGRY : ?
(*a*) HNUGRY (*b*) UNHGYR
(*c*) YRNGUH (*d*) UHGNYR

4. SSTU : MMNO : : AABC : ?
(*a*) GGHH (*b*) IJKK
(*c*) XXYZ (*d*) NOOP

5. ACE : FGH : : LNP : ?
(*a*) QRS (*b*) PQR
(*c*) QST (*d*) MOQ

6. UVW : SXU : : LMN : ?
(*a*) JOL (*b*) KNM
(*c*) JKL (*d*) MLO

7. EIGHTY : GIEYTH : : OUTPUT : ?
(*a*) UTOPTU (*b*) UOTUPT
(*c*) TUOUTP (*d*) TUOTUP

8. TSR : FED : : WVU : ?
(*a*) CAB (*b*) MLK
(*c*) PQS (*d*) GFH

9. CJDL : FMGR : : IKJR : ?
(*a*) OQPT (*b*) RSTU
(*c*) OQRT (*d*) KRMO

EXPLANATORY ANSWERS

1. (*b*) : The letters of the first group are reversed.

GFC : CFG : : RPJ : JPR

2. (*a*) : The three letters are moved 2, 2 and 1 steps forward respectively.

BCF : DEG : : MNQ : OPR
+2, +2, +1

3. (*d*) : The word is divided in sections of two letters and the letters are reversed.

NATION : ANITNO : : HUNGRY : UHGNYR

4. (*c*) : The first letter in each group is repeated and followed by two consecutive letters.

5. (*a*) : The three letters are moved 5, 4, and 3 steps forward respectively.

ACE : FGH : : LNP : QRS
+5, +4, +3

6. (*a*) : The three letters are moved –2, +2 and –2 steps respectively.

UVW : SXU : : LMN : JOL
–2, +2, –2

7. (*d*) : The word is divided into two sections and the letters are written backwards.

EIGHTY : GIEYTH : : OUTPUT : TUOTUP

8. (*b*) : The letters are consecutive and written in reverse order.

9. (*a*) : In each set of letters, the 1st and 3rd letters are consecutive.

CJDL : FMGR : : IKJR : OQPT

SEMANTIC ANALOGY

In Analogy Tests the relationship between two given words is established and then applied to the other words. The type of relationship may vary, so while attempting such questions the first step is to identify the type of relationship, which can be any one of the following.

MULTIPLE CHOICE QUESTIONS

Directions : *In the questions given below establish the relationship between the two words. Then from the given options select one which has the same relationship as of the given two words.*

1. HUNGER : FOOD : : THIRST : ?
(*a*) Water (*b*) Drink
(*c*) Tea (*d*) Coffee

2. HUNTER : GUN : : WRITER : ?
(*a*) Book (*b*) Pen
(*c*) Poem (*d*) Page

3. WOOL : SHEEP : : SILK : ?
(*a*) Saree
(*b*) String
(*c*) Silkworm
(*d*) Moth

4. FOOD : STOMACH : : FUEL : ?
(*a*) Engine (*b*) Automobile
(*c*) Rail (*d*) Aeroplane

5. WATER : SAND : : OCEAN : ?
(*a*) Island (*b*) River
(*c*) Desert (*d*) Waves

6. ADULT : BABY : : FLOWER : ?
(*a*) Seed (*b*) Bud
(*c*) Fruit (*d*) Butterfly

7. WRITER : READER : : PRODUCER : ?
(*a*) Creator (*b*) Contractor
(*c*) Creature (*d*) Consumer

8. ENTRANCE : EXIT : : LOYALTY : ?
(*a*) Treachery (*b*) Patriotism
(*c*) Fidelity (*d*) Reward

9. MOTHER : MATERNAL : : FATHER : ?
(*a*) Eternal (*b*) Detrimental
(*c*) Paternal (*d*) Formidable

10. PEARL : NECKLACE : : FLOWER : ?
(*a*) Plant (*b*) Garden
(*c*) Petal (*d*) Bouquet

11. ALPHABET : WORD : : WORD : ?
(*a*) Sound (*b*) Music
(*c*) Sentence (*d*) Dictionary

12. LIFE : DEATH : : HOPE : ?
(*a*) Cry (*b*) Pain
(*c*) Despair (*d*) Sad

13. GOOD : BAD : : VIRTUE : ?
(*a*) Blame (*b*) Sin
(*c*) Despair (*d*) Vice

14. BIRD : FLY : : SNAKE : ?
(*a*) Timid (*b*) Clatter
(*c*) Crawl (*d*) Hole

EXPLANATORY ANSWERS

1. (*a*) : Hunger is satiated by food, thirst by water.
2. (*b*) : Weapon of a hunter is a gun, weapon of a writer is a pen.
3. (*c*) : Wool is obtained from sheep, silk is obtained from silkworm.
4. (*a*) : Food is consumed in stomach, fuel is consumed in engine.
5. (*c*) : The related words are near opposites.
6. (*b*) : The youngone of an adult is a baby and that of a flower is a bud.
7. (*d*) : A writer aims to please the readers by his writings, a producer aims to please the consumers by his products.
8. (*a*) : The related words are opposites.
9. (*c*) : Relations on the mother's side are maternal and on the father's side paternal.
10. (*d*) : Many pearls make a necklace, many flowers make a bouquet.
11. (*c*) : More than one alphabet make a word, more than one word make a sentence.
12. (*c*) : The related words are opposites.
13. (*d*) : The related words are opposites.
14. (*c*) : Birds fly, snakes crawl.

CHAPTER 2

Number Classification

ODD ONE OUT—NUMBERS

In this type of classification, different numbers are given as options. These numbers have some commonness; except one which is the odd one. One has to identify the similarity and then strike the odd one out as answer option. The number can be odd/even/consecutive, prime numbers, multiple of some number, single, square or cubes of different numbers, plus/minus of some other number or combinations of any mathematical calculation.

MULTIPLE CHOICE QUESTIONS

Directions : *In each of the following questions, there are four options. Three numbers, in these options, are alike in certain manner. Only one number does not fit in. Choose the one which is different from the rest.*

1. (*a*) 1948 (*b*) 2401
(*c*) 966 (*d*) 1449

2. (*a*) 182 (*b*) 169
(*c*) 130 (*d*) 158

3. (*a*) 129 (*b*) 130
(*c*) 131 (*d*) 132

4. (*a*) 3215 (*b*) 9309
(*c*) 4721 (*d*) 2850

5. (*a*) 1776 (*b*) 2364
(*c*) 1976 (*d*) 3776

6. (*a*) 64 (*b*) 84
(*c*) 16 (*d*) 36

EXPLANATORY ANSWERS

1. (*a*) : Other numbers are divisible by 7.
2. (*d*) : Other numbers are multiples of 13.
3. (*c*) : 131 is a prime number.
4. (*b*) : In other numbers, no digit is repeated.
5. (*b*) : In other numbers the last two digits are same.
6. (*b*) : All other numbers are perfect squares.

ODD ONE OUT—LETTERS

In this classification of letters, four groups of letters or a series of letters is given as options. One has to select the option as answer which does not share the commonness of the others.

MULTIPLE CHOICE QUESTIONS

Directions : *In each of the following questions, four out of five alternatives contain alphabet placed in a particular form. Find the one that does not belong to the group.*

1. (*a*) BXCW (*b*) OTPS
(*c*) GQHR (*d*) JNKM

2. (*a*) BVPS (*b*) OLMZ
(*c*) RPSR (*d*) XTCD

3. (*a*) RNJH (*b*) SOKG
(*c*) QMIE (*d*) MIEA

4. (*a*) QLJS (*b*) GVTI (*c*) KRPM (*d*) ONMP

5. (*a*) PEAR (*b*) TORE (*c*) REAP (*d*) TEAR

6. (*a*) ECA (*b*) JHF (*c*) OMK (*d*) UWY

7. (*a*) ACE (*b*) PRT (*c*) UWY (*d*) MNO

EXPLANATORY ANSWERS

1. (*c*) : In all other groups, first and third letters are consecutive and second and fourth letters are in reverse alphabetical order.

2. (*c*) : No letter is repeated in any other group.

3. (*a*) : In all other groups, there is a gap of three letters between two consecutive letters.

4. (*d*) : In all other groups, first and third letters are moved two steps forward to obtain fourth and second letters respectively.

5. (*b*) : All other groups contain E, A and R.

6. (*d*) : All other groups contain alternate letters from right to left.

7. (*d*) : All other groups contain alternate letters from left to right.

ODD ONE OUT—WORDS

In this type of classification, five words are given out of which four are almost same in matter or meaning and only one word is different from the common four. One has to find out the word which is different from the rest.

MULTIPLE CHOICE QUESTIONS

Directions : *In each of the following questions, four words are alike in some manner. Spot the odd one out.*

1. (*a*) Green (*b*) Red (*c*) Colour (*d*) Orange

2. (*a*) Stable (*b*) Hole (*c*) Canoe (*d*) Sty

3. (*a*) Nose (*b*) Eyes (*c*) Skin (*d*) Teeth

4. (*a*) Venus (*b*) Moon (*c*) Pluto (*d*) Mars

5. (*a*) Happy (*b*) Gloomy (*c*) Lively (*d*) Cheerful

6. (*a*) Cone (*b*) Circle (*c*) Triangle (*d*) Rectangle

7. (*a*) Lead (*b*) Mercury (*c*) Copper (*d*) Iron

8. (*a*) Kite (*b*) Bird (*c*) Radar (*d*) Jet

9. (*a*) Knee (*b*) Shoulder (*c*) Ankle (*d*) Palm

10. (*a*) Deluge (*b*) Calamity (*c*) Catastrophe (*d*) War

EXPLANATORY ANSWERS

1. (*c*) : All others are types of colour.

2. (*c*) : Canoe is a boat. Others are resting places of birds/animals.

3. (*d*) : All others are sense organs.

4. (*b*) : All others are planets.

5. (*b*) : All others are expressions of joy

6. (*a*) : All others are geometrical figures.

7. (*b*) : All others are solid metals.

8. (*c*) : All others are flying objects. Radar traces the objects in sky.

9. (*d*) : All others are joints in human body.

10. (*d*) : All others are nature-bound. Only war is man-made.

CHAPTER 3

Small & Capital Letters/ Numbers Coding-Decoding and Classification

TYPE - I

Coding is a secretive language which is used to change the representation of the actual term/word/value. This coded language can be framed by *(i)* moving the letters one or more steps forward or backward; *(ii)* substituting numbers for letters and vice–versa; *(iii)* writing the letters of the given word in reverse order in part or in whole; and *(iv)* replacing the letters in their natural series by the same positioned letters in their reverse series.

Alphabet in natural series are :

A B C D E F G H I J K L M N O P Q R S T U V W X Y Z

A ↓ 1st, E ↓ 5th, J ↓ 10th, O ↓ 15th, T ↓ 20th, Y ↓ 25th

Alphabet in reverse series are :

Z Y X W V U T S R Q P O N M L K J I H G F E D C B A

Z ↓ 1st, V ↓ 5th, Q ↓ 10th, L ↓ 15th, G ↓ 20th, B ↓ 25th

Note : On reaching Z, the series restarts from A and on reaching A, it restarts from Z.

MULTIPLE CHOICE QUESTIONS

Directions : *In the following questions select the right option which indicates the correct code for the word or letter given in the question.*

1. If CHAIR is coded as FKDLU, then RAID is coded as :

(*a*) ULGD (*b*) ULKG
(*c*) ULDG (*d*) UDLG

2. If CONDEMN is coded as CNODMEN, then TEACHER is coded as :

(*a*) TEACHER (*b*) TAEECHR
(*c*) TCAEEHR (*d*) TAECEHR

3. In a code language COME is written as XLNV and ABLE as ZYOV. How will MOLLY be written in that code?

(*a*) NLOBO (*b*) NLBOO
(*c*) LNOOB (*d*) NLOOB

4. In a certain code PROFESSION is written as EFORPNOISS. In the same code DICTIONARY will be written as :

(*a*) YRANOITCID (*b*) ITCIDYRANO
(*c*) ITCIDYRNAO (*d*) ITCDIYARNO

5. JUNE is coded as NXPF, how will STAY be coded in the same manner?

(*a*) WWCZ (*b*) WVCZ
(*c*) WWDB (*d*) VWZC

6. If in a certain code GENIUS is coded as IGPKWU, then IDIOT will be written in the same code as :

(*a*) JEJPU (*b*) KFKQV
(*c*) LGLRW (*d*) HCHNS

7. If ACTION is coded as ZXGRLM, then HEALTH will be coded in the same way as :

(*a*) SVZOGS (*b*) TVZOGT
(*c*) RUZPGR (*d*) QVGOZQ

8. If THOUSAND is coded as SGNTRZMC, then FUMING will be coded as :

(*a*) GVNJOH (*b*) ETHLMF
(*c*) EVLJMH (*d*) ETLHMF

9. If EARTHQUAKE is coded as MOGPENJOSM, then EQUATE will be coded as :

(*a*) MENOPM (*b*) MENOMP
(*c*) MJOGPM (*d*) MNJOPM

10. In a certain code language HJIZT code is deciphered as MONEY, in the same way NOVGZ will be deciphered as :

(*a*) STUMP (*b*) STALE
(*c*) STICK (*d*) SPIRE

EXPLANATORY ANSWERS

1. (*d*) : The word is coded by moving the letters three steps forward.

C H A I R F K D L U
+3, +3, +3, +3, +3

Similarly,

R A I D U D L G
+3, +3, +3, +3

2. (*d*) : In this word, the second and third letters interchange their places and the fifth and sixth letters do the same. Other letters retain their position.

C O N D E M N C N O D M E N

Similarly,

T E A C H E R T A E C E H R

3. (*d*) : The letters of the word are coded by their represented letters in the reverse series.

C O M E → letters in natural series
X L N V → letters in reverse series
↓ ↓ ↓ ↓
3rd 15th 13th 5th → position of letters

A B L E → letters in natural series
Z Y O V → letters in reverse series
↓ ↓ ↓ ↓
1st 2nd 12th 5th → position of letters

Similarly,

M O L L Y → letters in natural series
N L O O B → letters in reverse series
↓ ↓ ↓ ↓ ↓
13th 15th 12th 12th 25th → position of letters

4. (*b*) : The word is divided into two equal parts and the letters of each part are written backwards.

PROFE SSION EFORP NOISS

Similarly,

DICTI ONARY ITCID YRANO

5. (*a*) : The word is coded by moving the letters +4, +3, +2, and +1 steps respectively.

J U N E N X P F
+4, +3, +2, +1

Similarly,

S T A Y W W C Z
+4, +3, +2, +1

6. (*b*) : The word is coded by moving the letters two steps forward, *i.e.*,

G E N I U S I G P K W U
+2, +2, +2, +2, +2, +2

Similarly,

IDIOT → KFKQV

+2, +2, +2, +2, +2

7. (a) : The letters of the word are coded by their represented letters in the reverse series.

A C T I O N → letters in natural series

Z X G R L M → letters in reverse series

1st 3rd 20th 9th 15th 14th → position of letters

Similarly,

H E A L T H → letters in natural series

S V Z O G S → letters in reverse series

8th 5th 1st 12th 20th 8th → position of letters

8. (d) : The word is coded by moving the alphabet one step backwards, *i.e.,*

THOUSAND → SGNTRZMC

−1, −1, −1, −1, −1, −1, −1, −1

Similarly,

FUMING → ETLHMF

−1, −1, −1, −1, −1, −1

9. (d) : The alphabet in word EQUATE are taken from the given word EARTHQUAKE. Tally the letters from the coded word to get the answer code.

E A R T H Q U A K E → letters

M O G P E N J O S M → codes

E Q U A T E → letters to be coded

M N J O P M → answer codes

10. (b) : The coded alphabet are deciphered by moving five steps forward, *i.e.,*

HJIZT → MONEY

+5, +5, +5, +5, +5

Similarly,

NOVGZ → STALE

+5, +5, +5, +5, +5

TYPE - II

Column coding is a very complex form of coding. It needs a lot of attention and swift eye movement to decode the code for each letter of the given words. Proper words in capital letters are given in one column and the codes in small letters are given in another column. Based on the information given in both columns the candidate has to arrive at the correct answer option.

MULTIPLE CHOICE QUESTIONS

Directions: *The following questions are based on the column pattern. Understand the coding pattern and answer the questions.*

	Column I		Column II
(1)	FAMOUS	(a)	jcqhxp
(2)	SATIRE	(b)	hqdbyn
(3)	FRIGHT	(c)	ybcnke
(4)	TANGLE	(d)	zewhnd
(5)	ROVING	(e)	epbmyw
(6)	HUNTER	(f)	wdnbxk

1. What is the code used for the letter U?
(*a*) d (*b*) n
(*c*) b (*d*) x

2. What is the code used for the letter N?
(*a*) e (*b*) p
(*c*) m (*d*) w

3. What is the code used for the letter A?
(*a*) h (*b*) q
(*c*) b (*d*) n

4. What is the code used for the letter F?

(*a*) w (*b*) p
(*c*) d (*d*) c

5. What is the code used for the letter E?

(*a*) d (*b*) n
(*c*) b (*d*) k

Column I	Column II
(1) WRONG	(a) cklxd
(2) GRANT	(b) pdqkc
(3) STEAM	(c) qpuns
(4) CROWS	(d) lxnvk
(5) CEMET	(e) usqvs
(6) TERMS	(f) nukqs

EXPLANATORY ANSWERS

1. (*d*) : From statements (1) and (6), U = X.

2. (*d*) : From statements (5) and (6), RN = bw. From statement (4), N = w.

3. (*a*) : From statements (2) and (4), ATE = hdn. From statement (6), TE = dn. Therefore, A = h.

4. (*d*) : From statements (1) and (3), F = c.

5. (*a*) : From statements (2) and (4), ATE = hdn. From statement (6), TE = dn. From statement (3), T = n. Hence E = d.

TYPE - III

There is variety in ways of coding. Coding language is not only for words and numbers but also for hiding a group of words, statements or even sentences. This form of coding pattern may appear to be confusing but after solving only a few questions it is very easy to understand. Questions based on this coding pattern require no moving of steps or straining efforts of calculations, but only quick tallying or comparing ability. The codes can be letters or numbers.

MULTIPLE CHOICE QUESTIONS

Directions : *In the following questions study the coded patterns and then select the right option from the given alternatives.*

1. In a certain language, (a) 'go ju mi' stands for 'plenty of money'; (b) pao ju go nei vu' for 'money creates lots of problems'; (c) 'kol vu nei' for 'problems create tension'; and (d) 'sol tun ju haw' for 'still money is needed'. Which of the following words stand for 'money'?

(*a*) nei (*b*) ju
(*c*) haw (*d*) go

2. In a certain language, (a) 'FOR' stands for 'old is gold'; (b) 'ROT' stands for 'gold is pure'; (c) 'ROM' stands for 'gold is costly'. How will 'pure old gold is costly' be written?

(*a*) TFROM (*b*) FOTRM
(*c*) FTORM (*d*) TOMRF

3. In a certain code '415' means 'milk is hot'; '18' means 'hot soup'; and '895' means 'soup is tasty'. What number will indicate the word 'tasty'?

(*a*) 9 (*b*) 8
(*c*) 5 (*d*) 4

4. In a certain code '643' means 'she is beautiful', '593' means 'he is handsome', and '567' means 'handsome meets beautiful'. What number will indicate the word 'meets'?

(*a*) 5 (*b*) 3
(*c*) 7 (*d*) 6

5. In a certain code language, (a) 'dugo hui mul zo' stands for 'work is very hard'; (b) 'hui dugo ba ki' for 'Bingo is very smart'; (c) 'nano mul dugo' for 'cake is hard', and (d) 'mul ki qu' for 'smart and hard'. Which of the following words stand for 'Bingo'?

(*a*) jalu (*b*) dugo
(*c*) ki (*d*) ba

6. In a certain code language, (a) 'pic vic nic' stands for 'winter is cold'; (b) 'to nic re' for 'summer is hot'; (c) 're pic boo' for 'winter and summer' and (d) 'vic tho pa' for 'nights are cold'. Which of the following word is the code for 'summer'?

(*a*) nic (*b*) boo
(*c*) to (*d*) re

7. In a certain language, (a) 'mx das sci' means 'good little frock'; (b) 'jm coz sci' means 'girl behaves good'; (c) 'ngv drs coz' means 'girl makes mischief'; and (d) 'das gp coz' means 'little girl fell'. What is the code for 'frock' in this language?

(*a*) mx (*b*) das
(*c*) sci (*d*) gp

8. In a certain language 'mu mit es' means 'who is she' and 'elb mu es' means 'where is she'. What is the code for 'where' in this language?

(*a*) es (*b*) elb
(*c*) mu (*d*) mit

9. In a certain code language '069' means 'grapes are sweet', '476' means 'very sweet fruit' and '509' means 'grapes are ripe'. Which of the following digits means 'ripe' in that language?

(*a*) 0 (*b*) 5
(*c*) 9 (*d*) 7

10. In a certain code language 'roi ja kyo twa' means 'Moody is writing letters', 'pok ju ja twa' means 'Woody is writing cards', 'trn kyo pos un' means 'they are writing letters', and 'koi rus pok' means 'gifts and cards'. What is the code word for 'Moody'?

(*a*) ja (*b*) twa
(*c*) roi (*d*) kyo

EXPLANATORY ANSWERS

1. (*b*) :

Code	*Sentence*
1. go *ju* mi	plenty of *money*
2. pao *ju* go nei vu	*money* creates lots of problems
3. kol vu nei	problems create tension
4. sol tun *ju* haw	still *money* is needed

In 1st, 2nd and 4th codes and their sentences the word 'ju' is repeated and so is 'money'.

2. (*a*) :

Code	*Sentence*
1. FOR	old is gold
2. ROT	gold is pure
3. ROM	gold is costly

Therefore,

F stands for old
O stands for is
R stands for gold
T stands for pure
M stands for costly

So, 'pure old gold is costly' will be written as 'TFROM'.

3. (*a*) :

Code	*Sentence*
1. 415	milk is hot
2. 18	hot soup
3. 895	soup is *tasty*

From 3rd code and its sentence neither number '9' is repeated nor the word 'tasty'.

4. (*c*) :

Code	*Sentence*
1. 643	she is beautiful
2. 593	he is handsome
3. 567	handsome *meets* beautiful

From 3rd code and its sentence, neither number '7' nor the word 'meets' is repeated.

5. (*d*) :

Code	*Sentence*
1. *dugo hui* mul zo	work *is very* hard
2. *hui dugo* **ba** *ki*	**Bingo** *is very smart*
3. nano mul *dugo*	cake is *hard*
4. mul *ki* qu	*smart* and hard

From 2nd code and its sentence, neither 'ba' nor 'Bingo' is repeated.

(Words repeated are in italics)

6. (*d*) :

Code	*Sentence*
1. pic vic nic	winter is cold
2. to nic *re*	*summer* is hot
3. *re* pic boo	winter and *summer*
4. vic tho pa	nights are cold

The word 'summer' is common in 2nd and 3rd sentences and so is the code 're'.

7. (*a*) :

Code	*Sentence*
1. **mx** *das sci*	*good little* **frock**
2. jm coz *sci*	girl behaves *good*
3. ngv drs coz	girl makes mischief
4. *das* gp coz	*little* girl fell

Word 'frock' is only in the 1st sentence. The code word 'das' is repeated in 4th sentence and 'sci' in 2nd sentence. So, 'mx' is the code for 'frock'.

8. (*b*) :

Code	*Sentence*
1. *mu* mit *es*	who *is she*
2. **elb** *mu* es	**where** *is she*

The code words 'mu' and 'es' are repeated in Ist sentence. The only code left is 'elb' which means 'where'.

9. (*b*) :

Code	*Sentence*
1. *069*	*grapes are* sweet
2. 476	very sweet fruit
3. **5**09	*grapes are* **ripe**

The code numbers '0' and '9' are repeated in 1st and 3rd sentences. The only code remaining is '5' which stands for 'ripe'.

10. (*c*) :

Code	*Sentence*
1. **roi** *ja kyo twa*	**Moody** *is writing letters*
2. pok ju *ja twa*	Woody *is writing* cards
3. trn *kyo* pos un	they are writing *letters*
4. koi rus pok	gifts and cards

'Moody' is in 1st sentence only. The code words 'ja' and 'twa' are repeated in 2nd sentence and 'kyo' in 3rd sentence. Only code word 'roi' remains which stands for 'Moody'.

CHAPTER 4

Semantic Series

MULTIPLE CHOICE QUESTIONS

1. ADG, XVT, BEH, WUS, ?
(*a*) VTR (*b*) CFI
(*c*) DFJ (*d*) STU

2. GMSY, IOUA, KQWC, ?
(*a*) MSYE (*b*) NSYE
(*c*) MTYE (*d*) MSYF

3. ADG, GJM, ?, SVY
(*a*) MPS (*b*) MQR
(*c*) MQS (*d*) SPM

4. KNQ, TWZ, CFI, ?
(*a*) KOR (*b*) LOR
(*c*) MNQ (*d*) JLM

5. AEI, BFJ, CGK, ?
(*a*) DLH (*b*) EGF
(*c*) EFL (*d*) DHL

6. CFI, IKM, OPQ, ?
(*a*) UUU (*b*) UST
(*c*) VUS (*d*) TUV

7. LAZ, NEX, PIV, ?
(*a*) SLS (*b*) QNS
(*c*) RMT (*d*) RMS

8. DED, EFE, FGF, ?
(*a*) HGH (*b*) GHG
(*c*) EFE (*d*) FHF

9. XYZ, UVW, ?, OPQ
(*a*) RST (*b*) STU
(*c*) QRS (*d*) TUV

10. VCL, UEI, TGF, ?
(*a*) SJC (*b*) THI
(*c*) SIC (*d*) RHD

11. ABC, EFG, HIJ, ?
(*a*) IJK (*b*) KLM
(*c*) LMN (*d*) JKL

12. PQR, HIJ, DEF, ?
(*a*) DEF (*b*) CDE
(*c*) ABC (*d*) BCD

EXPLANATORY ANSWERS

1. (*b*) : There are two alternate series.

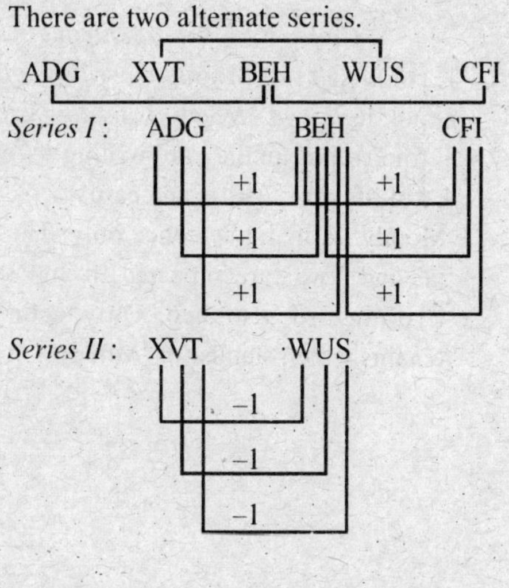

2. (*a*) : The series is formed by moving each letter two steps forward from one group to the next.

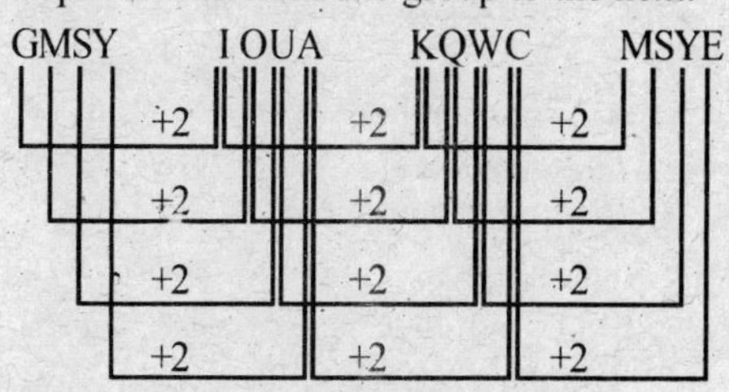

(The series restarts from A on reaching Z)

3. (*a*) : In each group of three letters the alphabet is in the succession of +3. The next group begins with the last alphabet of the previous group.

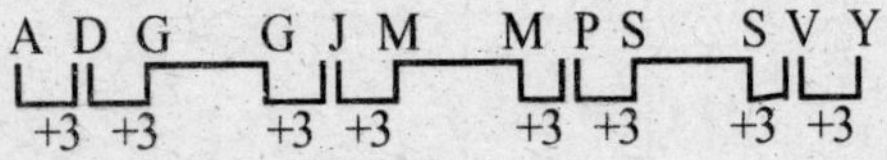

4. (b): All the alphabet in this group series is in succession of +3. The alphabetical series repeat from 'A' on reaching 'Z'.

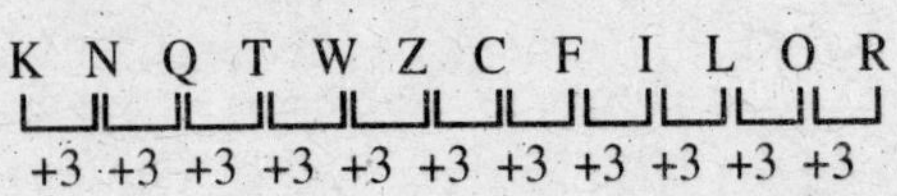

5. (d): Each of the three alphabet in one group corresponds to the alphabet in the next group in the succession of +1, *i.e.*,

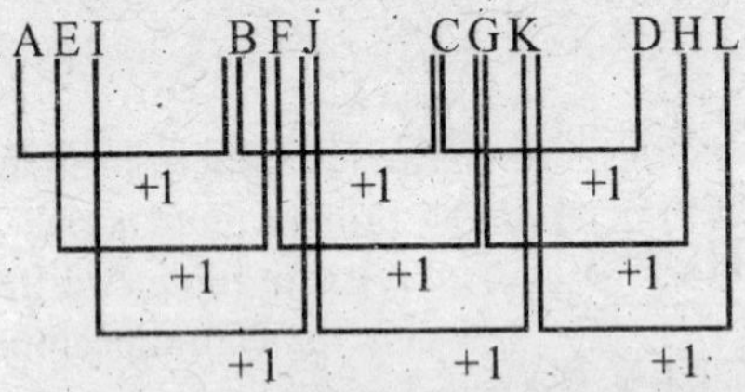

6. (a): The three alphabet in one group correspond to the alphabet in the next group in the manner +6, +5, +4 respectively, *i.e.*,

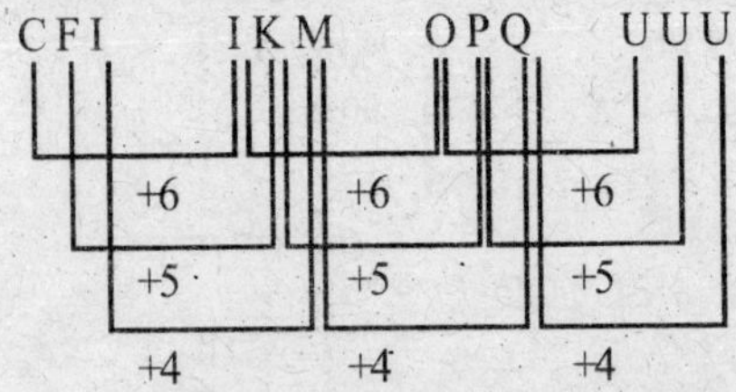

7. (c): The three alphabet in one group correspond to the alphabet in the next group in the manner +2, +4, –2 respectively, *i.e.*,

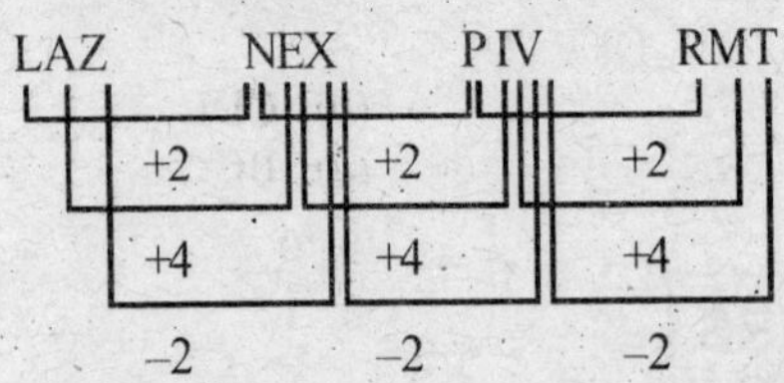

8. (b): The alphabet from one group to the next are in succession of +1, *i.e.*,

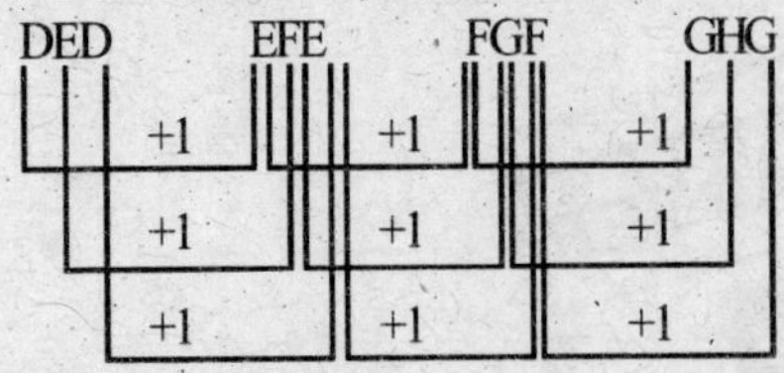

9. (a): The alphabet from one group to the next are in recession of –3, *i.e.*,

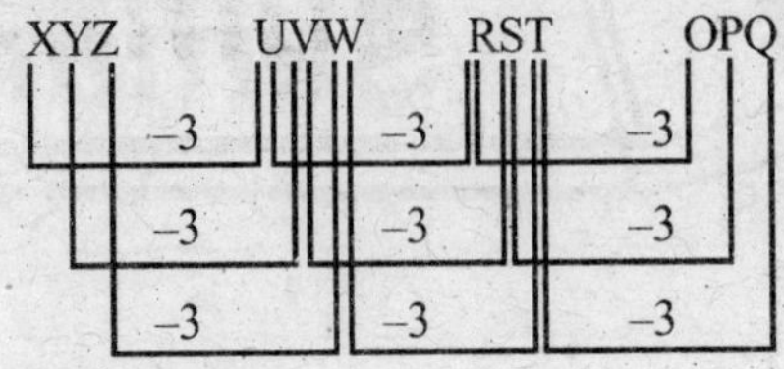

10. (c): The alphabet in one group correspond to the alphabet in the next group in the manner –1, +2, –3 respectively, *i.e.*,

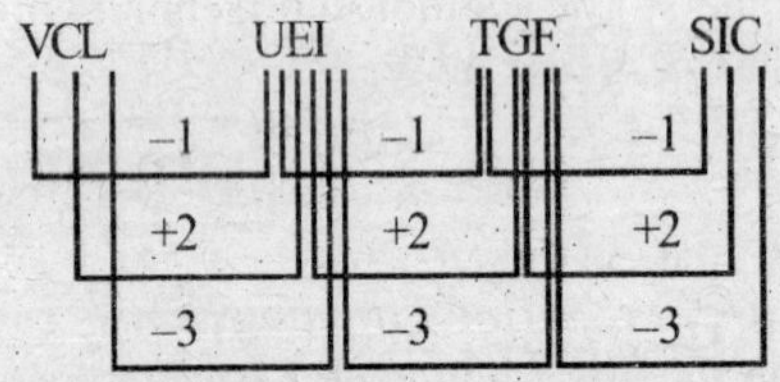

11. (d): The difference between the last letter of the preceding group of alphabet and the first letter of the next group is decreasing by 1, *i.e.*,

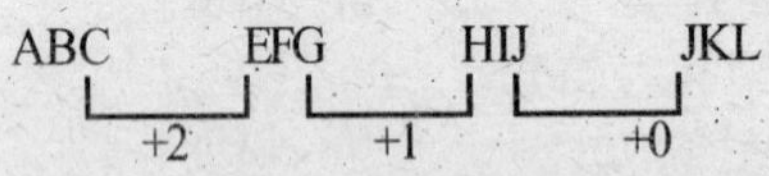

Otherwise the three letters in each group are in their natural order.

12. (d): The letters in each group of alphabet are in the recession of –8, –4, –2 respectively.

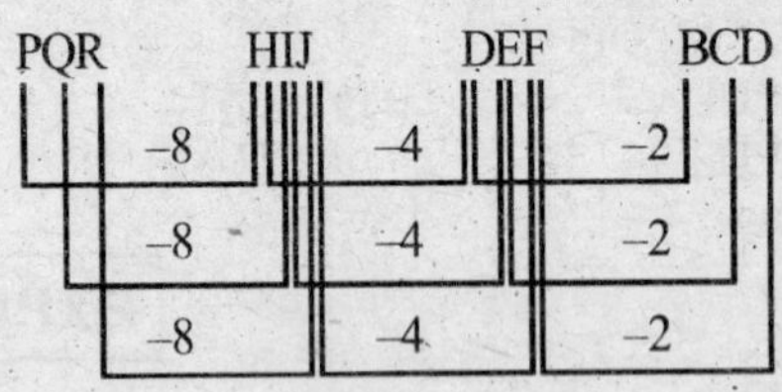

CHAPTER 5

Number Series

In this type of series, the set of given numbers in a series are related to one another in a particular pattern or manner. The relationship between the numbers may be (i) consecutive odd/even numbers; (ii) consecutive prime numbers; (iii) squares/cubes of some numbers with/without variation of addition or subtraction of some number; (iv) sum/product/difference of preceding numbers; (v) addition/subtraction/multiplication/division by some number; and (vi) many more combinations of the relationships given above.

MULTIPLE CHOICE QUESTIONS

Directions: *In the following questions, select the number(s) from the given options for completing the given series.*

1. 3, 9, 27, 81, 243, ?
(*a*) 486 (*b*) 729
(*c*) 972 (*d*) 359

2. 1, 6, 12, 19, 27, ?
(*a*) 38 (*b*) 35
(*c*) 36 (*d*) 54

3. 2, 6, 14, 30, 62, ?
(*a*) 126 (*b*) 128
(*c*) 120 (*d*) 130

4. 8, 48, 16, 96, 32, ?
(*a*) 192 (*b*) 150
(*c*) 64 (*d*) 288

5. 2, 8, 14, 24, 34, 48, ?
(*a*) 66 (*b*) 62
(*c*) 58 (*d*) 64

6. 4, 9, 19, 34, 54, ?, 109
(*a*) 89 (*b*) 84
(*c*) 74 (*d*) 79

7. 3, 15, 35, 63, 99, ?
(*a*) 144 (*b*) 143
(*c*) 121 (*d*) 169

8. 2, 3, 6, 18, 108, ?
(*a*) 1944 (*b*) 1658
(*c*) 648 (*d*) 1008

9. 1, 2, 3, 2, 3, 5, 4, 5, ?
(*a*) 9 (*b*) 6
(*c*) 10 (*d*) 7

10. 7776, 1296, 216, 36, 6, ?
(*a*) 6 (*b*) 0
(*c*) 3 (*d*) 1

11. 1, 8, 27, 64, 125, ?
(*a*) 172 (*b*) 176
(*c*) 216 (*d*) 189

12. 2, 3, 5, 7, 11, 13, ?
(*a*) 19 (*b*) 57
(*c*) 31 (*d*) 17

13. 80, 64, 48, 32, 16, ?
(*a*) 4 (*b*) 0
(*c*) 8 (*d*) 1

14. 3, 8, 13, 24, 41, ?
(*a*) 65 (*b*) 75
(*c*) 70 (*d*) 80

15. 9, 81, 90, 810, 819, ?
(*a*) 7371 (*b*) 900
(*c*) 8100 (*d*) 1638

16. 0, 8, 24, 48, 80, ?
(*a*) 110 (*b*) 96
(*c*) 120 (*d*) 140

17. 2, 4, 8, 3, 9, 27, 4, 16, ?
(*a*) 64 (*b*) 32
(*c*) 48 (*d*) 24

EXPLANATORY ANSWERS

1. (*b*) : The numbers in the series are multiplied by 3 to get the next numbers.

2. (*c*) : The difference between the numbers in the series increases by 1, after beginning from 5, *i.e.*,

1 6 12 19 27 36
+5 +6 +7 +8 +9

3. (*a*) : The difference between the numbers in the series doubles each time, after beginning from 4, *i.e.*,

2 6 14 30 62 126
+4 +8 +16 +32 +64

4. (*a*) : *Explanation I* : The sequence in the series is × 6, ÷ 3 which is repeated.

8 48 16 96 32 192
×6 ÷3 ×6 ÷3 ×6

Explanation II : There are two alternate series and the numbers are multiplied by 2.

×2 ×2
8 48 16 96 32 192
×2 ×2

Series I : 8, 16, 32

Series II : 48, 96, 192

5. (*b*) : The sequence in the series is :

2 8 14 24 34 48 62
+6 +6 +10 +10 +14 +14

The difference increases by 4 at alternate step.

6. (*d*) : The difference between the numbers increases by 5, after beginning from 5, *i.e.*,

4 9 19 34 54 79 109
+5 +10 +15 +20 +25 +30

7. (*b*) : The series follows the sequence of the squares of even numbers beginning from 2, minus 1.

8. (*a*) : Every third number in the series is the product of previous two numbers.

2 3 6 18 108 1944
2 × 3
3 × 6
6 × 18
18 × 108

9. (*a*) : In this series three numbers form a set. The first two numbers of each set are in natural order and the third number is the sum of first and second numbers. The first number of the next set begins with double the first number of the previous set.

× 2 × 2
1 2 3 2 3 5 4 5 9
1 + 2 2 + 3 4 + 5

10. (*d*) : The numbers in this sequence are divided by 6 each time.

11. (*c*) : The sequence in the series is cube of numbers in their natural order.

12. (*d*) : The series consists of prime numbers in increasing order.

13. (*b*) : The numbers in the series are decreasing with the difference of 16 at each step.

14. (*c*) : The sequence in the series is (number + next number) + addition of natural number increasing by 1 at each step, after beginning from 2.

3 8 13 24 41 70
(3+8) + 2
(8 + 13) + 3
(13 + 24) + 4
(24 + 41) + 5

15. (*a*) : The sequence in the series is × 9, + 9 which is repeated.

16. (*c*) : The sequence of the series consists of the product of 2 even numbers in natural order, *i.e.*,

0	8	24	48	80	120
↓	↓	↓	↓	↓	↓
(0 × 2)	(2 × 4)	(4 × 6)	(6 × 8)	(8 × 10)	(10 × 12)

17. (*a*) : In this series 3 numbers form a set. The first number is in natural order. The second number is the square of above number. The third number is the cube of first number.

CHAPTER 6

Arithmatical Reasoning

MULTIPLE CHOICE QUESTIONS

Directions (1–5) : *The following questions are based on the information given below :*

Data of 450 candidates, who took part in an examination in Social Science, Mathematics and Science is given below:

Passed in all the subject	167
Failed in all the subject	60
Failed in Mathematics	199
Failed in Social Science	175
Failed in Science	191
Passed in Science only	52
Passed in Mathematics only	48
Passed in Social Science only	62

1. How many passed in at least one subject?
(*a*) 450 (*b*) 390
(*c*) 304 (*d*) 167

2. How many failed in two subjects only?
(*a*) 56 (*b*) 61
(*c*) 152 (*d*) 162

3. How many passed in Mathematics and at least in one more subject?
(*a*) 210 (*b*) 203
(*c*) 170 (*d*) 94

4. How many failed in Social Science only?
(*a*) 15 (*b*) 21
(*c*) 30 (*d*) 42

5. How many failed in one subject only?
(*a*) 152 (*b*) 144
(*c*) 61 (*d*) 56

6. A, B, C, D and E play a game of cards. A says to B, "If you give me three cards, you will have as many as E has and if I give you three cards, you will have as many as D has." A and B together have 10 cards more than what D and E together have. If B has two cards more than what C has and the total number of cards be 133, how many cards does B have?
(*a*) 22 (*b*) 35
(*c*) 25 (*d*) 23

7. A bus starts from city X. The number of women in the bus is half of the number of men. In the city Y, 10 men left the bus and five women entered. Now, number of men and women is equal. In the beginning, how many passenger entered the bus?
(*a*) 15 (*b*) 30
(*c*) 36 (*d*) 45

8. I have a few sweets to be distributed. If I keep 2, 3 or 4 in a pack, I am left with one sweet. If I keep 5 in a pack, I am left with none. What is the minimum number of sweets I can have to pack and distributed?
(*a*) 25 (*b*) 37
(*c*) 54 (*d*) 65

9. A, B, C, D and E play a game of cards. A says to B, "If you give me 3 cards, you will have as many as I have at this moment while if D takes 5 cards from you, he will have as many as E has", A and C together have twice as many cards as E has B and D together also have the same number of cards as A and C taken together. I all together they have 150 cards, how many cards has C got.
(*a*) 28 (*b*) 29
(*c*) 31 (*d*) 35

10. At the end of a business conference, ten people present shake hands with each other once. How many handshakes will be there all together?
(*a*) 20 (*b*) 45
(*c*) 90 (*d*) 55

EXPLANATORY ANSWERS

1. (*b*) : Candidates passed at least in one subject = (Candidates passed in only one subjects) + (Candidates passed in only two subjects) + (Candidates passed in only all subjects). (Candidates failed in only two subjects) + (Candidates failed in only one subject) + (Candidates passed in all the subject)
= 162 + 61 + 167
= 390.

2. (*d*) : Candidates failed in two subjects only
= Candidates passed in one subjects only
= 62 + 48 + 52
= 162.

3. (*b*) : Candidates failed in science only
=191 – (62 + 60 + 48)
= 21
Candidates failed in one social science only = 15
Therefore, candidates passed in maths and at least one more subject
= (21 + 15 + 167)
= 203

4. (*a*) : Candidates failed in social science only = (candidates failed in social science) – (candidates failed in all subjects + candidates passed in science only + candidates passed in maths only)
= 175 – (60 + 52 + 48)
= 175 – 160
= 15.

5. (*c*) : Candidates failed in one subject only
= (total number of candidates) – (candidates passed in all subjects + candidates failed in all the subjects + candidates passed in one subject only)
= 450 – (167 + 60 + 62 + 48 + 52)
= 450 – 389
= 61.

6. (*c*) : From the questions, we have
B – 3 = E ...... (i)
B + 3 = D ...... (ii)
A + B = D + E + 10 ...... (iii)
B = C + 2 ...... (iv)
A + B + C + D + E = 133 ...... (v)
From (i) and (ii)
B – E = D – B ⇒ E + D = 2 B ...... (vi)
From (iii) and (vi)
A + B = 2B + 10 ⇒ B = A – 10
or, A = B + 10 ...... (vii)
From (v), (vi), (iv) and (vii) we have
(B + 10) + (B) + (B – 2) + 2B = 133
5B = 133 – 8 = 125
= 25.

7. (*d*) : In the city X let the number of men be x
Then the number of women be $\frac{x}{2}$.
In the city y, $x-10=\frac{x}{2}+5$
or, $\frac{x}{2}=15$ or, $x-30$ and $y=15$.
Therefore, total number of passenger at the beginning were 30 + 15 = 45.

8. (*a*) : The required number will be obtained by taking LCM of 2, 3 and 4 and adding 1 into it. The number so obtained is 25.

9. (*a*) : From the questions it is clear that
B – 3 = A ...... (1)
D + 5 = E ...... (2)
A + C = 2 E ...... (3)
A + C = B + D ...... (4)
A + B + C + D + E = 150 ...... (5)
From (3), (4) and (5) we get
5E = 150 ∴ E = 30
Now from (2) D = 30 – 5 = 25
and from (4) A = 32
Now from (3) 32 + C = 2 × 30
C = 60 – 32 = 28.

10. (*b*) : Total number of handshakes = (9 + 8 + 7 + 6 + 5 + 4 + 3 + 2 + 1) = 45

CHAPTER 7

Problem Solving

Number problems consists of number sequences, problems with algebraic expressions, mathematical calculations and other compatiable problems.

MULTIPLE CHOICE QUESTIONS

1. How many 6's are there in the following series of numbers which are preceded by 7 but not immediately followed by 9?

   6 7 9 5 6 9 7 6 8 7 6 7 8 6 9 4 6 7 7 6 9 5 7 6 3

   (*a*) One (*b*) Two
   (*c*) Three (*d*) Four

2. In a chess tournament each of six players will play every other player exactly once. How many matches will be played during the tournament?

   (*a*) 12 (*b*) 15
   (*c*) 30 (*d*) 36

3. How many 4's are there in the following series which are preceded by 7, but are not preceded by 8?

   3 4 5 7 4 3 7 4 8 5 4 3 7 4 9 8 4 7 2 7 4 1 3 6

   (*a*) 1 (*b*) 2
   (*c*) 3 (*d*) 4

4. How many even numbers are there in the following series of numbers, each of which is immediately preceded by an odd number, but not immediately followed by an even number?

   5 3 4 8 9 7 1 6 5 3 2 9 8 4 3 5

   (*a*) Nil (*b*) 1
   (*c*) 2 (*d*) 3

5. If all the numbers from 1 to 51 which are exactly divisible by 3 are arranged in descending order, which of the following numbers will come at the seventh and tenth places from the top?

   (*a*) 33 & 27 (*b*) 33 & 21
   (*c*) 21 & 30 (*d*) 33 & 24

6. Nitin was counting down from 32. Shasank was counting upwards, the numbers starting from 1 and he was calling out only the odd numbers. Which common number will they call out at the same time if they were calling out at the same speed?

   (*a*) 21
   (*b*) 22
   (*c*) 19
   (*d*) They will not call out the same number

7. In the following list of numerals, how many 3s are followed by 3, but NOT preceded by 3?

   2 4 6 3 3 1 5 7 8 3 3 3 4 6 2 3 3 3 3 9 7 2 3

   (*a*) 1 (*b*) 2
   (*c*) 3 (*d*) 4

8. If in a given number 5 8 9 4 3 2 7 6 1 4, we interchange the first and the second digits, the third and the fourth, the fifth and the sixth and so on, then counting from the right end, which digit will be sixth?

   (*a*) 3 (*b*) 2
   (*c*) 4 (*d*) 5

9. Aparna cuts a cake into two halves and cuts one-half into smaller pieces of equal size. Each of the small pieces is twenty grams in weight. If she has seven pieces of the cake in all with her, how heavy was the original cake?

   (*a*) 140 grams (*b*) 280 grams
   (*c*) 240 grams (*d*) 120 grams

10. In the following number sequence how many such even numbers are there which are exactly divisible by its immediate preceding number but not exactly divisible by its immediate following number?

    3 8 4 1 5 7 2 8 3 4 8 9 3 9 4 2 1 5 8 2

    (*a*) Two (*b*) Three
    (*c*) Four (*d*) More than four

11. How many 7s are there in the following series which are not immediately followed by 3 but immediately preceded by 8?

8 9 8 7 6 2 2 6 3 2 6 9 7 3 2 8 7 2 7 7 8 7 3 7 7 9 4

(*a*) Nil (*b*) One
(*c*) Two (*d*) Three

12. How many 9's are there in the following sequence which are neither preceded by 6 nor immediately followed by 3?

9 3 8 6 9 9 5 9 3 7 8 9 9 9 3 9 6 3 9

(*a*) One (*b*) Two
(*c*) Three (*d*) Four

13. If a number is five times as great as another number which is four less than forty, then the number is :

(*a*) 220 (*b*) 180
(*c*) 144 (*d*) 200

14. If 2/3rd of a number is 96, what will be the 3/4th of that number?

(*a*) 108 (*b*) 198
(*c*) 128 (*d*) 48

15. If such numbers which are divisible by 5, and also those which have 5 as one of the digits are eliminated from the numbers 1 to 60, how many numbers would remain?

(*a*) 53 (*b*) 47
(*c*) 40 (*d*) 45

EXPLANATORY ANSWERS

1. (*c*) : 6795697$\underset{1}{\underline{768}}$$\underset{2}{\underline{767}}8694677695\underset{3}{\underline{763}}$

2. (*b*) : When all the players have to play with each other then the method of calculating the number of matches to be played is $\frac{n(n-1)}{2}$ where '*n*' is the number of players playing the match. So, the number of matches played will be :
$(6 \times 5) \div 2 = 30 \div 2 = 15$

3. (*d*) : 3457$\underset{1}{\underline{743}}$$\underset{2}{\underline{748}}543\underset{3}{\underline{749}}8472\underset{4}{\underline{741}}$36

4. (*c*) : 5348971$\underset{1}{\underline{653}}$$\underset{2}{\underline{298}}$435

5. (*d*) : The numbers divisible by 3 in descending order are:
51, 48, 45, 42, 39, 36, $\underset{7th}{\underline{33,}}$ 30, 27, $\underset{10th}{\underline{24,}}$ 21, 18, 15, 12, 9, 6, 3.

6. (*d*) : When Nitin is on count 22, Shasank is on 21 and when Nitin is on count 21, Shasank is on 23.

7. (*c*) : 246331578333462333397 23
1 2 3

8. (*b*) : The new number after interchanging the digits is :
8549236741
↑ (6th)

9. (*c*) : There is one bigger piece and six smaller pieces. One small piece weighs 20 gm. Total weight of six smaller speices is 120 gm.
∴ Weight of the bigger piece = 120 gm
∴ Weight of the original cake = 240 gm

10. (*a*) : 3841 5$\underset{1}{\underline{728}}3\underset{2}{\underline{48}}$939421582

11. (*c*) : 89$\underset{1}{\underline{87}}6226326973\underset{2}{\underline{287}}$2778737794

12. (*d*) : 93869959378999396 39 — 1 2 3 4

13. (*b*) : Number four less than forty is $40 - 4 = 36$
Five times the number is $= 36 \times 5 = 180$

14. (*a*) : If the number is *x*, then

$$\frac{2}{3}x = 96$$

$$x = \frac{96 \times 3}{2} = 144$$

$\frac{3}{4}$ th of the number is $144 \times \frac{3}{4} = 108$

15. (*c*) : The eliminated twenty numbers are : 5, 10, 15, 20, 25, 30, 35, 40, 45 and 50 to 60. The remaining numbers are $60 - 20 = 40$.

CHAPTER 8

Numerical Operations/ Symbol Substitution

Questions in this category are easy to attempt. Candidates must be quick in substituting symbols and calculations. The common pattern of questions asked are given below.

SOLVED EXAMPLES

1. If '+' stands for '×'; '×' stands for '÷'; '÷' stands for '–' and '–' stands for '+' then
$2 - 8 \times 2 + 6 \div 7 = ?$
(*a*) 32 (*b*) 19 (*c*) 23 (*d*) 9
Ans. (*b*) : After substituting the symbols in the given expression the new expression will be :
$2 + 8 \div 2 \times 6 - 7$
The solving steps will be :
$2 + 4 \times 6 - 7$
$2 + 24 - 7$
$26 - 7 = 19$

2. If ▲ stands for '+'
■ stands for '–'
● stands for '÷'
∗ stands for '×' then
13 ▲ 5 ∗ 20 ● 10 ■ 9 = ?
(*a*) 26 (*b*) 37 (*c*) 14 (*d*) 55
Ans. (*c*) : After substituting the symbols the new expression will be :
$13 + 5 \times 20 \div 10 - 9$
The solving steps will be :
$13 + 5 \times 2 - 9$
$13 + 10 - 9$
$23 - 9 = 14$

MULTIPLE CHOICE QUESTIONS

Directions : *Each of the following questions is followed by four alternatives. Select the most appropriate answer.*

1. If "+" means "–"; "–" means "×"; "×"means "÷" and "÷" means "+", then
$15 \times 5 \div 10 + 5 - 3 = ?$
(*a*) 9.5 (*b*) 0
(*c*) – 2 (*d*) 24

2. If "+" means "–"; "–" means "×"; "×"means "÷" and "÷" means "+", then
$15 \times 3 \div 15 + 5 - 2 = ?$
(*a*) 0 (*b*) 10
(*c*) 20 (*d*) 6

3. If "+" means "÷"; "×" means "–"; "÷"means "+" and "–" means "×", then
$16 \div 8 \times 6 - 2 + 12 = ?$
(*a*) 22 (*b*) 24
(*c*) 23 (*d*) 20

4. If "+" means "×"; "–" means "÷"; "÷"means "+" and "×" means "–", then what will be the value of $20 \div 40 - 4 \times 5 + 6 = ?$
(*a*) 60 (*b*) 1.67
(*c*) 150 (*d*) 0

5. If "+" means "×"; "–" means "÷"; "×"means "–" and "÷" means "+", then
$5 + 8 - 4 \times 2 \div 9 = ?$
(*a*) 15 (*b*) 13
(*c*) 17 (*d*) 11

6. If × stands for addition, ÷ stands for subtraction, + stands for multiplication and – stands for division, then $(20 \times 6 \div 6 \times 4)$ is equal to
(*a*) 5 (*b*) 24
(*c*) 25 (*d*) 80

7. If "+" means "×"; "÷" means "–"; "×"means "÷" and "–" means "+", what will be the value of the following expression?
$4 + 11 \div 5 - 50 = ?$
(*a*) 79 (*b*) –11
(*c*) 91 (*d*) 89

8. If "+" means "÷"; "÷" means "–"; "–"means "×" and "×" means "+", then
$10 \div 2 - 15 + 3 \times 5 = ?$
(*a*) 10 (*b*) 15
(*c*) 25 (*d*) 5

9. If A stands for add, B for subtract, C for multiply and D for divide, then for what does 4A 3B 3A 2 stand?
(*a*) 2 (*b*) 4
(*c*) 6 (*d*) 8

10. If × stands for add, *y* stands for subract, *z* stands for divide and *p* stands for multiply, then what is the the value of $(7\ p\ 3)\ y\ 6 \times 5$?
(*a*) 5 (*b*) 10
(*c*) 15 (*d*) 20

11. If "+" means "÷"; "÷" means "–"; "–"means "×" and "×" means "+", what will be the value of $8 + 2 \div 3 - 4 \times 6 = ?$
(*a*) –2 (*b*) $-15\frac{1}{3}$
(*c*) 12 (*d*) 15

12. If "+" means "÷"; "×" means "–"; "÷"means "×" and "–" means "+", what will be the value of the following expression?
$9 + 3 \div 4 - 8 \times 2 = ?$
(*a*) $6\frac{3}{4}$ (*b*) $-1\frac{3}{4}$
(*c*) $-6\frac{1}{4}$ (*d*) 18

13. If "–" means "÷"; "+" means "×"; "÷"means "–" and "×" means "+", then which of the following must be true?
(*a*) $1 \div 2 + 3 \times 6 - 8 = 12$
(*b*) $2 + 3 - 5 \times 8 \div 4 = 7$
(*c*) $5 + 6 \times 8 - 2 \div 3 = 31$
(*d*) $6 \div 1 + 2 - 8 \times 4 = 31$

14. If "÷" means "+"; "+" means "×"; "–"means "÷" and "×" means "–", then
$5 + 8 - 4 \times 2 \div 9 = ?$
(*a*) 13 (*b*) 15
(*c*) 11 (*d*) 17

EXPLANATORY ANSWERS

1. (*c*) : $15 \div 5 + 10 - 5 \times 3$
$3 + 10 - 15 = -2$

2. (*b*) : $15 \div 3 + 15 - 5 \times 2$
$5 + 15 - 10 = 10$

3. (*c*) : $16 + 8 - 6 \times 2 \div 12$
$16 + 8 - 1 = 23$

4. (*d*) : $20 + 40 \div 4 - 5 \times 6$
$20 + 10 - 30 = 0$

5. (*c*) : $5 \times 8 \div 4 - 2 + 9$
$10 - 2 + 9 = 17$

6. (*b*) : $20 + 6 - 6 + 4 = 24$

7. (*d*) : $4 \times 11 - 5 + 50$
$44 - 5 + 50 = 89$

8. (*d*) : $10 - 2 \times 15 \div 3 + 5$
$10 - 10 + 5 = 5$

9. (*c*) : $4 + 3 - 3 + 2 = 6$

10. (*d*) : $(7 \times 3) - 6 + 5$
$21 - 6 + 5 = 20$

11. (*a*) : $8 \div 2 - 3 \times 4 + 6$
$4 - 12 + 6 = -2$

12. (*d*) : $9 \div 3 \times 4 + 8 - 2$
$12 + 8 - 2 = 18$

13. (*c*) : (*a*) $1 - 2 \times 3 + 6 \div 8 = 12 \Rightarrow \frac{-17}{4} = 12$
(*b*) $2 \times 3 \div 5 + 8 - 4 = 7 \Rightarrow \frac{26}{5} = 7$
(*c*) $5 \times 6 + 8 \div 2 - 3 = 31 \Rightarrow 31 = 31$
(*d*) $6 - 1 \times 2 \div 8 + 4 = 31 \Rightarrow \frac{-39}{4} = 31$

14. (*d*) : $5 \times 8 \div 4 - 2 + 9$
$10 - 2 + 9 = 17$

CHAPTER 9

Word Building

These are spellings, word order and dictionary related questions. The candidate is given a word and asked to select the word that can/cannot be formed from its spellings. He/she may be asked to decide the meaningful order of the given words. He/she may also be asked to arrange the given words in the sequence in which they occur in the dictionary.

MULTIPLE CHOICE QUESTIONS

Directions (Qs. No. 1 to 12): *From the given alternatives select the word which* ***cannot*** *be formed using the letters of the given word.*

1. REPUBLICAN
(*a*) CLIP (*b*) PURE
(*c*) ANKLE (*d*) BANE

2. ESTRANGE
(*a*) GENERATE (*b*) SERGEANT
(*c*) REAGENTS (*d*) GREAT

3. DETERMINATION
(*a*) DETENTION (*b*) DESTINATION
(*c*) TERMINATE (*d*) DOMINATE

4. CHRISTMAS
(*a*) CHRIST (*b*) SMART
(*c*) CRUST (*d*) HARM

5. LEGALIZATION
(*a*) ALERT (*b*) ALEGATION
(*c*) GALLANT (*d*) NATAL

6. CHARACTER
(*a*) CRATE (*b*) CHARTER
(*c*) HEARTY (*d*) TRACER

7. ADMINISTRATION
(*a*) Station (*b*) Minister
(*c*) Ration (*d*) Mind

8. ORGANISATION
(*a*) ORGAN (*b*) ORGANISE
(*c*) NATION (*d*) ORATION

9. PERAMBULATOR
(*a*) RAMPANT
(*b*) LABOUR
(*c*) MARBLE
(*d*) RAMBLE

10. POSSESSION
(*a*) SESSION
(*b*) POSE
(*c*) POISE
(*d*) OBSESS

11. PRINTINGS
(*a*) SAINT (*b*) PRINT
(*c*) STING (*d*) RINGS

12. QUALIFICATION
(*a*) LIAR (*b*) FIAT
(*c*) LION (*d*) FICTION

13. From the given alternatives select the word which can be formed using the letters given in the word.
ULTRANATIONALISM
(*a*) ULTRAMONTANE
(*b*) ULTRAMODERN
(*c*) ULTRAIST
(*d*) ULULATE

14. A meaningful word starting with R is made from the first, second, fourth, fifth and eighth letters of the word CREATIVE. Which of the following is the middle letter of the word?
(*a*) E (*b*) T
(*c*) C (*d*) A

Directions (Qs. No. 15 to 18): *Which one of the given responses would be a meaningful order of the following words?*

15. 1. Amoeba 2. Oyster
3. Worm 4. Cow
(*a*) 1, 3, 2, 4 (*b*) 1, 2, 3, 4
(*c*) 4, 3, 2, 1 (*d*) 3, 2, 4, 1

16. 1. Birth 2. Death
3. Childhood 4. Infancy
5. Adolescence 6. Adulthood
7. Old age
(*a*) 2, 6, 7, 5, 4, 3, 1 (*b*) 1, 4, 3, 5, 6, 7, 2
(*c*) 1, 4, 3, 6, 5, 7, 2 (*d*) 2, 7, 6, 4, 5, 3, 1

17. 1. Police 2. Punishment
3. Crime 4. Judge
4. Judgement
(*a*) 3, 1, 2, 4, 5
(*b*) 1, 2, 4, 3, 5
(*c*) 5, 4, 3, 2, 1
(*d*) 3, 1, 4, 5, 2

18. 1. Orange 2. Indigo
3. Red 4. Blue
5. Green 6. Yellow
7. Violet
(*a*) 7, 2, 4, 5, 6, 1, 3 (*b*) 7, 2, 4, 6, 5, 1, 3
(*c*) 7, 2, 6, 4, 5, 1, 3 (*d*) 7, 2, 6, 4, 1, 5, 3

Directions (Qs. Nos. 19 and 24): *Arrange the given words in the sequence in which they occur in the dictionary.*

19. 1. Clone 2. Climate
3. Clutter 4. Create
5. Clapped
(*a*) 52143 (*b*) 51234
(*c*) 52134 (*d*) 53124

20. 1. Lasted 2. Loop
3. Lake 4. Litter
5. Listed
(*a*) 31542 B. 31254
(*c*) 31245 (*d*) 31452

21. 1. Intricate 2. Interview
3. Intransigent 4. Interrogation
5. Intravenous
(*a*) 2, 4, 5, 3, 1 (*b*) 5, 3, 1, 2, 4
(*c*) 4, 2, 3, 5, 1 (*d*) 3, 5, 2, 1, 4

22. 1. Forge 2. Forget
3. Forgo 4. Forgive
5. Format
(*a*) 1, 2, 4, 3, 5
(*b*) 5, 2, 4, 3, 1
(*c*) 1, 4, 3, 2, 5
(*d*) 3, 4, 5, 2, 1

23. 1. Forecast 2. Forget
3. Foreign 4. Forsook
5. Force
(*a*) 3, 5, 1, 2, 4 (*b*) 5, 1, 3, 2, 4
(*c*) 5, 1, 3, 4, 2 (*d*) 5, 1, 2, 3, 4

24. 1. Fenestration 2. Feather
3. Feed head 4. Feature
5. Feminine
(*a*) 2, 4, 3, 5, 1 (*b*) 4, 2, 3, 1, 5
(*c*) 2, 4, 1, 5, 3 (*d*) 4, 2, 3, 5, 1

25. Arrange the given words in the sequence in which they occur in the Dictionary and locate the last word.
(*a*) Frankenstein (*b*) Frankincense
(*c*) Frankalmoign (*d*) Frauendienst

26. Grouping of words are given. Choose the next word in the series from the given options.
AFGHAN, INDEFINITELY, SYNOPSIS, STUPENDOUS, BURST
(*a*) GLACIAL (*b*) COMPANION
(*c*) RESCRIPT (*d*) HIJACKER

ANSWERS

1	2	3	4	5	6	7	8	9	10
(*c*)	(*a*)	(*b*)	(*c*)	(*a*)	(*c*)	(*b*)	(*b*)	(*a*)	(*d*)
11	**12**	**13**	**14**	**15**	**16**	**17**	**18**	**19**	**20**
(*a*)	(*a*)	(*c*)	(*d*)	(*a*)	(*b*)	(*d*)	(*a*)	(*c*)	(*d*)
21	**22**	**23**	**24**	**25**	**26**				
(*c*)	(*a*)	(*b*)	(*a*)	(*d*)	(*d*)				

CHAPTER 10

Relationship Concept

While attempting questions on blood relations, one should be clear of all the relation patterns that can exist between any two individuals. These type of questions are given mainly to test one's relationship ability.

Very well known relations are :

Mother	Grandmother
Father	Grandfather
Son	Grandson
Daughter	Granddaughter
Brother	Brother-in-law
Sister	Sister-in-law
Niece	Father-in-law
Nephew	Mother-in-law
Uncle	Son-in-law
Aunt	Daughter-in-law
Husband	Cousin
Wife	

The patterns of some relationships which help in solving questions in these tests are :

Father's *or* Mother's Father	—	Grandfather (Paternal *or* Maternal)
Father's *or* Mother's Mother	—	Grandmother (Paternal *or* Maternal
Father's *or* Mother's Son	—	Brother
Father's *or* Mother's Daughter	—	Sister
Father's Brother	—	Paternal Uncle
Father's Sister	—	Paternal Aunt
Mother's Brother	—	Maternal Uncle
Mother's Sister	—	Maternal Aunt
Uncle *or* Aunt's Son *or* Daughter	—	Cousin
Son's Wife	—	Daughter-in-law
Daughter's Husband	—	Son-in-law
Husband's *or* Wife's Brother	—	Brother-in-law
Husband's *or* Wife's Sister	—	Sister-in-law
Brother's Wife	—	Sister-in-law
Sister's Husband	—	Brother-in-law
Brother's Son	—	Nephew
Brother's Daughter	—	Niece

MULTIPLE CHOICE QUESTIONS

Directions : *In each of the following questions keenly study the relationship mentioned between the persons, and then from the given options select the right relationship as the answer.*

1. 'A' is the father of 'B' and 'C'. 'B' is the son of 'A' but 'C' is not the son of 'A'. What is 'C's' relation with 'A'?
(*a*) Daughter (*b*) Son
(*c*) Niece (*d*) Nephew

2. A lady said, "The person standing there is my grandfather's only son's daughter". How is the lady related to the standing person?
(*a*) Sister (*b*) Mother
(*c*) Aunt (*d*) Cousin

3. Ravi is the brother of Amit's son's son. What is Amit's relation to Ravi?
(*a*) Cousin (*b*) Father
(*c*) Grandfather (*d*) Son

4. Mayank said, "My mother is the sister of Rajat's brother." What is Rajat's relation with Mayank?
(*a*) Cousin
(*b*) Maternal uncle
(*c*) Uncle
(*d*) Brother-in-law

5. Introducing Lily, Raghav said, "Her father is my mother's only son". How is Lily related to Raghav?
(*a*) Aunt (*b*) Daughter
(*c*) Mother (*d*) Sister

6. Ajay is the brother of Vijay. Mili is the Sister of Ajay. Sanjay is the brother of Rahul and Mehul is the daughter of Vijay. Who is Sanjay's Uncle?
(*a*) Rahul
(*b*) Ajay
(*c*) Mehul
(*d*) Data inadequate

7. Adity is Bhavi's brother, Bharat is Jayant's father. Ella is Bhavi's mother. Aditya and Jayant are brothers. What is Ella's relationship with Bharat?
(*a*) Sister
(*b*) Mother
(*c*) Daughter
(*d*) Wife

8. A man introduced the boy coming with him as "He is son of the father of my wife's daughter". What relation did the boy bear to the man?
(*a*) Son-in-law
(*b*) Son
(*c*) Brother
(*d*) Father

9. A and B are two brothers. C is sister of B. D is sister of E. E is son of A. Who is D's uncle?
(*a*) D (*b*) E
(*c*) B (*d*) C

10. Varun said pointing towards Arun, "He is my sister's only brother's son". How is Arun related to Varun?
(*a*) Son (*b*) Brother
(*c*) Nephew (*d*) Data insufficient

11. Pointing to a man, a lady said, "His brother's father is my grandfather's only son." How is the lady related to the man?
(*a*) Mother
(*b*) Sister
(*c*) Daughter
(*d*) Aunt

12. Vidya is the wife of Gopi and Gopi is the brother of Akhil. Akhil is the uncle of Vijay. What is Vijay's relation with Vidya?
(*a*) Son
(*b*) Nephew
(*c*) Brother-in-law
(*d*) Brother

EXPLANATORY ANSWERS

1. (*a*) :

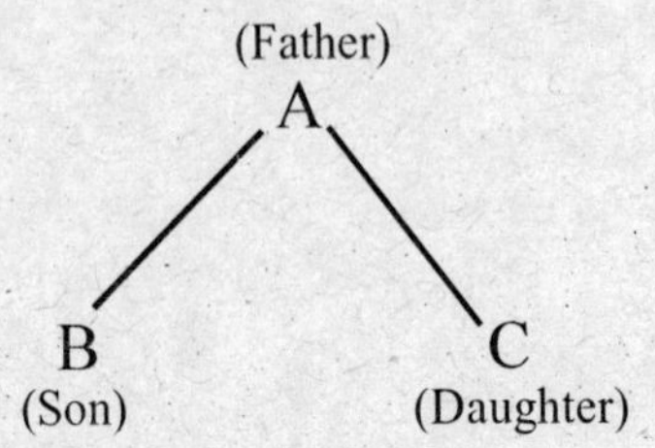

'C' is not the son of 'A', but 'A' is the father of 'C'. So, 'C' is the daughter of 'A'.

2. (*a*) :

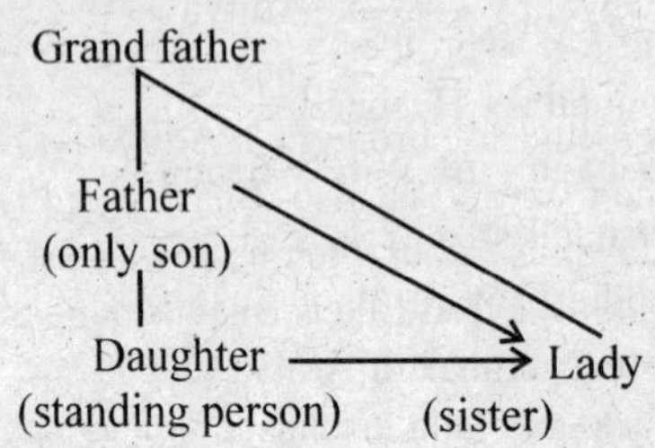

Lady's grandfather's son is lady's father and father's daughter will only be lady's sister.

3. (*c*) :

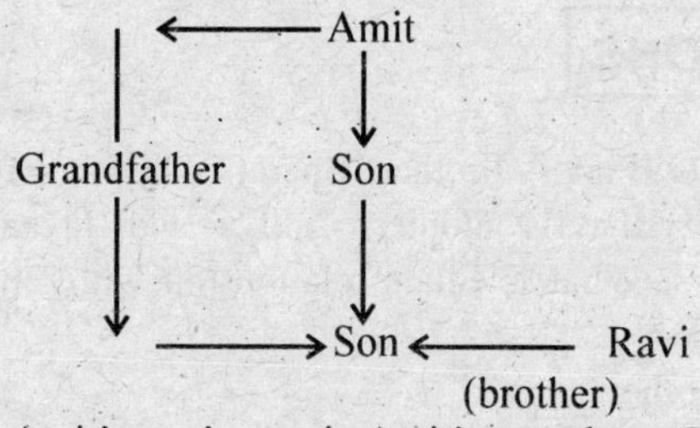

Amit's son's son is Amit's grandson. Ravi is the brother of Amit's son's son. So, Amit is also the grandfather of Ravi.

4. (*b*) :

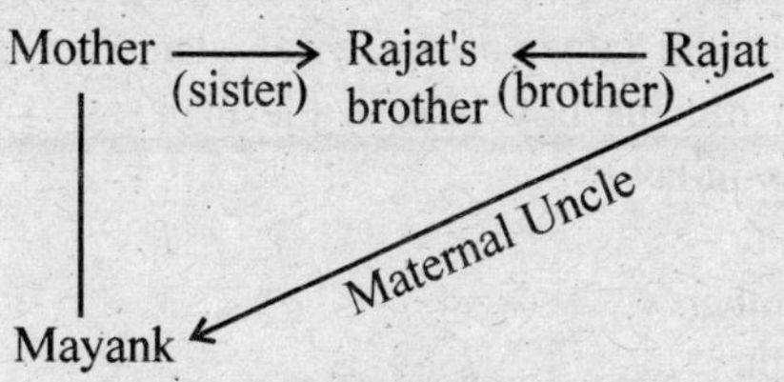

Mayank's mother is the sister of Rajat's brother. So Rajat is also the brother of Mayank's mother. Relation of the brother with his sister's child is maternal. So Rajat is Mayank's maternal uncle.

5. (*b*) : The relation is :

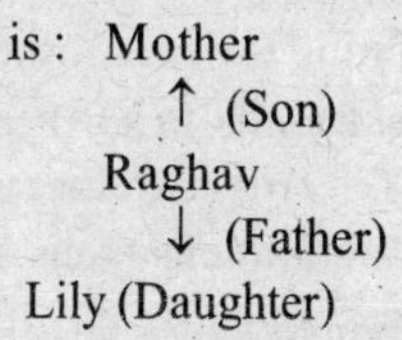

'My mother's only son' means Raghav himself. 'Her father' means Lily's father; *i.e.* Raghav and so, Lily is Raghav's daughter.

6. (*d*) :

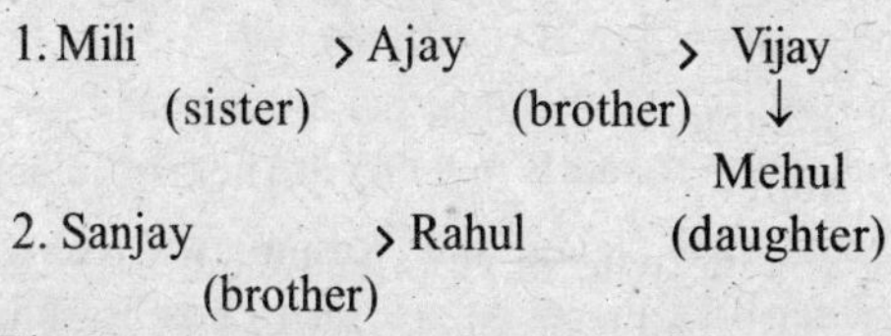

There are two sets of relationship. Information given is incomplete and no relation can be established between the two sets.

7. (*d*) : The relationship chart based on problem is :

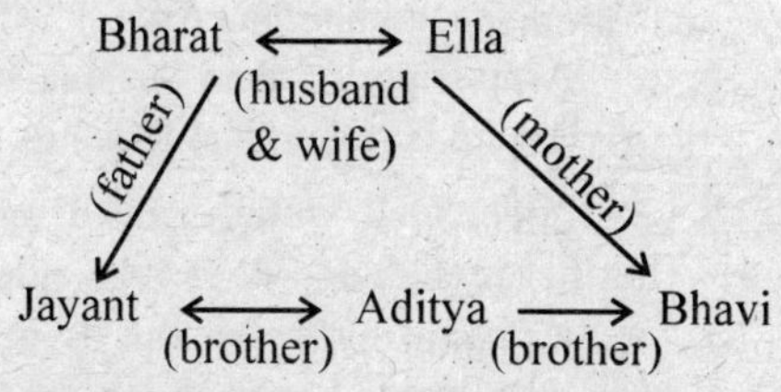

Jayant and Aditya are brothers. If Aditya is Bhavi's brother, then Jayant is also Bhavi's brother. If Bharat is Jayant's father, then he is also the father of Aditya and Bhavi. If Ella is Bhavi's mother, then she is also the mother of Aditya and Jayant. This means Bharat and Ella are husband and wife and the parents of three.

8. (*b*) : The relationship chart based on problem is :

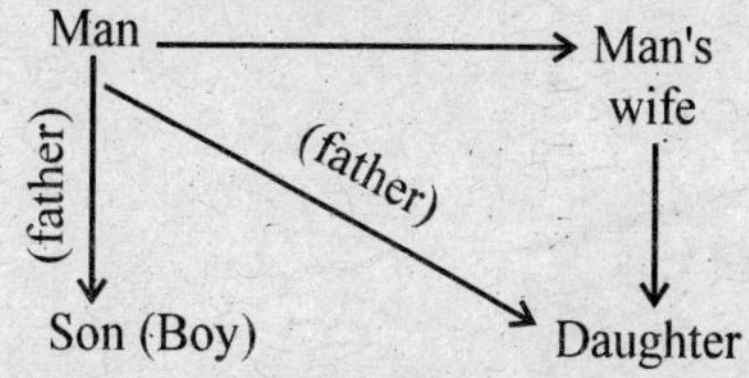

'Father of the man's wife's daughter' is the man himself and the boy in question is the man's son.

9. (*c*) : The relationship chart based on the problem is :

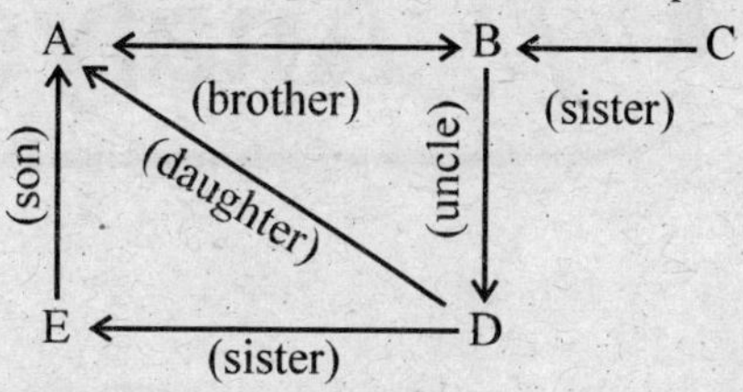

When D is sister of E, who is son of A then D is daughter of A. Brother of A is B and so, B is D's uncle.

10. (*a*) :

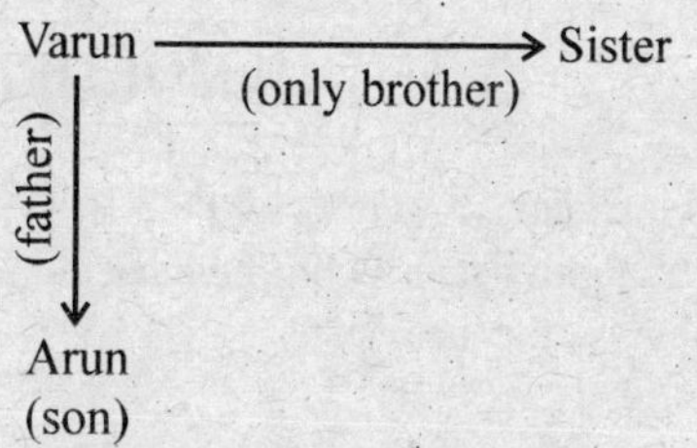

Varun's sister's only brother is Varun himself and Arun is his son.

11. (*b*) :

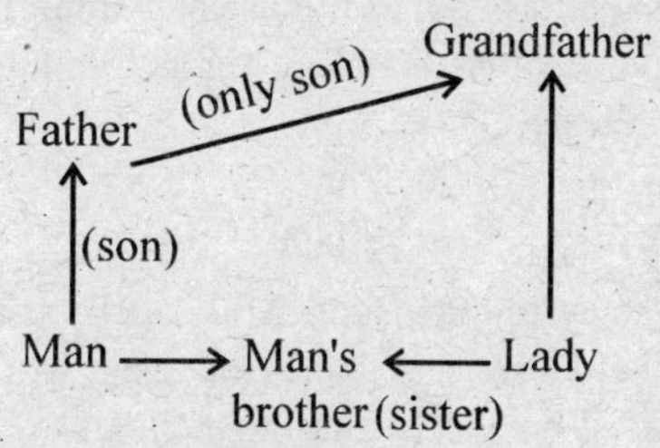

Man's brother's father is also the lady's father as he is the only son of lady's grandfather. So, the lady is man's sister.

12. (*b*) : The relationship chart based on problem is :

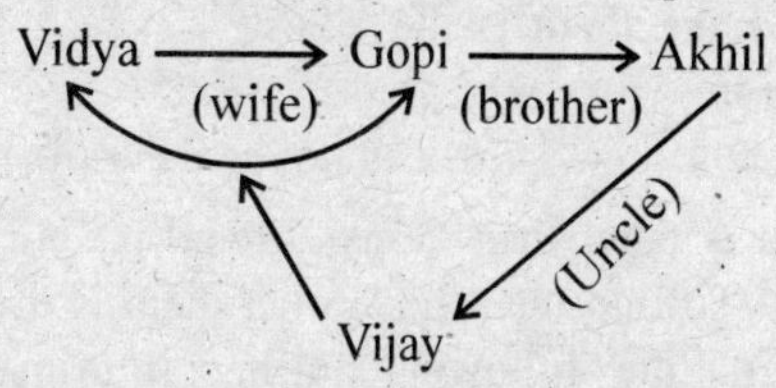

Vidya is wife of Gopi who is brother of Akhil. So, Vidya is sister-in-law of Akhil. If Akhil is uncle of Vijay then Gopi will naturally be the uncle of Vijay as it is not specified that any of the mentioned persons are Vijay's parents. Now, when Vijay is Gopi's nephew then he will also be Vidya's nephew.

CHAPTER 11

Analysis

In these type of questions, a few statements are given. Certain facts are broken up and mentioned in these statements. What is required is to analyse the statements, arrange and sort out the given facts and then answer the questions related to the given statements.

MULTIPLE CHOICE QUESTIONS

1. Among five friends, A is heavier than B; C is lighter than D; B is lighter than D but heavier than E. Who among them is the heaviest?

(*a*) B (*b*) C
(*c*) A (*d*) Can't say

2. Pune is bigger than Jhansi, Sitapur is bigger than Chittor. Raigarh is not as big as Jhansi, but is bigger than Sitapur. Chittor is not as big as Sitapur. Which is the smallest?

(*a*) Jhansi (*b*) Pune
(*c*) Chittor (*d*) Sitapur

3. Ajay works more than Ram. Alok works as much as Raju. Pankaj works less than Alok. Ram works more than Alok. Who works the most of all?

(*a*) Ajay (*b*) Ram
(*c*) Alok (*d*) Raju

4. Vipul is taller than Hans. Hans is taller than Anand. Alok is taller than Ashok. Ashok is taller than Hans. Who among them is the tallest?

(*a*) Vipul (*b*) Alok
(*c*) Ashok (*d*) Cannot be determined

5. Pramod is taller than Gopal. Gopal is shorter than Madhu. To find out who among them is the tallest, which of the following further informations is necessary?

(*a*) Madhu is taller than Gopal.
(*b*) Madhu is shorter than Pramod's brother
(*c*) Pramod is taller than Madhu.
(*d*) Pramod is taller than Madhu's brother.

6. Among five friends P, Q, R, S and T, who is the youngest? To arrive at the answer which of the following information given in the statements (A) and (B) is sufficient?

(A) R is younger than P and T.
(B) S is younger than Q.

(*a*) Only A alone is sufficient
(*b*) Either A or B is sufficient
(*c*) Both A and B together are needed
(*d*) Both A and B together are not sufficient

7. Sushma is richer than Rashmi whereas Anand is richer than Priya. Arun is as rich as Rashmi. Shoba is richer than Sushma.

Which of the following statements is correct according to the above propositions?

(*a*) Rashmi is poorer than Priya.
(*b*) Priya is richer than Arun
(*c*) Arun is poorer than Sushma.
(*d*) Anand is richer than Rashmi

8. A is elder to B while C and D are elder to E who lies between A and B. If C be elder to B, which one of the following statements is necessarily true?

(*a*) E is elder to B (*b*) A is elder to C
(*c*) C is elder to D (*d*) D is elder to C

9. Vikram is taller than Rajan but shorter than Annie. Jamal is taller than Annie. Sita is taller than Vikram. Rajan is shorter than Sita. Who is the shortest of all in the group?

(*a*) Sita (*b*) Rajan
(*c*) Vikram (*d*) Cannot be determined

10. Suresh is as much older than Kamal as he is younger than Prabodh. Navin is as old as Kamal. Which of the following statements is wrong?
(*a*) Suresh is older than Navin
(*b*) Kamal is younger than Suresh
(*c*) Prabodh is not the oldest
(*d*) Navin is younger than Prabodh

11. Ashok is heavier than Gopal. Mahesh is lighter than Jayesh. Prashant is heavier than Jayesh but lighter than Gopal. Who among them is the heaviest?
(*a*) Gopal (*b*) Jayesh
(*c*) Prashant (*d*) Ashok

12. Subodh's marks in English are as much more than Gopal's marks in History as less than Pramod's marks in English. To find out Subodh's marks in English, which of the following informations given in the statements (A) and (B) is/ are sufficient?
(A) Gopal's marks in History.
(B) Pramod's marks in History.
(*a*) Both A and B together are needed
(*b*) Only B is sufficient
(*c*) Either A or B is sufficient
(*d*) Both A and B together are not sufficient

Directions (Qs. 13-14) : *(A) Gopal is shorter than Ashok but taller than Kuhav; (B) Navin is shorter than Kuhav; (C) Jayesh is taller than Navin; (D) Ashok is taller than Jayesh.*

13. Who among them is the tallest?
(*a*) Gopal (*b*) Ashok
(*c*) Jayesh (*d*) Navin

14. Which of the following informations is not necessary to answer the above question?
(*a*) A (*b*) B
(*c*) C (*d*) D

Directions (Qs. 15-16) : *Five men A, B, C, D and E read a newspaper. The one who reads first gives it to C. The one who reads last had taken from A. E was not the first or last to read. There were two readers between B and A.*

15. B passed the newspaper to whom?
(*a*) E (*b*) B
(*c*) A (*d*) None of these

16. Who read the newspaper last?
(*a*) E (*b*) B
(*c*) D (*d*) Cannot be determined

EXPLANATORY ANSWERS

1. *(d)* : The five friends in descending order of weight are : A/D, B/C, E or A/D, B, C/E. Either A or D is the heaviest.

2. *(c)* : The order of cities in descending order of size is : Pune, Jhansi, Raigarh, Sitapur, Chittor.

3. *(a)* : On the basis of doing work, the descending order will be : Ajay, Ram, Alok/Raju, Pankaj.

4. *(d)* : On the basis of height, the descending order will be Vipul/Alok, Ashok, Hans, Anand. Either Vipul or Alok is the tallest.

5. *(c)* : According to the information both Pramod and Madhu are taller than Gopal. Option (c) decides who is the tallest.

6. *(d)* : Statements are not inter-related.

7. *(c)* : On the basis of wealth, the descending order will be :
1. Shobha, Sushma, Rashmi/Arun
2. Anand, *and* Priya
(The two statements are not inter-related.)

8. *(a)* : The order in descending seniority will be : A/C/D, E, B.

9. *(b)* : On the basis of height the descending order will be :
Jamal/Sita, Annie, Vikram, Rajan.
or
Jamal, Sita/Annie, Vikram, Rajan.

10. *(c)* : On the basis of age the descending order will be : Prabodh, Suresh, Kamal/Navin.

11. *(d)* : On the basis of weight, the descending order will be : Ashok, Gopal, Prashant, Jayesh, Mahesh.

12. *(d)* : Comparison in marks do no clarify Subodh's marks in a subject.

13. *(b)* : On the basis of height the descending order will be :
Ashok, Gopal/Jayesh, Kuhav, Navin
or
Ashok, Gopal, Kuhav/Jayesh, Navin.

14. *(c)*

15. *(d)* : The men read the newspaper in this order : B, C, E, A, D, and B passed the newspaper to C.

16. *(c)* : The men read the newspaper in this order : B, C, E, A, D, and B passed the newspaper to C.

CHAPTER 12

Judgement

MULTIPLE CHOICE QUESTIONS

1. Eileen is planning a special birthday dinner for her husband's 35th birthday. She wants the evening to be memorable, but her husband is a simple man who would rather be in jeans at a baseball game than in a suit at a fancy restaurant. Which restaurant below should Eileen choose?

(*a*) Alfredo's offers fine Italian cuisine and an elegant Tuscan decor. Patrons will feel as though they've spent the evening in a luxurious Italian villa.

(*b*) Pancho's Mexican Buffet is an all-you-can-eat family style smorgasbord with the best tacos in town.

(*c*) The Parisian Bistro is a four-star French restaurant where guests are treated like royalty. Chef Dilbert Olay is famous for his beef bourguignon.

(*d*) Marty's serves delicious, hearty meals in a charming setting reminiscent of a baseball clubhouse in honor of the owner,Marty Lester, a former major league baseball all-star. Answer & Explanation

2. The film director wants an actress for the lead role of Lucy who perfectly fits the description that appears in the original screenplay. He is not willing to consider actresses who do not resemble the character as she is described in the screenplay, no matter how talented they are. The screenplay describes Lucy as an average-sized, forty something redhead, with deep brown eyes, very fair skin, and a brilliant smile. The casting agent has four actresses in mind.

1. Actress #1 is a stunning red-haired beauty who is 5'9" and in her mid-twenties. Her eyes are brown and she has an olive complexion.
2. has red hair, big brown eyes, and a fair complexion. She is in her mid-forties and is 5'5".
3. is 5'4" and of medium build. She has red hair, brown eyes, and is in her early forties.
4. is a blue-eyed redhead in her early thirties. She's of very slight build and stands at 5'.

(*a*) 1, 2 (*b*) 2, 3
(*c*) 1, 4 (*d*) 2, 4

3. The school principal has received complaints from parents about bullying in the school yard during recess. He wants to investigate and end this situation as soon as possible, so he has asked the recess aides to watch closely. Which situation should the recess aides report to the principal?

(*a*) A girl is sitting glumly on a bench reading a book and not interacting with her peers.

(*b*) Four girls are surrounding another girl and seem to have possession of her backpack.

(*c*) Two boys are playing a one-on-one game of basketball and are arguing over the last basket scored.

(*d*) Three boys are huddled over a handheld video game, which isn't supposed to be on school grounds. Answer & Explanation

4. Mrs. Carson took a taxi to meet her three friends for lunch. They were waiting for her outside the restaurant when she pulled up in the car. She was so excited to see her friends that she left her tote bag in the taxi. As the taxi pulled away, she and her friends took notice of the license plate number so they would be able to identify the car when they called the taxi company.

1. The four women seem to agree that the plate starts out with the letter J.
2. Three of them agree that the plate ends with 12L.
3. Three of them think that the second letter is X, and a different three think that the third letter is K.

The four license plate numbers below represent what each of the four women thinks she saw. Which one is most likely the license plate number of the taxi?

(*a*) JXK 12L (*b*) JYK 12L
(*c*) JXK 12I (*d*) JXX 12L

5. Zachary has invited his three buddies over to watch the basketball game on his wide-screen television. They are all hungry, but no one wants to leave to get food. Just as they are arguing about who should make the food run, a commercial comes on for a local pizze-ria that delivers. The phone number flashes on the screen briefly and they all try to remember it. By the time Zachary grabs a pen and paper, each of them recollects a different number.

1. All of the men agree that the first three numbers are 995.
2. Three of them agree that the fourth number is 9.
3. Three agree that the fifth number is 2.
4. Three agree that the sixth number is 6; three others agree that the seventh number is also 6.

Which of the numbers is most likely the telephone number of the pizzeria?

(*a*) 995-9266 (*b*) 995-9336
(*c*) 995-9268 (*d*) 995-8266

EXPLANATORY ANSWERS

1.(*d*) : Since Eileen's husband does not enjoy fancy restaurants, choices (*a*) and (*c*) can be ruled out. Choice (*b*), although casual, doesn't sound as though it would be the kind of special and memorable evening that Eileen is looking for. Choice (*d*), which is owned by a former baseball star and is described as "charming" and "reminiscent of a baseball clubhouse", sounds perfect for Eileen's husband, who is described as a baseball fan and a man with simple tastes.

2.(*b*) : 2 and 3 possess most of the required traits. They both have red hair and brown eyes, are average-sized, and are in their forties. 1 is very tall and is only in her mid-twenties. She also has an olive complexion. 4 is of very slight build and is in her early thirties. She also has blue eyes.

3.(*b*) : Seeing four girls surrounding another girl, while in possession of her backpack, is the most suspicious of the incidents described.

4.(*a*) : The four women seem to agree that the plate starts out with the letter J. Three of them agree that the plate ends with 12L. Three of them think that the second letter is X, and a different three think that the third letter is K. The plate description that has all of these common elements is "Option A".

5.(*a*) : All of the men agree that the first three numbers are 995. Three of them agree that the fourth number is 9. Three agree that the fifth number is 2. Three agree that the sixth number is 6; three others agree that the seventh number is also 6. "Option A" is the best choice because it is made up of the numbers that most of the men agree they saw.

DECISION MAKING

MULTIPLE CHOICE QUESTIONS

Directions (Qs. 1 to 2) : *Read the following information carefully and answer the questions given below it.*

Following are the criteria for admitting a student in the first year engineering course in a college.

The student must—

(*i*) have passed XII standard examination in science with at least 80% marks.

(*ii*) not be more than 20 years old as on 1. 8. 1998.

(*iii*) have secured at least 90 marks in the entrance test out of a total of 150 marks.

(*iv*) be able to pay ₹ 15,000 as tuition fees for the first semester and ₹ 5,000 admission charges at the time of taking admission.

In the case of a candidate, who satisfies all other criteria except at—

(*a*) (*iv*) above but can pay at least 60% of the stipulated fees, the case may be referred to the Admission Committee.

(*b*) (*iii*) above but has secured more than 95% marks in the XIIth standard examination, the case may be referred to Chairman–Admissions.

You are given the following cases as on 1. 8. 1998. Depending upon the information provided in each case and based on the criteria mentioned above, recommend your decision. You are not to assume anything. If the information provided is not adequate to take a decision, mark 'Data inadequate' as the answer.

1. Subodh Mohaptara was 19 years old as on 20th December, 1997. He has secured 98% marks in XIIth standard examination with science and 80 marks in the entrance test. He can pay the requisite tuition fees and admission charges.
(*a*) Admit
(*b*) Refer to Admission Committee
(*c*) Data inadequate
(*d*) Do not admit
(*e*) Refer to Chairman–Admissions

2. Reema Jaiswal was born on 20th July, 1978. She has secured 85% and 75% marks in XIIth standard with science and entrance test respectively. She can pay the requisite tuition fees and admission charges.
(*a*) Refer to Chairman–Admission
(*b*) Refer to Admission Committee
(*c*) Data inadequate
(*d*) Do not admit
(*e*) Admit

Directions (Qs. 3 to 4) : *Read the following information to answer the given questions :*

Following are the criteria for selecting candidates for Research Fellowship :
The candidate must—
(*i*) be a post–graduate with minimum of 65% marks.
(*ii*) not be more than 30 years as on 15. 10. 1993.
(*iii*) have at least 3 years research experience.
(*iv*) have diploma in Statistics.
(*v*) have secured at least 50% marks in the entrance test.
(*vi*) have finalised the topic for research.

However, in case a candidate who fulfills all other criteria except
(*a*) (*iii*) above, but has M. Phil degree, should be referred to Dean.
(*b*) (*iv*) above, should be referred to Chairman.
(*c*) (*i*) above, but has at least 55% marks in post–graduation and 65% in the entrance test, should be given fellowship.
(*d*) (*v*) above, but has at lest 45% marks, should be wait–listed.

Based on these criteria and information provided below, decide the course of action in each case. You are not to assume anything. If the data provided is not adequate to decide the given course of action, your answer will be "data inadequate". These cases are given to you as on 15. 10. 1993.

3. 26 years old, Mamta Deo is a post graduate with 58%. She has got four years' research experience and has finalised topic for research. She got 70% marks in diploma in Statistics and 54% marks in the entrance examination.
(*a*) Fellowship not to be granted
(*b*) Refer to Dean
(*c*) Refer to Chairman
(*d*) Grant Fellowship
(*e*) Data inadequate

4. Shushila Nair has 65% marks in her post–graduation and is M. Phil. She has 5 years research experience. She has secured 65% in the entrance test and has finalised the research topic. Her date of birth is 11. 8. 65.
(*a*) Grant fellowship (*b*) Wait–list
(*c*) Refer to Dean (*d*) Refer to Chairman
(*e*) Data inadequate

Directions (Qs. 5 to 6) : *Read the following information to answer the given questions :*

Following are the conditions for selecting candidates for Research Fellowship :

The candidate must—
(*i*) be a post-graduate with minimum of 60% marks.
(*ii*) not be more than 30 years as on 1. 9. 1993.
(*iii*) have at least 3 years' research experience.
(*iv*) have diploma in statistics.
(*v*) have secured at least 55% marks in the entrance test.
(*iv*) have finalised the topic for research.

However, in the case of a candidate who fulfills all other criteria except—
(*a*) (*iii*) above but has M. Phil degree, should be given fellowship.
(*b*) (*iv*) above should be referred to Dean.
(*c*) (*i*) above but has atleast 55% marks in post-graduation, should be wait-listed.
(*d*) (*v*) above but has atleast 50% marks, should be referred to Chairman.

Based on these criteria and information provided below, decide the course of action in each case. You are not to assume anything. If the data provided is not adequate to decide the given course of action, your answer will be "data inadequate". These cases are given to you as on 1. 9. 1993.

5. Vijay Gupta is 24 years old and has got 58% marks in the entrance examination. He has secured 63% marks in his post-graduation and 55% marks in M.

Phil. He has got diploma in Statistics and has also finalised the topic for research.

(a) Grant Fellowship (b) Refer to Dean
(c) Refer to Chairman (d) Wait-list
(e) Data inadequate

6. Ajoy Dwivedi has secured 65% marks in the post-graduation and has secured 5 years research experience. He has secured 65% marks in the entrance test and has finalised the research topic. His date of birth is 11. 8. 1965.

(a) Grant Fellowship (b) Wait-list
(c) Refer to Dean (d) Data inadequate
(e) None of these

Directions (Qs. 7 to 8) : *Read the following information carefully and answer the questions given below :*

Following are the criteria of promotion from Junior Officer's Cadre to Senior Officer's Cadre in an organisation:

The candidate must—

(a) have completed atleast 5 years in the organisation.
(b) have secured 65% marks in the written test for promotion.
(c) have secured 60% marks in the Group Discussion.
(d) have secured 70% marks in the interview.
(e) have good record of his work performance.
(f) have good communication skill and get along well with his colleagues.
(g) not be more than 40 years and less than 30 years as on 1. 9. 93.
(h) have good academic record with an average of at least 65% marks.

However, in the case of a candidate who—

(i) satisfies all other conditions except (d) above but has secured 75% marks in the written test and 65% marks in he Group Discussion, the case is to be referred to the General Manager (Personnel)–GM(P) for the decision.
(j) satisfies all other criteria except (h) above but has secured an average of more than 60% marks, the case is to be referred to the Managing Director (MD) of the organisation.

Now read the information provided in the case of each candidate in each of the questions given below and decide on the basis of the information provided and based on the above conditions, which of the courses of action you would suggest. These cases are given as on 5. 9. 1993. (Remember you are not to assume anything which is not provided in the question). If complete information is not provided, the answer would be Data inadequate.

7. 38 years old Rajesh has secured 65% marks in the written test for promotion, 73% marks in interview and 62% marks in Group Discussion. He has good record of his work performance, good communication skills and gets along well with his colleagues. He has good academic record with an average of 61% marks and has completed 7 years in the organisation.

(a) Refer to GM(P) (b) Refer to MD
(c) Promote (d) Do not promote
(e) Data inadequate

8. 34 years old Sudha has secured 60% marks in the written test for promotion, 72% marks in interview and 69% marks in Group discussion. She has good communication skill and gets along well with her colleagues. Her record of work performance is good and she has completed 6½ years in the organisation.

(a) Refer to MD (b) Do not promote
(c) Refer to GM(P) (d) Promote
(e) Data inadequate

EXPLANATORY ANSWERS

1. (e) : Criterion *(iii)* is not satisfied but Criterion *(b)* gives the decision.

2. (d) : Both Criterion *(iii)* and Criterion *(b)* are not satisfied.

3. (a) : Both Criterion *(i)* and Criterion *(c)* are not satisfied.

4. (d) : Criterion *(iv)* is not given but Criterion *(b)* gives the decision.

5. (a) : Criterion *(iii)* is not satisfied but Criterion *(a)* gives the decision.

6. (c) : Criterion *(iv)* is not satisfied but Criterion *(b)* gives the decision.

7. (b) : Criterion *(h)* is not satisfied but Criterion *(j)* gives the decision.

8. (b) : Criterion *(b)* is not satisfied.

CHAPTER 13

Statement Conclusion

In this reasoning pattern, a statement is given followed by two conclusions. The statement is to be taken as the fact. Then based on it one has to decide which of the conclusion(s) definitely follows or does not follow from the given statement.

MULTIPLE CHOICE QUESTIONS

Directions (Qs. 1 to 20): *In the following questions, each question has a statement followed by two conclusions. Taking the statement to be true, decide which of the given conclusions definitely follows from the given statement. Indicate your answer as (a) if only I follows; (b) if only II follows; (c) either I or II follows; (d) if neither I nor II follows; and (e) if both I and II follow.*

1. *Statement* : The Principal humiliated the teacher in the presence of students.

Conclusions I: The Principal did not like the teacher.

II: The teacher was not popular amongst his students.

2. *Statement* : Good health is dependent on right eating habits. Most of the people do not follow any rule regarding eating.

Conclusions I: Most of the people have poor health.

II: People are ignorant of proper eating habits.

3. *Statement* : Until our country achieves economic equality and political freedom, democracy would be meaningless.

Conclusions I: Political freedom and democracy go hand in hand.

II: Economic equality leads to real political freedom and democracy.

4. *Statement* : Black cloud follows thunder. Rains follow thunder.

Conclusions I: Thunder is the cause of rain.

II: Black cloud is the cause of thunder.

5. *Statement* : Practice is better than precept. Most doctors are heavy smokers.

Conclusions I: Most doctors cannot advise people not to smoke.

II: Doctors do not regard smoking as injurious.

6. *Statement* : Workers feel highly motivated when they get sense of involvement by participating in the management of companies.

Conclusions I: Workers should be motivated to produce more.

II: Workers should be allowed to participate in the management of companies.

7. *Statement* : Industrial revolution which first of all started in Europe has brought about modern age.

Conclusions I: Disparity between rich and poor results in revolution.

II: Revolution overhauls society.

8. *Statement* : America's defence secretary reiterated that they would continue to supply arms to Pakistan.

Conclusions I: Pakistan is incapable of manufacturing arms.

II: It would ensure peace in the region.

9. *Statement* : Poor people are more trust-worthy as compared to the rich. They can do wonders if they are taken into confidence.

Conclusions I: Poor people are wonderful people.

II: By and large rich people are not trustworthy.

10. *Statement* : Government has spoiled many top ranking financial institutions by appointing bureaucrats as Directors of these institutions.

Conclusions I : Government should appoint Directors of the financial institutes taking into consi-deration the expertise of the person in the area of finance.

II : The Director of the financial institute should have exper-tise commensurate with the financial work carried out by the institute.

Directions (Qs. 11 to 15): *In the following questions, the symbols* $*$, $\stackrel{*}{=}$, $=$, @ *and* $\underset{=}{@}$ *are used with the following meanings :*

(*a*) * (*b*) means (*a*) is greater than (*b*),

(*a*) $\stackrel{*}{=}$ (*b*) means (*a*) is either greater than or equal to (*b*).

(*a*) = (*b*) means (*a*) is equal to (*b*).

(*a*) @ (*b*) means (*a*) is smaller than (*b*) and

(*a*) $\underset{=}{@}$ (*b*) means (*a*) is either smaller than or equal to (*b*).

Answer is given as:

(*a*) If only conclusion I is true;

(*b*) If only conclusion II is true;

(*c*) If either I or II is true;

(*d*) If neither I nor II is true;

(*e*) If both I and II are true.

11. *Statements* : T $\stackrel{*}{=}$ P, P @ S, P = M
Conclusions : *I.* S * M *II.* T @ S

12. *Statements* : R $\underset{=}{@}$ M, M * P, R $\stackrel{*}{=}$ L
Conclusions : *I.* M = L *II.* P = L

13. *Statements* : M = T, T $\underset{=}{@}$ Z, S * M
Conclusions : *I.* Z * M *II.* Z = M

14. *Statements* : L @ C, C * Z, Z $\underset{=}{@}$ F
Conclusions : *I.* C * F *II.* F = C

15. *Statements* : Z @ B, N $\stackrel{*}{=}$ S, B @ N
Conclusions : *I.* B = Z *II.* S $\underset{=}{@}$ B

EXPLANATORY ANSWERS

1. (*a*) : Only conclusion I follows. Conclusion II is not confirmed by the given statement.

2. (*a*) : Conclusion I definitely follows. Conclusion II is not confirmed by the given statement.

3. (*b*) : Only conclusion II follows. Conclusion I cannot be drawn from the given statement.

4. (*b*) : Only conclusion II follows. Conclusion I is wrong as rains are the cause of thunder.

5. (*e*) : Both conclusion I and conclusion II follow from the statements as the doctors who are heavy smokers indicate that they do not regard smoking as injurious and thus, cannot advise people not to smoke.

6. (*e*) : Both conclusions I and II follow from the statement as involvement of workers boosts production and benefits the companies.

7. (*b*) : Only conclusion II follows. Conclusion I is not related the statement.

8. (*d*) : Neither conclusion I nor conclusion II follows. Both the conclusions are unrelated to the statement.

9. (*b*) : Only conclusion II follows. Conclusion I is not related to the statement.

10. (*e*) : Both conclusion I and conclusion II follow.

11. (*a*) : $T \geq P, P < S, P = M$
$\therefore S > M$

12. (*d*) : $R \leq M, M > P, R \geq L$
$\therefore L \leq R \leq M$

13. (*c*) : $M = T, T \leq Z, Z = M$
If $T = Z$, then $Z = M$
If $T < Z$, then $Z > M$

14. (*d*) : $L < C, C > Z, Z \leq F$
No relation can be established between C and F.

15. (*d*) : $Z < B, N \geq S, B < N$
No relation can be established between B, S and Z.

CHAPTER 14

Syllogistic Reasoning

In this reasoning pattern two statements are followed by few conclusions drawn. Four options (*a*), (*b*), (*c*) & (*d*) are given as answers. Based on the statement the candidate has to select the right answer in each question.

MULTIPLE CHOICE QUESTIONS

Directions (Q. 1–4) : *In each question given below two statements are followed by four conclusions numbered I, II, III and IV. You have to take the two given statements to be true even if they seem to be at variance from commonly known facts. Read the statements and conclusions and decide which of the conclusions logically follows from the two given statements, disregarding commonly known facts.*

1. Statements: All the phones are scales. All the scales are calculators.

Conclusions:

I. All the calculators are scales.
II. All the phones are calculators.
III. All the scales are phones.
IV. Some calculators are phones.

(*a*) Only I and IV (*b*) Only III and IV
(*c*) Only II and IV (*d*) Only I and II

2. Statements: No door is dog. All the dogs are cats.

Conclusions:

I. No door is cat.
II. No cat is door.
III. Some cats are dogs.
IV. All the cats are dogs.

(*a*) Only II and IV (*b*) Only I and III
(*c*) Only III and IV (*d*) Only III

3. Statements: Some tables are T.V. Some T.V. are radios.

Conclusions:

I. Some tables are radios.
II. Some radios are tables.
III. All the radios are T.V.
IV. All the T.V. are tables.

(*a*) Only II and IV (*b*) Only I and III
(*c*) Only IV (*d*) None of the four

4. Statements: All men are vertebrates. Some mammals are vertebrates.

Conclusions:

I. All men are mammals.
II. All mammals are men.
III. Some vertebrates are mammals.
IV. All vertebrates are men.

(*a*) Only IV (*b*) Only II
(*c*) Only III (*d*) Only I

Directions (Q. 5–9) : *Every question below has a few statements, followed by four conclusions numbered I, II, III and IV. You have to consider every given statement as true, even if it does not conform to the well known facts. Read the conclusions and then decide which of the conclusions can be logically derived.*

5. Statements: Some keys are staplers. Some staplers are stickers. All the stickers are pens.

Conclusions:

I. Some pens are staplers.
II. Some stickers are keys.
III. No sticker is key.
IV. Some staplers are keys.

(*a*) Only I and II
(*b*) Only II and IV
(*c*) Only II and III
(*d*) Only I and IV and either II or III

6. Statements: All the locks are keys. All the keys are bats. Some watches are bats.

Conclusions:

I. Some bats are locks.
II. Some watches are keys.
III. All the keys are locks.
IV. Some keys are locks.

(*a*) Only I and II (*b*) Only I and IV
(*c*) Only II and III (*d*) Only I and III

7. Statements: All the papers are books. All the bags are books. Some purses are bags.

Conclusions:

I. Some papers are bags.
II. Some books are papers.
III. Some books are purses.
IV. Some papers are purses.

(*a*) Only I and IV (*b*) Only II and III
(*c*) Only I and II (*d*) Only I and III

8. Statements: All the bottles are boxes. All the boxes are bags. Some bags are trays.

Conclusions:

I. Some bottles are trays.
II. Some trays are boxes.
III. All the bottles are bags.
IV. Some trays are bags.

(*a*) Only III and IV (*b*) Only I and II
(*c*) Only II and III (*d*) Only I and IV

9. Statements: Some rats are cats. Some cats are dogs. No dog is cow.

Conclusions:

I. No cow is cat. II. No dog is rat.
III. Some cats are rats. IV. Some dogs are cats.

(*a*) Only I and IV (*b*) Only I and II
(*c*) Only I and III (*d*) Only III and IV

EXPLANATORY ANSWERS

1. (*c*)

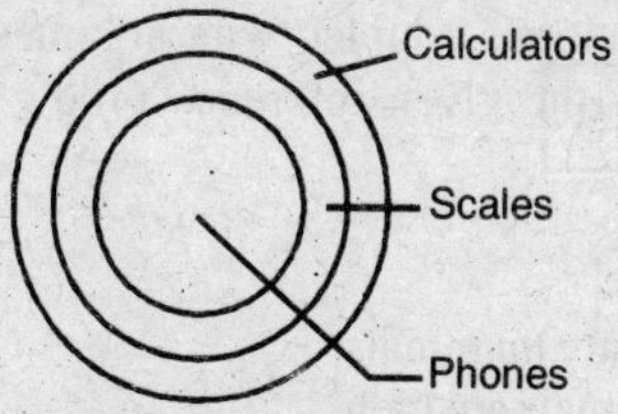

2. (*d*)

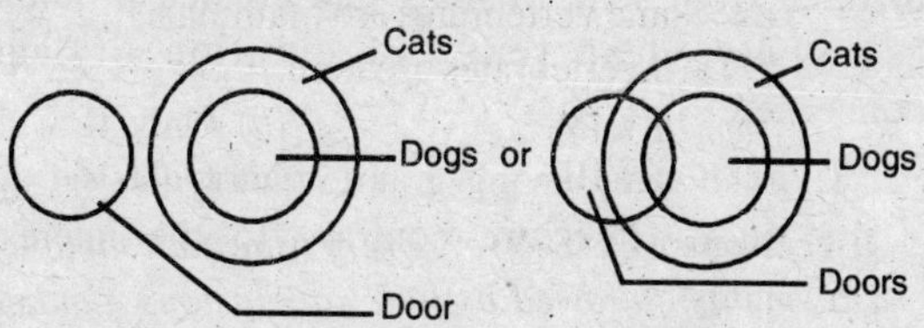

3. (*d*)

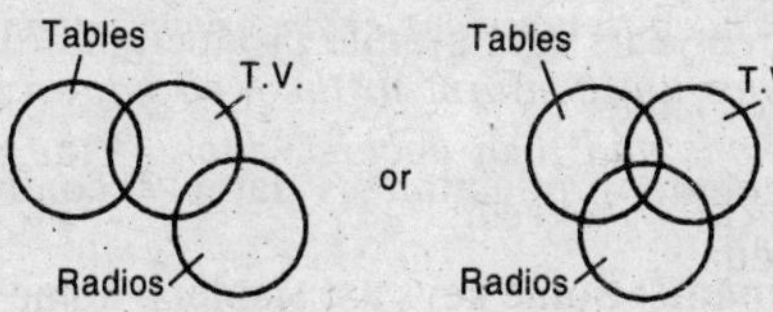

4. (*c*)

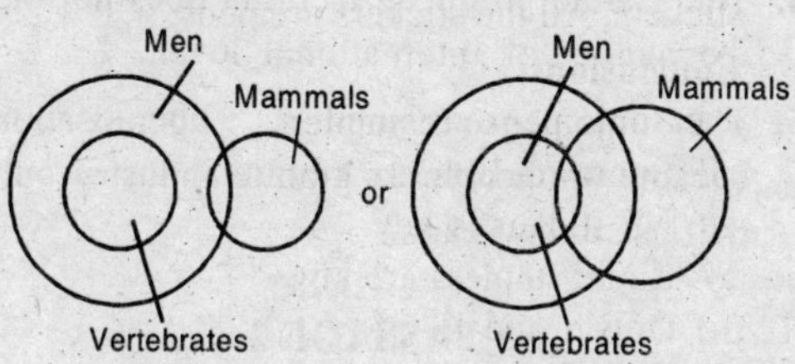

5. (*d*)

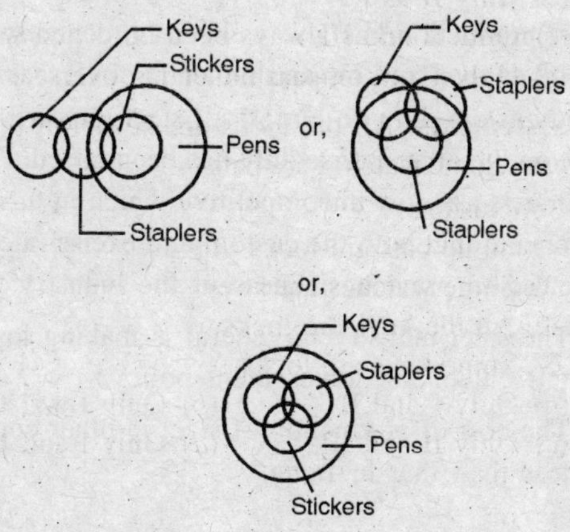

6. (*b*)

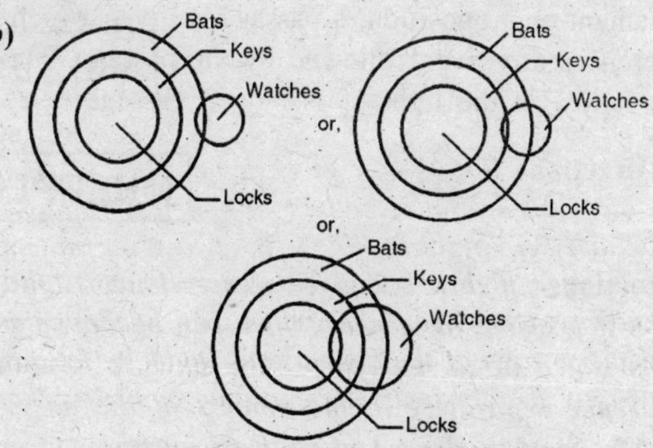

7. (*b*)

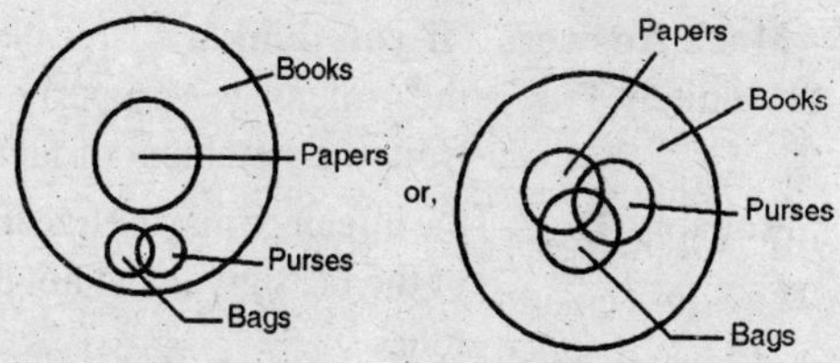

8. (*a*)

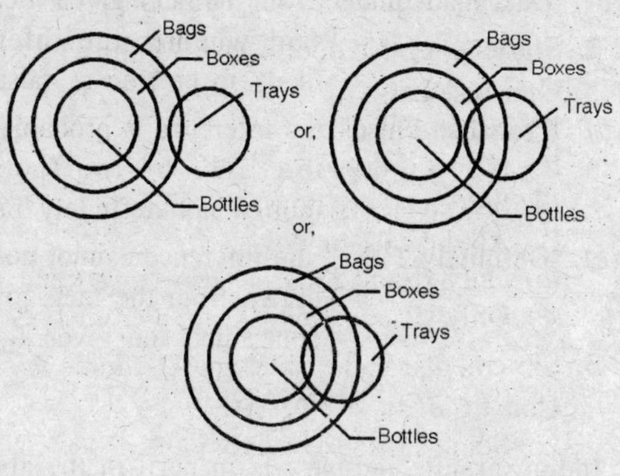

9. (*d*)

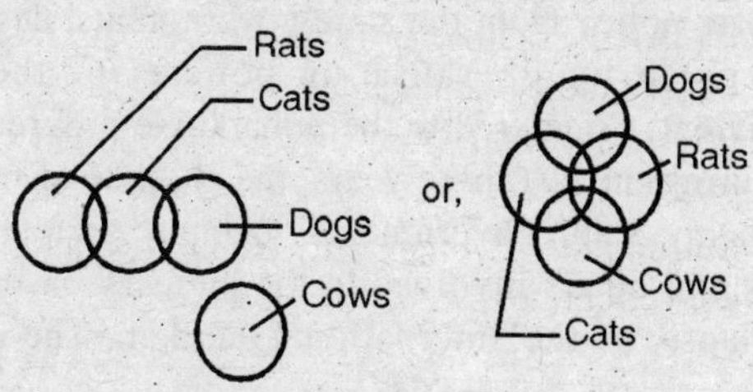

CHAPTER 15

Drawing Inferences

Questions on this type of reasoning have become quite common in competitive examinations. In this test, instead of a statement or proposition, a passage is given which is a congregation of many propositions coupled with arguments. Some inferences are given followed by the passage. The candidate has to decide whether the given inference follows, or does not follow in the light of the given passage.

MULTIPLE CHOICE QUESTIONS

Directions : *Below are given some passages followed by several possible inferences which can be drawn from the facts stated in each passage. You have to examine each inference separately in the context of the passage and decide upon its degree of truth or falsity.*

	Mark Answers	If you think...
(a)	"Definitely True"	the inference properly follows from the statement of facts given.
(b)	"Probably True"	the inference may be true in the light of the facts given but not definitely true.
(c)	"Data Inadequate"	from the facts given it cannot be said whether the inference is likely to be true or false.
(d)	"Probably False"	the inference is probably false in the light of the facts given though not definitely false.
(e)	"Definitely False"	the inference cannot possibly be drawn from the facts given or it contradicts the given facts.

PASSAGE 1

Indian granite industry is in peril in the absence of a uniform policy from the state governments, despite the thrust given by liberalisation policies of the union government. Compared to the remarkable progress in the field during the last three years, the absence of matching policies by state governments had put granite quarry owners and others involved in the industry on the verge of collapse in the international market. The policies differed from state to state, had created problems as far as loyalty, dead rent and duration of lease were concerned.

1. Each state having granite quarry has set up its own rules which are contrary to the interest of the industry.

2. Till three years ago, granite production in India was not profitable.

3. The granite production is largely controlled by individuals.

4. The granite produced in India does not match with the quality of international level.

5. The union government's liberalisation policy became applicable to granite industry only during the last three years.

PASSAGE 2

Steel production has always been burdened with costs much higher than in comparable plants overseas. On the one hand custom duty on almost all steel imports has been reduced, on the other excise duty has been raised. Domestic steel products are now uncompetitive which in turn has led to the demand that both the custom and excise rates should be reviewed to prevent sickness in the industry.

6. The steel industry in general is making losses as a fall out of the government policy.

7. The cost of production of steel in other countries is less than that in India.

8. India can compete with the foreign countries in re gard to the price of steel with a favourable government policy.
9. Foreign steel has become cheaper comparative to domestic steel.
10. The government is considering lowering of excise duty on steel products.

PASSAGE 3

The annual domestic consumption of plastics in India is expected to grow between 2.5 and 3 million tonnes by the end of the Ist balls of the century from the current level of about one million tonnes. The global consumption of plastics now stands at 100 million tonnes. To sustain the present growth pattern, India would need two additional polymer plants of 1,000 tonnes every year till the turn of the Ist half of this century. Entrepreneurs should now think in lines of globalisation and promote projects of international capacity and they would have to look at technology transfer as well as upgradation and strategic and creative alliances.

11. The total domestic consumption of plastics in India is about one per cent of the global consumption.
12. At present India does not import plastics.
13. India lacks in technological capabilities in producing plastics.
14. There is an expected growth of about .2 per cent in the plastic consumption every year.
15. Potentially India can be one of the major players in the production of plastics in the international market.

EXPLANATORY ANSWERS

1. ***(a)*** **:** The policies differed from state to state.

2. ***(c)*** **:** Remarkable progress during the last three years is mentioned in the paragraph but nothing suggests that the production was not profitable.

3. ***(a)*** **:** There is absence of a uniform policy from the state Governments.

4. ***(c)*** **:** According to the paragraph, absence of matching policies had put the quarry owners and others involved in the industry on the verge of collapse in the international market. Nothing is mentioned about the granite quality produced in India or of the international level.

5. ***(e)*** **:** The inference does not relate to the facts given in the statement.

6. ***(d)*** **:** Government policy alone may not be responsible for the losses. Cost or quality factor may also be responsible.

7. ***(c)*** **:** The paragraph mentions that steel production in India has always been burdened with costs much higher than in comparable plants overseas. But nowhere in the paragraph it is mentioned that the cost of production of steel is less in other countries.

8. ***(a)*** **:** If the government reviews its policy, India can definitely compete with the foreign countries in regard to the steel price.

9. ***(a)*** **:** Customs duty on almost all steel products has been reduced.

10. ***(b)*** **:** There is a demand that both the customs and excise rates should be reviewed.

11. ***(a)*** **:** The global consumption of plastics is 100 million tonnes and current level of consumption in India is 1 million tonnes.

12. ***(c)*** **:** The paragraph does not mention about the import or export of plastics.

13. ***(a)*** **:** Entrepreneurs would have to look at technology transfer as well as upgradation and strategic and creative alliances.

14. ***(a)*** **:** The expected growth by end of the Ist half of this century is between 2.5 and 3 million tonnes. India needs 2 additional polymer plants of 1,000 tonnes per year.

15. ***(a)*** **:** By thinking in lines of globalisation and promoting projects of international capacity India can be one of the major players in the production of plastics in the international market.

CHAPTER 16

Trends

This type of questions are asked to assess the thinking pattern or mental trends of the candidate. These are simple questions but should be answered honestly and carefully.

MULTIPLE CHOICE QUESTIONS

Directions : *In the questions given below four alternatives have been given below each one of them. You have to select the right alternative according to your mind and mark it in your answer sheet.*

1. I like pre-defined rules and regulations.
(*a*) Sometimes (*b*) No
(*c*) Yes (*d*) No idea

2. I found a purse full of money in college premise. I:
(*a*) donated the amount among poor
(*b*) gave it to the principal
(*c*) offered it at temple
(*d*) None of these

3. I am punctual regarding
(*a*) going to bed (*b*) time
(*c*) meals (*d*) dating

4. I was travelling on a boat which capsized. Firstly, I:
(*a*) rescued others (*b*) saved myself
(*c*) closed my eyes (*d*) cursed my luck

5. When someone asks you for help in odd situations then:
(*a*) you give him/her all possible help
(*b*) you promise him/her help
(*c*) you do not help him/her
(*d*) you turn a deaf ear

6. In case my wristwatch is out of order, I:
(*a*) would try to repair it myself
(*b*) would give it to watchmaker
(*c*) would buy a new watch
(*d*) would throw it away

7. Often I change my opinion in the last moment.
(*a*) Yes (*b*) No
(*c*) Sometimes (*d*) No idea

8. Generally I am extrovert and well behaved.
(*a*) Yes (*b*) No
(*c*) Sometimes (*d*) No idea

9. I like to use new technique of work.
(*a*) Yes (*b*) No
(*c*) Sometimes (*d*) No idea

10. When someone considers you wrong then:
(*a*) you do not react
(*b*) you consider him/her wrong
(*c*) you try to ward off the misunderstanding on proper occasion.
(*d*) you pick a fight

11. The secret of my success is:
(*a*) hard labour (*b*) awakening in night
(*c*) gossiping (*d*) luck

12. If you are a female and you are talking with a male:
(*a*) You hide your age
(*b*) You are afraid
(*c*) You talk without hesitation
(*d*) You avoid talks

13. I do like rules and regulations.
(*a*) Yes (*b*) No
(*c*) Sometimes (*d*) No idea

14. Excellent ideas come to my mind:
(*a*) while working alone
(*b*) while working in a group
(*c*) while in sleep
(*d*) while in bathroom

15. Whenever my little baby cries loudly, then I
(*a*) beat him/her
(*b*) feed milk to him/her
(*c*) make him/her sleep
(*d*) ask my husband to handle him/her

16. When I see a mad person, I :
(*a*) approach towards him/her
(*b*) maintain distance from him/her
(*c*) throw stone at him/her
(*d*) start laughing at him/her

17. While driving my car I offer lift to people who ask for lift.
(*a*) Always (*b*) Sometimes
(*c*) Never (*d*) If she is a girl

18. When someone tries to convince you then:
(*a*) You get convinced
(*b*) You do not get convinced
(*c*) You hear him/her passionately
(*d*) You turn a deaf ear

19. Whenever someone knocks on my closed door then firstly I
(*a*) open the door
(*b*) peep through the lens fitted in the door
(*c*) do not open the door
(*d*) yell at him/her

20. I speak to others about my expectation and dreams.
(*a*) Rarely (*b*) Often
(*c*) Sometimes (*d*) Never

21. Any dispute can be solved by :
(*a*) quarrelling (*b*) court
(*c*) dialogue (*d*) money

22. When I do any foolish work then :
(*a*) I feel ashamed (*b*) I feel proud of myself
(*c*) Nothing happens (*d*) I weep

23. If I were correspondent of any newspaper then I would write on the following subject :
(*a*) Cinema and theatre
(*b*) Political events
(*c*) Sports
(*d*) Stock market

24. If I were not human being then :
(*a*) I wish to be a bird (*b*) I wish to be a horse
(*c*) I wish to be God (*d*) Can't say

25. Suppose, you have worn a new shirt and your friend passed a comment that it is not looking good on you. You :
(*a*) will change the shirt immediately
(*b*) will take it lightly as it is your style
(*c*) will not change the shirt but feel offended
(*d*) will start quarrelling

26. I wish to live alone always.
(*a*) Yes (*b*) No
(*c*) Sometimes (*d*) Never

27. I want to spend my spare (extra) time :
(*a*) in reading interesting books
(*b*) in reading comics
(*c*) in viewing films
(*d*) in gossiping

28. Before doing any work I ask myself 'Is it appropriate'?
(*a*) Yes (*b*) No
(*c*) Sometimes (*d*) Never

29. If I see the GOD, I will ask for
(*a*) huge wealth (*b*) honesty
(*c*) love (*d*) heaven

30. People call you selfish.
(*a*) Always (*b*) Sometimes
(*c*) Never (*d*) No idea

31. While talking to friends I do not like to express my very personal matters.
(*a*) Yes (*b*) No
(*c*) Sometimes (*d*) Never

32. Consultation with others helps me to take a decision.
(*a*) Yes (*b*) No
(*c*) Sometimes (*d*) Never

33. After failure:
(*a*) One repents
(*b*) One tries again to succeed
(*c*) Nothing special is happened
(*d*) Nothing in life remains

34. I want to be convinced by arguments.
(*a*) Yes (*b*) No
(*c*) Sometimes (*d*) Never

ANSWERS

1	2	3	4	5	6	7	8	9	10
(*c*)	(*b*)	(*b*)	(*b*)	(*a*)	(*b*)	(*b*)	(*a*)	(*a*)	(*c*)
11	**12**	**13**	**14**	**15**	**16**	**17**	**18**	**19**	**20**
(*a*)	(*c*)	(*a*)	(*a*)	(*b*)	(*b*)	(*b*)	(*a*)	(*b*)	(*a*)
21	**22**	**23**	**24**	**25**	**26**	**27**	**28**	**29**	**30**
(*c*)	(*a*)	(*c*)	(*a*)	(*b*)	(*c*)	(*a*)	(*a*)	(*c*)	(*c*)
31	**32**	**33**	**34**						
(*c*)	(*a*)	(*b*)	(*a*)						

CHAPTER

17

Critical Thinking

In this type of reasoning, a statement is given and assumptions are drawn from it. An assumption is something assumed, supposed and taken for granted. The implicity of the two assumptions is in question. The implication means the hidden meaning, something which is derived from and as such based upon the statement.

MULTIPLE CHOICE QUESTIONS

Directions (Qs. 1 to 6): *In each question below are given two statements followed by two conclusions numbered I and II. You have to take the two given statements to be true even if they seem to be at variance from commonly known facts and then decide which of the given conclusions logically follows from the two given statements, disregarding commonly known facts. Read both the statements and—*

Give answer (a) if only conclusion I follows; give answer (b) if only conclusion II follows; give answer (c) if either I or II follows; give answer (d) if neither I nor II follows and give answer (e) if both I and II follows.

1. *Statements* *I*: All tomatoes are red.
II: All grapes are tomatoes.
Conclusions *I*: All grapes are red.
II: Some tomatoes are grapes.

2. *Statements* *I*: All painters are smilling.
II: Some authors are painters.
Conclusions *I*: All smiling authors are painters.
II: Some authors are smiling.

3. *Statements* *I*: All peons in this office are efficient.
II: Ramu is not efficient.
Conclusions *I*: Ramu is not peon in this office.
II: Ramu should be more efficient.

4. *Statements* *I*: All weavers are hard working.
II: No hard working men are foolish.
Conclusions *I*: No weavers are foolish.
II: Some foolish are weavers.

5. *Statements* *I*: All fishes are cars.
II: All cars are vegetables.
Conclusions *I*: Some vegetables are cars.
II: Some vegetables are fishes.

6. *Statements* *I*: Some dogs are pups.
II: All horses are pups.

Directions (Qs. 7 to 10): *In each question below is given a statement followed by three assumptions number I, II and III. An assumption is something supposed or taken for granted. You have to consider the statement along with the assumptions and decide which of the assumptions is implicit in the statement. Then decide which of the alternatives is the correct answer.*

7. *Statement* :
"Use Riya Cold Cream for fair complexion"—an advertisement.
Assumptions :
I. People like to use cream for fair complexion.
II. People are easily fooled.
III. People respond to advertisements.
(*a*) Only I is implicit.
(*b*) Only II is implicit.
(*c*) Only I and III are implicit.
(*d*) Only I and II are implicit.
(*e*) All are implicit.

8. *Statement* :
"Slogans against smoking in office should be put on the notice board"—an employee in an office suggests.
Assumptions :
I. The employee felt that his suggestion will be considered.
II. People smoke in the office.
III. Some people will stop smoking after reading the slogans.
(*a*) Only I is implicit.
(*b*) Only I and II are implicit.
(*c*) Only II and III are implicit.

(*d*) None is implicit.
(*e*) All are implicit.

9. *Statement :*
"I want to present him a book on techniques of yoga on his birthday"—A tells B.
Assumptions :
I. A and B will be invited for the birthday celebrations.
II. The person to whom the book is to be presented, is not keeping good health.
III. Book is the best gift for birthdays.
(*a*) Only I and II are implicit.
(*b*) Only II and III are implicit.
(*c*) Only I and III are implicit.
(*d*) None is implicit.
(*e*) All are implicit

10. *Statement :*
Keeping in view the financial constraint, the management institution has decided to charge at the time of providing employment in various organisations, a placement fee of ₹ 25000 from the organisation in which the student will be provided the employment.
Assumptions :
I. It will help in increasing the demand of the students belonging to the management institution.
II. The amount collected in this way will be purposeful.
III. It may be possible that the organisation providing employment may select less number of students in future.
(*a*) None follows.
(*b*) Only II and III follow.
(*c*) Only I follows.
(*d*) Only I and II follow.
(*e*) None of these

EXPLANATORY ANSWERS

1. (*e*) : When all tomatoes are red and all grapes are tomatoes, then all grapes are also red. When all grapes are tomatoes, then some tomatoes must be grapes. Therefore, both conclusions I and II are correct.

2. (*b*) : When all painters are smiling and some authors are painters, then some authors are smiling. Therefore, only conclusion II is correct.

3. (*a*) : When all the peons of the office are efficient, then Ramu cannot be a peon in this office. Therefore, only conclusion I is correct.

4. (*a*) : When all weavers are hardworking and no hardworking men are foolish, then no weavers are foolish. Therefore, only conclusion I is correct.

5. (*e*) : When all fishes are cars and all cars are vegetables, then all fishes will naturally be vegetables. This means that some vegetables are fishes. And when all cars are vegetables, then some vegetables will be cars naturally. Therefore, both the conclusions I and II are correct.

6. (*d*) : No relationship can be established between the two statements. Therefore, neither conclusion I nor conclusion II is correct.

7. (*c*) : The advertisement itself denotes that people like to use cream for fair complexion and they do respond to advertisements. Advertisements are for awareness of the product not for fooling people.

8. (*e*) : Suggestion for putting up the notice is made because some people must be smoking in office. Notice board is read by people in office and some may stop smoking after reading the slogans.

9. (*c*) : According to A presents are best gifts for birthdays and when A has bought the book he expects to be invited for the birthday celebration. Nothing is mentioned about health of the birthday person.

10. (*b*) : The amount collected will lessen the financial constraint and there is every possibility for selecting less number of students because of the fee charged.

CHAPTER 18

Emotional Intelligence

Emotional intelligence (EI) refers to the ability to perceive, control, and evaluate emotions. Emotional intelligence (EI) is the area of cognitive ability involving traits and social skills that facilitate interpersonal behaviour. Intelligence can be broadly defined as the capacity for goal-oriented adaptive behaviour; emotional intelligence focuses on the aspects of intelligence that govern self-knowledge and social adaptation.

Emotional Intelligence that is also called Emotional Intelligence Quotient or (EQ) narrates the capability, capacity, or deftness to understand. It evaluates and manages one's emotions.

MULTIPLE CHOICE QUESTIONS

Directions: *Answer the following questions by selecting the appropriate option.*

1. In my group of friends, I am generally aware of how each person feels about the other people in our social circle.
(*a*) Strongly Agree (*b*) Agree
(*c*) Disagree (*d*) Strongly Disagree

2. When I am upset, I can usually pinpoint exactly why I am distressed.
(*a*) Strongly Agree (*b*) Agree
(*c*) Disagree (*d*) Strongly Disagree

3. While there are some things that I would like to change, I generally like who I am.
(*a*) Strongly Agree (*b*) Agree
(*c*) Disagree (*d*) Strongly Disagree

4. When I make mistakes, I often berate and criticize myself and my abilities.
(*a*) Often (*b*) Sometimes
(*c*) Rarely (*d*) Almost Never

5. I feel uncomfortable in emotionally charged situations.
(*a*) Strongly Agree (*b*) Agree
(*c*) Disagree (*d*) Strongly Disagree

6. I tend to avoid confrontations. When I am involved in a confrontation, I become extremely anxious.
(*a*) Strongly Agree (*b*) Agree
(*c*) Disagree (*d*) Strongly Disagree

7. I am generally aloof and detached until I really get to know a person.
(*a*) Strongly Agree (*b*) Agree
(*c*) Disagree (*d*) Strongly Disagree

8. I tend to overreact to minor problems.
(*a*) Often (*b*) Sometimes
(*c*) Rarely (*d*) Almost Never

9. I feel confident about my own skills, talents, and abilities.
(*a*) Strongly Agree (*b*) Agree
(*c*) Disagree (*d*) Strongly Disagree

10. I would describe myself as a good judge of character.
(*a*) Strongly Agree (*b*) Agree
(*c*) Disagree (*d*) Strongly Disagree

11. When I am facing an unpleasant task, I tend to:
(*a*) Make a plan and work on it a little each day
(*b*) Get it over with as soon as possible
(*c*) Put it off until the last minute
(*d*) Don't do it at all

12. During a heated argument, I am more likely to:
(*a*) Stop the fight and agree to a short break before resuming the discussion.
(*b*) Shut down and stop responding to the other person.
(*c*) Give in and apologize in order to quickly end the argument.
(*d*) Start insulting the other person.

13. When making an important decision, I tend to:
(*a*) Follow my instincts
(*b*) Rely on direction from other people
(*c*) Go with the easiest option
(*d*) Guess randomly

14. Which of the following statements best describes you?
(*a*) I have an easy time making friends and getting to know new people.
(*b*) I get along well with others, but I have to really get to know someone before they become a true friend.
(*c*) I find it difficult to meet people and make friends.
(*d*) I cannot make friends.

15. You have invested a lot of time and energy into a project for one of your classes. While you feel confident about your work, your instructor gives you a C+ on the project. How do you deal with this situation?
(*a*) Decide the class is stupid and stop putting forth your best efforts.
(*b*) Berate and criticize your own work.
(*c*) Confront the instructor and ask for a better grade.
(*d*) Think about ways you could improve the project and apply these ideas to future schoolwork.

16. One of your best friends has suffered a miscarriage. How do you respond?
(*a*) Allow your friend to express her feelings and offer your support.
(*b*) Spend time with her, but avoid talking about her loss.
(*c*) Convince her to go out with some friends to get her mind off it.
(*d*) Give her some time to herself.

17. One of your co-workers has a habit that annoys you. The problem seems to be getting worse each day. How do you respond?
(*a*) Tell your co-worker what is bothering you.
(*b*) Make a complaint about the behaviour to your supervisor.
(*c*) Talk about your co-worker behind his back.
(*d*) Suffer in silence.

18. You've been feeling stressed out at work and haven't finished projects as quickly as you should. When your boss suddenly assigns you another large project, how do you feel?
(*a*) Anxious about getting all the work done.
(*b*) Overwhelmed by the task before you.
(*c*) Angry that your boss hasn't noticed how overworked you are.
(*d*) Depressed and sure that you can never finish it all.

19. If I am scheduled to meet a loved one at a certain time and that person is late, I get worried and eventually start to panic:
(*a*) Frequently (*b*) Sometimes
(*c*) Rarely (*d*) Never

20. Others do not want to spend time with me in public because my behaviour embarrasses them.
(*a*) Frequently (*b*) Sometimes
(*c*) Rarely (*d*) Never

21. I prevent being in situations where I need to show compassion and affection because I feel uncomfortable comforting others.
(*a*) Frequently (*b*) Sometimes
(*c*) Rarely (*d*) Never

22. When I am angry, I do not care about what I say or do and end up saying and doing things I regret later and need to apologize for.
(*a*) Frequently (*b*) Sometimes
(*c*) Rarely (*d*) Never

23. I feel frequently depressed and unhappy without really knowing why.
(*a*) Frequently (*b*) Sometimes
(*c*) Rarely (*d*) Never

24. If others point out my mistakes or give me negative feedback about myself, I feel ashamed, embarrassed and then become offensive and angry.
(*a*) Frequently (*b*) Sometimes
(*c*) Rarely (*d*) Never

25. Crying makes me feel better so I frequently cry when I am angry, ashamed, or embarrassed.
(*a*) Frequently (*b*) Sometimes
(*c*) Rarely (*d*) Never

ANSWERS

1	2	3	4	5	6	7	8	9	10
(*b*)	(*b*)	(*a*)	(*b*)	(*d*)	(*d*)	(*c*)	(*d*)	(*a*)	(*b*)
11	**12**	**13**	**14**	**15**	**16**	**17**	**18**	**19**	**20**
(*a*)	(*a*)	(*a*)	(*a*)	(*d*)	(*a*)	(*a*)	(*a*)	(*c*)	(*d*)
21	**22**	**23**	**24**	**25**					
(*d*)	(*d*)	(*d*)	(*d*)	(*d*)					

CHAPTER 19

Social Intelligence

Questions on social intelligence are asked to assess the common sense of the candidate in various social situations.

MULTIPLE CHOICE QUESTIONS

Directions : *Each of the following questions is followed by four alternatives. Select the most appropriate answer.*

1. In the examination hall, you find that your question paper is too tough to be answered satisfactorily by you. The best thing you can do is:
(*a*) try cheating from your neighbouring candidate.
(*b*) leave the paper and walk out.
(*c*) try attempting those questions first of which you know something.
(*d*) complain to the examiner about the toughness of the question paper.

2. Your best friend is annoyed with you for certain reasons. You will :
(*a*) try your best to reason out your friend's annoyance.
(*b*) go out and make new friends.
(*c*) show indifference.
(*d*) remind the friend of your good friendship.

3. You were invited to a party, but on the day of the party you are informed that the party has been cancelled. You will :
(*a*) try to find out the reason for its cancellation.
(*b*) decide that you will never go to that place ever again.
(*c*) not discuss the matter with anyone.
(*d*) hold the party at your place instead.

4. You find that the cooking gas cylinder is leaking. The first thing you would do is :
(*a*) switch off the light.
(*b*) close the knob of the cylinder.
(*c*) call the fire brigade for help.
(*d*) alert all the members at home.

5. While returning home from a far away place you find that your pocket has been picked. You will :
(*a*) try to hitch-hike to home.
(*b*) hire a taxi and pay on reaching home.
(*c*) go to the nearest police station and lodge an FIR.
(*d*) call home and ask someone to pick you from the place you made the phone call.

6. Your friend has not invited you to his marriage party, you will :
(*a*) ignore the whole affair.
(*b*) send him your best wishes.
(*c*) attend the ceremony.
(*d*) hold it against him.

7. You are interviewed for a new job. Which of the following questions is most important to you?
(*a*) Remuneration you will be paid.
(*b*) Opportunities for promotion.
(*c*) Scope to develop your ideas and use them to improve the working of the organisation.
(*d*) All the above are equally important.

8. You are walking down the street and suddenly you see two hundred-rupee notes on the pavement. What action will you take?
(*a*) Give the money to beggar.
(*b*) Pocket it yourself.
(*c*) Deposit it in the nearest police station.
(*d*) Leave it as it is.

ANSWERS

1	2	3	4	5	6	7	8
(*c*)	(*a*)	(*a*)	(*b*)	(*b*)	(*b*)	(*d*)	(*c*)

INDEXING ADDRESS MATCHING

Directions : *In each question below a combination of name and address is given in the first column at the left, followed by four such combinations, one each under the columns (a), (b), (c) and (d). You have to find out the combination which is exactly the same as the combination in the first column. The number of that column which contains that combination is the answer. If all the combinations are different, the answer is '(e)'.*

1. Triveni Atma
Opp Lal Banglow
Varanasi -221002

(*a*) Triveni Atma
Opp Lal Bangalow
Varanasi -221002

(*b*) Triveni Atma
Opp Lal Banglow
Varanasi -220012

(*c*) Triveni Atma
Opp Lal Banglow
Varanasi -221002

(*d*) Triveni Athma
Opp La! Banglow
Varanasi -221002

2. Tara Lal Appa
Javagal street
Calicat 673005

(*a*) Tara Lal Appa
Javagal Street
Calicat 673005

(*b*) Tara Lal Appa
Javagal street
Calicut 673005

(*c*) Tara Lal Appa
Javagal street
Calicat 670035

(*d*) Tara Lal Appa
Javagal streat
Calicat 673005

3. Iqbal Rehman
Bhandri Gali
Post Box No -3097

(*a*) Iqbal Rehman
Bhandri Ghali
Post Box No -3097

(*b*) Iqbal Rehman
Bhandri Gali
Post Box No -3097

(*c*) Iqbal Rehman
Bhandri Gali
Post Box no -3097

(*d*) Iqbal Rahman
Bhandri Gali
Post Box No -3097

4. Jaganpa Shinde
Christ phot co.
Tel no -27363

(*a*) Jaganpa Shinde
Christ photo co.
Tel no -27363

(*b*) Jaganpa Shinde
Christ phot co.
Tel no -27363

(*c*) Jaganpa Shinde
Christ phot co.
Tel no -273633

(*d*) Jaganna Shinde
Christ phot co.
Tel no -27363

5. N.R. Savitri
Giri Girls hostal
Anapuram-167951

(*a*) N.R. Savitri
Giri Girls hostal
Anapuram-167951

(*b*) N.R. Savitri
Giri Girls hostel
Anapuram-167951

(*c*) N.R. Savitri
Giri Girls hostal
Anapuram-167851

(*d*) N.R. Savithri
Giri Girls hostal
Anapuram-167951

6. Madam Brulopher
Jung villa
Banjaram Hills

(*a*) Madam Bruloper
Jung vilia
Banjaram Hills

(*b*) Madam Brulopher
Jung villa
Banjaram Hill

(*c*) Madam Brulopher
Jung Villa
Banjaram Hills

(*d*) Madam Brulopher
Jung villa
Banjaram Hills

7. Samartha sen
C 20/05 Guftga Bldg
B. No. - 1631

(*a*) Samartha sen
C 20/05 Guftga Blg
B. No. - 1631

(*b*) Samartha sen
C 200 Guftga Bldg
B. No. - 1631

(*c*) Samartha sen
C 20/05 Guftga Bldg
B. No. - 1631

(*d*) Samartha sen
C 20/05 Guflga Bldg
B. No. - 1631

8. Phiroz Gherabl
Harmit palace
Samaita nagar

(*a*) Phiroz Gerabi
Harmit palace
Samaita nagar

(*b*) Phiroz Gerabl
Harmit place
Samaita nagar

(*c*) Phiroz Gerabl
Harmit palace
Samaita nager

(*d*) Phiroz Gherabl
Harmit palace
Samaita nagar

9. Nitu gajadhar
Shersing Haveli
Jaipur -302006

(*a*) Nitu gajadhar
Shersing Haveli
Jaipur -302006

(*b*) Nitu gajadar
Shersing Haveli
Jaipur -302006

(*c*) Nitu gajadhar
Shersing Haveli
Jaipur -303006

(*d*) Nitu Gajadhar
Shersing Haveli
Jaipur -302006

ANSWERS

1	2	3	4	5	6	7	8	9
(*c*)	(*a*)	(*b*)	(*b*)	(*a*)	(*d*)	(*c*)	(*d*)	(*a*)

CHAPTER 20

Venn Diagrams

In these type of questions diagrammatic representation presents a logical illustration of particular class or statements based on which the questions are asked. A clear view of the diagram makes the concept clear for attempting such questions.

SOLVED EXAMPLE

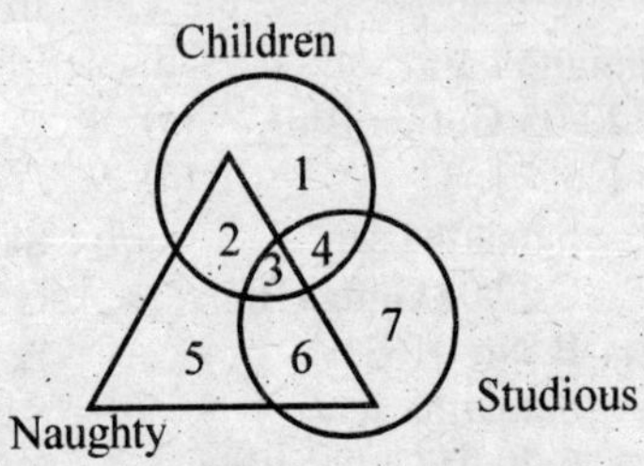

Study the above diagram and specify the region representing children who are naughty as well as studious.

(*a*) 3 and 6 (*b*) 2 and 4
(*c*) only 3 (*d*) only 4

Ans. (*c*) : The explanation depicting children who are naughty as well as studious will be :

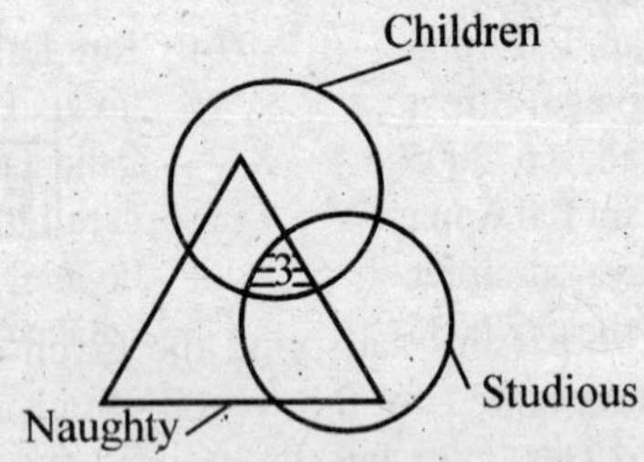

It is now clear that only region 3 represents all the three classes.

MULTIPLE CHOICE QUESTIONS

Directions (Qs. 1–3) : *In the following diagram, there are three figures interlocking each other – a rectangle, a square and a triangle. Each figure represents the class mentioned against it.*

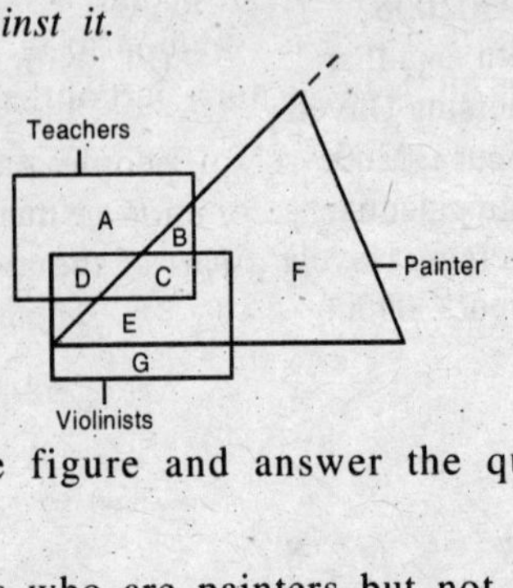

Study the figure and answer the questions that follows.

1. Teachers who are painters but not violinists are represented by

(*a*) B (*b*) C
(*c*) D (*d*) F

2. The region which represents painters and violinists but not teachers, is denoted by

(*a*) B (*b*) D
(*c*) E (*d*) F

3. Which letter represents teachers who are painters as well as violinists?

(*a*) B (*b*) C
(*c*) D (*d*) E

Directions (Qs. 4–6) : *In the figure given below, there are three interesting circles each representing certain section of people. Different regions are marked a-g. Read the statements in each of the following questions and choose the letter of the region which correctly represents the statements?*

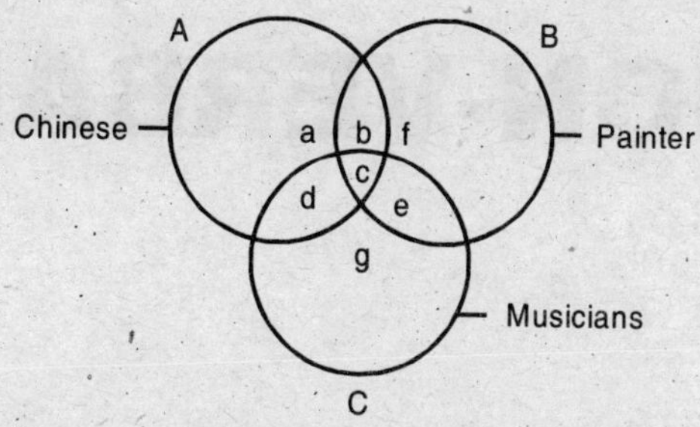

4. Chinese who are painters but not musicians?
(*a*) b (*b*) c
(*c*) d (*d*) g

5. Chinese who are musicians but not painters.
(*a*) d (*b*) c
(*c*) b (*d*) a

6. Painters who are neither Chinese nor musicians.
(*a*) b (*b*) c
(*c*) f (*d*) g

Directions (Qs. 7–10) : *In the following figure, the circle stands for employed, the square stands for hard-working, the triangle stands for rural and the rectangle stands for intelligent. Study the figure carefully and answer the questions that follow.*

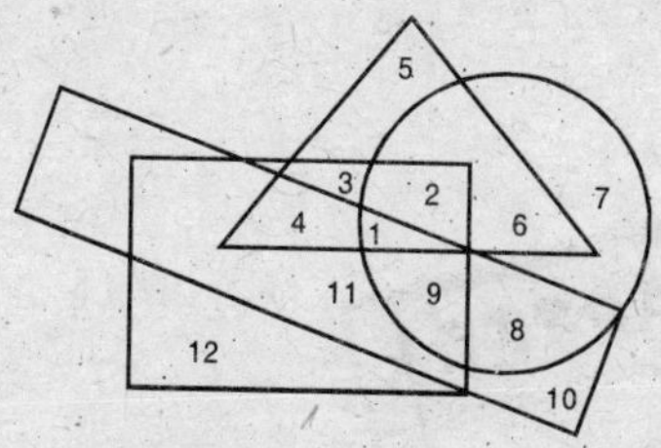

7. Rural employed people who are neither intelligent nor hard-working are indicated by region.
(*a*) 10 (*b*) 9
(*c*) 6 (*d*) 4

8. Unemployed rural hard-working and intelligent people are indicated by region.
(*a*) 1 (*b*) 2
(*c*) 3 (*d*) 4

9. Rural people who are hard-working and employed but not intelligent are indicated by region.
(*a*) 1 (*b*) 2
(*c*) 3 (*d*) 4

10. Rural employed people who are neither intelligent nor hard-working are indicated by region.
(*a*) 2 (*b*) 4
(*c*) 6 (*d*) 9

EXPLANATORY ANSWERS

1. (*a*) : The persons satisfying the given conditions are represented by the region which is common to the rectangle and the triangle but not the square *i.e.*, B.

2. (*c*) : The persons satisfying the given conditions are represented by the region which is common to the triangle and the square but is not a part of the rectangle *i.e.*, E.

3. (*b*) : The required set of persons is represented by the letter denoting the region common to the rectangle, triangle and the square *i.e.*, C.

4. (*a*) : The required region is the one which is common to the circles A and B and lies outside circle C *i.e.*, b.

5. (*a*) : The required region is the one which is common to the circles A and C but is not a part of circle B *i.e.*, d.

6. (*c*) : The required region is the one which lies inside the circle B but is not a part of either circle A or circle C *i.e.*, f.

7. (*c*) : The required set of people is represented by the region which is common to the triangle and circle but is not a part of either the rectangle or the square *i.e.*, 6.

8. (*d*) : The required set of people is represented by the region which lies outside the circle and is common to the triangle, square and rectangle *i.e.*, 4.

9. (*b*) : The required set of people is represented by the region which is common to the triangle, square and circle but is not a part of the rectangle *i.e.*, 2.

10. (*c*) : The required set of people is denoted by the region which is common to the triangle and the circle but is not a part of the rectangle *i.e.*, 2.

NON-VERBAL

CHAPTER 1

Series/Figural Series

MISSING SERIES

This form of series is almost identical to the one mentioned earlier. Here too are given two sets of figures, the Problem Figures and the Answer Figures. The problem figures follow a particular pattern of movement which constitute the series. The only difference from the earlier mentioned set of series is that instead of depicting the last figure that continues the pattern here one of the middle figures needs to be depicted from-the answer figures. This type needs a little more concentration and brain work as the continuity is broken and has to be set right. Understand the set up of elements, pattern and figures in each set and try different styles and rules to find the answer.

MULTIPLE CHOICE QUESTIONS

Directions : *In each of these questions, there are two sets of figures. The figures placed first are Problem Figures, and those follows are Answer Figures indicated by the letters (a), (b), (c), (d) and (e). A series is established if one of the five Answer Figures is placed at the question-marked space. Figures form a series if they change from left to right according to some specific rule. The letter of the Answer Figure which should be placed in the question-marked space is the answer. All the figures, i.e. three Problem Figures and one Answer Figure placed in the question-marked space should be considered as forming the series.*

1. Problem Figures

Answer Figures

(a) (b) (c) (d) (e)

2. Problem Figures

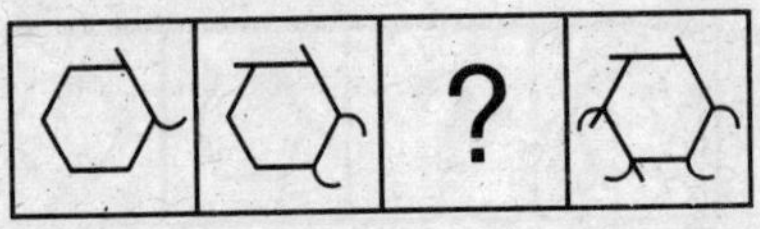

Answer Figures

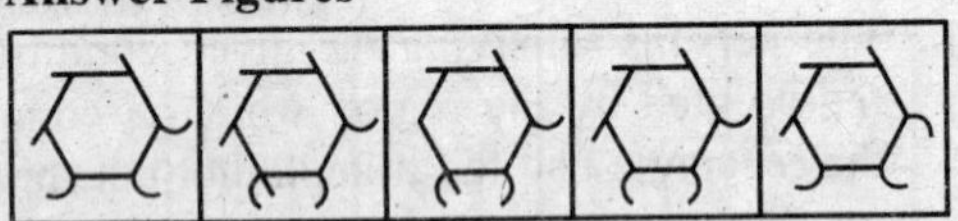

(a) (b) (c) (d) (e)

3. Problem Figures

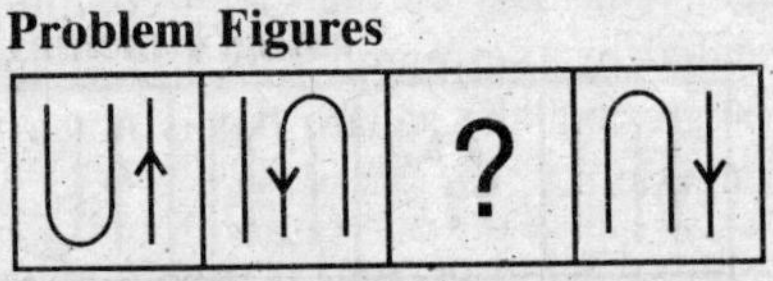

Answer Figures

(a) (b) (c) (d) (e)

4. Problem Figures

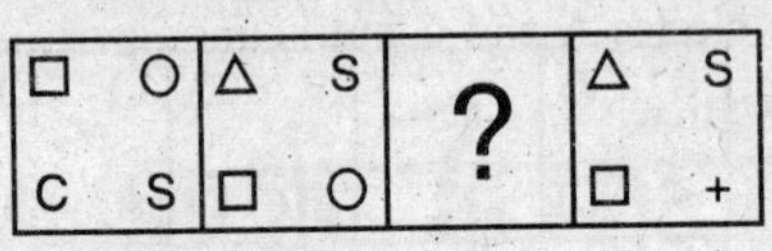

Answer Figures

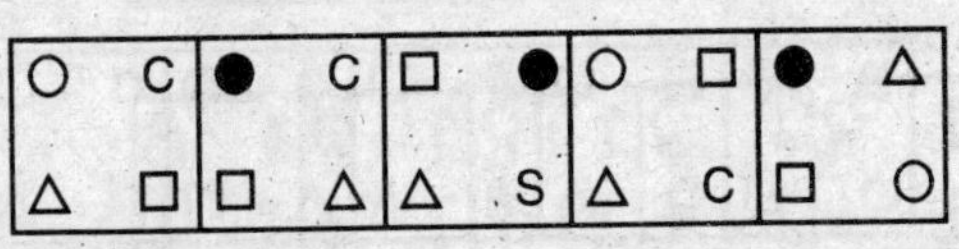

(a) (b) (c) (d) (e)

5. Problem Figures

Answer Figures

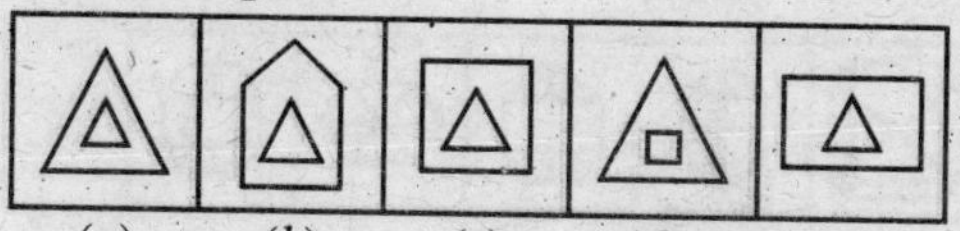

(*a*) (*b*) (*c*) (*d*) (*e*)

6. Problem Figures

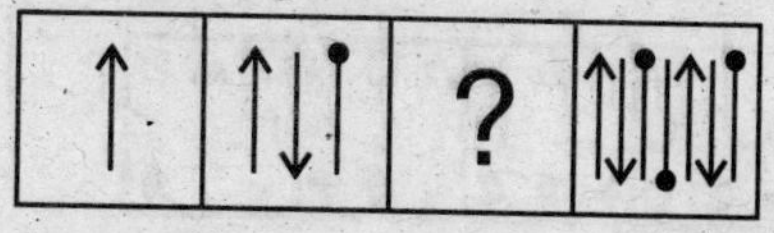

Answer Figures

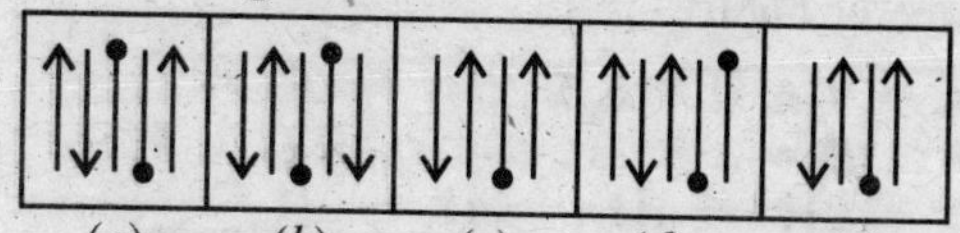

(*a*) (*b*) (*c*) (*d*) (*e*)

EXPLANATORY ANSWERS

1. (*c*) : From first problem figure to the second the elements on the top are shifted down and vice versa. In fourth problem figure there are three elements which, as per rule, are also shifted. So, in question marked space only option '(*c*)' can be considered as forming the series.

2. (*d*) : Anticlockwise one of the sides of the hexagon is extended and clockwise one arc is added. The direction of the arc is changed at each step. Answer figure 'D' is the right answer.

3. (*e*) : Both the elements are turned upside down, their places interchanged and the arrow head moved left from one element to the other. In the question marked space the 'U' shape and the arrowhead should be facing upwards, the line segment should be on the right and the arrowhead should be on the extreme left. To continue the series the next figure has the 'U' shape and the arrowhead facing downwards, the line segment on the right and the arrowhead on the extreme right. Option '(*e*)' fits into the question marked space.

4. (*c*) : At each step the places of two elements on the horizontal are interchanged and clockwise one element is made new. Option '(*c*)' fits in the pattern to complete the series.

5. (*b*) : At each step the enclosed figure is enlarged in the next and a new figure is placed inside the enlarged figure. Option '(*b*)' fits into the question marked space.

6. (*a*) : The arrow and the line with the dot are increased in a set pattern in opposite directions. The series they form is two arrows and two lines with the dot which is repeated. Answer figure '(*a*)' is the right choice.

FIGURAL SERIES

In this form of non-verbal series, which are the most common, four or five consecutive problem figures form a definite sequence and one is required to select the one figure from the given set of Answer Figures that will continue the same sequence.

One has to try different set of moves, changes, replacements, rotations, repetitions and a lot more variations to arrive at the logical pattern making the series. Practising alone will sharpen one's skill of solving such sequences.

MULTIPLE CHOICE QUESTIONS

Directions : *In each of the following questions which one of the five answer figures given below should come after the problem figures if the sequence are continued?*

1. Problem Figures

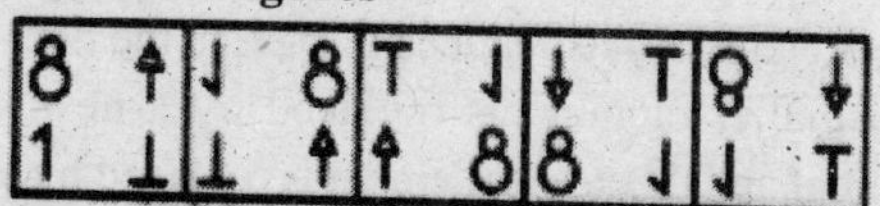

Answer Figures

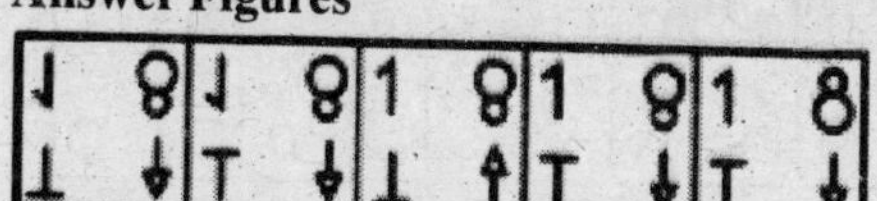

(*a*) (*b*) (*c*) (*d*) (*e*)

2. Problem Figures

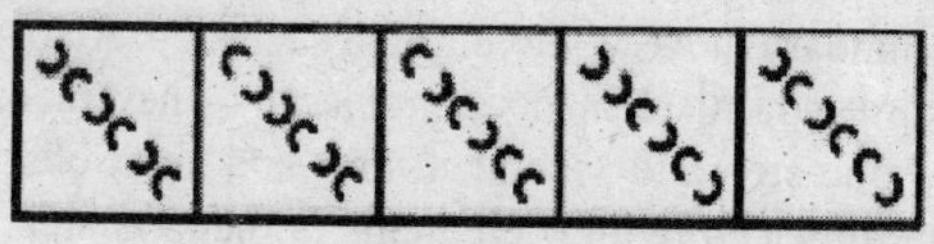

Answer Figures

(*a*) (*b*) (*c*) (*d*) (*e*)

3. Problem Figures

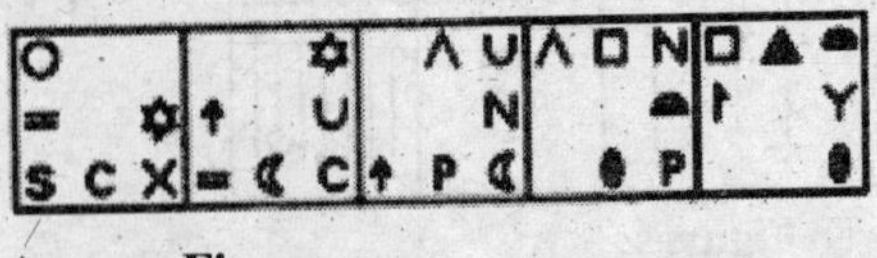

Answer Figures

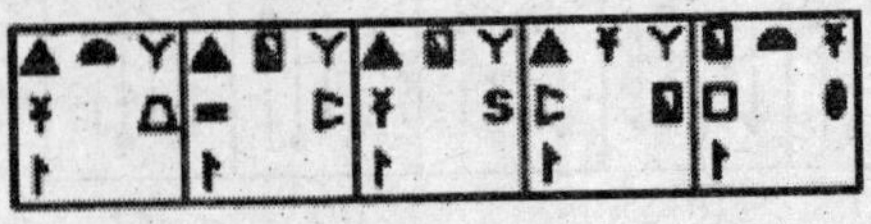

(a) (b) (c) (d) (e)

4. Problem Figures

Answer Figures

(a) (b) (c) (d) (e)

5. Problem Figures

Answer Figures

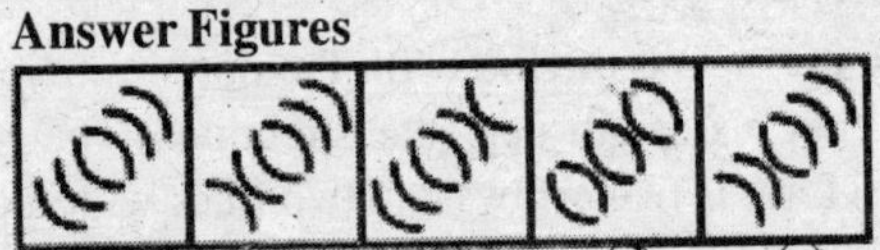

(a) (b) (c) (d) (e)

6. Problem Figures

Answer Figures

(a) (b) (c) (d) (e)

7. Problem Figures

Answer Figures

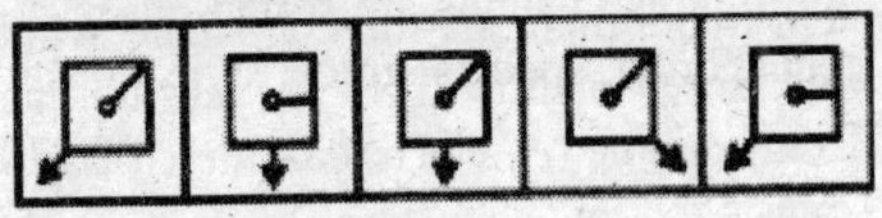

(a) (b) (c) (d) (e)

8. Problem Figures

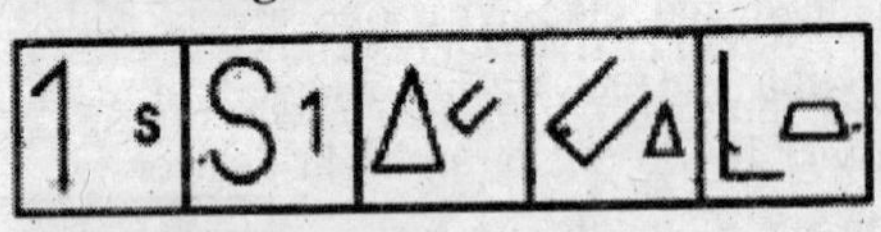

Answer Figures

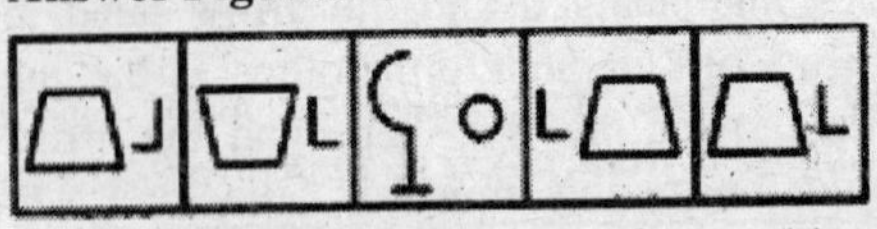

(a) (b) (c) (d) (e)

EXPLANATORY ANSWERS

1. (*d*) : In each step, all the elements move to the adjacent corner (of the square boundary) in a CW direction and the element that reaches the upper-left corner gets vertically inverted.

2. (*c*) : We can label the arcs as shown . The arcs get inverted in the sequence (1 & 2), (3, 4 & 5), (6 & 1), (2, 3 & 4), (5 & 6), ...

3. (*d*) : All the elements move half-a-side of the square boundary in ACW direction in each step. Also, first, third and fifth elements are replaced by new elements in one step and second, fourth and sixth elements are replaced by new elements in the next step. The two steps are repeated alternately.

4. (*a*) : In each step, the dot moves one space CW and the arrow moves two spaces CW.

5. (*c*) : One arc and four arcs get inverted alternately.

6. (*e*) : The number of parts increases by one along with the number of sides in the figure.

7. (*c*) : The pin rotates 45°CW and 90°CW alternately and moves one space (each space is equal to half-a-side of the square) and two spaces CW alternately. The arrow rotates 90°ACW and 45°ACW alternately and moves two spaces and one space.

8. (*e*) : In one step, the two elements interchange positions and the smaller element gets enlarged while the larger element gets reduced in size. In the next step, the smaller element is replaced by a new small element and the larger element is replaced by a new large element.

CHAPTER 2

Semantic Classification

Classification means arranging the given content in groups or classes having qualities of same kind. In classification type questions, the figures or items are sorted out in groups on the basis of their similarities in qualities in shapes, size, pattern, structure, genus, order, species, grade, style, constituents and other specifications, and thus the answer is found out.

TYPE-I

Classification of this type does not have two sets of figures known as Problem Figures and Answer Figures; instead they have only one set of four or five figures known as Problem Figures. One of these Problem Figures is not like the other four figures. In other words, three or four of the Answer Figures belong to a class while one which is the odd figures, does not belong to it.

MULTIPLE CHOICE QUESTIONS

Directions : *In each of the following questions one of the figures is different from the rest. Spot the figure.*

1. 

(a) (b) (c) (d) (e)

2. 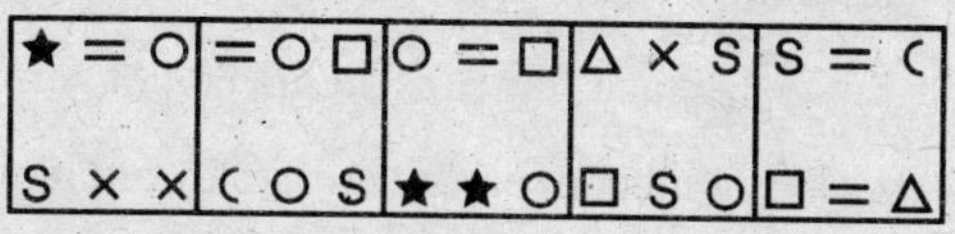

(a) (b) (c) (d) (e)

3. 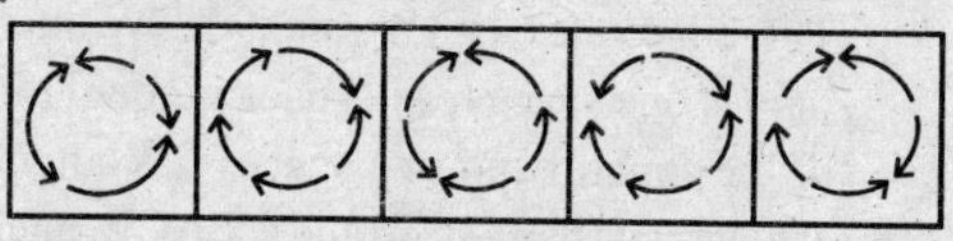

(a) (b) (c) (d) (e)

4. 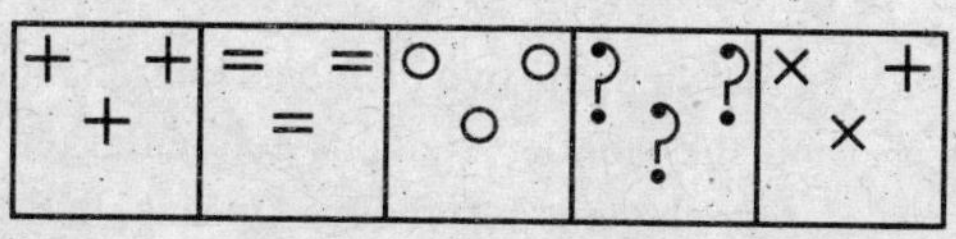

(a) (b) (c) (d) (e)

5. 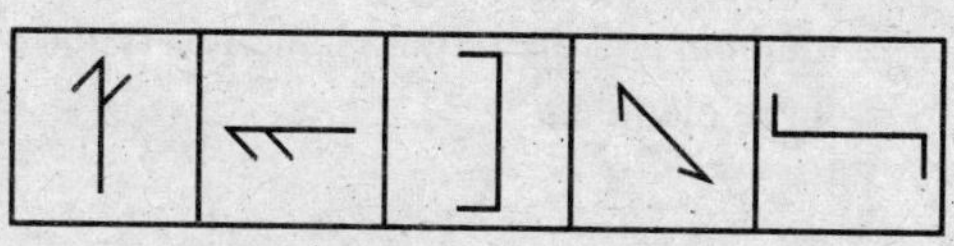

(a) (b) (c) (d) (e)

6. 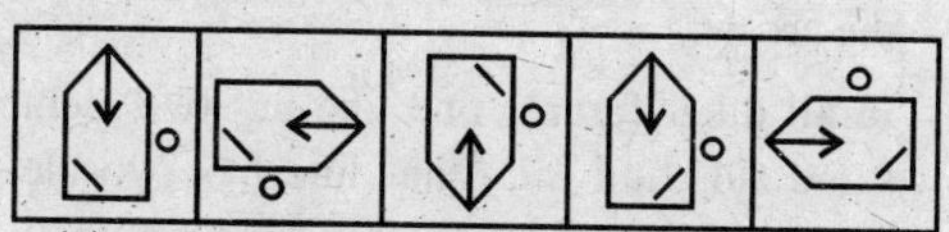

(a) (b) (c) (d) (e)

7. 

(a) (b) (c) (d) (e)

8. 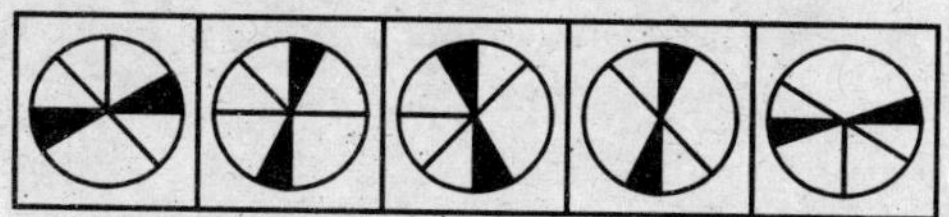

(a) (b) (c) (d) (e)

9. 

(a) (b) (c) (d) (e)

10. 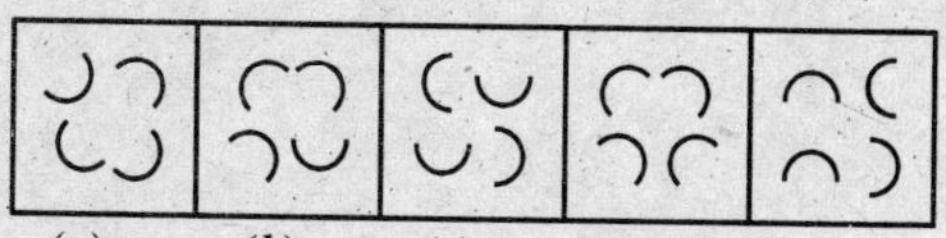

(a) (b) (c) (d) (e)

11. 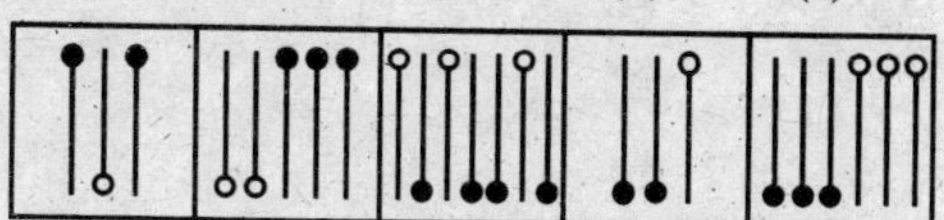

(a) (b) (c) (d) (e)

12. 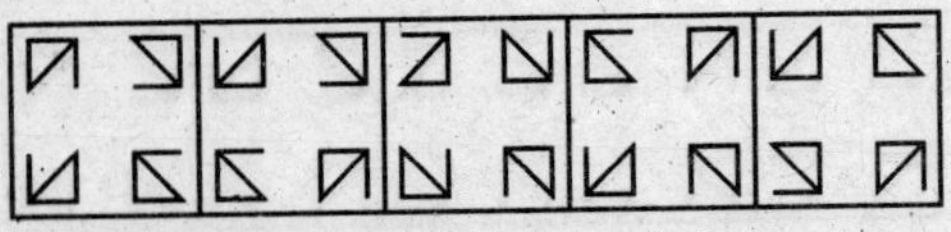

(a) (b) (c) (d) (e)

13. 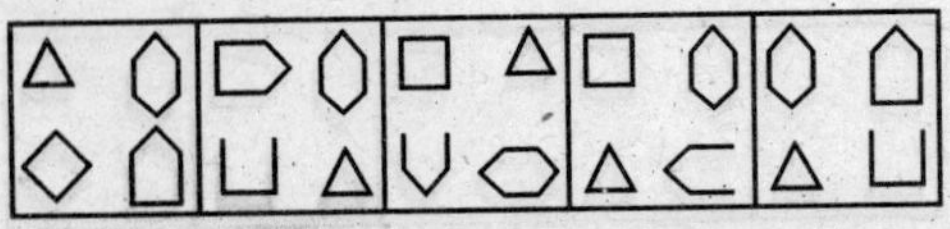

(a) (b) (c) (d) (e)

14. 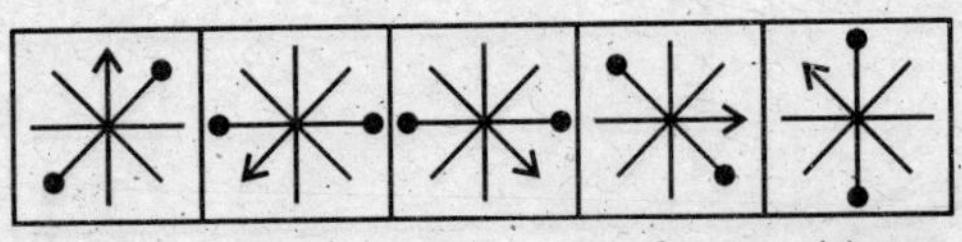

(a) (b) (c) (d) (e)

15. 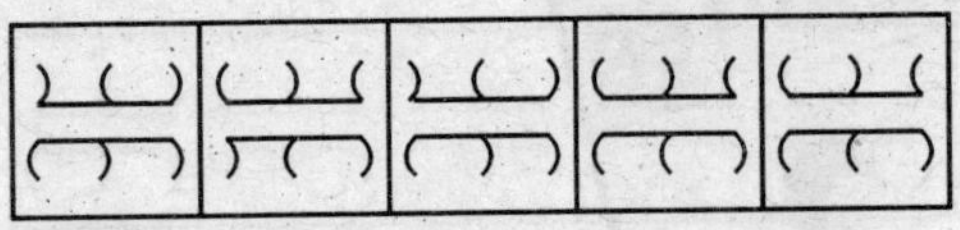

(a) (b) (c) (d) (e)

EXPLANATORY ANSWERS

1. (*d*) : Only in this figure all the lines making the hands and legs of the human shape are drawn downwards.

2. (*c*) : In all other figures only one set of elements is identical.

3. (*b*) : Only in this figure four arrows are pointing in same direction, and one arrow in its opposite direction. In other figures three arrows are in same direction and two in the opposite direction.

4. (*e*) : All other figures have three identical elements.

5. (*d*) : In all other figures two lines are parallelly drawn.

6. (*c*) : In all other figures the circle is on the left side of the arrow.

7. (*c*) : In all other figures one line has two elements on same side and the other line has two ele-ments, one on either side. In this figure both the lines have two elements on same side.

8. (*d*) : Only in this figure one of the three sections in between the shaded sections is not marked.

9. (*e*) : In all other figures the elements inside as well as outside the hexagon are placed at equal distance. In this figure the outside element at the top is wrongly placed (It should be near the other corner of the same line).

10. (*d*) : In all other figures two elements are in same direction and the other two elements are opposite to each other.

11. (*e*) : Only in this figure the two types of elements are equal in number.

12. (*c*) : In all other figures the diagonal line in all other elements is drawn from the right end.

13. (*a*) : In all other figures one of the four elements has one open side.

14. (*c*) : In all other figures the arrow is to the left of the dot.

15. (*b*) : In all other figures two of the three curves on one of the lines are in the same direction and are adjacent.

CHAPTER 3

Figural Analogy

Figural Analogy is a process of reasoning between two parallel cases. It relates to agreement or correspondence in certain respects between two things. It is a process whereby the underlying relationship that exists between two figures, designs or patterns is determined. Under the process, one has to discover the features common to the two figures or designs. This common feature is a model or base. The question seeks solution on the basis of this model or base.

In non-verbal analogy questions, there are two sets of figures which are known as *(i)* Problem Figures, and *(ii)* Answer Figures. The Problem Figures are divided into two parts. The Answer Figures are given below the Problem Figures.

MULTIPLE CHOICE QUESTIONS

Directions : *The second figure in the first unit of the Problem Figures bears a certain relationship to the first figure. Similarly, one of the figures in the Answer Figures bears the same relationship to the first figure in the second unit of the Problem Figures. Locate the figure which would fit the question mark.*

1. Problem Figures

Answers Figures

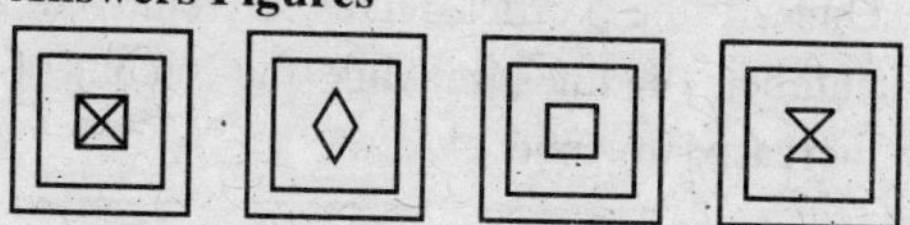

(a) *(b)* *(c)* *(d)*

2. Problem Figures

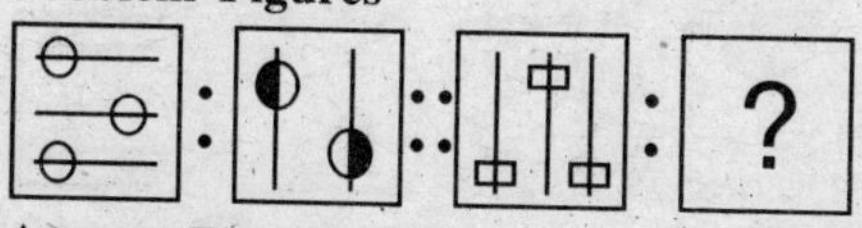

Answer Figures

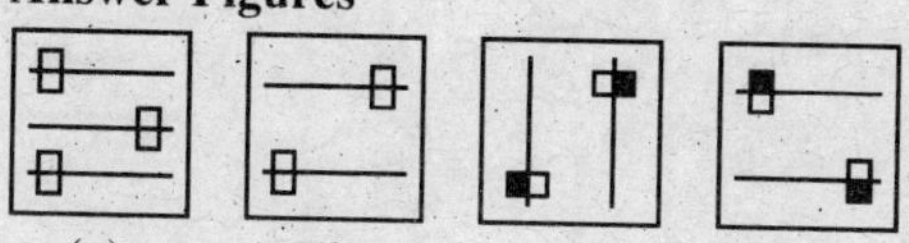

(a) *(b)* *(c)* *(d)*

3. Problem Figures

Answer Figures

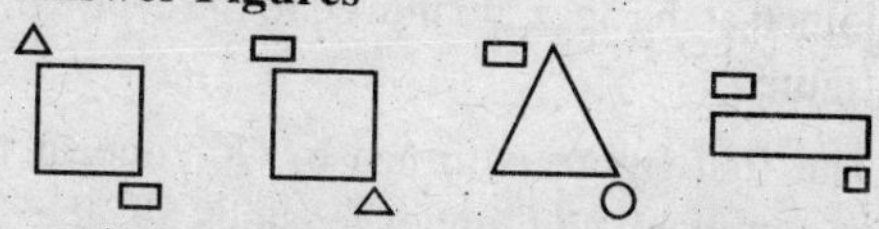

(a) *(b)* *(c)* *(d)*

4. Problem Figures

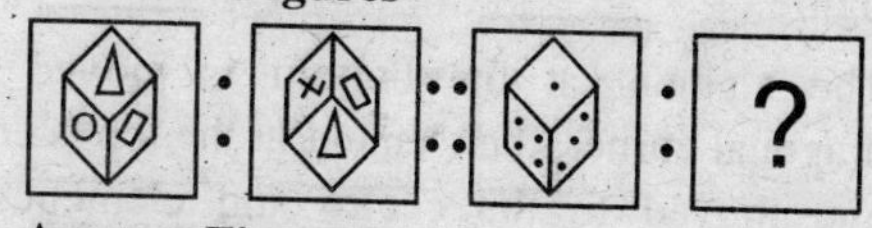

Answer Figures

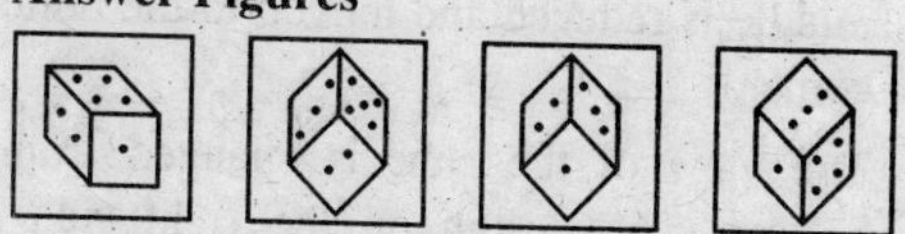

(a) *(b)* *(c)* *(d)*

5. Problem Figures

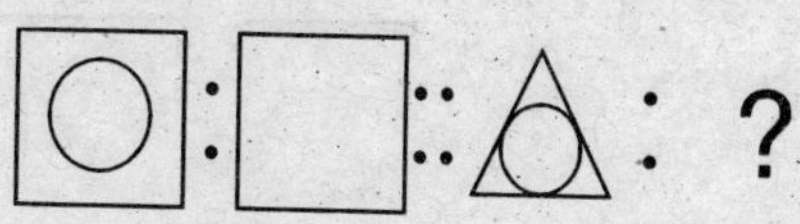

Answer Figures

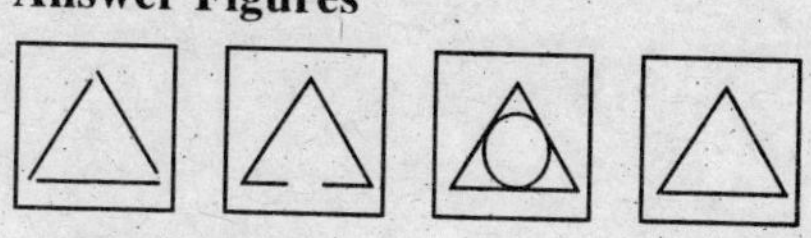

(a) *(b)* *(c)* *(d)*

6. Problem Figures

Answer Figures

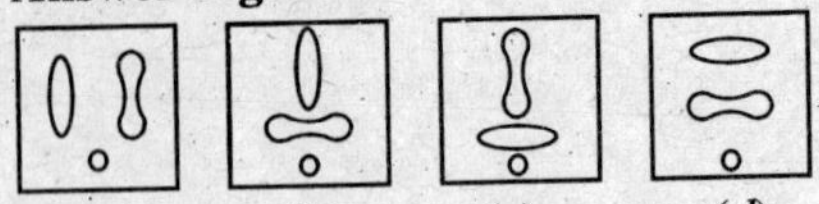

(a) (b) (c) (d)

7. Problem Figures

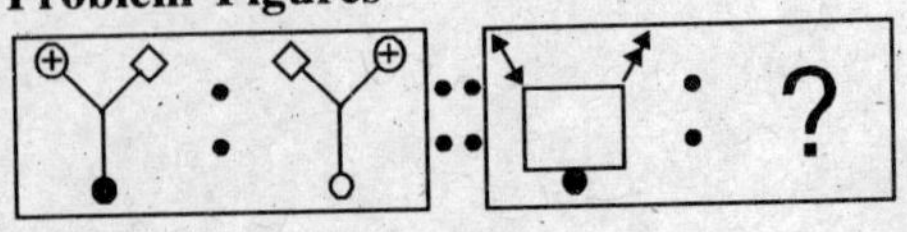

Answer Figures

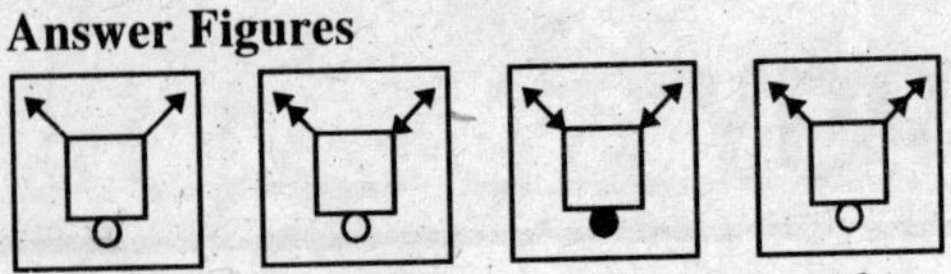

(a) (b) (c) (d)

8. Problem Figures

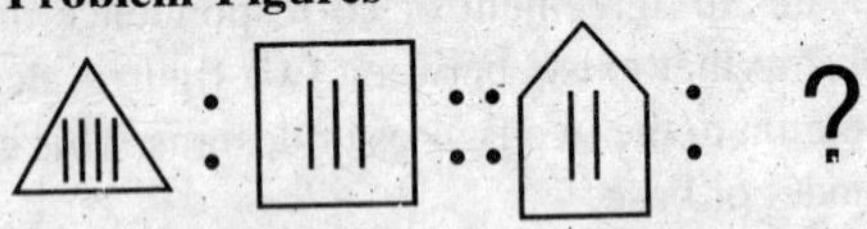

Answer Figures

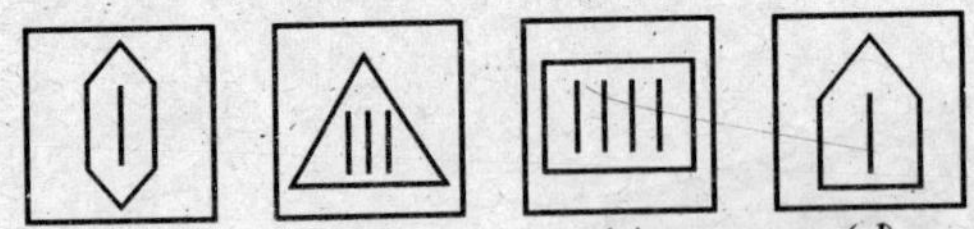

(a) (b) (c) (d)

9. Problem Figures

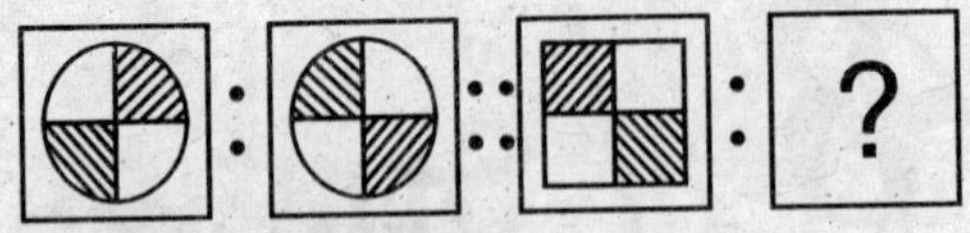

Answer Figures

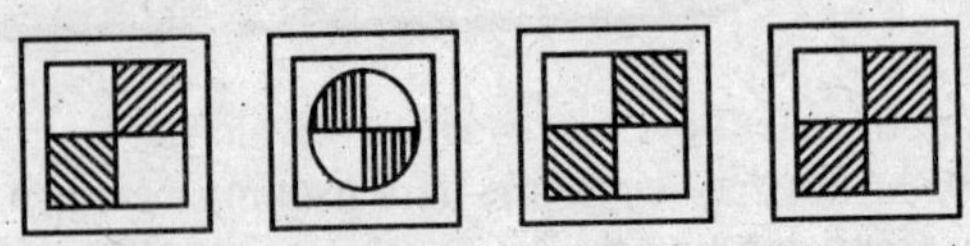

(a) (b) (c) (d)

EXPLANATORY ANSWERS

1. (*d*) : The triangle in the first figure is moved to the centre of the second figure. Similarly, the two triangles joined at the apex are moved to the centre in answer figure.

2. (*d*) : The first figure is turned by 90° one of the bars is removed and opposite sides of the element attached to the bar are shaded to get the second figure.

3. (*a*) : The element at the bottom is moved to the diagonal corner, the element in the top is enlarged and moved to the centre and element in the middle is reduced and moved to the bottom right corner.

4. (*c*) : The view of the cube is changed from top to bottom. The design on the right side remains unchanged while the design on the left side is changed.

5. (*d*) : The inner shape in the first figure is removed to get the second figure.

6. (*b*) : The two half shapes placed vertically are turned upside down and joined, and this new shape is moved to the top. The two curved shapes placed horizontally are joined and this new shape is moved to the centre. One of the two remaining corner shapes is moved to the bottom.

7. (*b*) : The places of elements on the top are interchanged and the shade inside the circle is removed.

8. (*a*) : One of the vertical lines is removed and the number of lines making the second figure is increased by one.

9. (*a*) : First figure is rotated 90° anticlockwise to get the second figure.

CHAPTER 4

Spatial Visualization

In such questions, cut-out pieces are given alongwith the whole figure, that is the figure out of which the figures have been cut. By looking at the cut-out figures one has to find out the figure which may be constituted by putting the pieces together, i.e., one has to find out the figure of which the pieces have been cut. One has to be very imaginative and has to use space perception in finding out the solution. The whole process is mental and requires special skill in visualising different spatial patterns. It is not easy to develop this skill overnight but it can certainly be cultivated by practice and the method of trial and error.

MULTIPLE CHOICE QUESTIONS

Directions (Qs. 1-5) : *Which one figure can be made out of given paper cut-outs?*

1. 

(a) (b) (c) (d)

2. 

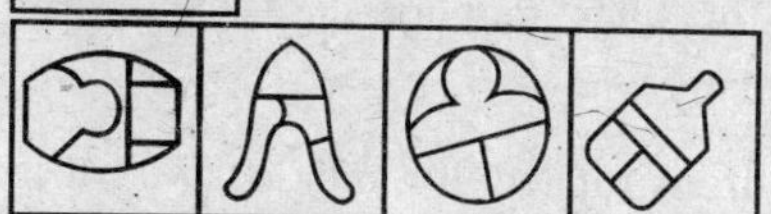

(a) (b) (c) (d)

3. 

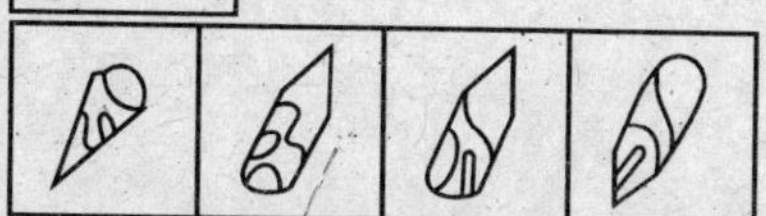

(a) (b) (c) (d)

4. 

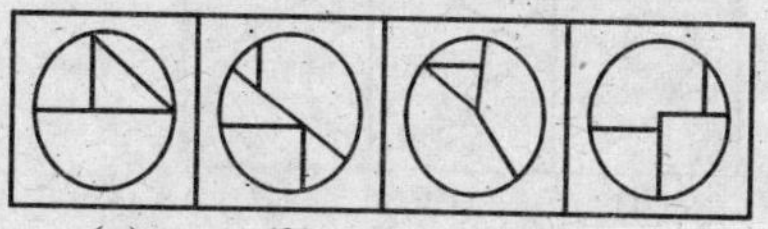

(a) (b) (c) (d)

5. 

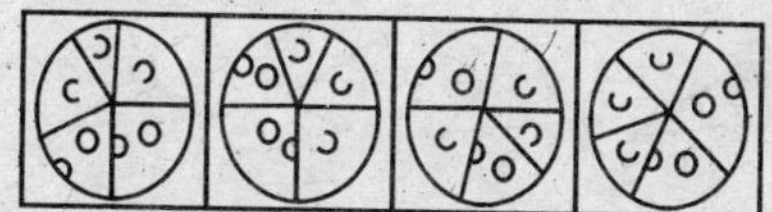

(a) (b) (c) (d)

Direction (Qs. 6-10) : *In each of the following questions an irregular piece of paper has been cut into two pieces. One piece has been shown on the left while the other piece has been given as one of the four alternatives against it. Find the correct alternative:*

6. 

(a) (b) (c) (d)

7. 

(a) (b) (c) (d)

8. 

(a) (b) (c) (d)

9. 

(a) (b) (c) (d)

10. 

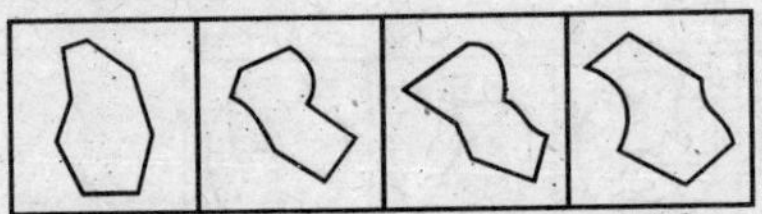

(a) (b) (c) (d)

Directions (Qs. 11-15) : *In each of the following questions five diagrams marked A to E are given. Three of these when put together form an equilateral triangle and have been given as one of the four alternatives under the question. Find the correct alternative in each case.*

11. 

A B C D E

(a) ABE (b) BCE
(c) ADE (d) BDE

12. 

A B C D E

(a) ABC (b) BCD
(c) CDE (d) BDE

13. 

A B C D E

(a) BCD (b) CDE
(c) ABD (d) ABE

14. 

A B C D E

(a) ABD (b) ACD
(c) BDE (d) CDE

15. 

A B C D E

(a) ABC (b) ACE
(c) BDE (d) CDE

Directions (Qs. 16-20) : *In each of the following questions five diagrams A, B, C, D and E have been given. Three of these diagrams make a complete square which have been given as one of the four alternatives under it. Find the correct alternative in each case.*

16. 

A B C D E

(a) ABC (b) BDE
(c) CDE (d) BCD

17. 

A B C D E

(a) ACD (b) BDE
(c) BCE (d) CDE

18. 

A B C D E

(a) ACD (b) BCD
(c) ACE (d) CDE

19. 

A B C D E

(a) ABC (b) ACE
(c) ADE (d) CDE

20. 

A B C D E

(a) BDE (b) ABC
(c) ACD (d) BCD

ANSWERS

1	2	3	4	5	6	7	8	9	10
(b)	(d)	(c)	(a)	(b)	(b)	(c)	(a)	(d)	(c)
11	12	13	14	15	16	17	18	19	20
(c)	(d)	(d)	(b)	(b)	(d)	(b)	(c)	(c)	(d)

CHAPTER 5

Space Visualization

In these type of questions, a template or a layout of a cube, dice or a box is given, which can be folded to produce different patterns. To solve these questions what is required is a clear study of the given layout and the selection of one figure, from the alternative patterns which can be made from the given layout. To attempt such problems understand the unfolded patterns given below:

Layout 1. 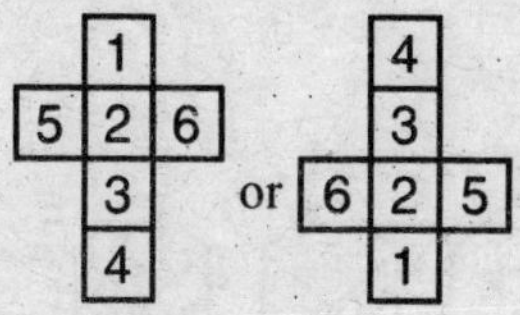

The opposite sides are :
1—3, 2 — 4 and 5 — 6

Layout 2. 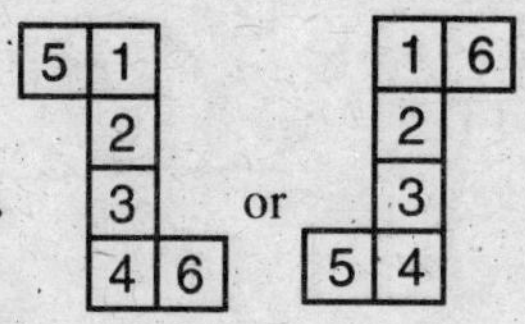

The opposite sides are :
1 — 3, 2 — 4 and 5 — 6

Layout 3. 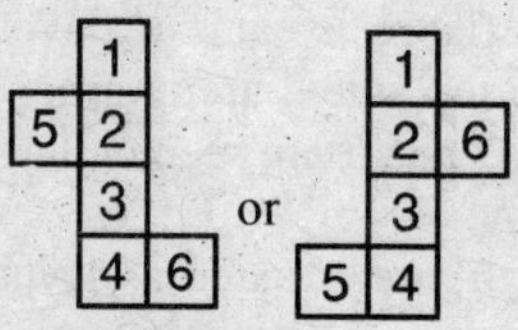

The opposite sides are :
1 — 3, 2 — 4 and 5 — 6.

Layout 4. 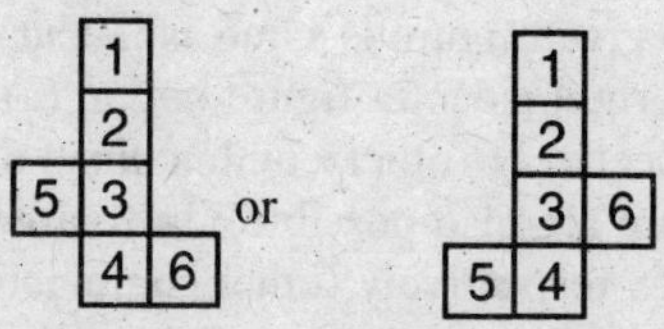

The opposite sides are :
1 — 3, 2 — 4 and 5 — 6

Layout 5. 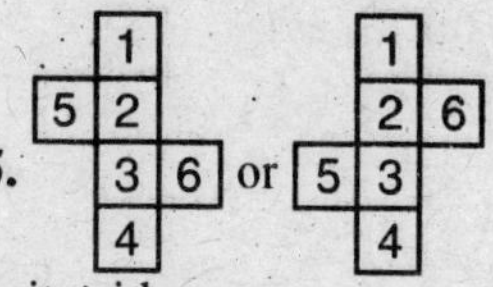

The opposite sides are :
1 — 3, 2 — 4 and 5 — 6

Layout 6. 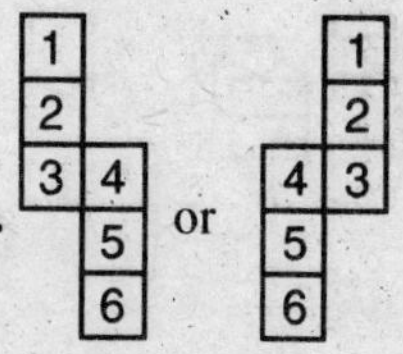

The opposite sides are :
1 — 3, 2 — 5 and 4 — 6

Layout 7. 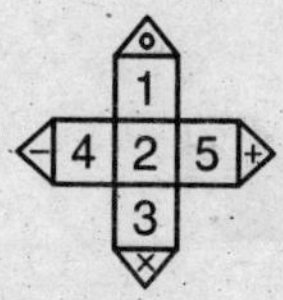

The opposite sides are :

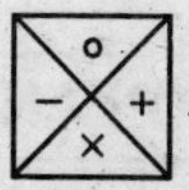 — 2, 1 — 3 and 4 — 5. Here, side 6 is divided into four parts

Layout 8. 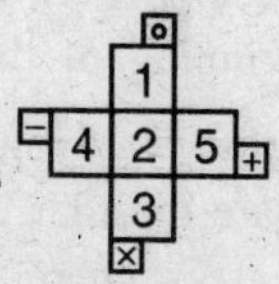

The opposite sides are

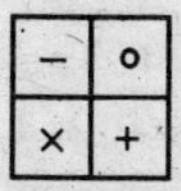 — 2, 1 — 3 and 4 — 5. Here, side 6 is divided into four parts.

Observe from the above layouts that all sides except the opposite side are adjacent sides. Also keep in mind that the three visible sides of the option figures are one of the opposite sides of each opposite pair.

MULTIPLE CHOICE QUESTIONS

Directions : *The figure is folded to produce different box patterns. Study the pattern to know if they can be produced from given figure and select the answer from the alternatives.*

1. 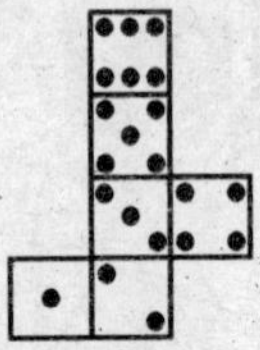

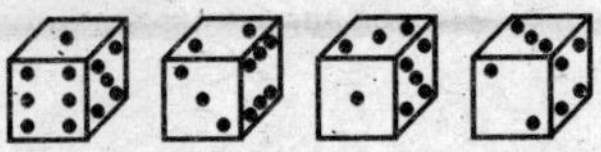

(*a*) (*b*) (*c*) (*d*)

2. 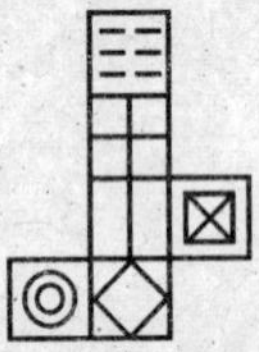

(*a*) (*b*) (*c*) (*d*)

3. 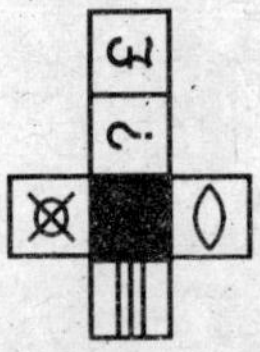

(*a*) (*b*) (*c*) (*d*)

4. 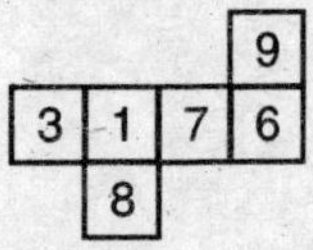

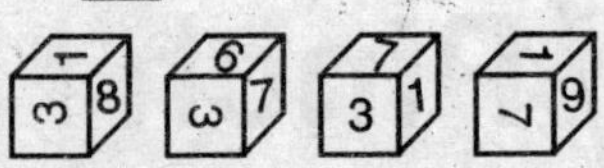

(*a*) (*b*) (*c*) (*d*)

5. 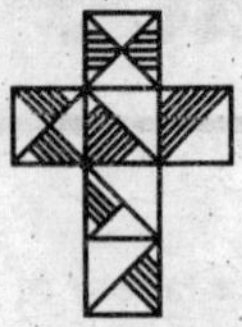

(*a*) (*b*) (*c*) (*d*)

6. 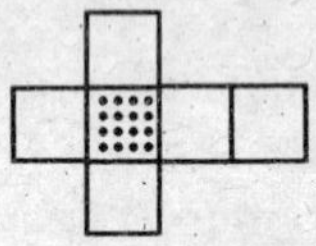

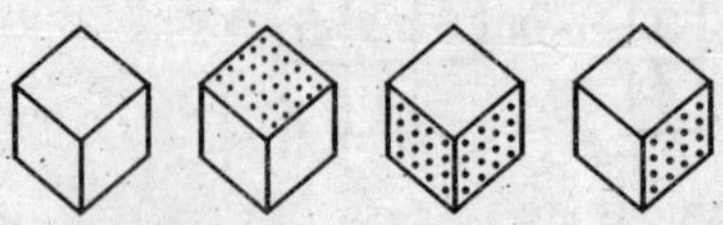

A B C D

(*a*) A, B and D
(*b*) B and D
(*c*) B, C and D
(*d*) A and D

EXPLANATORY ANSWERS

(All answers are based on number pattern of the sides as in the layout given in the beginning of this section)

1. (*d*) : The given figure is same as layout 4. The sides adjacent to top side 3 are in order 2, 5, 4, 6 — of these sides, 4 and 6 are seen on left and right sides respectively.

2. (*b*) : The given figure is same as layout 4. The sides adjacent to top side 5 are in order 4, 3, 2, 1 —of these sides 1 and 4 are seen on left and right sides respectively.

3. (*d*) : The given figure is same as layout 1. The sides adjacent to top side 5 are in order 4, 3, 2, 1 — of these sides 2 and 1 are seen on left and right sides respectively.

4. (*a*) : The given figure is same as layout 3. The sides adjacent to top side 2 are in order 1, 5, 3, 6 — of these sides 1 and 5 are seen on left and right sides respectively.

5. (*c*) : The given figure is same as layout 1. The sides adjacent to top side 6 are in order 1, 2, 3, 4 — of these sides 2 and 3 are seen on left and right sides respectively.

6. (*a*) : The given figure is same as layout 1. The top, left and right sides in figure option (a) are 1, 4 and 5 respectively (other combinations of sides for this figure are also possible); in figure option (b) 2, 1 and 5 respectively (other combination of sides for this figure are also possible; and in figure option (d) 1, 5 and 2 respectively (other combinations of sides for this figure are also possible).

CHAPTER

6 Pinch Hole/Paper Folding & Unfolding

These type of questions are based on a piece of paper which is folded and cut or punched in a particular manner. One of the option figures either resembles the pattern that would be formed when the paper is unfolded or resembles the form in which the paper is folded and cut or punched.

MULTIPLE CHOICE QUESTIONS

Directions (Qs. 1-5) : *In each one of the following problems, a square transparent sheet with a pattern is given. Figure out from amongst the four alternatives as to how the pattern would appear when the transparent sheet is folded at the dotted line.*

1. 

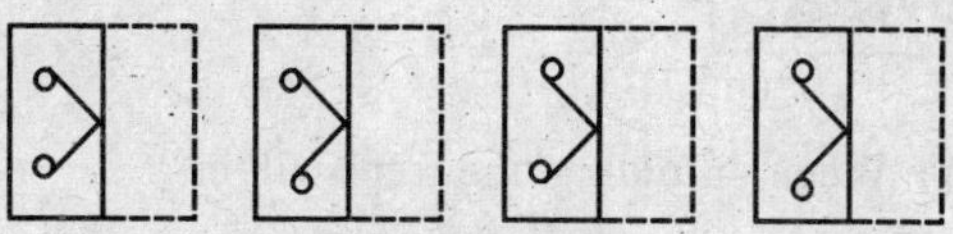

(*a*) (*b*) (*c*) (*d*)

2. 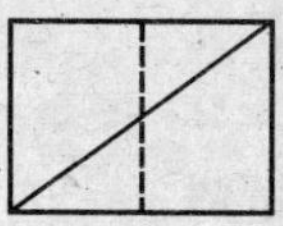

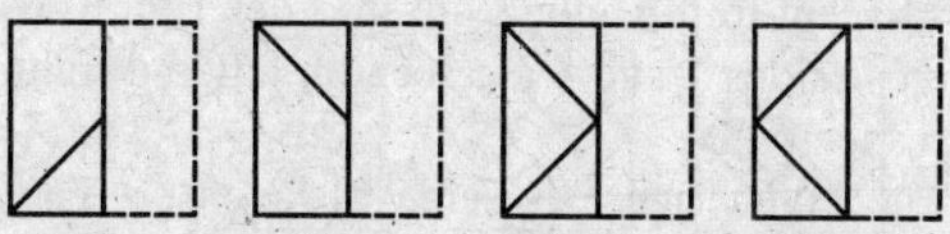

(*a*) (*b*) (*c*) (*d*)

3. 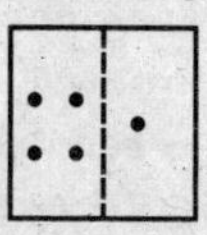

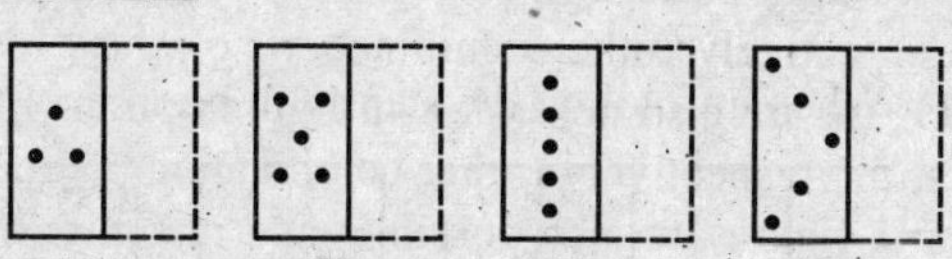

(*a*) (*b*) (*c*) (*d*)

4. 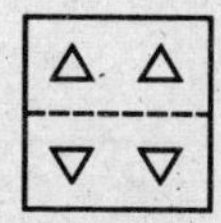

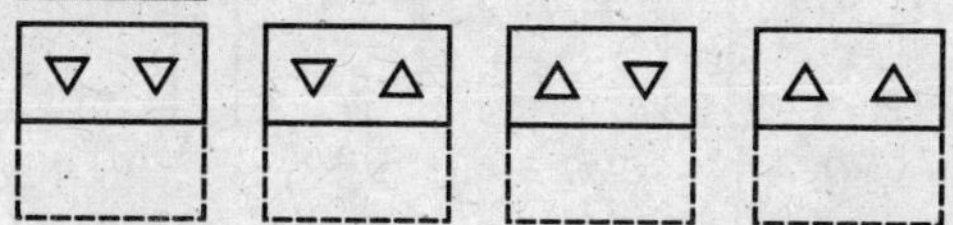

(*a*) (*b*) (*c*) (*d*)

5. 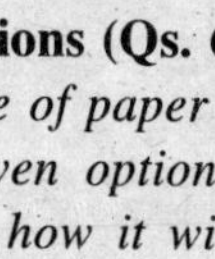

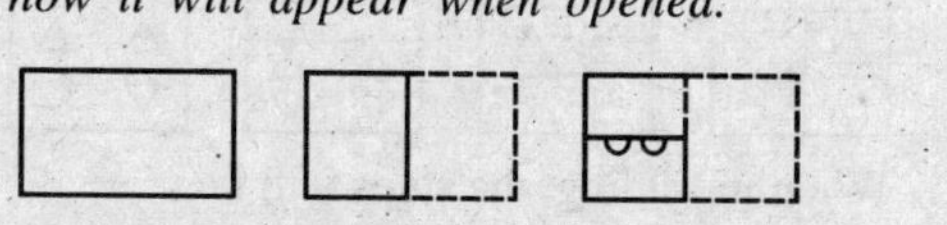

(*a*) (*b*) (*c*) (*d*)

Directions (Qs. 6-13) : *In each of the following questions a piece of paper has been folded and then punched. From the given options figure out the correct response which shows how it will appear when opened.*

6. 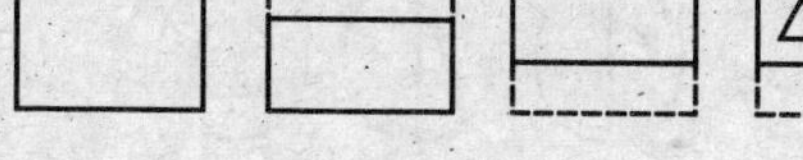

(*a*) (*b*) (*c*) (*d*)

7. 

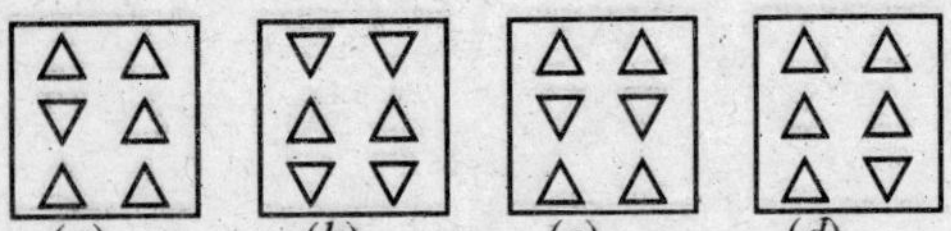

(a) (b) (c) (d)

8.

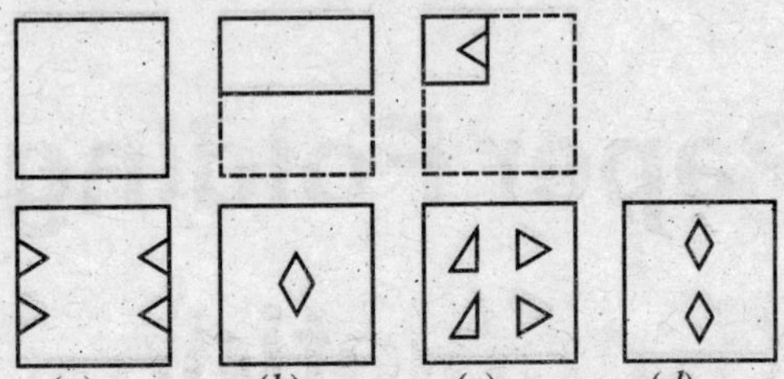

(a) (b) (c) (d)

9.

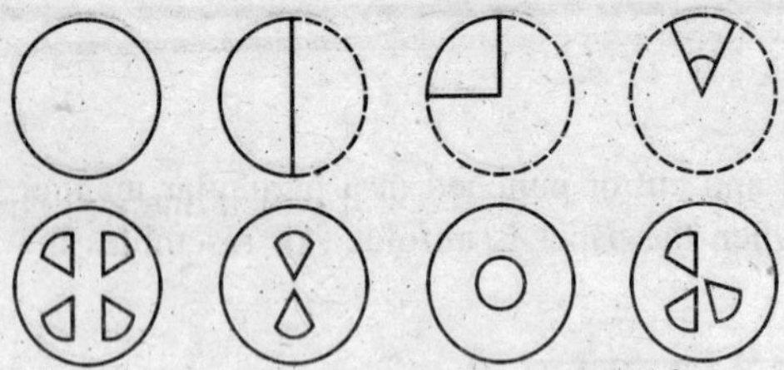

(a) (b) (c) (d)

10.

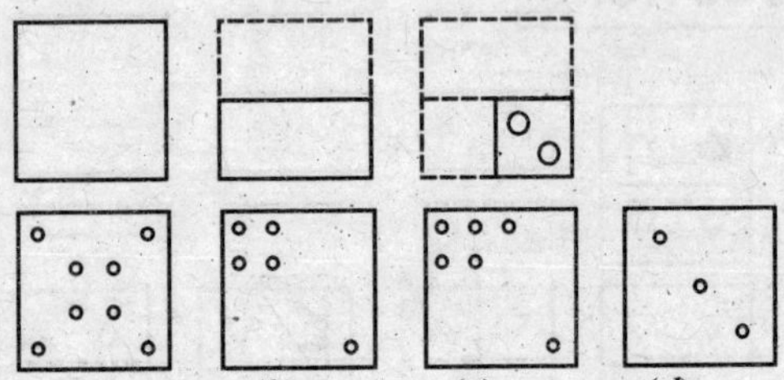

(a) (b) (c) (d)

11.

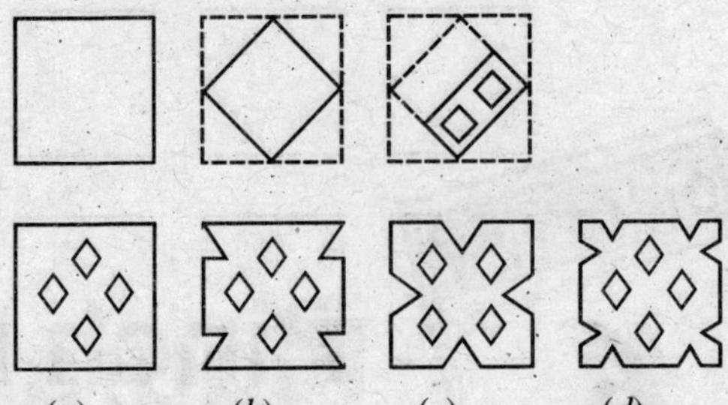

(a) (b) (c) (d)

12.

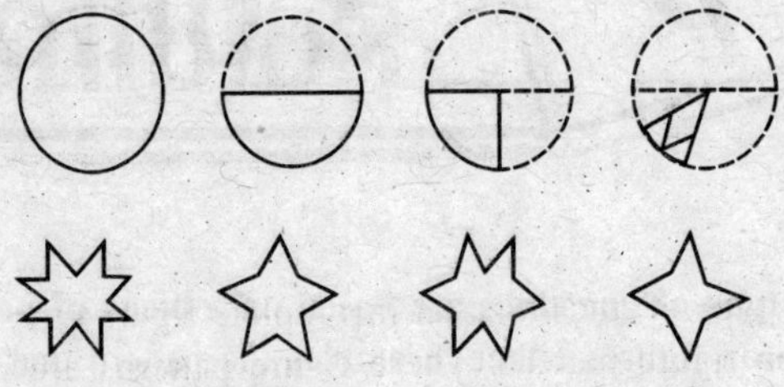

(a) (b) (c) (d)

13.

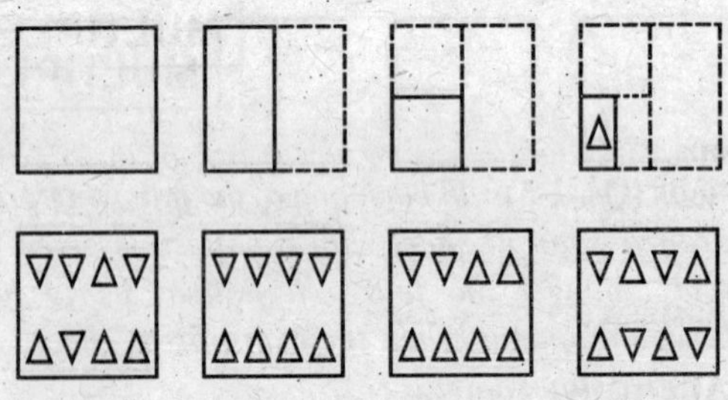

(a) (b) (c) (d)

EXPLANATORY ANSWERS

1. (*d*) **2.** (*c*)
3. (*b*) **4.** (*d*)
5. (*b*)

6. (*c*) : When unfolding, the steps will be :

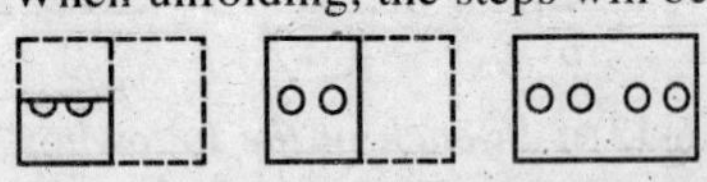

7. (*b*) : When unfolding, the steps will be :

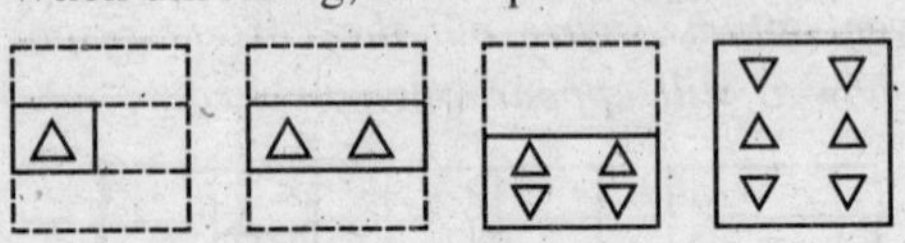

8. (*d*) : When unfolding, the steps will be :

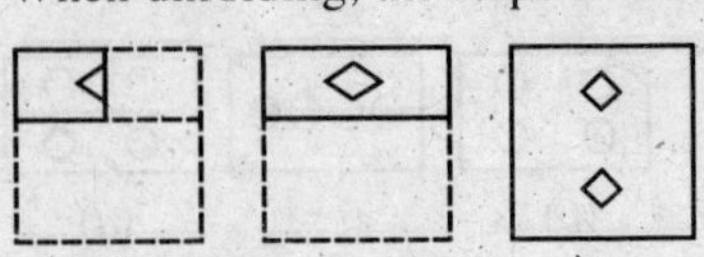

9. (*c*) : When unfolding, the steps will be :

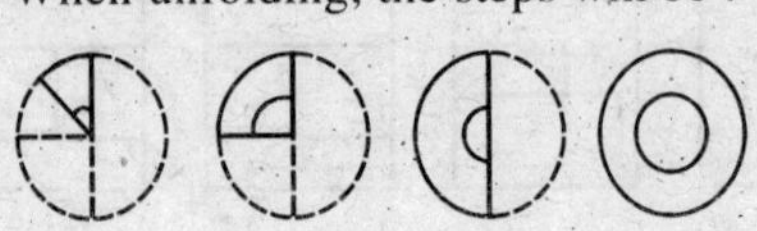

10. (*a*) : When unfolding, the steps will be :

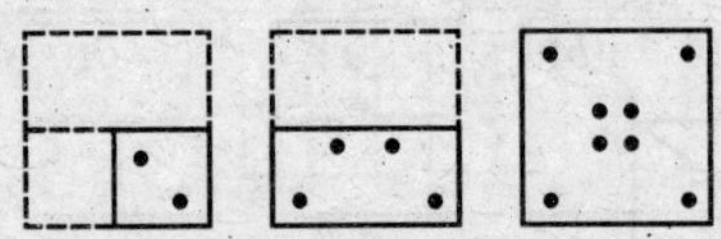

11. (*d*) : When unfolding, the steps will be :

12. (*a*) : When unfolding, the steps will be :

13. (*b*) : When unfolding; the steps will be :

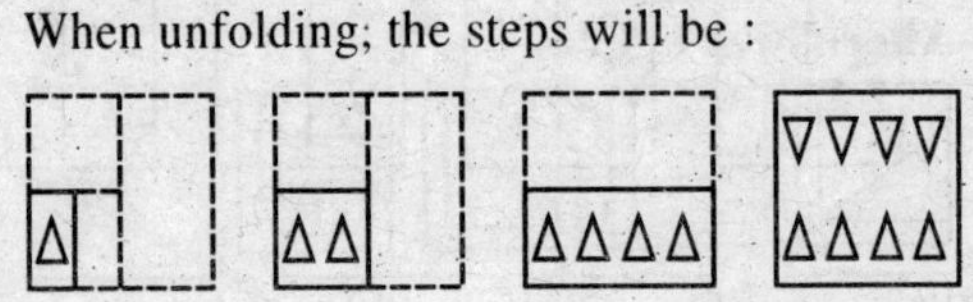

CHAPTER 7

Figural Pattern Folding and Completion

In these type of questions an incomplete figure pattern is given followed by alternative figures of which one will complete the given figure pattern. These figure patterns are mainly based on symmetries.

MULTIPLE CHOICE QUESTIONS

Directions : *In each question, which one of the alternative figures will complete the given figure pattern?*

1. Pattern 

Alternative figures

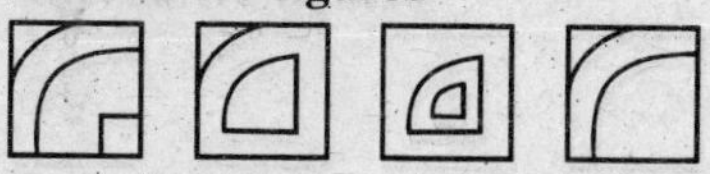

(*a*) (*b*) (*c*) (*d*)

2. Pattern 

Alternative figures

(*a*) (*b*) (*c*) (*d*)

3. Pattern 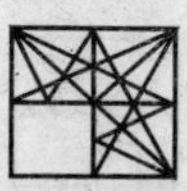

Alternative figures

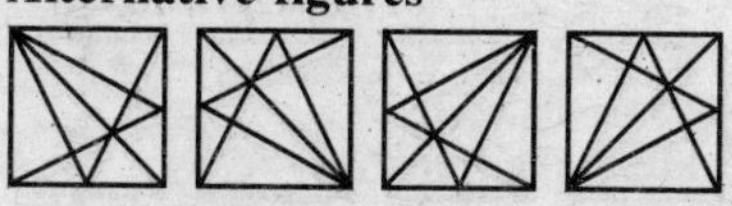

(*a*) (*b*) (*c*) (*d*)

4. Pattern 

Alternative figures

(*a*) (*b*) (*c*) (*d*)

5. Pattern 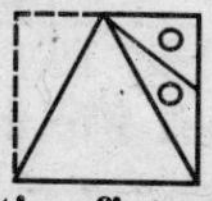

Alternative figures

(*a*) (*b*) (*c*) (*d*)

6. Pattern 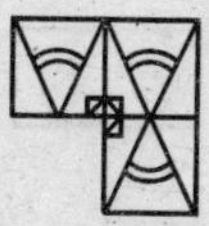

Alternative figures

(*a*) (*b*) (*c*) (*d*)

7. Pattern 

Alternative figures

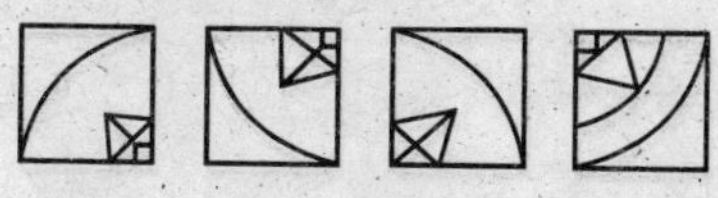

(*a*) (*b*) (*c*) (*d*)

8. Pattern 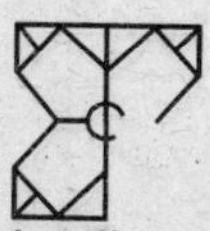

Alternative figures

(*a*) (*b*) (*c*) (*d*)

9. Pattern 

Alternative figures

(*a*) (*b*) (*c*) (*d*)

10. Pattern 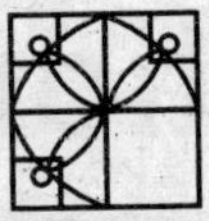

Alternative figures

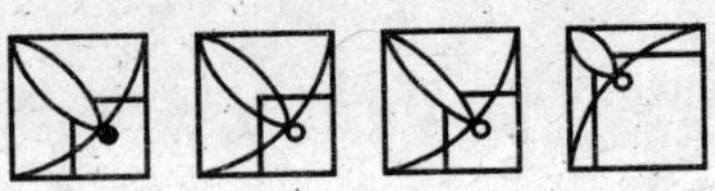

(*a*) (*b*) (*c*) (*d*)

11. Pattern 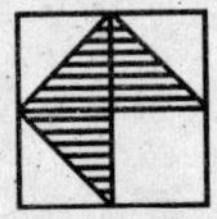

Alternative figures

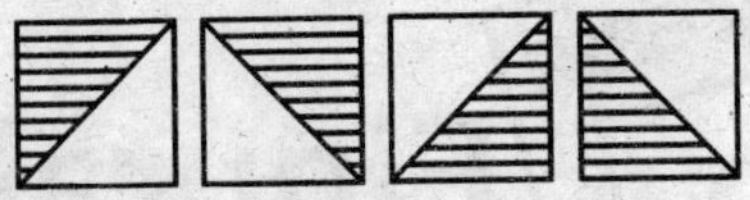

(*a*) (*b*) (*c*) (*d*)

12. Pattern 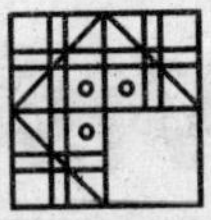

Alternative figures

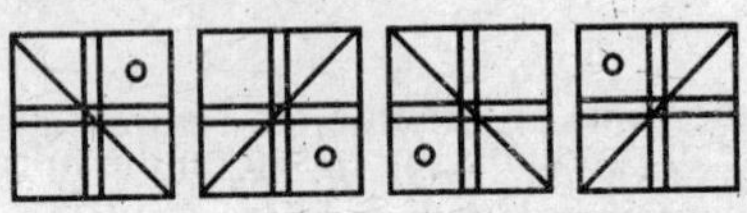

(*a*) (*b*) (*c*) (*d*)

EXPLANATORY ANSWERS

All the completed figures will look like this:

1. (*b*) : 

2. (*a*) : 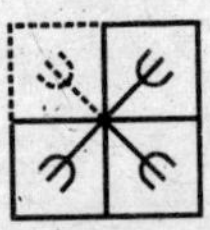

3. (*d*) : 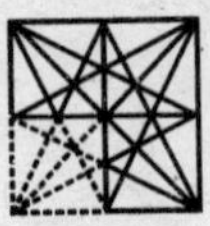

4. (*d*) : 

5. (*a*) : 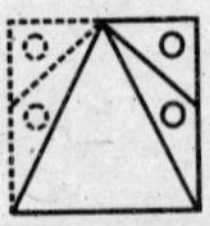

6. (*a*) : 

7. (*b*) : 

8. (*c*) : 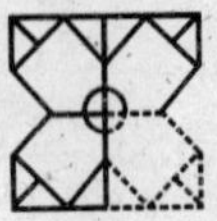

9. (*a*) : 

10. (*b*) : 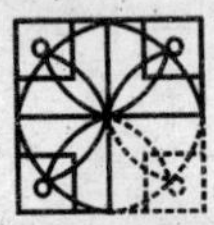

11. (*a*) : 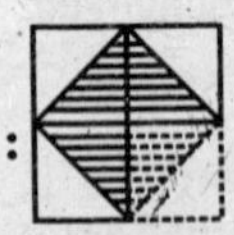

12. (*d*) : 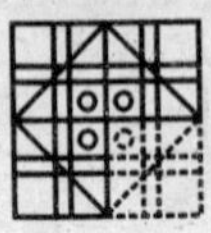

CHAPTER

8

Visual Memory

These type of problems are based on the mirror images or reflections of number, letters and figures. While attempting such questions one must be able to visualise clearly the questioned reflections, be they on vertical plane or on horizontal plane. Study the chart and information given below. The visualisation of letters and numbers is easier than the visualisation of figures for the simple reason that the figures have many forms and all cannot be summed up.

Horizontal Mirror Images (HMI) of Numbers

Number	*HMI*	*Number*	*HMI*
0	0	5	ꙅ
1	I	6	∂
2	ᘔ	7	⅂
3	Ɛ	8	8
4	ᔦ	9	୧

Note : HMI of 0 and 8 remain unchanged

Vertical Mirror Images (VMI) of Numbers

Numbers : 0 1 2 3 4 5 6 7 8 9

VMI : 0 I ᘔ 3 ᔦ ꙅ ୧ ⅃ 8 ∂

Note : VMI of 0, 3 and 8 remain unchanged.

Exceptions in style need caution. Example 3 will be 3, or 8 will be 8.

Horizontal Mirror Images of Capital Letters

Letter	HMI	Letter	HMI	H letter	HMI
A	A	J	Ⴑ	S	Ƨ
B	ᗺ	K	ꓘ	T	T
C	Ɔ	L	⅃	U	U
D	ᗡ	M	M	V	V
E	Ǝ	N	И	W	W
F	ꟻ	O	O	X	X
G	Ә	P	ꟼ	Y	Y
H	H	Q	Ϙ	Z	Ƹ
I	I	R	Я		

Note : HMI of A, H, I, M, O, T, U, V, W, X and Y remain unchanged.

Exceptions in style need caution. Example : A will be A, or X will be X.

Vertical Mirror Images of Capital Letters

Letters : A B C D E F G H I J K L M

VMI : ∀ B C D E Ⅎ ⅁ H I ſ K Γ W

Letters : N O P Q R S T U V W X Y Z

VMI : ᴎ O b Ό ʁ ƨ ⊥ ∩ Λ M X ⅄ Z

Note : VMI of C, D, E, H, I, K, O and X remain unchanged.

Horizontal Mirror Images of Small Letters

Letter	HMI	Letter	HMI	Letter	HMI
a	ɒ	j	ꞁ	s	ƨ
b	d	k	ʞ	t	ɈT
c	ɔ	l	l	u	u
d	b	m	m	v	v
e	ɘ	n	n	w	w
f	ɟ	o	o	x	x
g	ǫ	p	q	y	y
h	ʜ	q	p	z	ƹ
i	i	r	ɿ		

Note : HMI of o, v, w and x remain unchanged.

Vertical Mirror Images of Small Letters

Letter : a b c d e f g h i j k l m

VMI : ɐ p c q ǝ ɟ ƃ ɥ ! ɾ ʞ l ɯ

Letter : n o p q r s t u v w x y z

VMI : u o b d ɹ ƨ ʇ n ʌ ʍ x λ z

Note : VMI of c, o and x remain unchanged. Letter l has exceptions: if it is a straight vertical line – l then it remains unchanged.

MULTIPLE CHOICE QUESTIONS

Directions (Qs. 1 to 15) : *In each question below which is the exact horizontal mirror image?*

1. DuST
   (a) ꓷuSꓕ (b) TSnD
   (c) TSuD (d) ꓷuST
2. CHAIR
   (a) ЯIHAƆ (b) ЯIAHƆ
   (c) ЯIAHC (d) ƆHAIЯ
3. WHOM
   (a) MOHW (b) WOHM
   (c) ʍHOW (d) ʍOHM
4. plaque
   (a) ǝupɐlq (b) ǝuqblp
   (c) qlapue (d) ǝuqɐlp
5. brows
   (a) dɹowƨ (b) drows
   (c) ƨwoɹd (d) ƨword
6. flying
   (a) gniylf (b) gnilyf
   (c) gniylf (d) gniylf
7. 4379
   (a) 9734 (b) 4379
   (c) 9734 (d) 9734
8. 57182
   (a) 28175 (b) 57182
   (c) 28175 (d) 28175
9. 69430
   (a) 03469 (b) 03469
   (c) 03469 (d) 03469
10. 2JKS
    (a) ƧKJ2 (b) ƧKJ2
    (c) ƧKJ2 (d) ƧKJ2
11. P9Yf3
    (a) ƐfY9P (b) ƐfY9P
    (c) Ɛ3Y9P (d) ƐfY9P
12. GZ5QRh
    (a) hRQ5ZG (b) hRQ5ZG
    (c) hRQ5ZG (d) hRQ5ZG
13. 2$%CH
    (a) HC%$2 (b) HC%$2
    (c) HC%$2 (d) HC%$2
14. 7↑FN8
    (a) 8NF↑7 (b) 8NF↑7
    (c) 8NF↑7 (d) 8NF↑7
15. yk19G
    (a) G91ky (b) G91ky
    (c) G91ky (d) G91ky

ANSWERS

1	2	3	4	5	6	7	8	9	10
(c)	(b)	(a)	(a)	(c)	(d)	(b)	(a)	(d)	(c)
11	**12**	**13**	**14**	**15**					
(d)	(b)	(c)	(a)	(d)					

CHAPTER 9

Discrimination

In these problems one has to count the geometrical figures in a given complex figure. A little bit of systematic approach is needed to get the correct number of the asked figure. The shapes of all geometrical figures must be clear in mind.

MULTIPLE CHOICE QUESTIONS

1. How many triangles are there in the figure given below?

(*a*) 24 (*b*) 27
(*c*) 25 (*d*) 26

2. How many parallelograms are there in this figure?

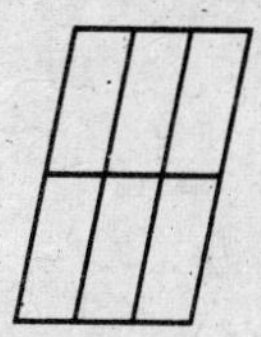

(*a*) 9 (*b*) 13
(*c*) 15 (*d*) 18

3. How many triangles are there in this figure?

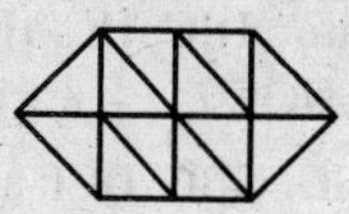

(*a*) 16 (*b*) 17
(*c*) 18 (*d*) 19

4. The number of rectangles in this figure are.

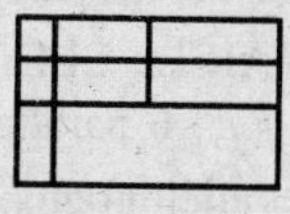

(*a*) 21 (*b*) 24
(*c*) 23 (*d*) 25

5. How many squares are hidden in this figure?

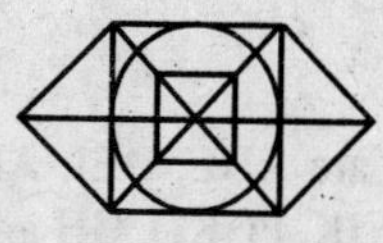

(*a*) 7 (*b*) 8
(*c*) 9 (*d*) 10

6. The number of triangles in this figure are.

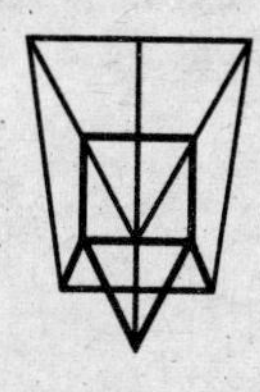

(*a*) 19 (*b*) 16
(*c*) 21 (*d*) 15

EXPLANATORY ANSWERS

1. (*a*) :

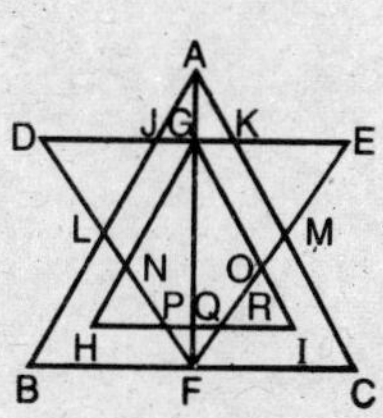

- The main triangles making the figure are ABC, DEF and GHI *i.e.,* – 3 triangles
- The simplest triangles are AJG, AGK, KEM, DJL, NHP, PQF, QFR and ORI *i.e.,* – 8 triangles

- The triangles formed by the bisecting line AF are ABF, AFC, GHQ, GQI, DGF and GFE *i.e.,* – 6 triangles
- The triangles formed inbetween the three triangles AJK, ALF, AMF, DGN, DGF, LBF, MFC, GEO, GNF and GOF – *i.e.,* 10 triangles
- So, the total number of triangles is
  3 + 8 + 6 + 10 = 27

2. (*d*) :

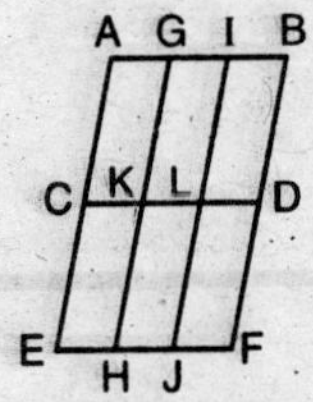

- The main parallelogram is ABEF *i.e.,* 1 parallelogram
- When divided into half by line CD the main figure has ABCD and CDEF *i.e.,* 2 parallelograms
- When further lines GH and IJ are drawn, the parallelograms are AGEH, GIJH and IBJF *i.e.,* – 3 parallelograms.
- The simplest parallelogram are AGCK, CKEH, GIKL, KLHJ, IBLD and LDJF *i.e.* – 6 parallelograms
  Other parallelograms are AICL, CLEJ, GBKD, KDHF, AIEJ and GBHF – *i.e.,* 6 parallelograms
  So, the total number of parallelograms is
  1 + 2 + 3 + 6 + 6 = 18

3. (*a*) :

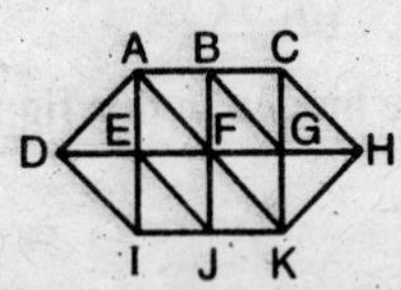

The simplest triangles are ADE, DEI, AEF, ABF, EIJ, EFJ, BFG, BCG, FJK, FGK, CGH and GHK – *i.e.,* – 12 triangles
The bisected triangles are ADI and CHK – *i.e.* – 2 triangles
Other triangles are AIK and ACK *i.e.,* – 2 triangles
So, the total number of triangles is
12 + 2 + 2 = 16

4. (*c*) :

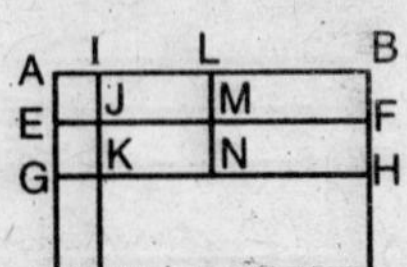

The main rectangle is ABCD – *i.e.,* – 1 rectangle
The simplest rectangles are AIEJ, ILJM, LBMF, EJGK, JMKN, MFNH, GKCO and KHOD *i.e.* – 8 rectangles.
The rectangles which have two parts are ALEM, IBJF, EMGN, JFKH, AIGK, IKLN, LBNH, EJCO and GHCD *i.e.* – 9 rectangles.
The rectangles which have three parts are AICO, ABEF and EFGH *i.e.* – 3 rectangles
The rectangles which have four parts are ALGN and IBKH *i.e.* – 2 rectangles
So, the total number of rectangles
1 + 8 + 9 + 3 + 2 = 23

5. (*d*) :

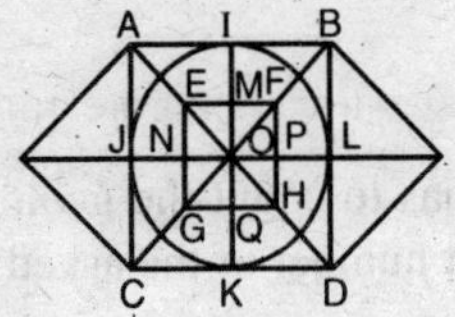

The main squares are ABCD and EFGH *i.e.,* – 2 squares
The simplest outer squares are AIJO, IBOL, JOCK and OLKD *i.e.,* – 4 squares
The simplest inner square are EMNO, NOGQ, MFOP and OPQH *i.e.,* – 4 squares
There are no other squares formed in the figure
So, the total number of squares is
2 + 4 + 4 = 10

6. (*b*) :

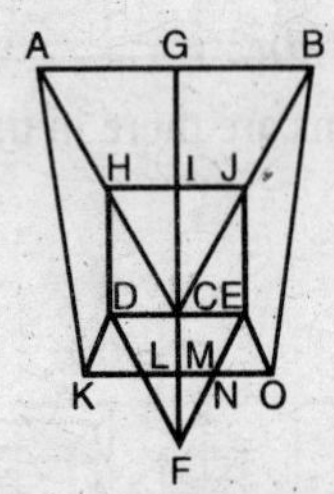

The main triangles are : ABC, DEF, LNF, and HJC *i.e.* 4 triangles
The simplest triangles are : HIC, IJC, HDC, JCE, DKL, LMF, MFN and NOE *i.e.* – 8 triangles
Other triangles are : AGC, GBC, DCF and CEF – *i.e.* 4 triangles
So, the total number of triangles is 4 + 8 + 4 = 16

CHAPTER 10

Embedded Figures

In these type of questions a figure form is given followed by alternative figures. In one of these figure options the given form is embedded. Practice of visualisation comes handy in attempting such easy questions.

MULTIPLE CHOICE QUESTIONS

Directions (Qs. 1 to 6) : *In the questions given below a figure is given. From the given alternatives select the one in which the given figure is embedded.*

1.

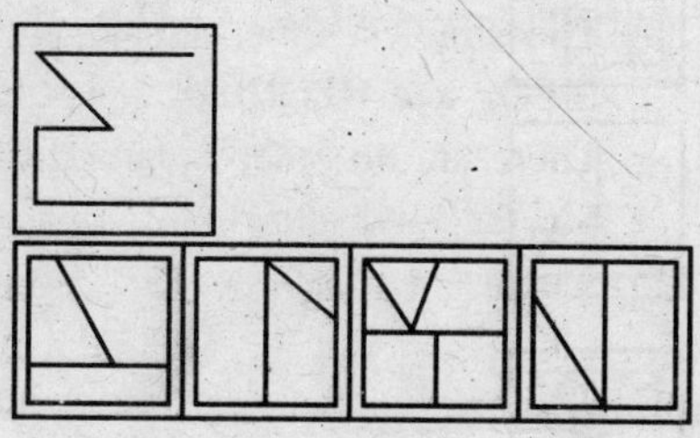

(a) (b) (c) (d)

2.

(a) (b) (c) (d)

3.

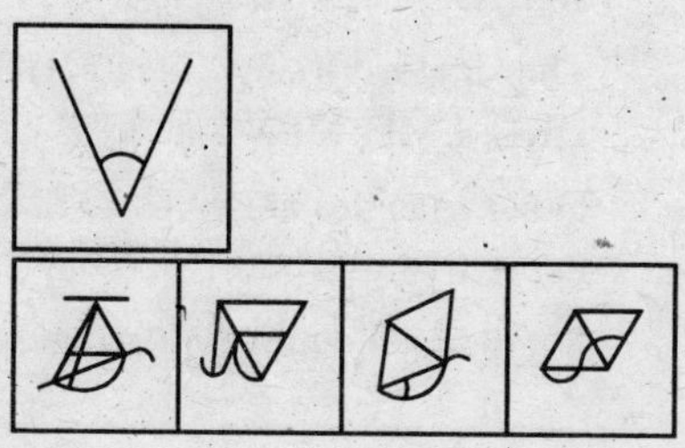

(a) (b) (c) (d)

4.

(a) (b) (c) (d)

5.

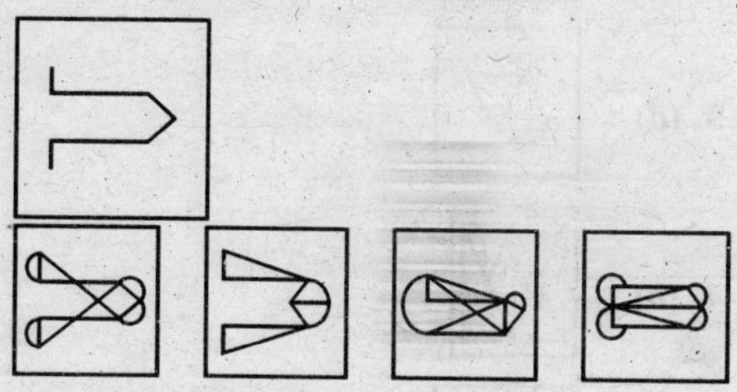

(a) (b) (c) (d)

6.

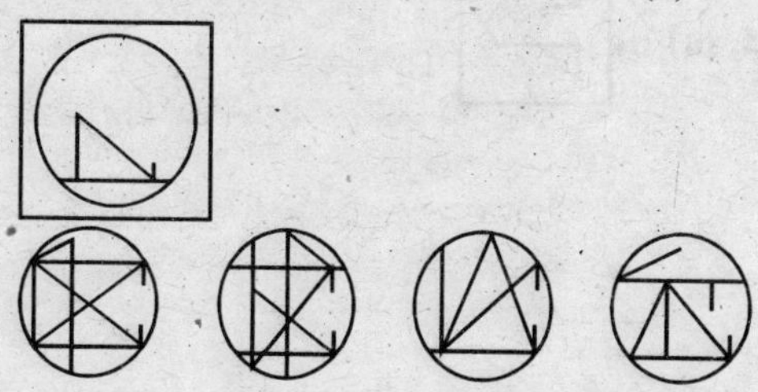

(a) (b) (c) (d)

Directions (Qs. 7 to 10) : *In each question given below find the figure form which is embedded in the given pattern.*

7.

(a) (b) (c) (d)

8. 

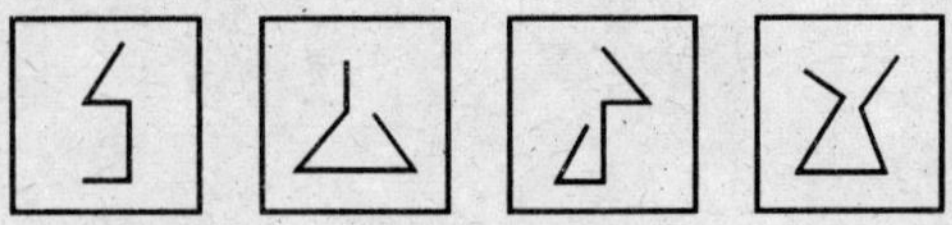

(a) (b) (c) (d)

9. 

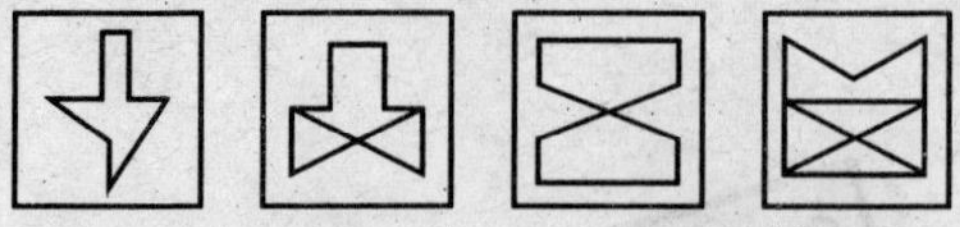

(a) (b) (c) (d)

10. 

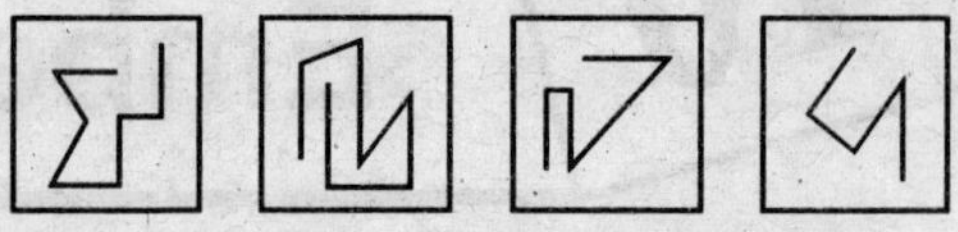

(a) (b) (c) (d)

EXPLANATORY ANSWERS

1. (*a*) : 

2. (*a*) : 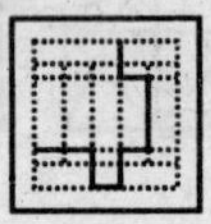

3. (*d*) : 

4. (*b*) : 

5. (*a*) : 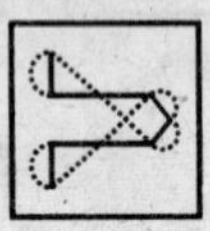

6. (*b*) : 

7. (*d*) : 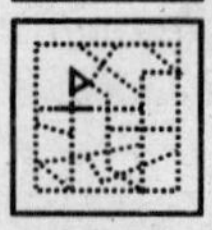

8. (*b*) : 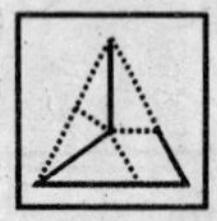

9. (*c*) : 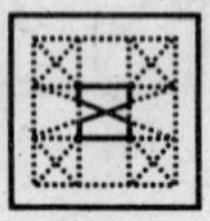

10. (*d*) :